POST-SECULAR PHILOSOPHY

Philosophical discussion of theology has usually been determined by secular assumptions, a disposition that has often resulted in a philosophical rejection of God. But the destruction of theology at the hands of secular reason no longer seems so certain. Recent work in philosophy has questioned the modern exclusion and denial of God, returning theology to the centre of current debate.

Post-Secular Philosophy: Between Philosophy and Theology is a major anthology that describes the relationship between theology and the foremost thinkers of the modern philosophical tradition. By locating this relationship in terms of contemporary philosophical debate, *Post-Secular Philosophy* goes to the heart of the current discussion about the role of God in modern philosophy and thought.

Beginning with Descartes, Kant and Hegel, continuing with Levinas and Derrida, ending with Irigaray and Baudrillard, *Post-Secular Philosophy* provides a clear focus, enabling the reader to follow how the modern philosophical tradition has constituted God. By discussing each thinker in separate chapters, a clear picture emerges of how figures as diverse as Heidegger, Freud or Wittgenstein approach and configure the question of God. In a compelling introduction Phillip Blond positions each contribution in respect of the modern philosophical tradition, and suggests where theology might seek to challenge its secular constitution.

A controversial feature of this book is its call for a rethinking of religiosity in face of the nihilism that dominates much of contemporary Western thinking. Rescuing the importance of religion from both fundamentalist assertion and liberal erasure, *Post-Secular Philosophy* transcends the determinations of modern philosophy and post-modern thinking by articulating an entirely different possibility.

Phillip Blond is at Peterhouse, University of Cambridge.

POST-SECULAR PHILOSOPHY

Between philosophy and theology

Edited by
Phillip Blond

London and New York

First published 1998
by Routledge
11 New Fetter Lane, London EC4P 4EE

Simultaneously published in the USA and Canada
by Routledge
29 West 35th Street, New York, NY 10001

Typeset in Baskerville by
BC Typesetting
Printed and bound in Great Britain by
Creative Print and Design (Wales), Ebbw Vale

British Library Cataloguing in Publication Data
A catalogue record for this book is available from the British Library

Library of Congress Cataloguing in Publication Data
Post-secular Philosophy: Between philosophy and theology/edited by
Phillip Blond.
Includes bibliographical references and index.
1. Philosophy and religion–History.   I. Blond, Phillip
B56.P67   1997
211–dc21   97-8952

ISBN 0–415–09777–0 (hbk)
0–415–09778–9 (pbk)

For Francis Xavier Wilson
and Mary Frances Atkins

God's Grandeur

The world is charged with the grandeur of God.
   It will flame out, like shining from shook foil;
   It gathers to a greatness, like the ooze of oil
Crushed. Why do men then now not reck his rod?
Generations have trod, have trod, have trod;
   And all is seared with trade; bleared, smeared with toil;
   And wears man's smudge and shares man's smell: the soil
Is bare now, nor can foot feel, being shod.

And, for all this, nature is never spent;
   There lives the dearest freshness deep down things;
And though the last lights off the black West went
   Oh, morning, at the brown brink eastward, springs –
Because the Holy Ghost over the bent
   World broods with warm breast and with ah! bright wings.

Gerard Manley Hopkins

CONTENTS

NOTES ON CONTRIBUTORS

Editor

Phillip Blond is at Peterhouse, Cambridge and is a research student completing his PhD in Theology in the Faculty of Divinity at the University of Cambridge. He previously held a prize fellowship in philosophy at the New School for Social Research in New York. He has published articles on phenomenology, aesthetics and theology. This is his first published volume. He is currently working on a monograph on theology and perception.

Contributors

Alison Ainley is a Senior Lecturer in Philosophy at Anglia Polytechnic University. She has published essays on Irigaray, Levinas, Kristeva, Nietzsche and Heidegger, and is currently working on a book on Irigaray and feminist philosophy.

Philippa Berry is a Fellow and Director of Studies in English at King's College, Cambridge. Her publications include articles on renaissance literature, feminist theory and contemporary thought. She is the co-editor of *Shadow of Spirit* (Routledge 1992), the author of *Chastity and Power: Elizabethan Literature and the Unmarried Queen* (Routledge 1989) and *Shakespeare's Feminine Endings: Figuring women in the tragedies* (Routledge forthcoming).

Howard Caygill is Professor of Cultural History at Goldsmiths College, University of London, and is the author of *The Art of Judgement* (Blackwell 1989), *The Kant Dictionary* (Blackwell 1995) and *Walter Benjamin: The Colour of Experience* (Routledge 1997).

Michel Haar teaches Contemporary Philosophy and Aesthetics at the University of Paris XII. Among his published works are two volumes on Heidegger, *Heidegger and the Essence of Man* (SUNY 1993) and *The Song of the Earth* (Indiana University Press 1993), and also *Nietzsche and Metaphysics* (SUNY 1996).

Kevin Hart is Professor of English and Comparative Literature at Monash University, Melbourne. His critical works include *The Trespass of the Sign: Deconstruction, Theology, Philosophy* (CUP 1989), *A.D. Hope* (OUP 1992), *The Oxford Book of Australian Religious Verse* (OUP 1994) and *Losing the Power to say 'I'* (Art School Press 1996). His latest collection of poetry is *New and Selected Poems* (HarperCollins 1995). He has recently completed a study of Samuel Johnson and is now writing a monograph on Maurice Blanchot.

Fergus Kerr is an Honorary Senior Lecturer in the Department of Theology and Religious Studies at the University of Edinburgh. He is the editor of *New Blackfriars*, author of *Theology after Wittgenstein* (OUP 1986, 2nd edition SPCK 1997), and of *Immortal Longings: Versions of Transcending Humanity* (SPCK 1997).

Jean-Luc Marion was a student at the Ecole Normale Supérieure. He was a Professor at the University of Poitiers and the University of Paris X, Nanterre and he is now Professor of Philosophy at the University of Paris, Sorbonne and visiting Professor at the University of Chicago department of philosophy. His recent books and publications include *Etant donné: essai d'une phénoménologie de la donation* (P.U.F. 1997). *God without Being* (University of Chicago Press 1991), *Réduction et donation* (P.U.F. 1989) *La Croisée du visible* (La Différence P.U.F. 1996), *Sur le prisme métaphysique de Descartes* (P.U.F. 1986).

John Milbank is a Reader in Philosophical Theology at Cambridge University and a Fellow of Peterhouse, Cambridge. He is the author of *The Religious Dimension in the Thought of Giambattista Vico* (Edwin Mellen 1991), *Theology and Social Theory: Beyond Secular Reason* (Blackwell 1990), and *The Word Made Strange; Theology Language Culture* (Blackwell 1997).

John Peacocke is a Lecturer in Philosophy and Literature at Bolton Institute of Higher Education. His interests and publications include Heidegger, Indo-Tibetan Studies and French psychoanalytic thought. He is currently editing a collection of papers entitled *Lacan on Narcissism* (Curzon Press forthcoming).

Regina M. Schwartz is a Professor of English at Northwestern University, and Director of the Institute of Religion, Ethics and Violence. She is the author of *The Curse of Cain: The Violent Legacy of Monotheism* (University of Chicago Press 1997), *Remembering and Repeating: On Milton's Theology and Poetics* (University of Chicago Press 1990) editor of *The Book and the Text: The Bible and Literary Theory* (Basil Blackwell 1990) and co-author of the *Postmodern Bible* (Yale University Press 1995).

Graham Ward is Dean of Peterhouse, Cambridge, where he teaches theology, philosophy and literary analysis. He is author of *Barth, Derrida and the*

Language of Theology (CUP 1995) and *Theology and Contemporary Critical Theory* (Macmillan 1996) as well as being editor of *Michel de Certeau S.J.* (New Blackfriars 1996) and *The Postmodern God* (Blackwell 1997). His essays have appeared in several academic journals and books. He is the senior editor of *Literature and Theology* (OUP).

Andrew Wernick teaches Cultural Studies at Trent University, Ontario, and directs a graduate programme in Methodologies for the Study of Western History and Culture. He has published many essays on social theory and contemporary culture. He is the author of *Promotional Culture: Advertising, ideology and symbolic expression* (Sage 1991), the co-editor of *Shadow of Spirit* (Routledge 1992) and co-editor with Mike Featherstone of *Images of Ageing: Cultural representations of later life* (Routledge 1995).

Rowan Williams has been the Anglican Bishop of Monmouth in Wales since 1992. He was previously the Lady Margaret Professor of Divinity at Oxford and was prior to that a University Lecturer in Divinity at Cambridge. His recent publications include *Arius: heresy and tradition* (Darton Longman Todd 1987), *Teresa of Avila* (Chapman 1991) and *After Silent Centuries* (Perpetua Press 1994).

Charles E. Winquist is the Thomas J. Watson Professor of Religion at Syracuse University. He is the author of numerous works including *Desiring Theology* (University of Chicago Press 1995) and *Epiphanies of Darkness: Deconstruction in Theology* (Fortress Press 1986).

ACKNOWLEDGEMENTS

First of all, my sincere thanks and appreciation are due to all those whose work appears in this book, all of whom stayed with the project durings its long inception. I am very grateful to them for being a part of this collection.

I would like to thank all those who have had an intellectual influence on me. At the University of Hull during those strange and beautiful halcyon days, I would like especially to thank the late R.N. Berki, and Noel O'Sullivan. At the University of Warwick I owe a debt of gratitude to Andrew Benjamin and David Wood. Of others whom I have met, studied under, or talked with I would like to thank Michel Haar, Robert Bernasconi, Howard Caygill, Andrew Bowie and Peter Dews. Gillian Rose was a great presence and influence – I wish her all the very finest things. I would like in addition to thank Kevin Hart, Andrew Wernick, Charles Winquist and Regina Schwartz who as well as being colleagues I hold in high esteem, are also my friends. Others with whom I have spoken and would like to thank include Bettina Bergo, Simon Jarvis, Alison Milbank, Constantin Boundas, Johnathan Bordo, Toby Foshay, Paul Morris, Jeanette Cossar, Edith Wyschogrod, Arthur Gibson and Don Cupitt.

During my time in New York and at the New School for Social Research I would like to thank for an abundancy of friendship and conversation Timothy Benjamin, Peggy Zita, Mick Calhoun, Jim Luchte, Emma Bianchee, Sharin Elkholy, Felix Ensslin and James Harris. I would like also to thank the late Reiner Schürmann, a man whose intellectual presence and influence is much missed, and Pierre Adler who was one of the best minds on the faculty. Finally from New York, I would like especially to thank and acknowledge Brent Hopkins and Caitlin Dempsey, friends possessed of a wonderful intelligence whose engagements with theology at brunch on Sunday mornings in Manhattan were a great delight and a joy sadly forgone.

As to the book itself I would like to thank Maria Stasiak who did an incredible job copy-editing a huge pile of disparate manuscripts in tiny fonts. At Routledge I would like to thank Barbara Duke my desk editor without whose efficiency I would still be at proof stage, Tony Bruce my editor who has carried through and supported the book marvellously, and finally Adrian

Driscoll who all those years ago saw the potential of the collection and helped me bring it together.

In terms of lifelong friends who have in various and manifold ways helped me beyond all expectation, I would like to thank Adam Richards, Mark Kenbar, Suzie Labinjoh and Joanne Mallabar. I would also like to thank Gabrielle, Patrick, Oliver, Adriana, Henry and Massimo – a glorious and grace-filled family all of whom I love, intellectually respect and admire.

Concerning Cambridge, I would like to thank Oliver Soskice for all our wonderful conversations about painting and seeing, and Ben Quash and Graham Ward, two of the finest priests that I know. To my glorious and radically orthodox colleagues Catherine Pickstock, Conor Cuningham, Simon Oliver and Michael Hanby, I wish to convey my deep appreciation and thanks for discussion, support and an intellectually demanding religious life. I would like especially to thank Christ Horner – one of the finest and most engaged minds that I know in Cambridge. Finally and most importantly, my greatest intellectual thanks and acknowledgement go to John Milbank.

Phillip Blond
Peterhouse
August 1997

The editor and publisher also wish to thank the following for permission to reprint previously published material:

Chapter 1: Jean-Luc Marion (1982) 'Descartes et l'Onto-théologie,' *Bulletin de la Société Française de Philosophie*, t. LXXVI, 1982, pp. 117–71. Translated by Bettina Bergo. Reprinted with permission of the Société Française de Philosophie.
Chapter 4: John Milbank (1996) 'The Sublime in Kierkegaard' in *The Heythrop Journal*, 37 (1996) 298–321. Reprinted with permission from Blackwell Publishers Ltd.
Chapter 5: Michel Haar (1996) 'Nietzsche and the Metamorphosis of the Divine'. Reprinted from *Nietzsche and Metaphysics* by Michel Haar, translated by Michael Gendre, by permission of the State University of New York Press.
Chapter 13: Philippa Berry (1995) 'Kristeva's feminist refiguring of the gift' in *Paragraph*, 18, No. 3, 1995. Reprinted with permission from *Paragraph* and Edinburgh University Press.

INTRODUCTION

Theology before philosophy

Phillip Blond

Contra Mundum

For not all have faith.
(2 Thess 3.2)[1]

We live in a time of failed conditions. Everywhere people who have no faith in any possibility, either for themselves, each other, or for the world, mouth locutions they do not understand. With words such as 'politics', they attempt to formalise the unformalisable and found secular cities upon it. They attempt to live in the in-between and celebrate ambiguity as the new social horizon, always however bringing diversity into accord with their own projections. Always and everywhere, these late moderns make competing claims about the a priori, for they must be seen to disagree. Indeed such thinkers feel so strongly about the ethical nature of their doubt that they argue with vehemence about overcoming metaphysics, about language and the dangers of presence. Since God is committed to presence, they assume that theology is no longer an option sustainable by serious minds.[2] These secular scholars accept without question the philosophical necessity of their position (they are happy autonomous creatures these atheists), even though with a certain magnanimity of gesture they might concede in an informal discussion that God could perhaps exist in some possible world, but they tell us in all likelihood it is not this one. To an external observer such gestures might suggest that these minds are grasping for enemies in a world that they are no longer sure of. But of course such external positions are now no longer considered possible. Blind to the immanence[3] of such a world, unable to disengage themselves from whatever transcendental schema they wish to endorse, these secular minds are only now beginning to perceive that all is not as it should be, that what was promised to them – self-liberation through the limitation of the world to human faculties – might after all be a form of self-mutilation.

1

Indeed, ever since Kant dismissed God from human cognition and rele-gated access to Him to the sphere of practical ethics and moral motivation, human beings have been very pragmatic indeed. They have found value in self-legislation and so see no reason for God. For after all, they now maintain, there can be no moral realism, the good cannot possess any actuality outside the conditional and conditioning nature of the human mind. Nor apparently, according to these late moderns, can a transcendent value escape any of the contemporary surrogates – language, pragmatics, power – which transcen-dental thinking has engendered in order to preserve itself. These proxies, which are viewed as the ruling a prioris of the day, supposedly determine or foreclose upon any other possibility. No, their advocates say, 'your values are ancillary to this, in respect of this discernment everything else is subordi-nate, this is the prior discourse that secures our descriptions, and we, we who ascertained this, we are the authors and judges of this world and there is no other'. Perhaps unsurprisingly this state of affairs is viewed as a cause of much joy and self-affirmation.

And what a world it is that is so blithely affirmed. Every day in the contem-porary polis new beings are unearthed, new subjectivities are claimed as excluded, with fresh litigations being initiated on their behalf for mutual and communal benefit. The pious speak righteously to each other about the Other, about how they are keeping faith with the world, about the need to be vigilant against the illegitimacy of hierarchies. For we are told there can be no discrimination in this secular city. In this polis the lowest has become the highest, and equality names itself as the only value that cannot be deva-lued.

However, without true value, without a distinction between the better and the worse, of course the most equal and the most common will hold sway. Of course the lowest common denominator will be held up to be the foundation of human civic life. What yardstick then for such a society, what measure do the public who must measure themselves require? If they themselves now realise, as some do, that human beings cannot (and indeed must not), provide their own calibration, where do they look?

Not surprisingly, most still attempt a modern solution; either they seek the path of immanence or they accept the necessity of a transcendental method-ology. The latter turn away from the world as if it were too fearful a thing to confront, and seek safety in allying the formal conditions of thought with those of behaviour; whereas the former, too convinced by the hopelessness of their position, deduce themselves to be avid powerless creatures, and as beings who desire nothing but the affect of their own potency they throw themselves into the void, embracing the anonymity therein as if it were a true destiny and a real proof of their ultimate autonomy.

Those who seek to refrain from such extremes of philosophical candour do so by turning away and celebrating and debating their own immanent social order. They will deny that the preceding positions mark the outermost

2

boundaries of their own possibilities. They will speak of thinking beyond these binaries, and not consider the possibility that these oppositions might merely think them. In consequence, though these creatures of perspicacity and unconcealment speak almost endlessly about difficulty, inherent paradox and suddenly discovered aporia, they cannot bring themselves to acknowledge the conditions that gave rise to their world. Oscillating without resolution or recognition between transcendental hope and immanentist conjecture, they lack a perception of their position. Holding the middle of a lie, they feel profoundly comfortable with themselves and even more so with their enemies.

Always and everyday those trapped in such worlds practise the violence of denial. They deny that any world or order might precede them; through turning away from the transcendent they violate that which is present alongside and before them, and with the intoxicating compulsion of *ressentiment* they complete it all with the refusal of a future, taking being-towards-death (*Sein zum Tode*) as the definitive mark of the only subjectivity to come. Death, they say, is the only future that both you and I can authentically have as individuals. As they sadly ponder the reality of their own deaths (no doubt by casting themselves into the role of the tragic), these thinkers return almost unthinkingly to the positivism that has authored their whole lives: 'After all beyond one's life how could one know anything else?' Or they might say, with a smile accompanied by a slight incline of the neck, 'no other possibility has ever made itself known to me'. Happy in their respective oppositions, they will indeed be, until their deaths, unaware of that which they never sought to address.

Another possibility

Look, there he stands – the god.
Where? There. Can you not see him?
(Kierkegaard, *Philosophical Fragments*)[4]

This however, is not to say that that which remains unaddressed does not address us. Somehow it is part of reality, part of the nature of the unaddressed, to announce itself despite its proscription. After all it was Hegel who in the *Phenomenology* cautioned us that the mode of approach to an object would in part determine the way that object would present itself. If this is so, then those who claim that they have never experienced anything but their own potency and ability (or lack thereof), have perhaps failed to understand the very thing they feel so confident about – their world. For it is the claim of theology that other possibilities abound in the world for its inhabitants, possibilities that are presented to those who would care to address them. 'For the one who asks always receives; the one who searches always finds' (Matt. 7:8). If this is true then the task appears to be a simple one. Theology merely has to recover its object, discern its own sensorium and locate this dimension of objectivity in the world so that all might see it. For does not St Paul suggest that this realm is present for those that would look? Does not St Paul call for a new faculty of perception, for a subjectivity not blinded by its own potency, since for Paul at least, God 'however invisible has been there for the mind to see in the things he has made' (Rom. 1:20). Moreover, this call for a recovery of perceptual ability, for a theological aesthetics, has once again in the twentieth century found its advocates, from Von Balthasar's adherence to theological perception, to the latest works in French theology which discern a theological dimension in (or more precisely a crossing of), all phenomena as such.[5] If there are then theological modes of perception, might there also be a theological dimension to objects, present there for all to see?

Yet this perception encounters easy refusal. Those who do not see will say 'I do not see', and there seems little weight, though every importance, in asking them to look again. Self-evidently there is only so much that one can say or show to an atheist, as the atheist has already made a decision about what is possible for him, what he can know and what he cannot. Too fearful of any possible experience that lies beyond his own desire to accompany it, and claim it as his own, the atheist has already concluded that he is a natural animal with only two options. Either he must dominate nature through elevating his own subjectivity, or he must deny himself by positing his consciousness as a consequence of other less human structures, structures which it is suggested only the strong can bear to endure.

In respect of those whose only options appear to be an affirmation or denial of themselves, one experiences a strange kind of silence. A silence moreover whose dreadful acquiescence impels one to speak about it. From a theological perspective one would want to displace this whole secular oscillation, cast doubt on its self-evident ascendancy, refuse the very terms of its self-assertions and denials. And certainly there are a number of strategies available to the contemporary mind to enable at least some of these goals to be attained. Nowadays, it seems one can displace systems and cast doubt upon self-evidence without much difficulty. Yet is there not now a common feeling that these resources alone are still too weak a force to confront the present with its ownmost possibilities? These deconstructive strategies lack what Merleau-Ponty called perceptual faith (*la foi perceptive*); they do not understand the import of even the merest brush of sensation – that there is a world, and in all its paradoxical certainty it calls forth for description.[6] To lack faith in the external world, or even to doubt that there is any knowable external to the synthetic activities of the human mind, is to be complicit with the modern oscillation between subjectivity and its indifferent denial.

Scepticism may help us to displace the high edifices of modernity in all their self-sufficiency, but it can, if it affirms nothing but itself, only lead us to an even more dreadful and Gnostic immanence, a universe where indifferent and diverse principles preside over the denials that any other option might pertain. To begin (or rather to end), in scepticism, to doubt wholly the evidence of the senses, is to warp human life and hand us over to a curious form of despair. Theology must be braver than this. None the less, in the attempt to displace the secular economy, theology appears to face a curious dilemma. It seems that religion must either join forces with scepticism and doubt the foundations of atheism, thereby producing a dangerously chimerical form of worship (which finds itself allied with everything and therefore respects nothing); or, on the other hand, if theological scepticism is not endorsed, must theology commit itself to an ugly form of ontic fundamentalism regarding revealed experience? A position that would be for all those who did not care to share it a form of religious solipsism.

To think on this is perhaps to move closer to the heart of the issue. There are those who think that theology can only be defended in a negative fashion and indeed that this form of negation or doubt concerning grounds is the only discourse that will allow a theology at all. However, these theological sceptics (if I can call them that), lack a cataphasis. They lack an understanding that the *via negativa* itself requires a positum, a positum reserved for theology alone. However, this positum is not simply there as a fully replete phenomenon, it is rather more correctly conceived of as an inexhaustible plenitude and negation which expresses our inadequacy of reception (our inability that is to be equal to what we are given) and hence our need for further negation in order to ascend to an ever greater and ever more mediated account of what we have indeed been given. Negative theology requires a positive discourse about God, if, that is, this form of negation is to be recognisably about God at all. Only then can negative theology take its place in the peculiar grammar and comportment of religious affirmation.

To my mind, for these reasons, and for many others, it is necessary to be a theological 'realist'. Unfortunately however, modern philosophers and theologians who have attempted to resist scepticism in theology, who have attempted to be realists concerning God, have commonly done so by means of a 'natural theology'; that is, they have attempted to discern, or infer, the nature of God from a secular construal of the nature of the world. These natural theologians connected the realm of nature (*physis*) with the realm of God for good reasons. They wished to give to human cognition the possibility of knowing God, and since all commonly accept that we have sensible intuitions, it seemed appropriate to argue that God was capable of being known (though perhaps not comprehended), through the sensible apprehension of his effects – his creations. To attain such a correspondence between cause and effect necessitated that some term (we can leave unresolved for now what this term might be), be given in due proportion to both the Creator and his creatures in order that each could know the other. For it is a classical and cardinal point that the utterly dissimilar would have great difficulty in attaining any knowledge of one another, for mutual knowledge can only be achieved if 'like is known by like'.[7]

The crucial moment in the development of 'natural theology' (which I understand as the surrender of theology to secular reason's account of nature), seems to occur in England between the time of Henry of Ghent (1217–93) and Duns Scotus (1266–1308). Henry maintained that any knowledge held of any created thing by the human intellect is at the same time a knowledge of God. However, for Henry this apparent similarity is actually a failing of the human eye, for there are in fact two concepts of being at work. In creatures being is determinable, whereas with God His being is indeterminable. For Scotus the distinction between the two concepts was tenuous at best. In the eyes of Scotism 'the distinction between knowing God in Himself and knowing Him in a creature' was not 'the point'.[8] It was the same God who would be known. Regardless of the route taken to know Him, either you reached a knowledge of God Himself or you did not. Since Scotus in his discussion of Henry's position held 'that one thing can be known through another only by reason of the similarity existing between the two', then it will not surprise us that Scotus found Henry's distinction to require a prior unity if knowledge of God was to be possible at all.[9]

It was for this reason that Duns Scotus, when considering the universal science of metaphysics, elevated being (*ens*) to a higher station over God, so that being could be distributed to both God and His creatures. This prior discourse of being then assigns to God that mode of being appropriate for His being (infinity), and that mode of being appropriate to other beings (finitude). The rationale for this was that such an elevation was constituted in order that God could be known. As Scotus puts it in his *De Metaphysica*, which was probably written in the earliest years of the fourteenth century, 'we argued that God cannot be known naturally unless being is univocal (*univocum*) to the created and the uncreated'.[10]

This univocity of God and creature therefore marks the time when theology itself became idolatrous. For theologians had disregarded what Thomas had already warned them against, that nothing can be predicated univocally of God and other things. For Thomas in the *Summa Contra Gentiles*, that which is predicated of God can only be participated in by finite creatures via analogy. This analogical mode, whilst it accepts that we only come to have knowledge of God via His effects, understands that the reality of these effects belongs by priority to God, even though we only uncover God as the source of these effects after having experienced such effects without initially recognising their antecedent cause.[11]

It is here that I can perhaps offer the first simple remark concerning the shape of modern idolatry. For it appears that a discourse about God, philosophical or theological, is idolatrous in nature when it understands the ground of objects as being utterly synonymous, and hence exchangeable with, the ground of God. Moreover, if one wishes to say that the relationship with God is analogous to the relationship one has with an object, then unless the source of the object or the thing (*res*) is understood as lying only in God

6

then this analogy will, as Thomas pointed out, only point at some higher third entity which both God and creature will have to share as derivative terms.[12] In short, if one wishes to avoid idolatry it must be understood that God's reality has to be seen to lie at the source of any created object's reality. Which is to say that insofar as any object or thing has reality, it only does so because all reality owes its origin not to itself but to God. Ontologically this means that entities are not self-subsistent, simply existent objective things, nor are they quiescent amalgams of matter and abiding form awaiting animation and recognition by human intelligence. No, neither of these forms of realism capture the nature of things themselves, for the things themselves belong to God; they are utterly donated givens, gifts whose phenomenology is saturated with their origin in God. In this sense, theological realists have to be absolute anti-realists when discussing the very idea of any reality existing outside and apart from God. Not least because secular realism commits its adherents to the idea of a world of self-sufficient independent ontological entities whose phenomenology reflects only this. If this is true, then those theologians who claim to be realists, and who feel that the proof of the existence of God rests upon some ontic proof of an external world, lack a certain perception. They lack the recognition that ontic description fails to see the phenomenology of creation, and so forbids access to the reality of theology.

To be a realist with respect to God means that one understands that He is the source and origin of all that claims to be; correspondingly this means that every other created thing, however real it might be, is utterly contingent, relying upon Him for any substance that it might possess. Perhaps the most developed formulation of this position in Christian philosophy was that of Meister Eckhart, the fourteenth-century German Dominican. Eliding for now the internal complexity of Eckhart's position, it is worth noting that Eckhart's thesis as to the pure nothingness of creatures, endorsed as it is by the famous passage from the Johannine Prologue – 'through him all things came to be, not one thing had its being but through him' (John 1:3) – was condemned by the Papal Bull 'In agro dominico', albeit with reservation, along with some twenty-seven others on 27 March 1329.[13] For surely, the theologians of the Roman Curia argued, created beings are also in some sense something. Of course in a limited way this is true, but for Eckhart this limitedness cannot be a ground for the creature (as it will be for modernity), since for Eckhart what limits a creature forbids that creature any abiding self-sufficiency, or its origin lies beyond its own powers, in the act of donation whereby God grants creatures their being as a gift.[14]

Moreover, Eckhart is hardly alone in maintaining the singular insufficiency of creatures when they seek to maintain themselves apart from God. Aquinas writes that every 'created thing has being only from another, and considered in itself it is nothing'.[15] Indeed, in his commentary upon John, Eckhart quotes from the first book of Augustine's *Confessions*, 'existence and life flow into us from no other source Lord, than from the fact that you create us . . .

for you are the supreme existence and supreme life'.[16] Augustine himself, in seeking a distance from the Manichaean heresy, drew upon the Plotinian teaching that evil is not a power in the world, but rather a privation of the good. He wrote of *magis esse*, a plenitude of being that the soul encounters when it turns towards God and *minus esse*, a privation of being, its lessening when the soul turns away from its origin in God and risks thereby becoming nihilated (*inanescere*). For Augustine the soul that turns away from God consorts with the lowest level of bare existence, a life that leads to nothingness (*tendere ad nihilum*).

However, this understanding of the created world as insufficient in respect of itself is not to suggest that theology is coextensive with any disregard or contempt for the world. To view the created world as a donation, as a loving act of salvific providence, would hardly permit such an attitude. Conversely the fear on the part of those who wished to maintain the integrity of creatures did not derive from any concern to maintain the dignity of the creation; but rather, as I have already suggested, from the mistaken belief that if creatures were rendered wholly contingent then there would be no possibility of articulating any relationship between their arbitrariness and the (deemed) necessity of God.

I do not wish to underplay this issue for it foregrounds exactly the contemporary theological situation. As is by now no doubt obvious, I do not wish to offer either an exegesis or a history of modernity and its denial of God, rather what I would like to do is to describe the philosophical shape of the modern denial of revelation and its specific warrant. To this end I have suggested, and indeed it is one of Aquinas's more cardinal points, that one of the most consequent factors in the loss of the uniqueness of the theological warrant is the elevation after Duns Scotus of a third term over and above the relations between the Creator and His creatures. Whilst this was done in order to explain how the latter might come to know the former, has not the actual result of this been a complete erasure of God by the creature?

For instance, have we not shown that the creature, wishing to assure itself of its status, predicated something that it held as pertaining to itself, of God. Whatever the creature held, God, if He is to be God, must obviously hold more of it. If the term that was elevated above God and His creatures was 'being', then God must have an absolute plenitude of being whilst we must thus hold our derived being in diminished quantities. At first sight one sees nothing to object to here, indeed it appears somewhat classical, but we must be aware that something catastrophic has happened.

The qualitative analogical perception of God's difference from us has been supplanted by a quantitative understanding of His differentiation from us. For of course since both God and His creatures are derived from some other prior term, then the only difference between us and Him can be that God quite simply has more of what we have less of. As soon as this quantitative differentiation became conflated with power (as it does with Ockham), then we have the characteristic setting for the nominalist conjectures as to the possibility of God's malign will, and our utter defencelessness in the face of such deception. It should not surprise us then that in the wake of Duns Scotus and his univocal account of God, William of Ockham should have so stressed the power and potency of God and His lack of debt to us that God became an object of fear and trepidation for human life.[17] For once the nothingness of creatures has been figured as a lack (of power) formed in reference to a corresponding fearsome (and utterly powerful) whole, then we can already see the path to modernity's demand for human self-assertion.[18]

Self-assertion and construction

> I am an object of myself and of my representations.
> That there is something outside me is my own
> product. I make myself.
> (Immanuel Kant, *Opus Postumum*)[19]

Our description of events has now taken us to the beginning of the anthology proper. I will withhold, for the moment, my comments on the path a theology should take, in order to describe some of the more characteristic properties of modernity itself. David Rapport Lachtermann was surely correct to discern, apart from all the semantic vagaries of its meaning, a common shape to modernity. The word he chose for this shape was construction. For Lachtermann the modern marks its beginning via 'the identification of mind as essentially constructive'.[20] This identification extends beyond the recognition that in modernity the mind is thought of as being self-constituting, for the crucial aspect is that now consciousness is thought to construct the phenomenal world. For me the notion of the modern mind as essentially constructive follows from the usurpation of creation by the creature which I had previously described. It is not just that the *conatus* so conceived is necessarily self-divinising, but also that this emphasis on the constructive mind tends to eliminate any mind-independent account of ontology (a feature which helps to give modernity its characteristic immanence). Whilst I would not wish to endorse here any happy concordat between theology and an Aristotelian account of an independent though informed finite *ousia* (as in the end I think this relation tends to fall into some variant or other of natural theology). I would like to suggest that this 'mind-independent account' allows us to consider how things might present themselves if we forgo the bizarre idea of having to offer an account of ourselves before offering an account of anything else. And this situation, though pervasive, constitutes a strange inheritance, for even in that most foundational of modern texts, *The Critique of Pure Reason*, there is never a moment where Kant holds that the mind could dispense with the independence of the world. After all, the Kantian refutation of idealism depends upon the realisation that outer experience is a necessary

9

corollary for internal representations. Happily, it is precisely the structure of this attempted elimination, and reduction of ontology that concerns our first chapter.

In 'Descartes and onto-theology', Jean-Luc Marion returns to an issue that has marked much of his earlier work. To whit, how is it that with Descartes the manner of being of the ego, or rather the manner in which being most clearly presents itself to the ego, comes so utterly to supplant any other inquiry into the manner of being *qua* being. Marion discerns the origin of this absence of ontology (*néant d'ontologie*), as lying within a certain methodology: a methodology first located by him in one of Descartes's earliest works, the Rules for the Direction of the Mind, the *Regulae*. Here we find under Rule VI the demand that entities be ordered and classified not according to their own internal form, or being, but rather and only 'in accordance with the order of their clarity' in respect of the ego.[21] Once the order of natural priority passes from something which adheres in the things themselves to the ego, which will sort them according to its own standards of clarity, then Marion is surely right to suggest that 'knowledge begins when the thing (*res*) loses all essence proper to it'.

After this act of elimination Marion discerns a necessity for a reduction because the *ens philosophicum* has not been thoroughly eliminated; it still apparently admits of a residue. The ego being aptly described as *cogito me cogitare rem* (the I constituted as an I thinking itself thinking a thing), must still in some sense direct itself towards a thing even if the thing is only a thing insofar as it is viewed as such by the ego. This *res repraesenta* cannot be simply nothing; if it were, then thought would have nothing to work with. Here being (*ens*) 'indicates purely and simply the minimal object of the imaginative regard of the mind. . . . Ens retains nothing, here, of an essence or *genus* (*entis*) of the categories.' This loss of all form by *ousia* coupled with the Cartesian requirement for objectivity means that being (*ens*) is 'reduced to that, precisely, which the elimination aimed to bring out – that is, to a pure, simple empty and uniform objectivity'. This elimination of ontology as an enquiry into the meaning of the being of being, and the reduction of being to a simple empty and formless objectivity, or possibility thereof, produces what Marion calls Descartes's grey ontology (*ontologie grise*).

The question as to why this elimination of ontology occurs then provides Marion with the means to ascertain, and also perhaps to date for our epoch, an onto-theological character to modern metaphysics in this, its decisive Cartesian form. Marion locates two forms of this structure of thought in Descartes, and thus he postulates the presence of a double onto-theology. The first Marion discerns operating under the principle of thought (*cogitatio*); the second, which supersedes and encapsulates the first, is that of causality. In respect of the former he ascribes the elevated role of being *par excellence* to the ego, in the case of the latter this site is given to God.

For Marion, working within the Heideggerian rubric, onto-theology discerns that structure of thought that obliterates the difference (and now I introduce the capitalised typography) between Being and beings by seeking their twofold, asymmetrical but none the less reciprocal, unity. The encompassing side of this structure of thought is found when Being comes to ground and found all beings as such, whilst in addition, as a reversing and completing moment, those grounded beings elevate that which gave them ground to the station of the most excellent and perfect entity - an entity from which henceforth they will all consider themselves to be derived. All of which begs the question as to what allows Being to move forward in the first place and claim for itself this unique role. For Heidegger this requirement is fulfilled when God enters philosophy in the shape of the *causa sui*, that is as a cause pertaining to cause itself. But Marion is surely right to claim that it is really Descartes who first calls God by this name, and Descartes who introduces the idolatrous name of *causa sui* into philosophy's consideration of theology.

Of course, ever since Heidegger appropriated and utilised the term onto-theology, the precise etymology of the phrase and indeed its critical scope has been in debate. Heidegger himself tells us we can detect his own use of the term as early as 1929, and that its scope reaches back to the decline of philosophy in ancient Greece. However, it might be argued that when Heidegger, in Todtnauberg on the 24 February 1958, declared that the unthought unity of metaphysics lay in the relation between ontology and theology and its failure to think the difference between Being and beings, he was manifestly referring to a non-Christian, or better still, to an idolatrous philosophy. For though, 'Western metaphysics since its beginning with the Greeks has eminently been both ontology and theology', Western theology has not necessarily complied with, nor endorsed, the relationship between theology and ontology that Heidegger goes on to describe as 'onto-theological'.[22] Prior to God entering philosophy under the name of *causa sui* (and here I agree with Marion's argument that the *causa sui* did not enter philosophy as the decisive thought of God until Descartes), I would suggest that theology was not necessarily onto-theological in the Heideggerian sense, even if we can already see the preparation of the ground for the *causa sui* from Scotus onwards.

In Heidegger's account of onto-theology, if I read it correctly, Being approaches being in order to give to being its ground (*ergründen*). On the other hand beings account for (*begründen*) Being by elevating Being to the highest station – Being *par excellence*. Now if *gründen* governs (as Heidegger tells us that it does) the relationship between *ergründen* and *begründen* then a relation appears to dominate the configuration of onto-theology that theology itself would call idolatrous. Configuring the characteristically double and crossed relation of onto-theology through ground and elevation, whilst pertinent in cases of secular metaphysics, is I would suggest, absolutely unrecognisable in any (properly conceived) theological relationship that pertains between the giving of Being and its acceptance and acknowledgement (or not) by beings.

For it seems as though the onto-theological nature of metaphysics falls, although not neatly, at least somewhat squarely, into a position that we have already rejected for theology! I have already suggested that the relationship between ontology and theology cannot be one of foundation or ground (*gründen*). For theology there can be no self-sufficient account of any ontological entity whatsoever; there can be no wholly grounded entity, as everything comes from God, the eminent source of all reality and all entities whatsoever. Moreover, have we not already denounced the idea that any term can function so as to found the relationship between God and his creatures other than what He Himself gives – and let us be absolutely clear, God certainly, and most of all, does not give us ground.[23] The relationship then that pertains for theology with respect to ontology must be one of absolute superiority. By this I mean that theology is the discourse about the origin of being. For this reason ontology cannot account for theology; ontology can offer no discourse as to its own origin. Being will always, as Heidegger himself noted, find itself already there, already distributed in beings. Being is not accessible except through beings. Just as Hegel was never actually able to buy fruit itself; that is, he was unable to purchase a fruit that was not also an apple or a pear, so ontology will never be able to grasp Being apart from beings.[24] Ontology, as Aristotle himself acknowledged, can never grasp or account for Being in its most general (and most specific) form; such a horizon is quite simply beyond its scope. For it is here that ontology, unable to give an account of the ground of its own system of classification, betrays itself, as it must, to a theological account of its origin.

Just as ontology cannot ask for foundation from theology, theology must utterly refuse to give ground to ontology. If ontology is the discourse of being *qua* being, an investigation of being in its most general and universal form, then without God, I would suggest, it is a discourse that cannot grasp its own essence. The undoubted profundity and weight of a secular ontology will consist only in its perpetual marking of aporias and paradoxes. For only theology can give an account of these disjunctures that allows thinking to move beyond them. Just as the opening lines of Genesis can be read so as to place God before the act of creation that brought about individuated beings, so the opening lines of the Gospel of St John give the presence of the Father and the Son (begotten and not made), before anything else came to be. The New Testament is on this point unequivocal; being (being in general; *ens commune* as Aquinas termed it) did not precede, nor is it equiprimordial, with the Most High. Because theology precedes ontology, ontology must always be open, non-immanent, or indeed aporetic. To suggest this is to maintain that the path to a fundamental ontology leads, if properly followed, to the transcendent and nowhere else, or to argue that what is fundamental to ontology is not its own modes of self-presencing and concealment, but prior modes which it assumes and ignores: the modes of 'creation *ex nihilo*'.

But let me try to make these points more specific. Why is it antithetical to theology to hold that finite entities are self-sufficient? The answer to this question is perhaps best illustrated via a focus on the second figure that concerns us: that of Immanuel Kant. Kant concerns us because he more than anyone else sought to secure a finite realm wherein a cognitively self-sufficient sphere could be articulated that would make possible knowledge. Now let me say first of all that the Kantian division between sensibility and the understanding, between the impingement of the external world and the space of rationality, suggests that Kant never endorsed the idea, let alone the possibility, of a fully immanent self-sufficient cognition. None the less, and here I follow Max Scheler and Merleau-Ponty, for Kant sensibility seems never to have any role other than to deliver over an acquiescence of the empirical domain to the human mind. For though Kant separated cognition into spontaneity and sensibility, he always sought to show that sensibility had conceptual content.[25] Indeed the only way Kant could hope to secure the possibility of knowledge was by unifying the divide between receptivity and spontaneity through the use of the transcendental a priori. This ideality was inserted behind all empirical manifestation, with the additional Copernican provision that all empirical appearances (if they wish to become known), conform with this prior requirement. The Kantian reformation of the empirical world would not necessarily be a cause for theological concern, if God had not been at first banished from, and *only then* thought through this atheistic account of sensibility.

For it is at this juncture, with *The Critique of Pure Reason*, that theological knowledge finds its own possibility prohibited. From the side of sensibility, transcendental knowledge – so conceived – is conditioned knowledge, for it is wholly conditional upon empirical sensibility conforming to the ideality of the a priori. God, being of course absolutely unconditional, is thereby proscribed from human sensibility. One would think though that God could be saved through reason, that the intellect could at least accept the necessity of a necessary being. It is Kant's secular genius both to accept the practical necessity of this belief and yet deny us a concept of God that would have any import for experience: in Kant the concept of God is empty, since there is no empirical intuition that could provide its content. For even though reason when it separates itself from sensibility, and flies above the senses, seeks a being fully realised as to all its possibilities, a supreme being – an *ens realissimum* – this idea, or more precisely ideal, constitutes a transcendent violation of transcendental philosophy. Though we can think it we can never know such a being as it has no correlate in experience. Pure thought cannot produce real objects: as Kant writes, 'all existential propositions are synthetic'.[26]

For Kant – the ideality of a priori knowledge notwithstanding – human cognition is such that we require a union between spontaneity and receptivity to produce knowledge. God, having been denied existential import, is transferred to the status of a mere regulative idea for practical (and to a lesser extent scientific), reason. As an empty formal horizon for a universal ethics, God assumes the only mantle left for Him. He becomes a merely 'sublime' phenomenon for a self-sufficient subject that has no genuine cognitive requirements in respect of anything external to itself.

However, this was not Kant's intention. For surely he sought to 'make room for *faith* [*Glaube*]'.[27] As Howard Caygill points out, 'faith is not cast as the affective antithesis to knowledge'. Finding a parallel between the antinomy of faith, in *Religion within the Limits of Reason Alone*, and the antinomy of judgement as to the sublime and the beautiful in *The Critique of Judgement*, Caygill recasts Kant's theology in terms of the latter distinction. If this antinomy of faith (its retrospective mode of loss and restitution, and its prospective economy of life-giving pleasure) rests upon the earlier conceived antinomy of judgement, then the question for us to ascertain is whether God is thought by Kant through the figure of the sublime or the form of the beautiful? Caygill quite rightly points to a certain hesitation in the *Third Critique*, where Kant, unable to decide between these two modes of judgement, develops both.[28]

This hesitation is crucial, as it suggests that Kant's earlier denial of God to sensibility was a cause of subsequent regret. For the empirical world by the time of the *Third Critique* is the site of both the sublime and the beautiful. If indeed it was the *First Critique* that determined God as having no existential manifestation, at least not one that was capable of being taken up by the understanding, then God readmitted in the *Third Critique*, through the figure of the beautiful, seems to give Himself to the world of sense. This would seem to suggest that after the *Critique of Pure Reason*, Kant appears to have realised that his privileging of subsumptive judgement precludes any discernment of the transcendent. In subsequent works one can detect an attempt to limit the potency and range of subsumptive judgement, or at the very least bring it into a less antagonistic relationship with the desire to discriminate with equity. This perhaps can be attested, as Caygill points out, via a concern expressed in the *Lectures on Ethics* for a forgotten accord between judgements as to the sublime and those as to the beautiful. The accord finds itself present in the *Third Critique* as a perfected judgement, wherein there is an 'attunement' (*stimmung*) between the interests of subsumption and those of discrimination. This attunement reaches its fullest expression only in the encounter with beauty. Immanent to judgement, this 'contemporaneity of the kingdom' expresses itself via a disengagement with the logic of the sublime. Here for Kant the beautiful is now no longer thought under the aegis of the understanding. As a form of sensibility it has freed itself from the categories, expressing itself apart from concepts and their felt content; the beautiful is cognised without being subsumed by the understanding. Now beauty brings with it a form which though not created by us, finds itself, as Kant writes, 'preadapted to our judgement', whereas the sublime does 'violence to the imagination'.[29]

The sublime, though it has its corollaries in the external world in the sense of might and measure, does not, like the beautiful, have its source there, 'for no sensible form can contain the sublime'.[30] The source of the sublime does not lie in external objects, but originates rather within the sphere of rationality with the ideas of reason. It is of course wholly in line with our immanentist charge against Kant that that which exceeds the understanding should in fact not be anything sensible, but rather something immanent to rationality. This follows since for Kant the sublime functions so as to bring any sensible form which might escape the purview of the understanding back under the sway of the a priori. In this way the feeling of the sublime in nature 'makes intuitively evident the superiority of the rational determination of our cognitive faculties to the greatest faculty of our sensibility'.[31] The sublime figured in this way is the final denial of the transcendent; a denial that Kant had argued for as early as the *First Critique* when he denied God to us via a refutation of the ability of the most high to preserve His form in sensibility.[32] Now through the sublime, even though we are presented in intuition with forms that exceed our own (a situation that perhaps ought to initiate reflection on dependency and participation), we are told that this experience is 'like an abyss' in which the imagination 'fears to lose itself'.[33] This situation provokes a return to an account of our own greater potency where the sublime in nature becomes inverted into a 'respect for our own destination'.[34] And it is in this form that one could suggest that the Kantian theory of the sublime completes the secular dismissal of God from the realm of experience. Conceived in this way, the sublime then provides a uniquely successful synthesis of both the nominalist fear of God and the Scotist emphasis on a prior and determinate sphere of knowledge (an emphasis that actually ends with the dismissal of God from cognition). The peculiar though understandable result of all this is that God becomes both unknowable and yet deeply feared.

Earlier I had asked, why is it antithetical to theology to hold that finite entities are self-sufficient? Or better still, why is it inappropriate for theology to accept the idea of a cognitively self-sufficient finitude? In many ways the answer is obvious: a self-sufficient finitude denies itself any relationship with infinity; a self-sufficient account of an entity would seem to deny any need to give an account of God. But leaving these and other responses aside, it seems to me, at least, that the true risk of such a position goes something like this. Anyone who wishes to hold on to a finite account of cognition, in short anyone who would hold to a secular epistemology, will recognise, to use the Hegel of *Glauben und Wissen*, 'something higher above itself from which it is self-excluded'.[35] This situation (whether acknowledged or not) has produced in all subsequent secular thought a relationship with the higher which can perhaps only be described as sublime.

The pejorative import of this claim applies because it seems that secular thought cannot, despite its best efforts, dispense with the higher possibilities of transcendence. Whether this is because any attempt to offer an egalitarian ontology seems hopelessly relativistic if not counter-intuitive, it is a characteristic of these late modern times that when most secular political, social and philosophical movements seek to legitimise themselves they seek to embrace that which transcends them. Of course they cannot fully embrace or accept the transcendent, not least as this would invalidate the secular world picture which it is their task to establish. But still, to echo Hegel, they recognise that they require, at the very least, the appearance of a higher external warrant. Now whilst the earlier account of onto-theology might have explained the form that this mutated relationship with the higher might take, it does not perhaps explain the potency of the idolatrous phenomenology that is operative here. Because the impact of the transcendent must be constrained so that it does not shatter the attempts to appropriate it, the secular attempt to deploy the higher on behalf of the lower repeats of course the construction and form of onto-theology. Yet the previous account of onto-theology does not by itself explain why this idolatrous structure is able to hold such a sway over its participants. What is required is an account of the phenomenology that this structure licenses and issues forth. If onto-theology acts so as to initiate a crossed and reciprocal account of mutual foundations, then it appears that the sublime as an idolatrous form perhaps best explains how the nature of this relation is concealed from its participants. For whilst sublimity claims to deliver the experiences from which finite life has self-excluded itself, the encounter with these experiences only returns the secular to itself as the sublime is, in reality, not an encounter with the truly transcendent but an error of subreption, a reflex of finite thought which can only project the beyond as a negative image of its own (self) limitation.

As a consequence, one can sense the difficulty in ever unmasking the sublime as an idolatrous rather than transcendent form. Indeed, as an idolatrous form it has a double potency. The sublime delivers what is taken to be, for modernity, the transcendent experience *par excellence*, the congruence of terror and vacuity. This experience fulfils the demands of finite self-sufficiency by delivering the legitimation of an external encounter, with, however, the immanentist shape of this encounter being both concealed and completed (and perhaps even secured), when the sublime experience is returned to the thought which undergoes it.[36] I do not pretend that the sublime is the only idolatrous shape that has currency in the world, nor do I think that the sublime is necessarily and for all time an idolatrous form. However, in terms of its function within this context, the sublime reveals itself in much of what I see as idolatrous in modern thought, and thus it remains for my purposes suitably indicative.

If the origin of the sublime in Kant can be located in Kant's sundering of thought from reality, then perhaps I would not be mistaken if I suggested that it was the hope of Hegelianism that thought could be reconciled with reality and thereby also with the absolute. As such Hegel offers an alternative way to recover transcendence from 'subjectivism and formal thinking'.[37] In the words of Rowan Williams, this aspect of Hegel's thought produces 'a trust in the thinkable (and thus reconcilable) character of reality'. But this reconciliation, this convergence of the universal and the particular, is not the act of cognitive finality that it is often taken to be. On the contrary, to reconcile oneself with the absolute is 'to enter into an infinite relatedness'. For Williams, Hegel is less the thinker who elides otherness, than he is the thinker who dissolves the finite self-sufficiency of perceptions and isolated objects, in order to move thought beyond the diversity (and antagonism), of the merely contingent, into a relationship of complementary otherness. A relationship that since it refuses the finite, is already in commerce with the absolute through its motion towards reconciliation with infinite otherness.

Williams gives a radical and brilliant theological reading of this motion of dialectic and power. For him Hegelian understanding (*Verstand*) is God's goodness. This goodness is marked by thinking a thing not in abstraction, but rather in and through its self-defining uniqueness. This particularity however is superseded by the dialectic and 'dialectic is what theology means by the power of God'. The dialectic provides the means to transcend particularity and ascend to its greater, or rather its more elevated source. For, as Williams shows, Hegel's theological skill lies in his refusal to allow any discrete predicates to stand solely for God. God cannot be simply reduced to this goodness or that beauty – rather Hegel shapes his theology around the greater truth – that of God's self-relatedness, simplicity and indivisibility.

At first sight, to think God in these terms suggests that the world is collapsed into divine self-relation, that somehow God stands apart from the world and negates its complexity into His divine simplicity. But Williams uses the doctrine of the Trinity to show how Hegel thinks God's self-relation and his relation to the world as wholly inseparable from each other. Furthermore, Williams links this Trinitarian grammar with the Christian doctrine of love, and he uses this to show that when Hegel thinks of God, he does so within the classic theological economy of Father, Son and Spirit. This Trinitarian economy of love has 'no remainder' – there is no unmediated God standing over and apart from the world He created. Indeed, to say that God is love is to say, in Hegelian terms, that God is not thinkable apart from His relation to the world. For Hegel this Trinitarian economy has already been accomplished by history. It has already happened on earth and the task of mental life is to achieve full consciousness of what has already occurred. As a result, in contra-distinction to Kant, Hegel held that God was no abstract and unknowable deity. The reconciliation between humanity and the absolute had already been achieved, in history, with the incarnation of Christ and his subsequent path to Calvary.

Obviously, there is much to celebrate here. There is a fidelity to the reality of the Christian narrative, a rendering of God as one who affirms the ultimately reconcilable aspects of all that will occur to human life, and an emphasis on discerning a Trinitarian grammar in the dialectic between God and man. In many ways a Christian thinker, or rather a thinker who would bear fidelity to the nature of the Christ event, must endorse this. What has happened, what is happening, demands nothing less. Indeed, how could it be otherwise?

However, I would like to draw back a little from such an affirmation. Not because I disagree with any of what has been outlined here, but really because it seems that a true Trinitarian grammar requires something more. For is it not the case that the Trinity is futural and not teleological, since surely our participation in it has no end or finality. For me the inexhaustibility of the Trinity, its infinity, requires that being (and it need not necessarily be being, it could be beauty or goodness) is not fully exhausted in being known, not even in being known as infinite negation. And for Hegel what is not known does not matter. Another way of putting this is that *God cannot be exhausted by being known*. To suggest that He is, to maintain that that which stands apart from our thinking cannot be thought, is to risk, despite all the protestations to the contrary, reducing God to the level and shape of our own mental life. To avoid a simple immanentism such a position would have to claim that mental life can indeed come to a full knowledge of the absolute without constructing that absolute, as the absolute has already fully actualised itself in history. Since God does not stand apart from us, He stands for Hegel as already fully present and historically completed. Human cognition, rather than constructing this objectivity, has merely to come to an awareness of it being already existent. In this sense mental life is not futural, and as Williams points out for Hegel, 'we can't think necessity forwards without falling into fantasy'. But to base a religious life on this is to have a theology without a future. For human life would be denied the possibility of the new, the promise of renewal. Though a certain type of immanentism is avoided by making knowledge of God a retrospective matter for the mind (a position that has the advantage of denying the mind any constructive power over God), another immanentist shape is restored by reducing God to all that the human mind can retrospectively acknowledge. This adequation of God and history has two undesirable consequences: mental life is forced to acknowledge what should never be acknowledged, and the mind is denied any possibility of its own reversal, or more precisely any possibility of its own futurity. For Christianity, all that has occurred in history, all the satanic negations of human life, all the death and crushed possibility, is not a negative that can be turned into a positive (and here I make a Christian reading of Bataille's critique of Hegel), but is rather the utter privation and nothingness that I spoke of earlier. The Christian response to these events is that they are not the final word. They have no defining role in theology. For there are some events, some death events, that one should never be reconciled with. And what is Christianity if it is not this, this refusal to accept death. And what is the message of the New Testament, all the discussion of sin and *metanoia*, of reversal and mercy and resurrection, if it is not the possibility of a future which is not dictated by any need to assume the wickedness of what has passed. The promise and hope of the new rests upon both an acceptance (as we shall go on to show with Kierkegaard), and also a refusal of what has passed.

But this religious refusal of simple historical objectivity seems to introduce an unavoidable evaluative and judgemental aspect to the religious problematic. I have pursued religious objectivity and yet I now find that its actualisation requires some sort of contribution from its human participants. This is to say that suddenly in my pursuit of the objective dimension of theology we find ourselves in the realm of the subjective. For we have found ourselves talking of futurity, of upholding what might be possible against what is actual. And it seems that this critique of what is simply existent requires the consideration of certain unavoidably subjective dimensions. For in selecting one possibility over another we will abruptly find it necessary to speak of issues like orientation, judgement and recognition. Leaving aside for now the question as to whether this realm would invalidate the universality that we seek, a more pressing question asserts itself. How would it be possible to bear fidelity to the subjective dimension of theology, the nature of theology as a possibility, a possibility that in a certain sense is a choice, without losing theology by reducing this occasion to a mere caprice of happy contingency – an understanding that would destroy theology by conceiving it as just one option amongst many.

Kierkegaard means to negotiate this traverse. Ontologically he offers us no easy conciliation; the world is such that everything is both unique and arbitrary. Each event stands in no necessary relation to any other. There is only the differential play of contingent series upon contingent series, of singular events upon differential moments. Whilst this world appears to invite and make possible every inclination of secular interpretation, such an arbitrary universe does not appear ontologically to allow any religious account which privileges providence over chance. Fortunately however, we are provided with an ingenious reading of how Kierkegaard accepts this sceptical situation and yet still manages to affirm a religious metaphysic.[38] None the less, it often seems as though Kierkegaard's solutions are, as John Milbank points out in respect of repetition, 'chronically aporetic'. Indeed Kierkegaard acknowledged that evil and error can be repeated along with the good and the true.[39] Yet as Milbank attests, for Kierkegaard this 'abyss can be traversed by a decision'. And it is in the character of this decision that for Milbank Kierkegaard's path away from sceptical atheism lies.

Repetition, the stance that the subject takes amidst the differential indifference of the world, confers a radical sense of possibility on the individual that practises it. It is genuinely futural in that its account of human possibility rests on its account of human origin. A point Kierkegaard himself makes: 'the dialectic of repetition is easy, for that which is repeated has been – otherwise it could not be repeated – but the very fact that it has been makes the repetition into something new'.[40] Yet repetition as a response to the seeming indifference of time is not simply Nietzsche's eternal return foretold. It is not the return of the same together with the knowledge of this fact, nor is it the simply new. The peculiar character of repetition lies rather in its affirmation of what has been and its orientation as to what might be. The orientation and fidelity to what has been (the incarnation for example), corrects the pagan demand for the simply new. And this is where repetition distinguishes itself from any secular performative. Secular minds might indeed embrace repetition out of some sort of frustrated hope for finite consistency. For the late moderns this need to embrace hope stems from the failure of their own antecedents to establish a secular sphere within which human projects could find their truth. Having turned away from any soteriology associated with the object, those who nowadays profess themselves to be agnostic cannot embrace any idealism, as their own critiques now find no rest or comfort there. As a consequence, in many works of today, one can find, in one shape or other, essays concerning hope. Yet what can those whose futurity rests only with hope do? As they have no anterior faith in what has preceded them, they can affirm nothing but the new as utterly new. This relationship to the new is therefore both violent and false, because each time the new arrives it loses its value the moment it is accepted.[41] Like a token of some terrible pagan religion, the new conceived in this way demands the abasement and sacrifice of all that has previously been for the sake of what might be. As Kierkegaard writes, 'hope is a beckoning fruit that does not satisfy'. Or again, 'Who would want to be a tablet on which time writes something new every instant. . . . Who would want to be susceptible to every fleeting thing, the novel, which always enervatingly diverts the soul anew?'[42] Differentiating itself through what it affirms, separating itself from those who refuse to share its assumptions, repetition avoids being appropriated by the secular. For by blessing what has been ('repetition is the daily bread that satisfies with blessing') there is no need to deny the past in the search for some new experience or encounter.[43] Yet this past fidelity confers on the individual a genuine futurity because the maintenance of a consistent past for the 'subject' gives this figure consistency, repetition gives this 'subjectivity' as performance – the promise of a future. In this way a 'just proportion' between time and eternity is maintained as a figure for the human, a form which repeats the similar wager made by Christ. And in the emphasis on subjective decision in the name of what has been and what will be, Kierkegaard outlines the anterior priority of the figure of faith. It is this very prioricity which distinguishes repetition from other movements and charts the path back for the subject to what is ownmost for it – the solicitude that the most singular has with the most high. A situation, where at the end of *Fear and Trembling*, 'the single individual stands in an absolute relation to the absolute', as an absolutely unique yet utterly dependent creature.[44] Yet this decision is only possible because of God. The creature cannot will the results of repetition, a prior commitment of love must actually be there for repetition to repeat it. This is not just the abstract postulation of a 'pre-established harmony' by an individual, a subjective meta-narrative; if it were simply this there could be no healing of anxiety by faith. And faith is able to do this because, once again in Milbank's words, 'faith is not a decision but a gift'. For Kierkegaard, 'repetition is and remains a transcendence', because it repeats the actual giving of the gift of the Son, a fact which can never be appropriated to immanence as immanence is not capable of understanding 'the gifts that he has given us' 1 Cor. 2:13.[46]

On theological vision

It seems to be a general pretence of the unthinking herd that they cannot see God.

    (Bishop Berkeley, *Principles of Human Knowledge*)[47]

When your eye is sound, your whole body too is filled with light; but when it is diseased your body too will be all darkness.

    (Luke 11:34)

In the opening to this introduction I described the peculiar phenomenology of the current age, its happy disjuncture of objectivity from subjectivity and its indifferent oscillation between immanentist materialism and transcendental agency. Indeed I have already discerned within this movement, with its loss of faith in the highest human possibility, the shape of a nihilism that completes itself with the belief in the death of God; moreover, the account of this situation will be deepened when we enter Michel Haar's reading of Nietzsche. However, due to the demands of both exigency and space I cannot proceed down the line of figures presented in the anthology in the manner of a disinterested exegesis. Up to this juncture I have already articulated various reservations and refusals, and by so doing I have uncovered a position that can only be described as theological. As this account is one that I will maintain in respect of the subsequent developments in twentieth-century philosophy that the anthology goes on to describe, it may well be more appropriate at this point to become even more explicit about my own position.

In my efforts to discern God and recover Him for human cognition, I described the results of His erasure from human experience. In addition, I contended that this deletion was a result of the endorsement by modernity of various conceptual and perceptual configurations, arrangements whose adoption in the name of clarity has initiated an astonishing regime of human self-mutilation and blindness. I have sought to disengage from these understandings, arguing that they conceal the manifestation of transcendence. To this end I thought that there should be an attempt to recover the theological sensorium (or theological 'objectivity' if you will), from a world-picture that does not acknowledge it. However, in this approach I have learnt that any account which seeks to recover God from objective denial cannot dispense with the realm of the subjective. For though I have been pursuing the objective dimension of theology as a means to escape from both transcendentalism and immanentism, we have now begun to realise that any attempt to recover God's 'objectivity' for human experience requires an approach that is quite different from that required to rescue the objectivity of any ontic object. For God's objectivity is not the same as any secular object and so does not stand over and against human subjectivity as some ultra-real entity whose potency dissolves our own. Indeed, though I had spoken of a theological realism, we had to immediately distinguish this from the disastrous secularisation of realism by natural theology and idolatry. For there is no onto-theological communality between the realm of the Creator and that of His creatures. As the Creator does not offer our world a foundation in order to elevate Himself above it, it would be ill-advised to seek to account for Him in this manner. Indeed, many of my criticisms of secular realism have and will centre on the recognition that the world cannot provide its own foundations.

However, what path could possibly allow us to proceed further on this issue? How can we embrace a theological realism without falling into a purely ontic account of the real? For whilst it is a profound error to put the reality of the world and that of God on the same plane, this is not to say that God and the world do not have reality, nor is it to say that human cognition is necessarily denied access to either of these dimensions. If the error of natural theology lies in the attempt to know God from a nature initially cognised apart from God, then one path immediately suggests itself. If we unknow nature, that is if we give up trying to offer accounts of nature that serve only to confirm knowledge of ourselves, then we might perhaps see the relation between God and nature in a new light. Now though it is hardly a new path against the pretensions of human mental life to propose an orientation towards empiricism, I would suggest that the experience of a thing does not reduce the thing, or its existent possibilities, to my sensation of it. It is here that we can begin to get a sense of how immanentism might be avoided and a perception of how something else becomes possible. As I have said before, it is the first brush of sensation that teaches us that cognition might not be a wholly mind-dependent affair. As G.E. Moore put it, 'there is, therefore, no question of how we are to "get outside the circle of our own ideas and sensations." Merely to have a sensation is already to be outside that circle.'[47] Now even though Moore may have gone on to defend common sense and deny certain forms of argumentation that sought to maintain that reality was spiritual, thereby unfortunately giving credence to Hegel's claim as to the emptiness of sense certainty, he none the less reveals for me my task.[48] For if an empiricism is the best stage upon which to deny the foundational pretensions of the modern mind, then it might also be the best platform from which to divest the more insidious, and recently revived, secular accounts of the

real. If the secular account of mental life (transcendentalism) has been superseded in certain quarters by a revitalised secular account of both the mental
and material world (immanentism) then the terrain has shifted and a revived
materialism should be combatted not by a self-satisfied conceptual theology
but by a theological account of the real. What is being suggested here is that
if cognition and perception can be disengaged from their ontic approaches to
reality, then nature itself might suddenly show itself as the created spiritual
reality which it is. Whilst it is not unusual to use an empiricism to deny knowledge, it is perhaps rarer for this to be done in order to affirm theology. For I
still have to show why this orientation leads to a revitalised account of God
and not to a revitalised account of nature. In spite of this it seems at least
that we have grasped the gravity of the issue, for if human life is to ascertain
that higher actualities are possible for it, then these promises must not be lost
but placed before human perception so that all might see what it is possible
to become.

Heidegger writes 'higher than actuality stands *possibility*' (*Höher als die
Wirklichkeit steht die Möglichkeit*).[49] This statement stands in a peculiar alliance
with the position that I have been attempting to describe.[50] For me the existent secular world has to be revealed as an illusory actuality that denies its
own possibility. On the empirical stage in the realm of perception this means
that theology has to show how the experience of actuality, the experience of
common existence (*Wirklichkeit*), can be displaced and exceeded by a religious mode of perception (*Wahrnehmung*).[51] But by positioning ourselves
against atheist actuality in the name of perceptual possibility, we break with
the idea that there can ever be a secular foundational account of reality.
Now though I agree with Berkeley's opposition to 'sceptics and atheists',
and though I will for instance focus on an account of vision in order to deny
immanentist materialism, the matter will not be resolved by simply claiming
to see God.[52] I have not advocated a critique of secular positivism in order to
become a positivist about theological perception; theology cannot simply
replace secular objectivity with its own supplanted variant. In this respect
the account I will offer will differ from most accounts of phenomenological
transcendence. It will not be a question of elevating one phenomenon over
another but of a focus on phenomena as such. As a consequence, there will be
no endorsement of the suffering human face as there is in Levinas, no opposition of an iconic as opposed to an idolatrous manifestation as there is in some
of Marion's work, nor will the phenomena of the most high be experienced
as an encounter with the absolute in all its supremacy as in Scheler.[53] No one
phenomenon will be put forward as the sole vehicle of transcendence. If it
were, then religion would simply be the ugly ontic fundamentalism that its
detractors (and unfortunately some of its advocates) allege it to be. In this
respect human beings are not passive in the face of higher phenomena; any
higher cognition requires human perceptual activity as higher cognition
calls us to fulfil and recognise our own form. My focus on phenomena then

speaks to the Trinitarian harmonic that theological perception can initiate, and this harmonic with its focus on mutual joy, solicitude and love calls human beings to participation in the possibilities that God as the highest reality gives and donates to human life, an activity that is unrecognisable by any mere human passivity in the face of ultimate experience.

Any simplistic adequation between perception and secular objectivity must be rejected for another reason. *Percipi* (perception) cannot equal *esse* (being) because, as I have long argued, modern ontology cannot provide the model for theology as it cannot be the equal of theology. Earlier I had argued that ontology rests on theology, that ontology has no account of its origins and that only theology can offer this original narrative. If in terms of the contemporary world I am focusing on perception to suggest that we can – as it were – see through ontology to theology, and if modernity only provides us with a secular account of ontology, then for our purposes we cannot make this modern idolatrous account of *esse* equal to all our possible perceptions of it – because quite simply we see beyond secular *esse*. Since, if we can have theological perceptions (and I believe we do), it would repeat the error of natural theology to frame theological perceptions within the terms of the perception of the modern accounts of *esse*. To put this more clearly, I have chosen to speak of theology as a higher possibility for human life (a possibility that is of a greater reality), and I maintained that this possibility is not a conceptual abstraction but a phenomenal appearance of a genuine higher reality. Now to elevate human cognition such that one can see these possibilities over and above any construction of secular actuality means that these perceptions should no longer be equated with the idolatrous reality that they rise above. One can certainly concede to secular vision its 'truth', as perception can see that which is simply existent. But one may also contemplate the thought that a higher possibility may supervene on this onlic certainty, in this sense *percipi* is more then *esse* because quite simply the existent construction of modern *esse*, its brute objective idolatrous facticity, does not determine all of *esse*'s corporeal possibilities. To say this is to suggest conversely that modern secular objectivity was always wrong about its construal of *esse*, it is to say that *esse* always offers more possibilities to sight than any secular attempts to objectify it as a godless materiality. Which is to say that perception sees more than self-sufficient being, because beings themselves show more than self-sufficiency.

Of course, to hold this position is already to depart from secular actuality. Perhaps only now have I begun to write theologically. For in many ways one cannot understand theology, or rather faith, until one embraces it. Faith gives over its content after one has already become faithful. Or as Paul puts it, 'faith leads to faith' (Rom. 1:17). If this is true, then our inquiry moves to the possibility of a higher phenomenology because we have become faithful to its promise. This promise is not abstract but actual; when one embraces the higher possibilities of faith the higher potentialities of perception become manifest. One suddenly discerns that this conjunction of perception and faith discloses a world whose origin lies beyond itself. However, before one attempts any description of this situation one requires some new vocabulary. I will speak of the *visible* and the *invisible*, not only because these terms have already had some deployment in contemporary work on phenomenology and theology, but because they speak to the current perceptual situation. The contemporary secular gaze can only discern the visible adumbration of the given. Since it approaches the visible universe as a subject approaches its object, the secular gaze objectifies the visible world into its ontic possession and yet it will – in a moment of sublimity – doubt the veracity of this external objectified phenomena without the presence of its unifying consciousness. For it will look into the heart of phenomena and partially glimpse the truth – that there is no possibility of secular knowledge there. However, as I have said, this experience of sublimity functions so as to give the illusion of threatening externality, whilst in reality it actually only engenders for the perceiver an ever-greater internal stability. As a result, when looking at the visible a point of security will be found for the secular gaze and its doubt will pass. An ontic account of reality will then be advocated, the world will be secured, gold will once more be seen as gold and even trees will be allowed to fall in forests without anyone hearing them. For such approaches the higher dimensions of the visible world are quite simply invisible, not even recognised nor aimed at by subjective intention. Which perhaps is why Jean-Luc Marion coins the phrase *invisable* (a play on the negation of the French verb *viser* which means to aim at or intend) to describe this precipitation off and separation of the invisible from the visible and its subsequent denial to sight by the secular gaze.[54] In truth, however, the invisible is not separable from the visible; in fact (and here I get ahead of myself), the visible is but a dimension of invisibility and indeed the very clarity of the visible world rests upon the profiles and adumbrations of this higher discernible.[55]

In *Le Visible et l'invisible*, Merleau-Ponty moves to a point where he also phenomenologically acknowledges the presence of the invisible in visibility. Like Berkeley, Merleau-Ponty distances himself from conceptual abstraction, yet he does not denounce the reality of immanent bodies, since for him transcendence is not a departure from the world but an immersion in it. For Merleau-Ponty pursued the *esse* of the phenomenal world in the phenomenal world, and in this pursuit of immanent sensibility he determined the world to be 'one body' or flesh (*chair*), a body moreover whose being (*esse*) grants to the things themselves (*les choses elles-mêmes*) the plenitude of always being more than the look which perceives them.[56] Yet in the heart of this immanent world the perceiver is not absorbed by its flesh. The individuated human maintains itself: in all its singularity, even as it is incorporated by the generality of the sensible in-itself (*sensible en soi*) the perceiving body is a sensible for-itself (*sensible pour soi*). This generality of being constitutes the flesh of the world from which individuated beings segregate and singularise themselves in a reciprocal and reversible fashion. The world flesh then is unlimited (*illimité*) and as the most terminal notion (*une notion dernière*) it sustains all subsequent beings who derive their corporeality and singularity from it.[57] Now, the general and specific visibility that Merleau-Ponty describes seems at first sight the most specific and compelling picture of a phenomenology that has been led to immanentism and not transcendence. Its strength lies in the fact that here we find no easy absorption of the world into a transcendental subject but rather an immanentism that does not consume singularity but claims to give rise to it. If secular perception was correct, then we could never on this model see more than this immanent universe sustaining itself via its own internal acts of individuation.

Yet this Deleuzian settlement does not satisfy Merleau-Ponty; for him such a description is not true to the phenomena of the world. If flesh (*chair*) is the sustaining midpoint for Merleau-Ponty between the individual and the ideal it does not explain why ideality seeks to consummate itself in singularized lived reality. For Merleau-Ponty begins to discern in the heart of all this massing of corporeality, a disjuncture between the 'subject' and the 'objective world'. The irreducible distance between 'my flesh' and the world begins to speak to him of a second visibility (*une visibilité seconde*), a form of visibility that accompanies the massiveness of flesh such that it grants to this flesh the possibility of being a specific body not a Being-in-general but a particular living being; as such this second visibility reveals itself to be not a 'second positivity' of the flesh but rather the invisible ideality that shapes formless matter and makes it into a body, a something as opposed to a nothing, a glorified body (*un corps glorieux*) created out of the massiveness of indifferent Being-in-general.[58] This discernment brings with it the consequent implication of an order which is higher than that of mere immanence. He sees in the heart of immanence that which will forever forbid visibility from believing itself to be the only description of the world; he sees what makes a world the higher order of the invisible.

This higher order or ideal is for Merleau-Ponty not an absolute invisible (*qui n'aurait rien à faire avec le visible*) cut off from this world; on the contrary it is 'the invisible *of* this world'.[60] This ideality comes to the immanence of flesh, giving it all its dimensions, axes and depths. In earlier times the concept would claim this ideal role in respect of empirical content, but for Merleau-Ponty this concept is not an abstract formulation of the mind but a carnal presence in the body; as a form this presence enshrines itself in all singularised beings, indeed it is what allows these beings to assume their individuated natures in the first place. Merleau-Ponty surmised that this ideal was perhaps the animating presence of the intelligible in corporeal life. Indeed, the contemporary pathos of the non-sensate concept, its relegation to the status of a melancholy science pursued by northern Europeans, speaks to the inability of a conceptual ideality, an ideality separable in principle from the body, to ever be true to experience. Consequently the invisible ideality which covers all differentiating and plural life is not a category of subsumption or prior necessity, just as a form does not stand apart from what it informs, so there is no possibility here of deducing any a priori knowledge of this ideal apart from its adhesion to the real. This ideal is not an abstract conceptualisation by a mental life that has sundered itself from reality, it is reality at its profoundest level.

I have argued that though this ideal is not visible it is not separated from sight. Though it is in a sense invisible, this is not for it a noumenal quality: invisibility has a look. The ideal as an invisible look upholds what it sees and sustains all visibles as such.[60] And in respect of this invisibility, 'sensation is literally a form of communion' (*la sensation est à la lettre une communion*).[61] As an invisibility this *eidos* does not negate the ontic visibles that it creates. Though existent beings stand in seeming independence and brute facticity, they are in truth all enveloped in an invisible penumbra which they can either deny or acknowledge. The invisible shapes and hollows out visibility from the general undifferentiated mass. From the perspective of ontic visibility the invisible need not be perceived, but the transcendent gratuity of the invisible, its formless donation, clings to all the singularised beings it holds together not as an internal *ousia* but as a transcendent form inseparable from that which it informs. Spread along the surface of each being, flowing along its contours, this a posteriori ideality grants creation existence through adhering to the ownmost potential of each creature.

Finally I can now sketch out what I have been trying to approach. The seeming independence of the external world, its apparent indifference to and denial of the highest values lies at the source of a now exhausted transcendentalism and a now revitalised and more horrific immanentism. Yet both these positions are false. Though the world does not depend on the human mind, the world is not as a consequence independent nor indeed is it self-sufficient. Its being is real, yet it is not an ontic reality, but a created one, and the reality of the created order is that it is created and any reality it has comes from its participation in, and donation by, God. As such, any being possessed by an existent is granted as a gratuity by a charity that could not be fully grasped by the human mind until it was made incarnate in Christ. In consequence a return to the natural order, via an epoché of all these false and dreadful idolatries does not lead us to a pantheistic world of non-identical self-identities. In truth all secular discourses, all the ontic claims made about reality and correct description are not even wrong, they are just weak. Reality is real, but if configured only within the secular or pagan rubric it is reality at its lowest power. Like confining oneself to the most privated level of Neo-Platonic emanation, to think reality only at this tier is to consort with drained matter and nothingness, and only those who fail to see any rank above this imagine themselves stronger and more honest as a result. In truth all beings are a combination of both the actual and the manifestly possible (the manifestly possible being nothing but a possibility of a higher plenitude of actuality). Each actualised creation hovers then in its moment of formation and all the possibles, all the best possibles are born with it and come to it. This is what one means by this earth being the best possible world – not reducing the world to its most privated state but arguing for its highest power. Here is what it means for a possibility to supervene on an actuality and for it not to be an oppressive act. In John we find Christ saying the following, 'I tell you most solemnly, unless a man is born from above he cannot see the Kingdom of God' (John 3:3). And the glory is that *man is born from above*, his possibility stems from the fact that he is born from the highest actuality and it is this and our participation in it that alone allows human beings to transfigure themselves and their world.

From the above we can see how the fullest truth retains its visual component. Perception as a strange and beautiful combination of activity and passivity, spontaneity and reception, is what allows us in these denuded times not to be wholly authored by our environment. It is granted to perception to see and grasp those possibles, which are given to us at birth, as potentials that can be made actual. In the realm of the visual, beings retain a diaphanous quality such that the possibility of the good and the beautiful and the true can shine into them and cohere their bodies with the highest values.

And this description also provides the shape of an answer to our questions as to how the subjective relates to the objective. The created being is not absorbed by any false objectivity; there is nothing foreign in the highest shapes that coalesce around the created form. The subject ascends to the highest shapes of actuality as the hope of both the creature and the Creator. For this is no simple reductive henology or Neo-Platonic emanation from simplicity to complexity and back again. If Plotinus was never able to answer why the One had to create, if he was never able to ascertain why the One was not satisfied with itself, this is not true for Christianity, for Christ taught that God creates only out of love. Similarly the solicitude of the invisible for the visible arises only from love, and because nothing is created so that it might die, this love does not negate what it creates. Instead it raises it to the highest level of being that it can occupy. In this way the most high utterly abandons itself to us, its kenosis consists in that 'the Word was made flesh' (John 1:14) and we remain forever transfigured as a result. The Johannine transparency of the Son in respect to the Father, 'The Father is in me and I am in the Father' (John 10:39) is an elevation that is also given to us: 'I shall draw all men to myself' (John 12:32). Perception draws us into this Trinitarian harmonic – in which we participate without negation – and we embrace the objective because we are for it and it is for us.

Furthermore, the error of natural theology is avoided. Indeed I have almost restored something closer to Henry of Ghent's original recognition that the human eye can determine two different types of being. But I have done this by arguing that no thing is in fact determinable, that all beings, being a combination of actuality and possibility, are incapable of finite determination, not least because they are capable of so much more. And whilst I have avoided natural theology by denying any knowledge founded on finitude, I have perhaps reformulated the relation between nature and theology. Because we have discerned that every natural visible rests on an infinitude of participation and possibility, we have in a curious and unexpected way recovered nature for God. Since knowledge of nature apart from God no longer provides the model for knowledge of God, and since God's glory and ideality is now revealed to cover every creature, every substantial surface and every visible body, we have perhaps recovered the correct alignment and perception of God's relationship to the world. For by accepting the adumbration of existent actuality and by refusing the ability of this ontic account of actuality to determine what is actually possible, we have prevented the reduction of invisibility to visibility and preserved the qualitative uniqueness of God's transcendence and prevented its reduction to immanence. Moreover, since it has been contended that this invisibility is not thinkable apart from visibility we do not have a transcendence that takes place at the expense of immanence. As invisibility as a possibility represents a higher dimension of actuality, then immanence is simply life at its lowest power. Without a cognisance of the invisible, immanence remains trapped in untruth, for it is impossible to enclose visibility from its invisible and then claim truthful knowledge of it. All of which is to say that the plenitude of the Trinitarian harmonic retains a phenomenological presence, a presence that can be perceived, even if it is not necessarily seen.

The fall of the modern and the rise of pagan discordance

You worship what you do not know; we worship what we do know.

(John 4:22)

'Truth?' said Pilate. 'What is that?'

(John 18:38)

I will not enter the world of each chapter to the extent that I did before. Because the late modern situation is so diverse and so diffuse, and as I have already taken a position on that plurality, it would be disingenuous of me to enter this realm with ever more precise and searching exegesis, as if I were looking for something that I believed I had not already found. What I will discern in what follows is the operation of the various forms of concealment and idolatry that I have already described. The sublime celebration of the decline of objectivity and the fall of the modern has ushered in a world of false variables, dreadful affirmations and ever more peculiar claims to transcendence. Of course to a certain extent theology must walk with those who displace false objectivity, criticise science and seek to free the plenitude of the world from some falsifying totality. It need have few problems with any of the contemporary epochés or destructions. They should strike it as liberating.

However, the trouble lies with what is – or is not – affirmed after these liberating disavowals of metaphysics and essentialism. Many of these strategies never again emerge from their own negativity. Or if they do, what is affirmed seems to occupy some strange parasitical half-light. Perhaps this is because these discourses feel that to affirm anything would be a pejorative imposition upon some originally aporetic quality. Avoiding this contemporary vacillation between the necessity for overcoming and its perceived impossibility is for me a prerequisite for any genuine experience of transcendence. To say this is to suggest that these pagan discourses perform the function of sublimity, and only deliver the subjects of their narratives outside themselves in order to maintain themselves. As false forms of desire and refusal, they prevent transcendence from manifesting itself and they thus represent a much more pervasive and dangerous form of idolatry. For *they conceal the most holy by claiming to pursue it.*

In accepting the necessity of the pursuing of the holy, Nietzsche was no exception. Like most post-Kantian thinkers Nietzsche accepts the absence of higher perceivables and indeed he discerns this lack of perception as lying at the origin of nihilism. He famously observes 'What does nihilism mean? That the highest values devaluate themselves. The aim is lacking; "why?" finds no answer.'[62] Moreover, this lack of aim, this inability to see that the highest values are in fact capable of discernment stands at the origin of the situation that Nietzsche's work speaks to. From the madman of *Die Fröhliche Wissenschaft* and the forlorn cry of 'I am looking for God, I am looking for God', to Heidegger's recognition that these words were indeed sincere, Nietzsche's work expresses a profound sense of spiritual nihilism together with a recognition of the necessity of overcoming it. Indeed as Michel Haar points out in his astute and detailed contribution, 'Nietzsche's declared "atheism" is relative to a particular definition of God.' The pejorative God is the God of morality, the God of consciences, and his death – celebrated by Nietzsche – brings about, as Haar tells us, not only the death of the God of metaphysics, but also the possibility of a rebirth of the divine essence.

Furthermore, Nietzsche's rejection of the idolatrous configuration of God mirrors our own earlier refusal of idolatry. Nietzsche's atheism arises, as Haar points out, because he configures God as a 'principal of totalisation . . . which governs the totality of the world from above and beyond', for 'this amounts to demoting the world because it amounts to measuring it against an external quantum'. This Nietzschean rejection of God, is, however, not a rejection of the God of the theologians but that of the philosophers. As I have already argued, the idea of an external governing moralising deity does not arise from theology, but from the vicissitudes of modernity which made the world so ontic that God could only be thought of as being external to it. Despite this false caricature of Christianity, Nietzsche does acutely discern the nihilistic consequences of an idolatrous imposition of totality upon the world. For these totalised values are unable to disguise their human origin and historical genealogy. As a consequence those who invested so heavily in them face as Haar puts it 'the complete de-divinization of the world'. As his ameliorative response, Nietzsche denies any possibility of totality and affirms instead that all that is existent, all the oppositional contraries, all the joy and suffering; he affirms that all of this can be unified together in an affirmation of eternal return.

Given this, and given also that we may agree with Nietzsche's critique of idolatrous totalities, we cannot avoid the immediate recognition that Nietzsche's understanding of God as being analogous to such totalities is blatantly mistaken, not least because we have already explicated this error and laid it at the door of the philosophical attempts to appropriate and govern reality. Our theological distinction becomes even more explicit when we enter the metaphysics of the Nietzschean alternative to the 'external oppressive deity'. As Haar points out, this new form of divinity has no name and it does not go under the aegis of Dionysius because 'ignorance of the name is tantamount to a negative condition for a new blooming or a free re-deployment of the religious instinct'. But this free religious instinct manifested outside of any external oppressive code or tradition, though it has its momentary instances of transcendence, and though indeed it seeks the link with all things, can in its completion only end up obeying the vicissitudes of its own figuration, which having destroyed all idols, remains seduced only by its own force and by its ability to embrace the all. To exemplify then a religious instinct through the maximisation of the *Wille zur Macht*, to claim thereby to embrace the all without negating any of its parts, looks not like a divine pantheism but an immanentism which negates the true possibilities of the world. Haar summarises this concern: 'Isn't the feeling of the divinity of the world tantamount to a blinding and narcissistic projection of subjectivity which sees nothing else but itself in the mirror of the world.' For even though we are subsequently shown that there is a Nietzschean understanding of religious interiority which would mitigate against such a projection (in Nietzsche's accounts of Christ for example), there is still no recognition that a transcendent exteriority could be the affirmation not the negation of this interiority. In a world where everything is affirmed (and yet made horizontal), we are made to suppose that all formulas and traditions are impositions unless they emanate from the supervening *puissance* and intoxicating acceptance of the overman. Indeed, however much Nietzsche celebrated the withdrawal of Christ from the world of institutional reality as being in some way allied to this project, the distance Christ took from the world was by contrast not a withdrawal into the self-positing glory of the overman and his sublime acquiescence to the eternal return of actuality; rather it was a public affirmation of another possibility for the world, a possibility that only God's love and glory can bring and make actual. For Christianity saves lived actuality because it refuses to allow any false account of the actual to speak for what is really possible; as a result human life is not simply abandoned to repeat its fate in order to find its true profundity. On the contrary, with Christianity human actuality is reconciled with its highest possibility and this reconciliation consists in the resurrection and reality of human life beyond circular time. As a result human beings are not hopelessly condemned to repeat who they are, what they have done, nor indeed what they have undergone. We are saved from this because God loves us not only for who we are but also for what we might and should be.

To say all this is to suggest that however compelling and liberating Nietzsche's critique of idolatry and its motives are, in the end his account fails to transcend itself because it fails to think that there could be a possibility for mankind beyond the intoxicating and self-glorifying acceptance of all surface actuality. What is needed here is a critique of any assertion of an immanent and coextensive continuum between the human and the divine. As Barth writes in his *Epistle to the Romans*,

> So long as religious as well as anti-religious activities fail to draw attention to that which lies beyond them, and so long as they attempt their own justification, either as faith, hope and charity, or as the enthusiastic and dionysiac gestures of the Anti-Christ they are assuredly mere illusion.[64]

The illusion consists in thinking that in order for daily life and the divine to coincide, the divine must be reduced to all that life consists of. Not only would this falsify human life in that it appears imperative in any existence to accept some things and deny others, but it falsifies God into a beyond that is external to us, and accepts nothing of Him unless He accepts all of us. And this is a falsification of the most high because the task of human life is to distance ourselves from our lowest powers and possibilities in order that we can move to an acceptance of what we have been given and an acknowledgement of Christ who 'sacrificed himself for us' (Titus 2:14). And to take this seriously is to discern that behind the truth of the *Übermensch* lurks a greater truth – the Nietzschean affirmation of becoming cannot really affirm what man can become.

And if our direction is aligned around just this question, the question of what man can be as opposed to what he is, then it is instructive for us to consider the meaning of Heidegger's epitaph to the ontical priority of the question of Being. For if fundamental ontology is conducted on behalf of Dasein, as a result of Dasein being a being which 'in its very Being, that Being is an *issue* for it', then what does the claim that Heidegger makes at the end of his career mean?[64] For if 'only a God can save us now' (*Nur noch ein Gott kann uns retten*), then why pursue the question of Being rather than that of God?[65] Of course I am being facetious here, since I am not only juxtaposing sentences which may not be opposed, but I am also suggesting that there is an absolute opposition between an inquiry into Being and an inquiry into God. Now in terms of theology such an opposition would be an obvious error, yet in the paradigm of contemporary philosophy this opposition seems perfectly acceptable – an inquiry, they tell us, into Being, is quite independent of any inquiry into God. Since the Heideggerian account of onto-theology has already been discussed, and since I have already refused the applicability of this thesis to the God of theology, I can accept along with Heidegger that onto-theology conceals the truth of Being without disturbing the true focus of my question – why Being rather than God?[66] And indeed, if God does not conceal Being, does Being conceal God?

John Peacocke's sophisticated and rigorous paper takes us directly to the question at issue. Peacocke writes 'it is my contention that the essence of the religious is for Heidegger the very project that he is engaged in: thinking the truth of being as a place of admittance to the holy'. In this Peacocke is commenting on the following passage from Heidegger's *Letter on Humanism*: 'Only from the truth of Being can the essence of the holy be thought. Only in the light of the essence of divinity can it be thought or said what the word "God" is to signify.'[67] For me of course this raises a question, a question we will benefit from, despite the fact that it cannot be answered here. Does the inquiry into Being conceal and mutate the inquiry into God? If it is the truth of Being that admits one into the province of the holy (*das Heilige*), and if it is this truth that licences and makes possible the truth of God, then is not this the idolatry which allows ontology to speak for theology? Having said this, we have to acknowledge that there is in Heidegger no simple elevation of an ontic understanding of Being over God as there was for instance in Scotus. No, the difficulty consists in the fact that it is Heidegger (and he most of all) who has decisively rejected any ontic understanding of ontology. And was it not earlier suggested that such a rejection is a prelude, and should indeed be a precursor, to an ontological recognition of the superiority of theology? And if the concern in the face of Heidegger's *œuvre* is that one discerns a failure to make that transition, then it will have to be shown – albeit at another time – how the manifestation of the ontico-ontological priority of Being conceals the prior priority of God for Dasein. To suggest this is to doubt that when one stands in the presence (*Anwesenheit*) of the Being of beings one stands in the presence of something holier than God.

Since I have already raised certain questions about a phenomenological approach to theology, I will stay with those thinkers (Levinas and Marion) who in the collection attempt to approach transcendence via the phenomenological method. Now as I have perhaps already indicated, my fears about certain phenomenological approaches to transcendence and theology lie with their seeming positivism and reductionism. By this I mean that in these approaches we find that one phenomenon is selected, be it the phenomenon of a human face or that of the religious icon, and to this one phenomenon are given all the qualities of a positive revelation. This revelation is apparently simply there, unconditioned by any subjective approach or situation, as such transcendence is understood to be present only in this one phenomenon, and the sole response appropriate for the subject in respect of this manifestation is absolute acceptance and submission. Yet not only do these characteristics appear to bear an unpleasant resemblance to the form and shape of various bad ontic arguments about essentialism and truth, they also argue for a bad form of phenomenology. For this position appears to reduce all phenomena to one phenomenon without phenomenological authorisation. By this I do not mean to suggest that phenomena cannot present themselves in a hierarchical fashion; I think they can and I think they do, but I do not believe that higher phenomena present themselves in such a way that their own ascendancy involves the negation of all other phenomena. For whilst we can accept Husserl's point in *Ideas I* that primordial intuition 'is a source of authority', we must recognise that Husserl also thought that the authority of this intuition pertains 'only within the limits in which it then presents itself'.[68] As the limits of a phenomenon appear to extend no further than the phenomenon itself, it seems in this respect unphenomenological to allow one phenomenon to reduce all other phenomena to itself.

Having said all this, my concerns regarding Levinas's approach to transcendence perhaps appear obvious. Whilst I would not deny that the human face can be the bearer of transcendence, I do not necessarily think that it is its only phenomenological representative on earth. Nor do I think that transcendence needs to be approached via an otherness that assumes that all other phenomena are the phenomena of totality. Leaving aside any question as to why one would assume that otherness could be so quickly identified with goodness (i.e., it is not immediately obvious to me that alterity is good), it is striking that a methodology that refuses God access to the world, except through the suffering and wounded face of only one of His creatures, should have gained such a wide acceptance among religious thinkers. For we see in Levinas's work an absolute restriction of God's invisibility to that 'invisibility' engendered by the destitute human face, and as such we appear to see an almost stunning reduction of God's invisibility to that human phenomenon. Quite apart from the shocking anthropocentric limitation of God's sovereignty to human phenomenology, the rest of the visible world appears utterly abandoned by God. The remaining world can apparently only offer us a vision of totality, a totality that is engendered for Levinas solely as a response to the Manichaean sway of the *Il y a*.[69] For of course since goodness is understood as being commensurate with otherness, then God must now achieve the transcendence proper to Him via 'his absolute remoteness' (*son éloignement absolu*) from us.[70] This absolute distance between God and the world, whilst it preserves the qualitative distinction between us and the most high, does so at the price of violently withdrawing God from 'objectivity, presence and being' (*Dieu est arraché à l'objectivité, à la presence et à l'être*).[71] And yet how can I disagree with this argument for an absolute distance between God and man? Have I not been arguing for a qualitative distinction between God and nature since the beginning of this paper? Well obviously yes, but I have never argued for a distinction that is so extreme that it prevents communion. For Christianity love is the first name of God, and this implies that the distance between us and the Father is a distance undertaken only out of love. This distance is initiated not so that He can separate himself from us, but so that He can come to us as our most intimate and genuine possibility. Qualitative distinction is a condition of subsequent intimacy and solicitude, not its destruction. The Levinasian reduction of God to the distance and alterity of the self–other relation, even if this distance is thought at the most intimate and corporeal level, destroys the possibility of a non-violent communion with God, not least because God is thought of as an absolute term in respect of which one can only be utterly passive. This configuration of the relation between the Creator and his creatures is violent because the creature must surrender and deny its singularity (a singularity thought of by Levinas only as the wholly pejorative world of the ego) in order to participate phenomenologically in God's universality. And as I have said, the 'phenomenological manifestation' of Levinas's God – this appearance of non-appearance in the human face – risks denying the communion that transcendence has with the rest of the created world, since it understands God's transcendence from the world via a sublime rupture by the Other from the rest of God's visible creation. The resulting phenomenological chasm that alterity opens up between itself and nature has the curious effect of restoring atheistic totality in the name of overcoming it – not least because the Other drains the whole world of value in the name of value and denies God's phenomenal presence in order to testify to His absence. All of which leaves the phenomenal world very much as both modernity and atheism have described it. For the sublime fracture that Levinas proposes in order to overcome this atheistic world only functions, as we might expect, to confirm it.

Jean-Luc Marion also defends the idea that it is the distance between God and man that allows their intimacy and communion. He writes in *L'Idole et la distance* that it is only the incommensurability between God and man (the *distance du Père*) that makes possible the intimacy between them (*de Dieu à l'homme, l'incommensurable rend seul possible l'intimité*).[72] And for Marion it is the icon that alone possesses the ability to convey this distance and bring its incommensurability to visibility.[73] But is not this reduction of all higher appearance to the form of the icon problematic, and indeed in Graham Ward's analysis of Marion we find a profound engagement with – and a sincere suspicion of – the way in which the incommensurability of the icon's presence is thought. For it is not that Ward is anti-theological, far from it; rather it is that he discerns an unthinking theological absolutism behind the figure of the icon, an absolutism that eclipses any other account of revelation and visibility. For Ward, writing from a certain rejection of phenomenology, Marion's elevation of the icon represents little more than an attempt by dogmatic ecclesiastical authority to claim visibility for itself.

However, I have not rejected phenomenology, nor do I view it as a method which is necessarily committed to dogmatic assertion and positivism. Indeed, at first it appears that Marion's insistence on a phenomenological presence for theology sounds very like the project that I have been advocating; none the less, his reliance upon the use of one visible (the icon) to reduce all others (the idols) in order to maintain the qualitative distinction of iconic phenomenality over idolatrous appearance, causes one concern. For example, whilst Marion's recent theological work relies upon visibility, he uses, as he himself puts it, 'a conflict between two phenomenologies' to distinguish a theological from an idolatrous phenomenality.[74] But in spite of all the arguments for distance and incommensurability, it appears that these two phenomenologies require a conflictual relationship with each other in order to recognise and articulate themselves. At the very least this conflictual relationship is engendered by Marion's reliance on the same model of intentionality to define and yet distinguish both the idol and the icon. In *Dieu sans l'être*, the idol and the icon are understood only by virtue of a finite as opposed to an infinite intentionality; 'Whilst the idol results from the gaze that aims at it', the icon summons a vision (*l'icône convoque la vue*) which is boundless, as the icon results not from the limited intention of the finite gaze but from the infinite gaze and intention of God.[75] Now Graham Ward's concern speaks to my own, for by defining the icon by virtue of a reversal of idolatrous intentionality, do we not find that the distinction between the idol and the icon becomes unstable? And does not this instability result in a collapse of the distinction between the finite and infinite worlds, leaving us with a world of infused but silent phenomena, all of which only speak in order to bear testimony to an authority beyond themselves?[76]

Marion's predicament in this regard does not appear dissimilar to that of Levinas, for by taking such an extreme position against so-called 'idolatrous visibility', or 'the same', both Marion and Levinas leave God without any appearance whatsoever. For they both oscillate between an arbitrary positivistic privileging of one phenomenon (the face, the icon) and the conveyance by this one phenomenon of a phenomenality which is actually *trans phenomenal*, in that both the face and the icon depart from manifestation altogether in order to transcendentally appeal to a subject who intends beyond appearance. To say the least, this is an invidious situation for those who still use a phenomenological method, as it means that both thinkers must return to the visibility they denigrated in order to give themselves the presentation they require. For example, as early as 1963, Levinas wrote of departing from phenomenology with his notion of the trace, yet he still situated this trace in respect 'of the phenomenology that it interrupts' (*de la phénoménologie qu'elle interrompt*).[77] Similarly, even in one of Marion's more recent theological works, *La Croisée du visible*, we still find the invisible being brought to the visible by intentionality (*comment coïncident donc le visible et l'invisible? Nous l'avons déjà dit, intentionnellement*) even though this intentionality – albeit the intentionality of the finite gaze – remains the mark of the idol.[78]

In a certain way the aforementioned looks perilously close to a type of Platonic dualism (one though that Plato himself would not have endorsed), with the iconic standing over and against a world of idols, a world that is subsequently negated when the divine makes its appearance in it. For as I have already made clear, even though I consider it quite possible that an icon, through being graced by God's illumination, can represent the divine, I see no reason why it is the only phenomenon that is allowed to do so. Moreover, and more seriously, the elevation of this one visible (even if the iconic is a phenomenon in general and not just one phenomenon) over all the others aestheticises God self-expression, now we are told that only the icon (like the Levinasian face) can testify to the 'presence', of God. Unfortunately and similarly, this devalues all other visibility, making it necessarily blasphemous. Moreover, and as a consequence, not only does this seem a bad phenomenology, it seems a bad theology. It is a modernist flaw to uphold a universal over any particular, for as we have already suggested (and as Rowan Williams's chapter on Hegel has already shown us), the kenotic nature of Christ and Christian universality means that a theological universal does not give or show itself except through the singularised beings that it brings into being, for Christian universals do not negate that which they inform, but seek to bring them to their highest shapes. In the words of Christ, 'I have come so that they may have life and have it to the full' (John 10:10). This is the true message of the incarnation, and the true nature of God's love. All of which brings me to my final point about Marion. At his most brilliant there is in Marion a glorious and beautiful endorsement of a theological communality and reciprocity around visuality and its objects, and indeed *La Croisée du visible* begins and ends with exactly these affirmations.[79] However, the question is whether Marion's methodology can lead us there, for one may wonder if his phenomenology is Trinitarian enough. Quite simply, in Marion's account of visuality there seems to be little recognition of the third person of the Trinity, in spite of all appearances to the contrary; in spite of all the remarks on or about the gift (and here I take St Augustine's point that gift is the most appropriate name for the Holy Spirit), *I do not see or perceive* in Marion's phenomenology any decisive manifestation or infusion of grace.[80] Consequently since it is through the Third Person that we are brought up to participation in the most high, Marion's failure to give us a phenomenological account of grace means that though we are always brought to cognition of the qualitative distinction of the Father and the Son from us, we are not brought up to participate in them. In Marion's work the Father and the Son appear to offer us as a salvation nothing but our own negation and submission. But this account of the most high seems wholly at odds with Christianity. For if indeed it is by virtue of the Holy Spirit that we are raised up to participate in our highest possibility, this is because each of us 'has been given his own share of grace' (Eph. 4:7). And since the ascension of Christ marks the possibility of our own, I cannot believe that Christ negates us: 'I have come not to condemn the world but to save the world' (John 12:47); Christ saves us for who we are, because of what we might be. And Marion's phenomenological duality bespeaks a failure to discern that Trinitarian thinking arises principally to avoid a dualistic negation of subjective life by objectivity. Moreover, a theology that would be phenomenological might be better served if it followed St Augustine and abandoned any Neo-Platonic resolution of plurality into simplicity, for Augustine attempted to uncover a Trinitarian seeing that might mirror a Trinitarian phenomenality of the world.[81] To say this is to say that theology should be truer to what is presented to it. The world cannot be thought to transfigure itself through a violent and dualistic struggle between good and evil since for Christianity evil can be given no defining power over creation. Thus, icons do not need to be opposed to a world that has already been gnostically surrendered to idolatry. Grace and salvation always already mark the phenomenal world, and though idolatry can and does conceal the world's advocacy of God, idolatry can never be thought to destroy the highest possibilities of creation, because to cede the world to idolatry is to deny the world and to deny that 'God saw that it was good' (Gen. 1:10). And though this is done so that a conservative objectivity can negate all the plurality and diversity of life, it is a false abstraction. God created everything that is out of love, and this love does not reduce the plenitude of the earth, it alone sustains it.

If part of this refusal of positivism in phenomenology stems from a reciprocal and mutual account of the relationship that pertains between those that see and the phenomena themselves, and if one can articulate this position because one has refused to accept that Kant's account of silenced and blinded phenomena captures the visibility of the visible world, then perhaps we can see where this refusal to divorce phenomena from language and conceptuality might lead. For modernity has accepted the strange idea that phenomena are, at best, passive positives – brute factual existences whose presence in temporal succession and spatial juxtaposition stems not from themselves but from some abstract transcendental that arranges and coheres appearances according to its interests. Now apart from the fact that language is commonly taken to fulfil the role of this abstract transcendental and that language is presumed thereby to refute any phenomenological presence and positivity, it does seem that when contemporary thought speaks of 'language', it almost always does so by repeating the terms of the Kantian opposition between the conceptual and the empirical. It appears that contemporary thought, when considering language, simply places the 'play of language' in the vacated space of the conceptual, with the result that this account of 'language' now occupies much the same position over and above the empirical world as did the concepts that preceded it. Which is why so many of the contemporary reflections on the innate ability of language to undermine phenomenal presence represent little more than another species of transcendentalist meta-physics, and if this is for me a pejorative, that is because something other than the phenomenal world is being allowed to stand over appearance and speak against it. No doubt this is because language claims for itself the ability to speak for phenomena, as the secular model of brute phenomenological posi-tivity seems so obviously unable to speak for itself. But as I have said before, this reduction of the phenomenal to the level of an a-conceptual brute positiv-ity is false; unfortunately however, it is such an understanding of the phenom-enal that is common to both phenomenological positivism and to those transcendental accounts of language that claim to render such a positivism unthinkable. And if this attempt to describe a world undivided by the opposi-tion of rationality and sensibility invites refutation by contemporary trans-cendental thought, then one needs to offer an account of language that ties discursivity to the phenomenal such that transcendental thought can never again use language to depart from the world in order to explain it.

In respect of which, Wittgenstein's remarks on language and its relation to the world seem for theology highly advantageous; for instance he writes in the *Philosophical Investigations* that '[P]hilosophy is a battle against the bewitchment of our intelligence by the means of language'.[82] And if for me language bewitches us, it does so because it makes us believe that the explana-tions for phenomena lie beyond the phenomena themselves, and inasmuch as language does indeed force us into this belief it assumes – as Wittgenstein again points out – that '*essence is hidden from us*'.[83] All of which is to say that lan-guage can, via its very grammatical structure, induce us to locate the essence of phenomena either behind the appearances themselves, or indeed above them, in the structures of conceptuality that claim to make appearances pos-sible. It is Wittgenstein's critique of the various obfuscatory consequences of an overemphasis on disembodied language and abstracted mental life that reveal for Fergus Kerr the explicit implication: that 'our inner mental life is rooted in our interaction with the world as physical beings'. And of course it is exactly this refusal to divorce the mental from the phenomenal that interests me, for as Kerr's adroit demonstration shows, as soon as language departs from engagement with the world in order to search for the essential substance of a grammatical form (the pronoun I for instance), then language enters the illusory world of ideal substances that have no reality (for example the bodi-less subject cannot be found, as the I only seems to exist in an incarnate form). If indeed the errors and illusions of metaphysics arise in part from the grammar that causes us to depart from the only world in which this language is applicable, perhaps this is because as Wittgenstein put it '[W]e feel as if we had to *penetrate* phenomena'.[84]

However, inasmuch as this refusal to use language to go behind phenomena produces a renewed account of the relation between the mental and the mate-rial without giving an account of what is subsequently seen, it displaces our theological concerns onto a new stage without necessarily meeting them. For although religion might subsequently break free of all the intellectualist and transcendental attempts to explain it by reference to some external non-religious or metaphysical criteria, and although, as Kerr points out, we are offered the opportunity of understanding religion on its own terms, there is a danger here and it is the risk that accompanies any situation where theology finds its possibility secured in advance by a secular philosophy. As Wittgenstein's methodology can be seen to free accounts of the natural world from abstraction in favour of an account of human engagement with nature itself, this can have, and indeed has had, the consequence of reinventing a pragmatist variant of ontic realism, and if it is this sort of realism that grants theology its own encounter with reality, then theology has been displaced from an objective account of what God has done for us (creation, revelation and redemption for example) to an account of what people are doing in respect of Him (engaging in externally odd but internally meaningful rituals in Church). Now I am not suggesting here that Wittgenstein's work is simply secular; indeed, much of Kerr's work claims that his greatest insights arose out of a reflection on religion; nor indeed am I saying that those who reduce Wittgenstein to a form of analytic realism are in direct correspondence with his writings, but I am saying that Wittgenstein's work should not be accepted by theologians simply because it makes a certain sort of theology possible.[85]

Not least because a world where an account of nature can be given independently of an account of God is for theology a wholly idolatrous domain. Furthermore, this situation appears thoroughly analogous to that of Duns Scotus, who first initiated the thinking that held that an account of God's presence in nature required a prior account of an ontology without God. For theology, or rather a theological realism, cannot accept any naturalist account (of the world and its interconnection with human beings) that prevents or prohibits a theological account of the origin and nature of nature itself. Not only does this position defend the naturalism of theology (if you will) from any natural theology, it also prevents there being any account of nature that isn't at the same time an account of its dependency on God. So to Wittgenstein's rather melancholic observation that '[W]e can only describe and say, human life is like that',[86] theology would say that not only does this appear to assume that there is still a position that one could exhaustively consult in order to describe 'the way things are' but also from the position of theology you could only hope to give a description of human life that would be equal to that life, if that description also gave an account of the God who created that life and the Son who will redeem it. Whilst I would indeed agree with Wittgenstein's injunction to not 'look for anything behind the phenomena', as 'they themselves are the theory',[87] I would also caution that it would be an error to see only the visible phenomena, and a falsehood to describe only the ontic reality that one found there, as this would be a denial of the true nature of the visible and its communion with invisibility. All of which would be to say that though Wittgenstein may have turned us away from

metaphysical abstraction to an account of physical presence, he failed to give
an account of what the physical itself gives an account of – God. And by so
doing Wittgenstein himself repeats a metaphysical account of the physical in
that he also actualizes the ontological and transcendental occlusion of the
possibility that God is also to be seen in the visible world.

And in respect of this question, the question as to what makes phenomena
possible and what, as a consequence, these phenomena can be expected to
convey, Kevin Hart presents us with a continuation of his work on Derrida.[88]
In a piece of rare quality and distinction we are treated to a full examination
of the implications of Derrida's work for theology. Hart however accepts the
veracity of Derrida's early position that 'God is the name and the element of
that which makes possible an absolutely pure and absolutely self-present self-
knowledge'.[89] In consequence the possibility of an alternative account of
theology, an account that might escape this Derridean assumption, is not
considered. Instead Hart chooses the path of 'negative theology' (as opposed
to any supposed metaphysical theology) in order to think the distinction
between God and Derridean conceptuality. However, Hart shows that it
would be an error to think that Derrida was simply opposed to theology;
rather it is that Derrida's work is opposed to the operation in theology of
certain philosophical structures, structures that cannot escape being metaphysical. Furthermore Hart accepts that *différance* does indeed place itself
before any operation of language and conceptuality such that as soon as
theology makes its conceptual beginning it cannot avoid repeating and
reauthorising *différance* even as it attempts to argue otherwise. Which perhaps
is why the issue for theology is a question as to the status and 'originality of
différance'. The problem, however, with a theological acceptance of the originality of *différance* is that we are left with the conundrum of how negative theology might attempt to differentiate itself from *mere* negativity, because the
secular negativity of *différance*, of indefinite postponement and the *via negativa*
do appear to be different. A point that Hart himself addresses:

> 'the God of negative theology' is the ground of Being which can be
> approached only by using a syntax of neither-nor. It is transcendent
> and transcendental, which means it forms the condition of possibility
> for the world and human beings to have meaning while also
> surmounting that world. *Différance* by contrast is a condition of
> possibility which as 'meaningless play' is incapable of forming a
> solid ground; it is transcendental though not transcendent.

Whatever distinction one can make between negativity and negative theology, this distinction will have to have (if one wishes to preserve theology),
the character of a theological affirmation. However, it seems questionable
whether this affirmation is possible or even thinkable under the aegis of
différance. Whilst for Hart 'it would be quite possible to grant that *différance*

provides the condition of possibility for all discourse and still to believe in a God who abides above or beyond being', for me this would be only to allow a transcendental to place and define the transcendent, since if a theology (negative or positive) allows its affirmation to be thought through *différance*, then it will have accepted that a name which is not God can stand over and against God: in that *différance* claims to frame even the name of God leaving it no longer 'the name above every other name' and the name of God as no longer ultimate. In this sense there is no difference between a positive idolatry and a negative one. Just as it would be an error to think that a positive predicate can stand for God, so it must be an error to think that a negative predicate can stand against him. Moreover, whilst theology must accept the unstable nature of its names, that does not mean that theology is reduced to instability, nor does it mean that theology must smuggle in a covert metaphysics to maintain this stability. For as I have already argued, no a priori discourse can take precedence over God without de-throning Him. And here we must be very clear: Derrida installs an a priori precedence into thinking; even though this a priori is one that breaks into its Kantian elements as soon as it is constituted, these elements still dictate the possibilities for experience. *Différance* still constitutes a form of conceptual idolatry because it still seeks to understand what can be said only in terms of itself. Instead of asking how things can be such that they have come to be, *différance* closes the question of its own origin by claiming itself to be 'already there'. As a result *différance* as a transcendental fails to investigate its own conditions of possibility and so fails to discern what is truly possible. Gillian Rose makes much the same point:

> The definition of writing as 'all that gives rise to inscription in general' implies a priori that writing is pre-scription: that it prescribes or commends and that it is the precondition of inscription. In this way Derrida closes the question of form itself.[90]

And the question of form, the question as to why there are transcendental structures, the question as to why there does appear to be order and shape in the world, should lead us to the paradox of creation and the question of who formed the first form. The erasure of this possibility by *différance* prevents there being any understanding that forms are not full self-sufficient ontic presences but rather participatory attendances of the highest shapes that beings can fulfil. And though Hart tries to rescue God from absorption into a human consciousness structured by *différance* – by preserving a distinction between human mental life and the divine reality and materiality of God – the reality and materiality of the divine enters a noumenal void, where its sacredness only consists in the fact that we cannot speak of it without affirming the superiority of a transcendental prohibition over God's transcendence.

And it is this wholesale elevation of transcendentalism above transcendence that stands as the supreme exemplar of the passage from transcendentalism to immanentism. For modernity has declined to such a point that many of those who claim to differ so profoundly from each other occupy more or less the same territory. Obviously, I have spoken earlier of the modern oscillation between transcendentalism and immanentist materialism, but the fact that contemporary transcendental thought can no longer refrain from postulating an ever-widening influence for its various a prioris speaks even more strongly to the failure of transcendental idealism to save any external faith and so keep itself within finite bounds. As a consequence, in its current forms transcendentalism has become a relentlessly internalising project of rationality, which neither recognises nor accepts any internal bounds or outer limitation. Since it was external faith (or rather faith in the external) that always limited the scope of the Kantian project, the loss of this empirical externality has meant that the totalising ideas of reason have left the regulatory realm of the imaginary and demanded full actualisation in the world. This passage from transcendentalism to immanentism has its source in Kant's decision to deny God's mode of being phenomenal purchase; by consigning God to a purely noumenal realm Kant denied God's indeterminacy any determinacy and as a result he fatally limited the ability of the infinite reflexively to contain and control the relentless impulses and drives of finite secular rationality.

For what we have been seeing in the last one hundred years or so is the fracturing of the Kantian vocabulary and the increasingly strange and bizarre structuration and arrangement of its parts. Nowadays concepts break from intuitions and from each other with their consequent elements (empiricality and ideality), relentlessly diverging without either believing itself to be blind or empty as a result. On one side of this now failed divide we have the raw upsurge of empiricality and undifferentiated pregnant intuition, on the other we find, wholly unlimited by experience, a relentless totalisation and competition of concepts. And as an exhausted and dysfunctional transcendentalism becomes the immanentism that it is, we can even see the attempt to pass from confusion to an ever more dreadful clarity taking shape, as the distinction between concepts and empirical content fades into a new materialism that claims both ideality and empiricality for itself in the vacated space of a universality that knows no limits. If this all sounds rather unrecognisable, it is perhaps because our own understanding is now so close to this position that we lack the perspective to see where we truly are.

In this respect psychoanalysis codifies for contemporary subjects their current scenario. For here it is wholly accepted that differential antagonistic transcendentals and their warring empirical contents should be placed at the origin of subjects who desire nothing but unification and reconciliation. Moreover, not only are these transcendental/empirical structures constituted so as to fracture any attempt at human unity, they are even placed beyond the reach of consciousness in the noumenal world of ids and superegos. The resulting tragic schisms – resolved only by pathological drives or utopian illusions – do nothing, however, to challenge the vaunted universality and originality of these transcendental/empirical fractures and consequently there is little that those who operate under such aegises can do except map the discrepancy between their desires and their own lives. Which in many ways is exactly the path that Regina Schwartz describes for Freud. Freud, according to Schwartz, had decried earlier in his career any hope that religious convictions might be anything but 'illusions', yet we find at the end of his life nothing but the fantasy of *Moses and Monotheism*, and as Schwartz's admirable depiction shows us, a methodology whose ambivalence and aporetic quality cannot be resolved within the borders of the psychoanalytic discipline. If psychoanalysis is so constructed, then it is within these epistemic wounds and between the discrepancy of the real and the Lacanian symbolic that Charles Winquist hopes to establish and articulate a 'theology of desire'. For Winquist it is only these disjunctures that provide the possibility for a communion of a non-totalising theology with alterity. However, despite an elegant and sustained account of a theology conducted out of these subjective aporias, it remains unclear why theology has anything to do with such discrepancies at all. Moreover, to speak of a theological desire arising from a more primordial and non-theological lack seems once again to allow a fractured transcendental to position and speak for theology. All of which would be to deny that theology finds its origin in fracture and dispersal, since, one might suggest, fracture and dispersal arise from the failure of a secular picture of reality to be adequate to what is truly present. In this sense, epistemic fractures represent the inadequacy of idolatrous attempts to capture reality, not the condition of possibility for theology.

Obviously, in this regard, my phenomenological approach experiences certain profound methodological problems with the psychoanalytic sphere. For the phenomenological, anything that sets up the noumenal as being more decisive for consciousness than that which is phenomenal is problematic. Moreover, if psychoanalysis understands consciousness solely via what is hidden or separable from consciousness, it risks (despite any Lacanian collective constitution of the symbolic), pushing arguments and visual disclosure back from the public realm into a relentlessly private and ultimately solipsistic discourse. For even if, after Lacan, the unconscious is now rendered as a symbolic refracted through a cultural imaginary, the symbolic itself is still thought through, and still thought of, as an antagonistic and unreconcilable relation of unconsciousness to consciousness. All of which would be to say that however the relation between consciousness and unconsciousness is configured, whether unconsciousness occupies an ever more noumenal world or whether this noumenal quality is transferred to a public sphere that necessarily thwarts any private desires, what is to be questioned is the idea that the resolution of the interior life of consciousness is still fractured by an a priori transcendental that has no interest or desire for human reconciliation or elevation.

However, this is not to say that psychoanalysis is reducible to phenomenological concerns. For not only does psychoanalysis have its own truth-
revealing phenomena (in the sense of the realm of discernible symptomatic
effects), but from a theological perspective psychoanalysis retains our interest
because it still represents a redemptive project that seeks a reconciliation for
human consciousness. It is this aspect that perhaps explains why psychoanalysts are increasingly taking on theological language and conceptuality
to articulate the possibility of human redemption. Indeed, in Philippa Berry's
chapter we are taken to Julia Kristeva's account of the pre-oedipal *chora* and
her attempt to give a Trinitarian reworking of its origin. Taking on board
Kristeva's intention of restoring 'to illusion its full therapeutic and epistemological value', we are presented with the contemporary imperative of constructing a new subjective capacity for idealisation and love. In *Tales of Love*,
Kristeva introduces us to a psychic space that was destroyed by modernity
(the ternary psychic structure of father, mother and child), to show in sharp
relief how the destruction of this space has initiated the contemporary crisis
of subjectivity and the resultant inability of narcissism to engender a productive encounter with otherness. Kristeva attempts to re-enter this realm via
the notion of gift, which she uses, as Berry carefully describes, to challenge
the traditional models of desire – models which have reduced subjectivity to
the binary and unsatisfying opposition of self and other. The gift is that of
love, and it comes as a passivity to a subject previously only described by
psychoanalytic models of projection. This gift, to quote Berry, 'is very much
oriented to an unspecified "open future" which is multiple rather than singular'. Such a future is genuinely open, as it has, according to Berry's reading
of Kristeva, a structure 'that is not tragic in its implications, since seemingly
it has the capacity to transform the relationship of the emergent individual
to abjection and hence to the death drive'. This is possible because Kristeva
re-enters the pre-oedipal psyche and recovers a third position (that of the
father). Moreover, Kristeva identifies this imaginary father with the source
of a mysterious and unconditional love. As a result Berry's hope is that psychoanalysis can begin to lose its tragic element via a 'sublation of narcissism
through love'.

Evidently, the positing of an unconditional love at the origin of consciousness repeats religious accounts of human creation. Similarly, the trinodal
situation that Kristeva uncovers at the heart of the child's constitution has
an obviously Trinitarian structure. But the question would be whether
psychoanalysis can internally reconcile a theological conceptuality with an
essentially a-theistic discourse without allowing that atheistic discourse to
prioritise itself at the expense of any genuine theological import. For example,
in Alison Ainley's elegant paper we are taken to Luce Irigaray's attempt
to open up, for the feminine, a site of subjectivity that could escape the
patriarchal positioning of Lacan and Freud. In this regard the theological
for Irigaray is the site of the construction of subjectivity and also therefore a

site for female recovery and transcendence. And by questioning the alignment between masculinity and the transcendent, Irigaray's work, as Ainley puts it, 'is not only an interrogation of the exclusive constructions of onto-theology but an attempt to develop a notion of what a feminine gender might mean – the creation of a still as yet hypothetical space for women to become'.

Now what is both compelling, and ultimately most problematic, is the extent to which Irigaray's account of the divine assumes a materialist and carnal positionality to articulate a divine feminine self-image for woman. This materialist account is so compelling – and in parts so beautiful – because it too graces matter with spirit and like the earlier account I offered of phenomenology, it also refuses to accept that transcendence is divorced from the physical and sensate world. None the less, what renders this project so problematic is that the recovery of an incarnate transcendence is conducted under the auspices of the assumption that in Irigaray's words 'as such nothing is more spiritual than female sexuality' (*[R]ien de plus spirituel, à ce titre, que la sexualité féminine*).[92] For Irigaray the assertion of this superlative is necessary, since as she makes quite clear, as 'long as woman lacks a divine made in her image she cannot establish her subjectivity'.[93] However, this claim that woman can establish her subjectivity via a recovery of the divine remade in her image appears almost immediately to repeat all the errors of idolatry. And this seems idolatrous not least because Irigaray appears to accept as legitimate one of the cardinal principles of modernity and onto-theology – that God is used to found subjectivity; moreover, not only is this belief not objected to, it is duplicated by Irigaray who revises its modern structure (in the light of the arrangement's exclusive masculine configuration), and claims it for feminine subjectivity. For example we read in *An Ethics of Sexual Difference*, that '[M]an sets the infinite in a transcendent (*transcendant*) that is always deferred to the beyond', a move which engenders for the male (in for example Irigaray's reading of Levinas), a situation where man invokes God 'but does not perceive him in the here and now', whereas God 'already finds and loses himself (*il se tient-retient déjà*) in the sensibility of the female lover'.[94] What appears to have happened here is that Irigaray has exchanged a model of a modern masculine subjectivity grounded by the sublimity of the beyond for a feminine subjectivity grounded by the sublimity of the near; in so doing she has reduced the idolatrous modern model of transcendence (God as the utterly beyond in respect of which I constitute myself as an aggressive finitude) to its more pervasive and acceptable contemporary advocate (God as the utterly near in respect of which I deny any external limits and immanentise infinitely for myself). For here, as so often before, early modern noumenal transcendence appears to have collapsed into late modern immanence.

Evidently of course, Irigaray aspires to avoid an immanentist appropriation of the divine, and she attempts to do this through the evocation of the *transcendental sensible*, the *transcendental sensible* being a means to bear fidelity to

the corporeal uniqueness of sexed bodies by gracing such bodies with a transcendence specific only to them, which would then hover above such a sensibility, conferring on it a horizon of its own possibility. In consequence Irigaray
would hope to avoid any abstract transcendence negating embodied specificity (and any embodied particularity claiming for itself transcendent universality), a situation which has, according to her, normally reduced the
uniqueness of the feminine subject to the same order as male identification.
But if, to repeat a prior quotation, 'nothing is more spiritual than female sexuality', and if this is because (as Irigaray tells us in an interview when asked
about this phrase), female sexuality corresponds 'to the generation of a sensible transcendental', then we are left with the question of who generates this
salvation of the female subject – who creates this *transcendental sensible* – such
that a feminine identity becomes possible?[94] Irigaray leaves us in little doubt
that this generation arises from women themselves, since for women there is
'a lack of a transcendental to which they correspond' thus 'they have to discover one for themselves'.[95]

And yet theologically speaking the last thing humans are capable of is the
manufacture or discovery of salvation by themselves. Indeed, as I have
already stated, this sort of claim is hardly the revolutionary statement that it
is commonly taken to be, and in truth it appears both deeply modern and
utterly masculine. Feminine self-salvation on the basis of an image bequeath-
ing self-sufficiency reappropriated from the male order, mimics the modern
construction of this (male) order when subjectivity appropriated all its
powers from the God that it made noumenal. Indeed it appears that Irigaray
remains so sociologically dedicated to a participation in secular politics that
she allows this fundamentally atheistic anthropology to determine both God
and concomitantly any theory of the 'feminine subject' that she wishes to
advance.

We find, for example, in her account of Jesus's incarnation in *Equal to
Whom*, a claim that 'God made man or God the father are not enough to sanc-
tify the female sex', for apparently all subjectivities have 'the right to a
divine identity'.[97] This claim for a divine identity, this belief that God must
be made woman in order for women to truly become women, seems utterly
at odds with almost everything about Christianity and Christ's incarnation.
For the Christ enfleshed by his mother Mary blesses not one human incarnation, but all human form as such. Moreover, the whole message of Christ was
that the grace that he both fully instantiates and makes possible cannot be
restricted nor made the exclusive property of any ontic form. To allow
Christ to be appropriated by a male symbolic, to accept that God has been
reduced to male form, is to allow Christ's humanity to determine Christ's
divinity, rather than permitting this divinity to 'personify' Christ's human
nature in such a fashion that it includes in advance all *possible* humanity
(male and female). Irigaray's position only revives the blasphemy of Arius
and the Arians (who denied the divinity of the Son); it accepts a view of

transcendence and of grace that stands wholly at odds with Christian tradition but wholly in line with the modern self-sufficient subject that arose from the denial and displacement of God.

For what we are given from Christ is not any assertion of divine preference for a particular masculine form, but the gracing of all incarnate form as such, and moreover the gift of the Holy Spirit and the promise that all can participate in it. The nature of the Christian universal is that it can only express itself in and through the creation of singulars, for God is not an abstract universality that proceeds to phenomenality by negating His creations, nor indeed do we only participate in Him via deficient similarity, for God's highest self-expression is those whom he creates and each of God's creatures stands on its own as an utterly unique and *non-negatable* testimony to God in the sense that *in* God it most fully is and *is* most fully affirmed. And the reduction of this relation to a model of Kantian subsumption where the universal negates the particulars that are its representations is a definitive sign of secular immanentism. But now, in an immanentist reversal of this failed transcendental vocabulary, Irigaray has allowed the particular sexate form of the incarnate Christ – his body – to stand over and against his universality and his divinity, with the not unpredictable consequence that his divinity is not thought now to be able to transcend nor speak beyond his embodied particularity.

By contrast with this double static limitation of spirit and body stands Catholic eucharistic reality. For since Christ's divine nature is not determined by his particular body, it divinises all bodies as such. In this way the relationship of the divine nature to Christ's particular embodied incarnation indicates the superlative extreme of a theological relation whereby the most high does not negate its most particular creations. And this refusal to negate that which has been created is so radical that Christ promises the resurrection of all bodies that participate in him, in the realm of the eternal beyond the time and space of secular reality. Thought in this way, Christ's embodiment does not represent a partial manifestation of divinity in one specific form, but the participation of each and every specific form in the Trinitarian recovery and redemption of finite dependent life. Indeed, it is Irigaray's failure to understand that Christian universality is not reduced or nihilated by the specific form that it takes that makes her reduce Christ's divinity to his humanity. Likewise, this failure to comprehend the non-violent extension of Christian universality over specificity bespeaks a failure to understand – once again – that it is the Holy Spirit which allows a full participation by all creatures in the Son, for it is the Spirit that enables all flesh to be graced with the possibility of absolute participation in the reciprocal love of the Father and the Son. And if it is grace that enables all singular creations fully to participate in the Son then it is the absence of a corresponding account of grace that makes Irigaray's engagement with theology an immanentist one. Not least because she allows the incarnation to be read not as the possibility of participation in the divine hypostastis but as a general human identity with it: for instance she writes that the incarnation represents 'nothing more or less than each man and each women being virtually gods'.[97] The evident danger of this pagan mimicry of Christ and the Christian message is that it allows the human self-image to govern the relationship that the body (both female and male) undoubtedly has with transcendence.

Now I recognise that Irigaray's accounts of sensibility risk escaping from the very conditions that she imposes on them, but in her attempts to avoid the horrific undifferentiated non-sexed immanence of the neuter (an idea which incidentally is a creation of secular philosophy and not of God), Irigaray retreats from the possibility of a truly theological account of sexed incarnate singularity to an almost ontic account of the female body and feminine anthropology, and she allows this ontic caricature to stand over and against the divinity of the Paraclete who graces all incarnate form with a possibility that cannot be captured by any particular determination.[98] To venture this implies that Irigaray has not yet understood that Christ's incarnate embodiment tells us that both men and women are already in the image of God and that neither men nor women should attempt to manufacture any higher image for themselves, not least because this portrays a failure to discern that these highest images have already been given to us as our own embodied actuality. And this gift given to women and men is not capable of being destroyed or denied by any length of human idolatry or blindness, quite simply because we ourselves are always born into a relationship with truth and transcendence. And enfleshed as we are, we always bear the imprimatur of that which is not reducible to our own horizon. For let me be very clear, any patriarchal or matriarchal appropriation of God is also an idolatry, since neither men nor women can manufacture a God for their own foundation without foreclosing on any genuine relation with transcendence. If Irigaray has indeed – despite all appearances to the contrary – accepted rather than challenged the modern appropriation of God, if she has claimed from men their idolatrous relation to God, then any resultant divinity accorded to women can only be false and idolatrous also. Not least because only God can give divinity and only God can give men and women their true image.

All of which should lead theology to take a certain distance from psychoanalysis and its modernist noumenology. The reason being that God is and must be thought to be *entirely phenomenal* (even if His full appearance is not apparent to us). For as soon as we accept like Lacan that 'God is not dead but unconscious' then we make God noumenal, and as a consequence we force transcendence to function in a sublime manner.[99] Moreover, the assent given by psychoanalysis to modernity's denial of God's phenomenality means that psychoanalytic consciousness can never achieve reconciliation with God, since God (consigned to the noumenal edge of cognition) can only ever mark the chimerical limit of a consciousness that is driven relentlessly to determine itself against that always receding constraint. Thought in this way, a consciousness that claims to pursue its own salvation in transcendence, when that transcendence can only have a sublime form, only succeeds in attaining an ever-greater self-expansion. Against which it might be suggested that a true account of Trinitarian consciousness (or rather personhood) forbids any subjective interiority at all. For in truth there can be no private realms for theology, not least because nothing can be considered to be separate or apart from God, and since God does not give one thing to one person without also allowing another to participate in it, any solipsistic realm would find itself eclipsed by a theology of the endless relationality of creatures. In this sense Hegel was perhaps right in his insistence that a fully reconciled consciousness (a consciousness that would love what it was and what it was not), should have no internal unthought dimensionality, since all the complexity and differentiation of fulfilled identity would need to be fully actualised, present in the world in history, if it was to inhabit a true as opposed to an abstract universality. Now whilst for theology there would never be any final fulfilment of being (as the religious world would have no Hegelian end nor indeed one single consciousness within which to express it), but rather a life of infinite participation, this participation would not be subsumable by any interior world of private occult gestures, which means that theology cannot accept any reduction of the visibility it thematises to explanations of a private pathology. This means again that theology cannot accept psychoanalysis, unless, that is, psychoanalysis abandons noumenal investigation and surrenders itself to an account of the mystery and translucent glory of phenomenality. For the phenomenality that theology wishes to speak of is not reducible to the mundane static caricatures of positivistic empiricism nor indeed is it amenable to the realist naivety of scientific description. No: an adequately theological account of such phenomenality would crucially liberate depth from the privatised interiority of psychoanalysis, for the *depth* that theology seeks in phenomena is not behind the surface but rather is that ineliminable possibility of the surface which is the appearance yet-to-come and the phenomena which are possibilities yet-to-be.

In speaking of the possibility of phenomenality, I earlier denied the modern assumption that language and phenomena were to be thought of as necessarily opposed, for not only was any ontic account of phenomena that denied appearance its own form as language refused, but also any divorcing of the mental from the phenomenal realm in order to subsume visibility under the abstract universality of the mind. And if in contemporary philosophy language or mental mediation has taken a distance from phenomenal reality, this is because secular construals of language have been permitted to hand over the sensible realm to the descriptions that modernity has prepared for it. The costs of this denial of language to the visual and its images are obvious but no less harmful for that, for as our final contribution shows, Jean Baudrillard has described in the most exquisite detail the representational void into which the image idolatrously divorced from language has descended.

For now language is thought to mitigate against the claims of the visual as soon as it speaks of it, and as a consequence images as soon as they are mediated by language become, apparently, sundered from their original, and our modern culture (founded upon the idea and hope of a certain referentiality) seems to face an ever-deepening inability to refer to anything outside of itself. Yet Andrew Wernick tells us that this nihilistic situation might not constitute the last moments of civilisation before our general absorption into the undifferentiated mass of consumption. Apparently Baudrillard, in spite of endorsing such an account of language and phenomena, does offer 'a salvific opening' – 'a challenge to the powers of the world, including the gods, to appear once more'. For Baudrillard, according to Wernick's deeply insightful account, takes the collective, or rather the social, to occupy the now displaced and defunct site of God in the modern epoch. In which case we are looking at, according to him, a second death of God. For this second death was prefigured by the first, and the first death was the loss of the God who guaranteed the subject its foundation and its objective reality. Whilst the original Marxist critique of the loss of the object to alienated work and labour was mitigated in some sense by the rise of a social agency that sought its recovery, the consequent loss of the real object and the rise of a specular mass society testifies to the death of the social as well. Indeed, it is the loss of this emancipatory space that defines Baudrillard's work, because for him the social remains in this epoch the sole – and unavoidably religious – horizon of redemptive possibility. As Wernick writes,

> on the one hand, then, the God term projected onto the human subject, whether as Man, the revolutionary proletariat, or Society, disappears along with its simulacrum. But on the other hand, the gestural place for pointing towards 'that' beyond 'this' is preserved. It lives on in the irrepressibility of the counter-gift, of the sacrifice, of the violence that makes sacred.

Baudrillard's question, given all this, is 'Can the gods be made to reappear?' In the hope of this manifestation, Wernick suggests that Baudrillard embraces a form of Catholic realism – the Baroque – and becomes an iconolater who celebrates and defends the image against its Protestant prohibition, because for Baudrillard the image and its inherent structural failings represent the condition for the glorious profusion of signs and mediated signification that he adores. None the less, in spite of this purported 'realism' of the image, Baudrillard does not accept any idea of the sacred participation of the divine in images. In fact, he maintains the divine non-reference of the image and stresses the ability of the oversimulated copy to occlude the real whose image it originally was. As such Baudrillard enacts a kind of performative endorsement of the images of failed mediation, and in a manner not unlike Nietzsche's account of the overcoming of nihilism, Wernick contends that this knowing embrace of a failed mediation might offer to such idolatry its own completion and culmination, such that a resacralisation of all images would be possible.

But the embrace of idolatry cannot here enable one to go past it, not least because nothing other than idolatry is ever considered possible. And if Baudrillard can at best only offer us descriptions of a life lived in knowing absence of the divine, this post-modern sociology has only succeeded in concealing the truth of its own deeper blindness. For if Baudrillard as disillusioned revolutionary has still remained faithful to a certain transformative impulse, then what he should have transformed was the secular model of the world that allowed reality to be considered apart from God in the first place. Since one can only sunder an image from its original if the image is thought to be capable of standing apart from what it participates in, then as soon as one speaks of images 'representing' their originals, then in some way one has allowed images to deny their dependency and become self-sufficient copies. Now of course Baudrillard accepts the idea that the image is that which can represent its original, but he accepts this model of the image because it is a model that can only fail. A self-sufficient image, an image that wishes to be a copy, can only fail to depict its origin as its relation to that original has to be mediated by another term which would adjudicate the accuracy of its reproduction. This spatial and temporal adjudication (which is language), though it is not a part of the image, contaminates the image, since it is what allows an image to articulate itself as what it is; as such the necessary mediation of language inevitably prevents any perfect visual reproduction from emerging, because this mediation has now become part of what that image is. All of which leaves Baudrillard claiming to embrace the abyss between phenomena and language as some sort of nihilistic prevention of nihilism.

However, from a theological perspective Baudrillard's original assumption is false, since a theological image can never represent nor copy its original! Not least because the original of the image is nothing but a plenitude of images itself (for God's 'originality' is his creativity and as the Father only is his expression in the Son, we find that God's image does not stand apart from our own, because not only are we made in His image, His image, which contains us, is only an image of all the other images – those that have been, those that are and those that will be). This 'original' then is nothing but the glory and possibility of an infinite engendering surface, and any image which attempts to be adequate to the God who is the source of this unlimited inundation of image and phenomena necessarily fails. For a finite image is incapable of ever copying or ever representing this boundless source. For just as the Creator eminently 'contains' all his creations, whilst at the same time always producing more, so the infinite originality of the original is precisely the promise of further creation and appearance, and a copy cannot supplant this original source without idolatrously denying this possibility of infinite creation and renewal.

And unfortunately this denial of the original in the sense of an eternal plenitudinous source of appropriate images and providential forms is exactly the form of 'realism' that Baudrillard embraces, as the 'Catholic realism' that Baudrillard speaks of is really only that of onto-theology, a form of realism that believes that God can be reduced to what is simply real (an onto-theological form that is by the way precisely emergent in the Baroque epoch), and this form of realism is idolatrous as it allows that which is real to stand for, rather than stand within, God. Moreover, if the true blindness of Baudrillard's position is that it repeats the theological acceptance of secular realism by allowing Being in general to stand over God and distribute self-sufficiency to all particular beings, then to embrace the model of the image that holds that the image is a self-sufficient signification of the divine is again to allow instantiated particulars to stand over and against the universality that created them. This is despite the fact that Baudrillard accepts this model of the image only in order to denigrate and celebrate its subsequent failure.

For the reason that created beings or created images cannot be self-sufficient representatives of the divine is that they are indeed created, and as created, their being consists only in being related to the Creator. All of which means that one can only speak of images through ideas of their participation in and dependency on an infinite giving origin, rather than through ideas which assume that images can adequately represent their origin, and so have as a result the possibility of independence from it. In Christianity one cannot, in the end, speak of copies and originals at all, because copies always live in fear of being negated by originals and as the source of all origination God does not create beings in order to negate them. Hence *there can be in Christianity no acceptance of the language of copy and original*, as each and every being is an 'original' created image whose singularised look and form cannot copy its origin in the abundant solicitude and gratuity of God. And because no created image is adequate to the light that passes through it, our reception of such gratuity becomes a celebration not of our failure to copy its dimensions but rather of our glorious participation in it. Moreover, this is a celebration that is imparted and shown to others, for we 'all grow brighter and brighter as we are turned into the image' (2 Cor. 3:18).

Here indeed then is a genuine excess and supplementarity beyond anything that post-modernism can dream of. For post-modernism requires this illusion of the 'copy of the original' since all of these dreadful contemporary claims that the original stands apart from its mediation and consequently falls prey to it fail to understand that the Creator does not stand apart from what He creates, and that his voice and presence are the gifts that transform and transfigure our own voice and presence. The origin in all its non-noumenal phenomenal plenitude, its hidden glory of infinite manifestation, is nothing but gift and giveness – an infinite infusion of the being that we have with the promise of the creation and possibility to come. And this promise and potentiality of the original is exactly what post-modernism denies; but by this denial, by this removal of the original, post-modernity denies also any possibility of a value outside or external to the copy that contains it. Consequently, this erasure of the original removes any value, permanence or novelty from the copy and indeed any 'originality' as well. It is not surprising then, that when copies are abandoned to self-sufficiency, they discover themselves to be adrift in a void, hopelessly seeking the possibility of the new; but of course this novelty is now no longer possible for them, since these copies without originals have cut themselves off from the only possibility that could provide such a thing. Consequently this Baudrillardian and post-modernist realism of originless images and fatherless phenomena expresses uniquely the dreadful bankruptcy of the age, as images that once claimed to represent the divine now claim to represent nothing but themselves, and in taking this modern separation of finitude from infinity to its logical outcome, this bankruptcy represents the true inheritance of idolatry and modernity.

The end of the secular and the beginning of perception

> But we see this Matter shewes it self to us, in abundance of *varieties* of *appearance*; therefore there must be another principle besides the Matter to order the motion of it so, as may make these *varieties* to *appear*: And what will that prove but *a God*?
>
> (Henry More, 'An Antidote against Atheism')[100]

> [O]ur investigation however, is directed not towards phenomena, but, as one might say, towards the *'possibilities'* of phenomena.
>
> (Ludwig Wittgenstein, *Philosophical Investigations*)[101]

To say we should now bring an end to the secular is to say that we should reverse the dreadful consequences of the liberal erasure of God and take myth back from out of the hands of the fascists where it has all too often fallen.[103] If we do not, if we as an advanced culture have as our highest value only a form of self-reference, then we will only ever become more primitive as we develop. For not only will we hand over religion to the fundamentalists, we will hand over ourselves and our futurity as well. To speak against fundamentalism is to say at the same time that it is not possible to give the highest account of ourselves without religion and what it discloses. And it is Christ's incarnation of the Word into flesh, that alone grants us the possibility that our highest descriptions might actually be the case. For Christ binds together in his own body the invisible and the visible, and as a result He incarnates the transcendent in the flesh and prevents any subsequent account of human materiality divorcing itself from theology. And if it was the desire to give an account of this materiality before giving an account of God that initiated the whole despicable idolatry of the modern, then it is only an account of matter's absolute and utter dependence upon God that can overcome the dreadful vacuity and despair that this age has fallen into.

For the celebration of this vacuity and its endless self-serving acts of negation and denial has become the new weak mysticism of the age. Indeed, now people quite happily disavow any possibility that their own melancholia and desperation might be attended by a form and a shape that could transfigure them and their world. And this characteristic of contemporary nihilism – the indifference of those who face the extinction of their own and others' possibility – is but the middle ground of the passage from a failed transcendentalism to the horrors of the sublime surrender to immanentism. And if this has all come about because the modern quest for knowledge and foundation denied the dependency of objects on God and claimed instead that it was objectivity in general that made both God and knowledge of objects possible, we should perhaps not be surprised that atheistic subjectivity has suddenly found – at the end of modernity – that objectivity without God is nothing at all. Which again is perhaps why modern transcendentalism has culminated so explicitly in immanentism, for if nothing can be objective, then objectivity itself must be nothing, which means correspondingly that there is nothing above, beyond or other than simple ontic actuality. Whilst the modern project tried to found its own self-referential account of value on the absolute lack of external value and the apathy and indifference of matter, the failure of this foundational enterprise has left us abandoned on a Godless world with no other alternative account of it and consequently ourselves. It is little wonder then that people choose to accept that brute immanence and human inclusion in its listless dimensionality and force constitute all that is possible for them. For the blind and hopeless acceptance of this falsified actuality and its consequent denial of the transcendent possibility of a higher actuality is what marks the most pernicious and final consequence of God's erasure from experience. And if the final consequence of the rise of atheistic subjectivity is the sublime surrender of that subjectivity to a dehumanized pagan materiality, we should not be surprised. Not least because the sublime always plays itself out at the expense of the subject that it was once thought to guarantee. This idolatry of the sublime plays itself out because the vacuity and terror that once marked and preserved the borders of human finitude when it faced infinite non-human reality can now, after the end of foundational reflexive man, no longer mark the distinction between what is human and what is not. Now in fact terror and vacuity mark the point at which those without God surrender themselves to that which originally they had thought themselves so opposed – a violent and nihilistic nature. A nature which is indeed both terrible and vacuous because it absorbs human beings without accounting for them, and does so without any meaning or rationale whatsoever.

55

Which is why it is so important to refuse to surrender the world and its phenomenal beauty and materiality to Gnostic and idolatrous denials of God's creation. Which again is why the whole stress and hope of this introduction is to say that reality is indeed spiritual, that matter is indeed intertwined with spirit, and that matter is as result not in essence a noumenal materiality but rather a wholly phenomenal language of futurity. For both nature and humanity have and show a futurity and a possibility that is not reducible to each being absorbed by the other. In a theological vision both man and nature, mind and world, have their origin in God, and both testify to and celebrate what is possible for them as a result. Mind and world are indeed meant to come together in knowledge, but the only knowledge that can genuinely come from this union is that of the Father and the Son. And it is this possibility that I have been attempting to describe. From the perspective of man this means that though 'no one has ever seen God' (John 1:18) 'whom no man has seen and no man is able to see' (1 Tim. 6:16), Christ is the one 'who has made him known' (John 1:18) since as Christ himself says, '[T]o have seen me is to have seen the Father' (John 14:9), for we are told that 'whoever sees me sees the one who sent me' (John 12:45). And this inconceivable sight is possible for us, because Christ represents the Word, and 'the Word was made flesh' (John 1:14) and as a consequence our reality has forever been transfigured because now 'the reality is Christ' (Col. 2:18). As a result of this unimaginable event, God has been reconciled with man such that the created world is restored in and to its mediated alignment with the Creator, and in its most truthful consort with its highest possibility, the phenomena of the world testify to nothing but their dependency in the glory and love of God.

To say this is to reconsecrate our world; it is to say that no created thing stands apart from its creator and that each and every existent creation reveals its origin in the Father through showing and revealing the phenomenology of its own given form. In respect of this I feel then that it is no act of idolatry to believe that theology finds its possibility here – etched in the phenomenal world of perception and in the look and appearance of the created world. Not least because this claim that we see God in the glory of the perceptual world necessarily prohibits any visible from being both self-determinate and determinative of God, since, as I have shown, God is only seen when every being and each and every visible surrenders idolatrous self-determination to enter into the beauty and light of infinite participation. In this way a phenomenal indeterminacy reveals an utter dependence upon, and an absolute determination by God. Perhaps then this is why phenomena cannot show any self-sufficient secular object, perhaps this is why secular knowledge always has to retreat from and dissolve the phenomenal world in order to explain it. All of which is to say that when modernity made God noumenal by claiming that there was no empirical impression equal to His concept, it was operating with a false concept of Him – because an impression's glorious inequality in respect of divinity is exactly how the divine shows itself!

And this inequality – even though it reveals the inadequacy of the given in respect of the superlative extent and range of God's phenomenal gifts to us – is beautiful and not sublime. Beautiful, because though we see and acknowledge the inadequacy and in-determination of the visible given, when its visibility is fractured by the invisible possibilities that the giver makes manifest, this excess of visible invisibility does not stimulate us (as does the sublime) to give an account of our own greater potency – a potency that would fill in this gap in the visible with our own projections. No: the relation of the invisible to the visible is beautiful because it is a phenomenality that binds together what cannot be reduced to the same; indeed this co-presence of materiality and transcendence is beautiful because it delights apart from any opposition. To say this is to say that a sensible form can carry the beautiful, but that this containment spills over to the conceptuality of the subject and carries the mind and its delight in the world to an acknowledgement and recognition of the mutual origin of mind and world in the solicitude of God. Since the beautiful is the phenomenality of the Creator for its creatures, we can never define nor reach the limits of that which delights in harmonising our mind and our world. Indeed, when mind and world touch the recognition that each is present in the other, when they both recognise that neither can determine the parameters that modernity claimed defined and separated them, they both become celebratory of the resulting harmony that pertains. Moreover, since the beautiful takes us beyond the secular opposition and antagonism of concept and intuition, the beautiful gives itself to us without any threat of a subsequent redetermination or indeed negation. Because that which is not determined, but always given, is never taken away; not least because we return the unlimited love of the Father with a love for Him and a love for what He has created: as such we reconsecrate what we have been given, we become more beautiful, we create and make possibility actuality as we make the beautiful appear and become real; as such our subjectivity participates in the objective and indeed becomes part of that order. But as I have said, this theological objectivity does not assimilate our created singularity to itself; this becoming objective preserves us as we are and as we can be, because when we enter into our own form and make its ideality ever more real we return the gift of the given by remaking ourselves and our world according to the highest images that attend us. As a consequence human gifts – works of beauty, truth and goodness – cannot for theology ever be degraded by time, as they already participate in the eternal by initiating and creating a reciprocity that will forever celebrate what is granted to human perception.

And this is why I have focused on perception, because to perception is given, as Merleau-Ponty recognised, the paradoxical and wondrous gift to see both immanence and transcendence, to discern in the heart of what is most material what is most transcendent, which is to say that perception always goes beyond its objects because objects always go beyond themselves.[103] For immanence is founded on a transcendence that is more intimate than itself, and that which is transcendent distinguishes itself from every immanent thing only in order to give itself wholly, without noumenal reserve, to every single thing. And for human beings it is perception that has first encounter with this wholly phenomenal gift. But this phenomenon does not stand above us as a transcendence hovering in negation beyond a world that it cannot embrace. No – as soon as we open our eyes, as it were, we find ourselves wholly embraced and already inscribed, we find the ideal already running over us, and the invisible already there streaming over our bodies. And all of the shapes that we see, all of the depth, perspective, colour and form, are figures and contours that the invisible brings forth for the visible; it pulls visibility into attendance with its highest form and possibility, and in the end we cannot separate the one from the other, we cannot see in this kenotic consort of the invisible and visible where one ends and another begins. This is perhaps why perception, with its inability to separate intuition from concept, with its account of passive reception and active contribution, cannot discern where the intellectual begins and the phenomenal ends. Because in truth perception takes us beyond any secular opposition, it affirms us and our objects and it affirms them both as participation and as culmination of God, and God's glory. And in respect of this utter reality and beauty, only a theological realism can properly acknowledge and affirm what is presented there. For God grants to perception both the invisible and the visible, and when we colour in the adumbrations and transcendent shapes of the invisible and make it seen, and when we judge that we are for it and it is for us, and when we act in the name and are named in the act, then we see the phenomenal presence of the ideal in the real. And this ideality has the effect of calling forth from us a contribution such that we might make it so and make manifest that it is so. In this way our actuality consorts with its own possibility, a possibility that has itself been given to human beings in the hope and faith that we will make it real.

Notes

1 This quote is taken from the opening to Schleiermacher's *On Religion, Speeches to its Cultured Despisers*, tr. R. Crouter, Cambridge: Cambridge University Press, 1988. All other biblical references are taken from *The Jerusalem Bible* unless otherwise indicated. All translations from French texts are my own unless I indicate otherwise.

2 The use of the term theology is intended to refer only to the theology of the Christian tradition. The Greeks had a theology, and there are indeed many theologies, but when I use the word theology I do not intend to refer to anything but the tradition of thinking that grew up out of the Jewish blessing and the incarnation of Christ.

3 When the word immanence or immanentist is used, I deploy it in opposition to transcendence. As a pejorative, it refers for me to a world that believes itself to

be wholly sufficient unto itself, an atheistic world or account that neither asks nor requires anything external to itself. And inasmuch as these immanentist accounts do not often recognise themselves as relentlessly internalising projects which occlude consideration of the transcendent, I will approach them as forms of blindness that claim the ability to see.

4 Søren Kierkegaard, *Philosophical Fragments/Johannes Climacus*, ed. H.V. Hong and E.H. Hong, Princeton: Princeton University Press, 1987, p. 32.

5 See Hans Urs Von Balthasar's *Herrlichkeit*, Einsiedeln: Johannes Verlag, 1961, and also Jean-Luc Marion's *La Croisée du visible*, Paris: La Différence, 1991.

6 Maurice Merleau-Ponty, *Le Visible et l'invisible*, hereafter *VI*, ed. C. Lefort, Paris: Editions Gallimard, 1964, p. 17.

7 Aristotle, *De Anima*, Bk I, 404b17.

8 Duns Scotus, 'Cognitio Naturalis De Deo', in *Philosophical Writings*, tr. Allan Wolter OFM, Indianapolis: Hackett, 1987, p. 16.

9 *Ibid.*, p. 18.

10 Scotus, *De Metaphysica*, *ibid.*, p. 5. Of course Scotus was anxious to avoid charges of pantheism and attempted to do so by constructing his doctrine of formal distinction, by virtue of which he hoped to maintain a qualitative distinction between God and His creatures, but one that still allowed of a natural knowledge of God without the necessity of divine illumination. Obviously my point is that without divine illumination all claims of knowledge are immanentist.

11 See *Summa Contra Gentiles*, Vol. 1, especially Chapter 32, part 2, tr. Anton C. Pegis, London: University of Notre Dame, 1975. For Thomas one cannot predicate anything of God univocally with other things, for this would disturb the order and priority of God with respect to his creations. One can only predicate by assigning priority to God and allowing other things to participate in Him via diminished perfection.

12 *Summa Contra Gentiles*, Vol. 1, Chapter 34.

13 The Bull contained condemnation of twenty-eight of Eckhart's articles, dividing them into seventeen which were definitely heretical, and eleven any approval of which would be enough to bring about a suspicion of heresy.

14 Reiner Schürmann makes this point beautifully:

> Eckhart considers the being of created things in its provenance – their being belongs first to God. Creatures receive being as a loan, not as their own. Their being resides in God, it is a gift; but he who gives can also take back. Their being is precarious, it comes to them from another. The created in itself is nothingness: what deserves attention in creatures is the origin of the gift, which is greater than its term.
> (*Meister Eckhart: Mystic and Philosopher*, Bloomington: Indiana University Press, 1978, p. 62)

15 *Summa Theologiae*, Part Ia IIae, question 109, art. 2.

16 Eckhart, *Meister Eckhart*, tr. Edmund College and Bernard McGinn, New York: Paulist Press, 1981, p. 140.

17 It is interesting to note that the Curia at Avignon also condemned fifty-one propositions of Ockham in 1326. I will leave it to others to decide whether this represents astute judgement on the part of the theologians of the Babylonian captivity or not. Incidentally, it is probable that Ockham witnessed some or all of Eckhart's own defence; unfortunately he apparently thought the latter was quite made.

18 Hans Blumenberg also detects a similar connection. He writes:

> it may seem insignificant that while the nominalistic discussion of Ockham's thesis of the possibility of intuition of a nonexistent thing does not arrive at Descartes's *Cogito*, it does anticipate his assertion of the incontestability of man's freedom not to have to let himself be deceived.

In this separation of a sense perception that could be deceived by God, and a judgement by finite humanity that this need not be so, Blumenberg perceives that 'the nominalists already saw the narrow solid ground of self-assertion'. See Hans Blumenberg, *The Legitimacy of the Modern Age*, tr. R.M. Walker, Cambridge, Mass.: MIT Press, 1985, pp. 193ff.

19 Immanuel Kant, *Opus Postumum*, ed. E. Föster, tr. E. Föster and M. Rosen, Cambridge: Cambridge University Press, 1993, p. 189.

20 David Rapport Lachterman, *The Ethics of Geometry: A Genealogy of Modernity*, London: Routledge, 1989. See Chapter 1, 'Construction as the Mark of the Modern'.

21 Jean-Luc Marion, *Graduate Faculty Philosophy Journal*, Vol. 11, No. 1, 'On Descartes' Constitution of Metaphysics', p. 23.

22 Martin Heidegger, 'The Onto-theo-logical Constitution of Metaphysics', in *Identity and Difference*, hereafter *ID*, English: German edition, tr. J. Stambaugh, New York: Harper and Row, 1969, p. 54. *Die onto-theo-logische verfassung der metaphysik*, p. 121.

23 Which is why, to a religious mind, the Heideggerian idea of being towards death as the singularising event in the life of Dasein is somehow to miss the point of such a finitude. For theology death is not how one thinks the futurity of the creature.

24 I draw this remark from Heidegger's discussion of Hegel's predicament in *Identity and Difference*.

25 This of course is a matter of intense debate. For even though sensibility has its own formal a priori dimension that is space and time, Kant was always at pains to show that this formal element was not a creation of the understanding. Moreover, a strict Kantian interpretation would say that it would elide the difference between sensibility and the understanding if it was suggested that merely because intuition also has its own a priori forms that it could be then conflated with the understanding. None the less, it remains my claim that Kant did construe the interests of sensibility as lying in conforming with the demands of the understanding. For instance, even though Kant might have written the following: 'The categories of understanding, on the other hand, do not represent the conditions under which objects are given in intuition. Objects may, therefore, appear to us without their being under the necessity of being related to the functions of understanding; and understanding need not, therefore, contain their a priori conditions' (Immanuel Kant, *Critique of Pure Reason*, hereafter *CPR*, tr. Norman Kemp Smith, London: Macmillan, 1933, §A90: B123), he resolved this possibility – at least in the A deduction – through negating it: for instance, he writes that intuitions 'are nothing to us, and do not in the least concern us if they cannot be taken up into consciousness' (*CPR*, §A116).

26 *CPR*, A598: B626.

27 *CPR*, Bxxx.

28 For an excellent discussion of the sublime and the beautiful, and its relationship to judgement in Kant, see Howard Caygill's *The Art of Judgement*, Oxford: Basil Blackwell, 1989. See also by the same author an extremely useful guide to

the complexities of Kant's lexicon, *A Kant Dictionary*, Oxford: Basil Blackwell, 1995.

29 Immanuel Kant, *The Critique of Judgement*, hereafter *CJ*, tr. J.H. Barnard, New York: Hafner, §23, p. 83.

30 *CJ*, §23, p. 84.

31 *CJ*, §27, p. 96.

32 This becomes especially clear when one reads Kant's attempt to ascertain whether 'a determinate experience' can provide us with 'an assured conviction of a supreme being' (*CPR*, A620: B648). This section, 'The Impossibility of the Physio-theological Proof', is perhaps the most interesting of Kant's refutations of speculative theology, insofar as it appears to be the argument that he finds the weakest, yet the one he has most sympathy for. It is here in the world of empirical nature that he finds the purposiveness of nature that he will, in the *Critique of Judgement*, find to be definitive of beauty, and also a recognition of nature's lack of purpose, an experience which he later determines to be symptomatic of the sublime. However, despite any presumed equivocation, Kant ends this discussion with the conclusion that the God pursued by the physico-theological proof is an 'object that has refused itself to all their empirical enquiries' (*CPR*, A630: B658).

33 *CJ*, §27, p. 97.

34 *CJ*, §27, p. 96.

35 G.W.F. Hegel, *Faith and Knowledge*, tr. W. Cerf and H.S. Harris, Albany: SUNY Press, 1977, p. 61.

36 This description is somewhat analagous to that which Jean-Luc Marion uses concerning the invisible mirror in *Dieu sans l'être*. See Marion, *Dieu sans l'être*, hereafter *DE*, Paris: Quadridge/PUF. For instance, pp. 32–3: 'Tandis que l'idole se détermine toujours comme un réflexe, qui la fait venir d'un point fixé, à partir d'un original dont fondamentalement, elle revient.' See also Marion's *L'Idole et la distance*, 'Les marches de la métaphysique', Paris: Le livre de poche, 1991, pp. 15–24. However, whilst the origination of the mirror is explained in Marion's work as a product of the fatigue of the idolatrous gaze, it seems to me, at least, that the potency of the idolatrous structure is also explained by the power of finite thought. Whilst Marion does argue that the idol represents the high-water mark of secular thinking, he contrasts it with an iconic manifestation where (to my mind at least) he opposes finite intentionality with infinite intentionality and so I think risks failing to distinguish adequately the phenomenological modes of idolatrous and iconic appearance. To put this more simply, it seems to me that Marion's account of the icon risks, as I will show later, a certain sublimity.

37 Hegel, *Faith and Knowledge*, p. 67.

38 In a way this understanding of Milbank's paper on Kierkegaard reflects a similar concern in Milbank's own work. See his ground-breaking *Theology and Social Theory: Beyond Secular Reason*, Oxford: Basil Blackwell, 1990. In the introduction to this work Milbank speaks of breaking with 'realism in favour of linguistic idealism and a variant of pragmatism', p. 5. However, a need to establish theology as a meta-discourse again confronts him with the necessity of being 'theologically realist', p. 6. Whilst the concluding chapter of *Theology and Social Theory* does offer us an 'ontology of peace', it does not give this ontology any phenomenology. My concern with this position would be that such an ontology would be hopelessly noumenal unless this ontology could be shown to have a phenomenal presence in the world. To say this is to suggest that a pragmatic account that wishes to be theologically realist requires some sort of theological account of the real. Otherwise it is difficult to see how a theological realism could differ, or escape from, a

pragmatic and possibly voluntaristic account of what is realisable for human experience.

39 However, the repetition of evil and error can only be that of identical repetition, i.e., evil repeating itself as simply evil, and identical repetition denies the futural aspect of genuine repetition which never simply repeats itself. For instance, see his open letter to Professor Heiberg, where Kierkegaard resists the absorption of the individual spirit which wills repetition into the self-identical world of repeating and thus self-realising nature, *Fear and Trembling and Repetition*, *Kierkegaard's Writings*, Vol. V, ed. and tr. H.V. Hong and E.H. Hong, Princeton: Princeton University Press, 1983, p. 290.

40 *Ibid.*, *Repetition*, p. 149.

41 At this moment I am thinking of the various attempts by French thinkers to evince some sort of faith in the sublime event of the new. For example, see Lyotard's attempt to construct a political theory out of the differend – Jean-François Lyotard, *Le Différend*, Paris: Les Editions de Minuit, 1983. Also see Gilles Deleuzes's attempt to conduct a transcendental empiricism around a materialist theory of the event: Deleuze, *Différence et Répétition*, Paris: Presses Universitaires de France, 1968.

42 Kierkegaard, *Repetition*, pp. 132–3.

43 *Ibid.*, p. 132.

44 Kierkegaard, *Fear and Trembling*, p. 120.

45 Kierkegaard, *Repetition*, p. 186.

46 Bishop Berkeley, *Principles of Human Knowledge*, ed. R. Woolhouse, London: Penguin, 1988, §148, p. 109.

47 G.E. Moore, 'The Refutation of Idealism', in *Selected Writings*, ed. T. Baldwin, London: Routledge, 1993, p. 42. See also his response to the English Hegelian F.H. Bradley in 'External and Internal Relationships', reprinted in the same volume.

48 See G.W.F. Hegel, 'Sense Certainty', in *The Phenomenology of Spirit*, tr. A.V. Miller, Oxford: Oxford University Press, 1977, pp. 58–66.

49 Martin Heidegger, *Being and Time*, hereafter *BT*, tr. J. Macquarrie and E. Robinson, Oxford: Basil Blackwell, 1962, p. 63. Martin Heidegger, *Sein and Zeit*, hereafter *SZ*, Gesamtausgabe, vol. 2, Frankfurt: Vittorio Klostermann, 1977, pp. 51–2.

50 I say peculiar here because I believe that Heidegger is fundamentally wrong about his account of what our possibilities are and what actuality is. See for example the first section of my paper 'God and Phenomenology', in this collection.

51 This project again echoes Hans Urs Von Balthasar's; see Vol. 1 of his *Herrlichkeit: Eine theologische Asthetik, Band I: Schau der Gestalt*, Einsiedeln: Johannes Verlag, 1961.

52 Of course I am not suggesting that this is the position that Berkeley intended to propound.

53 There are sufficient references to Marion's and Levinas's use of phenomena in the anthology. However, this may not be the case for Scheler, so in respect of these matters see Max Scheler, *On the Eternal in Man*, tr. Bernard Noble, London: SCM Press, 1960. I am grateful to Sonya Sikka for directing my attention to this work.

54 *DE*, p. 29.

55 I have argued elsewhere that this invisibility marks the relationship of the theological to the ontological and so indicates the point at which perceptions can transcend the secular and become truly theological. See my 'Prolegomena to Theological Perception', in *Religion, Modernity and Postmodernity*, ed. D. Martin, P. Heelas and P. Morris, Oxford: Basil Blackwell, 1998.

56 *VI*, p. 178: 'On comprend alors pourquoi, à la fois, nous voyons les choses elle-mêmes, en leur lieu, où elles sont, selon leur être qui est bien plus que leur être-perçu.' Indeed this discrepancy between the subject and the object in matters of perception, their always being in excess of each other, testifies to a (theological) recognition that neither side of this divide can ever foreclose on the other. The object will always have more perspectival profiles for the intending gaze of the subject, and the subject will always bring more cognitive desires to the object than the object can ever satisfy. For this type of disjuncture speaks to the higher eros of cognition and it marks therefore the passage to a genuinely theological perception.

57 *VI*, p. 185.

58 *VI*, p. 195; p. 196

59 *VI*, p. 198.

60 By using the phrase 'invisible look', I am attempting to account for the relationship of the intelligible to the phenomenal. In point of fact I take this phrase from Plato and Platonic scholarship; see for example Jacob Klein, *Plato's Trilogy: Theaetetus, the Sophist, and the Statesman*, Chicago: University of Chicago Press, 1977. It has often been noted that the Platonic use of the word from (*eidos*) is conjoined in Greek with verbs of visibility and vision. In the *Republic* 510d Plato writes, 'they make use of the visible kinds' (*tois horómenois eidesi proskhrôntai*); similarly, if one thinks of a form as an idea, *idea* also means to see a visual aspect and to exhibit a kind; an idea then is a family of the visual cast, usually, it is 'very beautiful to look at' (*tên d'oun idean panu kalos*) (Protagoras 315e).

However, *tas d'* . . . *ideas noeisthai men horasthai d'ou*; the ideas are thought of but not seen (*Republic* 507b). The intelligibles at their most universal do not exhibit themselves visually, they are invisible. Hence I have taken the Platonic universal to be 'an invisible look'. Moreover, it is questionable as to what extent this invisible universal is separable from its particulars. As Gregory Vlastos has shown, Plato never uses the Greek word for separation, *chōrizein*, in respect of the forms and their relations; moreover, when discussing how the ontological status of the forms (e.g., do they exist by themselves, together or in combination) could be approached from the perspective of their participants (that which partakes of them) the word Plato uses is *diairein* or dialectics. Indeed when Plato does use *chōrizein* it is to suggest a pejorative divide, a harsh opposition between the soul and the world, a separation engendered only by death (*chōrisei, Republic* 609d7 and *choris einai, Phaedo* 64c6–8, 67aI). See Gregory Vlastos, 'Separation in Plato', in *Oxford Studies in Ancient Philosophy*, vol. 5, Oxford: Oxford University Press, 1987, pp. 187–96. It is perhaps more in subsequent interpretations of Plato that one finds arguments that suggest that the Platonic universal was separate from its participants. For instance, Simplicius wrote of a form described as separate from its matter, see *Physics* 544.23, incidentally even Aristotle, who based much of his critique of Plato on the argument that the forms are separate from that which they inform, acknowledges that Plato's teacher Socrates 'did not treat universals as separate' (*Met* 1078b30).

61 Maurice Merleau-Ponty, *Phénoménologie de la Perception*, Paris: Librairie Gallimard, 1945, p. 246.

62 Friedrich Nietzsche, *The Will to Power*, ed. W. Kaufmann, tr. W. Kaufmann and R.J. Hollingdale, New York: Vintage Books, Random House, 1968, Book 1, aphorism 2, p. 9.

63 Karl Barth, *The Epistle to the Romans*, tr. E. Hoskyns, Oxford: Oxford University Press, 1968, p. 136.

64 *BT*, p. 32; *SZ*, p. 16.

65 Martin Heidegger, *Der Spiegel*, No. 23, 1976, pp. 193–219.

66 For me of course the truth of Being does not lie in Being but rather in God, as God is the origin of Being and all Being is – as it were – dependent upon Him.

67 Martin Heidegger, *Basic Writings*, ed. D.F. Krell, 'Letter on Humanism', tr. Frank A. Capuzzi, London: Routledge & Kegan Paul, 1978, p. 230. Martin Heidegger, *Wegmarken*, Gesamtausgabe, vol. 9, Frankfurt: Vittorio Klostermann, 1976, p. 351.

68 Edmund Husserl, *Ideas*, tr. W.R. Boyce Gibson, London: Collier Macmillan, 1962, p. 83.

69 This for example appears to be the thesis of Levinas's first major publication, *De l'existence à l'existant*, Paris: Vrin, 1947.

70 Emmanuel Levinas, 'Dieu et la philosophie', hereafter *DP*, in *De Dieu qui vient à l'idée*, 2nd edn, Paris: Vrin, 1986, p. 115.

71 *DP*, p. 115.

72 Jean-Luc Marion, 'La Distance et son icône', in *L'Idole et la distance*, Paris: Editions Grasset & Fasquelle/Livre de Poche, 1977, p. 247.

73 This, however, is not to say that there are not other possibilities in Marion's work, indeed in his consideration of the saturated phenomena we can see and begin to ascertain a different modality and way to think the relationship between phenomena and theology, one that is not simply subsumable under the thought of the icon and the idol. See Jean-Luc Marion, 'Le Phénomène saturé', in *Phénoménologie et Théologie*, ed. J.F. Courtine, Paris: Criterion, 1992, pp. 79–128.

74 *DE*, p. 15.

75 *DE*, p. 28: 'Tandis que l'idole résulte du regard qui la vise.'

76 Marion recognises the danger of defining the icon in terms of an intention. He writes in *Dieu sans l'être*, 'a superficial listener may object, in defining the icon by the aim of an intention, therefore by a gaze does one not rediscover (*retrouve*) exactly the terms of the definition of the idol?' *DE* p. 31. For Marion however, opposing a finite intentionality with an infinite one is enough to prevent the icon from falling back into idolatry.

77 Emmanuel Levinas, 'La Trace de l'autre', in *En découvrant l'existence avec Husserl et Heidegger*, Paris: Vrin, 1967, p. 199.

78 Jean-Luc Marion, *La Croisée du visible*, hereafter *CV*, Paris: La Différence, 1991, p. 148.

79 *CV*. For example when speaking of the need for theological interest in the question of painting, 'Elle appartient à la visibilité elle-même, donc à tous – à la sensation commune' ('It belongs to visibility itself, to communal sensation, thus to all'), p. 7. Or as in the last chapter when writing about the object, 'l'image devient alors le lieu d'une transition réciproque, donc l'instrument d'une communion' ('then the image becomes the place of a reciprocal transition, thus the instrument of communion'), p. 152. This aspect of Marion's work has been somewhat neglected by English-speaking audiences who tend to see objectivity as a necessarily pejorative thought for theology. For an interesting indication of just how hostile the English reception to Marion's work has been, see the journal *New Blackfriars*, 'Special issue on Jean-Luc Marion's *God without Being*, July/August 1995. As I have said, I like the emphasis on an objective theological dimension in visibility, but many others feel that the presence of such a dimension mitigates against the essentially unencompassable character of creation. Obviously I do not necessarily think that either of these positions correctly captures the nature of the relation between theology, universality and phenomenality.

80 *De Trinitate*, Book V, 12–16.

81 In this regard see *De Trinitate*, Book XI.

82 Ludwig Wittgenstein, *Philosophical Investigations*, hereafter *PI*, tr. G.E.M. Anscombe, Oxford: Basil Blackwell, 1968, §109.

83 *PI*, §92.

84 *PI*, §90.

85 See Fergus Kerr's *Theology after Wittgenstein*, Oxford: Basil Blackwell, 1986.

86 Ludwig Wittgenstein, *Remarks on Frazer's Golden Bough*, ed. R. Rhees, tr. A.C. Miles, Doncaster: Brynmill Press Ltd, 1991, p. 3e.

87 Ludwig Wittgenstein, *Remarks on the Philosophy of Psychology, Vol. 1*, ed. G.E.M. Anscombe and G.H. von Wright, tr. G.E.M. Anscombe, Oxford: Basil Blackwell, 1980, §889.

88 See for example his book, now a contemporary classic, on the relationship between Derrida and negative theology: Kevin Hart, *The Trespass of the Sign: Deconstruction, Theology and Philosophy*, Cambridge: Cambridge University Press, 1989.

89 Jacques Derrida, *Of Grammatology*, tr. G. Spivak, Baltimore: Johns Hopkins University Press, 1976, p. 98.

90 Gillian Rose, *Dialectic of Nihilism*, Oxford: Basil Blackwell, 1984, p. 137.

91 Luce Irigaray, *Ethique de la différance sexuelle*, hereafter *ED*, Paris: Les Editions de Minuit, 1984, p. 57. See also the translation, *An Ethics of Sexual Difference*, hereafter *ESD*, tr. C. Burke and G.C. Gill, London: Athlone Press, 1993. I have however used my own translations, as I find Burke and Gill's at times a little misleading, see for example note 96 below.

92 Luce Irigaray, *Sexes and Genealogies*, tr. Gillian C. Gill, New York: Columbia University Press, 1993, p. 63.

93 *ED*, p. 67; *ED*, p. 182ff.

94 Luce Irigaray, 'Women Amongst Themselves: Creating a Women-to-Women Sociality', tr. D. Macey, in *The Irigaray Reader*, ed. M. Whitford, Oxford: Basil Blackwell, 1991, p. 190.

95 '[A] défaut d'un transcendental qui leur corresponde, et qu'il leur faudrait découvrir', *ED*, p. 71. The translators of the English edition have rendered this phrase in the following manner: 'since there is no transcendental made to their measure, since they have to make one for themselves.' I find the latter half of this a little too creative, even if this translation would as it turns out strengthen my argument. See *ESD*, p. 69.

96 Luce Irigaray, 'Equal to Whom', hereafter *EW*, tr. R.L. Mazzola, in *Differences* 1 (1989): pp. 59–76, hereafter *EW*.

97 *EW*, p. 64.

98 For a more sympathetic account of Irigaray's relation to the incarnation see two excellent articles by Graham Ward, 'Divinity and Sexuality: Luce Irigaray and Christology', *Modern Theology*, Blackwell, Vol. 12, No. 2, April 1996, pp. 221–37. And 'In the Name of the Father and of the Mother', *Literature and Theology*, Oxford University Press, Vol. 8, No. 3, September 1994.

99 Jacques Lacan, *Four Fundamental Concepts of Psychoanalysis*, tr. A. Sheridan, Harmondsworth: Penguin, 1979, p. 59.

100 Henry More, 'An Antidote Against Atheism', in C.A. Patrides (ed.), *The Cambridge Platonists*, Cambridge: Cambridge University Press, 1980, p. 246.

101 *PI*, §90.

102 My reference for this is taken from Gillian Rose's use of Thomas Mann's book *Joseph and his Brothers*; see Gillian Rose, *The Broken Middle*, Oxford: Basil Blackwell, 1992, pp. 115–33.

103 See M. Merleau-Ponty's *Le Primat de la perception*, Paris: Verdier, 1996, p. 49. 'Il y a donc dans la perception un paradoxe de l'immanence et de la transcendence.' In English the text of this 1946 discussion can be found in 'The Primacy of Perception and its Philosophical Consequences', tr. J.M. Edie, in *The Primacy of Perception*, ed. J.M. Edie, Chicago: Northwestern University Press, 1964.

1

DESCARTES AND ONTO-THEOLOGY

Jean-Luc Marion
Translated by B. Bergo

An absence of ontology[1]

"[P]rimus enim sum"[2] (for I am the first) declares Descartes about himself in 1647. Under the circumstances, it is a question here of the primacy that he asserts for having determined the *cogitatio* (thought) as the principal attribute of incorporeal substance. For us, however, this primacy essentially brings to light a more radical innovation and one, curiously, less emphasized by critics [critiques] of Descartes. *Primus sum* (I am the first): the verb *to be* occurs first. First must here be understood in two senses: it occurs first, as it were immediately, almost at the beginning. And especially, it occurs as the first person singular, *sum*; Descartes conducts his philosophy in this, then, that for him *to be*, *esse* (even therefore εἶναι) is said first under the figure of *sum*; it is declined firstly under the first thinkable inclination, the inclination of and toward the *ego*. Aristotle defines τό ὄν τοντο ἐστι τὶς ἡ οὐσία (being, which is – which [is] the substance) as that which, originally (and thus, equally now as for the following), proposes itself as to be sought and slips away each time as inaccessible.[3] Descartes responds to this injunction, in a sense that we shall have to consider carefully, and he himself eludes this same sense, for "enim" (for) for him (and fairly we cannot introduce this "point of view: for him" except as precisely for *him*, that is for the first *ego* or sooner the first, first *ego*), for him then, primordially, *esse* is said as *sum*. The question τὶ το ὄν [ἡ ὄν] (or: how is it with being *qua* being?), is no longer oriented upon the path of οὐσία (substance), and this at the inevitable risk of an errancy measured on the infinity of diverse beings. The question ceases, completed, from the moment of its first enunciation: *primus enim sum*; as soon as the *ego* intervenes the cause of *esse* is found to be understood: viz. *esse* amounts to *sum*. It is incumbent upon him who says *sum*, to claim of *esse* its modern sense or, rather, to declare it in its modern sense. *Sum* pronounces the understood cause of *esse*, "primus enim sum": thereafter, everything shall be only in as much as it comes out of *sum*.

A short-circuit: parting from *esse*, the question no longer runs its course freely, far off; its course cuts shortest, and is stopped at the first to come: "primus enim sum". Short-circuit, in the way we speak of "short-circuits", for indeed it is as much the cause of the *ens* (being) – and still more the cause of the ὄν (being) which remains obstinately and obscurely attached to it – this cause will no longer be understood except in finding itself cut short. Eventually therefore, in finding itself precisely *not* understood as such. For if *primus sum* can, to a prepossessed ear, respond to the question τὶ τό ὄν? (what is being?), if indeed it must in all rigour maintain the *rapprochement* which makes the one text speak in the other of the two texts [of Aristotle and Descartes], then immediately the *sum* is shown to be invested with a redoubtable dignity, for itself that is. *Sum* responds not only, nor even first, to the question: "Am I, I who think?" It responds to that which Aristotle is unable to consider and confront except in saying οὐσία, that is to say [in asking] the question τὶ τό ὄν? But what of the *ens in quantum ens* (being qua being)? Descartes responds "primus enim sum". The first manner through which *esse* is said has a name – *sum*. "[P]rimus enim sum" does not so much indicate a primacy of existence – i.e. the first being for him who philosophizes in the order, "ordine philosophanti"[4] – as it does a primacy of essence. Or rather, as it is not yet a question here of the distinction between *existentia/essentia*, this concerns a response to the interrogation τίσ ἡ οὐσία, viz. how is it with the essencing of the being [*l'estance de l'étant*]?

One will not fail to raise, immediately, several objections. Indeed I anticipate these objections all the more readily, as they appear perfectly justified to me. In the first place I am overestimating an isolated formula pulled out of a text habitually considered minor, and taken from its very context. But the overestimation itself would not have occasion to intervene if the formula did not lend itself, as if miraculously, to a turn of meaning [*effet de sens*] which the formula supports, nourishes and, as it were, calls forth. Yet, as one will again insist more firmly, Descartes never explicitly takes up the programmatic and nodal questioning that Aristotle articulates in *Metaphysics Z*, 1. Never does Descartes unfold an analysis of *sum* that sets forth the primacy of the point of view of οὐσία, of the essencing [*l'estance*] of all beings [*étants*]. This objection can but only reinforce my undertaking, because it is perfectly exact. For if, as all the critiques can but admit, Descartes ends by beginning with the *ego*, and thus ends by positing the *sum* as the first *meaning of esse*, and this from one end to the other of his path of thought, then the surprise appears to us inevitable, that Descartes never thought it necessary to devote his effort to explaining how it is that [*en quoi*] the manner of being of the *ego* deserved this primacy. In other words, that the ego intervenes at the head of the order is a point established by the *Meditationes* (and already, doubtless, by the *Regulae*). There remains the second point: this *ego* is, and the verb to be is certainly, in the first place, only said under the figure of the *sum*. Being does not enter into certitude except first under the figure of *sum*. Why and how is it that Descartes never approached the manner of being not only of the *ego* (he treats of this abundantly as the *res cogitans*, as *substantia*, etc.), but indeed that of the *sum* as well? The objection thus touches home so justly that, far from contradicting our manner of questioning, it comes instead to support it with a new force, fixing the question ever more profoundly within the body of the Cartesian text. This question was in fact posed by Heidegger from the time of the "destruction of the history of ontology" in 1927:

> With the "*cogito sum*," Descartes laid claim to the founding of a ground both new and sure for philosophy. But what he left indeterminate in this "radical" beginning is the manner of being of the *res cogitans*, more precisely the *meaning of being of the "sum"*.[5]

That the *ego* be, and that it be the first – this still says nothing about the meaning of being of this peculiar figure of *esse* which is said as *sum*. The more the demand for a primacy of the *ego* is established, the more a questioning as to the meaning of being of the *sum* ought to appear urgent. Now it seems that Descartes has consistently failed to respond to this question, for the reason that he, doubtless, could not hear it [*l'entendre*]. But we [today], can we hear it, even after *Sein und Zeit*? This silence around the meaning of being of the *sum* resonates all the more dully that the announcement "primus enim sum" rings forth clearly. But this silence leads us still further: if Descartes was first to posit the *ego sum* as the first being, while dodging the question of the meaning of the being of the *sum*, we immediately perceive that he, firstly, had to desert the question of the manner and the meaning of being of *all* other beings. The absence of ontology – if the word is appropriate – of the *sum* constitutes the reason, secret but sufficient, for the extraordinary desertion of the ontology of beings in general which characterizes, in the explicitness of the debates and the visible body of the texts, the Cartesian inauguration. Nothing has more oriented me, personally, toward the study of Descartes – may I be pardoned for this too subjective interpolation – than the absence of any word on the Being of the being, whatever might have been the contrary indications that my teachers did not cease to give me. Inversely it is apparent that, contrary to all of his predecessors, including and especially those from the second scholasticism, and contrary to his immediate successors (to whom, precisely, we owe the term of *ontologia*),[6] Descartes never treated of the *ens* and the *entia*, other than to step away from them. Formally, his philosophy is expressly constituted as a non-ontology [*non-ontologie*]. This paradox can be established in a few results and analyses.

The explicit non-ontology is marked by three operations carried out continually: an elimination (and diversion), a reduction and a postulation of evidence. (a) The elimination concerns that which the *Regulae* stigmatize under the name of *entia philosophica* or *entia abstracta*, and which at the other extreme of Descartes' career in letters, the *Recherche de la Vérité* will again call *entia scolastica.*[7] In what way do these beings deserve such an exemplary philosophical definition? *Regula VI* specifies this: in that they belong, each respectively, to such and such a *genus entis*, which genres of being are themselves constituted (as in Porphyry's tree mentioned elsewhere)[8] according to the categories of the philosophers, thus according to the κατηγοριαι τον όντοσ (categories of being). The initial and constant decision of the *Regulae*, and also of all the thought which will follow, shall consist in never considering those things susceptible of being made into objects of the *intuitus* (well known) according to the categorial figures of the *ens*; this decision, concerning which Descartes announces solemnly that: "[Although the message of this] Rule [may not seem very novel], it contains nevertheless the main secret of my method; and there is no more useful Rule in this whole treatise" consists in this: "[For it instructs that] all things can be arranged serially in various groups, not in so far as they can be referred to some ontological genus (such as the categories into which philosophers divide things), but in so far as some things can be known on the basis of others".[9] A similar operation is repeated frequently in the *Regulae*, however, without ever identifying as clearly the categorial *ens* thus eliminated, but on the contrary underlining the instance toward which the *res* are to be found diverted – diverted in the precise sense of a diversion of a flow of water, or, better, of a diversion of funds [fonds]. Thus in *Regula XII*: "when we consider things in the order that corresponds to our knowledge of them, our view of them must be different from what it would be if we were speaking of them in accordance with how they exist in reality". In effect, "since we are concerned here with things only in so far as they are perceived by the intellect, we term 'simple' only those things which we know so clearly and distinctly that they cannot be divided by the mind into others which are more distinctly known".[10] There results from this simple natures, which are not simple, better, which quite simply are not, in as much as diverted from that which they are *revera*, which are not, in a word, except "respectu intellectus nostri" (by reference to our understanding) (418, 9; 419, 6–7). This diversion far from the *categoriae* that determine the *genera entium* (390, 10) refers the *res* to the *Mathesis Universalis* (378, 1–2), "nempe ad ordinem vel ad mensuram" (order or measure) (451, 8),[11] without taking account of the differences introduced by the slightest "specialis materia" (378, 6). Knowledge begins when there disappears, as determinant instances, the matter and thus the form which, each time, "specializes" it, specifies it and gives it *forma* and therefore *essentia*, είδοσ and thus ousia. Knowledge begins when the *res* loses all essence proper to it, thus when the order imposed by the *ens*, and its different meanings, is erased. Each time the *Regulae* evoke the *genus entis*,[12] they eliminate it as radically as possible. Why? Because a genus of being implies a new term, the "*novum* genus *entis*" (435, 15), and therefore also a "*novum ens*" which is therein inscribed and installed (413, 12). Now this new being demands its recognition, by virtue of an *essentia* irreducibly imbricated in the categories. It thus demands first of all an admission of ignorance, for the mind that has not yet acceded to this new (Categorial) region of the being: all *novum ens* displays its novelty under the figure of "some new kind of entity previously unknown to him".[13] Ten years after the *Regulae*, Descartes will again say "a philosophic being which is unknown to me."[14] Let us understand this well: this being remains unknown, as long as one obstinately persists in viewing it as the philosophers take it, according that is to the *categoriae entis*, instead of taking the being as the order demands, *respectu intellectus nostri*. To put it plainly, Descartes asks that one leave philosophy in as much as philosophy considers beings according to their *genera entium* and thus according to the categories of the *ens*, in short he asks that one give up philosophy as ontology.

This elimination allows for the passage (b) to the reduction. Reduction, because the elimination of the *ens philosophicum* remains tangential, and still admits a residue. Two occurrences of *ens* in the *Regulae* – the only ones that do not connote any disqualification – allow us to specify the status of this residue. Supposing, in the first case (*Regula XIV*, 446, 3–10), a *subjectum* understood such as it presents itself in its quite particular essence of a being, that is the being appropriated to the requirements of geometry; according as the mind intends a figure in it, it [the mind] will only consider the character of a *figuratum*. If, in that being, the mind focuses on a body, it will consider the three dimensions of Galilean space in that body; if the mind intends, in the being, its surface, then it will consider only two dimensions. If it intends a line, a single dimension; and finally, if it intends a point therein, the mind will consider "we should leave out every other property save its being an entity".[15] *Ens* thus intervenes, finally irreducible, in order to connote position pure and simple, without any measurable extension; an unextended position, but also an unreal position (to speak like Husserl): there intervenes here no *res* doted with individuality, existence, nor even with essence. What then is it that merits the title of *ens*, and why, here precisely, does it not undergo any disqualification? This double question easily receives its single response: *ens* indicates purely and simply the minimal object of the imaginative regard of the mind and the *ens* is ordered to this regard all the more perfectly since it results from the mind. *Ens* retains nothing, here, of an essence, of a *genus* (*entis*), of the categories. It will not even appear once the initial *subjectum* has disappeared and, with it, all "unknown philosophic being".

As to the second occurrence, taken from the same *Regula*: "we perceive [very distinctly that combination of familiar] entities or natures".[16] The knowledge of any question, here that of the magnet, is summed up in the combination of beings already known; why speak positively here of beings, and why call them known, since prior to this (and afterward) they will be said to be unknown and, for this very reason, disqualified? The evident response: "notorum entium *sive naturarum*;" (known being or natures) in other words, the privilege results here from their equivalence with simple natures, which consist entirely in the knowledge that the constitutive mind takes of them.

Thus the *ens* remains accepted, at the end of the elimination, only to the exact degree to which it is reduced to that, precisely, which the elimination aimed to bring out – that is, to a pure, simple, empty and uniform objectivity. Uniform because absolutely destitute of all *forma* as of the slightest *essentia*. In brief, an *ens* with none of the determinations of the *ens*: neither categories, nor *potentia/actualitas*, nor *substantia/accidens*.[17] Or, rather, of the Aristotelian senses of ὄν, only a single one remains, and hypertrophied: "[T]here can be no truth or falsity in the strict sense except in the intellect alone".[18] But, as a striking confirmation however bedazzling, what remains, even under this derived formulation, one of the senses of the ὄν for Aristotle and his successors, reappears here in a terrain expressly conquered over all *Seinssinn* (sense of being) and against all *genus entis* (sort of being). The truth is not situated only in the understanding; truth issues from it by virtue of a certitude that dispenses the understanding from the very question of the meaning of the *ens*. The *ens*, reduced and known, disqualifies the interrogation on the meaning of being of the being [*le sens d'être de l'étant*]. *Ens non in quantum ens* [being not *qua* being].

The elimination of ontology and the reduction of the *ens* to pure objectivity permits our conceiving, finally, (c) how ontology could have become the place, blind and yet uncircumventable, of a postulation of evidence strangely not criticized. Since the *Regulae* and that which we believed possible to discern therein under the title of a grey ontology, for Descartes, the question and the task of an ontology is no longer posed. To put it precisely, after the *Regulae*, the question continues not to be posed any more explicitly than before or after. Now in order to respond to other needs, the inquiry shall be able to find again one or another fragment (for example, the treatise sketched of substance in the *Principia Philosophiae I*), yet Descartes will never question that ontology departs of itself to such an extent that he might not only eliminate it in his own text, but likewise, as if not seeing the contradiction herein, suppose ontology as definitively won and well known: "The distinction between essence and existence is known to everyone,"[19] he retorts superbly to an objection of Hobbes (AT VII, 194, 11), adding in a letter doubtless written later: "As concerns the distinction between essence and existence, I do not remember where it was that I spoke of this"; to which responds, finally, the *Recherche de la Vérité*: "I would never have believed that there has ever existed anyone so dull that he had to be told what existence is."[20] It is necessary to recognize that, to avoid what he calls a stupidity, Descartes presupposes, in fact, that "Existence is contained in the idea or concept of every single thing, since we cannot conceive of anything except as existing."[21] But whence this presupposition, which he fails to trouble himself with so much as to declare it a-hypothetical as such? From the original assumption of *existentia* among simple natures, from the *Regulae* on (AT X, 368, 22; 419, 22, etc.). If *existentia* is imposed with such ease as an object of *intuitus* (without the *essentia* moreover), then one must no doubt suspect that the very question of the ontological stake of a distinction between essence and existence simply does not come to thought: Descartes only sees the *existentia* with such evidence as he does, because he fails to see of what stake (among others, the interpretation of *oúsía*) it remains the witness and the result. As proof we note the equal mis-appreciation [*méconnaissance*] of the *esse potentiale* (in fact the couple ἐνεργείᾳ ον/δυναμει ὄν), held to be pure nothingness: "potential being, which strictly speaking is nothing".[22] The question of being is strictly lacking, in no longer posing the question in any manner. Each term taken from the ontological tradition amounts to nothing, *nihil*. Here one text rings strangely. Although taken from the *L'Entretien avec Burman*, we shall readily privilege it: "V. in Metaphysica nihil intelligitur per ens."[23] In his excellent edition of the text, J.-M. Beyssade establishes the obvious and, doubtless, incontestable sense of this text: "See in metaphysics, where nothingness is only understood by reference to being."[24] We would read it in another manner, however, as this doubtless remains possible; to the question posed – "sic nihil deberet prae-supponere ens?" [thus nothing ought to presuppose the being] – Descartes can neither respond affirmatively, nor negatively, since for him, in his "meta-physics" (principally the *Meditationes*), he says nothing of the *ens*, unless he says it to be equal to nothing. It is not here a question of a radical meditation on the relations between being/beings and nothing, but, on the contrary, of the very powerlessness to distinguish the one from the other term, equally use-less and inoperative in the new "metaphysics." Descartes appears to us indeed as the first – "nemo ante me" (nobody before me) (AT VIII–2, 347, 13)[25] – to believe himself able and obliged to dispense, from among the philo-sophers, with thinking the *ens in quantum ens* (being qua being), except as a "novum ens inutiliter [admittendum]" (AT X, 438, 12).[26] By *ens*, there is nothing to understand – because there is nothing to await.

Principle and *causa sui*

Ineluctably our first question returns: if Cartesian thought is characterized in its most proper inauguration by an utter absence [*un néant d'ontologie*] of ontol-ogy, if moreover, according to Heidegger's words, "each metaphysical thought is onto-logy or is quite simply nothing,"[27] then is it not fitting to admit that Cartesian thought *does not* belong to metaphysics? As provocative as this might appear, and paradoxical, such a supposition has nothing unten-able about it, nor anything extravagant. Besides the fact that this supposition would certainly, radically take account of the originality to which Descartes himself lays claim, the supposition would rejoin the views of certain famous critiques, celebrating the end of all "realism" and the setting forth of a pure reign of "consciousness."[28]

In fact, except if we would keep a vague acceptance of the notion of meta-physics – which after the gains of Heidegger seems neither reasonable nor rigorous – we must recognize that the metaphysical status of Cartesian thought becomes worthy of question, and even highly problematical. To hold ourselves to simple textual analysis, it is moreover necessary to note the extreme, and quite conscious, reserve demonstrated by Descartes before the very term "metaphysics." On two occasions, he specifies, at the moment of delivering the manuscript for definitive printing, that the *Meditationes* do not aspire, properly, to a metaphysics, but only to a first philosophy:

> I had not even given [it] a title, but it seems to me that the most appropriate thing will be to write *Renati Descartes Meditationes de Prima Philosophia*; for I am not treating at all of God and the soul in particular, but in general of all the first things which one can know in philosophizing.

Further on, "I believe that one shall be able to call it *Meditationes de Prima Philosophia*, for I do not treat therein, only of God and of the soul, but in general of all the first things that one can know in philosophizing by order."[29] The title also of the French translation does not begin by *Metaphysical Meditations* except to correct itself, immediately thereupon, with this specification: *concerning first philosophy*. This restriction, since it is indeed one, must be understood on the basis of the warning that, in the same year 1647, the preface-letter of the French translation of the *Principia Philosophiae* brings with it:

> the true Philosophy, of which the first part is Metaphysics, which contains the Principles of knowledge, among which is the explication of the principal attributes of God, of the immortality of our souls, and of all the simple and clear notions within us.[30]

In brief, Descartes does not undertake a metaphysical task except in restricting *metaphysica* to what one will call later on *metaphysica specialis* (special metaphysics), inflecting the latter into a science of first principles (protology), themselves finally understood [as being] the primacy accorded to the order of (the simplest) knowledge. If "metaphysics" remains a term in the Cartesian lexicon, it can only remain so in a considerably reduced meaning, since ontology remains, as such, radically absent.

However, Descartes claims, in 1630, to access (by demonstration) to the "metaphysical truths" (AT I, 144, 15). And this demand provokes nothing less than the first emergence of the doctrine of the creation of eternal truths. Thus Descartes claims that he is also engaging in a work of metaphysics. It remains to be grasped why he intends to arrive at metaphysics without producing an ontology. In order to advance on this Cartesian aporia, let us return to the sentence of Heidegger which, in appearance, closes the path to us: "each metaphysical thought is onto-logy or indeed is nothing at all."

Heidegger is not writing, in a word, ontology in the sense of the *ontologia* of Clauberg, Goclenius or C. Wolff; he writes onto-logy. Why? In order to underscore that all metaphysics, if it speaks of the ὄν, precisely *speaks of it*, thus utters in its regard a *lógos*; in the *ontologia* of the treatises, there speaks, in fact, more profoundly than the ὄν, the *lógos*. For the *lógos* does indeed offer a mode, even the mode of modes, for all deployment of the ὄν ἦ ὄν. Now – and this deepening will demand nothing less than the gap which separates *Holzwege* from *Identität und Differenz* – the *lógos*, which precedes and utters all ontology as onto-logy, redoubles its priority with a theo-logy: the *lógos* which states the being in its being, states it as much in an indissoluble and double cohesion, as supreme. Doubtless metaphysics is stated as ontology, but for this indeed, "metaphysics, thought more exactly and more clearly, is onto-theo-logic,"[31] Onto-theo-logic constitutes the "fundamental trait" of metaphysics, in such way that "Being founds the being, and the being as being *par excellence* founds and supports Being, "*gründet Sein das Seiende, begründet das Seiende als das Seiendste das Sein.*"[32] The being is founded according to Being, and Being lets itself be as if confirmed, and in this sense, founded, by the being in its excellence. The double quality of the founding demarcates the redoubling of the *lógos*. This redoubled priority of the *lógos*, as much over the *ens in quantum ens* as over the *summum ens*, attests the authentically metaphysical character of a thought. We can thus take up anew the primitive question and ask: does Cartesian thought satisfy, despite its desertion of ontology, the "fundamental trait" of metaphysics, that is its essentially onto-theo-logical constitution?

Without prejudicing the analyses which remain to be carried out, two remarks immediately give to the renewed question a pertinence which we divine to be essential: for the illumination might well not remain unilateral, and Descartes' thought, illumined by the [above-mentioned onto-theo-logical] constitution, could, in return, also place that constitution in a just light. (a) The onto-theo-logical constitution implies a double, although dissymmetric, foundation of Being by a being (*begründen*), and of a being by Being (*gründen*). Now protology, which Descartes privileges in fact over metaphysics, rests upon a strange but essential re-duplication of the notion of principle:

> the word *principle* can be taken in diverse senses, and . . . it is one thing to search for *a common notion* which be so clear and so general that it might serve as principle for proving the existence of all Beings [les Estres], the *Entia*, that we shall know afterward; and another thing to seek a Being [*un Estre*], whose existence be better known to us than that of any others, in such a way that it might serve as *principle* by which to know them.[33]

Principle, *principium* (but not *fundamentum* here), ἀρχή can be understood – be practised, display "itself" to take up again a Cartesian *hapax* (AT X, 496, 14) – just as well by an "Estre"; that means: a being taken in all the excellence of its "existence," that by a notion which precedes and makes possible "all the Estres, the *Entia*," that is, a notion which states that by which beings are what they are, or, in a more Cartesian terminology, which can exist such as they are, in a word, in as much as they are. It is not an accident, moreover, but a confirmation, that there appears here one of the rare positive occurrences of *ens/entia*. We ask: how does this doubleness of the principle play out in Cartesian thought? Can this play be located in a precise conceptual figure, or even in several? In this eventuality, what relation do these figures entertain first of all among themselves, but thereafter and especially with the onto-theo-logical constitution of all metaphysics? What argument could be thus formulated in favour of the authentically and very precisely metaphysical character of Cartesian thought? For the moment it will have to satisfy us to formulate the following questions. (b) In the immediate, a second remark incites us to pursue the *rapprochement*. In effect, Heidegger marks, as a decisive trait of the onto-theo-logy of *all* metaphysics (and not only of its Hegelian completion), the determination of the name and of the function of "God" as *causa sui*: "The Being of beings becomes, once it is taken in the sense of a foundation, fundamentally presented as *causa sui*, and uniquely thus. With this is named the metaphysical concept of God."[34] *Causa sui* does not indicate one function among others, nor one denomination among others of "God" as a being among others; *causa sui* effects an essential moment in the unfolding of the ontological difference such that metaphysics marks it [the ontological difference] indissolubly, and misses it, finishes it and forgets it; this moment gives rise to the being in the erection of its excellence, excellence which finds its irrefragable figure in the return to itself of efficiency, *causa (efficiens) sui*. We will not here discuss, even in the form of a sketch, the implications or the complications of this decisive thought of Heidegger. We shall simply call attention to an evidence of fact: the first thinker to consciously name God *causa sui*, at the end of a meditation on causality – not final, but altogether efficient – was none other than Descartes.[35] We ask, consequently: how is it that the thinker who first made a radical concept of onto-theo-logy rise to the surface of the lexicon – how should he not, on his part, understand an intimate rapport [here] with the essence of metaphysics, thus also with its history? How could one reduce this encounter, in the first place and without examination, either to an anachronism of Heidegger generalizing over time a concept historically outdated, or to a happy discovery of a Descartes pressed by objectors too clairvoyant but also too scholastic?

We believe, not without hesitation, that there remain to us no other paths than this: to re-read Descartes on the basis of the onto-theo-logical constitution of metaphysics, or more exactly, to re-read him in the intention of letting rise anew, in suspension, from deep within the densities of the text, the figure – sketched but certainly visible – of one of the apparitions of metaphysics, original but fulfilling the common destiny of metaphysics.

The first word on the Being of the being: *cogitatio*

Our inquiry, aiming to evince a Cartesian ontology (thus a metaphysics) failed, in its first effort, before the disqualification of all *novum ens* (new being), by virtue of all *ens* as such, to the benefit of that which, whatever it be, offers itself to knowledge, to its laws and its exigencies. We must therefore take up our attempt at this point. We dispose of a positive indication at least: Descartes names, in one case, the residue thus fully knowable *ens notum* (AT X, 439, 8). We understand this certainly in the obvious sense of the known being, but especially and likewise in the exact sense that the known, as purely and simply known, remains a being. Thus to remain as known amounts to remaining as a being, in the sense that the epistemic reduction [which is] pure of all occurrence (*ea omnia quae occurrunt*, say the *Regulae* in the first title, AT X, 359, 6)[36] to that which ultimately could be known of it, repeats – while displacing the reduction that, according to Aristotle, "a certain science" effects when it reduces – or better leads the ὄν back to itself in so far as it is, and nothing more. Decisive point: the Cartesian reduction of the world, coming to its reduced and conditional status as object, does not desert the reduction of the world to its status of a being, but repeats it on a level slightly displaced. Or, sooner, this displacement, in its very violence, attempts to recapture originarily the Aristotelian move, from which issues all subsequent metaphysical ontology. When the "things can serve as objects to true thoughts" (AT II, 597, 15–16), when therefore the thing is used up in the operation which makes of it a "res repraesentata" (AT VII, 8, 23), when the world must thus pass by the Caudine Narrows, or when it must bow before the tribunals of the *objectum purae Matheseos* (the object of pure Mathesis) – of which we could not overemphasize that it forms the essential gain that passes from the *Regulae to the Meditationes*[37] – it is a question, again and finally, of the *ens in quantum ens*. Otherwise stated, being known gives a manner, precisely, of being. The manner of being which leads the being back to its status of pure being is pronounced in the Cartesian inauguration – to be in the mode of the *objectum*. Descartes declares this explicitly: "[T]he mode of being by which a thing exists objectively (or representatively) in the intellect by way of an idea, imperfect though it may be, is certainly not nothing, and so it cannot come from nothing."[38] Objective reality remains, by all rights without which it would not claim any cause, an *esse objectivum* [objective being].[39] When Descartes, therefore, responding to Burman, defines once again the "totum et universum Matheseos objectum [whole and entire object of the Method]," he can legitimately assimilate it to a 'verum et reale ens" [true and real being] in the very sense in which he accords equally to physics an "objectum suum verum et reale ens" [true and real object of its own].[40]

Physics does not reach the *ens* any more than does the *Mathesis*, for Descartes at least and contrary to an Aristotelian conception; because for him, the *ens* is in no way defined in its relation to the φυσις, but solely and sufficiently according to objectivity. And this, in such way that the *objectum purae Matheseos* [object of pure Method] does not remain a veritable *ens*, *in spite of* its separation from the object of physics (in the sense, for example, of the *ens diminutum* of Scotus). We must say, all to the contrary, that the more perfect purity of its objectivity qualifies it as an *ens* of the first rank. All the other objects, however less imperfect they appear to the readers, remain beings, by right and by fact, but less perfectly so because less certainly objects. The proof: in order to arrive at them, we must first pass by the *objectum purae Matheseos*. The object is, in so far as it is an object, indeed.

In acceding to objectivity, each thing is led back to that which it is, in as much as it is. But this reconduction, holding the place of ontology, would remain impossible without the intervention of another instance – other than the thing, but not foreign to the manner of being to which it attains *qua* object. The thing does not, in effect, become an object, but the object of an understanding: "[T]he intellect can never be deceived by any experience, provided that when the object is presented to it, it intuits it in a fashion exactly corresponding to the way in which it possesses the object."[41] *Res objecta* [object-thing] because *objecta intellectui* [object of the intellect]: objectivity implies the objectity [*l'objectité*] which objectifies the thing for understanding. Or, according to another vocabulary: "[there is] always a particular thing which I take as the object of my thought".[42] The thing attains objectivity, which alone can establish it as a being, to the strict degree to which it yields to the exigencies of the *cogitatio*. The *Regulae* remain perfectly operative in the *Meditationes*, and the grey ontology does not disappear into the white theology which, on the contrary, presupposes the former.[43] Nevertheless the second formulation indicates that a new step forward is taken: the thing yields not only to the *cogitatio* in general – in the sense in which the *Regulae* say *intellectus* here – but more precisely to "*meae* cogitationis." Such mention of the possessive does not betray some unhappy, pre-critical naïveté, confounding the "empirical subject" with pure and constitutive thought; the possessive defines here the very essence of the pure *cogitatio*. The *cogitatio*, as such, implies this possessive adjective, exactly in the sense in which, as such, it implies its reflexivity [son réfléchi]. *Cogitatio mea*, and *cogito me cogitare*[44] – since it belongs properly to the *cogitatio* to reflect back upon itself, since it reverts properly to the *cogitatio* to belong to itself. *Cogitatio* is not equivalent, despite the consecrated use by translations, to *thought*; even were we to suppose that "pure thought" offers itself as a mirror of, and to evidence, it would still be necessary to envisage the *cogitatio* as a type of convergent mirror, which reflects light rays by focusing them upon a unique point. In this unique point we recognize the *objectum*, that toward which finally all occurrences are concentrated. But this very concentration, which assures to its result the high luminosity of a rational object by exposing it in full light, this concentration depends upon the curve of the mirror. If the objectivity of knowing depends upon the object, the object depends upon the objectivity of its being brought into evidence, which depends in its turn, finally, upon the curvature of cogitative thought. Curvature of thought, the *cogitatio* implies a reflecting appropriation, of which the ultimate implication has a name – *ego*. The *ego* does not come to be added to the *cogitatio* as an adjacent specification, eventually superfluous, because too intermixed with psychology or with "subjectivity." The *ego* delivers the proper name of the *cogitatio* in manifesting its reflecting and appropriating essence – the curvature of thought. Just as an *objectum* does not exist if it lacks a *cogitatio* which assures it objectivity, so too a *cogitatio* could not insure the certitude of its object without a curvature, which has as name – *ego*. A *cogitatio* without the *ego* would again become thought, albeit motionless, stale thought and impotent to produce an object. That which we call currently "the Cartesian *cogito*," that is, that which Descartes rather calls "the first principle [which] is *that our soul exists*, for the reason that there is nothing whose existence be more notorious to us," or again: "This piece of knowledge – *I am thinking, therefore I exist* – is the first and most certain of all,"[45] is implied by right directly, in the exercise of all *cogitatio*; better, in the reconduction of each thing to the status of an *objectum*. No new operation of thought is necessitated hereby, since it itself, and it alone, makes thought possible as a *cogitatio* effectuating the *objectum*. If we allow for this liaison (that we will confirm immediately), one consequence is sketched. We have established that the being is *qua* object. Now the object does not thus become *ens* except as *cogitatum*, and with the *cogitatum*, in question is a manner of being. Likewise the *cogitatum* implies, in its turn, the *ego* (*cogitans*). Thus the *ego* intervenes in the meaning of being which permits the *cogitatum* to be as a being in its being [*d'être à titre d'étant dans son être*]. Thesis: any object, as such, and thus as *cogitatum*, is – and this implies in turn: the *ego*, with and more essentially than any other being, and in as much as it cogitates, it exists. The *ego* exists before and more certainly than any other being, because and uniquely because no being exists except in so far as it is an *objectum*, thus as *cogitatum*. Inversely, the *ego* exists, *par excellence* and in priority, only because all the other beings exist only as objects of a *cogitatio*, they are not except as *cogitata*: "[N]othing can be known prior to the intellect, since knowledge of everything else depends on the intellect, and not *vice versa*."[46] An utterance on the manner of being of beings (onto-logy) maintains a reciprocal relation of foundation with a proposition on the singular existence of a being *par excellence* (theo-logy). The existence of the *ego* grounds and supports [*begründet*] the manner of being of the *cogitata*. The manner of being which manifests itself in the *cogitata*, by revealing them as beings, founds [*gründet*] the *ego* in its privileged existence. Such a foundation as this, double and crossed, literally satisfies the characteristics of what Heidegger disclosed under the name of the onto-theo-logical constitution of metaphysics. We can even specify easily the nature of the "-logic" in Cartesian thought. The λόγοσ is brought into play as *cogitatio*, curvature of thought; starting from the "logical" decision which is accomplished by the *cogitatio*, ontology envisages beings as such *qua cogitata*, and theology sets out the being *par excellence* in the *cogitans*, the *ego*. We must thus conclude that Cartesian thought belongs fully to metaphysics, if, at least, metaphysics admits an onto-theo-logical constitution.

From a strictly Cartesian point of view, this conclusion raises at least two ineluctable objections, however. First, our analysis of the relation of implication between the object and the *ego* appears to deduce the existence of the *ego* from the very nature of objects, thereby contradicting the fundamental order of Descartes' approach. More than this, however, analysis leads to the existence of the *ego* without passing by doubt, nor without expressly admitting that a new operation of thought, or a particular reasoning, be required to attain this effect. Now precisely, the existence of the *ego* demands a reasoning comparable to none other. To this is added a second objection: such an onto-theo-logical restitution of Cartesian thought is conducive to identifying the being *par excellence* with the *ego*, thus with a finite being, and not with God. Apart from the fact that this distortion reduces to nothing an entire section of the explicitly deist intention of Descartes, it receives a massive textual contradiction: the syntagma *summum ens* appears frequently in the *Meditationes*, but it always designates God, never the *ego*.[47] Let us attempt to respond. (a) As to the procedure which leads directly back from objects to the *ego*, it ought in no way to surprise us, since it is a matter of the deployment of beings *qua cogitata* up to the *cogitans*, the existence of which, alone, renders the *cogitata* thought, thus rendering their being possible. A canonic text confirms this factually: the analysis of the piece of wax. Apparently, the thing is, and the *cogitans* remains only as an undecided, "[But it still appears . . . that the corporeal things . . . which the senses investigate, are known with much more distinctness than] this puzzling 'I' which cannot be pictured in the imagination."[48] In final reality, it is indetermination [that] shall characterize the wax, "extensum quid, flexible, mutabile" (31, 2–3). Whence comes this reversal? From the reduction, as if by degrees, of the wax, thus of all things, first to the status of an *objectum*, then and indissolubly to the status of a *cogitatum*, which results, beyond (but also thanks to) sense perception and the imagination, from *solius mentis inspectio* [perceived by the mind alone] (31, 25). *Inspectio* is equivalent to the *cogitatio*, just as *mens* goes for the *ego* (*cogitans*). This analysis, like its parallels in the *Regulae* and in the *Principia Philosophiae*,[49] altogether disengages the *ego* (*cogitans*) from the *cogitatum*, or rather from the interpretation of the *objectum* as *cogitatum*, here of the wax as "nihil aliud quam . . . quid" [merely something as . . . which (31, 3). The *cogito* disengages itself from the analysis of the *objectum* as "piece" of *cogitatio*, as *cogitatum quid*, as a target for an aiming. Now we must specify immediately, this strict implication of the *cogito* in every *cogitatum* does in no way contradict the specific moment which, just before the analysis of the piece of wax, is given as a demonstration of the existence of the *ego*. In fact the texts remain strictly parallel. Just as the said analysis of the piece of wax effects in fact an analysis of the wax as *cogitatum* and of the *cogitatum* as supposing, more essentially, a *cogito* cogitating it, so too the demonstration of the existence of the *ego* remains indifferent to the occasional identity of the *cogitatum* relative to which the *cogitans* discovers itself as *ego*. Doubtless the demonstration mobilizes a formula: "*Ego sum, ego existo*" (AT VII, 25, 12; 27, 9); but this formula owes its privilege more to the ancitipation of the result – that which exists has a name: *ego* – than to its particular pertinence. The proof of this is that any action, as Descartes will expressly recognize, allows us access to the existence of the *ego*. At least under a single condition: that this action find itself, *qua objectum*, renewed or prolonged to the status of a *cogitatum*, and thus that it make the *ego cogito* stand out in it [the action]. I take a walk, therefore I am, at least "in so far as the awareness of walking is a thought at all".[50] Thus the meaning of the formula cogitated has little import; the only important thing is the analysis of this formula in as much as it is a *cogitatum*, and the reconduction of this *cogitatum* directly to the·*ego cogito*. In like manner, the canonic texts of the *Meditatio II* do not make the existence of the *ego* arise from the formula "*Ego sum, ego existo*," but rather from the actually cogitative thought of this formula. Moreover, in order to underscore the fact that the conquest of the *ego* depends upon the *cogitatio* at work (and not of one or another *cogitatum*), these texts go to the point of introducing the cogitative performance: "[T]his proposition . . . is necessarily true whenever it is put forward by me or conceived in my mind."[51] The meaning of the *cogitatum*, even here, decides nothing, the reduction of the indifferent and ordinary *cogitatum* to the *cogitatio* in its living effectivity [en oeuvre vive] decides it all. Thus, as the two *cogitata* – "piece of wax" and "*Ego sum, ego existo*" – differ only as to their meaning, and as the essential is played out in the *cogitatio* which is therein acting and manifest, the two analyses come to the same – since they lead two *cogitata* back to the single *ego*, [the] being *par excellence* and whose primacy founds the *cogitata* as real and true objects.

There remains (b) a final difficulty: in the onto-theo-logical constitution that we are attributing to Cartesian thought, the being *par excellence* takes place in the *ego*, not in God. This distortion is not something we shall try to reduce, nor to mask, because it seems to us to fix at least *one* of the most decisive Cartesian initiatives. We shall here attempt only to specify this initiative with a few indications that avoid misconstrual. First, we must say again that the theo-logy of metaphysics remains, essentially, a the*io*logy; it focuses upon the being *par excellence*, without prejudging the ontic region in which it would appear. Greek philosophy teaches us sufficiently that these regions can vary. Limited in *this* sense, the Cartesian initiative should have nothing stupefying to it. Second, the being *par excellence* raised here is defined as *cogitans* and as *ego*; the deep reason for Descartes not identifying this being *par excellence* with God is due firstly to his original decision on the divine essence; God is not at all defined by the understanding, and again less by the *cogitatio* such as we are effectively (scientifically) putting it to work, but rather by (in 1630) "incomprehensible power", by the *potentia immensa, exuperans* et *inexhausta* [immense, overflowing and inexhaustible power].[52] God does not so much cogitate as He cannot cogitate. The exercise of the *cogitatio* neither reaches Him nor defines Him as much as does the exercise of power. The excellence of a being defined by the *cogitatio* would remain too little highlighted to [be able to] utter and think the infinite, whose radical incomprehensibility cannot, according to Descartes, make itself thinkable, except as power. God would not know to condescend to the *cogitatio*, and thus the being which derives from the *cogitatio* alone, its excellence, must not claim to be identified with God. Third, it should be noted that Descartes in no way ignored the path that he refused, however, to take; we shall only take one text as proof of this, unique to our knowledge, wherein he describes precisely:

> It is true only in the sense in which every operation of the intellect is a conceptual entity, that is, an entity which has its origin in thought; and indeed this entire universe can be said to be an entity originating in God's thought, that is, an entity created by a single act of the divine mind.
>
> (*PWD*, Vol. II, p. 97)[53]

The world, here envisaged as *ens rationis divinae*, might have been able to come from the divine *mens*, just as objects cogitated come from the *cogitatio* and depend upon it. If this position were laid out, it would certainly permit the resorption of the gap between God and the supreme (cogitating) being, but it would impose that we conceive God as a conceiving understanding – in a word, as the place of possibles, ultimately identical and/or subject to them. This is what, from 1630 onwards, Descartes refused radically. The gap which provoked the objection thus flows less from a misled interpretation than from an authentically Cartesian decision: nothing less than the doctrine of the creation of eternal truths.

We shall therefore attempt neither to skirt nor to blur the difficulty: the *cogitatio*, if it utters a being as such in saying it as *cogitatum*, indissolubly denounces the *ego cogitans*, alone, as the being which, *par excellence*, responds to a being taken as such. If we admit – and how could we not? – that the *ens ut cogitatum* [being as thought] fulfils an ontology, we must concede that the *ego cogito*, as *cogitatio sui*, completes the corresponding theo-logy, by virtue of being an *ens par excellence*. We must recognize the textual fact and conceptual confirmations of this fact, [viz.] that the God of the Christian religion, though always explicitly and sincerely confessed, does not ensure, in this onto-theo-logy, the function of the being *par excellence*. Only then can the authentic question be formulated: does the *ego* find itself invested with the role of being *par excellence* by virtue of an arbitrary decision (subjective, non-conceptual, in brief, vain) of Descartes, or is this the consequence of an imperious compulsion of the *cogitatio* itself? The *cogitatio* arranges two figures of beings, the being as *cogitatum* and the being *par excellence* as *cogitatio sui*, which [together] suffice to design an onto-theo-logical constitution, and yet the God that Descartes confesses never intervenes. For if the *cogitatio sui* (*ego cogito*) does not apply to God, but precisely to the *ego* which fulfils the human mind, then we must suppose that, already more essentially, from the region of the being as such, God let Himself be approached neither as *cogitans*, nor as *cogitatum* (but only as "incomprehensible power"). That from the point of view of an onto-theo-logy of the *cogitatio*, God should not hold the role of the being *par excellence* (and that He abandons it to the *mens humana*, at the price of a strange distortion), indicates a characteristic and unsurpassable limitation of the *cogitatio* itself. A fundamental trait of beings, the *cogitatio* allows at least one region, and not the least [of them], to escape from what we must, precisely, not call being – since the *cogitatio* does not allow us to think it as a being – namely that whose name is God. The infinite, "incomprehensible power," overflows the constitution of beings according to the *cogitatio*. This overflowing thus places us, if we do not attempt to reduce it too quickly, on the path of a new question: this fundamental trait of beings, the *cogitatio*, could it surpass itself toward a trait *more* fundamental still? To pass outside the *cogitatio*, toward a word still more radically metaphysical because more constitutively onto-theo-logical, would this not indeed define the ultimate task of Cartesian thought?

The second word on the Being of the beings: *causa*

A being allows itself also, and, in effect, more fundamentally, to be said, as such and without exception, from the standpoint of causality. We must set out here, with all possible clarity, the multiform and constant declaration which, without reservation from 1641 on, subjects all existence (thus any being in as much as it is) to causality, a causality erected to the rank of principle and onto-logical reason. Let us raise the principle statements of the second Cartesian word on the most fundamental trait of a being: "However, the light of nature does establish that if anything exists we may always ask why it exists; that is, we may inquire into its efficient cause, or, if it does not have one, we may demand why it does not need one."[54] Or again:

> Concerning every existing thing it is possible to ask what is the cause of its existence. This question may even be asked concerning God, not because he needs any cause in order to exist, but because the immensity of his nature is the cause or reason why he needs no cause in order to exist.
>
> (*PWD*, Vol. II, p. 116)[55]

And finally:

But I think it is clear to everyone that a consideration of efficient causes is the primary and principal way, if not the only way, that we have of proving the existence of God. We cannot develop this proof with precision unless we grant our minds the freedom to inquire into the efficient causes of all things, even God himself. For what right do we have to make God an exception, if we have not yet proved that he exists?

(*PWD*, Vol. II, p. 166)[56]

These three canonic texts, respectively advanced by the *Responsiones I, II* and *IV*, match each other almost to the letter. It may suffice here to underline the common saliencies of their superimposed profiles. (a) The *causa* does not govern only the rigour of intelligibility, but rather the proof of the *existentia*; the *causa* is not limited to an epistemological function already dominant (to know implies knowing by causes), but takes into account, sufficiently and exclusively, all of the *existentia*. Now the *existentia* marks, in Cartesian terms, the meaning of the being of a being, [and this] *par excellence*. Thus, by *causa*, a being plays its very being, and thus appears *qua* being. Existing in as much as caused, the being manifests itself *qua* being to the strict degree to which it appears under the angle and in the light – or rather the shadow – of the cause of its existence. More essentially as *ens qua cogitatum*, the *ens* declares itself in its being *qua causatum*. The advance of the *ens qua causatum* over the *ens qua cogitatum* is precisely marked in that one can remain within [the domain of] possibility or the *ens rationis*, which, for Descartes is confused almost with the *nihil*, whereas the other alone opens the access to existence, the royal sense of being. Here disappears the necessity, where we were constrained by the empire of the *cogitatio*, to reinterpret with care and sometimes subtlety, any *cogitatum* as an *ens cogitatum* [i.e.] any object of cogitation as still yet and always a being considered as such under the mode of cogitation itself (grey ontology). Here causality manifests directly the *ens in quantum ens* since its explicit and unique stake has the name, the *existentia*. (b) This direct advance into the question of the meanings of being is doubled by a second advance: the *causa* deciding existence governs all that pretends to accede to it. Now the dignity of existence appears such, among the other manners of being (or rather of not being), that none among beings can, nor may, exempt itself from recognizing the *causae dignitas* [the dignity proper to the cause] (AT VII, 242, 5).[57] No more than it might excuse itself from existing, a being will not be able to hold the *causa* as optional. And even non-existence demands a cause. Whence an unstoppable consequence: while the *cogitatio* could not pretend to treat God as an *ens cogitatum* by common right, the *causa* may legitimately approach God as *ens causatum*. Doubtless, this reduction is accomplished neither so directly, nor so brutally: God has no *causa* distinct from himself; but this absence of a heterogeneous *causa*, resting on the particular excellence of the divine essence (its inexhaustible power), imposes anew a

causa sive ratio: there is always a cause for which God has not a cause heterogeneous to himself, that is his proper essence, taking the place of a cause. Far
be it that this particular case marks some kind of weakening of the *causa*, it
permits Descartes, on the contrary, to make it play out in all its purity as
causa sive ratio; and thus to mark for the first time that efficient causality takes
into charge all the *ratio* of things. These two advances of the *ens qua causatum*
divide themselves in two compatible directions: direct access to the question
of the meanings of Being, and recuperation of the divine residue which resisted
the *ens qua cogitatum*. (c) The dignity of the most fundamental trait of beings
is found recognized by the *causa* (*sive ratio*) as an imperious evidence ("Dictat
autem," "omnibus esse manifestum"). Here, in effect, Descartes can still
only practise what we called above a postulation of evidence: the placing at
the principle of the *causa* (*sive ratio*) does not itself remain a principle except
to the precise degree that no other cause can intervene to account for it.
Alone this unreason makes a principle of the cause of the *ratio*. Or again: that
all existence must account for its cause, this only becomes a principle by
imposing itself without reason or cause. We shall leave, then, to the Latin its
secondary effect of signification [*effect de sens secondaire*], and so will indeed
hear the formula: "Dictat . . . lumen naturae" [statement or precept of . . .
natural reason] (AT VII, 18) as a *dictat* of reason, which dictates to the *ens in
quantum ens* [being in as much as it is a being] that it shall not be except as
caused: *ens ut causatum* [being as caused].

We have just stated that the empire of the *causa* over the being passes
beyond that of the *cogitatio* over the being. It is worthwhile specifying the
stages of this appropriation of dominance and position. This course alone
will make thinkable for us, at least in sketch form, the decisive scope of the
ultimate Cartesian word on a being in its being. Firstly, we raise the fact
that, from the *Regulae* on, the *causa*, among all the notions said to be absolute,
benefits from an uncommon privilege. In effect, according to the *Regula VI*,
the *ordo rerum cognoscendarum* [order of things known] overturns, among other
things but principally, the order issued from the Aristotelian categories in
that it dissociates the couple, held up until now to be strictly correlative, of
cause and effect: "Philosophers, of course, recognize that cause and effect are
correlatives; but in the present case, if we want to know what the effect is, we
must know the cause first, and not *vice versa*."[58] Stated otherwise, if it is a question of knowing – and in principle, here, it is never a question but of knowing
– the correlation is undone, and the *causa* gains an indisputable priority: it
accounts for its effect, in that it makes it knowable.[59] This is a primacy set up
very consciously, "de industria" (by intention) (AT X, 383, 3)[60] in the
manner of one single other priority, that of equality over inequality. These
two priorities suffice, moreover to fix the two parameters of the *Mathesis Universalis*, the order and the measure – in other words, to make the only two
operators of Cartesian science work in full light the *series* (or succession) and
the equation. The *Meditationes* will again take up this gain anew, asking "For

where, I ask, could the effect get its reality from, if not from the cause?"[61] One difference, however, summons us to force the assimilation: in 1627, the anteriority of the *causa* is tied to the intention of knowing (*Cognosci*), whereas in 1641, this anteriority also concerns the *realitas*. This gap confirms the fact that the directly ontological pertinence of the *causa* is not acquired immediately. Why this gap, one will perhaps object, since with the *Regulae* already, the *causa* precedes, as an absolute element, all the other notions and simple natures? The answer: the *causa*, precisely, only precedes other *notions*, and limits its priority to the domain that defined and granted by an element still more absolute than any absolute notion, i.e. the understanding itself, which refers all things to itself: "[W]ith regard to its possible usefulness to our project,"[62] thus containing in advance "in what way particular things may be susceptible of investigation by the human mind."[63] The *causa* no longer depends on the *effectus*, but depends all the more on the *mens* in that it owes to the *mens* itself its first and unique property. One term at least does not depend on the absolute *causa*, the *mens* which makes use of it, or again the *cogitatio* which, alone, comprises *res omnes* in its *universitas* (398, 15).[64] Thus we verify our interpretation: the priority of the *causa* is reliant upon the *cogitatio*, the sole absolute term in the *Regulae*, and it subordinates itself therefore to the onto-theo-logy of the *ens qua cogitatum*, whose limits, especially, the *causa* – distinguished and industrious labourer that it is – does not contest.

Thus the cause cannot become the principle and *dictat* of reason except by going beyond the very priority that the *cogitatio* acknowledges it as having. Up to what point? Up to inverting the relation of comprehension between *cogitatio* and *causa*: no longer assuring the priority of the *causa* by the *cogitatio* under its aegis, then, but indeed subjecting the *cogitatio* itself to the *causa*, thanks, eventually, to the *cogitatio* itself. Logically, it will not appear possible and thinkable to subject God to the *causa sive ratio*, except from the moment at which, firstly, the *cogitatio* in all its dimension (thus also the *ego cogito*) admits the *causa* as its *ultima ratio*. On the path of this reversal, the three *Lettres à Mersenne* of 1630, declaring the creation of eternal truths by God, mark, without a doubt, a decisive stage. In this regard a single indication will suffice:

> You ask me *in quo genere causae Deus disposuit aeternas veritates* [into what sort of cause did God place the eternal truths]. I answer you that it is *in eodem genere causae* [in the same sorts of cause] that He creates all things, that is to say *ut efficiens et totalis causa* [as efficient and total cause]. For it is certain that He is just as well the Author of the essence, as of the existence, of creatures: now this essence is nothing other than these eternal truths.
>
> (*PWD* III p. 25, AT I, 151, 1–152, 5)

Existences are created by the efficient causality of God; altogether banal. But there is nothing, on the contrary, less banal than the creation by efficient causality of the eternal essences of things; these essences also comprising, moreover, the mathematical truths, logical principles, ethical values, etc. Thus truths, thoughts, *cogitationes*, although imposed upon our understanding as necessary and unconditional evidences, remain created according to efficient causality. The *cogitatio*, in all that it holds moreover as most necessary, is discovered as bypassed by the cause; and the latter, according to an inevitable consequence, thus escapes the *cogitatio*, which henceforth can no longer apprehend it except as an "incomprehensible power" (AT I, 150, 22; 146, 4–5). Independently of its significance for Cartesian thought, the brilliant stroke of 1630 marks the first and definitive subversion of the *cogitatio* by the *causa*. From this moment on, the sometimes subterranean work of the *Meditationes* is made more easily discernible. At a precise theoretical moment, in effect, it is found explicitly posited, as a principle without reason since, precisely, it gives a universal account of everything, that: "Now it is manifest by the natural light that there must be at least as much ⟨reality⟩ in the efficient and total cause as in the effect of that cause."[65] In question once again is causality in its entire splendour, total *qua* efficient, and therefore such as, in 1630, it first subverted the *cogitatio*. Why then does it intervene, if it is expressed already as admitting no exception, only in the middle of the *Meditatio III*? Why does causality not introduce its principle from the origin? The response arises inevitably: because at the origin is found the *cogitatio*, whose proper function consists in leading from doubt to the *ego* (*cogito*). Causality, as much efficient as total, must not intervene except at the precise moment where the *ego* itself sets off in quest of the foundation of its own cogitative existence. And in order to transit from an existence of a cogitative being to an absolutely founded existence, the *ego* ceases to define itself from the essence of the *ens ut cogitatum* (being as thought), and lays claim to a more essential word upon the being in its being: the *ens ut causatum* (being as cause), for which the exact formulation intervenes, then and then alone, as an unavoidable evidence. Posited as new principle, indeed as the second beginning of the *Meditationes*, the *causa* unfolds its authority immediately and directly, upon that which it is a question of surpassing, the *cogitatio* itself. Whence this audacity, which Descartes, first, no doubt, risks: "[And this is transparently true] not only in the case of effects which possess ⟨what the philosophers call⟩ actual or formal reality, but also in the case of ideas, where one is considering only ⟨what they call⟩ objective reality."[66] Any being is, in so far as it is a *cogitatum*, as the *Meditatio II* had established. The *Meditatio III* confirms this, but completes it, adding: "any *cogitatum* depends upon a *cogitatio*, which itself is, only insofar as it is caused, as a *causatum*. More essential to a being is that its status of *cogitatum* reveals to itself its dignity as a *causatum*. And the dignity of a *causatum* is more profound, in effect, than the 'affectus indignitas' (indignity of the effect)" (AT VII, 242, 6),[67] for it is directly produced by the *causa* as such. This redoubling leads first, exemplarily, to the so-called proof of the existence of God by the effects. It should be more precisely defined: proof, by the status of the *causatum*, of the *idea Dei*, an idea which "I cannot in any way grasp, and perhaps cannot even reach in my thought."[68] The highest *cogitatio*, which gives the idea of God, cannot deliver the existence of God, except if it lets itself be taken up anew by the *causa* efficient and total, *ut causatum*. Now if even this *cogitatio* can be interpreted *ut causata*, how much more so may all the others ("Caetera autem omnia," AT VII 45, 2) "as for all other elements",[69] since they only lay claim to the *ego*, a finite substance, as their sufficient cause. There thus remains no *cogitatio* that must not be understood as caused, and so be included in the interpretation of the being as such *ut causatum*. However, despite this gain, there is yet a final obstacle to overcome. That the *cogitationes* be submitted to causality constitutes one point, which is considerable, but which decides nothing about the *cogito* itself. In as much as the *ego cogito* remains an autonomous and sufficient principle, the *cogitatio* eludes, in its function if not in its products, the sway of the *causa sive ratio*. As seductive as it might appear, this position of withdrawal offers nonetheless no security. For the *ego* itself is inscribed in a *causa*, which has as its name, God: "Deus mei causa est, ego ejus effectus [God is the cause of me, I am his effect]."[70] The ego is no exception to the universality of the divine creative cause, since the very idea of God as *summe potens* implies that: "[W]hich created both myself and everything else."[71] Essences, but also the *ego* have God for their cause, as much as do existents. We must push still further: the *idea Dei* intervenes at least as *causatum* without another, possible cause than God. Now Descartes specifies the resemblance of God "[And that I perceive that likeness] which includes the idea of God, by the same faculty which enables me to perceive myself."[72] The same faculty makes me perceive myself and perceive the *idea Dei*; this faculty has as name: *cogitatio*; by it, I at once perceive myself and I perceive the *idea Dei*. I propose to comprehend this: the *cogitatio* can either understand itself, according to the *ens ut cogitatum*, and deliver the *ego*, or it may – the same – let itself be taken up again according to the *ens ut causatum*, and lead to the existence of God. The divergence of the end points depends solely upon the subversion of the *cogitatio* by the *causa*.

Having reduced all exceptions and resistances, the *causa*, therefore, may henceforth be given legitimately as the most fundamental trait of a being. That is, of a being, conceived as such, according to the express formula of 1641: "What does seem to me self-evident is that whatever exists either derives its existence from a cause or derives its existence from itself as a cause."[73] In this *omne id quod est* [all that which is] we can read nothing other than the being taken universally as such. We must therefore translate: the being as such and universally is only by virtue of a cause; little matter if this cause is different from itself or identical to itself. The *causa* becomes a principle of an onto-logy strictly founded in reason. Whatever might be, it shall be founded in its being in as much as it is caused, "omne id quod est esse a causa [all that which is from a cause]." Since this foundation in reason unfolds itself universally, why does Descartes add, "vel a se tanquam a causa [or derives its existence from itself as a cause]"? Before advancing any other factual and doctrinal explication, let us recall again the onto-theo-logical constitution of all thought (wishing to constitute itself as) metaphysics: the being [*l'être*] of a being [*l'étant*] as such founds therein all beings (onto-logy), and indissolubly, the being *par excellence* therein founds and supports the being of the being [*l'être de l'étant*] (theo-logy). The being of a being as such entertains with the being *par excellence* a relation of reciprocal foundation – although, in the one and the other case, the modes of foundation (*gründen/begründen*) differ. According to this figure, it becomes quite intelligible that Descartes states twice the tie which unites "omne id quod est" (all which is) to the *causa*. For, in fact, the two formulas do not remain parallel, in spite of the stylistic appearance. The first, which ties "omne id quod est" to "esse a causa," articulates an onto-logy which brings to light the manner of being of all beings, founded by it because by right, in Cartesian terms, common to all finite beings. The second, on the contrary, which rests the "omne id quod est" upon "esse a se tanquam a causa [being deriving from itself its cause]," only concerns a single being, the being *par excellence*. This formula operates the reversed foundation (not the inverse) of all the other (finite) beings by way of the excellence of an exceptional being. In fact, the second formulation is pronounced upon the theo-logy that fulfils the onto-theo-logy of the *causa*.

Proving this claim does not present us with insurmountable difficulties. By hypothesis, if the onto-theo-logy of the *causa* overrides that of the *cogitatio*, the corresponding being *par excellence* must be displaced from the *ego* to God; or more exactly, from the cogitative foundation of the *ens ut cogitatum* to the causal foundation of the *ens ut causatum*, thus from the *ego* (*cogito*) to a causal God who, first, causes himself just as the *ego* first self-cogitates, as *causa sui* afterward and as the *cogitatio sui*.[74] As to this displacement, Descartes not only accomplishes it explicitly in the *Meditatio III*, but he performs it in a text which, first, announces the hypothesis of a positive aseity, such as Caterus and Arnauld will take it up again in order to oblige Descartes to publish the decision about God as *causa sui*.[75] The text itself states: "Yet if I derived my existence from myself, then I should neither doubt nor want, nor lack anything at all; for I should have given myself all the perfections of which I have any idea, and thus I should myself be God."[76] We have read rightly! (a) It is thus a question of searching for a being *par excellence* from the onto-logy of the *causa*, of which the hypothesis comes to be advanced a few pages prior to it (40, 21–25), and which contains expressly the version "a se tanquam a causa" (from itself, as from a cause); or rather, since this formula only appears in the *Primae Responsiones* to comment on this very text, here the ontology of the *ens ut causatum* undertakes for the first time to fulfil itself in a being *par excellence*. (b) The *ego* is indeed what is in question; in effect, the thought of the *causa* only intervenes on the basis of what was established by the thought of the *cogitatio*; just as after having fulfilled the *cogitatio* in the *ego*, Descartes subjects each of these to the more fundamental recovery of the *causa*. He begins here by again taking up the ultimate point at which the onto-theo-logy of the *cogitatio* culminated: the *ego*, being *par excellence cogito*. To this *ego*, taken as this being, he applies the onto-theo-logical hypothesis imposed by the second word on the being of the being [sur l'être de l'étant], and tries, on the *ego*, the experiment of determining whether it satisfies the *causa par excellence*. Conceptually this crucial question is articulated: can the *ego* be conceived and thus be *a se*, understanding thereby, positively *a se, tanquam a causa* [from itself, as from a cause]? (c) The retreat of the onto-theo-logy of the *cogitatio* before the onto-theo-logy of the *causa* is accomplished by the very fact of the *ego*, which, examining itself, ascertains its incapacity to satisfy the causal excellence, although it can always illustrate cogitative excellence. This avowal of impotence (impotence in the strict sense, which will determine the true being *par excellence* as infinite potency) is made with the recognition that I doubt. In effect, the *dubitatio* can be understood in two manners, with two opposed consequences: as the *cogitatio*, the doubt assures, despite the uncertainty of its own modality, the certitude of the *cogito* and the ontic excellence of the *ego*; but, considered as requiring a cause, this same *dubitatio* attests that the *ego* does not entertain a relation of cause to effect with all of its thoughts, and thus that in certain cases it does not exercise totally the *causa efficiens*, required nevertheless *etiam de ideis* [even concerning ideas]. In the doubt, the *ego* confirms its ontic primacy *qua cogitatio*, but it invalidates all pretension to ontic excellence as *causa*. In a word, it ascertains of itself that "I am nothing but a thinking thing":[77] the admission of this reduction indicates that the *ego* renounces, in this second moment, the fulfilment of the excellence of the being.[78] The onto-theo-logy of the *ens ut causatum* will thus be completed in God, conceived as *causa sui*. The audacity of this ultimate, Cartesian name for God must not dissimulate another, and primary, audacity: God may not admit positive aseity (against Saint Thomas and his disciples) and bend back upon Himself the imperative of a *causa sive ratio*, except in so far as, in any event, the being *par excellence*, whatever it might be, would have to satisfy the *causa sui*. If the *ego* had been able to hold the role of this being *par excellence*, it should have taken, itself, the name of *causa sui* – for there is none other to be found, in the heavens or upon the earth, indeed not even in the inferno. Only God comes to fill, after the insufficiency of the *ego*, the function of *causa sui* – a function which is not imposed upon Him except in as much as it precedes Him following the necessities proper to the onto-theo-logy issuing from the *causa*. The figure of the *causa sui* – as model of any being *par excellence*, founded upon and the founder of the *ens ut causatum* – is decided and evinced before the identity of this being (*ego*, God) is specified; which specification, thereafter and as a consequence, will make this identity effective.[79] Only in this sense can it be conceived, moreover, that after 1641 the *ego* attempts again to imitate tangentially that which makes of God a being *par excellence*, the *causa sui*. This imitation leads to a reinterpretation of morality and liberty as a manner of enacting, within a limited field and by the perfect mastery of self that the free will guarantees the *ego*, independence; for "independence, conceived distinctly, contains infinity within itself" (AT III, 191, 15–16).[80] Thus is fulfilled the second word of Descartes on the most fundamental trait of the being: the being is as it is *qua* caused; this manner of being founds beings by unfolding them as *causata*, and, indissolubly, founds itself in a being *par excellence* which marks itself as *causa sui*. The onto-theo-logical constitution unfolds the being of the being according to the *causa*, and thus identifies the dignity, definitively metaphysical, of Cartesian thought.

Reduplicating the onto-theo-logy

Our task, however, is not yet at its end. On the contrary, we encounter here the difficulty which is doubtless the most considerable of all. We wished to establish the strictly metaphysical character of Cartesian thought, in recognizing in it a figure of the onto-theo-logical constitution of all metaphysics. Now, in wanting to prove our claim, we seem to have proven too much. We have located not one, but two figures of this constitution, the one according to the *cogitatio*, the other according to the *causa*. What relationship do these maintain? Do they contradict each other? Ought we not, before this proliferation, simply place in doubt the operations and rigour of the very concept of onto-theo-logical constitution and indeed of the notion of "metaphysics," supposed imprudently to be univocal?

These questions have nothing to do with rhetoric, and cannot receive, even in the form of a sketch, definitive answers here. But we can at least attempt to formulate them with greater exactitude. We concede first, that Heidegger only introduces the thesis of an onto-theo-logical constitution of metaphysics at the end of his reflection on Hegel: a study seminar on the *Science of Logic* (WS 1956/57) precedes the lecture given on 24 February 1957 at Todtnauberg. Doubtless we must also add to this background the courses given during the preceding semester (WS 1955/56) at the University of Fribourg on Leibniz and the *Satz vom Grund* [*Principle of Reason*]. In this sense, and without the prejudice of a more exact textual examination (which the *Gesamtausgabe* alone shall make possible), we hold that the onto-theo-logical constitution only imposes itself on the thought of Heidegger from the basis of the two figures of metaphysics who most massively bring out this constitution and put it to work: Leibniz and Hegel. However, just as we must allow for "a time of incubation of the principle of reason," which itself depends on the "incubation of Being,"[81] it seems to us that we must allow a time of incubation for the onto-theo-logical constitution. This constitution is, moreover, not so much a reverse effect permitting a retroactive hermeneutics as a reflective and non-determinative judgement of sorts – since from Plato and Aristotle on, metaphysics lets itself be read as an onto-theo-logy – than it is a slow emergence, in figures often very complex, of that which in the Leibnizian and Hegelian achievements takes on the brilliance of a simple constitution because therein it is definitively fulfilled. Hegel himself was perfectly aware of a decisive, Cartesian kinship. From 1807 on, he places the moment of absolute freedom under the aegis of the "concept of Cartesian metaphysics . . . that is, that in itself being and thought are the same, *daß an sich Seyn und Denken dasselbe ist*."[82] This equivalence, which goes to the point of requiring the Same between being and thought, characterizes not only Hegelian onto-theo-logy (and Leibnizian), but also, provided one understands thought as *cogitatio*, the first figure of Cartesian onto-theo-logy. Far from this Hegelian inscription forbidding us any properly metaphysical approach to Cartesian thought, it leads us back to it rather imperatively. A similar confirmation could very easily be found, starting from Leibniz, whose "great principle," which alone allows us to "rise up to Metaphysics" – that is, "Ratio est in Natura, cur aliquid potius existat quam nihil [Reason is in Nature, why does something exist rather than nothing]"[83] – literally, if not expressly, refers back to that which we recognized, in the *Responsiones*, as the *dictat* of reason. Historically, no insurmountable difficulty is offered in establishing filiation between the two Cartesian figures of onto-theo-logy and its completed figures. The metaphysics of the *ens ut cogitatum* refers back to Hegel, the metaphysics of the *ens ut causatum*, to Leibniz; the gaps, which remain no less massive, merely indicate the path, leading from Descartes, to the later fulfilments of the destiny of metaphysics. Our difficulty is thus transformed: it is not so much a question of determining *if* the onto-theo-logical constitution operates pertinently for Cartesian thought (and is not limited to later moments reached by Leibniz and Hegel), than it is one of determining *which* destiny modifies, with Descartes, this constitution. In these two figures is it a question of a contradiction, of a concurrence or of an incoherence due to a metaphysical oversight? No doubt none of these responses are appropriate, for nothing founders, in the case of the great thinkers, in non-thought. We ought perhaps to return the question, and ask: can, first, the complexity of the figure(s) of Cartesian onto-theo-logy be thematized in a single framework and, in this case, what does Descartes teach us about the onto-theo-logical constitution? The simple figure of the constitution that Heidegger thematizes, *à propos* Hegel (and Leibniz), might only offer one case, privileged certainly but neither normative nor unique. The complication of this simple figure, as imposed by Descartes, could on the contrary become the rule, or at least the most probable hypothesis for the examination of the metaphysical character of philosophical thoughts in general. In other terms, the onto-theo-logical complexity of Cartesian metaphysics would amount less to an exception, relative to the primordial but elementary figure of onto-theo-logy as laid out by Heidegger in Hegel (and Leibniz), than to the contrary. Heidegger's elementary figure, then, would not offer the exceptional design of a game elsewhere more complex and eventually, infinitely varied but no less onto-theo-logical. The Cartesian exception to Heidegger's elementary figure could, in fact, give the index of a rule: that without exception, the onto-theo-logical constitution

takes in metaphysics, a complexity greater than that of the Hegelian achievement. This hypothesis shall not be verified (or therefore invalidated), except
by works pursuing the onto-theological constitution in one or another thinker
of metaphysics (such as we have attempted here, as in prior studies, in the
case of Descartes), or those pursuing the very history of the concept of metaphysics. Here it may suffice to mark the inversion of the question, the laborious anticipation of elements toward the response.

We can henceforth return to Descartes, and attempt to fix the structure
wherein come together the two figures assumed by the onto-theo-logical
constitution. We are postulating that these two figures no more oppose each
other than they contradict one another, but rather that they subordinate
each other in a sort of onto-theo-logy which is not double, but redoubled.
Let us spatialize this schema in a figure since, as Descartes repeats, the figure
suits the imagination, and the *imaginationis adjumenmentum* [imagination as an
aid] (AT X, 438, 12) permits that the question "[B]e perceived much more
distinctly by our intellect."[84]

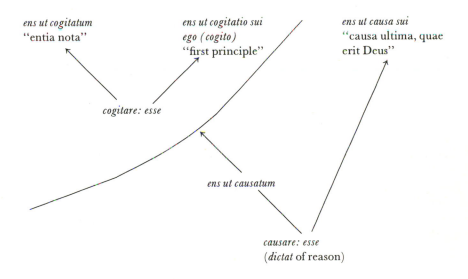

ens ut cogitatum   ens ut cogitatio sui   ens ut causa sui
"entia nota"   ego (cogito)   "causa ultima, quae
                   "first principle"   erit Deus"

cogitare: esse

ens ut causatum

causare: esse
(*dictat* of reason)

We are not here juxtaposing two onto-theo-logical constitutions, we are
redoubling a first constitution with a second, the one and the other unfolding
separately, but completely, a thesis on the *ens in quantum ens* (or: *ens ut cogitatum*,
or indeed *ens ut causatum*) and a thesis on the being *par excellence* (respectively,
cogitatio sui and *causa sui*). Thus it is a question of a redoubling, and not of an
incoherent or conflictual splitting into two parts, because all of the first constitution is found, over and above its own articulation, and taken up within the
second constitution as a region of being in general. The onto-theo-logical constitution, according to the *dictat* of reason, thinks as *ens causatum* (therefore

according to an ontology) the totality of the onto-theo-logical constitution deployed according to the first word on being (*cogitare*), thus just as much the *ens ut cogitatio sui* (*ego*, theology) as the *ens ut cogitatum* (ontology). Descartes redoubles his onto-theo-logy in reinterpreting the first meaning of *esse, cogitare*, with a second, *causare*.

This redoubling calls for several remarks by way of commentary. (a) The onto-theo-logy which is deployed first from the *cogitare*, in the combined play of the *ens ut cogitatum* and the *ens par excellence ut cogitatio sui*, is thus accomplished before the explicit (and limited) enterprise of special metaphysics presented in the *Meditationes*. In fact this enterprise is set up from the time of the *Regulae*; and if the *Meditationes I* and *II* are all the more strictly attached to it in that they arrive at the highest formulation of the *ens par excellence* appropriate to the *cogitatio sui*: viz. the *ego*, we must not underestimate for all that the prior sketches, approaches and formulations of the *ego*. (b) Reciprocally, the second figure of the onto-theo-logy, which unfolds from the *causare*, in the combined play of the *ens ut causatum* and of the *ens par excellence ut causa sui*, does not coincide with the field of the *Meditationes*. This second figure only expressly reaches its being *par excellence* with the *Responsiones I* and *IV*; it does not determine the being as *causatum* except from the *Meditatio III*. In effect, a double lexical fact must hold our attention here, one which confirms the redoubling (and finds its meaning therein): *substantia* does not intervene in the order of reasons before the *Meditatio III* (precisely, AT VII, 40, 12).[85] Now, by an accident which amounts to a necessity (albeit somewhat concealed), the same page offers also the first, theoretically significant occurrence of *causa* in the *Meditationes*; an occurrence which is found at the centre of nothing less than the first formulation of the *dictat* of reason: "Now it is manifest by the natural light that there must be at least as much (reality) in the efficient and total cause as in the effect of that cause."[86] Thus the transition from one onto-theo-logy to another is inscribed in the very text of the *Meditationes*, and, one might add to specify exactly, in AT VII, 40, which appears as a decisive recasting of the speculative impetus. Moreover, we find here a break in that order of reasons long highlighted by the most authoritative of critics.[87] We venture here that the hypothesis of the redoubling of the onto-theo-logical constitution contributes no small amount toward making this break intelligible and thinkable. (c) That the onto-theo-logical domain of the *causare* does not coincide with the *Meditationes* allows us to raise another precise difficulty. One could object, in effect, that all properly, and purely ontological, consideration abstracts the being, by definition, from all determination – *ens in quantum ens*, in particular from the determination of a transcendence and a creation: *ens creatum* excludes from the first the *ens in quantum ens*. Duns Scotus and Suarez, among many others, have underscored this.[88] Thus, if *causare* appeared only in the first philosophy aligned with, or devoted to God, and thus became the synonym of *creare*, then no ontology would remain possible. Now *causare* is not equivalent to *creare* (all the while including it): the primacy of the *causa* is exercised between finite terms from the *Regulae* and supports the physics of the *Discourse on Method* as well as the *Essays*, without reference to a creation nor to a transcendent causality. *Causa* determines directly the science of the common being, without reducing it for all that to an *ens creatum*. As proof of this, the submission of the creator God himself to the exigency of causality: *causa sui* attests, by the redu lication of the *causa*, that even the creator must be submitted to the *causa*. Now if God can be thought as *causa sui*, He could not be understood as *creator sui*, even for Descartes. Therefore the *ens ut causatum* is in no way reduced to the *ens creatum*. (d) The most considerable difficulty issues from the status of the *ego* (*cogito*). In the present schema, the *ego* intervenes in two opposed acceptations; from the point of view of the *esse: cogitare*, it fills the function of the being *par excellence*, while from the point of view of the *esse: causare*, it has to do with the *ens in quantum ens, ut causatum*. This real duplicity allows, however, for the resolution of another, purely textual, difficulty. In effect, the *ego cogito* receives expressly the title of first principle:

> remarking that this truth: *I think, therefore I am*, was so firm and so assured, that all the extravagant suppositions of the Sceptics were not capable of shaking it, I judged that I could receive it, without scruples, as the first principle of Philosophy, which I was seeking.
>
> (AT VI, 32)

In the other sense, the first principle is *that our Soul exists*, for the reason that there is nothing whose existence is to us more notorious:

> considering that he who would doubt all things cannot doubt, all the same, that he not be while he doubts, and that which reasons in such a way that, in not being able to doubt itself though nonetheless doubting all the rest, this thing is not what we say to be our body but what we call our soul or our thought, I have taken the being or the existence of this thought as the first principle, from which I have deduced very clearly the following things: that is, that there is a God, who is author of all that which is in the world.[89]

How can this "first principle," which submits to itself the existence of God itself, recognize itself, moreover, as *ens creatum* (AT VII, 45, 14), *res ab alio dependens* (51, 24–25; 53, 10–11). In a word, how can it admit to not meriting the title of *summum ens* – "nos non esse summum ens et nobis deesse quamplurimum" (374, 13–14) (we are not the highest being and we lack a great)? This distortion reveals, in fact, no contradiction; it only shows that the *ego* can be read from the two Cartesian claims about the being as such. Considered from the *cogitatio*, the *ego* amounts to the "first principle," precisely in as much as it is the "most notorious," in as much as it is "truth . . .

firm and assured," in brief as "the being or the existence" of a "thought," therefore of a first *cogitatio*, and existing with the status of *cogitatio* (*sui*). But this does not keep the one and same *ego*, this time from the standpoint of the *causa*, which is introduced by the prodigious recast of the *Meditatio III*, from becoming an *ens causatum* by common right: the reduplication of the onto-theo-logy assures this and imposes a second metaphysical site, at the same time that it establishes God for the first time in the site of the being *par excellence*, of the *summum ens* (see n. 47). The double status of the *ego* – a major difficulty for all modern interpreters but also for the ancient ones – only reflects, albeit exemplarily, the redoubling of the onto-theo-logical constitution of Cartesian metaphysics. (e) The *causa sui* has meaning, finally, only in response to the exigency of thought that seeks, according to the *dictat* of reason, the cause of all beings, up to this, that "ad causam ultimam deveniatur, quae erit Deus" (50, 6) (comes back to a last cause which will be God). More than to Spinoza, who takes up this formulation without – here, as frequently – placing it in question, or perhaps even thinking about it, the Cartesian *causa sui* refers to that which Leibniz will meditate as the "great principle" of sufficient reason, or more exactly, the *principium reddendae rationis*, the principle that reason, in all beings, must be furnished in order to found its existence. In this sense, the Cartesian God remains indeterminate, as fundamentally so as the *ego*: the latter only playing as *first* principle, and not yet as *causa ultima*; the former amounting already to a final reason and cause, but without taking back into its midst the *cogitatio* (*sui*), which is still first. Better than Malebranche and Spinoza, Leibniz alone arrives at making the *cogitatio* conspire with the *causa* in a single foundation: the *cogitatio*, as *ratio sive causa* assuring the foundation, the thought of the cause completing the rationality of the principle.

Cartesian thought thus belongs strictly to metaphysics since it twice fulfils its onto-theo-logical constitution. This duality betrays no incoherence, but rather reveals a decisive recasting of the *cogitatio* by the *causa*. And if this restart nonetheless opens an abyss, this very abyss defines the properly metaphysical task of post-Cartesian thought, illustrated by Spinoza, Malebranche and to a wholly other degree, Leibniz, among others. This task is to make coincide with one another, the two Cartesian claims on the being in its being [l'étant dans son être]. It might even be that, in Descartes, their separation remains one of the charms which, as metaphysics is today brought to completion, still attracts us to reading him. For metaphysics is only accomplished once *causa* and *cogitatio* are perfectly identified, in such way that their separation offers us the trace of a more secret disquiet.

Notes

1 TN. Marion is here referring to the deliberate absence of ontology in the work of Descartes. As he points out, this constitution of a philosophy as explicitly non-

ontological, in reaction to scholasticism, is effectuated by means of conceptual operations of elimination and reduction. This Cartesian procedure is first inaugurated in his *Regulae*.

For further discussion of Marion's thesis concerning Descartes' substitution of an implicit, anti-metaphysical ontology starting from the *ego cogito*, and taking the place of Aristotle's concept of the Being of beings *on hé on*, see J.-L. Marion, *René Descartes: Règles utiles et claires pour la direction de l'esprit dans la recherche de la vérité* (The Hague: 1977). The above-mentioned thesis is most fully developed in J.-L. Marion, *Sur l'ontologie grise de Descartes: Science cartésienne et savoir aristotélicien dans les Regulae* (Paris: Librairie Philosophique J. Vrin, 1975; 1881, 2nd edn). For an English-language introduction to Marion's discussion of Descartes, see also "On Descartes' Constitution of Metaphysics" (paper delivered at Columbia University, October 1985) in *Graduate Faculty Philosophy Journal*, 11/1, 1986, pp. 21–33; in this essay, see the editor's note, fn. 12 for a discussion of the significance of "grey ontology," as that which "conceals itself under an epistemological discourse," thereby "maintaining the thing in the greyness of the object [qua mental construction], and thus bears testimony to the intoxication . . . of the *ego*, 'master and owner' of the world reduced to evidence". Pierre Adler, editor of this essay points the English speaker to the implicit play on words in "ontologie *grise*" – as, on the one hand, a literally colourless, indistinct ontology and, on the other hand, in the sense of "*griserie*" – which bespeaks a state of intoxication, here of the Cartesian first being, the *ego cogitans*, see Adler's note 12, p. 31. A further elaboration of this argument, with additions and improvements, was published as Chapter 2 of *Sur le prisme métaphysique de Descartes* (Paris: PUF, 1986); the English translation of this book will be published by the University of Chicago Press in Spring 1998.

2 *Oeuvres de Descartes*, ed. Ch. Adam and P. Tannery, revised edn (Paris: Vrin/CNRS, 1964–76); *Notae in Programma quoddam* (1647), AT VIII–2, 348, 15. See 543, 20–21 and AT V, 9/16. English translation: *The Philosophical Writings of Descartes*, trans. J. Cottingham, R. Stoothoff and D. Murdoch (Cambridge: Cambridge University Press, 1985). This quote Vol. I, p. 297. Hereafter *PWD*, Vol. I and *PWD*, Vol. II respectively and also *PWD* III (Cambridge: 1991).

3 *Metaphysics Z*, 1, 1028b1–4. For the interpretation of this precise text, consult the study of R. Brague in *Du temps chez Platon et Aristotle* (Paris: 1982).

4 "Ac proinde haec cognitio *ego cogito, ergo sum*, est omnium prima et certissima, quae cuilibet ordine philosophanti occurat," *Principia Philosophiae 1*, §7, and §10 (see §12). "Accordingly, this piece of knowledge – *I am thinking therefore I exist* – is the first and most certain of all to occur to anyone who philosophizes in an orderly way."

5 *Sein und Zeit*, §6, p. 24. See "Descartes, to whom one attributes the discovery of the *cogito sum* as the ground of departure of the modern philosophic question, directed his research on the *cogitare* of the *ego* – within certain limits at least. On the other hand, he left the *sum* totally unexposed (*unerörtet*), although it was as originarily established as was the *cogito*" (*Sein und Zeit*, §10, S. 46) and *Wegmarken*, in *Gesamtausgabe* (Frankfurt am Main: Klostermann, 1975), 9, 89–90. Hereafter referred to as G.A. On Heidegger's reading of Descartes, see other indications in my note on "Heidegger et la situation métaphysique de Descartes," *Bulletin Cartésien IV*, *Archives de Philosophie*, 38/2, 1975.

6 The term appears , in Latin, under the pen of Clauberg, from 1647 – thus in Descartes' lifetime – in the *Elementa Philosophiae sive Ontosophia*, published in Groningue, in the United Provinces then; this text, reprinted in 1660 (Duisbourg, *Ontosophia Nova, quae vulgo Metaphysica*), in 1664 (Amsterdam, *Metaphysica de ente, quae rectius Ontosophia*), resulted finally in the *Opera Philosophica* (Amsterdam: 1691, p. 281), in the following formulation: "Sicuti autem θεοσοφία vel θεολογία dicitur quae

circa Deum occupata Scientia; ita haec, quae non circa hoc vel illud ens speciali nomine insignitum, vel proprietate quadam ab aliis distinctum, sed circa ens in genere versatur, non incommode *Ontosophia* vel *Ontologia* dici posse videatur. [Just as *theosophia* or *theologia* designate the science that treats of God; thus the science which treats not of one or another being, marked by a special sign, or distinguished from other beings by some property, but of being in general, seems able to be named without inconvenience, *Ontosophia* or *Ontologia*.]"

Formulated otherwise, "Est quaedam scientia, quae contemplatur ens *quatenus ens* est, hoc est in quantum communem quandum intelligitur habere naturam vel naturae gradum, qui rebus corporeis et incorporeis, Deo et creaturis, omnibusque adco et singulis entibus suo modo inest. Ea vulgo Metaphysica, sed aptius *Ontologia*, vel scientia Catholica, *eine allgemeine Wissenschaft* et philosophia universalis nominatur (p. 283). [There exists a certain science which contemplates a being *in as much as it is*, that is, in as much as it is understood as having a nature or a degree of nature, which is in corporeal or incorporeal things, in God and in the creatures, in all and each according to its mode. This science is habitually called metaphysics, but also by preference *Ontologia*, or scientia catholica.]"

In fact, in Greek, ὀντολογία, the term is found already at work in J. Miscrealius, *Lexicon Philosophicum* (Jena: 1653, p. 654), A. Calov, *Metaphysica divina* (Rostock: 1639) (*Praecognita II*, p. 4), and J.H. Alsted, *Curcus Philosophiae Encyclopaedia* (Herborn: 1620, p. 149). Now Alsted, himself, refers to the *Lexicon Philosophicum* of Goclenius, published by 1613 in Frankfurt, which, examining the different types of abstraction, defines one as of the abstraction "ὀντολογία," idest Philosophiae de ente seu Transcendentibus" (p. 16). And in the margin, one reads "ὁι'τολογία" et philosophia de ENTE." See the classic article of E. Vollrath, "Die Gliederung der Metaphysica Specialis," *Zeitschrift für philosophische Forschung*, 1962, 16/2, pp. 258–284. In fact, it is above all important that Goclenius define first a "Scientia . . . ex consideratione ὀντῶν – Universalis, quae considerat simpliciter ὀντα seu ὁν ἠ ὁν. Prima philosophia" (*ibid.*, p. 1011). Thus, at the very moment at which Descartes is writing, the impetus given by Suarez (among others) to a science of the *ens in quantum ens* has in no way wavered. Thus the Cartesian abstention therefrom becomes all the more significant. Or again independently of the lexical question, whose importance remains only symptomatic, it must be stated that Descartes did not write a text responding to *De ente et essentia*, to the two first *Disputationes Metaphysicae* of Suarez (*De natura primae philosophiae seu metaphysicae*, to the *De ratione essentiali seu conceptu entis*) or to the *De conceptu entis* of Cajetan.

7 "[E]ntia philosophica, quae revera sub imaginationem non cadunt" (AT X, 412, 27–28), *Entia abstracta* (AT X, 443, 6 and 444, 23). Finally, "omnia entia Scholastica, quae ignorabam et de quibus nunquam aliquid inaudiveram, quaeque, ut existimo, in sola tantum eorum, qui ae invenerunt, Phantasia subsistunt" (AT X, 517, 22–26); this latter reproach contradicts the preceding ones moreover: Descartes excludes the *entia* of the philosophers because they do not fall under the imagination (the auxiliary of the understanding in the *Regulae*) and because all their reality resides in the imagination of the philosophers. *Ens*, for Descartes, does not always, nor first, designate the abstract concept of *ens commune* (which precisely Descartes does not thematize, or thematizes little), but rather the genus, the species, the specific difference, and the definitions which follow (constant criticism of the definition of *homo* as *animal rationale*, AT VII, 25, 26–31; AT X, 517, 6–33).

8 The *arbor Porphyrii*, evoked by Epistémon, attracts in response, the criticism of the *Metaphysici gradus* (AT X, 516, 12, then 517, 13, 19). It might, moreover, be possible that, in positing that "all Philosophy is as a tree, the roots of which are Metaphysics" (*Preface* to the French translation of the *Principia*, AT IX–2, 14, 24–25),

Descartes wishes precisely to take up again the tree of Porphyry. Concerning the translation and the meaning of the *Regula VI*, in particular AT X, 381, 7–16, I take the liberty of referring to Marion, *René Descartes*; pp. 17 sq., as well as to Marion, *Sur l'ontologie grise*, §§12–14.

9 *PWD*, Vol. I, p. 21: "praccipuum . . . continet artis secretum, nec ulla utilior est in toto hoc Tractatu," "res omnes per quasdam series posse disponi, non quidem in quantum ad aliquod genus entis referuntur, sicut illas Philosophi in categorias suas diviscrunt, sed in quantum unac ex aliis cognosci possunt (AT X, 381, 9–13)."

10 TN. *PWD*, Vol. I, p. 44: "aliter spectandas esse res singulas in ordine ad cognitionem nostram, quam si de iisdem loquamur prout revera existunt" (418, 1–3), "hic nos de rebus non agentes nisi quantum ab intellectu percipiuntur, illas tantum simplices vocamus, quarum cognitio tam perspicua et distincta est, ut in plures magis distincte cognitas mente dividi non possint" (418, 12–17).

11 TN. "[V]iz. order or measure," *PWD*, Vol. I, p. 64.

12 *Genus entis*, AT X, 390, 10; 438, 15; 439, 2; 447, 12.

13 TN. *PWD*, Vol. I, p. 49. "aliquod genus entis (mihi) ignotum" (427, 9–10).

14 *A Morin*, 12 September 1638, AT II, 364, 4–5 and 367, 19–20. The best examples of such "philosophic beings," eliminated because held to be unknowable, come from the *Regulae*: disqualification of movement (AT X, 426, 16–25) and of place (AT X, 426, 9–16 and 433, 14–434, 1). See Marion, *Sur l'ontologie grise*, §24, pp. 146 sq., as well as §28, and Marion, *René Descartes*, pp. 248–249 (other references).

15 TN. *PWD*, Vol. I, p. 61. "omisso omni alio, praeterquam quod sit ens" (446, 9–10).

16 TN. *PWD*, Vol. I, p. 57. "notorum entium sive naturarum mixturam" (439, 8).

17 The *ens* does not merit this name until it is in act, since "esse potentiale . . . proprie loquendo nihil est" (AT VII, 47, 21–22). The separation between substance and accident loses, on its side, all its importance once *species* and *genus* can only count as *respectiva* (AT X, 382, 25–383, 1).

18 See *Metaphysics E*, 4, 1027b25–27 (text already obscured, as we know, by *Metaphysics θ* 10, 1051b17, which alone reaches the true as the meaning, and as the first meaning, of the ὄν). The *rapprochement* with the *Regulae* is found indicated by Heidegger, *Wegmarken*, G.A. 9, p. 233. TN. *PWD*, Vol. I, p. 30: "veritatem proprie vel falsitatem non nisi in solo intellectu esse posse" (396, 3–4).

19 TN. *PWD*, Vol. II, p. 136: "Nota est omnibus essentiae ab existentia distinctio."

20 TN. *PWD*, Vol. II, p. 416: "Neminem enim unquam tam stupidum exstitisse crediderim, qui (. . .) quid sit exsistentia edocendus fuerit."

Respectively perhaps, *AX*, 1645? 1646?, AT IV, 348, 7–9 and *Recherche de la Vérité*, AT X, 524, 10–11. To which we will add, taken from the same indeterminate letter, a confirmation *a contrario*: "de triangulo extra cogitatione in quo manifestum mihi videtur essentiam et existentiam nullo modo distingui, et idem est de omnibus universalibus" (AT IV, 350, 7–9).

From this point of view, one of the "Axiomata sive Communes Notiones" of the *Ilae Responsiones* becomes significant and questionable: "X. In omnis rei idea sive conceptu continetur *existentia*, quia nihil possumus concipere nisi sub ratione existentis; nempe continetur existentia possibilis sive contingens in conceptu rei limitatae, sed necessaria et perfecta in conceptu entis summe perfecti" (AT VII, 166, 14–18). It appears clearly (a) that existence constitutes the name of the *ens* given that the *res* (this *ens*) enters into play only from its *idea*, itself understood not as εἶδος, but as *conceptus*. In other words, when ontology becomes grey (i.e. depends upon methodical knowledge), the *ens* turns toward the *existentia*; (b) that this turn admits no exception, since even the simple possibility, thus strictly speaking non-existence (*essentia*, or δυνάμει όν), is understood as *existentia possibilis*; this strangely contradictory syntagma is imposed, once the *esse potentiale* is reduced to nothing ("proprie loquendo nihil est," AT VII, 47, 21–22); (c) that the *existentia* is imposed univocally to all beings, God included, as is confirmed moreover by the equivalence between *être* and *exister* in the proof of the existence of God: "God who is this perfect Being, is or exists" (D.M., AT VI, 36, 28), "God is or exists" (*ibid.*, 38, 19).

21 TN. *PWD*, Vol. I, p. 117: "in omnis rei idea sive conceptu continetur existentia, quia nilhil possumus concipere nisi sub ratione existentis" (AT VII, 166, 14–16).

22 *PWD*, Vol. II, p. 32: "esse potentiali, quod proprie loquendo nihil est" (AT VII, 47, 21–2).

23 TN. John Cottingham's translation, *Descartes' Conversation with Burman* (Oxford: Clarendon Press, 1976), §V, reads,

since we are composed partly of nothingness and partly of being, we incline partly towards being and partly towards nothingness. As for God, on the other hand, he cannot incline to nothingness, since it is supreme and pure being. This consideration is a metaphysical one and is perfectly clear to all those who give their mind to it.

24 AT V, 153, 32 and *L'Entretien avec Burman*, edited, translated and annotated by J.-M. Beyssade (Paris: 1981), §13, pp. 44–45. Beyssade rests his translation on *A Hyperaspiste*, August 1641, n. 6, AT III, 426, 27–427, 20; to which we shall add: "Ego enim, qui per falsum nihil aliud intelligo quam veri privationem" (Therefore, I don't understand by falsity anything else than to be deprived of truth) (AT VII, 378, 21). The nothingness of ontology is confirmed (doubtless for other motives) with Pascal: "One cannot undertake to define a word without beginning by the words, *it is*, either one expresses it, or one understands it. Thus to define being, we must say *it is*, and thus employ the word defined by the definition" (*De l'esprit géométrique*, in *Oeuvres complètes*, ed. L. Lafuma (Paris: 1963), p. 350. This same text criticizes the Aristotelian definitions of *man*, of light and of time – exactly as Descartes has done.) That which authenticates a parallel: "Who knows indeed what it is to be which it is impossible to define, since there is nothing more general, and that it would be necessary, in order to explain it, to first use this very word, saying: *It is*, to be . . .?" (*Entretien avec M. de Saci, ibid.*, p. 294). Despite the separation between intentions, we are pleased to place the expression of "nullity of ontology" [néant d'ontologie] under the aegis of F. Alquié, "Descartes et l'ontologie négative," *Revue Internationale de Philosophie*, Brussels, Vol. 4, no. 12, April 1950, pp. 153–159.

25 TN. "No one before me," *PWD*, Vol. I, p. 296.

26 TN. Cottingham's translation of AT X, 438 reads, "whenever we deduce something unknown from something already known, it does not follow that we are discovering some new kind of entity," *PWD*, Vol. I, p. 56.

27 Heidegger, *Holzwege*, G.A. 5, p. 210, 1950 edn, p. 194.

28 We think here of L. Liard: "That which characterizes his [i.e. Descartes'] physics and makes of it an entirely novel thing, without precedent, is the absence of any metaphysical idea." By consequence: "In the entire work of Descartes, the method and the sciences form a distinct and independent work. That which is found there inserted from metaphysics can be detached from it without harm" (*Descartes*, Paris: 1882, pp. 69 and 141). There is the same analysis, played in the opposite direction, by J. Maritain: "Descartes is a metaphysician unfaithful to metaphysics, and who voluntarily turns away toward the plains, toward the vast,

flat country that the river Mathematics waters," therefore "Descartes appears to us as having, properly speaking, *degraded* metaphysics" (*Le songe de Descartes et autres essais* [Paris: 1927], pp. 132 and 133). It remains for L. Brunschvicg to formulate the motive of this supposed desertion of metaphysics, the indifference or even the rejection of being: "Descartes challenges (. . .) the *universals of the dialecticians* and he abandons to its illusory destiny the entity of the concept of being" (*Les Progrès de la conscience dans la philosophie occidentale* [Paris: 1927], Vol. 1, p. 138), that is to say "the illusory preoccupation with the principles of being" (*Écrits Philosophiques* [Paris: 1950, Vol. 1, p. 72).

29 Respectively, *A Mersenne*, 11 November 1640, AT III, 235, 13–18, then 239, 2–7.

30 AT IX–1, 14, 7–12 (see 16, 13–16). On the use, by the title, of "metaphysics," see my study "L'ambivalence de la métaphysique cartésienne," in *Les Études Philosophiques*, 1976/4, reprinted in *Sur l'ontologie grise de Descartes*. In a strict sense, Descartes sometimes even reduces metaphysics to theology (*A Regius*, January 1642, AT III, 505, 10–11).

31 Heidegger, *Identität und Differenz* (Pfullingen: 1957), p. 50. French translation in *Questions I* (Paris: 1968), p. 293 (modified). English translation by Joan Stambaugh, *Identity and Difference* (New York: Harper and Row, 1969).

32 Heidegger, *Identität und Differenz*, p. 62. *Questions I*, p. 304 (modified). *Grundzug*, "fundamental trait" ["traite fondamental"], *Identität und Differenz*, pp. 50 and 51, *Questions I*, p. 294.

33 *A Clerselier*, June/July 1646, AT IV, 444, 4–12. This distinction is evidently applied to *cogito, ergo sum, Principia Philosophiae I*, §10 and *L'Entretien avec Burman*, AT V, 147, 8–18 (ed. Beyssade §3, pp. 18–19). It remains that one can understand it on the one hand from the *ego cogito* (principle: a being), on the other hand from any proposition (common notion, "in order to think, it is necessary to be," or, to put it as well, "all that which is has a cause").

34 Heidegger, *Identität und Differenz*, p. 50. *Questions I*, p. 294 (modified); see pp. 64 and 65ff. in the German original.

35 For it must be underscored that Spinoza does not innovate here. He supposes established the Cartesian concept of *causa sui* ("ut *vulgo* dicitur, causa sui," *De Intellectus Emendatione*, §92), only to modify thereafter the concept's domain of application (*Éthique 1*, def. 1 and §7, demonstration preparing only §25, dem.). In the scholastic realm, the refusal of the *causa sui* seems unanimous, at least to our knowledge and in the greatest of the scholastics. Thus Suarez, *Disp. Mét*, I, s. 1, n. 27, *XXVIII*, s. 1, n. 7, *XXIX*, s. 3, n. 1; thus also Duns Scotus, *De Primo Principio III*, Conclusions 2 (*causa sui*) and 3 (*incausabile*). Thus Saint Thomas , *De Ente et Essentia V, Summa Theologiae, Ia*, q. 2, a. 3, c., q. 19, a. 5, c., q. 45, a. 5, *ad 1 m, Contra Gentiles I*, 18 and 22; *II*, 15, etc.; thus also Saint Anselm, *Monologion VI* ("summa natura nec a se nec ab alio fieri potuit"). Doubtless, Saint Thomas admits *one* acceptation of *causa sui*, "Liberum est quod causa sui est" (*Contra Gentiles II*, 48), but it is only a commentary of the formula of Aristotle, ἐλεύθερος ὁ αὑτοῦ ἕνεκα καὶ μὴ ἄλλου ὤν (*Metaphysics A*, 2, 982b25–26, see *De Veritate*, q. 24, a. 1). We would in no manner manage to rediscover, there, the withdrawal of efficiency into itself [le repliement sur elle-même de l'efficience]. The same reserve is imposed before the users by Plotinus (*Enneads VI*, 8, 14 and 20) or those of Proclus (*Elements*, §46). All research for eventual "sources" of the Cartesian theme must at least be oriented upon its fundamental trait: not only, or even first, does Descartes innovate in saying *causa sui*, but in thinking the *causa* (*sui*) from efficiency and its absolute privilege over all other types of causality.

36 TN. The title of Rule One reads "[The aim of our studies should be to direct the

mind with a view to forming true and sound judgements] about whatever comes before it," *PWD*, Vol. I, p. 9.

37 *Objectum purae Matheseos* (AT VII, 71, 8 and 15; 74, 2; 80, 9–10) refers, more than to the "object of the geometers" (*Discours de la méthode* (*D.M.*), AT VI, 36, 5), to what the *Regula IV* calls a *Mathesis valde diversa a vulgari* (Mathesis deeply different from the vulgar) (AT X, 376, 4), the *Mathesis universalis* which is given as *objectum* (378, 3) "illa omnia tantum, in quibus aliquis ordo vel mensura examinatur" (377, 23–378, 1). When the path of the *Meditationes* again finds the *verae et immutabiles naturae* (true and immutable natures) (AT VII, 64, 11) which the doubt had revoked ("simplicia et universalia vera," 20, 11), it in fact covers over all the gains of simple natures, thus of the *Regulae*.

38 *PWD*, Vol. II, p. 29: "iste *essendi* modus, quo res est objective in intellectu per ideam (. . .) quantumvis imperfectus sit . . . non tamen profecto plane nihil est, nec proinde a nihilo esse potest" (AT VII, 41, 26–29).

39 *Esse objectivum ideae* (AT VII, 47, 20–21), see the Latin translation of the *D.M.*, AT VI, 551 (in the margin). One should not confound this with the much more current locution, *realitas objectiva*, which, precisely, omits the intervention of *esse*. Access to existence passes by the *Cogitatio*, thus by the *ens cogitatum*: "prius quam inquiram an aliquae tales res extra me existant, considerare debeo illarum ideas, quatenus sunt in mea cogitatione" (AT VII, 63, 12–14), or: "jam ad minimum scio illas [*sc.* res materiales], quatenus sunt purae Matheseos objectum posse existere, quandoquidem ipsas clare et distincte percipio" (AT VII, 71, 14–16), or finally: "Quippe per ens extensum communiter omnes intelligunt aliquid imaginabile (sive sit ens rationis, sive reale, hoc enim in medium relinquo)" (*A.H. More*, 5 February 1647, AT V, 270, 1–3).

40 *L'Entretien avec Burman* (AT V, 160, 17–19), §26, pp. 72–73. On this text see G. Brown, "*Vera entia*: The Nature of Mathematical Objects in Descartes," *Journal of the History of Philosophy*, Vol. 18, no. 4, 1980.

41 TN. *PWD*, Vol. I, p. 47: "intellectum a nullo unquam experimento decipi posse, si praecise tantum intueatur rem sibi objectam" (AT X, 243, 1–3).

42 TN. *PWD*, Vol. II, p. 26: "semper quidem aliquam rem ut subjectum meae cogitationis apprehendo" (AT VII, 37, 8–9).

43 It would remain for us to attempt, on the other hand, to read the *Meditationes* from the *Regulae* as starting point, as is authorized moreover by the principle of generic interpretation defended by F. Alquié. It is not a question of reducing 1641 to 1627, but rather setting out the consistent models of the presentation – a consistency which certainly does not exclude the gap between the questions and the heterogeneity of the two discourses.

44 On this formula, introduced by Heidegger and his relation to Cartesian texts, see my analysis in *Sur la théologie blanche de Descartes* (Paris: Presses universitaires de France, 1981), pp. 388–392, esp. fn. 32.

45 Respectively, *A Clerselier*, June/July 1646, AT IV, 444, 23–25 and *Principia Philosophiae I*, §7. *PWD*, Vol. I, p. 195: "*haec* cognitio, *ego cogito, ergo sum* (. . .) omnium prima et certissima,"

46 TN. *PWD*, Vol. I, p. 30: "Nihil prius cognosci posse quam intellectum, cum ab hoc caeterorum omnium cognitio dependeat, et non contra" (AT X, 395, 22–24).

47 *Summum ens*: AT VII, 54, 17–19, 22; 67, 21, 27; 135, 4; 144, 3; 374, 13; 428, 12, etc.

48 TN. *PWD*, Vol. II, p. 20: "nescio quid mei, quod sub imaginationem non venit" (AT VII, 29, 23–24).

49 In the *Regulae*: "Si vero eadem via ostendere velim, animam rationalem non esse corpoream, non opus erit enumerationem esse completam, sed sufficiet, si omnia simul corpora aliquot collectionbus ita complectar, ut animam rationalem ad

nullam ex his referri posse demonstrem" (AT X, 390, 13–18), or: "Neque immensum est opus, res omnes in hac universitate contentas cogitatione velle complecti, ut, quomodo singulae mentis nostrae examini subjectae sint, agnoscamus; nihil enim tam multiplex esse potest aut dispersum, quod per illam, de qua egimus, enumerationem certis limitibus circumscribi atque in aliquot capita disponi non possit" (398, 14–20). In the *Principia*, not only *I*, §11, but also *II*, §§4, 9 and 11.

50 TN. *PWD*, Vol. II, p. 244: "quatenus ambulendi conscientia cogitatio est" (AY VII, 352, 12–13).

51 See Marion, *Sur la théologie blanche*, §16, esp. pp. 378–386. *PWD*, Vol. II, p. 17: "hoc pronuntiatum . . . quoties a me profertur vel mente concipitur, necessario esse verum" (25, 11–13).

52 Respectively AT I, 146, 4–5 and 150, 22, completed by "immensa et incomprehensibilis potentia" (AT VII, 110, 27); then AT VII, 237, 8–9, 110, 27 and 112, 10, 109, 4 and 236, 9.

53

Neque enim hoc eo sensu verum est, quo per *ens rationis* intelligitur id quod non est, sed eo tantum quo omnis operatio intellectus *ens rationis*, hoc est ens a ratione profectum; atque etiam totus hic mundus ens rations divinae, hoc est ens per simplicem actum mentis divinae creatum, dici potest.

(AT VII, 134, 21–26)

54 TN. *PWD*, Vol. II, p. 78: "Dictat autem profecto lumen naturae nullam rem existere, de qua non liceat petere cur existat, sive in ejus causam efficientem inquirere, aut si non habet, cur illa non indigeat, postulare" (AT VII, 108, 18–22).

55 TN. "Nulla res existit de qua non possit quaeri quaenam sit causa cur existat. Hoc enim de ipso Deo quaeri potest, non quod indigeat ulla causa ut existat, sed quia ipsa ejus naturae immensitas est causa sive ratio, propter quam nulla causa indiget ad existendum" (AT VII, 164, 28–165, 3).

56 TN.

Atqui considerationem causae efficientis esse primum et praecipuum medium, ne dicam unicum, quod habeamus ad existentiam Dei probandam, puto omnibus esse manifestum. Illud autem accurate persequi non possimus, nisi licentiam demus animo nostro in rerum omnium, etiam ipsius Dei, causas efficientes inquirendi: quo enim jure Deum inde exciperemus, priusquam illum existere sit probatum?

(AT VII, 238, 11–18)

We note that the expression "puto omnibus esse manifestum" is not translated in the English.

57 TN. "I have attributed to God the dignity of being a cause [in such a way as not to imply that he has any of the indignity of being an effect.]" *PWD*, Vol. II, pp. 168–169.

58 TN. *PWD*, Vol. I, p. 22: "apud Philosophos quidem causa et effectus sunt correlativa; hic vero si quaeramus qualis sit effectus, oportet prius causam cognoscere, et non contra" (AT X, 383, 5–7).

59 Marion, *Sur l'ontologie grise*, §14. This privilege of the *causa* alone gives its weight to the curious expression of "effectus indignitas" (AT VII, 242, 6), as well as to the formula of Spinoza: "Cognitio effectus nihil aliud est, quam perfectiorem causae cognitionem acquirere [knowledge of an effect is nothing other than the

acquisition of more perfect knowledge of its cause]" (*De Intellectus Emendatione*, §92 (in C. Gebhardt, *Spinoza Opera II, De Intellectus Emendatione Tractatus* (Heidelberg: Carl Winters, 1924), p. 28. English translation by R.H.M. Elwes, *The Chief Works of Benedict de Spinoza*, Vol. 2 (London: G. Bell, 1884), p. 34); see *Tractatus theologico-politic:* (in Gebhardt (ed.), *Spinoza Opera III*, Caput IV), pp. 57–69).

60 Cottingham *et al.* translate with "deliberately," *PWD*, Vol. I, p. 22.

61 *PWD*, Vol. II, p. 28: "undenam posset assumere realitatem suam effectus, nisi a causa?" (AT VII, 40, 24–25).

62 *PWD*, Vol. I, p. 22: "eo sensu quo ad nostrum propositum utiles esse possunt" (AT X, 381, 18–19),

63 *PWD*, Vol. I, p. 31: "quomodo singulae mentis nostrae examini subjectae sint" (398, 16–17).

64 Cottingham *et al.* translate the statement: "Nor is it an immeasurable task to seek to encompass in thought everything in the universe," *PWD*, Vol. I, p. 31.

65 TN. *PWD*, Vol. II, p. 28: "jam vero lumine naturali manifestum est tantumdem ad minimum esse debere in causa efficiente et totali, quantum in ejusdem causae effectu" (AT VII, 40, 21–23).

66 TN. *PWD*, Vol. II, p. 28: "hoc non modo perspicue verum est de iis effectibus, quorum realitas est actualis sive formalis, *sed etiam de ideis*, in quibus consideratur tantum realitas objectiva" (AT VII 41, 1–4).

67 TN. Cottingham *et al.* translate: "It should also be noted that I have attributed to God the dignity of being a cause in such a way as not to imply that he has any of the indignity of being an effect," *PWD*, Vol. II, pp. 168–169.

68 TN. *PWD*, Vol. II, p. 32: "nec comprehendere, nec forte etiam attingere cogitatione, ullo modo possum" (AT VII 46, 20–21; see 52, 5–6 which confirms, and does not correct this).

69 TN. "As for all the other elements . . ." *PWD*, Vol. II, p. 31.

70 *L'Entretien avec Burman* (AT V, 156, 8), §17, pp. 54–55 (which closes thereafter on God as *causa totalis*! *Ibid.*, §11, AT V, 153, 2, p. 41). God appears as *causa ultima* (AT VII, 50, 6), *Author* (48, 27; 62, 17, etc.) who produces me (50, 9), or makes me (61, 19). Doubtless the *ego* recognizes itself as *creatus* (AT VII, 45, 14; 51, 19; 54, 19; 55, 11, etc.), but not less than *effectus*, and in this precise sense, Descartes unfolds less the *ens* as *creatum*, than he reduces (and abolishes) the thought of the creation to that of efficiency, become the unique cause (TN. AT VII, 50, 5–6 "ad causam ultimam div . . . quae erit Deus").

71 TN. *PWD*, Vol. II, p. 31. "tum ego ipse, tum aliud omne . . . est creatum" (45, 13–14).

72 TN. *PWD*, Vol. II, p. 35. "in qua Dei continetur, a me percipi per eandem facultatem, per quam ego ipse a me percipior" (51, 21–23).

73 TN. *PWD*, Vol. II, p. 80: "Per se autem notum mihi videtur, *omne id quod est*, vel esse a causa, vel a se tanquam a causa" (112, 3–5).

74 I hazard this expression, despite its Latin quality and the absence of reference, in virtue of the parallel *causa (sui)/cogitatio (sui)*, and of the formula *idea mei ipsius* (AT VII, 51, 14).

75 The point of departure of Caterus is found precisely in the citation of the *Meditatio III*, 48, 3–10 (in AT VII, 94, 8–13). Arnauld also takes up AT VII, 48, 7–10, in express reference to the first citation by Caterus of the same text (AT VII, 207, 25–208, 11). The debate over the divine *causa sui* begins thus explicitly by a debate on the positive aseity of the *ego* (certainly refuted by Descartes, but for this same reason, first envisaged and formulated).

76 TN. *PWD*, Vol. II, p. 33: "Atqui, si a me essem, nec dubitarem, nec optaren, nec omnino quicquam mihi deesset; omnes enim perfectiones quarum idea aliqua in me est, mihi dedissem, atque ipsemet Deus essem" (48, 7–10).

77 TN. *PWD*, Vol. II, p. 33: "nihil aliud sim quam res cogitans" (49, 15).

78 In fact, it is in an indisputably late text that the existence of the *ego* is deduced from the doubt, as if the *cogito* was repeated under the light of another principle (God, starting from the cause): "Nos non posse dubitare, quin mens nostra existat, quia ex hoc ipso quod dubiteremus, sequitur, illam existere" (*Notae in programma quoddam* 1647, AT VIII–2, 354, 19–21). This might lead us to give an equally late date to the parallel text: "ita ut possimus simul ac dubitare sum adgressus, etiam cum certitudine me cognoscere experire" (*Recherche de la Vérité*, AT X, 525, 4–5). We know that these texts, placed together with *Regulae XII*, "Sum, ergo Deus est" (I am, therefore God is)(AT X, 421, 29) allowed the forging, with some foundation, of the shortened, "Dubito, ergo Deus est" (I doubt, therefore God is): which allows us to mark the decentring of the *cogito* when it passes under the jurisdiction of the second Cartesian claim [parole] on the *ens in quantum ens*.

79 See Marion, *Sur la théologie blanche*, §18. One will note however, that another register subsists, among the acceptations of *causa/cause* applied to God, "haec Caritas, hoc est, sancta amicitia, qua Deum prosequimur, et Dei causa etiam omnes homines, quatenus scimus ipsos a Deo amari" (AT VIII–2, 112, 22–24); "surtout à cause que c'est la cause de Dieu que j'ai entrepris de défendre" (because it is God's cause that I undertook to defend) (AT III, 238, 5–7).

80 On this turn about of the *similitudo Dei* into independent vis-à-vis God, see Marion, *Sur la théologie blanche*, §17, 411 sq.

81 "Aus der Incubation des Seins und ihrer Epochen stammt die Incubationszeit des Satzes vom Grund," *Der Satz von Grund* (Pfullingen: 1957), p. 114. [TN. In German in the text. Translated as "From out of the incubation of Being and its epochs stems the incubation time of the principle of reason."] From an historiographic point of view, the same conclusion comes from E. Vollrath, commenting on AT VII, 164, 25 sq., "Dies ist geradezu eine Vorform des Satz vom Grunde bei Leibniz" (Vollrath, "Die Gliederung der Metaphysica Specialis," p. 281). [TN. "This is plainly a prior form of the principle of reason in Leibniz."] But this pertinent judgement loses validity if one supposes, besides, that it be the *Mathesis Universalis* which receives a foundation here. The *Mathesis Universalis* already itself sketches a principle, in virtue of the *Cogitatio*, according to a completed onto-theology, which the passage to the *causa* does not complete, but rather takes over and overdetermines.

82 G.W.F. Hegel, *Gesammelte Werke*, Bd. 9, *Phänomenologie des Geistes* (Hamburg, 1980), pp. 313, 25–26, French trans. Jean Hyppolite (Paris: Aubier Montaigne, 1941), vol. 2, p. 125. [TN. English trans. A.V. Miller, *Phenomenology of Spirit* (Oxford: Oxford University Press, 1977), p. 351.]

83 Sources of Leibniz's remarks are, respectively: *Theodicy*, §44, in C. Gehrhardt (ed.), *Die philosophischen Schriften vom Gottfried Wilhelm Leibniz* (Hildesheim: Ohms Verlagsbuchhandlung, 1960–1), VI, 127; *Principes de la Nature et de la Grâce*, §7, *ibid.*, 602; and *24 Propositions*, in Gehrhardt (ed.), *Leibniz*, VII, 289 (= *Opuscules et fragments inédits*, ed. L. Couturat, p. 533).

84 TN. *PWD*, Vol. I, p. 56: "longe distinctius ab intellectu percipietur" (AT X 438, 11).

85 See A. Becco, "Première apparition du terme de substance dans la *Meditation III* de Descartes" ["First appearance of the term, substance, in the *Third Meditation* of Descartes"], in *Annales de l'Institut de Philosophie*, 41/4, 1978.

86 *PWD* II p. 28: "Jam vero lumine naturali manifestum est tantumdem ad minimum esse debere in *causa* efficiente et totali, quantum in ejusdem *causae* effectu" (40, 21–23). To our knowledge (in anticipation of a general index established by computer), before AT VII, 40, 21–23, the term *causa* does not appear anywhere

except in 33, 17 ("vel quavis alia ex causa"; "or some other cause whatever it be"), and in 33, 21 ("pluribus ex causis innotuit"; "and many causes besides"), where precisely the cause is never clearly identified, neither with a being, nor with a *Ratio*. As to 39, 18 ("exempli causa"; "for example"), besides its banality, it does not belong to the register of the cause, strictly understood, and still less to efficiency. The two occurrences from the *Synopsis* (14, 27: "a causa summe perfecta" (a supremely perfect cause); and 15/2: "habere Deum ipsum pro causa" (to have God himself as a cause)), belong precisely to the summary of the *Meditatio III*. One will note, finally, that the *Discours de la Méthode* [*D.M.*] never uses *cause(s)* in its fourth part which is, nevertheless, metaphysical (*à cause que*, in AT VI, 38, 27 and 39, 22, does not constitute a real contradiction.) See P.-A. Cahné, *Index du Discours de la Méthode de René Descartes* (Rome: 1976).

87 F. Alquié, *La découverte métaphysique de l'homme chez Descartes* (Paris: 1950, 2nd edn, 1960, p. 226). M. Gueroult, *Descartes selon l'ordre des raisons* (Paris: 1953), vol. 1, p. 229. W. Halbfass, *Descartes Frage nach der Existenz der Welt* (Munich: 1968), p. 72.

88 Marion, *Sur la théologie blanche*, §§6–7. I cite, among others, Duns Scotus, "Intellectus viatoris potest esse certus de Deo, quod sit ens, dubitando de ente finito vel infinito, creato vel increato" (*Ordinato I*, d. 3, p. 1, q. 1–2, n. 17; Charles Balic (ed.), *Ioannis Duns Scoti Opera Omnia* (Civitas Vatican: Typis Polyglottis Vaticanis, 1950), vol. 3, p. 18), or again "Deus non est cognoscibilis a nobis naturaliter nisi ens sit univocum creato et increato" (*Ordinato I*, d. 3, p. 1, q. 3, n. 139, in *ibid.*, p. 87). [(a) The understanding of man still in development can be certain that God is a being, while doubting whether this being is finite or infinite, created or uncreated."]

The same for Suarez: "per conceptum formalem entis, neque Deus, neque substantia creat, neque accidens repraesentantur, secundum modum quo in re sunt, neque prout inter se differunt, sed solum prout aliquo modo inter se conveniunt, ac similia sunt" (*Disp. Met. II*, s. 2, n. 17, in Francisco Suarez, *R.p. Francisci Suarez Opera Omnia* (Paris: Apud Ludovicum Vives, 1856), vol. 25, p. 76); or "nam *ens* in vi nominis sumptum commune est Deo et creaturis, et de Deo affirmari vere potest" (*Disp. Met. II*, s. 4, 11, *ibid.*, p. 91). [(a) By the formal concept of being, neither God, nor the created substance, nor the accident are represented according to their real mode of being, but [they are represented] only in so far as they agree in a certain manner among themselves and are thus similar. (b) "[F]or *ens/being* taken in the sense of a name is common to God and to the creatures and can be affirmed in truth of God." Finally, see the second text of Goclenius, cited in n. 5.

89 Respectively, D.M., AT VI, 32, 18–23 (where "que je cherchais" ["that I looked"] displaces the Aristotelian δητούννον from the ὄν ἥ ὄν to the *ego*), *A Clerselier*, June/July 1646, AT IV, 444, 23–25 and *Lettres-préface* to the French translation of the *Principia Philosophiae*, AT IX-2, 9, 29–10, 8. On the contrary, *fundamentum* is applied only indirectly and rarely to the *ego cogito* (AT VII, 144, 24, compared with 145, 24–27; AT VI, 558, 28, translating "premier principe" [first principle] from AT VI, 32, 23).

2

KANT AND THE KINGDOM

Howard Caygill

At a crucial point in the argument of *Religion within the Limits of Reason Alone* (1793) Kant describes the advent of the 'Kingdom of God' in terms of a 'gradual transition' from 'ecclesiastical faith' to the 'sovereignty of pure religious faith'.[1] The former is *doctrinal* and partial, 'having as its end the transformation of ecclesiastical faith for a given people at a given time into a definite and enduring system' while the latter is *authentic* and universal, based on the 'natural predispositions' of truth and goodness and 'valid for the whole world'.[2] On first reading such distinctions seem justifiably to situate Kant within the tradition of modern liberal theology, the same whose progressive rationalism provoked the violent critiques of first Kierkegaard and then Nietzsche. Yet such an affiliation squares uneasily with the destructive impulse of the critical philosophy which, by showing that human reason was incapable of knowing a being such as God, unleashed a crisis not only in philosophy, but also in the traditions of thought informed by its *logos* – psychology, cosmology and above all theology.

Kant's status as a progressive, liberal theologian might be secured by an appeal to his claim to have 'found it necessary to deny *knowledge*, in order to make room for *faith*'.[3] The destructive impulse of critique may either be limited to the field of knowledge without prejudice to faith, or, in a more subtle theological inflection, it may destroy the claims of ecclesiastical doctrine in favour of the authentic faith of reason. Yet on closer examination Kant eludes such readings through the internal complexity of his understanding of faith. For him, faith is not cast as the affective antithesis to knowledge but is a complex and internally differentiated phenomenon, one which, furthermore, does not necessarily exclude the claims of reason.

In *Religion Within the Limits of Reason Alone* Kant identifies two elements involved in 'saving faith':

> the one having reference to what man himself cannot accomplish, namely, undoing lawfully (before a divine judge) actions which he has performed, the other to what he himself can and ought to do, that is, leading a new life conformable to his duty. The first is faith

107

in an atonement (reparation for his debt, redemption, reconciliation with God); the second, the faith that we can become well-pleasing to God through a good course of life in the future.[4]

Each of the two elements of 'saving faith' possesses distinct temporal orientations: the former operates retrospectively in the undoing of past acts, the latter prospectively with regard to what must be done in the future. Furthermore, each of these elements follows a distinct economy of operation: the former involves an economy of loss and restitution, the latter one of giving pleasure, in this case, of causing God to be pleased. Finally, the two elements of faith, far from testifying to an intuitive, immediate feeling, both involve an exercise of judgement; the recollection and repetition of saving faith, to usurp Kierkegaard's terms, are both performed in accordance with the law.

Kant proceeds immediately to consider the ways in which the two elements of saving faith may be related to each other. Although he claims that 'both conditions constitute but one faith and necessarily belong together'[5] he does not regard them as yielding any form of dialectical synthesis. The way in which they 'necessarily belong together' is extremely problematic, and cannot easily be stated. The necessity of their belonging together, however, can be comprehended by 'assuming' that one is derived from the other, 'that the faith in the absolution from the debt resting upon us will bring forth good life-conduct, or else that the genuine and active disposition ever to pursue a good course of life will engender the faith in such absolution'.[6] But the circularity shows only that the elements *must* belong together, and not *how* they in fact do so. The question of the relation between the two elements of 'saving faith' arrives at 'a remarkable antinomy of human reason with itself', one which is possibly without solution and which can yield only a series of potential 'adjustments' between the terms. The two forms of faith are in relation, but the character of this relation betrays an antinomy: faith too, in other words, does not escape the antinomies which afflict reason.

The implications of the antinomy of faith may be explored by means of further reflection upon the terms of the 'opposition' between a faith which atones before and one which pleases God. It has already been noted that the 'opposition' is couched in terms of the retro- and prospective times of recollection and repetition as well as in terms of the economies of loss and restitution and the giving of pleasure. This and the observation that both elements of faith involve exercises of judgement suggests an alignment between the properties and the antinomy of faith and Kant's earlier discovery of an irresolvable difficulty in the notion of judgement in the *Critique of Judgement* (1790). There Kant not only distinguished between different temporal orientations of judgement, one which was retrospective and associated with the mourning of loss, the other prospective and associated with hope, but also related to differing economies of operation, the one with loss and restitution, the other with excess and vivification. In the guise of judgements of the sublime and of the beautiful, Kant explored the 'difficulty of judgement' in terms which parallel, extend and supplement his later discussion of the antinomy of faith in *Religion Within the Limits of Reason Alone*.

In the *Critique of Judgement* Kant is more interested in stating the difficulty of the principle of judgement than in offering a solution to it. The terms of this difficulty had already been stated in the *Critique of Pure Reason* (1781/1787) as 'subsumption under a rule' and the discrimination of whether or not something stands under that rule. There can be no rule to guide discriminations as to whether something comes under a particular rule. This formal problem is extended to the relation between the subsumed particularities of intuition and the subsuming rules of the understanding. In the *Critique of Judgement* the problem of subsumption and discrimination is generalised into one of the place of pleasure and imagination in judgement, and leads to a distinction between two modes of judgement. The first views judgement as resting on the sublime sacrifice of meaning which is restored in and by God, while the second sees judgement as the giving and enhancement of life in the beautiful, as 'excessive' and not founded in loss. However, as with the two elements of 'saving faith' the relationship between these two modes of judgement is not easily stated, but bears witness to an irreducible 'difficulty' in judgement itself.

The rehearsal of Kant's intricate yet allusive distinction between the two forms of judgement, and their implications for faith, God and the Kingdom, may begin with his definition of the Kingdom of God at the end of the *Lectures on Ethics*. There he says, 'The realisation of the full destiny, the highest possible perfection of human nature – this is the Kingdom of God on earth. Justice and equity, the authority, not of governments, but of conscience within us, will then rule the world.'[7] By describing the Kingdom in these terms Kant aligns it with a perfected judgement, one which would bring together the law or rule of justice with the respect for differences of equity. This perfected judgement – one in which subsumption and discrimination mutually co-exist rather than repeatedly undermine each other – justifies not only the judge but also the judged. In the *Third Critique* (the *Critique of Judgement*) Kant consistently describes this perfected judgement as 'life' and sees in it a freely established accord or 'attunement' [*Stimmung*] between judge, judgement-power and the judged.[8]

Already in the pre-critical *Lectures on Ethics* Kant points out that the attainment of such perfected judgement is by no means inevitable. It is possible for the power of judgement to become violent and destructive, for the judges to destroy both themselves and the judged in the giving of judgement: 'There could then be no certainty that humanity might not use their power to destroy themselves, their fellows, and the whole of nature.'[9] For 'freedom makes it possible for humanity to turn nature inside out in order to satisfy itself'.[10] On the one hand there is the satisfaction of perfected judgement in the life of the Kingdom, where the power of judgement accords between judge and judged.

On the other, there is the murderous satisfaction of a disproportioned judgement-power in which the judge violently subjects itself and the judged, a form of judgement which founds and obeys a logic of sacrifice.

The play between and across the forms of judgement is a structural feature of the *Critique of Judgement*. The crisis of judgement analysed in its pages arises from a disproportioned judgement, one manifest in the disjuncture between the law of the judge and the differences of the judged. But what is difficult to grasp is that Kant clearly regards the 'Kingdom as now' – we are 'in possession' of a perfected judgement, divinity is immanent to judgement. There are signs or portents of this perfected judgement of the Kingdom in the accord or attunement between judge and judged in the experience of beauty. And this experience offers not only a new space for judgement, but also another way of thinking God. Not only does this not bring God into historical time, but it also refuses the distinction between retrospective and prospective temporalities.

The main textual consequence of the contemporaneity of the Kingdom is that the accord or attunement of judge and judged cannot be stated in the prevailing meta-language of judgement – i.e. philosophy. Kant employs many artful textual strategies to deal with this difficulty, his most favoured being the *via negationis*. Kant systematically pursues and negates the attempts by philosophical judgement – logic – to 'analyse' the accord of judgement power revealed by beauty. The accord is indifferent to philosophy's demands that it show its quality, its quantity, its relation and its modality. Kant playfully sends up the learned folly of philosophy – he is of course the writer who modelled his authorship on Rabelais, Erasmus and Montaigne, not to mention Butler's *Hudibras*.

To philosophy's demand that beauty state its quality, Kant answers that the beautiful delights apart from any interest in the *existence* of its object – the beautiful is indifferent to philosophy's obsession with existence. The beautiful pleases universally, not by means of philosophy's beloved 'concept' but through a communion of the lovers of beauty. It stands in some relation of finality to an object, but not the sort of finality directed to an end avidly pursued by philosophers. Finally, the judgement of the beautiful is modally necessary, but it obeys its own peculiar necessity, not the conceptual necessity of the philosophers. The judgement of the beautiful is excessive, and cannot be bound by philosophy's table of judgements.

Kant shows through these elliptical formulations that the accord of judge and judged achieved in the judgement of the beautiful cannot be captured by the prevailing, logical structures of philosophical judgement. Yet access to this accord through beauty offers an intimation of a perfected judgement, one which is vivifying, one which gives life through the feeling of pleasure. It cannot be judged by philosophical categories because these, Kant will later show, are themselves founded on the violent sacrifice of the sublime, which negates life in the name of transcendence.

Kant further claims that the accord between the law of the judge and the differences of the judged revealed in beauty is 'there' in all judgements. It cannot be said to be 'present', since this would deliver us to the philosophical opposition of presence and absence, so Kant habitually describes this accord as 'forgotten'.[11] For without such an accord or attunement between the law of the concept and the differences of intuition, there could be no judgement whatsoever: even the most violent subsumption requires some community between the judge and the judged.

Kant writes in § VI of the Introduction to the *Critique of Judgement*, 'We do not, and cannot, find in ourselves the slightest effect on the feeling of pleasure from the coincidence of perceptions with the laws in accordance with the universal concepts of nature (the Categories)'. In other words, as we might expect, categorial subsumptive judgement is distinct from the judgement of the beautiful. But Kant goes on in § VI to severely qualify this view: 'Still it is certain that the pleasure appeared in due course, and only by reason of the most ordinary experience being impossible without it, has it become gradually fused with simple cognition, and no longer arrests particular attention.' In other words, the feeling of pleasure evoked in a perfected judgement is there but forgotten in every experience we have, in every judgement we make.

We can do nothing without this forgotten accord between judge and judged, understanding and intuition, one described in the *Lectures on Ethics* as a divine gift, and yet we are so fallen that we only experience its fullness in beauty – only the beautiful 'is directly attended with a feeling of the furtherance of life' (*Critique of Judgement* § 23). Thus Kant claims that judgement presupposes grace, for without the accord bestowed before judgement there would be no judgement.

Kant suggests that it is only in the judgements of the beautiful that we fully 'realise' our power of judgement, only there do we achieve the mutual vivification of judge and judged. Most judgement however, he goes on to show, privileges the sublime. Judgements of the sublime are structured around a desire for death, for the annihilation of self, world and ultimately God. The experience of the sublime is a pleasurable imagination of sacrificial death, 'a pleasure that only arises indirectly, being brought about by the feeling of a momentary check to the vital forces' (*Critique of Judgement* § 23). The experience of the sublime demands the sacrifice of the accord between judge and judged, an act of violence wrought upon both the subject and object of judgement.

The investment in sacrifice directs the experience of the sublime toward a peculiar dialectic of mystery and subjection, one which is both productive of power and yet utterly disempowering. The sublime sacrifice is

a feeling of imagination by its own act depriving itself of its freedom. . . . In this way it gains an extension and a might greater than that which it sacrifices. But the ground of this is concealed from it, and in its place it *feels* the sacrifice or deprivation as well as its cause, to which it is subjected.

(Critique of Judgement § 29)

Earlier Kant claimed that the accord of judge and judged signalled by pleasure in the beautiful was always there but forgotten in every experience. Now in the *Critique of Judgement* he claims the same for the experience of the sublime: the sacrificial simultaneity of subjection and mastery is ubiquitous. The experience may appear 'far-fetched and subtle' (at least to a man of the Enlightenment, today it is all too familiar), but it is, he adds, 'the foundation of the commonest judgements, although one is not always conscious of its presence' (§ 29).

The *Third Critique* claims that there are two opposed experiences informing all our judgements: one is the pleasure of life in the accord of judge and judged, while the other is the sacrifice of this accord, the desire to annihilate judge and judged. Every judgement we make, whether of the world, of the soul, or of God is implicated simultaneously in both experiences. The question then arises of how it is possible for both experiences to be present in every judgement, what is their mutual implication, how is it that they may both co-exist in this forgetful way? The difficulty here is directly analogous to that presented by the two elements of 'saving faith' discussed above.

One answer is to found the accord of the beautiful upon the sacrificial violence of the sublime. This brings the sublime and the beautiful into relation, but at the cost of inaugurating a 'tragic' dialectic between them. The relation of beauty and the sublime is aligned with the myth of foundational sacrifice; but this itself is sublime. In this view, the paradigmatic Kingdom is the *Polis* and the relation between sublime and beautiful cast in terms of the tragic dialectic of sacrifice – acknowledgement of error through loss, crisis and restoration.

There is considerable textual warrant for claiming that Kant brought the beautiful and the sublime into relation through sacrifice and atonement.[12] Yet there are also intimations of a different 'relation' between beauty and the sublime, intimations which have been made visible by Irigaray's work on the haunted and matricidal character of tragic sublimity and its persistence in the philosophical *logos*.[13] The implications of this reading are considerable. For if the experience of sublimity is inseparable from the foundation myths of the Greek *Polis*, and if these are today cryptically encoded in the philosophical *logos*, then theology's thought of God and Kingdom is locked into a historically specific economy. If this economy is suspended, then God and the Kingdom may be thought differently, apart from the spectral structures of the *logos* and judgement proper to the *Polis*.

Before proceeding to outline this other economy of judgement in Kant it is necessary to warn against seeking to make the harmony and peace of beauty into a new master. This would but replace the dominance of the sublime in the relation of beauty and sublime with that of beauty; the structure of dominance would persist. In the *Third Critique* Kant remains with the thought that the two forms of experience are 'there' in every judgement, but that they are irreconcilable, or rather their relation cannot be one of reconciliation.

The differences between the two experiences of judgement are most exposed in the judgement of God. Kant aligns the sublime thought of God to the origins of onto-theology: the crisis of judgement provoked by a fall from meaning is met by the imagination of God as a source of meaning beyond judgement, one able to reconcile judge and judged in a 'last judgement'. Conversely, the beautiful thought of God intimates a judgement which accords judge and judged in a mutual vivification, a self-augmenting charitable judgement which might be described as *agapic*. Here judgement is overcome immanently, without recourse to an external avenger God. The two experiences of judgement map directly onto the two elements of saving faith discussed above.

Kant explores the genealogy of the sublime thought of God in §88 of the *Third Critique*, where he narrates the story of the origins of metaphysics. He imagines a time when humanity 'enjoyed [nature] without imagining the presence of anything but nature's accustomed course'. Here there was no question of freedom, of imagination or of judgement – just a blissful pre-lapsarian enjoyment of the course of nature. But the imagination of an injustice, of a fall from meaning and a diversion of nature's course led to a fall:

> one undeniable judgement must have come into presence among them. It could never be that it was all the same whether a person has acted fairly or falsely, with equity or with violence, albeit to their life's end, as far at least as human eye can see, his virtues have brought him no reward, his transgressions no punishment.
>
> (*Critique of Judgement* §88)

Here arise, in one passage, the themes of justice and injustice, violence and equity, imagination and a consciousness of death, and all in the context of the advent of a judgement whose appearance marked a moment of crisis.

Judgement arrived as a voice which said 'it must go otherwise' as an 'obscure perception of something to which they were bound to strive, and with which such a result would not make any sense' (§88). Onto the voice and the 'obscure perception' is then grafted a distinction of just and unjust, and when this distinction fails at its moment of inauguration it is extended beyond this life and becomes a law. Death sets a limit to human justice at the very moment at which it is conceived. But this cannot be without making a mockery of justice, and so the law must extend beyond death – there must be a last judgement to restore meaning to the finite judgements of humanity.

And so there must also be an avenger, a being who is beyond finitude and capable of judging according to an absolute law.

In this account both metaphysics and theology are cast as attempts to 'restore' harmony between law and the way of the world, to reinvest the world with meaning. Their narratives seek 'the way in which such an irregularity (of which nothing is more repugnant to the human powers ...) could be put straight.' (§ 88) Both resort to a thought of God as the 'one principle upon which they could ever conceive it possible for nature to harmonise with the moral law dwelling within them' (§ 88). Yet this thought of God is purchased with the sacrifice of an existing harmony. The narrative moves from a sense of violation to a failed attempt to judge, and then postulates an eternal law and an eternal judge who makes the last, ineluctable judgement.

Kant's narrative of the origins of onto-theology does not exhaust the ways in which he thinks of God in the *Third Critique*. There is another thought of God in the margins of the text, one associated with a different genealogy of judgement. In this account, judgement is not founded in loss, violation or sacrifice, but in giving and sharing. Kant describes this experience with the word *Mitteilen* which combines a sense of sharing, communing and communicating. The life-enhancing pleasure of such a judgement arises from 'the estimate formed by one who has the bent and turn for communicating pleasure to others, and who is not quite satisfied with an object unless their feeling of delight in it can be shared in communion with others' (*Critique of Judgement* § 41). The move from having delight to sharing delight is expansive, and extends even to the thought of God.

The God of the last judgement, the remote avenger who stands surety for the accord of judge, judgement and judged; the one who gives eternal meaning to everything finite in the last judgement, this thought of God gives way to another. If judgement is communion of delight, and this communion becomes itself the supreme object of delight, then the fixed oppositions of the sublime judgement collapse upon themselves. Here there is no judge nor judged, not an act of judgement but a work of communion and sharing. With the collapse of sublime judgement also goes the necessity of an avenger God and his last judgement. The thought of God with the judgement of the beautiful, the God thought in communion, is other while not exterior. God is the shared thought of God itself, not an external avenger called to wreak judgement for the failure of judgement.

The thought of God under the auspices of the judgement of the beautiful is vivifying – it is not the imposition of an absolute meaning to finite beings, but their discovery of such meaning in communion with others. The God of the sublime judgement is called to restore meaning to the world through a last judgement; while the God of the beautiful is found in the giving of judgement in communion with others. This God is not the imagined compensation for finitude and death, but a source of life in the mutual play of judging and being judged. The God of sublime judgement is also the God of faith in atonement, the one who 'undoes' past deeds and restores justice. The God of beautiful judgement is the God who is pleased by the disposition to pursue a good course of life and the mutual vivification which this brings with it.

It would be good to end with this other thought of God, the immanent divinity far from the God of liberal progressive theology and the stern 'wholly other' God of its modern critics. This divinity born of the beautiful might be cast as the God of peaceful communion and respect for differences. It might be offered as a 'postmodern' thought of God, one beyond the modern sublime's obsession with fusing transcendence with the last judgement. But such conclusions would simplify Kant's thought of God, since for him judgement includes *both* the sublime and the beautiful, and especially in the case of our judgements of God. The sublime onto-theological God of judgement has to be thought with the beautiful God of grace and charity. For Kant the thought of God is never simple, it must always include its other without subordination or exclusion. Such a thought remains in suspension, refusing to incline toward either a sublime last judgement or a beautiful grace. Faith and judgement are thus suspended between the two thoughts of God, one based on law and atonement, the other on difference and vivification, and it is in their negotiation that Kant discerns the memory, presence and promise of the Kingdom of God.

Notes

1 Immanuel Kant, *Religion Within The Limits of Reason Alone*, tr. Theodore M. Greene and Hoyt H. Hudson, Harper and Row, New York, 1960, pp. 105–14.
2 *Ibid.*, p. 105.
3 Immanuel Kant, *Critique of Pure Reason*, tr. Norman Kemp Smith, Macmillan, London, 1978, p. Bxxx.
4 Immanuel Kant, *Religion Within The Limits of Reason Alone*, p. 106.
5 *Ibid.*, p. 106.
6 *Ibid.*, p. 107.
7 Immanuel Kant, *Lectures on Ethics*, tr. Louis Infield, Methuen, London, 1979, p. 253.
8 See my *Art of Judgement*, Basil Blackwell, Oxford, 1989, Chapter 5, for a detailed discussion of these points.
9 Kant, *Lectures on Ethics*, p. 122.
10 *Ibid.*, p. 123.
11 For a fine reading of Kantian forgetting and recollection, see Jay Bernstein, *The Fate of Art*, Polity Press, Oxford, 1992.
12 Compare with the conclusion of my earlier reading of Kant in *Art of Judgement* where I align the beautiful and the sublime within a tragic dialectic of loss and restitution, and call for the 'furies to be given their due'.
13 See Luce Irigaray, *Speculum of the Other Woman*, tr. Gillian C. Gill, Cornell University Press, Ithaca, New York, 1985, esp. pp. 203–13.

3

LOGIC AND SPIRIT IN HEGEL

Rowan Williams

What is difficult in reading Hegel is understanding what (for him) it is to *think*. He will not countenance a splitting of the world into active mind and passive matter, insides and outsides:[1] thought as a process, thought as something that 'falls upon' a reality otherwise undiscovered. Thinking is what we do; we can't think ourselves not thinking. And if we can't think ourselves not thinking, we can't think ourselves speechless and alone, engaged in or with or by nothing. In Hegelian terms, to think what is nothing but 'identity' is to think nothing – though if we grasp *that* we shall see that thinking nothing is importantly different from not thinking. This is where Hegel's logic takes off:[2] if, in trying to think what it-is-to-be, we recognise that we are thinking sheer emptiness, we encounter the most primitive of all contradictions, because we cannot think *away* what-it-is-to-be without thinking pure non-sense, yet we cannot think it as such. Shifting out of the purely Hegelian vocabulary, we should have to say that we can't *begin* to think, decide to take up a 'thinking' stance towards something called The World, analysing it into primitive components like essence and predicates. If 'thinking is what we do', thinking is contemporary with our being around in the first place. Yet we cannot think that bare fact of 'being around' without thinking a context for it – which means we cannot think what it is to think *in the abstract*; we think our being and our thinking in their concrete, time-taking actuality. We think in relation to particulars; but we cannot, quite strictly cannot, think particulars simply as particulars, because we can't concretely think a pure self-identity. To think a particular is to think 'this, not that; here, not there; now, not then': to map it on to a conceptual surface by way of exclu-sions or negations, yet in that act to affirm also its relatedness, its involvement; from empty identity, thinkable only as a kind of absence and indeterminacy, to the specific position, this not that, and by way of that 'contradictory' state to arrive at thinking the 'individual' as convergence of the universal and the particular.[3] Thus to think is, ultimately, to step beyond all local determina-tions of reality, to enter into an infinite relatedness – not to *reflect* or *register* or *acknowledge* an infinite relatedness, but to act as we cannot but act, if our reality truly is what we think it is, if thinking is what we (just) do.

Two of the themes that surface here (and without which we cannot begin to understand Hegel) are, first, that there is no concrete identity that is not 'mediated', i.e. realised and maintained by something other than itself alone, and, second, that really to think what is other is to discover its otherness as implicated in the act of thinking and the thinking implicated in the otherness: more briefly, that to think otherness is to be 'reconciled', to stop seeing what is other as a rival, a competitor with the thinker's reality and so a menace. These two theses are, of course, at heart the same point approached from different perspectives. And their implication, which consistently disturbs Hegel's readers, is that no otherness is unthinkable, that an unthinkable otherness would leave us incapable of thinking ourselves, and so of thinking about thinking – and so of thinking itself. If there is what is not and could not be thought, there would be some sort of life or reality with which consciousness could not be in relation. But what could it *mean* to say this? We should have no word or idea for such a 'reality' (we could not even call a reality what we could not in any way engage with). The idea of an absolute otherness is fundamentally confused.[4] Before we too rapidly conclude that Hegel offers a total and implicitly totalitarian scheme for which nothing is *in principle* inaccessible or indigestible, we need to reflect on what else we could possibly say that isn't nonsense. For Hegel, an otherness that couldn't be thought would not even be a negation, because it would not negate anything that *could* be thought (if it did, it would not be absolutely other; part of its definition would be given, as 'not *x*'). To say that there was thinking *and...* whatever, that there was no identity between nature, action, history, law, society or religion and thinking, would be to conclude that thinking is not what we do, and that therefore we cannot think what we are. And, once again, what could that actually mean?[5] We should, of course, note in passing that, within Hegel's framework, thinking and knowing are not opposed to sensation or emotion or love[6] in the crude way that a late twentieth-century reader might suppose; we are talking about the awareness of relation, and the awareness of relatedness as constituting identity. As we shall see, quite a bit can be said about love in this connection.

The comprehensive power of thinking is not a power exercised *on* something *by* something else. In the *Logic*, Hegel, having begun by discussing the nature of 'understanding' (*Verstand*),[7] proceeds to give an account of 'dialectic' in terms of power, which makes it clear that the power in question is essentially the irresistibility of the motion of thought.[8] Because there is no moment of pure, unmediated identity in the actual world, there are no discrete and simple objects for thought to rest in. No perceived reality is stable and self-contained for thinking: Hegel offers some rather weak analogies from physics and (anecdotal) psychology, but his argument is stronger than these might suggest. As the fuller statements of his long treatment of identity and difference in both versions of the *Logic*[9] make clear, the point is that thought is bound to dissolve the finite perception, the isolated object, as such, moving from the level of diversity (a contingent multiplicity of things) to that of complementary opposition: each 'thing' is defined by not being another, lives in and only in the absence of another, and so 'passes over' from being a discrete object to being a moment in a complex movement. Everything is what it is because of what it is not; it is what it is by *excluding* what it is not; being what it is entails exclusion of what is in fact intrinsic to it. Contradiction and collapse: the whole scheme has to be shifted to another level, since the self-identity/exclusion-of-the-other model can't be sustained. Thinking passes through this process as action that realises itself in 'emptying' itself: and its continuity is secured in and by its challenging or denying of itself. And this is why dialectic can be conceived as power, as that which outlives and 'defeats' stable, commonsense perception, not by abolishing it from outside, but by the penetration of its own logic and process.

What is interesting for our purpose is how this analysis of dialectic and power is given by Hegel a clear theological point of reference. Dialectic is what theology means by the power of *God*, just as *Verstand* is what theology means by the goodness of God.[10] *Verstand* says 'Everything can be thought', 'nothing is beyond reconciliation', every percept makes sense in a distinctness, a uniqueness, that is in harmony with an overall environment. It is, as you might say, a doctrine of providence, in that it claims that there can be no such thing as unthinkable contingency. But, as we have seen, thinking the particular in its harmonies, thinking how the particular makes sense, breaks the frame of reference in which we think the particular. God's goodness has to give way to God's power – but to a power which acts only in a kind of self-devastation. And, says Hegel, the 'speculative' stage to which dialectic finally leads us is what religion has meant by the mystical, which is not, he insists, the fusion of subject and object but the concrete (historical?) unity or continuity or followability of what *Verstand* alone can only think fragmentarily or episodically.[11]

The theology underlying the *Logic* has not perhaps been given its full weight. Hegel here anticipates some of what is said in the *Lectures on the Philosophy of Religion* about divine predicates:[12] considered as describing different 'qualities' of the divine life, they fall short of actually bringing God into speech because they deal with what look like multiple determinations; and since God is not (as all classical theology agrees) a determinate object, a member of a class, these predicates collapse upon themselves. And if they are interpreted as relating to God's action upon the world, they fall short once again of speaking of God *as God*. The divine predicates cannot express the concrete life of God when they are taken as denoting discrete properties subsisting alongside each other. In the light of this later discussion, what is said in the *Logic* acquires added depth and interest. The *Logic* addresses the fundamental question of what the process of thinking concretely is; and it is Hegel's contention all along – as we have seen – that to think about thinking is to think about, or rather to think *within*, an infinite relatedness, a comprehensive intelligibility. To say, as Hegel effectively does in the *Logic*, that this is to think God and to participate in God, is to acknowledge that a comprehensive and unitary metaphysic is unlikely to be able to dispense (certainly in the Western intellectual tradition) with the term that has historically grounded a trust in the thinkable (and thus reconcilable) character of reality. But when this slightly banal observation has been made, do we simply conclude that the explicit theological reference is window-dressing, concealing an underlying secularism?[13] No; because it is precisely the grammar (including the paradoxes) of classical pre-Cartesian theology that shapes the actual structure of thinking about thinking. To think about thinking must, for Hegel, bring us finally to the point to which theology directs us, to a reality that is determined solely as self-relatedness: the grammar of the God of Augustine, Anselm and Aquinas is the grammar of thought, and without the former the scope of the latter could not be apprehended. The *un*thinkability of God in the tradition, the recognition that discrete predicates are a clumsy vehicle for indicating divine simplicity, is skilfully transmuted by Hegel into the conviction that to think is to think ultimate simplicity, indivisibility and self-relation.

But the way this transmutation is achieved is first, by rethinking the divine predicates dialectically – as in the *Logic* – and second, by rethinking the divine simplicity and self-relatedness in terms of another crucial aspect of the classical Christian tradition, the doctrine of the Trinity, understood (importantly and surprisingly, given some textbook accounts of Hegel) as the elaboration of belief in God as love. To think what is real, in the *Logic*, which is, of course, to think a reconciled totality, is to affirm the thinkable character of contingent particulars, and, precisely in so doing, to think what is not any particular but that which 'holds' the flow of one particular into another. And if the intelligibility of the particular cannot be thought without the transition to 'dialectic' and speculative reconciliation, what we have is a transcription of the doctrine of divine simplicity into the terms of a process – a temporal movement, in one sense, but not anything that could usefully be described as a sequence of happenings; it is, rather, a structure that could only be talked about in the language of temporal sequence, yet *could not be* 'a' series in the world's history, and which certainly could not be talked of as 'happening' in the sense of 'happening to occur'. The time in question is the time of thinking, which is not a series of contingent occurrences. Thus we are pushed at last to say that this structure exists only as self-sufficient, self-related, independent or absolute; that its grammar is that of the word 'God'; but also that this traditional grammar is flawed to the extent that it thinks divine simplicity as the pure negation of complexity and thus thinks the divine predicates in static, discrete or world-dependent ways. What the *Logic* hints at is that, if the divine predicates are thought as they should be, they 'yield' the divine simplicity as a dialectical unity. To think God's goodness only in terms of the orderliness and intelligibility of an endless series of objects is to bind God to a shapeless or contingent multiplicity; yet theology cannot

rest in a picture of divine life moulded by an alien, unreconcilable otherness –
prime matter, raw indeterminacy. So to think the goodness of God must pass
into thinking the independence of God from particular determination, the
power of God as Hegel understands it; and that power must in turn be rescued
from a mythological, dualist construction (God imposing the divine will on
what is alien) and brought to speculative unity. In other words, God's 'God-
ness', God's difference from the world, is too radical to be expressed by any
formulation that rests content with some version of 'God *and* the world',
whether it is the world that determines God or God who defeats or overcomes
the world. To think the divine self-sufficiency, *aseitas*, is to think away any
boundary between God and the world as between two entities; and this,
Hegel might argue, is no more than an exegesis of the strict sense of classical
theology, God as the *non aliud*.[14]

This, however, cannot be the resting point for Hegel's philosophical transcription of the divine aseity. The inchoate remarks in the *Logic* about theological equivalences are unfinished business insofar as they still speak of God
in relation to the world by way of goodness and of power: the 'mystical' resolution remains sketchy. While it is clear that, in terms of the logic expounded,[15]
God's relation to the world is nothing other than God's relation to God, the
perfect self-relatedness of what Hegel calls 'the Idea', we have not yet fully
seen how the attempt to talk of God as God, rather than God in relation to
the world, prescribes this conclusion. We can begin, as in the *Logic*, with one
kind of talk about God, the interweaving of the grammar of *aseitas* with the
classical predicates, but we shall have done no more than establish that,
given the traditional language of God (autonomous and self-sufficient) and
the world (contingent but intelligible) we cannot think through what we are
saying without collapsing the distinction between the two terms in its conventional and unreflective form. However, there is a more basic question to be
addressed: is thinking *God-as-such* necessarily to think the form of the dialectic?
If not, if the analogies of the *Logic* are all that can be said, there remains an
unclarity in the conception of God, a something not reconciled: we are not
shown how God and the world must be thought together from the beginning.
We have to start again, and show that the end to which the *Logic* has brought
us is also the primitive condition for thinking. In short, we cannot be content
with starting from 'God and the world': the reconciliation arrived at means
that we must think 'back' to the grammar of God, so that God is no longer
given as a discrete entity or identity.

God cannot be unmediated self-identity because thinking cannot recognise
unmediated identity: and if God cannot be thought, nothing in our thinking
holds or anchors trust in unconditional or comprehensive reconciliation. But
a God whose identity is mediated *simply* through the world won't do. We
have first to think what it is in talking about God and the world that makes
God's self-relation and God's relation to the world inseparable: otherwise we
remain at the level of master–slave relationship, in which one discrete subject

uses another to secure its peace with itself.[16] Nor is God thought if God appears as merely identical with the world's process: this would leave the world with an unmediated identity, and God as non-subjective or pre-subjective reality, and therefore not in the strictest sense thinkable[17] – i.e. God becomes inferior to the thinking mind, something that has to be connected with and reconciled with mind so as to be thought; and the idea of a *universal* 'substance' that is pre-subjective is a nonsense in Hegel's terms, since what is pre-subjective cannot be universal. Hegel's repudiation of charges of pantheism is profoundly serious.

And so to the doctrine of the Trinity. It is quite specifically the Christian doctrine of God's triune being that here resolves our aporia in thinking God. The most summary statement of why this is so is to be found in the *Philosophy of Nature*,[18] where God is defined as 'the living process of positing His Other, the world, which, comprehended in its divine form is His Son'. But for its elaboration we have, of course, to turn to the *Lectures on the Philosophy of Religion*. The section on the 'consummate religion'[19] – that is, the religion that is properly related to itself, the religion that is transparent to itself, thinks itself – spells out the inseparability of thinking God and thinking the reconciled consciousness; it also, very importantly, explains why such a religion can only be an historically determined ('positive' or 'revealed') faith. Consciousness is necessarily the recognition of self in the other, and so no individual or timeless subjectivity could be actual, could think itself, the world, or God. To think myself is to discover my identity in the alien givenness of the past, and to think history is to find it in my consciousness (thereby discovering that there is no such reality as a consciousness that is 'privately' mine). Thus the supreme awareness of thinking, thinking reconciliation, God, must be an *historical* discovery or recognition. Yet the recognition issues in something more than mere historical narrative – or rather it must dispossess itself of the positive so as to recover it as the content of thinking. And in terms of the actual process of exposition in the *Philosophy of Religion*, this means dealing with the doctrine of the Trinity before proceeding to reflection on the positivity of Jesus Christ, and indeed on the whole realm of createdness: which leads to the full and mature thinking of God, as spirit in community.[20]

We have been led to begin to think what thinking is, and so we are able to say that the condition for thinkable reality is the fundamental 'process, movement, life' of self-differentiation and self-recovery.[21] To speak of this condition 'in itself', to speak of spirit beyond time, God before creation, is in one sense an impossibility, since it is apparently to try to think being without otherness; but in fact the structure of Trinitarian doctrine enables us to avoid talking plain nonsense here, because it speaks of an eternal, irreducible being-in-the-other. To try and think the condition for thinkable reality would be a contradiction if God were envisaged as an unmediated identity; but the Christian vision is of a God who is quintessentially and necessarily mediated in a divine selfhood that is simultaneously its own absolute other. And, Hegel concludes,[22] the complete transparency of self in the other that is God's act of being (as 'Father' and 'Son') is what constitutes God as 'Spirit', as living consciousness proceeding into the determinate otherness of the world. 'That this is so is the Holy Spirit itself, or, expressed in the mode of sensibility, it is eternal love.'[23]

The introduction of *love* at this point is likely to be a surprise to the casual reader of Hegel, or, more globally, to a readership disposed to assume that a philosophy of thinking is bound to devalue love. But Hegel's elaboration of how he understands what it is to define God as love makes it clear that his thinking here converges startlingly with an older tradition, represented, for example, by Aquinas' assertion that love is a reciprocal *inhaesio* and *ecstasis*:[24] in the background is Pseudo-Dionysius' account of divine love as ecstasy, being-in-the-other, and Aquinas stresses that this is the love to which the believer must be assimilated. Compare Hegel's words:

> I have my self-consciousness not in myself but in the other. I am satis-
> fied and have peace with myself only in this other – and I am only
> because I have peace with myself; if I did not have it, then I would
> be a contradiction that falls to pieces. This other, because it likewise
> exists outside itself, has its self-consciousness only in me, and both
> the other and I are only this consciousness of being-outside-ourselves
> and of our identity; we are only this intuition, feeling, and knowledge
> of our unity. This is love, and without knowing that love is both a dis-
> tinguishing and the sublation of the distinction, one speaks emptily
> of it. This is the simple, eternal idea.[25]

Our thinking, then, is ultimately radical loving: ecstasy, being-outside-ourselves. And it is manifest as such because of the way in which the specific Christian tradition instructs us to think God: prior to any *contingent* otherness in the world, beyond a supposed determinate otherness between 'God' and 'the world' (which, as we have seen, is not really thinkable) God as such, *in se*, is the positing and sublating of 'ideal' otherness. Traditionally,[26] all that can be predicated of the Father can be predicated of the Son, except that the Father stands to the Son in an irreversible relation of origination; yet that origination is necessarily and eternally what it is to be 'Father', and there is no 'remainder' in this relation; *nothing* of the source that is not real and actual in the utterance or positing of the issue, and nothing of that issue that is not the life of the source lived in reflection or response. In scriptural and classical terms, this is what it means to say that God is substantively and necessarily love; and the much misunderstood notion[27] that the Spirit is the mutual love of Father and Son as a subsisting reality functions, among other things, as an affirmation that the relation of Father and Son is not all that is true of the divine life; the 'ecstatic' nature of the divine love exceeds the symmetry of the mutual self-dispossession of Father and Son, in constituting a life productive of infinite otherness and reconciliation. Theologically, the Spirit is what makes possible the extension or repetition of the Father–Son relation for persons within the created order. So, for Hegel, if the pattern of identity-in-the-other constitutes a unity that is living, active, historical, productive, concrete, this establishes a necessary third term in the movement of thinking and of thinkable reality. Thought thinks itself, 'abstractly', thinks the concrete other, its alien but inseparable and necessary partner, and thinks itself ultimately as the productive historical life that issues from living-in-the-other – as the life of the subject in community. And insofar as the community is truly *thought*, it is a life in which reconciliation and freedom are actual:[28] it is 'ethical' life, in which sacred and secular are indistinguishable. What is more, thinking the life of the community in this sense is passing beyond the Enlightenment,[29] which conceives only of an abstract and non-historical reconciliation. The Enlightenment becomes aware of the power of thought *over against* externality, heteronomy, tradition or authority, so that its ideal of freedom remains fundamentally negative. It also is incapable of thinking God except as a determinate other (which is, of course, not *thinking* God at all): its God will either become the abstract and unknown deity of Kantianism or – as a twentieth-century reader is bound to conclude – disappear entirely. Enlightenment thought leaves the gulf open between two possible destinies for the spirit: an 'absolute' freedom that is in fact bondage because it is incapable of enactment in the concrete world, and a subjectivity without content, legislating for itself according to 'private' sensibility.[30] Concrete freedom is the development of selfhood in the otherness of what is given – at every level; and the concluding message of the *Philosophy of Religion* lectures is that concrete freedom is unimaginable, unrealisable, if thinking revolts against the triune God, against thought as self-love and self-recovery in the other, against thought as *ecstasis*.

The conclusion to which this points is, in effect, that politics is not thinkable apart from the trinitarian dogma as thought by Hegel. 'Concrete freedom' is the condition in which human selves have understood that they have no unmediated identity, and so (of course) no legitimate interests that are purely private or individual: they recognise the identity of their interests with the 'law' of the community (not necessarily the *de facto* law of a presently existing state[31]). Thought as *ecstasis* dictates the dissolution of any conception of rights as competitive assertion or safeguards against the claims of an alien collectivity, though the perception of rights in such terms is the necessary step away from the tyranny of an illegitimate collective power, the force of a corporate political entity that has not yet been thought or understood. The concrete freedom that lies beyond the Enlightenment assertion of rights 'against' authority is the action that follows on grasping that my welfare or fruition is attainable only in the welfare or fruition of all: I lose my conception of private right so as to negotiate with the otherness of other persons a good neither mine nor theirs. And to do this with understanding, not slipping back into the forms of primitive consciousness in which the otherness of the other is eroded, is the business of free political life – which is the life pointed to by the Christian Church, but conspicuously not realised in its history, since it has been historically guilty of reverting to pre-conscious patterns of power.[32] The Church itself has failed in its trinitarian witness, remaining at the historical point of Jesus' collision with the power of his day: it treats freedom as interior and spiritual, and so offers no reconciliation with the political; it does not understand its own belief in the resurrection and the Holy Spirit.

In the 1831 lectures on the philosophy of religion,[33] Hegel asserts that 'the reversal of consciousness begins' at Calvary. The beginnings of the Church have to do with the discovery of reconciliation, the discovery that freedom is realised on the far side of a dispossession so total that it is now impossible to think of a God who claims the 'right' to be separate from humanity. God repudiates an identity as God-over-against-us, in the fact of creation itself and then, with deepening intensity, in the history of Jesus, who proclaims the kingdom, the presence of God – but does so by proclaiming an absolute interiority; God-with-us can only be thought first as the negation of all external, politico-legal forms as they are historically constituted. This negative proclamation is appropriately consummated (the 1831 lectures add) in a death at the violent hands of external religious and political authority, a death entailing curse and humiliation.[34] The kingdom, in other words, can only appear initially as that which has no place in the 'normally' constituted world: it is first interiority, then death, death without any sanctioning glow of heroism or any consoling sense of resignation to natural mortality. The significance of this is twofold for Hegel. It means both that the life of God comes to its fullness in the world solely by the death, the stripping, of the human – the human, that is, conceived as something solid in itself, as the finite negation or contradiction of the divine, and that human fragility and mortal weakness are not 'outside' God, in the sense that they do not prevent union with God.[35] After Calvary, then, human self-awareness, the human knowledge of humanity as vulnerable and finite, becomes inseparable from awareness of God. If we affirm the human in its frailty as senseless or Godless, as unthinkable, as a reality in and for itself alone, we cannot think God; if we put to death that affirmation of our vulnerable and mortal being as a something-in-itself, we can understand that this weakness is a moment in the life of God. And on this basis the new community is established.

It needs to be emphasised that Hegel sees the possibility of the community of freedom as rooted in a highly specific historical transaction – the violent death of Jesus and the perception of Jesus as the agent or locus of the divine life.[36] Unless it is a tangible historical sequence it cannot be a reality in the world of spirit (since this is not 'another' world to that of history). For thought to lay hold of its own nature, it must think its own dispossession,[37] its emptying-out – otherwise we never get beyond the primitive stage of thinking about two different sorts of *thing*, things that understand and things that are understood. But how is thinking to be 'dispossessed'? For Hegel, the answer is 'Only through a *history* of the emptying-out or bringing to nothing of the fullness of Spirit'; so, only beyond such a history can thinking establish itself, because only in such an event can we definitively lose the pretensions of the individual consciousness. By knowing that the power of the individual consciousness, the mind at home in and with itself over a passive externality, is a fiction, we 'come to ourselves', recognise what life, mind, spirit, speech, reality actually are. In Jesus, the substance of this reality is realised – and it is recognisable as such precisely because it is realised as interiority: it is something at last independent of anything external, anything that is not Spirit. But equally, it is precisely *as interiority* (over against the 'external' order) that it must disappear. The absolute difference between Spirit's reality and what is humanly constructed must be shown not only in the retreat of Spirit into the inner life (as in the preaching of Jesus) but also in the violent repudiation of this interiority by positive, *de facto* authority. In this violence, positive authority displays itself as groundless, as unthinkable: it is what destroys thought. But the thought it destroys is thought isolated (privatised?), thought that cannot think the public sphere, the shared territory of social acts. And thus it is that, in the mutual subversion of positive, unthought externality and the divine as a purely interior or individual reconciliation, the way is cleared for the unillusioned consciousness of 'concrete freedom', and for the *community* of Spirit, the community that lives from the recognition not only that God is 'at hand' in human intellectuality, but that this being-at-hand is manifest in the historical order as a concrete possibility for all humanity, and thus manifest as a community without exclusion or faction in which the negotiation and bonds of social life are given a transfigured valuation.[38]

I said earlier that, for Hegel, an authentic politics was unimaginable without the doctrine of the Trinity, since the doctrine affirmed the impossibility of unmediated identity. What the concluding sections of the *Lectures on the Philosophy of Religion* further affirm is that the doctrine is not thinkable except through the narrative of incarnation, crucifixion, resurrection and Pentecost. This is not to identify the fundamental structure of thinking with what history happens to throw up, but to understand (as noted above) what it is to *think* history at all – to recognise it as the enactment of the basic human reality, the dispossession and recovery that is mental life. But history would not make this recognition possible if it did not contain the narrative of divine dispossession: the idea of God as ultimate reconciliation is not established

> through speculative thinking. This presupposition [of the certainty of real reconciliation] implies the certainty that reconciliation has been accomplished, i.e., it must be represented as something historical, as something that has been accomplished on earth, in [the sphere of] appearance.[39]

So, from the fundamental analysis of mental life as relatedness, we are led first to understand what 'God' means, as the guarantor of the thinkable (reconcilable) nature of our world, and thence to the understanding of divine identity as complete and *inclusive* relation to self (thus dissolving the idea of an 'essential', relationless selfhood or mental/spiritual identity), as Trinity; and finally to the acknowledgment that our history has *already* told us all this, though in ways that have yet to reach full self-consciousness. Scripture and doctrine must be unveiled for what they truly are, and this is the destiny of philosophy.[40]

It is not my task here to discuss the 'compatibility' of Hegel's scheme with the traditional self-understanding of Christian doctrine – though it is important to register how very misleading some accounts of the areas of incompatibility can be. To say, for example, that Hegel neglects the tradition of God's perfect self-sufficiency and asserts a simple interdependence of God and the world (perhaps in the style of modern 'process' thought) is a bad misunderstanding. The basic structure of spirit is not dependent on, or a fact in, 'the world': it is what it is, identity, otherness, reconciliation. Because this is what mental life is, we can't think it apart from thinking ourselves; to think it as separate is to fail in thinking-as-such. 'But', we ask impatiently, 'would there be a God if there were not a world?' And Hegel simply refuses us the vocabulary and conceptuality to put such a question intelligibly. Insofar as God is the ungrounded or self-grounded reality without which there is nothing thinkable (and therefore *nothing*, if we seriously understand who and what we are), we can indeed deploy the traditional language of *aseitas*. Yet that reality is such that it refuses to be an object for thought, a life lived 'beyond' us that we can yet talk about. God's 'exceeding' of thought cannot itself be thought or spoken, and, in this regard, Hegel's convergence with Wittgenstein on religion is worth teasing our further.

Similarly, the idea that Hegel reduces the specificity of Christ to a speculative deduction[41] is fundamentally wrong. Necessity, for Hegel, is what history teaches if we think history, not an imposed or intruding destiny leading history by the nose. That the Christ *must* suffer before entering his glory, that this and this alone is the intelligible form that could reveal the kenotic quality of thought and set us free, is precisely what the record of cross and resurrection tells us, and it is what we could not think or structure in advance, because we can't think necessity *forwards* without falling into fantasy. While Hegel's reading of Christ's 'interiority' is quite unsustainable in the light of a more historically acute exegesis, this does not mean that his reading of the gospels was, by the standards of his day, fanciful or irresponsible; and it is a provoking question to wonder how much of his argument could be recast in the light of more recent versions of the original Jesus tradition, whether in terms of apocalyptic national regeneration or of popularised Cynic philosophy.[42]

My chief aim here has been to suggest two substantial points that should make us wary of any once-fashionable minimising of the theological impetus in Hegel. The first is connected to my caveats in the preceding paragraph. To say that Hegel is serious about history is a bit of an epic understatement: for him, history cannot ever be an *adjunct* to thinking. What we understand is what history has made it possible for us to understand; and what we understand is history, the story of mental life – which, for speaking and understanding subjects, is life or reality *tout court*. If Hegel's thought is dominated, as it unmistakably is, by the scriptural narrative, read through the Catholic doctrinal tradition in general and the specifically Lutheran emphasis on the revelatory significance of Christ's dereliction on the cross, it is no use saying that these things are a ladder he simply kicks away, let alone a bit of apologetic window-dressing. Hegel's thinking about thinking is, inexorably, a thinking of a narrative (incarnation and dereliction) and also, as we have seen, of a traditional theological grammar framing the narrative, of power and providence and simplicity. Again and again, his philosophical energy is roused by the unfinished business of both this narrative (the primitive self-consciousness of the Church impeding the freedom it portends) and this grammar (the need to think the divine simplicity in uncompromisingly trinitarian terms).

Second, I want to underline Hegel's commitment to the vision of thought as 'ecstatic' and 'kenotic'. Not enough is normally granted to Hegel's (admittedly tentative and undeveloped) assimilation of the process of thinking to love, understood as the self's being-in-the-other, but it must be allowed to modify any hasty judgements about the privileging of identity or the 'return to sameness' in his philosophy. It is precisely the model of thinking as a form of love that secures the real *otherness* of what is thought and thus the real voiding or negating of the self-identical subject and the final vision of thought as communal, its identity established only in the mediation of a shared language and in the recognition by each of the identity of the mental process in all (which means 'in history', and 'in the collaborative life of the community now', rather than being a recognition of parallel exemplifications of a process in separate individuals). That this puts in question any reading of Hegel as straightforwardly totalitarian should not need saying, but probably does:[43] 'concrete freedom' is not present if there is any coercion or any inauthenticity in the recognition of unity of interest. More serious is the tension in Hegel's thought between what the *Philosophy of Right* seems to say[44] about the empirical limits of community and the necessity of war as confirming a community's *Selbstgefühl*, and what is clearly laid out in the *Philosophy of Religion* as the optimal form of reflective human sociality, the form adumbrated but not realised by the Church: what is said here has to do with the life of *humanity* as such, and it is wholly unclear how, in the light of this, local loyalties (to this state as opposed to that state, instead of loyalty to *the* state as social form) could be said to be intelligible. We can grant that the discussion in the *Philosophy of*

Right remains at the level of what is actually negotiable in the political world; we do not pass beyond the 'maelstrom of external contingency'[45] in considering international relations, and international reconciliation remains an 'ought', external to the concrete life of real societies.[46] That the individual nation-state has in some sense to lose its being-in-itself by finding (at least) its legitimation in the recognition of such other entities[47] does suggest that there is no unreflective positivism about Hegel's view (let alone a glorification of military struggle as such); his concern is explicitly to think the identity of the state in a world of uncontrollable contingencies. Yet we are left with an uneasy tension which prompts some questioning of Hegel's account of the optimal relation of Church and state (insofar as *neither* realises what it portends or promises as possible). An 'ecstatic' politics remains as a teasing *marginale*, a convergence of Church and state that we cannot satisfactorily formulate.

Whatever needs saying about this, however, the theological force of Hegel's agenda and the theological idiom in which he thinks the nature of thinking are obstinate presences in the *oeuvre*. Certainly they challenge the theologian to be more consistently theological – oddly enough: to think God in more uncompromisingly trinitarian and incarnational terms. But at the same time they invite the theologian to abandon a theology-in-itself, a theology that refuses to be a way of thinking the nature of human sociality. They invite theology to enact what it talks about and so (*only* so) to become authentic thinking. To the cultured despiser of theology, Hegel's challenge is simpler and more radical: is a universally shareable, self-cognisant freedom possible for human beings? If not, we had better abandon all pretence to be thinking subjects or political subjects. This latter option has, apparently, found a good deal of favour in the twentieth century, by way of the cultural and political totalitarianisms of fascism, nationalism, enforced collectivism and the 'free' market; but that doesn't make it truthful.[48]

Notes

1 See particularly David Kolb, *The Critique of Pure Modernity: Hegel, Heidegger and After*, Chicago, 1986, p. 87.

2 See, for example, §24 of the Encyclopaedia Logic (*Hegel's Logic*, translated by William Wallace, with a foreword by J.N. Findlay, Oxford, 1975, pp. 39ff.): to think the nature of thought is to think a process that depends on nothing, in the sense that any formative contribution from my own contingent position or standpoint has to be denied. C.f. the discussion of 'beginnings' in the *Science of Logic*, translated by A.V. Miller, London, 1969, pp. 67–78; and §§86–8 of the Encyclopaedia Logic.

3 §§163–5 of the *Logic* explain the concept of a concrete notion, the particular as the object of thought in the strict sense, as opposed to mere abstract representation (generalities, class predications).

4 This is an area where the tensions between Hegel and 'postmodern thinking' come most clearly into focus – not because Hegel allows a timeless grasp of total presence

(on the contrary) but because *pure* absence or difference cannot be spoken; c.f. R. Williams, 'Hegel and the Gods of Postmodernity', in P. Berry and A. Wernick (eds), *Shadow of Spirit: Postmodernism and Religion*, London, 1992, pp. 72–80.

5 We should have to *think* that our thinking was systematically frustrated or distorted, to think away the possibility of thinking; this would have to be the ground for an Hegelian challenge to behaviourism of any kind, and it relates back to the point from §24 of the *Logic* – thinking has to think a process that is not dependent in *essence* upon contingencies, otherwise every possible mental operation is marked by unfreedom and alienation.

6 Such a misunderstanding is bizarrely in evidence in Hans Küng, *The Incarnation of God: An Introduction to Hegel's Theological Thought as Prolegomena to a Future Christology*, Edinburgh, 1987, pp. 235–7.

7 Hegel, *Logic*, §80, pp. 113–15.

8 *Ibid.*, §81, pp. 115–19.

9 Conveniently digested in Charles Taylor, *Hegel*, Cambridge, 1975, Chapter 10.

10 Hegel, *Logic*, pp. 114–15, 118–19.

11 *Ibid.*, p. 121. There is something here in common with the early Wittgenstein's definition of the mystical, in the sense that the *Tractatus* assimilates *das Mystische* to the sensation of the world as a (determinate) whole (*Tractatus Logico-Philosophicus*, translated by D.F. Pears and B.F. McGuinness, 2nd corrected edn, London, 1963, 6.45): the debate between them would be, I suspect, about the meaning of 'determinate'. Hegel would certainly repudiate any suggestion that the world could be thought of as a very large 'individual'; but it is not clear whether this is anywhere near what Wittgenstein means.

12 Reference will be made to the translation of the 1827 lectures edited by Peter Hodgson (*G.W.F. Hegel: Lectures on the Philosophy of Religion, One Volume Edition: The Lectures of 1827*, California, 1988), abridged from his excellent three-volume version of the entire corpus of texts (California, 1984, 1985, 1987). On divine predicates, see p. 419.

13 Not unfortunately an uncommon view. For an interesting recent study redressing the balance and offering a good account of the theological agenda of the work on logic, see J.W. Burbidge, *Hegel on Logic and Religion: The Reasonableness of Christianity*, New York, 1992 – though its conclusion fails, I think, to weigh the abiding importance in Hegel of the specificity of the narrative of divine self-negation in the incarnation (on which, see further in the present chapter).

14 The expression is associated with Nicholas of Cusa in the fifteenth century, but crystallises the doctrine of earlier mediaeval theologians: God is never an item numerable with others, and therefore is never *an* entity additional to the sum of entities in the universe.

15 §§213–15, 236–44 of Hegel, *Logic*; c.f. the *Lectures*, pp. 170–1.

16 C.f. *The Phenomenology of Spirit*, IV, A.

17 Hegel, *Lectures*, pp. 260–3.

18 From the second *Zusatz* of the Introduction: *Hegel: The Essential Writings*, edited by F.G. Weiss, New York/San Francisco/London, 1974, p. 209.

19 As Hodgson notes in his introduction to the *Lectures* (pp. 17–18), Hegel uses *vollendete* for the supreme form of religion, not *absolute*, the title imposed by his editors.

20 Hegel, *Lectures*, pp. 413–16, 460ff.

21 *Ibid*, p. 418.

22 *Ibid.*

23 Without this moment, consciousness remains alienated and contradictory; God would be 'frozen' in the contradictory position of externalising what he is without

there being a recognition of the *identity* between himself and himself in the other. Thus there could be no *real* identity, since the lack of recognition would introduce a moment of unthought differentiation.

24 Thomas Aquinas, *Summa Theologiae*, I.IIae, 28.ii and iii.
25 Hegel, *Lectures*, p. 418.
26 For example, Aquinas, *Summa Theologiae*, I.31.ii; and 29.iv on persons and relations.
27 Strongly criticised by some Eastern Christian thinkers on the grounds that it makes the Spirit less 'personal' than the Father and the Son. A closer reading of what, say, Augustine understands by this suggests a more nuanced picture; see his *De trinitate* Xv.xvii–xix.
28 Hegel, *Lectures*, pp. 475–9.
29 *Ibid.*, pp. 484ff.
30 C.f. Hegel's *Philosophy of Right* (translated by T.M. Knox, Oxford, 1952), Introduction and pp. 144–9, 185 etc.
31 *Ibid.*, pp. 189–208, 217, 260ff.
32 C.f. Gillian Rose, *Hegel Contra Sociology*, London/Athlone, 1981, pp. 112ff.
33 Hegel, *Lectures*, p. 463, n. 196, which gives the 1831 text.
34 *Ibid.*, p. 465, n. 199.
35 *Ibid.*, p. 468: 'finitude, negativity, otherness are not outside of God and do not, as otherness, hinder unity with God.'
36 *Ibid.*, p. 270:

it had to be a sensible certainty, which, however, at the same time passes over into spiritual consciousness, and likewise is converted into the immediately sensible – in such a way that the movement and history of God is seen in it, the life that God himself is.

37 Here above all is the point at which Hegel's thought converges with the Kierkegaard of the *Philosophical Fragments* – reason passionate for its own disabling; except that Hegel would insist that the equivalent of the Absolute Paradox of the *Fragments* is not something that reason meets as an external barrier. Reason's passion effects its own disempowerment through the thinking of the concrete and historical death of God (Søren Kierkegaard, *Philosophical Fragments* and *Johannes Climacus*, edited and translated by H.V. Hong and E.H. Hong, Princeton, 1985).
38 Hegel, *Lectures*, pp. 473–84.
39 *Ibid.*, pp. 471–2.
40 For example, Hegel, *Lectures*, pp. 399–404.
41 John Milbank's discussion of this point in his magnificent *Theology and Social Theory: Beyond Secular Reason*, Oxford, 1990, p. 163, does not completely avoid such a suggestion.
42 For the former, see N.T. Wright, *The New Testament and the People of God*, London, 1992; for the latter, J.D. Crossan, *The Historical Jesus: The Life of a Mediterranean Jewish Peasant*, San Francisco/Edinburgh, 1991.
43 And is said by Rose, *Hegel Contra Sociology*, especially Chapters 2 and 7, and Taylor, *Hegel*, Chapter 16.
44 §§ 209, 321–9.
45 *Ibid.*, § 340.
46 *Ibid.*, § 333.
47 *Ibid.*, § 331, *Zusatz*.
48 The challenge is articulated by Taylor, *Hegel*; also, with a better appreciation of the centrality for Hegel of the incarnational narrative, by Andrew Shanks, *Hegel's Political Theology*, Cambridge, 1991.

4

THE SUBLIME IN KIERKEGAARD

John Milbank

'Poststructuralist' writing, or shall I rather say, writing in the wake of Nietzsche and Heidegger, might well be characterized as a discourse 'on the sublime'. For it is a discourse 'about' the indeterminable, and seeks, in its very mode of utterance, to pay tribute to this ineluctable margin, rather than have this payment forcibly exacted from a determinate-seeming text. Whether or not this discourse on the sublime, which is also, by virtue of its idiom, sublime discourse, is properly described as 'postmodern,[1] it does represent a second phase in the enterprise of modern critical thought (though this is not to deny that one can find anticipators of the 'postmodern', before the commencement of the 'modern').[2] In the first phase, inaugurated by Kant, the sublime or the indeterminable was safely off limits for the proper exercise of theoretical reason, which is confined to notions that can be 'schematized' within finite space and time. In the second phase, by contrast, sublimity is perceived to contaminate even what is deceptively taken for finitude, so that it is precisely our 'here' and 'now' which cannot be finally characterized, but are only seized in their passing evanescence.[3]

Once sublimity ceases to mean that concerning which one must remain silent, and becomes instead that of which one cannot not speak, and yet cannot speak authentically, it is perhaps inevitable that it will be asked, is this 'sublime' merely old transcendence in (post)modern guise? Has God returned to haunt the ruins of ancient Christendom in a manner more eerie than the gothic shades which gave such agreeably sublime tremors to the heroines of Mrs Radcliffe in the ruins of ancient abbeys? Such questions may well occur to us.

In my opening sentence I mentioned the figures of Nietzsche and Heidegger, but I could easily have added a third: Søren Kierkegaard. He was the great forerunner of 'sublime discourse', the real inaugurator of the second phase of critique. From Kierkegaard, either have, or could have been borrowed (it makes no difference), a teasingly 'masked' mode of writing philosophy, which instead of straightforwardly communicating a propositional content, seeks to produce an unspecified effect, as if giving rough stage directions for performances which only the readers can realize, and will realize differently.

Also from Kierkegaard may be derived (in both possible senses), a series of philosophic categories of a new kind: categories which can only be said to 'represent' our indeterminable reality in a highly problematic sense, and so must be dubbed 'quasi-ontological'. They can be listed as 'Repetition', 'The Moment' (akin to Heidegger's *Das Ereignis*), *Inter-esse* and 'Anxiety'.

I shall advert to all of these in the course of my exposition, but let me begin here with the quasi-category of 'Repetition'. It is generally acknowledged that Kierkegaard was the instigator of the subversive, anti-metaphysical use of this *topos*, which plays such an important role in the writings of Heidegger, Derrida, Deleuze, Lacan, Lacoue-Labarthe and so forth. According to this usage, repetition, far from denoting monotonous sameness, or the literal reoccurrence of some supposedly 'original' event, indicates rather an 'originary repetition', or the constitution of an identity *only* through its reoccurrence. For Kierkegaard and his successors, we never have access to a single, isolated, original instance, and it follows as a corollary of this that the irreducible reoccurrence is nonetheless not an identical repetition, for otherwise one would be able to regard the second instance as a mere echo of a first that is free-standing in its own right. Thus the stress upon conjuncture, upon a trans-cendental necessity tying primary comprehension to the recognition of a *series* of instances, is nonetheless wrenched free from the 'realist' Platonic-Aris-totelian tradition of affirming 'universal' essences, and made paradoxically to depend upon an equally strong affirmation of the ontological diversity of each individual 'moment' or 'event'. The moment is not really an 'instance', a 'standing in' a larger category, such that it 'exemplifies' it; rather every moment introduces something new that has itself the weight of categorical uniqueness. Behind Kierkegaard's thinking lurked the Heraclitean and Leibnizian contentions that no two places or temporal moments can ever be precisely identical.[4]

So only when something happens again do we grasp that it has happened at all, yet this assumes that when it happens again, it always happens differently. But if that is the case, then while repetition may be inescapable, it is also chronically aporetic. Where every identity is a repetition, and every repeti-tion traverses a difference, then the identity can also be undone through the very movement which constitutes it. And the isolated moments which remain as the fragments of this deconstruction are not, of course, inviolable atoms, but themselves repeated identities which can in turn be undone, and so on *ad infinitum*. In the case of Kierkegaard, this sceptical implication is cer-tainly gestured towards, but not regarded as an inevitably engulfing abyss. The abyss can be traversed by a 'decision' – to affirm absurdly and without grounds such-and-such a repeated continuity. Yet the decision is never based upon any rational evasion of the *aporia*: I must repeat, but is *this* still the same? And have I *now* gone on to something else? Identity – 'my' identity, along with the identity and hence 'truth' of everything else – is precariously affirmed by Kierkegaard (in a manner which I must seek further to elaborate), yet he never denies that such identity must remain endlessly in question, endlessly liable to fracture and postponement.

Given this aporetic implication, it is not, however, surprising that, for the post-structuralists, 'Repetition' has becomes one of the tropes upon which humanism is made to turn and flounder. The human subject, far from being able to identify and command its own 'original' essence, is simultaneously preconstituted and deconstituted by a repetitious dynamic which permits only an illusory self-mastery. Something 'essential' for the subject's identity may be yet to happen to him, and every element of his selfhood which he regards as safely accumulated can be wrenched away from him by others who will easily demonstrate its alien origins and difference from his proper *persona*. This demise of humanism does not, of course, betoken any return of divinity, for the illusion of subjective self-identity is regarded by poststructuralism as something first borrowed from metaphysical constructions of Godhead, and supposedly transferred to its 'proper' site in finite humanity, whose stability is now exposed as an equally metaphysical illusion. Under the aegis of repetition, what is enthroned is not a transcendent God, but rather an alternately and indeterminately creative and destructive process, whose immanence subsumes the once-divine properties of infinitude and *comprehensio*.

What, therefore, is poststructuralism to make of Kierkegaard? – whose own philosophic usage of repetition it can only repeat by way of an immense rupture, since he not only upheld, above all else, a transcendent God and the ethically constrained human subject, but reaffirmed them precisely in connection with this quasi-category. Poststructuralism can only seek to demonstrate the forced and forged character of this linkage, and to prise apart Kierkegaard's usage of repetition from his theological interest; indeed to prise it apart from 'interest' (an inflection of Kierkegaard's quasi-category *inter-esse*), which assumes a subject, altogether. Hence, according to Gilles Deleuze, Kierkegaard deserts his critical insights to 'dream between a God and Self refound', and in the interiority of faith fraudulently claims to rediscover an essential *habitus* and stable memory which the analysis of repetition has already rendered insupportable. For this reason, the claimed interior presence must remain forever without issue or effect upon the surface flux of reality, dooming the Knight of faith to remain at best a 'comic simulacrum of himself'.[5] Likewise as writer, Kierkegaard can only don the guise of a humorist, ironically fragmented into his several authorial *personae*. These inscribe ceaselessly new versions of his own prematrimonial farce, while Kierkegaard 'himself' surveys these now alienated antics from the private box of his own reserved interiority. Within this enclosure, however, Kierkegaard secretly envisages a serious absurdity, a final eschatological repetition which is the salvation and resurrection of all humankind. Deleuze contends that this religious vision remains disjoined from the humorous discourses which disclose the only certifiable repetition, that of surface masks and disguises that present entirely assumed and conventional faces of 'identity'. It was left to Friedrich Nietzsche to will, not eschatological repetition, but the eternal return of this comic theatre of cruelty. Repetition receives its true ontological seal when this simulacrum of belief is perversely disclosed as the real kernel of truth, the unavoidable transcendental assumption, lurking within all religion.

In this reading of Kierkegaard, an unproblematic rupture is posed between his *scepticism* on the one hand and his *fideism* on the other: where reason comes adrift, there belief is anchored, and begins to restore by pure *fiat*, in an invisible world, 'present' and 'essential' entities. In what follows I wish to problematize this rupture, and to argue that, by attending to Kierkegaard's interweaving of his accounts of indeterminacy and repetition with a new articulation of 'God', 'the subject' and the inescapability of 'decision', we can point by contrast to a subjective 'decision' for atheism and anti-humanism, and so an ineradicable 'subjectivity' that poststructuralism is not owning up to.

This argument is made the more interesting and possible in so far as Kierkegaard himself incorporated, and never forgot or abandoned, precisely a demolition of the self-percipient Cartesian/idealist subject.[6] His 'deciding' subject, I shall argue, remained a 'textual' subject, and he was entirely aware of the moves one can make to show that one can never be sure of deciding, or having decided what one appears to have decided. However, as poststructuralism well knows, this 'appearing to decide' is itself inescapable; the (Kierkegaardian) question to be interposed here is whether dogmatic assertion of pure illusion operating at this point is nonetheless a disguised *decision* not to yield to the supposed seductions of this appearance, the always preinscribed necessity-to-decide. Perhaps it is significant that Kierkegaard is ancestor to two seemingly opposed twentieth-century discourses: on the one hand the 'existential' philosophy of the self-directing subject, categorically impelled to will beyond the reach of any universal law; on the other the structuralist/poststructuralist philosophy of the subject who always decides after it has been decided for her (and 'as her'), and never commands what she has decided. For it is arguable that Kierkegaard had already elaborated a broader problematic which shows the inescapability of both the decisionist and the textual aspects of subjectivity. Taking the hint from Kierkegaard's habitual balletic trope, one might dub this problematic of the inscribing figure who is also the figure inscribed, 'choreographic'. I shall claim that it is within this more and not less critical perspective that he is able consistently to conjoin his faith with his scepticism – without reverting to the kind of theoretical metaphysics he had so decisively abandoned.

The best way to commence is to indicate how all Kierkegaard's suspiciously 'Cartesian'-sounding categories – interiority, subjectivity, interest – which appear to allow a rupture between a sceptical science of surfaces and an inscrutable faith in promised presence, really denote different aspects of the same problematic crux, round which the more 'objective'-sounding cate-gories are also articulated. The crux arises from his *rejection* of 'the subject' of Cartesian, Kantian and German idealist philosophy, a subject which he takes to be but a variant (though an especially degenerate one) of the ancient Socratic knowing and self-knowing self, which he regards as constitutive of the very 'identity' of western philosophy.[7] This subject always mirrors an opposing object; it acquires its density through an adequate knowledge of the object, and therein negates itself. For Kierkegaard it makes relatively little difference that the idealist subject is able entirely to constitute itself out of its own native resources, for the same 'objectification' is the desired and achievable goal. Far from aiming, like idealism (and many successor philoso-phies) to overcome the subject/object divide, he insists that the rift must always remain in place, that there can never be any perfect correspondence between the two, precisely because their relationship is not one of mirroring, and therefore not of dialectical opposition and reunification either. The sub-ject cannot conform itself to the object, after the fashion of 'empiricism' (but this would here include 'realism'), because the object is in endless flux; any vauntedly exhaustive determination would mark instead an arbitrary stop-page and fixation. But neither can the object conform to the subject, after the manner of 'idealism', since reason is similarly in flux: necessary logical sequences and determinate sets of categories are but formalized and arbitrary abstractions (respectively), from an endless fictioning of possibilities which renders any attempted self-critique of reason, any attempt to know how we know, and thereby to acquire a standard to measure authentic knowledge – genuinely grasped objectivity – co-terminously infinite.[8] Such a critique could only take the form of *another* imagined possibility, it would never become the true fiction of how to fiction.[9]

However, not only is the rift negatively speaking unbridgeable, such that there can *be* no truth in the theoretical senses of correspondence or coherence, the rift is itself that which positively allows there to be either subject or object at all. They *are*, through their mutual exclusion and yet inter-reference; therefore through the unavoidable *posing* of the question of truth as correspondence.[10] Both subjectivity and the question of truth are unavoid-able, because things are only manifest within reflective representation: a 'doubling' of the object such that to grasp an actuality is simultaneously to grasp its indeterminate possibility (how it might become and still be itself, what sort of things might happen to it) through an entertained fiction. It is by no means the case that the fiction is a lens we must use to enhance our sight, although it also distorts it. On the contrary, the manifestatory expression-through-possibility belongs wholly within ontology, and does not merely mediate between Being and Knowledge. No abyss sunders us, the knowing subjects, from reality, but rather reality is itself incessantly fractured between the actual and the possible, and within this rift 'subjectivity' comes to be/becomes possible.[11]

Far from espousing Cartesian or even Kantian dualism, Kierkegaard seeks to find a place for subjectivity within the seamless spatio-temporal chain by exploiting (in a fashion exceeding that philosopher's own account of 'the soul') Aristotle's problematic admission of 'possibility' and 'becoming' (*kinesis*) within the categories of 'Being', which would seem hospitable only to 'the actual'. Thus he contends that the real exhibits infinitely many transitions from rest to motion, and from possibility to act, and that these transitions, despite the regional operation of habitual causal patterns, have the character of positive 'leaps' which display no logic outside that of their own occurrence. This kind of transition, which, not being a 'state', is an invisible vanishing point for thought (doomed to the effort of representation) he names 'the moment', and claims that the moment is the site of specifically human, spiritual existence – 'spirit' being that which binds soul (thinking possibility) and body (living actuality) together. To grasp the moment and ourselves as *out of* the moment, we can only repeat, and never represent it. Through reflection we endeavour to reproduce the vanished transition of possibility to act (which has always already passed by), but this reinvocation of becoming can only take the form of reconverting the moment in its completed, actual occurrence back into a possibility that can no longer be the same, original possibility, and therefore, although it *is* the possibility of this moment, is no longer identical with it, and already foreshadows something new.[12]

It follows that, for Kierkegaard, subjective consciousness arises as a kind of special permutation of material motion, in which *kinesis* bends back upon itself, feigns a recapitulation of its own possibility, and instead bifurcates itself between the actual world on the one hand, and the fictional world of expressive, linguistic imaginings which constitutes the *humanum*. Hence his category of subjectivity, so far from being predicated on a 'private' self-awareness, is necessarily suspended between material motion on the one hand, and symbolic, linguistic operations on the other: as if to say, humanity *is* the difference between nature and humanity, yet is *both*. The energies of the real themselves interpose this suspension. The same goes for Kierkegaard's category of 'inwardness': the subject itself is not the locus of interiority, but is rather 'within' a perpetual transition that it can never survey in a theoretical manner from without.[13] Such 'externality' would, on the contrary, be the stance of the Cartesian self-enclosed, self-sufficient subject. Finally, our human existence and relation to truth is, indeed, 'interested' in the sense that the question of truth is only resolvable by an unfounded decision concerning our own self-development; however, this interest is made possible by our (quasi)ontological situation *inter-esse*, the perpetual fracture between possibility and act, and again, possibility, which determines and undetermines all being. (It is significant that while Kierkegaard professed a Socratic disinterest in natural philosophy, he nonetheless intimates – despite Deleuze's denial – that there is a repetition and even a kind of anxiety within nature.[14])

So far I have been trying to show how Kierkegaard's apparently 'existential' categories are equally ontological categories (this tends to push him closer to Heidegger than the latter was perhaps prepared to acknowledge).[15] However, they are also 'anti-ontological' categories in so far as they seem to describe universal conditions which prevent us affirming any universal identities or even sites of identity. But for Kierkegaard the question of such identity (and so of truth), is displaced from the theoretical to the existential or practical plane. Neither given objects nor self-conscious subjectivity afford us any security, yet in all our actions and preferences we perforce establish our identities and sketch out the norms for our own truths. Repetition accordingly operates as a kind of suspended ontological category, which is equally a category of suspense, of *anxiety*: will we be able to repeat ourselves, establish ourselves, find a 'character' of stable self-inscription (which Kierkegaard declares to be the whole essence of the ethical life)?[16] To hope for a positive answer is to make a kind of wager on the reality of an invisible 'proportion' pertaining between our particular series of finite positions, and that entire indeterminate reality which impinges upon, and seemingly undoes, our most meagre theoretical reckonings. It is to venture that there might be 'proper' positioning within the very submission to sovereign mutability.[17]

Since the game of truth is no longer something played out between the 'subjects' and 'objects' of a divided finitude, it is not surprising that Kierkegaard makes a significant return to Plato here, and thinks again of truth as something at issue between temporal flux and the non-representable, eternal 'other' of time. He is able to argue that Socrates refounded philosophy in terms of this problematic, which engaged already, at the heart of *ancient* philosophy, the question of the subject as the point where an eternal 'identity' can be recaptured through 'internal' recollection.[18] However, the only antique philosophers with whom Kierkegaard was more or less thoroughly in sympathy were not the Platonists, but the Sceptics, and just as he ruins Cartesian/Kantian reason, so he claims to ruin the Greek *logos* itself.[19]

For here also, extinction in the object awaits the subject falsely conceived as its 'opposite'. Reason must fulfil its destiny to know, yet what there is to know, if anything, is this 'other to reason', the objective forms beyond time. But the only way to know this inherently unknowable other is contradictorily to identify it with something found within time, with this or that: hence, according to Kierkegaard, the polytheistic plurality of Greek gods. Hence also the recollective rescuing of vanishing 'moments' through embalming them as fragments of eternity. As nothing in its happening is knowable, everything knowable belongs in an eternal past, a past that is eternal, without decay. Yet for reason, the only authentic mark of eternity must remain its indeterminacy, and therefore it appears to be aporetically trapped between the flux of time with its uncapturable moments, and the equally ungraspable vastness of the eternal.[20] According to Kierkegaard, Greek reason overlooks this *aporia*, by repeatedly making its own redeterminations of the eternal through hypostasizations of moments snatched from the temporal flux. The infinitude of the eternal is finitized, but 'unconsciously' acknowledged in the never-completed accumulation or gods of Platonic forms. Through this confusion, which is nonetheless endemic to (Greek) reason, reason collapses into unreason, into 'absurdity' and 'paradox', which for Kierkegaard are terms denoting the identity of eternity with temporal flow. It is here that his philosophy appears most 'dialectical' (and close to Hegel?), for absurdity and paradox are *not*, in the first place, attributes of faith as opposed to reason, but on the contrary, the inner suppressed reality of (Greek) reason itself.[21] But this apparent ruination of reason is transformed by Christianity into its higher redemption. For here one espouses a *logos* which from the outset embraces the identity of eternity with time (albeit that its mode of repetition is not that of polytheistic proliferation), such that 'absurdity' and 'paradox' now become names *for* (a higher) reason, and what appeared acutely embarrassing for reason turns out, on the contrary, to disclose the true order and possibility of human thought. However, the transition from a ruinous to a positive paradox is not in Kierkegaard (as for Hegel) ineluctable and by way of negation: the new bridge thrown across the abyss is not the work of the abyss, but of willed, contingent subjectivity. And without the higher comprehension of reason *by* positively embraced paradox and absurdity, it is doomed either to sceptical ruin, or else the contradictory quest to conjoin eternity to time through 'recollection'.

Despite Christianity, this Platonism (as Kierkegaard understood it) has persisted. The force of its *logos* has, in Kierkegaard's diagnosis, doomed the West to perpetual necrophilia and melancholia.[22] According to the (absurd) logic of *inter-esse*, we should live in perpetual suspension between the actual human hero and his fictional celebration by the poet, who are *both* preconditions of each other, and together compose an endless, unfinished human work.[23] Instead, in our Platonic trance, we choose to live in enclaves of 'aesthetic' secrecy and closure, where we convert our disappointments into private theatrical spectacles for consolation, and enjoy plots where 'everything is tidied up in five acts'.[24] The hero is always dead, and embalmed in poetic 'perfection', while inversely one thinks of this poetry as just 'representing' a heroism complete in its own terms. This is why, for Kierkegaard, the 'theoretical' and the 'aesthetic' are mutually complicit aspects of the Platonic spectacle. One goes wildly astray if one assumes that his 'anti-aestheticism' sets him squarely at variance with the rampant aestheticism of the poststructuralists. Kierkegaard's 'aesthetic' does not have the normal range of connotation of the term, but denotes something more like 'visual fixation' and false desire for all-encompassing vision and temporal closure – the drama with all tidied up in the final scene. As such it is somewhat like Nietzsche's 'Apollonian' art, while, given the musical and choreographical terms by which they are most frequently designated, Kierkegaard's 'ethical' and 'religious' somewhat correspond to Nietzsche's 'Dionysiac'. In terms of its usual scope, they do not *at all* fall outside the range of 'the aesthetic'.[25]

Having ruined the Greek *logos* in *Philosophical Fragments*, Kierkegaard proceeds to reinvent, or to repeat, a different *logos*, associated not with the 'identity' of Socrates (attained through recollection), but with the 'identity' of Christ (established through repetition). But as I have already intimated, there is no simple leap from sceptical reason to believing faith occurring here, and still less any retreat from an aporetic exterior to inward religious affirmation. For the terms used to characterize the new, Christian *logos* – 'paradox', 'the absurd' – have already been used to describe the concealed aporetic heart of Greek reason as it struggles 'to identify' the eternal with the resources of time; thus the Christian *logos* remains in one respect a deconstructed Greek *logos*, although this denotes no Hegelian genetic dependency. Since the Christian *logos* persists in the general task of all reason, which is to establish 'identity' by mediating between time and eternity, when Kierkegaard says that he believes 'by virtue of the absurd', he means 'by virtue of the incarnation', and so for the best possible *reason*.[26]

Just as the self-collapse of Greek reason brought absurdity and paradox to light, so also it exposed our loss of identity in the vanishing 'moment', and the emergent problematic of 'repetition'. Yet despite the (anti)categorical, universal bearing of these terms on all human existence as such, they are also used (like the equally universal 'paradox' and 'absurdity') with apparently exclusive reference to Christ and his work of atonement. The double usage of all these terms is appropriate because, while one must sceptically persist in paradox and absurdity, their *aporia* itself leaves open the question of whether a repeated identity, that is to say a 'consistency' established despite and by way of difference, is possible. Such an identity, unlike that attained through backwards recollection, would remain always 'to be completed', and yet would not thereby be rendered incoherent. Indeed it would actually *save* the appearances of motion, for if all is flux without (non-illusory, non-arbitrary) identity, then this resolves into final monistic 'indifference', an abyssal *non-motion*.[27]

By exhibiting 'consistency', and yet remaining indeterminately open to the future, this new Christological identity reinscribes 'truth' in the Socratic sense of discovering a proportion between time and eternity. The tribute that reason must pay to the indeterminable is now ensured through a repetition that discovers inexhaustible variety in 'the same' (or rather the same *as* inexhaustible variety), rather than it being secretly exacted through polytheistic profusion – which bequeathed to the West another dark destiny, that of Don Juan, who repeats not the same as manifold but the manifold as the same. In the former case desire is ceaselessly renewed, whereas in the latter it is endlessly disappointed, in so far as it deserts every new moment, embalming it in the assumption of exhausted possibility, and thereby reducing it to a mere 'instance' of subjective fulfilment, which thanks to this repeated reduction, will never be realized.[28] For Kierkegaard, Christ is that universal identity which arises through its happening again, differently. If there is 'continuity' here, then it is traced by faith in the 'pattern' of transmission. But the same faith must vanquish anxiety by projecting this continuity indefinitely forwards. Thus 'Repetition' (as realizing identity) and 'the Moment' (as recoverable through alteration) only become fully-fledged ontological categories through the practical, existential affirmations of faith. Kierkegaard does not suggest that we abandon philosophy (ontology) for religion, rather he 'saves' philosophy by transforming it, *without remainder*, into theology.

It is, of course, at this point, where repetition is affirmed in order to uphold ethical 'continuity', consistent identity, divine transcendence and atonement, that Kierkegaard diverges most drastically from poststructuralism. In the case of the latter, if repetition denotes continuity, it equally denotes rupture, and the ceaseless contamination of every identity such that this quasi-category cannot be construed as an ethical imperative for the realization of 'character'. However, there are two ways in which this contrast of outlooks can be mediated.

First of all, Kierkegaard pushes the project of realizing 'character' to an almost nihilistic extreme. The continuity, or 'inwardness', that each of us is to realize, conforms to no universal norms and indeed embodies what is exceptional to us, our particular expenditure of 'infinite passion' upon a particular sequence of finite instances. Each one of us repeatedly occupies a unique 'position' from which we enjoy unmediated contact with the infinite. Yet despite this seemingly anarchic state of affairs, the project of repetition also represents the wager that a unity can pertain amongst human beings which surpasses in ordered perfection the unity achieved through the subsumption of particulars under a universal. The envisaged conditions for this unity include, first, a kind of pre-established harmony amongst all the myriad points of reflection; second, a historical and intersubjective project of imitation permitted by the intrusion of Christ. The second condition qualifies the possible implication of 'windowless' monads in the first.[29]

This postulation of a double transcendental precondition in no way provides us with any guidance in practice, closing the chasms between actions and between ethically earnest individuals, which must be negotiated by repeated 'leaps'. Though judgement needs the support of external advice and the perspectives of others, the individual alone, in the last analysis, is in the right position from which to make a judgement concerning himself. Hence we must 'judge for ourselves', and judge anew, beyond the guidance of habit, in each new moment.[30] Yet judgement may still claim to effect/ discover unique yet continuous chains persisting *as* and *through* the constant positive leaps (which represent Kierkegaard's substitute for Hegelian determinate negation, or what he deems to be the false subsumption of movement under a logical process).[31] If, with the poststructuralists, it is maintained that these judgements always and necessarily (as opposed to sometimes, or even 'nearly always'), conceal ruptures, betrayals, subterfuges, then one may ask, what is the ground of *that* judgement? Has it any ground beyond its own subjectivity?

In the second place, Kierkegaard himself provides an involved account of ruptures in continuity; that is to say of leaps which alone *make up* continuity. This account can itself be subdivided into three. First of all, Kierkegaard insists that all Christian communication is maieutic and Socratic in a new sense. Not that of recalling us to our own identity in recollection, but of preserving our unique 'inwardness' of position or perspective (again the Leibnizian echoes are strong). The fatal danger of language is that it appears to bind us together in terms of a common signified content – 'propositions' and 'laws' – to which we are all supposed to assent. If this is the case, then additions to language will assume the status of corrections, implying an endlessly renewed sceptical doubt about previous usage, and the previous perceptions which it expressed. Such a state of affairs is assumed by the philosophic *logos*, especially in its post-Cartesian guise, and for this reason Kierkegaard claims that it informs a murderous, sacrificial community. Your teacher teaches you respect for objective truth, for the precise communication of propositions, and the only way to respect his teaching is to slay him, destroy his work, and revise his proposals.[32] Here is imitation, or repetition, as a death-dealing imperative – Kierkegaard's 'death instinct' which in un-Freudian fashion turns to be inscribed not in the soul, but in a particular cultural practice.[33]

Rejecting this practice, Kierkegaard sought to invent a non-sacrificial mode of communication. Hence his own writings are ironically self-reserving, and he claims to read them as the works of another author for whom he acts as a scribe. This permits them to be also charitably self-effacing: the reader is not required to assent to them or even interpret them; rather he is to 'reflect' them again, as his own interiority.[34]

In the second place, rupture involves a vertical as well as a horizontal dimension. There is not only the anxiety of 'what comes next?' and 'how shall I charitably reserve my position?', but also the overwhelming anxiety in the face of the indeterminate in general: being 'anxious about nothing'.[35] In *The Concept of Anxiety*, Kierkegaard did an extraordinary thing: instead of leaving the modern problematic of the indeterminacy of the infinite as a matter for the foundations of theology, he made it *thematic* for the whole of dogmatics – placing it at the heart of his account of fall and redemption.

The modern notion of sublimity – which Kierkegaard describes derogatively as an 'aesthetic accounting' for transcendence[36] – leaves us in a still more 'Greek', or detached, contemplative relation to the unknown. Here terror is fused with the thrill of uncertain anticipation and relief at withheld destruction.[37] Kierkegaard's pejorative remark might lead us to expect that he seeks only to reinstate Christian transcendence against this sublimity, by insisting that the unknown is mediated to us in terms of moral norms and the regulation of desire. Instead, it is patently clear that Kierkegaard, like Kant, yet in a totally divergent and far more ingenious fashion (at once more radical and more conservative) sought to transfer the moment of sublime anxiety (the centrality of anxiety undoubtedly deriving from the discourse on sublimity)[38] from the realm of aesthetic spectatorship to that of ethical involvement, and through this procedure to infuse sublimity itself with the qualities of transcendence. To be precise: the sublime had already been substituted for transcendence; Kierkegaard reinscribes transcendence by taking up and subverting the *impasse* of the sublime.

He does this by rewriting the Augustinian account of human fallenness, arguing that the 'original', innocent relationship to God nonetheless included that uncertainty pertaining to relationship with the unknown/unknowable, though this then took the form of a 'pleasing anxiety' entirely devoid of terror; the erotic connotations are obvious. Kierkegaard here effectively forestalled nihilism, by opening a space for a non-violated subject which yet preserves the indeterminate within the indeterminable. The constitutive distance of subjectivity, its arising as a vista upon the sublime, may indeed be the terrible, may be suspended violence, yet may also be the distance of erotic mystery and promise. This faith that infinite distance will not destroy 'continuity', meaning the intense and harmonious realization of human desires, but prove to be the ground of possibility *for* such a non-formalizable and indefinite continuation, reconciles, beyond Burke and Kant, the sublime with the beautiful (see n. 38).

The alternatives – interruptive terror, or beguiling distance – remain subjective construals, decisive 'leaps' of human disposition. Kierkegaard describes how gradually a playful anxiety becomes a fearful one, and this disposition mutates into the state of sin: the imagining of God to be terrible, as possibly forbidding we know not what, on pain of we know not what punishments, is itself the first irruption of sin – which only later immures itself in the safety of *determinate* desires it thinks it can command, dominion it presumes it can achieve. Where Augustine located the transcendental sin as 'pride', which already thinks to subject the infinite to its own grasp, Kierkegaard substitutes fear, which swims in the medium of acknowledged uncertainty. The only way out of this condition is to travel to the end of despair, to discover that despair does indeed lurk beneath the indeterminate series of finite projects – and then paradoxically to invest our hope and love in infinite indeterminacy itself. A leap into the void by which faith heals anxiety.[39]

However, there is a crucial tension in Kierkegaard's thought at this point. How does this movement of faith, this belief in an eternal repetition of all that is lost in time, relate to the healing of anxiety from moment to moment which is the ethical project of continuity, the humanly universal as fully disclosed by Christianity. (It should be stressed that the ethical in its proper character of repetition only fully emerges for Kierkegaard with Christianity or 'Religiousness B').[40] It is in this connection that Kierkegaard displays intriguing qualms concerning the relationship between our love for God on the one hand, and our love for our neighbour on the other. Is it right to locate 'despair' at the heart of the latter love? To turn her (and for Kierkegaard it was of course 'her'), into a mere occasion for transition to the love of God? An anxiety, one might say (to employ Augustinian terminology) about *usus* in pursuit of *frui*. Much religiousness, claims Kierkegaard, is all too akin to the sad passion of aesthetic melancholia (our philosophic disease) in which one loves the beloved only in perpetual retrospect, and sacrifices her through secret idealization. Here one remains silent about one's desires, forswears their realization and appears to sacrifice *oneself* only because one confines one-self to this private theoretical theatre which snatches one away from the ethical continuum that is supremely embodied in the 'voluptuous variation'[41] of marriage. The aesthetic rupture is therefore culpable, close to that demonic 'inclosing reserve' or self-regarding solipsism, which unlike ironic reserve prevents a self-effacing 'communication'.[42]

However, Kierkegaard also speaks of a religious rupture, which for all its kinship with the aesthetic one, can nonetheless be justified. This is a total sacrifice of self and others which in turn permits a certain *secrecy*. We can never disclose to others a will to 'give them up', for once this will finds expression in public language its only apparent meaning will be the sundering of human relationship, at worst the sin of murder. However, this is *not* the meaning of such a will if it is preserved in its pure esotericity – which is sheerly negative sublime rupture, not a Cartesian 'interior space'. For as inexpressible rupture this will belongs to a different economy: not the ethical one which must operate within the constraints of human frailty, of possible death and the inequities of sexual attractiveness, but rather the economy of the love of God, in which even the physically or psychically mis-shapen are loved; where also there is no death, for this love can even love us into existence.[43] The interplay of the two economies is repeatedly dramatized by Kierkegaard in all his writings, but most convulsively in *Fear and Trembling*. Here the story of Abraham and Isaac is presented as the ultimate comic performance of Schleiermacher's 'absolute dependence'.[44] The 'ethical' which is 'suspended' (i.e. ruptured, plunged temporarily, for the space of an unglimpsable 'moment' into the sublime abyss) in this account, although representing morality in general, is, in the Danish, *Soedelighed*, the equivalent of the German *Sittlichkeit*, and the deployment of antique examples in this work, along with direct allusion to Hegel's *Philosophy of Right*, makes it clear that Kierkegaard does indeed here conceive the ethical in Hegelian (*not*, as one might expect, Kantian) fashion as the dutiful performance of certain socially specified roles, even if these are accorded a universal 'moral' force.[45] This ethical 'law of the city', of what is taken to be the highest – namely free human association – can only be 'suspended' because the drama of Abraham and Isaac is enacted within a divine economy rather like that of the American film cartoon *Tom and Jerry*, in which no death is final, and every destruction is retrospectively negated as playful recreation.[46] (The problem of sadism is clearly close at hand here.)

Abraham's sacrifice of Isaac is an anti-sacrifice because it is a completely pointless sacrifice: *not* the ancient sacrifice performed within the city to ensure its survival, like Agamemnon's sacrifice of Iphigenia, which Kierkegaard contrasts at length with the Abraham story. Rather the sacrifice on the mountain *before* (and not even 'on the occasion of') the institution of the *polis*. Not, therefore, a sacrifice to seal the city's future, not at all a foundational sacrifice, but rather the absurd sacrifice of the one individual who is absolutely irreplaceable, who uniquely and without possibility of substitution (he is the lone, late, miracle child) bears the whole future city in his loins. *This* sacrifice can only be the offering of the entire city itself, in all its temporal duration, which is only possible before it even exists.

A different and absurd sacrificial economy: instead of the mediating spatial sacrifice of the individual to the totality, the single but 'repeated' temporal sacrifice which is the offering up of the (indeterminate) totality itself. Is this, one might ask, the bloody surrender of all to God, an horrendous acosmism? Religion as sacrifice, transgression *à la* Bataille? But no. For Kierkegaard the giving up of the whole – one's own desire, the other, all the others – to God, is also the only *possible* salve against the usual sacrificial economy which surrenders the individual to the city. The offering of the whole rather than the parts is specifically represented as identical with the infinite non-sacrificial preservation and *return* of the individual and the fulfilment of all the individual's positive desires. Agamemnon's love for his daughter for Iphigenia, his love within the *oikos*, must, at times, be surrendered to the state and its false, generalizing morality, tied to fixed roles and places. This love, by way of that compensation which is philosophy, can only be inauthentically conserved within the ideal theatre of recollection. It follows that, within the Greek *logos*, *theoria* of the soul and *dike* in the city are finally incompatible (as Plato's *Republic* discloses). But Abraham's gesture of sacrifice, his refusal to give up on a desire for the infinite (for 'God'), that is not satisfied by any finite attachments, is equally and immediately a refusal to give up on the indeterminate promise of these finite attachments themselves. The gesture is homeopathic, since it anticipates the possible deaths of individuals and desires which nature or the state may bring about, yet can only be made as an offering to *God* – who is creative love – in the absurd belief that these deaths are never the last word. It is thereby also a self-cancelling will to sacrifice, since undertaken in the conviction that the moment of sacrifice will never arrive, or else will prove to be always already passed: that moment of the abyss, of the rationally ineliminable anxiety as to whether the infinite will prove benign, reinforced by the reality of death which can assume no face of benignity within the purely finite ethical economy. To believe that the sacrifice will never occur/is always already over, is to believe that the apparently ominous sublime 'surplus' of divine infinitude which imposes an imperative 'beyond' the ethical, will actually turn out to be *exhausted* in its will for ethical repetition, the return and realization of every individual desire.

So it turns out that there is, after all, nothing really 'beyond' the ethical. Our ultimate *telos* exceeds the aim of association in the city; but this is merely to re-express what has always been involved in the Christian notion of 'a supernatural end'. And for Kierkegaard, the civil aim is not in fact un-ambiguously surpassed, for we have seen that one thrust of his work is not at all to exalt love of God over love of neighbour, but rather to instil qualms about the possible ethical dubiety of such an attitude. Not surpassed, but 'suspended', and what are we to make of a *telos* that is accorded the name of a delay (pending inquiries)? If this delay occurs at the end ('teleological sus-pension of the ethical'),[47] then it never occurs at all, is always 'over'. As a purely transcendental delay it never visibly intrudes, but upholds from above (*suspends*) the ethical as its condition of possibility. It does so because the ban on murder, seemingly the most absolute of ethical commandments, so that it can stand for all the rest, is nonetheless complicit with the inexorabil-ity of death, which can stand for the unavoidability of pain and suffering. Death is inseparable from the feeding of life by life, so that the absolute upholding of 'life' which demands the ban on murder, will also tend contra-dictorily to demand sacrifice – of the few to the many, the person to the com-munity. By contrast, the 'final suspension' of the ban on murder is a faithful refusal of death, and the entire economy of death, in its apparent manifesta-tion. In positing the 'return of all', and the non-necessity of sacrifice through the reduction of sacrifice to absurdity, it alone makes possible the ethical, which is now 'transvalued' to exclude not murder alone, but also sacrifice. (The use of the term 'positing' here, should call to mind Kant's somewhat kindred arguments for the necessity of God, judgement and eternal develop-ment to complete the ethical imperative; as with Kierkegaard's suspension, these things are not included within the ethical imperative, which is human and autonomous, yet are not simply 'beyond' it either. But Kant's postulation does not issue in a transvaluation in the way that Kierkegaard's does.)

Therefore for Abraham to make the gesture of sacrificing Isaac is to know that he will not sacrifice him, or that Isaac will return. The Christian figures of the beloved within the city – Beatrice, Regine – can never be sacrificed to the city, *or* to God, because they are in themselves that 'supernatural' beyond the city that gives the city point and the possibility of justice. As Kierkegaard intimates, *Fear and Trembling* is a critical commentary upon Hegel's *Philosophy of Right*, which refuses to recognize the incarnation of the divine in the sacrificial laws of the political 'whole'. However, like Augustine in his criticism of the ancient city/empire, Kierkegaard does not thereby downgrade civic, social life; on the contrary he envisions a seamless sociality which at no point sacrificially negates itself. Moreover, he also repeats a Dante-esque concern with the intersection of city and gender, appearing to foreshadow Luce Irigaray's contention that religion has too often been a

male substitution of transcendent difference (and pleasure) for sexual difference (and pleasure). Yet perhaps like her also, he intimates a possible surpassing of *this* either/or. For the sacrifice of the woman is a political offering to
the city, or else a metaphysical offering to the melancholically recollected
ideal forms. This perennial patriarchal gesture *cannot* be the way to the
God of eschatological promise. Thus Kierkegaard has shown just why
Abraham's founding patriarchal gesture was not only (un)founding, but also
(anti)patriarchal in a unique fashion.[48]

In the Abraham story one sees how the ultimate vertical rupture of faith is
supposed transcendentally to found and guarantee the continuity of ethical
life, which is the life of the city. Only when we persist in continuity is salvation
realized, but sustaining this achievement requires a constant reckoning with
the unknown, a faith in the continued possibility of this continuity, despite
all disasters. Thus only those forever prepared to surrender their desire and
their beloved are ready for the married life, just as for Plato only those concerned with a vision beyond the city are fit to rule it. Kierkegaard's figure for
this strenuous synthesis is the 'leap of faith': a balletic movement in which
the return to the ground from an upwards leap is converted at once and without pause into a calm and horizontal walk, so that at a physically unreachable
extreme all trace of the leap would be obliterated, and it would attain the
purely transcendental status of the vertical suspension – every bourgeois
walk would consummate, in every instance, an acrobatic feat. Precisely, as
Kierkegaard quips, 'the sublime in the pedestrian'.[49] That performance
from which Kierkegaard was himself tragically excluded, either by his own
lack of faith, or else by Regine Olsen's premature re-engagement.[50]

The third respect in which Kierkegaard incorporates rupture, concerns his
account of original sin. We *cannot* of ourselves 'decide' in favour of the ethical
repetition, because we are always already within sin: that is to say, within a
perverse repetition that undoes repetition and induces self-enclosed anxiety.
We are inevitably prey to the idioms and examples of despair, for sin 'is its
own presupposition',[51] forever begun, yet always begun *as* sin, not by virtue
of any extraneous cause. If we cannot, in consequence, 'decide' for salvation,
it is rather a case of discovering that we are already within the genuine repetition. The truly virtuous life is made possible by the saving event of the
Incarnation, yet this, in Kierkegaard, is almost equivalent to the claim that
virtue, like sin, must presuppose itself. For virtue is defined as nothing other
than the paradoxical identity of eternity with time, permitting continuity
within time, and if this means that a past moment (the event of the paradox
in Christ), is constitutive of the possibility of virtue (whereas Socrates effaced
himself before the recollected Good), this is not at all to say that some particular past history must be *recollected*. On the contrary, according to Kierkegaard's extraordinary claim, we cannot maintain that *any* actual detail of
Christ's life is of final relevance for faith, other than the bare formality of
these three facts: he was born, was an outcast, died. This homeopathic reduc-

tion (salve against philological 'disproofs' of the gospels) constitutes a necessary 'destruction of the historical by the historical', since true historicity
resides in a suspended 'moment' that has already been, but is again, and
again ceaselessly repeated and postponed.[52] However one-sided and *possibly*
apolitical we may find this Christology, Kierkegaard's main point is that it is
the 'how' of Christian process, the 'style' of Christian life that is decisive, and
not propositions concerning past facts, which always invite a probabilistic
and speculative reduction.

Faith is not a decision but a gift. Herein lies the key to the way in which the
religious 'suspension of the ethical' appears somehow to recapitulate and
redeem 'the aesthetic'. Despite it being the case that the gift of faith must be
appropriated through ethical decision (revealing his continuing pietist preoccupation with sanctification), Kierkegaard denies that those who existentially live the Christian life, or preachers who expound it from pulpits,
present the truest *vision* of this life.[53] This is done better by poets, who are
aesthetically suspended from the continuum (i.e. subject to melancholia),
and reinvent Christianity as though it were their own fiction (the procedure
Kierkegaard himself explicitly follows in *Philosophical Fragments*). Hence
Kierkegaard's spokesman for ethical immediacy in *The Sickness unto Death*,
Anti-Climacus, who speaks on behalf of 'owning' one's decisions in one's own
proper voice, and not retiring behind them with aesthetic irony, is himself,
through an irony not underlined – in contrast to the endless, and apparently
unmasked injunctions, to read the 'aesthetic' authorship ironically in favour
of the religious/ethical – Kierkegaard's own poetic projection of a person he
would like to be. If the usual, advertised irony devalues the aesthetic expression in favour of an unstated 'inward' content, then this non-advertised irony
(we are told that Anti-Climacus is an 'ideal' mask, but no irony in relation to
his ethical-religious advocacy is pointed up) reverses the usual effect of irony
by situating the fissure that divides apparent from real meaning, not between
exterior expression and reserved 'intent', but rather between the content of
expression and its form. Where the *fictional* content, as with Anti-Climacus,
sides with ethical immediacy and interiority (in the non-Cartesian sense of
being 'within' a repeated process), then the ironic victor is (ironically) the
aesthetic mask itself. And then no longer does the 'aesthetic' enclose a private,
demonically self-enclosed private theatre; on the contrary, its excess with
respect to the ethical continuum regards the priority of projected vision (that
is, faith) over actual performance. This is none other than the religious suspension, which Kierkegaard describes, in contrast to 'aesthetic' fictions, as
'the illusion that comes after knowledge'.

In this way the aesthetic rupture of the self-possession of the subject, its
disintegration into a series of masks, is baptized and justified as a figure for
justification by faith alone. This Lutheran excess is of course the original
guise for the discontinuous sublime vision that transcendentally undergirds
the redeeming ethical *continuum*.

From these three instances we may conclude that Kierkegaard ascribes to no simple belief in the integrity of decision or of self-recognition in deciding. Our decisions are preinscribed in conditions of innocence, sin and redemption, which no single person invents. And yet, what is preinscribed here is the constant necessity for the event of decision. It happens . . . that we decide. This preinscription of subjectivity within the text, such that the marks of the text are also speaking 'characters', articulated through the *activity* of mimetic repetition, is increasingly admitted by Derrida and his followers, and in another fashion by a Lacanian like Slavoj Žižek.[54] Yet does not this admission undermine the pure transcendental character of their sublime discourse? Its freedom from the taint of wager? If we are always already within the event of decision, then we can never unproblematically claim to see what is decided behind our backs. We cannot, especially, 'see' that there is no finite/infinite, determinate/indeterminate proportion, which the tradition called 'analogy' and Kierkegaard temporalizes as 'repetition'. Instead, we can only 'characterize' the determinate/indeterminate, 'sublime' relationship, which includes 'acting it out', either as monism in which the infinite process is indifferent to finite instances (which 'stand in' categorical univocity, and therefore are not true 'moments') which it constantly negates – in the line of Eleatic denial of motion, despite its Heraclitean espousals. Or else as transcendence (reinscribed through a working through the sublime) in which finite moments are absurdly repeated as 'eternity'.[55]

To stress 'characterization' in this fashion may appear to confine us within the illusion of the 'present' decision, and return us to pre-Freudian naivety. By way of riposte, however, it can be suggested that poststructuralist attempts to arrive at a final, transcendental reading of the determinate/indeterminate ratio (as aleatory) which are supposed to rise above or ironically point beyond subjective decision, thereby risk lapsing back into *theoretical* presence. Between the presence of decision and the presence of 'pure' contemplation, how shall we decide? We do have to appear to decide, even if this decision is really taken for us. But the choice for immanentist (in)difference is a choice for the annihilation of significant choice, and thereby a nihilistic variant of melancholic recollection of the 'past' eternal reality. By contrast, if we persist in choosing, or 'identifying' ourselves, and do not refer backwards the excess of our choosing, but remain with its superaddition, then we choose transcendence. This, for Kierkegaard, who finds the exceptional everywhere, is just ordinary, but constitutively 'human' choice.

It has been shown that Kierkegaard did not desert the critical ontological *a priori* of repetition in order to rediscover God and the subject, but rather incorporated the God/subject ratio as his construal of that *a priori*. However, this *a priori* remained always an impure one, since in contrast to the poststructuralists he admitted only pseudo-transcendental claims, always contaminated by decision. That is to say, by ineliminable transcendental subjectivity inscribed by the text within the text. Kierkegaard concedes that there can 'legitimately', for merely universalizing, philosophic law, be another choice, a choice against choice for immanentism.[56] Yet if it happens to us that we continue to choose at all, then this is the choice of faith.

Notes

Unless otherwise stated, references to Kierkegaard's works are to the Princeton collected edition edited by Howard V. Hong and Edna H. Hong. All works listed without an author are by Kierkegaard.

1 By no means all its exponents would accept this designation, which appears to tie a stance to a period.
2 See my essay, 'Problematizing the Secular: the Post-Postmodern Agenda', in *The Shadow of Spirit*, ed. Phillipa Berry and Andrew Wernick (Routledge, London, 1992).
3 See J.-F. Lyotard, 'What is Postmodernism?', in *The Postmodern Condition* (Manchester University Press, Manchester, 1986), 71–82, and 'Defining the Postmodern', with 'Complexity and the Sublime', in *Postmodernism: ICA Documents*, ed. Lisa Appignanesi (ICA, London, 1989), 7–10, 19–26; 'The Sublime and the Avant-Garde', in *The Lyotard Reader*, ed. Andrew Benjamin (Blackwell, Oxford, 1989), 196–212.
4 This is probably why he cites Leibniz as 'the only modern philosopher who had an intimation' of the replacement of recollection by repetition: 'Repetition', in *Fear and Trembling/Repetition*, 131.
   The suggestions of the footnote in the Hong edition make little sense. For Heraclitus, see *Fear and Trembling*, 123. On repetition in Kierkegaard see *Repetition*; 'Johannes Climacus', in *Philosophical Fragments/Johannes Climacus*, 170–172; *Concluding Unscientific Postscript*, trans. David F. Swenson and Walter Lowrie (Princeton University Press, Princeton, NJ, 1974), 84, 110, 143, 194, 222, 235ff., 471; *The Concept of Anxiety*, 18. Also, of course, the whole of *Fear and Trembling*.
5 Gilles Deleuze, *Différence et Répétition* (PUF, Paris, 1968), 13–19, 126–128, 19.
6 See *Johannes Climacus*; *Concluding Unscientific Postscript*, 176ff. There is probably room for argument as to how far Kierkegaard's notions of selfhood are akin to the more 'romantic' of German speculative thinkers, for example Friedrich Schlegel. However, Kierkegaard considered that Schlegel's irony was exercised in the interest of disentangling the empirical 'I' from a Fichtean, eternal 'I': all authorship had to be 'retracted' so that historical actuality would make room for a self-created actuality. Whether or not this is accurate with regard to Schlegel, it underlines the point that Kierkegaard does not himself employ irony to protect some 'inward' point of contact with the eternal; even Socratic irony he will ultimately find too complicit with such a notion. See *The Concept of Irony*, 275–277, on Schlegel and Tieck.
7 *Johannes Climacus*; *Philosophical Fragments*, trans. David Svenson (Princeton University Press, Princeton, NJ, 1971), Chapter 2, 28–45; *Concluding Unscientific Postscript*, 'Truth is Subjectivity', 169–224.
8 *Concluding Unscientific Postscript*, 112, 169ff.; *Johannes Climacus*, 169–171.
9 See Philippe Lacoue-Labarthe, 'The Caesura of the Speculative', in *Typography* (Harvard University Press, Cambridge, MA, 1989), 214.
10 Lacoue-Labarthe, 'Typography', in *Typography*, 43–138.
11 *Concluding Unscientific Postscript*, 112, 169ff.; *Johannes Climacus* 169–171.

12 *Concluding Unscientific Postscript*, 280–285 and 169ff., 179, 288. See also *Johannes Climacus*, 171–172; *Philosophical Fragments*, 27, 53, 90–93; *The Concept of Anxiety*, 84–90.

13 On language, mediation and expression, see *Johannes Climacus*, 168. Although Kierkegaard says little elsewhere about language, this passage indicates his fundamental concurrence with Hamann (whom he explicitly admired) and Herder's view of understanding as external, linguistic construction, a view which avoids both empiricism and aprioristic idealism. Kierkegaard develops a kindred philosophy in other terms, often substituting 'fictional possibility' for 'language'.

On 'inwardness' see *Concluding Unscientific Postscript*, 182, 184–185, 216–218, 232ff., 247, 254–255; *Johannes Climacus*, 169. Kierkegaard's account of the *political* connotations of inwardness make it even clearer that it does not designate a 'modern' isolated interiority: on the contrary, 'interiority' is a concomitant of being 'within' a socially recognized position in relation to others, characteristic of a prebourgeois 'organic' society. This positioning permits 'distance' between individuals, and so a reflective relation to self, whereas lack of distance and established relations leads not only to mere egoistic self-seeking, but also mass consent to ideas without individual appropriation resulting in 'pointless externality' – that is to say a situation in which the individual has a 'liberal' *indifference* to social relations. It lacks that 'deep inward decency that decorously distances the one from the other', *Two Ages*, 63.

It should however be pointed out that Kierkegaard's political attitude is highly ambiguous and strenuous: though the abolition of organic hierarchy is regarded by him as a disaster, modern liberal society has the capacity to force people to turn away from the consolations of 'Christendom', and from earthly teachers and overlords, towards a direct dependence on Christ, the one teacher who is not effaced by his own message (*Two Ages*, 108). In this essay I am trying to show that this dependence in fact implies a new pedagogic/social practice which, while being linked only to a transcendental, not a humanly embodied authority, nonetheless incorporates the 'relational distancing' of which Kierkegaard speaks in relation to traditional organicism, and effectively 'democratizes' heroic virtue. This appears to have the potential of a social alternative to either 'the past' or 'the present' age, and accordingly to surpass the idea of an apocalyptic opportunity for individual religious redemption. Yet whether or not Kierkegaard envisaged such a radical dimension to his political advocacy is not clear: though he was no proponent of a return to absolutism, he seems to imply a somewhat Lutheran resignation to the disenchanted egoism and massification of 'the present age'. On the other hand, he becomes more and more critical of a Lutheran denigration of 'works' that has encouraged 'cheap grace' (Bonhoeffer's Kierkegaardian lineage is transparent here; he even seems to conserve the same ambiguity I am seeking to delineate) and thereby immured the world in its unredeemed wordliness. Kierkegaard's 'interiority' is inherently relational and linked to a continuous, 'ordinary' love of the neighbour (even if this is always transcendentally accompanied by a 'prior' faith, the vision of the possibility of love: *Works of Love*, trans. Howard and Edna Hong, (Columbia University Press, New York, 1962, 33)) yet it does not appear consistently to extend to genuinely *socio-political* relations. Nonetheless, to present Kierkegaard, as does Bruce Kirmmse, as an anticipator of a characteristically American Protestant (i.e. Reinhold Niebuhr) recommendation of liberal democracy on the grounds of a Lutheran sundering of 'the two cities', is to overlook all that is interesting and subversive in Kierkegaard's thought. (Kirmmse is nonetheless useful for positioning Kierkegaard in a political and intellectual milieu quite specific to Denmark: see Bruce H. Kirmmse, *Kierkegaard in Golden Age Denmark*,

Indiana University Press, Bloomington, 1990). For a 'political' reading of Kierkegaard that is much more appropriately nuanced and oblique, see Gillian Rose, *The Broken Middle* (Blackwell, Oxford, 1992).

14 On *inter-esse*/interest, see *Concluding Unscientific Postscript*, 279: Here Kierkegaard explains why, since thought occupies the medium of possibility which does not mirror the actual and is not precisely the true possibility of the actual (which can never be recaptured) such that it is always 'between being', it can only be 'interested', i.e. a manifestation of a subjective, 'fictional' preference. On repetition in nature, see 'Supplement' to *Repetition*, 302–305, 322.

15 See John D. Caputo, *Radical Hermeneutics* (Indiana University Press, Bloomington, 1987). Chapter 1, 'Repetition and *Kinesis*', 11–35.

16 'Morality is character, character is something engraved ($X\alpha\rho\alpha\sigma\sigma\omega$) ... character is inwardness', *Two Ages* 77–78.

17 As for Kierkegaard, so already in the Renaissance, *dance* became a figure for uniting the idea of motion, even apparently random motion, with the ideas of harmony and order, as best exemplified by Sir John Davies' astounding late Elizabethan poem 'Orchestra', where the new cosmology is one evident context. See *The Oxford Book of Sixteenth Century Verse*, ed. E. K. Chambers (Oxford University Press, Oxford, 1970), no. 385 and especially p. 756: 'Wherein that dancer greatest praise hath won/Which with best order can all orders shun.'

18 *Philosophical Investigations*, 28ff.; *Concluding Unscientific Postscript*, 74ff.

19 See, especially, *The Concept of Irony*, 101–102; *Johannes Climacus*, 166–172; *Concluding Unscientific Postscript*, 75.

20 *Philosophical Fragments*, 54–60.

21 *Philosophical Fragments*, 54–67.

22 See, especially, *Repetition*, 136ff.

23 *Fear and Trembling*, 15–16.

24 *Fear and Trembling*, Problema III, 82–93; *Concluding Unscientific Postscript*, 257.

25 See *Concluding Unscientific Postscript*, 232, 257, 311; *Fear and Trembling*, 39–41, 82–123; *Repetition*, 162–163. In the last-cited *locus* from the *Postscript*, Kierkegaard affirms the unity of the transcendentals in Being: 'the true and the good and the beautiful belong essentially to every human existence, are unified for an existing individual not in thought but in existence.' The true and the beautiful do not, therefore, simply represent 'phases', and earlier on the same page Kierkegaard has declared that 'the poetic' belongs intrinsically to 'a human form of existence', and that 'the unification of the different stages of life in simultaneity is the task set for human beings'. It can be suggested that, while 'the religious' for Kierkegaard exceeds the scope of the three philosophic transcendentals, it is also the true condition for their integration: the religious alone completes the ethical, and does so by 'bringing back' the poetic/aesthetic in a higher guise: see my account of *Fear and Trembling* below.

For a penetrating analysis of three modes of repetition that correspond closely to Kierkegaard's three stages (though without any explicit parallel being intended), see Regina M. Schwartz, *Remembering and Repeating: Biblical Creation in Paradise Lost* (Cambridge University Press, Cambridge, 1988), 91–111. Here Satanic repetition seeks exact ('aesthetic') recurrence in order to achieve an impossible, perfect revenge; this turns out to be only attainable in the mode of eternal confinement to the empty *gesture* of destruction, which in relation to the power that gives being, must be forever thwarted of the slightest attainment. By contrast Adamic repetition (ethical) is prepared to turn away in mourning and repentance from the losses of the past. And yet Schwartz glimpses some Miltonic inkling of a salvific repetition ('religious') in Satan's rebellious non-resignation to loss: redemption involves restoration (even Nietzschean 'eternal return') of every moment, though no longer for vengeful purposes. This chapter is theologically and philosophically suggestive in its linking of Augustinian, Kierkegaardian, Freudian and Nietzschean thematics.

26 Kierkegaard declares that the contention of 'offended' reason that the Paradox (the Incarnation) is absurd, is only an 'echo' of the contention of the Paradox that *Reason* is absurd: that is to say, absurd because it fails to see that the dependence of thought on recollection of the moment involves it in the inescapability of 'fictional' decision, and the constitutive belonging of the historical moment of decision to the concept itself (here Kierkegaard is *at one* with Hegel). In seeking to evade this 'absurdity', it nonetheless *succumbs* to it by pretending it can eliminate the occasion of thought, and convert the moment into eternal, observable 'presence'. See *Philosophical Fragments*, 65; also *Concluding Unscientific Postscript*, 183: 'the fact that the truth is objectively a paradox shows in its turn that subjectivity is the truth.'

Readings of Kierkegaard as a simple fideist altogether overlook the point that it is primarily reason, not faith, which is 'absurd' and 'paradoxical'.

Another nuance in 'by virtue of the absurd' is suggested by the opening passage of the 'Eulogy on Abraham' in *Fear and Trembling*, 15: 'if a vast never appeased emptiness hid beneath everything, what would life then be but despair?... But precisely for that reason it is not so.'

27 *Concluding Unscientific Postscript*, 277: 'the assertion that everything is in motion means that there is no motion.'

28 *Either/Or*, Part I, 285–445. Here Kierkegaard is distinguishing between 'ethical' repetition, which is resourceful variation within 'sameness', and 'aesthetic' repetition, which seeks to repeat the delight of novelty by passing to a new instance. (Although the desire for *exact* reproduction of the instant is *also* aesthetic repetition, in its melancholic guise.) The first is supremely 'marriage'; the second, 'seduction'. See also *Concluding Unscientific Postscript*, 254–255, where Kierkegaard contrasts 'the craving of the life-weary for diversion', with that 'change in the same [which] is inwardness'.

Obviously, this is the point at which it would appear most plausible to attempt a deconstruction of Kierkegaard: the distinction of 'variation in the same' from 'the same in variety' can only be maintained on the basis of a clear distinction between what lies on the side of the subject experiencing, and what lies on the side of the experience undergone. That is to say, why is 'the seducer' not subjectively variegated and repeated through his seductions? Why is he necessarily life-weary? And conversely, why is the same that is variegated not *identical* with 'various things' that nonetheless in some fashion manifest 'the same'. The distinction undergirding Kierkegaard's morality here does seem to depend upon a residual affirmation of ontological 'identity'.

This may be conceded, and yet one could still argue that, where every moment is equally arbitrary and equally valuable or valueless, as with poststructuralist levelling, then the resultant attitude of critical 'indifference' *does* fix the subject in the monotonous and jaded density of 'the seducer'. To avoid this, it would require that 'the many experienced as one' be balanced by 'the one experienced as many', a discovery of depth in *some* moments, which would involve discrimination and limitation of 'the many' in qualitative and quantitative terms. Nevertheless, it remains unclear why, critically speaking, 'the manifold in unity' bears the freight of the ethical, and 'unity in the manifold' does not: here Kierkegaard's exclusive obsession with the erotic example (which for him of course involves the moral supremacy of monogamy) arguably unbalanced his general ethical and ontological conclusions. And while I have just delineated a degenerate form of 'unity in variety' (which 'externalizes' repetition), could one not conceive also a degenerate version of variety in unity, in which the moment, the performance, the beloved object or person became *so fragmented* by the subject (knower/performer) as to lose all 'identity' in the face of his repetitive virtuosity, thereby dissolving into a mere emanation of his being?

29 *Fear and Trembling*, 45; *Concluding Unscientific Postscript*, 225ff., 232.

30 *Concluding Unscientific Postscript*, 225ff.; 'Judge for Yourselves!', in *Judge for Yourselves/For Self-Examination*.

31 See *The Concept of Anxiety*, Introduction, 9–14.

32 *Johannes Climacus*, 155.

33 This remark is certainly not intended to pre-empt a detailed comparison of Kierkegaardian repetition with Freudian repetition in *Beyond the Pleasure Principle*. In the latter the link of repetition with the sublime, 'pleasure beyond pleasure', is also conserved; it could be argued that both Kierkegaard and Freud realize the 'normality' and necessity of repetition, whereas traditionally it was associated only with the obsessive fixations of lunatics – for example by Edmund Burke, who cites insane repetition under 'the infinite', and 'the infinite' in turn under 'the sublime'. See Edmund Burke, *A Philosophical Inquiry into the Origins of our Ideas of the Sublime and the Beautiful*, Part II, viii. (From which it is apparent that the *topos* 'repetition', besides the *topos* 'anxiety', lies adjacent to 'the sublime' before Kierkegaard. On Anxiety see n. 37, below.)

34 *Concluding Unscientific Postscript*, 225ff.; 545–554. Despite Kierkegaard's statement in the *Philosophical Fragments* that, whereas Christ (unlike Socrates) is himself permanently part of his message, other teachers only stand in a Socratic, maieutic role to the truth which is Christ, other passages seem to suggest that Christ, as transcendental moment, only *is* through repetition, and so through communication. Indeed, were this not so, then Christ would be reduced to a recollected truth. Thus, although the human teacher effaces himself before Christ, and so allows the pupil his own particular act of appropriation, the repetition enacted by the pupil can only repeat/imitate Christ as communicated. An intersubjective dimension to repetition is essential here, and yet Kierkegaard never quite makes this explicit. There may after all be a residual individualism in his thinking at this point, which concentrates too exclusively upon repetition within the life of a single person. This may in turn be related to Kierkegaard's preference for 'variety in the same' over 'the same in variety': see n. 28, above.

35 *The Concept of Anxiety*, 41–46, 61.

36 *Journals: A Selection*, ed. Alexander Dru (Oxford University Press, London, 1938), 346.

37 See Burke, *A Philosophical Inquiry*, Part I, vii; Part IV, v–vi.

38 See *Repetition*, 155, where Anxiety finds a characteristic home, like the sublime sensation, 'in a mountain region', and *The Concept of Anxiety*, 61, where Kierkegaard says: 'Anxiety may be compared with dizziness: he whose eye happens to look down into the yawning abyss becomes dizzy.' A glance at Mrs Radcliffe's novels, especially *The Romance of the Forest* will confirm the pre-Kierkegaardian link between the psychology of anxiety and the aesthetics of sublimity. The mediating term between the two is 'suspense'. The sublime sensation arises before an abyss, a gulf, an ultimate edge, an interval without apparent end; before this suspension we must remain, temporally, 'in suspense', and so (ontologically) 'anxious'. There is also an evident echo of the Kantian contrast of the beautiful with the sublime, and association of the latter with the noumenal 'Idea', in Kierkegaard's description of the man fascinated from childhood by the Abraham story: 'for what occupied him was not the beautiful tapestry of the imagination, but the shudder of the

idea': *Fear and Trembling*, 9. However, the ideal of the 'author' of this work, Johannes de Silentio, is clearly the reconciliation of the sublime with the beautiful: 'To exist in such a way that my contrast to existence constantly expresses itself as the most beautiful and secure harmony with it – this I cannot do' (50). This ideal is 'the sublime in the pedestrian' – see below.

39 *The Concept of Anxiety*, 155–163; *The Sickness unto Death*.

40 This is clear because the Socratic stance, Religiousness A, remained captivated by 'recollection', which is the source of fixation in a merely 'aesthetic' stage.

41 *Concluding Unscientific Postscript*, 543.

42 *Concluding Unscientific Postscript*, 21; *The Concept of Anxiety*, 123–135; *The Sickness Unto Death*, 104–107: here 'eternity' is defined as 'the essential continuity' and the ethical as the attainment of 'an infinite self-consistency', which alone grants us sufficient *impetus* and *momentum* (= 'the moment').

43 *Philosophical Fragments*, 38; *Repetition*, 160; *Fear and Trembling*, 105–106.

44 This is not explicitly stated by Kierkegaard, but would seem to be manifestly the case. Like Schleiermacher, Kierkegaard seeks to define an explicitly 'religious' category in contradistinction to the ethical and poetic, although one which turns out to be a condition of possibility for the full instantiation of the latter two, and of their integration. In *The Concept of Anxiety* (20), Kierkegaard celebrates Schleiermacher as a 'thinker in the beautiful Greek sense' in contrast to Hegel, who was but a 'philosopher on a large scale'. And in the *Philosophical Fragments* Kierkegaard describes the Christian *logos* in terms of a reliance on the 'teacher' – God – not merely for initial assistance in learning (as with Socrates and the Greek *logos*) but for the entire capacity to learn, for one's entire existence. This seems akin to Schleiermacher's 'absolute dependence'.

45 *Fear and Trembling*, 54–55. This issue, however, is complicated: in his Journals, Kierkegaard contrasts ethics as 'custom' (i.e. *Sittlichkeit*) with proper, 'universal' morality, which has appeared twice in history: with Socrates and the Old Testament law: *Journals and Papers*, I, 530–532. And in *The Concept of Anxiety* (18–19), it is claimed that all Greek ethics 'contained an aesthetic factor', and so failed to envisage ethics as the pure confrontation of reality with the ideal, unconcerned with *raising* reality into the ideal. Both these passages sound 'Kantian', but the passage cited in *Fear and Trembling* finds Kierkegaard agreeing with Hegel that from the ethical point of view, 'morality', which concerns only the visitation of absolute imperatives upon the consciences of individuals, is 'a moral form of evil'. (For Hegel a duty reduced to 'sheer inwardness of the will' and lacking any specified context will cease also to have any content: *Philosophy of Right*, trans. T. M. Knox (Oxford University Press, Oxford, 1967), 92.) Thus the ethical 'universality' talked about in this work is one which is inseparable from the ultimacy of the civic community. Only the imperative of faith apparently restores a 'Kantian' supremacy of the individual, although now in terms of an anti-imperative to realize oneself as an exception: *Concluding Unscientific Postscript*, 423.

However, my interpretation of *Fear and Trembling* below will show that to constitute oneself as an exception only 'suspends' the ethical, and concerns a transcendental gesture never actually/already carried out. This gesture does, however, subordinate the city, the totality of ethical laws, as much as individuals within the city, to the divine infinite. Yet the result of this subordination actually turns out to be the *return* of all the individuals who can no longer be sacrificed to the city's future. Kierkegaard's supraethical imperative of faith suspends and then reinstates the ethical in transformed guise as a new social space in which there is room for all desires and all beloved individuals in a harmonious *continuum* (evil is defined for Kierkegaard as negation, and specifically as that which 'lacks continuity':

Johannes Climacus, supplement, 245). Thus the 'religious stage' arguably involves a re-envisaged *Sittlichkeit*, shorn of Hegelian sacrificial subordination of individuals to the civic whole.

To support this view, it can be added that for Kierkegaard religion, *unlike* morality purified of custom (Socratic ethics/Old Testament law), *does* involve the raising, by grace, of the real to the ideal. To be content merely with the 'recollected' vision of one's ideal desire, would be, for Kierkegaard, to remain in Socratic 'Religiousness A'; whereas Christianity involves either the present reality or the eschatological expectation of 'the return' of what is loved. The account of 'The Knight of Faith' who realizes the ideal anonymously in the harmonious and ever-fresh performance of an 'ordinary' life, would seem to be in *continuity* with Hegel's critique of a moral idealism which, in celebrating a perfection 'elsewhere', colludes in the further degradation of the actual: on this see Gillian Rose, *The Broken Middle* (Blackwell, Oxford, 1992).

One should conclude that Kierkegaard invented a third conception of the moral/ ethical which is neither exactly Kantian nor exactly Hegelian.

46 See Slavoj Žižek, *The Sublime Object of Ideology* (Verso, London, 1989), 134–135.

47 *Fear and Trembling*, 54–67. Kierkegaard took the notion of an ultimate suspense (*epoché*) from the Greek sceptics, and says that for them it meant the withholding of assent: *Johannes Climacus*, 261. For Kierkegaard this 'pause' is the transcendental acknowledgement of the non-surpassability of subjective commitment as the mani-festation of 'truth': see *Philosophical Fragments*, 53–54. It also has eschatological as distinct from teleological connotations: in *The Concept of Anxiety* (88, footnote), Kierkegaard declares that St Paul eludes to 'the moment' (Øiblikket) when he says that the world will pass away 'in the twinkling of an eye', i.e. in a transition that takes no time whatsoever. 'The moment is commensurable with eternity', according to Kierkegaard, because 'the moment of destruction expresses eternity at the same moment'. This ultimate suspense/destruction (whose possibility we constantly pass through in time) never 'occurs', because with the eschaton/eternity all 'returns'. Such linking of transcendental destruction (which without pause turns into re-creation) with an ultimate eschatological end lying beyond the teleological moral end, should be connected with the legitimation of the gesture of sacrificial murder in *Fear and Trembling*. As I try to argue below, this only makes sense in terms of the divine economy, where irreversible death never occurs except in a 'transcendental' instant.

48 Luce Irigaray, *Ethique de la Différance Sexuelle* (Minuit, Paris, 1984), 173–199; 'Sexual Difference' in *French Feminist Thought: A Reader*, ed. Toril Moi (Blackwell, Oxford, 1989), 118–133. I am not necessarily suggesting that the *akedah* in the Bible itself can as easily be read in this benign fashion: it may be that Kierkegaard's rendering 'redeems' it.

49 *Fear and Trembling*, 41.

50 At times Kierkegaard seems to say that in pretending to be a deceiver and precipi-tating Regine's marriage to another he has set her free, and protected her from proximity to his own scarred personality, at others that he really intended to marry her, but had to first 'renounce' her to become fit for marriage. In the second case he seems to accuse Regine of precipitant lack of patience; in the first he oscillates between celebration of his 'deception' as an act of faith, secretly incor-porating the 'absurd' conviction that we will get Regine back again, and self-accusation of 'lack of faith', a fixation in 'poetic melancholia' that withholds him from marriage, the *truest* embodiment of paradox and absurdity. In the latter oscillation one sees expressed the tension between faith as enjoyment of the eternal in the passing repeated moment, and faith as eschatological hope for a 'final

repetition'. It would seem that both belong together for Kierkegaard, yet his hesitation suggests that he found it difficult to bring both aspects together within a single vocation. See *Repetition*, and *The Concept of Anxiety*, supplement, 170–171, for evidence of this fundamental uncertainty within a single paragraph: 'If I had had faith, I would have stayed with Regine'; yet a few sentences later Kierkegaard explains how he has saved her from 'initiation' into terrible knowledge – 'my relationship to my father, his melancholy, the eternal night brooding within me, my going astray, my lusts and debauchery'. Kierkegaard's intensely refined scrupulosity still had a Victorian core.

51 *The Concept of Anxiety*, 25–80.

52 *Philosophical Fragments*, 27, and 'The Problem of the Disciple at Second Hand', 124–138. In *The Sickness unto Death* (120, footnote) Kierkegaard seems to criticize the idea in which 'the fallen race has been regarded as reconciled by Christ once and for all'. Of course he is not denying the efficacy of the atonement, but he dislikes any version of this according to which humans are united *en masse* round a 'common idea' which is 'the same' for them all. He accordingly refuses to think of original sin as a 'something' handed on that is prior to individual responsibility, but instead thinks of it as 'repeated anew' in that 'predecision' that constitutes fallen subjectivity. (See also *Concluding Unscientific Postscript*, 475.) A mid-course is steered between Pelagianism and essentialization of 'the sin of the race'. The footnote cited suggests a parallel mid-course with respect to salvation: atonement can only be appropriated if it is 'repeated' in every redeemed individual: its 'once and for allness' is not a substantive 'something' which each individual can 'possess' through mere affirmation; though it is once and for all because it 'has happened', this is also a transcendental moment which keeps on happening, and continues to be 'over' before one is aware of its presence. The identity of Christ with the categorically transcendental 'pass me by' (moment) is one of the trickiest notions in Kierkegaard's *oeuvre*.

53 *The Sickness unto Death*, 78–79.

54 Lacoue-Labarthe, *Typography*, 'Typography', 43–139, and 'The Echo of the Subject', 139–208. See also Jacques Derrida's introductory essay to this volume, 'Desistance', 1–43 and his 'How to Avoid Speaking: Denials', trans. Ken Frieden in *Languages of the Unsayable*, ed. Sanford Budick and Wolfgang Iser (Columbia University Press, New York, 1989), 53–63 and Zizek, *The Sublime Object of Ideology*, 151–233.

55 According to Kierkegaard, just as only Christianity recognizes the temporal 'fleeting' moment, so also, only Christianity allows eternity its due (as the unlimited, infinite repetition), because by hypostasizing the moment as 'eternal presence', the Greeks lost both time *and* eternity: *The Concept of Anxiety*, 84.

56 *Concluding Unscientific Postscript*, 203:

> For the only consistent position outside Christianity is that of pantheism, the taking of oneself out of existence by way of recollection into the eternal, whereby all existential decisions become a mere shadow-play beside what is eternally decided from behind.

> Notice that Kierkegaard considers this immanentistic pantheism to be still within 'Platonism', just as he thinks the contemplative access to the eternal (evading the repeated decision) is still within immanentism: *ibid.*, 507–508.

5

NIETZSCHE AND THE METAMORPHOSIS OF THE DIVINE

Michel Haar
Translated by M. Gendre

> The supremely original matter [*die ursprünglichste Sache*]... the
> *originary* cause [*Ursache*] as *causa sui*, this is the right name for
> the god of philosophy. Man can neither pray nor sacrifice to
> this god. Before the *causa sui*, man can neither fall to his knees in
> awe nor can he play music and dance before this God.[1]
>
> (Martin Heidegger)

To ask about "Nietzsche and the divine" means to assume from the start (an
assumption that remains to be verified) that the famous phrase "God is
dead," however one interprets it, does not put an end to questions about
God, gods, or the divine, but rather raises anew the question of the very
essence of divinity. It assumes that Nietzsche's declared "atheism" is relative
to a particular definition of God. His "atheism" is not concerned with the
simple possibility of God, but rather asserts a distinction between a heavily
conceptualized and domesticated God and a divinity free from the conceptual
weight of metaphysical theology. Nietzsche initiates a questioning, which
makes him, as Heidegger wrote, "the last German philosopher who was
passionately in search of God."[2] As always with Heidegger, the expression
"in search of God" is not an idle phrase but one rigorously coined in a specific
context. The statement is not a psychological conjecture about Nietzsche,
the man; nor is it an allusion to Dionysos (for in those contexts the god is not
searched for but found – or about to be found); nor a reference to some of his
famous sayings, such as "How many new Gods are still possible!"[3] or "Two
thousand years and not one new God!"[4] Rather, the context is that of
The Gay Science (Section 125), where for the first time, before *Thus Spoke
Zarathustra*, the phrase "God is dead" is uttered by a strange character, the
Madman (*der tolle Mensch* – a reference perhaps to Anselm's "*insipiens*"?).
For what does the Madman say, as he lights a lantern at high noon – or
rather what does he shout, while running across the market place? He
should, "I am looking for God, I am looking for God." As for Zarathustra,

his proclamation occurs at the beginning of a long inquiry during which the possibility of a God is not excluded at all. On the contrary, there are several allusions to the possibility of another god: "I like the one who chastises his God because he loves his God" (*Thus Spoke Zarathustra*, Preface, Section 4), "I would believe only in a God who could dance" (*ibid.*, "To Read and Write"), and "Could you create a god?" ("On the Blessed Isles"). One of the so-called "Higher Men," the Old Pope, makes an allusion to this other God that Zarathustra is searching for, when he says to him, "O Zarathustra, you are more pious than you imagine with such unbelief! There is some God present in you that is inspiring you in your impiety. Is it not your piety that prevents you from still believing in God? . . . You have eyes, hands, and lips made from all eternity for blessing." ("Available," "Out of Service").

Whatever Nietzsche's position with regard to God and the divine, it is nothing like the dogmatic and easy atheism of the kind encountered in Diderot or in Sartre. To be sure, the atmosphere surrounding the announcement of the death of God in *The Gay Science* is one of anxiety and terror in the face of a catastrophe of cosmic proportions. It is most certainly not a happy event. For while – at least in Section 125 of the text – God does not simply die, the text does not insist on the fact that this is a crime, a murder. The emphasis is not on human responsibility, even though it is asserted: "God is dead; *we* killed him," but rather on the terrifying and apocalyptic nature of the catastrophe. The ancient God was as sun to the earth. Man split them, tore one from the other and henceforth the earth, detached from the sun, is falling into an infinite night. The earth has no more center, neither intellectual nor sensible light. "What were we doing when we unchained this earth from its sun? . . . It is not night always, night closing in on us?" asked the Madman. This catastrophic event is represented as an unbearable crisis, whose continuance will result in our own death, the death of the human race. Nietzsche insists on the fact that this is a rupture, an event unique in history, but also that it is a transitory, incomplete phenomenon. This event will inevitably complete itself, introducing – after the crisis, after the schism, after the "caesura" (as he calls it) in universal history – a new form of time: "this tremendous event is still on its way,"[5] and again: "the greatest recent event, that God is dead, that belief in the Christian God has become discredited, is already beginning to cast its first shadows over Europe."[6]

But what kind of discredit is this? Can discredit kill? How did God actually die? As we shall see, two simultaneous versions of his death are given in *Thus Spoke Zarathustra*: one that he simply died of sickness; the other that he was killed, that there was an assassination. Both scenarios are spectacular, dramatic, but not in the least tragic. It is the same God who died: the moral God, the God of consciences. The other version of the ancient God, namely the God of metaphysics, of the other world, creator and governor of the universe, did not die in a spectacular fashion. Rather, he wore out and vanished along with metaphysics. Undoubtedly, Nietzsche attached greater importance to the end of morality than to the end of metaphysics. The death of the God of morality necessarily brought with it the death of the God of metaphysics. The God of morality is the one Kant defined as the "ruler of the kingdom of ends," distinguished from the "Author of the world." He is the supreme Judge who rewards and punishes not only at the Last Judgement, but who now and forever "fathoms the loins and hearts," sees into the souls and their intentions, and through His Providence guides the course of the world. It is these moral determinations that in the end have turned against the idea of God. The centuries-old religious practice of the examination of conscience gave birth to a spirit of scientific scruple, which itself engendered a methodological atheism, forbidding appeals to "hidden causes" to explain phenomena, requiring adherence to facts. Nietzsche, who did not particularly believe facts to be sacrosanct (in his day any more than we do in ours), thought that such a moral-scientific atheism, far from destroying the essence of the divine, would liberate it for a rebirth in a new – and as yet indeterminate – direction. In two later and posthumous fragments, which both differ and harmonize, he affirms, without additional precision, the reappearance of God or of a god, and the disappearance of the God of morality:

The refutation of God: finally only the moral God has been refuted.[7]

You call this the self-decay of God: but he is only shedding his skin; he is only casting off his moral epidermis! You will soon see him again, beyond good and evil.[8]

This affirmation obliges us to ask what this God stripped of moral determinations would be like. If a rebirth of God remains possible, is it not because some immemorial, trans-historical, or pre-religious divine dimension subsists? Can this divinity have personal expression, or is Dionysos simply a symbol of the sacred? If this divinity exists outside of any establishment or institution, outside of even any tradition, as a pure possibility, why did Nietzsche call it by the ancient name of Dionysos? What link is there between the Greek Dionysos of *The Birth of Tragedy* and the new Dionysos, the internal Dionysos, who – in Section 295 of *Beyond Good and Evil* – is called "the genius of the heart"? What suggests this continuity in the name of God? Is there a relation between this second Dionysis and Christ as conceived of by Nietzsche, a post-Christian Christ as innocent as Dostoevsky's, or a pre-Christian, quasi-Buddhist, Christ, identified with neither the moral nor the metaphysical God? Is Dionysos a god who has already come, or is he a symbol of the god or the divine still to come? Why is he not simply referred to as the "Nameless One" (*der Namenlose*), as in *Thus Spoke Zarathustra*, the One whom future hymns will name?

The death of god as the self-suppression of bad conscience

Each of the two versions of the death of God in *Thus Spoke Zarathustra* is linked to a symbolic character (of the category of the so-called "Higher Men," who are looking not for a completely new God but for an ideal to replace the old God): the Old Pope who says that he watched God as he died, and the Ugliest man, who says he is the murderer of God.

Through the intermediary of another very nihilistic character, the Enchanter, just where the drama of God's death takes place. The Enchanter is a poet-comedian who parodies and caricatures religious interiority. This character probably contains allusions to Wagner, as the founder of a pseudo-religion. In the manner of a cheap melodrama, the Enchanter acts out a masochistic relationship between God and the guilty conscience, a conscience that suffers for its sins, but wants to suffer even more than it wants to be seen suffering. God, its supernatural partner, is reduced to a purely sadistic divine stare that tortures it for no apparent reason (since the term "sin" is not even mentioned) while watching it suffer. This conscience both adores and detests its torturer: "Why are you still staring at me, you who are eternally hungry for human suffering, why do you strike me down with your divine and cruel eyes?"[9]

This strange God, a Voyeuristic God (recalling the Sartrian "stare"), "Tormentor God" and "hunter" of souls, is not explicitly identified with the Christian God, since he is called "the Unknown God," "Thought, Unnameable". The comedian acts out the soul's despair when God is absent or has disappeared. Suddenly, he is gone and the soul is left with nothing but nostalgia for the continual staring and torment, and regret for the token of love in the pain. The soul would now prefer the company of this "divine tormentor" to its loneliness.

> Disappeared!
> Flown away, even him,
> my last, my only companion...
> my divine tormentor!
> No! Come back, with all your tortures...
> Oh, come back!
> My tears stream
> towards you!
> The last flame of my heart
> flickers towards you!
> Oh, come back
> you, my unknown God, my pain, my last happiness![10]

What is the meaning of this text? Why the *acting out* of this perverse relationship with God? Nietzsche wants to show a moment of extreme crisis in the development of the bad conscience. It has discovered a cause of its suffering outside of itself, a cause whose absence it can then no longer bear. The Enchanter says to Zarathustra: "I played the role of the *Penitent of the Spirit* . . . the man who freezes on contact with his bad conscience." This text represents the passive version of what the chapter, "The Ugliest of Men," presents in its active form: the difficulty for man to accept the absence of a transcendent spectator of his suffering, a spectator whose constant presence is the very target of the assassin of God. Both versions represent the same morbid hypertropy of an interiority that refuses to accept its dereliction. The text also suggests that no one believes this play-acting any more, it cannot even be performed: "The distaste [for your performance] alone is true [*echt*]" says Zarathustra to the Enchanter. The impossibility of presenting God as a hypostasis of bad conscience, the disproportion of such an image, its unbelievable quality, foreshadow the imminent disappearance of such a God.

It is at this point that Zarathustra meets the Old Pope, who tells him that he was the last Pope and served the ancient God to the end. He also tells the story (which Zarathustra will immediately suspect of being a fable, a fiction) of the decline of the Judeo-Christian God: "Hard and vindictive in his youth . . . he ended up growing old and soft and limp and compassionate, more like a grandfather than a father. . . . One day he ended up dying, choked by his excessive pity."

Much earlier ("On Pitying"), this interpretation had been attributed to the Devil, who says: "God died of his pity for men." Why is pity so dangerous, why can it be fatal? For Nietzsche, pity is a shameful glance at the suffering of the other. This glance is bad in itself, because it weighs down the shame of the one who suffers, and then it weighs itself down and falls even lower under the weight of its own shame. "I was ashamed of his very shame when I saw the suffering one suffer" ("On Pitying"). Pity is shame at witnessing a suffering, which is already humiliating. As shame about shame, pity is a paralyzing backwash of subjectivity against itself, a backwash that causes a congestion, a choking. Pity can neither let be the suffering of the other nor assist it by means of what Heidegger calls "*Fürsorge*," so that he might overcome it. "If your friend is sick, give shelter to his suffering, but be a hard bed for him" (*ibid.*). Tenderheartedness belongs to a sentimentality enamored of itself and caught up in itself, so that pity loves itself and its own pitying more than it does the other. When taken to an infinite degree, this tenderheartedness, this suffocation, this narcissism become fatal. Through pity, God's love for men becomes infinite love of self.

This idea of suicide by pity, a self-decomposing of God from a surfeit of good feelings, is not presented by Nietzsche as something to take seriously as an interpretation of the nature of God. Rather, it is a psychologizing, human, all too human, interpretation borne in the mind of the Pope. He does not believe that God could support his own infinite pity. His version gives rise immediately to Zarathustra's ironic, doubting comment: "Did you see that with your own eyes? Surely, it might have happened this way, or another, for when Gods die, they always die several kinds of death." Zarathustra suggests that perhaps the Pope saw nothing, that he invented the whole story. A Pope who had lost the faith discovers that God is not viable, is sick unto death; but the idea that God is but a monster of pity and must die of it only demonstrates weariness and distaste for pity.

The succeeding chapter puts the theme of pity in the foreground once again. This time, pity is the direct cause of the murder. The "Ugliest of Men" wanted to suppress the witness to his shame. He killed him out of hatred, out of resentment for God's pity at his shame. Why is the murderer of God hideous, horribly ugly, without form ("he looked like a man, but had almost no human shape, an unnameable being")? One might think that his ugliness came simply from his shame before God, or his resentment of him. But for Nietzsche, just as all beauty is affirmation, so all ugliness originates in non-acceptance of self. The ugliness of the "Ugliest of Men" comes primarily from ressentiment for himself. He does not love himself; he does not love man; he does not love the world. He becomes a murderer because he cannot bear that an omniscient and always vigilant conscience should know and see constantly the mass of suffering and hatred within him. Thus, the murder is by a sick man, the act of someone unbalanced. There is something mad, something paranoid in the discourse of the murderer of God, a folly with an element of trust – namely, the fact that man, whose being is rooted in ressentiment, must finally deny himself: what man denies in God is in fact his own unbearable essence:

> But he, he had to die [*er müsste sterben*]: he saw with eyes
> that saw *everything*, he saw man's depths and ultimate
> grounds, all his concealed disgrace and ugliness.
> His pity knew no shame; he crawled into the dirtiest
> recesses, this most curious, over-obtrusive,
> overpitying one, he had to die.
> He saw me at all times. I wanted to have revenge upon
> such a witness, or to cease to live.
> The God that saw everything, even man, had to die [*er müsste sterben*].
> Man cannot bear to let such a witness live.[11]

At this point, metaphysics seems to have turned into a bad detective story. The idea that God's lack of discretion, the morbid pleasure he would have in scouring the deepest – necessarily dirty – recesses of the human heart, comes from psychopathology. It is the dysfunctional projection of a persecution complex and a delirium of self-accusation. God is only the hypostasis of a delirious bad conscience, magnified by the metaphysical dimension into a constant presence. What is unbearable about the "divine" look of pity is its metaphysical, tireless, and infallible constancy; that God is endowed with inexhaustible, unflagging attention: "He saw me at all times."

In § 16 of *The Genealogy of Morals*, Nietzsche defines bad conscience as the profoundly morbid state that occurs when the aggressivity of the subject, which a certain development of the social order prevents him from exteriorizing, turns against the Ego. God's murder, the hyperbole of aggression, is the desperate attempt by man, suffering from himself, to get rid of the cause of his suffering. The murder of God reveals the impasse represented by a certain fixation on the very essence of man. Without bad conscience, no humanization, no internalization would exist. But this internalization is now secured, and man must move on to a new stage in which bad conscience is no longer necessary. The hypostasis of bad conscience as God, and the suppression of that hypostasis, are man's clumsy efforts to free himself from his reactive essence. But that reactive essence is already bypassed, already dead. The theme of the death of God and the fiction of his murder are part of a mourning ceremony, mourning which has as its true object the traditional essence of man. Man must overcome the loss of himself, overcome grief for himself, lest he remain enclosed in his former essence. "If we do not make of the death of God a great self-denial and a perpetual victory over ourselves, we will have to pay for this loss."[12] Grief over God's death can only be overcome by a new affirmation, but an evaluative principle other than that of a moral conscience thought of as self-accusation. Nietzsche calls this new principle for evaluating the world as a whole "the innocence of becoming." It implies not only the death of the moral God, but also, as we shall see now, the death of the metaphysical God, that is, God conceived as the leading conscience of the universe, as the operator of universal finalism. The innocence of becoming means the exclusion of universal ends in nature, in the world, as well as in history. "Becoming must appear as justified at every moment, so that it is impossible to devalue it,"[13] justified without recourse to any global completeness or intention, or any "final state." The metaphysical God originated from reactive nihilism, from the post-Platonic denial of becoming (understood as the world of sense, whose "truth" is a "world of affects"), for the benefit of supposedly immutable true world. Totalization, finalism, absolute goodness and immutable truth, identical with God or rooted in God – all these depreciate becoming and relegate it to a passive role in the achievement of the Absolute.

Such a God cannot die a violent death. Does it contain some element of the divine essence that is changing, that is metamorphosing itself? The moral God was personal, yet neutral, "objective" with the pure gaze of total overview. The metaphysical God was simply an impersonal, universal organizing principle. Contrasting with these abstractions, it seems, Nietzsche calls his Dionysos "the genius of the heart" and gives him a secret, furtive, intimate, and totally individual, not to say incommunicable, character. Does this amount to abandoning any idea of a universal divine power, a power gathering all together, implying the participation of all beings, and of which the metaphysical God was an all too rational example? We will see that something of the universal element, something Pan-like, something of the Greek Dionysos, is retained.

The refusal of a God conceived as "universal consciousness of becoming," or as "total sensorium," or as "total process"

The criticism of the idea of God as "total consciousness of becoming" is addressed more to the principle of totalization than to the principle of the absolute supremacy of the consciousness hypostasized as God. The common error among philosophers is to make consciousness a supreme measure, a regulating principle of the living, whereas consciousness is an instrument, a simple organ (of superficial unification) in the service of life, a translation of the necessities of life into simple codes or abbreviations, a "numerical language."

> All philosophers instinctively tend to imagine a total consciousness, a conscious life and a conscious will of everything in existence, a "spirit," "God." But it must be said that such a hypothesis truly makes existence a *monster*; that a "God," a universal sensorium would be sufficient to *condemn* existence... To have eliminated this global consciousness which sets ends and means is our great *relief* – it is that which permits us to be *obligatory* pessimists.... Our strongest objection to existence was the existence of God.[14]

To admit the existence of God as an omniscient consciousness that governs the totality of the world from above and beyond, from the *geometric focal point*, i.e., from a fictional geometric point that serves as the focal point of all perspectives, that imposes an order on the totality, a necessity, a transparent finality – all this amounts to demoting the world because it is tantamount to measuring it against an external quantum. A point of view which from the outside could cast a gaze upon the totality does not exist. Given that there is a totality, it must contain all things including all interpretations that are given of it. Given that there is a necessity, it could not possibly be imposed from outside, like the necessity of the laws of nature, those laws which Descartes's God established as a monarch would in his kingdom. If there is a necessity, it could not certainly be an immanent rational necessity, as is the case in Spinoza. The only "admissible" necessity for Nietzsche would be one that embraces everything, that encompasses all contraries, suffering and joy, creation and destruction, chance and reasonable freedom, chaos and law. The necessity that appears in the idea of the Eternal Return, the "ring" uniting all things, the Divine Ring, a Circle "perfect" in its very defectiveness, *circulus vitiosus deus*, a defectiveness that is nothing else but the impossibility of totalization – this Nietzschean "necessity" is a category without contrary and, in addition, linked to an undecidable. Indeed, it is impossible to say whether this "necessity" is the self-affirmation of becoming, or whether my affirmation is what engenders this necessity; in other words, whether my affirmation inscribes itself in necessity, or whether it makes an originary appeal to it. Such is the ambiguity of the *ego fatum* of *amor fati* (or rather, the ambiguity resulting from the identity of these two contrary formulae).

> Symbol of necessity,
> Supreme constellation of Being,
> Eternal "Yes" to Being,
> Forever I am your "Yes."[15]

In any case, Nietzsche rejects a God who communicates a necessity of becoming while being himself outside of becoming.

> "Necessity" [is not to be represented] in the shape of an overreaching, dominating total force, or that of a prime mover; even less as a necessary condition for something valuable. To this end it is necessary to deny a total consciousness of becoming, a "God," to avoid bringing all events under the aegis of a being who feels and knows but does not *will*: "God" is useless if he does not want anything, and moreover this means positing a summation of displeasure and unlogic which would debase the total value of "becoming." Fortunately, such a summarizing power is missing (– a suffering and all-seeing God, a "total sensorium" and "cosmic spirit" would be the greatest objection to being).[16]

Here Nietzsche intends to refute theodicy by means of two arguments. In the first place, if God were not only omniscient, but also an omnisentient Absolute (absolute sensorium), he would suffer all the pains of the world. But the projection of suffering into an all-powerful sensibility would either annul it (which would suppress the problem of divine compassion) or would give to the suffering a hallucinatory and truly fantastic intensity. Nietzsche reverses the reasoning of theodicy. The existence of God as absolute will and consciousness of the good, as absolute feeling of evil and suffering, cannot diminish the "total" suffering (from a perspective where the suffering would be reconciled by being included within a universal compatibility), but can only intensify it and make it more absurd. There is only one way to exonerate God from evil, and that is to say that he knows nothing of it, that he can do nothing about it, even though he is "power," albeit power devoid of finality. Hence the surprising aphorism,

> Let us separate supreme goodness from the concept of God ... Let us separate supreme wisdom in the same way; it is the pride of

philosophers that has imagined this absurdity . . . No, God is *Supreme Power*. That is enough. From that, everything results, from that results the 'world!'[17]

But – and here comes the second argument against theodicy – a theodicy is in any case impossible a priori, not because, in Schopenhauer's words, the sum total of suffering is greater than the sum total of happiness, but because such a totalization does not make sense. There is no "process of the whole," there is no making compatible with the "whole," because there is no "whole."[18] The world is neither a system nor an organism. The depth of Chaos that it includes cannot be reduced or reabsorbed, no matter what the point of view.

The refusal to hypostatize finality into God, the criticism of a universal, transcendental teleology, is each time simply a corollary to the rejection of totalization. The finalistic, providential interpretation of the phenomena of nature, of history, or of individual existence appears to the scientific spirit – trained and brought up in the ascetic ideal of probity inherited from Christianity – as a mystification, as an edifying fiction whose goal is to explain everything, as being part of a total plan of God.

> Considering nature as if it were a proof of the goodness and the protection of God; interpreting history for the glory of divine reason as a permanent witness of the moral finality of universal order; interpreting one's own experiences according to the meaning given to them long ago by the pious, as if *everything* were merely aptitude and illustration of love and as if *everything* were conceived in order to lead to the salvation of the soul: this is what has come to an end, from now on, this is what consciousness has against itself.[19]

The paradox that Nietzsche underscores in *The Genealogy of Morals* is that this "atheism" of interpretations is the self-destructive consequence pure and simple of applying the Christian ideal of rigorous and unconditioned truth.

Nihilism as "psychological state" is thus for Nietzsche the manifestation of an enormous lie, of disillusion, and, ultimately, of despair in the face of the crumbling of universal meaning, which results from the absolutization of becoming taken as a whole by means of logic and the moral order. "Psychological nihilism manifests itself when one has presupposed a *totality*, a *system*, even an *organization* within facts and between *all* facts."[20]

The excessive meaning turns into an excess of meaninglessness. "The soul longing for admiration and veneration," which draws its strength and its self-confidence from its relationship with the whole, which thinks of itself as "a mode of the divine," loses "the faith in its own value"; it feels no longer connected to anything, no longer guided by anything, no longer held to anything. "We have arrived at the feeling of the nonvalue of existence, when we have understood that it can no longer be interpreted as a whole either with the aid of the concept of 'end,' or with the aid of the concept of 'unity,' or with the aid of the concept of 'truth' "[21] (in the sense of a world both true and moral in itself). The moment of the complete dedivinization of the world, the complete dissociation of becoming and the logico-moral divine, constitutes the gravest crisis in the history of humanity. With the disappearance of the true world, the apparent world initially loses all consistency.

The reaffirmation of the divine beyond such a crisis is everything but evident. Man has several possible "outcomes" – actually, however, all dead ends. He can wallow in pessimism and in a new "Buddhism," in forms of indifference and frivolity; he can take refuge in a mediocre search for happiness, as does the "Last Man," or, again, in the adoration of the mere surfaces of things, in the admiration of anything whatsoever lacking significant depth (which is simply a version of reactive nihilism, the nihilism of ressentiment against excess of meaning). "We will no longer take anything to heart, we will choose the mask as supreme divinity and as redeemer."[22] Nietzsche prophesies a long reign for the substitutes of the dead God, which since the nineteenth century have been Science, Progress, and Happiness for All. According to Nietzsche's prophecies, the nihilistic crisis (with such terrifying symptoms as, for example, the decomposing of intra-individual unity and the economic and political struggles for planetary domination) will last two centuries, the twentieth and the twenty-first!

One might ask to what extent the doctrine of the Eternal Return is itself prisoner to nihilism, caught up in the reactive cycle subsequent to the destruction of the ancient gods. At first glance, the doctrine *seems to reverse* the nihilistic conclusion of the death of God ("Nothing has meaning anymore," because there is no end to becoming, no universal and transcendental goal), by making the contrary affirmation: "All is perfect, divine, eternal."[23] The phrase, according to Nietzsche, is pantheistic, but is not that of the Eternal Return. There is indeed in the Eternal Return a dimension that comes close to pantheism, insofar as the Return is the self-justification at every moment of the world, as good, infinitely precious, infinitely worthy of being affirmed, and completely assured of returning. But Nietzsche expressly rejects the idea of the divinity of the world, or rather of the world as divinity. The world is not a new god. The process is "divine," but it is not guided by divine intentions, nor by the opposite intention to be without goals whatsoever. For we wish at all cost the movement of the world to be "controlled," even if it means that no end could ever be produced. We keep "this nostalgic need to believe that the world is at least at some point similar to that ancient and well-beloved god, that infinite God of unlimited created power."[24] This is precisely Spinoza's nostalgia for *Deus sive Natura*, which wants to believe that "the god of old still lives." For Nietzsche, the world must not be thought of as an infinite substratum, unlimited in extension, eternally new, but eternally repeated, resounding within itself. We must be able to affirm of everything that it is divine without affirming the divinity of the All, without even affirming that there is an All. For there is certainly no All, which would be a subject conscious of all and settling everything. Dionysos, so enigmatic and diversely present in the later texts, most often represents not a god but rather explicitly a *faith* and attitude which Nietzsche calls "a joyous fatalism." "The faith . . . that generally speaking everything is resolved and affirmed . . . this is the faith, the highest possible of all faiths, that I have baptized in the name of Dionysos."[25]

From the revelation of the divine to the naming of a god

In the period of nihilism, all new naming or determination of a god appears provisional, hypothetical, and multifaceted in its formulation. For between the long perishing of the metaphysical moral god and the upsurge of a new meaning of the divine or of the god, the most that can be hoped for is that a space of expectancy remain open, a period of latency and maturation in which, when it is capable of emerging, the new meaning will appear indeterminate and surrounded by many blanks and question marks. The divine undergoes a metamorphosis without reference to any destination and any decision. There is no question of a "controlled" transmutation by any sort of will whatsoever. In the interregnum, when nothing is fixed, when the divine is – as it were – indecisive, free-floating, scattered, the philosopher must above all know how to wait. "We must wait and prepare ourselves to spot the welling up of new springs, prepare ourselves in solitude for strange visions and unexpected voices,"[26] writes Nietzsche in those fragments which also refer to Dionysos. After the death of God, the divine is to be reinvented.[27] It is to be rediscovered according to its own, "wild" apparition that we must not rush to categorize under an already established name and identity. It is obvious that for Nietzsche, Dionysos is only a name for expectancy, and not at all the definitive and final name of God. Despite this name, the god remains "the unnamed god" evoked in *Thus Spoke Zarathustra*, or again the "unknown god," the "ungraspable god" (*Du Unfassbarer*) previously invoked in an early poem (1844). "Oh, you, the ungraspable . . . I want to know you and love you."[28]

The name Dionysos seems the most powerful Nietzsche could find to designate a divinity still to come and a sacred form, both surprising and beyond classification, ever abounding and beyond limit. One must emphasize that the path of polytheism, which he sometimes urges, never leads to any sort of naming. Apollo disappears, forgotten in the Apollonian principle. The ancient Dionysos is dead. No other god is named. The *epoche* of the unique Name seems demanded out of respect for the very force of the experience of the divine. Lack of knowledge of the Name is tantamount to a negative condition for a new blossoming or a free redeployment of the "religious instinct." "The religious instinct experiences a vigorous surge, but rejects with deep suspicion the pacification of theism."[29]

In his later years, after the positivist critique of religion as an aberrant form of causality (in *Human, All Too Human*),[30] Nietzsche forced himself to describe the primordial, elementary, or transcendental conditions of the religious instinct, when it manifests itself outside a determined tradition or revelation. For him, faith and piety rest above all on the feeling of a "necessary link" between all things, of an immanent unity, of an original cohesion of the world that can possibly include transcendent beings. "Piety towards God is piety towards the necessary link between all things and the belief that there exist beings superior to man."[31] Only on the basis of an ancient sacredness predating all revealed faith could a god arise. Contrary to Heidegger, this sacredness resides less in Being itself than in a *fundamental feeling*, the feeling of the necessity of the universal link, the *amor fati*. This is a paradoxical pantheism where it is not the all that is divine, but rather the feeling of the link, or the link itself, and where each thing is sanctified and transfigured insofar as it participates in this link. "In solitude, where I experience all things as necessarily linked, every being is divine for me."[32] The divine character of the cosmic cohesion might well be one of the primitive contents of religious "revelation" taken in its originary indeterminateness as pre-religious, predating every constituted dogma. The indissoluble feeling of a marvelous belonging-together of all beings would be the source of the "religious instinct." "I, in whom the religious instinct – namely the one giving rise to the shape of a god [*gottbildende*] – is sometimes set in motion inappropriately, in how many different ways have I not received the revelation of the divine!"[33] In how many different ways? Nietzsche remains rather discreet concerning these experiences, which he calls "encounters." But through all the different aspects he describes (joy, surprise, the uncanny, the *stopping of time*, and *instantaneousness* "I have experienced the sight of so many things in these moments out of time"),[34] the Revelation is that of a link at once supremely necessary and supremely harmonious. "Five, six seconds, no more – suddenly you experience the presence of eternal harmony."[35] This is an almost unbearable, overwhelming feeling of joy, approbation, a feeling "superior to love."

> In his mortal shell man could not withstand this: he must either transform himself physically or die. Clear and indisputable feeling. You have the feeling of contact with nature in its entirety and you tell yourself, "Yes, this is true!" When God created the world, at the end of each day he said, "Yes, this is true, this is good!" *This is no emotion, my friends, this is joy*. You forgive nothing because there is nothing to forgive. You love no longer – oh, this feeling is superior to love. Most terrible is the awesome certainty through which this is expressed, the joy that overwhelms you. If this lasted longer, the soul would not withstand it, it would depart.

And the end of this text is surprising. For Nietzsche talks about "the understanding of the symbol of resurrection." A feeling that "the goal has been reached." The divine appears as a break in ordinary time, an *ecstatic* sight when the veil of interpretations is removed and when the universal link reveals itself to understanding, that is to say, affirms itself with irresistible and unlimited evidence and force. The "saying-yes-and-amen" without measure, without limit (*das und geheure, unbegrenzte Jaund- und Amen-Sagen* from *Thus Spoke Zarathustra*, III, "Before the Dawn") imposes itself before one can even express it. This "yes" is indistinctly the "yes" of man and the "yes" of Being, as in the *Dithyrambs of Dionysos* already cited: "Eternal 'yes' of Being, forever I am your 'yes.'" This is not the revelation of a particular divinity – nor of an unchangeable, divine essence of things that would eclipse what is human – but rather of an irresistible inclusion in Being. For Nietzsche, only moments can contain this "revelation," and that is why it is destined to remain indefinitely wild and untamed, since it is part of no continuity and always appears in the flash and lightening of the moment. On the side of man, let us recall, the Dionysian attitude is defined as "*instantaneous* identification with the principle of life."[36] On the side of the Will to Power, the divine or god is an apogee (one can find several positive definitions), a climactic state of the forces: "'God' as culmination."[37] "The only possibility of retaining any meaning in the concept of God would be to represent God not as the moving force but as the *maximum gradient* of forces."[38] "God" would be a state of perfection of the Will to Power in which the superabundance of forces arrives to an equilibrium with respect to which earlier stages of perfection could later be understood and linked in a *history*: "God" is explicitly named as an "epoch."

But the divine in Nietzsche is not synonymous with a perfection that would preserve itself free of all possible degradation, fallenness or destruction. Supreme perfection includes imperfection, as the highest joy includes suffering. "Perfection is nothing else but the prodigious *expansiveness* of the feeling of power . . . (that would extend so far as wanting obstacles)."[39] Perfection is not in fact an objective state of affairs, but a *Stimmung*, specifically the very *Grundstimmung* of joy. Divine is the moment, *movimentum*, the movement of transcendence in immanence, the *apogee* when joy severs the links, reunites what was sundered, reaches the limits of existence, and without reducing them gathers the negative, evil, suffering, and all forms of imperfection. At this juncture, "The Drunken Song" of the fourth part of *Thus Spoke Zarathustra* must be recalled: "Said ye ever Yea to one joy? O my friends, then said ye Yea also unto *all* woe. All things are linked, enlaced and enamored." And also "All joy wants the eternity of all things, it wants honey, it wants the dregs, it wants drunken-midnight, it wants graves, it wants the consolation of mourners' tears, it wants the gilded splendor of sunset."

The affirmation of the *circulus vitiosus deus* in *Beyond Good and Evil* (Section 56) is only meaningful against the backdrop of the repetition of the transfiguring affirmation of joy, hence against the backdrop not of a temporary leap for joy, but of an "insatiable" call for a *da capo!* issued to existence *such as it was and such as it is.* The joy that renders possible the Eternal Return is thus transformed, to be sure, into a permanent, and in that sense metaphysical, will for repetition. But in itself Dionysian feeling is more the joyful feeling of the *necessity of a universal link* than the will that follows from it. The Dionysian feeling, which is also called "tragic wisdom," is that of the *necessity* of coexistence and mutual relativity of contraries such as perfection/imperfection, joy/suffering, creation/destruction: "the fact of experiencing the necessity of imperfection itself from the superabundance of the form-imposing, Dionysian force."[40] The Dionysian is defined elsewhere as "the great pantheistic participation in every joy and suffering, which blesses and holds as sacred even the most awe-inspiring and enigmatic properties of existence... the feeling of the necessary union of creation and destruction."[41]

Is this not Heraclitus transposed on the plane of feeling? For Nietzsche does not say: "God is night and day, winter and summer, famine and abundance" (Heraclitus Fragment 67), but rather: *the feeling* of this necessary unity of contraries is *divine.*

Does not such a displacement of the divine toward feeling, toward the interiority of man or of the Overman render all the more difficult the encounter with an identifiable and personal god? Isn't the feeling of the divinity of the world tantamount to a blinding and narcissistic projection of subjectivity which sees nothing else but itself in the mirror of the world (evoked by Novalis' disciple to Saïs)? The "unnamed god" of *Thus Spoke Zarathustra* is a "hidden god": the god is "veiled to us because of his own beauty," we read in the hymn called "Before Sunrise." In such a climate, which is so close to pantheism, the god seems to be located everywhere and nowhere. However, in a tone part serious and part humorous, Nietzsche, in his later texts, tells of some strange encounters with his Dionysos. He bears little resemblance to the Dionysos of *The Birth of Tragedy*, clearly he is now a god half Greek, half Asiatic (of the Mysteries), a God of sacred drunkenness at the same time beneficial and cruel, a god of nature. He seems to have experienced a Christian metamorphosis. In the version given in *Beyond Good and Evil* he has become in part a god of interiority. "The genius of the heart" is indeed a god of consciousness, "flute-player, enrapturing the consciousness," whose single message consists in being seductive for the sake of existence. But how does he become seductive? Not because of the attraction for the vital element, the surface appearances or the masks, but by dint of revealing to each one "the hidden and forgotten treasure" he carries in himself. Dionysos is the "tempting god," the "seducing god" inasmuch as he teaches man to discover and to follow what is divine *within himself.* Dionysos is the revealing agent of an internal dimension that makes possible "a new path toward the Yea."

We must stop here for a moment to mark the strange proximity and – at the same time – the distance between this interiority of Dionysos and that of Christ, at least such as Nietzsche describes it in *Antichrist.* For the message of

Christ, in Nietzsche's account a message that was subsequently falsified by Paul and diverted in the direction of ressentiment and the ascetic morals, was only that the "Kingdom of God" resides in the pure interiority of the heart, in the intimate feeling of joy and love. "My kingdom is not of this world" signifies no ressentiment whatsoever toward the world, no negation of the "world" in the ecclesiastical sense. "Negation is something of which it is quite incapable."[42] Christ is deemed to have taught withdrawal from the world of established reality and great institutions. The "Good News" is the affirmation of the internal kingdom of God. "What does the 'Good News' mean? True life, eternal life has been found – it is no longer promised, it is here, it is *within yourselves*: life in love, without exception and without preference, without any feeling of distance."[43] Thence Christ is an antirealist, a "symbolist" par excellence, who does not negate the "world," but who detaches himself from the entire institutional order. "Jesus attaches no importance to anything established: the letter *kills*, everything fixed kills." For him, true "life" is immediate, *internal life*, beyond every formula and every representation. "He only speaks of what is more internal: "life," "truth," "light" are the names that he gives to this internal world."[44] He holds all the rest as inconsistent. He considers every exteriority merely as sign or symbol. "He locates himself outside of any religion, of any idea of worship, of any history, of any science of nature ... of any politics, of any psychology, of all books, of all art."[45] What he calls "the reign of God" is the feeling of transfiguration of all things that produces the total acceptance of *oneself*. Every reality is eclipsed in the face of this feeling of happiness. The Gospel would then be the original sketch for a Buddhist peace – which would be a novelty in the West – and the announcement of happiness on earth, yet outside time and space.

> If I understand something in this great symbolist, it is the fact that he took as realities, as "truths" nothing but the *internal* realities and that he conceived the rest, everything natural, temporal, spatial, historical, as signs, as occasions for parables.[46]

There is a resemblance between Christ thus presented and "the genius of the heart," inasmuch as this genius is an intimate voice, a call (a sort of joyful, non anxiety-ridden *Gewissen*) leading the individual to turn away from the clatter and noisy hubbub of the world, teaching him or her to turn aside and to *divine* himself or herself. For in this rediscovered interiority there is an abyss of strangeness and dispossession, a profound inadequacy that translates – in the description of the Dionysian effect – into uncertainty, frailty, scattering and yet indeterminate hope. "The genius of the heart" – an expression that is used four times in *Beyond Good and Evil* – brings no marginal benefit nor any elaborate doctrine on "spirituality." Most especially, this "genius" *does* not provide us with a god-sent "grace." Everyone is not so much thrown into a state of grace... *fulfilled and oppressed with goods from elsewhere*, as enriched from his own being, renewed in his own eyes, fulfilled, bathing and wafting in a spring breeze, perhaps more uncertain, more tender, more frail, more strewn, but filled with still nameless hopes.[47]

Such a divinity resembles the purely internal Christ inasmuch as the identity proper to the god is dimmed, so to speak, behind this message. In the end, Dionysos is nobody but that voice. This demonic dimension of a "genius" that inspires now fades. He is the "Great Hidden One"[48] without a contour and without worship. The principal element that distinguishes the new Dionysos from Christ is that in the other late texts of Nietzsche, Dionysos is not only associated with an internal affirmation, but appears as the symbol of an unlimited affirmation, the symbol of the sacred character of the *yes* that can only repeat itself infinitely and eternally. Dionysos then means the "saying *yes* to the world as it is, without subtraction, exception, or selection."[49] Such a saying yes includes the acceptance of all deaths. This Dionysos – akin to the Great Pan and a double of creation/disappearance ("under the name Dionysos it is becoming that is experienced in active fashion")[50] – has nothing Christian about him. But is he a god? Do we know what a god is? Is he anything other than the *symbol* for a philolosopheme? Is he anything other than a *lived experience*? Anything other than the one *and* the other, the one *in* the other? "Becoming felt and interpreted *from within*, this would be the continuous creation... of a god."[51]

In a preliminary remark to the reduction of the transcendence of God, Husserl notes in Section 51 of *Ideas*: "A world-god [*Ein mundaner Got*] is evidently impossible," and he adds: "The immanence of God in absolute consciousness cannot be grasped as immanence in the sense of being as experience [*Erlebnis*] – which would be no less absurd."[52] Husserl excludes as absurd that the absoluteness of the phenomenological lived experience and the absoluteness of God could coincide in immanence. But mostly (in the first part of the remark) the immanence of God in the world seems to him as something to be excluded.

For Nietzsche, neither the immanence of a god in the world nor the coincidence of the lived experience and of the divine are absurd. In this he is heir both to the Greek tradition (the Greeks have thought their gods as immanent and as susceptible of appearing under familiar guise in the world) and to a certain mystical tradition, or one of negative theology, that conceives the coincidence of the soul and of the divine principle in a happy *ecstasy*, i.e., in a nontragic fashion and without the annihilation of man. Paradoxically, what Nietzsche calls "tragic" is this ecstasy or this ecstatic coincidence felt in the midst of joy. The paradoxical theme of "tragic joy" exalts a sacred link to the world, a *re-ligio* in the strong sense, yet without worship and dogma – a faith, yet one without a creed.

List of abbreviations

The texts most quoted by Michel Haar from the German or the French translations of Nietzsche are:

Kritische Gesamtausgabe Werke, the recently completed edition by G. Colli and M. Montinari, Berlin: Walter de Gruyter, hereafter *K.G.W.*

Oeuvres philosophiques complètes (henceforth *O.P.C.*), also contains the volumes of the *Fragments posthumes*, Paris: Gallimard. It is to this *O.P.C.* collection of Nietzsche's works in French that references are made, especially concerning *La Naissance de la tragédie* (hereafter *N.T.*). Also included is *La Vision dionysiaque du monde* (in *Ecrits Posthumes 1870–73*) – hereafter referred to as *V.D.*

For the posthumous fragments the other edition used by the author is Kröner, edited by Alfred Baümler (with the title, *Unschuld des Werdens*, The Innocence of Becoming, in which a different ordering and numbering system has been followed than the one adopted in *K.G.W.*), in Kröners Taschenausgabe, Stuttgart: Alfred Kröner Verlag, 1956, 2 volumes, hereafter *K.*

The two texts the author uses for *The Will to Power* are:
the German *Wille zur Macht*, Kröners Taschenausgabe, Stuttgart: Alfred Kröner, 1956, hereafter *W.z.M* (the numbering of the sections of *W.z.M.* corresponds to that of the English translation by Walter Kaufmann);
the French *La Volonté de puissance*, trans. G. Bianquis, Paris: Gallimard, 1948, hereafter *V.P.*

The Gay Science, trans. Walter Kaufmann, New York: Vintage Books, 1974.

On the Genealogy of Morals and *Ecce Homo*, trans. Walter Kaufmann, New York: Vintage Books, 1967.

Beyond Good and Evil, trans. Walter Kaufmann, New York: Vintage Books, 1966.

The Will to Power, trans. Walter Kaufmann, New York: Vintage Books, 1967.

Twilight of the Idols and *The Anti-Christ*, trans. R. J. Hollingdale, London, Penguin Books, 1968.

Human, All Too Human, trans. Marion Faber, Lincoln: University of Nebraska Press, 1984.

Thus Spoke Zarathustra, trans. Thomas Common, New York: The Modern Library.

Notes

1 *Identity and Difference*, trans. Joan Stambaugh, New York: Harper and Row, 1969, p. 72, modified.
2 *Discours du Rectorat* (Rectorial Address), ed. Granel, T.E.R., 1982, p. 12.
3 *K.G.W.*, 17(4), Section 5. See also *Fragments Posthumes*, 15: 272.
4 *Twilight of the Idols*, " 'Reason' in Philosophy."
5 *The Gay Science*, Section 125.
6 *Ibid.*, Section 243.
7 *K.*, 2: 239.
8 *K.*, 2: 337.
9 "The Enchanter," also translated as "The Magician" (see *Thus Spoke Zarathustra*, Section 65).
10 *Ibid.* One would have to wonder why Nietzsche inserts the same melodramatic complaint verbatim for Ariadne. "Does one know who Ariadne is?" See *Dithyrambes de Dionysos, "Lamentation d'Ariane")*"Dithyrambs of Dionysos," 'Ariadne's Lament'), *O.P.C.*, pp. 57–63.
11 "The Ugliest Man" (Section 67).
12 *V.P.*, 2: 133.
13 *W.z.M.*, Section 708.
14 *W.z.M.*, Section 707.
15 *Dithyrambes de Dionysos* ("Dithyrambs of Dionysos"), pp. 70–71.
16 *W.z.M.*, Section 708.
17 *V.P.*, 2: 387; *K.*, 12: Section 168.
18 *W.z.M.*, Section 711.
19 *The Gay Science*, Section 357. Also quoted by Nietzsche in *The Genealogy of Morals*, 3rd essay, Section 2. (Emphasis added.)
20 *V.P.*, 2: p. 46.
21 *Ibid.*, p. 47.
22 *Ibid.*, p. 105.
23 *Ibid.*, p. 13.
24 *V.P.*, 1: 300.
25 *Twilight of the Idols*, "Expeditions of an Untimely Man," Section 49.
26 *W.z.M.*, Section 1051; see also *V.P.*, 2: 374.
27 "It is only after the death of religion that the invention of the divine will take on all its luxuriance," *V.P.*, 2: 379.
28 Quoted by Morel, *Nietzsche*, Paris: Aubier-Montaigne, 1971, 3: 300.
29 *Beyond Good and Evil*, Section 53.
30 See especially Section 111 of *Human, All Too Human*, "Origin of religious worship;" see also *Twilight of the Idols*, "The Four Great Errors," where at the end of section three Nietzsche writes: "The error of spirit as cause mistaken for reality! . . . And called God!"
31 *V.P.*, 2: 234.
32 *K.*, 2: 98.
33 *V.P.*, 3: 379.
34 *Ibid.*
35 *Fragments Posthumes*, XIII, 325 (11 {337}, 1888).
36 *V.P.*, 2: 375.
37 *V.P.*, 1: 252
38 *V.P.*, 2: 294.
39 *V.P.*, 2: 372.
40 *K.*, 2 : 245.

41 *W.z.M.*, Section 1050.
42 *The Anti-Christ*, trans. R. J. Hollingdale, London: Penguin Books, 1990, Section 32, p. 154. Hollingdale translates: "*Denial* is precisely what is totally impossible for him."
43 *Ibid.*, Section 29, p. 151. "What are the 'glad tidings'? True life, eternal life is found – it is not promised, it is here, it is *within you* as life lived in love, in love without deduction or exclusion, without distance."
44 *Ibid.*, Section 32, p. 154. "He cares nothing for what is fixed: the word *killeth*, everything fixed *killeth* . . . He speaks only of the inmost thing: 'life' or 'truth' or 'light' is his expression for the inmost thing."
45 *Ibid.*, Section 32, p. 155. "[He] stands outside of all religion, all conceptions of divine worship, all history, all natural science . . . all psychology, all books, all art."
46 *Ibid.*, Section 34, p. 156. "If I understand anything of this great symbolist, it is that he took for realities, for 'truths,' only *inner* realities – that he understood the rest, everything pertaining to nature, time, space, history, only as signs, as occasions for metaphor."
47 *Beyond Good and Evil* (Section 295): "not full of grace . . . *not enriched and oppressed as though by strange goods*, but richer in himself, newer than before, cracked wide open, blown open and drawn out by a spring wind, more uncertain now perhaps, more delicate, fragile, and broken, but full of hopes that have no names as yet" (stress added).
48 *Ibid.*
49 *W.z.M.*, Section 1041.
50 *V.P.*, 2: 369.
51 *Ibid.*, stress added.
52 Edmund Husserl, *Ideas*, trans. W. R. Boyce Gibson, New York: Collier Books, 1962, note to Section 51, p. 142.

6

HEIDEGGER AND THE PROBLEM OF ONTO-THEOLOGY

John Peacocke

> Religion is something infinitely simple, simple-souled. It is not
> knowledge, nor the content of feeling (for every kind of content
> is admitted at the outset when a man enters into collusion with
> life), it is not duty and not renunciation, it is not a limitation:
> but, within the perfect amplitudes of the universe it is – a direc-
> tion of the heart.[1]
>
> (Rainer Maria Rilke)

What is called Religion? we ask in pastiche of Heidegger's many works and
essays calling upon us to think via the question "What is?": *What is called
Thinking?*, *What is Metaphysics?*, *What is Philosophy?*, he asks. In asking the
question "What is?" Heidegger calls upon us to enter upon a path of thinking
that will lead us to the essence or nature of whatever is under discussion such
that "To think is to be underway".

Our question is "What is called Religion?" and specifically Heidegger's
relationship to such a question. The title of this work could equally, and
with as much justification, be called "What is called Theology?" Both of
these questions serve as reminders and monuments to that which calls us into
a thinking experience with what remains seemingly *un*-thought in Heidegger's
work. Now the un-thought is in each case unique to a thinker and, as such, it
is not a lack inherent in that thinking, so Heidegger informs us in *Was Heisst
Denken?* The un-thought represents a rich untapped vein: the greater and
more original the thinking, the richer the un-thought. These questions that
we ask, above all, stand as signs and indicators to titles of works which
Heidegger did *not* write – perhaps, could not write. This *not* in our expression
"the works Heidegger did not write" represents here not negation and
privation but something fundamentally different in character from either.
That Heidegger did not subject either of these topics to his usual and rigorous
thinking bespeaks of a relationship that was problematic, perhaps even
aporetic.

177

It is my intention in this chapter to call attention to Heidegger's relation-ship to religion and the religious; to question his reluctance, and ultimate refusal, to write a theology. I shall site my discussion within the overall problematic of onto-theology (a problem to which Heidegger devoted consid-erable attention) in the wake of Nietzsche's declaration that "God is dead", and Heidegger's discussion of this proclamation.

Heidegger attempts to "think" the closure of metaphysics and he speaks of "The end of philosophy and the task of thinking". At the forefront of such an "ending" is the "overcoming" or surmounting of the hegemony of reason. Thinking only begins, claims Heidegger, when "we have come to know that reason, glorified for centuries, is the most stiff-necked adversary of thought".[2]

The metaphysics of the West, for Heidegger, finds its culmination in the thinking of Nietzsche whom he designates as "the last metaphysician". Nietzsche, in Heidegger's view, heralds us into the era of completed nihilism and the resultant technocratic debasement of the earth. Metaphysics, for so long thought of – particularly since Descartes – as "first philosophy", becomes in Heidegger's hands "onto-theo-logy". Onto-theology is a neologism, coined by Heidegger, to describe the nature of the metaphysical enterprise. It is the onto-theological character of metaphysics that will constitute one of the focal points of this examination.

But we ask once again, "What is called Religion?", aware that any genuine thinking of this question seeks not a substantiative definition but an experi-ence with the question; an experience that will bring us into the region wherein and wherefrom the question speaks. Moreover, when we ask the question "What is called Religion?" we ask of a relationship: the relationship between Heidegger and the questions concerning the nature of the religious and the theological.

Yet, in asking this question of Heidegger and his texts, do we not ask after that which is prima facie self-evident? Are there not many texts in the Heideg-gerian corpus burgeoning with reference to God and the gods, and the quater-nity, divinities, mortals, sky and earth? Do we not have in our possession a text which quite specifically presents Heidegger's views on the relationship between theology and philosophy, a text originally published in 1927 and republished in 1970, which speaks of "Phenomenology and Theology"? So does not our question "What is called Religion? seem strangely otiose in the context of Heidegger's philosophy? Is it not futile to persist in our question-ing? Perhaps we would be better advised to approach a philosopher whose work contains very little about the religious and the theological. However, upon examination, what seems self-evident turns out to have the character of at most an aporia and at least ambiguity. So let us proceed slowly with our questioning, letting *the* question "What is called Religion?" act as a *leitmotiv* to our investigations. The question will resound throughout this piece, calling us back to its enigma, its very intransigency serving as a block to the super-ficiality of the hastily assembled answer.

That Heidegger was deeply influenced by matters pertaining to the religious and theological we have on his own account. And as Jacques Derrida has recently pointed out in his work *De l'esprit*, Heidegger constantly refers to the spirit and the spiritual throughout his works, even if, as in *Being and Time*, this is only in avoidance (*vermeiden*). In 1959 Heidegger published an account, in the volume entitled *Unterwegs zur Sprache*, of a dialogue occasioned in 1953/4 by the visit of a Japanese scholar. In this dialogue, whilst discussing the term "hermeneutics", Heidegger makes the following remark: "The term 'hermeneutics' was familiar to me from my theological studies. At that time I was particularly agitated over the question of the relation between the word of Holy Scripture and theological-speculative thinking."[3] Heidegger follows up this remark by stating that: "Without this theological background I should never have come upon the path of thinking. But origin always comes to meet us from the future."[4]

Despite this acknowledged debt to his theological past Heidegger believes that were he addressed by the call of faith, for him the real subject matter of theology, he would have to close up shop on thinking. Thinking and theology are seen to be radically incommensurable. He claims that "thinking" is that which man can pursue on his own and this falters or comes to an end when man is addressed by revelation. Moreover, he believes that when theologians engage in "philosophical" thinking they show little trust in their own standpoint; faith and revelation. He exhorts theologians to abide in the exclusiveness of revelation. He claims likewise in the 1927 lecture "Phenomenology and Theology" that "there is no such thing as a Christian Philosophy; that it is an absolute 'square circle'",[5] a claim he reiterated in *An Introduction to Metaphysics*. There is on the other hand, however, no such thing as a phenomenological theology. Phenomenology remains firmly wedded to the domain of philosophical method: "Phenomenology is always the name for the procedure of ontology, which essentially distinguishes itself from all other positive sciences."[6]

The simplistic picture wherein philosophy and theology are appropriated to their own distinctive regions is one that needs further investigation. Firstly we have to understand what Heidegger means by "thinking" and how this relates to "philosophy".

"Thinking", as we have seen, in the sense of "philosophical thinking", is the sole prerogative of philosophy; neither theology or any other discipline (the positive sciences) can make pretension to its privileged position. Yet, for Heidegger, philosophy itself is deeply suspect. When Heidegger republished the lecture "Phenomenology and Theology" in 1970 he indicated this when he added a foreword in which he said: "This little book might perhaps be able to occasion repeated reflection on the extent to which the Christianness of Christianity and its theology merit questions; but also on the extent to which philosophy, in particular that presented here, merits questioning."[7]

Philosophy, from Socrates to Nietzsche, has been a consistent veiling of what for Heidegger is *the* question: the question of Being, or rather, the question of the sense of Being. Therefore, philosophy is in itself questionable; "questionable", that is, in the full ambiguity of that word: what is worthy of questioning and what is somehow suspect or dubious.

Heidegger attempts to raise anew the question concerning what is considered to be the most universal and indefinable of concepts within the history of Western philosophy:

> Do we in our time have an answer to the question of what we really mean by the word "being"? Not at all. So it is fitting that we should raise anew *the question of the meaning of Being*. But are we nowadays perplexed at our inability to understand the expression "Being"? Not at all.[8]

As is evidenced by the last two sentences, there has been a forgetting of "Being". We mortals are no longer "perplexed" and, for the most part, remain untouched by the power of the question "Why is there something rather than nothing?" All essential questioning, so Heidegger believes, must begin with the fundamental question of Being. The task of Heidegger's first major work, *Being and Time* was, as we have seen, an attempt to raise this question again by examination of the being who in its very Being has that Being as an "issue": Dasein. Dasein is the site wherein Being comes to unconcealment. That the question of the meaning of Being has been forgotten is not, however, something simply accidental but has its roots in the soil of Greece; in the thinking of Socrates, Plato and Aristotle.

"Thinking" and "philosophy", since the era of Socrates and Plato, have been logocentric in character and adversarial/dialectical in form. Rational argument since this era has become the wrapping or mode of presentation of all ideas; "thinking" has become synonomous with *Ratio*. Thus, thinking is that which gives reasons and explanations.

When philosophy donned its garb of respectability – the argument, this gave rise to the spectacle of the contest; "thinking" became "philosophy" and philosophy was about battle and war, winners and losers. The "lovers of wisdom" were those who joyfully did battle with irrationalism and ignorance to proclaim the "truth" of reason. "Thinking" which did not cover the nakedness of its insight with the proffered cloak of respectability was consigned to the depths of irrationalism and exiled from the respectable precincts of philosophy. The "thinking" which was exiled from philosophy was to be encountered only in poetry, literature, art and, we might venture, mysticism and the religious. The whispered insights gained in such diverse fields, were never to be deemed worthy of the name "philosophy"; and never were the figures from these realms to be hallowed with the name "philosopher". To quote a modern example of such prejudice: "[T]here are great individual thinkers who are great writers, whom I would not call philosophers, such as

Kierkegaard and Nietzsche" (Iris Murdoch in conversation with Bryan Magee).[9]

At this juncture it is incumbent upon us to ask whether Heidegger has exempted himself from such prejudicial attitudes? Prima facie the outlook does not appear promising. Heidegger *appears* to commit himself to the same attitudes which inform a vast proportion of the Western philosophical tradition. After all we have it on Heidegger's own authority that theology can never be philosophy and a Christian philosophy would be a "round square and a misunderstanding". Furthermore, from the standpoint of theology, philosophy can only be a madness, a foolishness to be overcome. In a passage from the essay "The Word of Nietzsche: 'God is Dead'" Heidegger once again seems to uphold these old prejudices:

> The comparison between Nietzsche and Kierkegaard that has become customary, but is no less questionable for that reason, fails to recognize, and indeed out of a misunderstanding of the essence of thinking, that Nietzsche as a metaphysical thinker preserves a closeness to Aristotle. Kierkegaard remains essentially remote from Aristotle, although he mentions him more often. For Kierkegaard is not a thinker but a religious writer.[10]

What is noteworthy in this passage is not simply the coupling of the names of Kierkegaard and Nietzsche once again but the characterization of these figures as "religious" and "metaphysical". It is hard not to be disconcerted by Heidegger's statement that Kierkegaard is a "religious writer" and Nietzsche a "metaphysical thinker". Again Heidegger seems to fall into the age-old prejudices of the tradition. However, before we jump to any hasty conclusions we need first to ponder further what Heidegger means by "thinking", especially when conjoined with the term "metaphysical".

Why does Heidegger consider Nietzsche to be a metaphysical thinker? Nietzsche is, after all, the madman in *The Gay Science* who proclaims the death of God. Nietzsche, the philosopher with the hammer, believed himself to be ushering us into the era of completed nihilism and the task of the "revaluation of all values". Nietzsche's project looks disarmingly like Heidegger's. Heidegger speaks of destruction (*Destruktion*) and deconstruction and Nietzsche of a smashing of that which does not ring true. But what is nihilism for Nietzsche? "What does nihilism mean? *That the highest values devaluate themselves*".[11] When the highest values have devalued themselves it is the task of the *Übermensch* to be the creator of new values. The death of God, the highest value hitherto (announced by Nietzsche) means specifically the death of the Christian God. The terms "God" and "Christian God" in the thinking of Nietzsche refer to a suprasensory world: "God" means the world of ideals and ideas. This suprasensory world has its origins in a late Greek and Christian interpretation of Platonic philosophy and is conceived of as the

181

"real world". The changing world which we access through our senses is somehow "unreal". The suprasensory world is the metaphysical and real world which is placed in opposition to the ephemeral and suffering world which we inhabit. When Nietzsche declares that "God is dead" his declaration means that the suprasensory, the metaphysical world has ceased to have any power over us. Thus understood, Nietzsche's philosophy is the counter-movement to Western philosophy understood as Platonism. Nietzsche announces an overturning of the Platonic world; the "real" world has at last become a myth:

> We have abolished the real world: what world is left? the apparent world perhaps? . . . But no! *with the real world we have also abolished the apparent world!*
> (Mid-day: moment of the shortest shadow; end of the longest error; zenith of mankind; INCIPIT ZARATHUSTRA.)[12]

Now that God is dead, and what hitherto has been regarded as the highest value has devalued itself, we are faced with the spectre of a pervasive and appallingly trenchant nihilism. To overcome nihilism means to confront it at its source. Nietzsche finds this source in the redundant moralities of the West. In future all moralities will be required to show their "genealogy", and the *Übermensch*, of which Zarathustra is the herald, will, through the will-to power, be a creator of new and powerful values. We now repose our question: why does Heidegger believe that Nietzsche is a metaphysical thinker when on the evidence of his most famous expression, namely, "God is dead", he attempts to overturn the Platonism that has dominated Western thinking for so long? We need once again to engage with the nature of the metaphysical.

In his inaugural lecture "What is Metaphysics?", delivered in 1929, Heidegger gives his definition of metaphysics: "Metaphysics is inquiry beyond or over beings which aims to recover them as such and as a whole for our grasp."[13] In a much later text, published in 1957, Heidegger claims: "The wholeness of this whole is the unity of all beings that unifies as the generative ground."[14] Heidegger points out that a thinking which attempts to think beings as such and as a whole is metaphysical, and that thinking is in turn onto-theo-logical. The metaphysical is, thus, synonomous with onto-theology. Now this seems a strange claim, particularly when we consider this in regard to the thought of Nietzsche, the last "metaphysical" thinker. If what is being claimed here is that Nietzsche as a "metaphysical thinker" is also an onto-theological thinker, then the situation looks decidedly odd. Nietzsche, we object, proclaims the demise of God and the effectiveness or power of any such notion. No longer are we compelled to watch the flickering shadows on the walls of Plato's cave. The real and apparent worlds have at long last fulfilled their mythical status. To unravel this puzzling aporia, to which Heidegger brings us, we need to think the further term "onto-theo-logy" and dwell longer in the proximity of its speaking.

It is Heidegger's contention that Western metaphysics since the age of the Greeks has been both ontology *and* theology. Theology in the secular sense of the ancient Greeks is a "mytho-poetic utterance about the gods, with no reference to any creed or ecclesiastical doctrine".[15] He further claims that theology is the science of God.[16] This claim, drawn from the same text as the above quotation, appears commensurate with his position stated in 1927, in the lecture "Phenomenology and Theology", where he asserts that theology is a positive science and as such irremediably divorced from philosophy. Heidegger's thinking, however, does seem to have gone through some transitions between the earlier and later texts. Whilst still main-taining that theology is a science, there appears to be a subtle slippage between the earlier and later phases of his thinking. In the earlier lecture theology is characterized as a *positive* science, and more akin to mathematics and chemistry than philosophy. This characterization, of course, runs con-trary to any popular notions regarding the relationship between theology and philosophy. According to such a conception theology and philosophy have, to a certain extent, the same area as their theme: human life and the world. They are, however, guided by different perspectives. Theology pro-ceeds from *faith*, and philosophy from *reason*. Heidegger's contention, as we know, is far more radical: theology as a positive science is *absolutely* different from philosophy. Moreover, theology is, on this earlier interpretation, *the science of faith*.

We are thus confronted with two definitions of theology from out of Heidegger's own works: the science of God and the science of faith. The former is closer to the dictionary definition and, I think, what we convention-ally understand by "theology" when we hear that term spoken: "Theology: The science treating of God, his nature and attributes, and his relation to man and the universe; any particular system of this" (The Pocket Oxford Dic-tionary). As to the question "What is called Theology?", we are in possession of two distinct answers as to its nature. Are we thus confronted by a paradox? Has Heidegger's thinking undergone such a radical change that he now sees theology only in terms of what we ordinarily and conventionally understand? Or is there something extremely important going on in this seemingly ambig-uous relationship with theology? Rather than trying to surmount this ambi-guity by trying to get a perspective from a higher vantage point, let us try to think from out of the very region of the ambiguity itself. Thus, we take up the challenge of a thinking offering us no easy answers. To accomplish this we need to take a step back into the proximity of the questions posed initially; "What is called Theology?"; "What is called Religion?" The "What is?", as we have already seen, called us into a thinking relationship with what is the "matter" (*Sache*) of our questioning. When we keep this matter firmly in view we hear the question speaking to us in different ways. "*Was heisst*

Theologie?", *"Was heisst Religion?"* we ask once more, this time in German: what *calls* for theology, and what *calls* for religion; what is this "thing" called theology and what is this "thing" called religion? Thus, out of the speaking of the question we have two disparate strands, two ways of asking the question "What is?".

Staying with the question "What is called Theology?" for the moment, we recall Heidegger's assertion that: "Western metaphysics... since its beginning with the Greeks has eminently been both ontology and theology."[17] This happens because metaphysics is about what unifies as a generative ground the wholeness of the whole. Given that one form of our question is "What is calling for theology?", we venture the tentative answer that we are called upon via a theology, to provide a systematic account, to speak of God as the creative and sustaining *ground* for all beings; in short, to provide a *Logos*. When we are called in this way the deity enters into philosophy as the *causa prima*, the ultimate *Ratio*; "the final accounting". What this comes to mean is that the Being of beings reveals itself as a ground that gives reasons for itself, thereby grounding itself. This ground, the reason for the essential origin of beings, is in turn *Logos*, the gathering and letting be of beings.

It is prima facie evident that the terms "ontology" and "theology" resemble other "ologies" such as biology, psychology, archeology, pathology. In each case in our list the "ology" broadly indicates that we are dealing with a science. Each example, within its own special area of ontic enquiry, attempts to give grounds and produce a systematic account. For example, pathology offers us a systematic and scientific account of disease. However, the "ology"

> hides more than just the logical in the sense of what is consistent and generally in the nature of a statement, what structures, moves, secures and communicates all scientific knowledge. In each case, the -Logia is the totality of a nexus of grounds accounted for, within which nexus the objects of the sciences are represented in respect of their ground, that is, are conceived.[18]

Thus, theology, becomes in this sense "onto-theo-logy"; the "Science of God". This "science", suggests Heidegger, is both metaphysics and logic. In addition, ontology and theology are pre-eminently "ologies" in that they attempt to provide the grounds for all beings as such and within the wholeness of the whole. The Being of beings becomes that which is *causa sui*. This, states Heidegger, is the metaphysical concept of God.

It would be as well at this point, before proceeding any further, to hear the words of Nietzsche from the famous passage in *The Gay Science* wherein he announces the death of God:

> Have you not heard of that madman who lit a lantern in the bright morning hours, ran to the market place, and cried incessantly: "I seek God! I seek God".... This madman jumped into their midst and pierced them with his eyes. "Whither is God?" he cried; "I will tell you. *We have killed him* – you and I.... God is dead."[19]

Heidegger suggests that it is rather strange that the madman, identified with Nietzsche, seeks God when he already knows of God's death at our hands. This passage merely reiterates for Heidegger that we find ourselves in a world without God; the gods have flown. That Heidegger finds himself in this condition merely echoes the feelings of Pascal in the seventeenth century who found himself with mere reminders that God had once been immanent.

God, the dead God, as we have seen already, represents for Nietzsche the demise of the suprasensory realm and the myth of the "real" world. As of yet we know very little about the death of God, for the stench of divine decomposition has yet to reach our noses. God the highest value hitherto, the *summum ens qua summum bonum* of Christian theology, has been devalued, nihilism ensues and "the wasteland grows".[20] Nietzsche, however, takes an affirmative attitude towards nihilism. If the highest value has been devalued there must be a revaluation of all values. Values that arise out of the revaluation must be underpinned in a manner quite other than the suprasensory; the supra-sensory must no longer be the guarantor and arbiter of value. The message that Nietzsche brings us is that now values have to be *created*. The underwriter for the creation of the new values is to be the will, which according to Nietzsche represents the enhancement and preservation conditions of all life. Moreover, it is will-to-power that is the *essentia* of anything real and the ground of "superabundant life". We thus find in Nietzsche's philosophy, says Heidegger, the juxtaposition of the two components that represent the essential elements of all metaphysical thinking in the West: value and ground.

Thus, for Heidegger, Nietzsche remains firmly wedded to the metaphysical tradition of the West: "When metaphysics thinks whatever is, in its Being, as the will-to-power, then it necessarily thinks it as value positing. It thinks everything within the sphere of values, of the authoritative force of value, of devaluing and revaluing."[21]

Being is thus reduced to a mere value. The announcer of the death of God remains therefore firmly enmeshed within the tradition of onto-theology and remains a mere "metaphysical thinker"; the last "thinker" of the West. This in turn places him close to Aristotle, the thinker of God as the primary instance of substance, and Aquinas and his doctrine of the unmoved mover. Whether this is a fair assessment and characterization of Nietzsche remains outside of the scope of this chapter. What we do know, however, is that with the death of God we have become godless, that is, the God of philosophy is no longer with us. That the God of philosophy is dead still has not been recognized: as Nietzsche says, "I have come too early."[22] That we still continue to think primarily in a logocentric, that is, a metaphysical mode, and whether this is immanent to Western language remains, for Heidegger, an open question. The philosophical God is the expression of this logocentric tradition *par exemplar*.

The iron grip of the *Logos* that has prevailed in Western philosophy, and which is to be found in its very foundations, so Heidegger believes, has to be loosened before we can begin to address the question of Being. To think the question of Being is the task of thinking. Thinking, so Heidegger believes, only begins when philosophy ends. To this effect he announces "The end of philosophy and the task of thinking".[23]

So what is the "end" of philosophy? The "end" of which Heidegger speaks is not to be confused with a mere stopping; a grinding to a halt, a petering out. The "end" of philosophy is its completion as a gathering. Heidegger in his text "The End of Philosophy and the Task of Thinking" advises us that an older and more originary meaning of "end" is "place", as in the locution, "from one place to another". Thus, the end of philosophy represents its culmination as place; that place in which "the whole of philosophy's history is gathered in its most extreme possibility".[24]

The "most extreme possibility" of philosophy is witnessed, for Heidegger, by the gradual fragmentation of philosophy since the seventeenth century into the specialist scientific disciplines: "This development of philosophy looks like the mere dissolution of philosophy, and is in truth its completion."[25] Moreover, this dissolution of philosophy into the various scientific disciplines is not merely accidental, it has its origins in Greece and the dawn of Western civilization. One might say that the opening for the possibility of logocentrism began with Heraclitus and his obsession with the *Logos*. This concern for the *Logos* and the logocentric spawned Western man's fanatical quest for the ultimate grounds of reality. One of the tasks of "thinking" in the wake of philosophy's disintegration is to think "what the Greeks have thought in an even more Greek manner".[26] The West's obsession with reasons and grounds can be seen as one manner of appropriating the thought of Heraclitus; an appropriation which paves the way for the dominance of the technological. This explosion of the scientific and the technological surely demonstrates that man truly is the *animal rationale?* But no, what is "Most thought-provoking is that we are still not thinking",[27] so Heidegger informs us. Thus, we are now in a position to re-examine a question posed, but not answered, earlier. Is Heidegger merely reiterating the prejudices of the Western philosophical tradition when he conceives of a Christian philosophy as being a "round square"? Clearly not, as philosophy has reached its end and the task of thinking is about to commence. Also, despite the fact that Western technological prowess has exhibited such striking advances, this apparently does not constitute demonstrable evidence that we are thinking. We can state, therefore, reasonably succinctly: "thinking" does not reside in the *Logos*; thinking is not to be equated purely with ratiocination. Thinking which has the character of logocentrism Heidegger calls "calculative", and is firmly married to the technological and the *Gestell*[28] of the present era. Technological or calculative thinking views the world as standing resource. Being, in the era of the *Gestell*, presences merely as standing reserve for industry and the technological. It is worth quoting in full a famous example from *The Question Concerning Technology*, as this illustrates strikingly how Heidegger views technological thinking:

> The hydroelectric plant is set into the current of the Rhine. It sets the Rhine to supply its hydraulic pressure, which then sets the turbines turning. This turning sets those machines in motion whose thrust sets going the electric current for which the long-distance power station and its network of cables are set up to dispatch electricity. In the context of the interlocking processes pertaining to the orderly disposition of electrical energy, even the Rhine appears as something at our command. The hydroelectric plant is not built into the Rhine river as was the old wooden bridge that joined bank with bank for hundreds of years. Rather the river is dammed up into the power plant. What the river is now, namely, a power water supplier, derives from out of the essence of the power station. In order that we may even remotely consider the monstrousness that reigns here, let us ponder for a moment the contrast that speaks out of the two titles, "The Rhine" as dammed up into the *power* works, and "The Rhine" as uttered out of the *art* work, in Holderlin's hymn by that name. But, it will be replied, the Rhine is still a river in the landscape, is it not? Perhaps. But how? In no other way than as an object on call for inspection by a tour group ordered there by the vacation industry.[29]

The technological thinking evidenced in this passage is clearly *not* what Heidegger means by "thinking". In contradistinction to the power-dominated "calculative thinking" of the technological Heidegger speaks of meditative thinking. "Thinking" in this special sense reserved by him is "meditative" as opposed to "calculative". Yet, we ask, is not the term "meditative" derived from the religious? Let us leave any answer to this question in abeyance for the moment and examine how "meditative thinking" (*besinnliches Denken*) is characterized for Heidegger.

Meditative thinking, above all, has the character of serenity – what might be termed a receptive reverence for things as they are in themselves. The serenity referred to is non-willed. In addition it is also a non-forced and non-concerned activity. Meditative thinking waits upon the call, whilst calculative thinking is concerned with dominance, manipulation and mere utility. This will-less "thinking" is a spontaneity that sets things free to be what they are. A "higher acting", so Heidegger writes, is found in this attitude of letting-be (*Gelassenheit*) than "is found in all the actions within the world and in the machinations of all mankind".[30]

Meditative thinking is, moreover, pious, receptive and reverential. It is the genuinely receptive response to Being's call or voice: authentic "hearing" is a hearing that hearkens to this call and is appropriated to it in a sense of belonging and obeying. For Heidegger there is a filiality between what he calls in one text "the piety of thinking", and "thanking". Thus a thinking which re-calls is a thanking. Heidegger, who regards the essence of language to be Saying, resorts frequently to metaphors drawn from the aural as opposed to the visual. Hearing, it might be argued, is by its very nature social; the hearer enters into a relationship of reciprocity with the speaker. The privileging of the aural allows Heidegger to exploit the etymological kinship to be found in the German words "to hear" (*hören*), "to hearken" (*horchen*), "to belong" (*gehören*), and "to obey" (*gehorchen*). Hearing is thus, at one and the same time, a hearkening, belonging and obeying. A thinking which hears the call of Being gives thanks to the arrival of the call and is appropriated to that call by belonging and obeying. The pious listener who is attuned to the call, through *Gelassenheit*, releases beings from the tyrannizing demand of the visual with its essential modality of narcissism, into the intrinsic nature of their being.

To return to the question that we posed a short while ago: is not the term "meditative", used by Heidegger as the *principium* to delineate "thinking" from the calculative and philosophical, derived from religious discourse? Do not all religions possess something akin to meditation? – although this obviously varies from religion to religion. Whilst admitting the cogency of this assertion Heidegger's claim is that human being are *essentially* meditative beings because they are thinking beings. Meditative thinking is by no means "high-flown"[31] and thus exclusive to the religious. It is, however, no accident that Heidegger describes the nature of "thinking" as being pious, receptive, open to the call, and, above all, a thanking. Moreover, he describes the outcome of such "meditative thinking" as resulting in letting-be (*Gelassenheit*),[32] a term derived from Meister Eckhart and thus clearly having its roots in the religious. But when Heidegger uses such terms as "pious", "meditative", "receptive" and "thanking", is he not merely using them for their heuristic value? Cannot Heidegger's project, and thus his use of such terms, be seen merely as a corrective to the age of the technological *Gestell* with its over-emphasis on scientific rationality? Is not Heidegger attempting a respiritualization of the secular by reawakening us to the language of the spiritual dimension of human existence? However, we might add, this reawakening process is entirely secular in its origins and goal and thus, in a theological sense, a godless form of thinking.

These questions bring us back, once again, within the province of our original question "What is called Religion?", and allow us to dwell within its intransigency. That we live in godless times is evidenced within the

Heideggerian corpus on numerous occasions. He tells us, for instance, that we are "too late for the gods"[33] and that we live in a "destitute time". We are bereft of the support of the God of theology. When Nietzsche proclaimed that "God is dead" he proclaimed the death of the metaphysical God; the God of the philosophers. It appears, however, that this is no loss for Heidegger, but has positive advantages as we can "neither pray nor sacrifice to this god. Before the *causa sui*, man can neither fall to his knees in awe nor can he play music and dance".[34]

Schelling, in 1841–2, called for a God, demanded by the will, before whom man can pray, and before whom all knees are bent. Such a call clearly has its resonances in Heidegger. The God of metaphysics as synonomous with the God of theology *obviously* does not satisfy such a demand. Are we therefore, we might ask, condemned to merely godless and secular forms of thought? With the death of the metaphysical God are we ineluctably propelled out of the religious into the realm of a purely secular society? But perhaps we view "godless" forms of thinking in a way which is wholly negative and, therefore in a way which does little justice to how Heidegger views the matter. In Heidegger's view the death of the God of theology is the liberation from yet another instance of the *Logos* seen in terms of *Ratio*, perhaps, *the* instance and sole reason. The God of traditional theology is a God of reason, the *causa sui*, the metaphysical *reason* and ground for all things. Yet,

> The godless thinking which must abandon the god of philosophy, god as *causa sui*, is thus perhaps closer to the divine God. Here this means only: godless-thinking is more open to Him than onto-theo-logic would like to admit.[35]

Quite clearly Heidegger wishes to block any suggestion that the death of God is necessarily a fall into atheism and nihilism. In a passage in the "Letter on Humanism" he makes this apparent when he says, in a somewhat ironic manner: "Because we refer to the word of Nietzsche on the 'death of God' people regard such as gesture as atheism. For what is more 'logical' than that whoever has experienced the death of God is godless?"[36] The hegemony of reason within the Western world is so pervasive that whatever disturbs "the habitual somnolence of prevailing opinion is automatically registered as a despicable contradiction".[37] We are so "filled" with logic, as Heidegger puts it, that we become incapable of listening to the matter; we are literally incapable of genuine thought, "reason" being the stiffest-necked adversary of thought. A thinking which only "thinks" "logically" is one that finds it impossible to escape the rigid confines of the bi-polar oppositions of negation and affirmation. It follows "logically" that any speaking which speaks against theism must, of necessity, be atheistic. Likewise any speaking against humanism *must* be against man. Whenever we think within the limitations of *pro* and *contra* we fail to be called to the task of thinking.

When, however, we abandon the mode of rational determination for the meditative, this does not imply a mere indifferentism. Rather, a thinking which tries to think the truth of Being, when confronted with questions concerning God, thinks in a manner entirely outside of the governance of theism and atheism. A thinking which truly thinks Being can no longer feel comfortable with the cosy appropriation to either of these categories. What is clear is that, for Heidegger, *any* questions concerning God can *only* be thought out of the truth of Being, for "Only from the truth of Being can the essence of the holy be thought. Only in the light of the essence of divinity can it be thought or said what the word 'God' is to signify."[38] The essence of the holy will remain a closed dimension if the open region of Being is not lighted via the open site that is man: Dasein. The metaphysical closes access to the open site of Being. The God of the metaphysicians, theologians and philosophers must die for the essence of the holy to unveil itself.

The linking of the projects of metaphysics, theology and philosophy is meant to show that they are appropriated to the rational. In the rationality of their rational pronouncements they are firmly wedded to the sciences. So what of our questions "What is called Religion?"; "What is called Theology?" Perhaps we can suggest an answer in the form of the negative: what religion and theology are not. Clearly from what has been indicated so far religion and theology *cannot* be allied to the sphere of rationality. Both religion and theology, in so far as they are to come to their essential nature, are to be liberated from the tyranny of reason; they have to become thoroughly unreasonable. Yet there still seems a large gap between how Heidegger conceives of theology and what I shall term "religious thinking". If we recall, Heidegger suggested that he would have to close shop on thinking if called by faith. It is my contention that the essence of the religious is for Heidegger the very project that he is engaged in: thinking the truth of Being as a place of admittance to the holy. It is a moot point whether this aligns with any conventional understanding of this term. This term indicates both the quest for the religious and the holy and also its appropriation to both. It is pre-eminently hermeneutic in its character. The religious in this sense, which I discern in Heidegger's work, in so far as it is to think the truth of Being, remains "thinking", albeit meditative. The religious, as we have described it, has something more akin to Rilke's "direction of the heart" and perhaps what is needed to access the holy is what Rilke describes as "heart's work".[39] But these must unfortunately remain pregnant suggestions. The claim I am making is that Heidegger's primary mode of thinking is in *essence* religious and it is in this sense more akin to the secularized religion of Buddhism than the theologized Christianity which is part of the tradition he is immersed in.

However, one can discern deep tensions in his relationship to theology. Because of these tensions strains of ambiguity surface from time to time. Theology has everything to do with faith; it is, according to Heidegger, the science which has as its *positum* faith. Yet, as we have seen, as a science it has little in common with the other positive sciences that use rationality as their mode of enquiry, despite remaining, for Heidegger, a positive science. For: "God is in no way the object of investigation in theology, as, for example, animals are the theme of zoology."[40]

It is Heidegger's contention that it is the work of theology to induce faith by the historical explication of revelation. Theology is to be conceived as a thoroughly historical and systematic project. In so far as it is the historical nature of the Christian occurrence that is being explicated it implies that this historicity is to be appropriated ever anew for the community of the faith-full. Let us now, to conclude, explore some of the tensions within Heidegger's work regarding this conception of theology.

That Heidegger is deeply suspicious and critical of the representational/ metaphysical nature of theology is plainly obvious from the above. Whilst agreeing with Nietzsche's statement that God is dead, Heidegger still wants to leave room for faith and belief. In the wake of the death of God godless thinking appears to be more open to the possibility of God than onto-theology which posits God in a representationalist and, therefore, metaphysical manner. In the essay "The Word of Nietzsche: 'God is Dead'" Heidegger says, when referring to the "madman" passage in *The Gay Science*, that the bystanders in the market place have given up belief in God not because he has become unworthy of belief, but because they have given up the possibility of belief. Why have they given up the possibility of belief? Because, we are told, they are incapable of *thinking*; they have abolished thinking, replacing it with the idle chatter (*Gerede*) of the market place. The madman on the contrary cries: "I seek God, I seek God."

> The madman . . . the one who seeks God, since he cries out after God. Has a *thinking* man perhaps here really cried out *de profundis*? And the ear of our thinking, does it still not hear the cry? It will refuse to hear it so long as it does not begin to think.[41]

Could this possibly be the voice of Heidegger himself, as opposed to that of Nietzsche? Is Heidegger unhappy with the stance of one who must wait with piousness, receptiveness and thankfulness? Has he become dissatisfied with listening for the call of Being? The thinking man who cries out *de profundis* "I seek God" is, I believe, Heidegger, who cannot tolerate living in a world possibly *without* God.

Although Heidegger seeks to leave open the question of the possibility of God, questions as to God's existence or non-existence he has ruled out as absurd in the "Letter on Humanism"; through godless thinking he strives in this passage to exhort us to a "thinking" that seeks God. If Heidegger is in the position of one seeking God, and let us recall that in the 1966 interview with *Der Spiegel* he said that "only a God could save us now",[42] he is engaged in a project that seems outside the boundaries of "meditative thinking". "Meditative thinking", it is true, remains *open* to the possibility of God in a non-theistic manner, but that is all. This quest would also lie outside the scope of theology, theology's task being the explication of revelation and the inducement to faith. Thinking, it appears, has now become the active search for the existence of God and a search that might conceivably lead us back into the precincts of speculative onto-theo-logy. Thinking, in the sense of meditative thinking, retains the character of openness, piety and receptiveness only so long as it does not intend an object of belief. If Heidegger is actively seeking God, then this undermines the open character of the meditative and what is genuinely, I believe, his religious thinking. The metaphysical God may be dead but Heidegger appears "anxious" when it comes to remaining in the proximity of the mere possibility of God. The non-theist, which given some of his pronouncements Heidegger appears to be, does not actively seek God but leaves that question in abeyance. Sadly Heidegger abandons his "openness to the mystery"[43] for the neurotic striving to find God.

Works by Heidegger

AED *Aus der Erfahrung des Denkens*, translated as "The Poet as Thinker" by Albert Hofstadter, in *Poetry, Language, Thought*, Harper & Row, New York, 1971.

EP "The End of Philosophy and the Task of Thinking", in *On Time and Being*, translated by Joan Stambaugh, Harper Torchbooks, New York, 1972.

G *Gelassenheit*, translates as *Discourse on Thinking* by John M. Anderson and E. Hans Freund, Harper Torchbooks, New York, 1966.

ID *Identity and Difference*, translated by Joan Stambaugh, Harper Torchbooks, New York, 1969.

LH "Letter on Humanism", translated by Frank A. Capuzzi, in *Basic Writings*, edited by David Farrell Krell, Routledge & Kegan Paul, London, 1978.

PT *The Piety of Thinking*, translated by James G. Hart and John C. Maraldo, Indiana University Press, Bloomington, 1976.

QCT *The Question Concerning Technology*, translated by William Lovitt, Harper Torchbooks, New York, 1977.

SZ *Sein und Zeit*, translated as *Being and Time* by John Macquarrie and Edward Robinson, Blackwell, Oxford, 1962.

UZS *Unterweg zur Sprache*, translated as *On the Way to Language* by Peter D. Hertz and Joan Stambaugh, Harper & Row, New York, 1971.

WHD Was Heisst Denken?, translated as *What is Called Thinking?* by J. Glenn Gray, Harper & Row, New York, 1968.

WM "What is Metaphysics", in *Basic Writings*, edited by David Farrell Krell, Routledge & Kegan Paul, London, 1978.

Works by Nietzsche

GS   *The Gay Science*, translated by Walter Kaufmann, Vintage Books, New York, 1974.

TI   *Twilight of the Idols*, translated by R.J. Hollingdale, Penguin, Harmondsworth, 1968.

WP   *The Will to Power*, translated by Walter Kaufmann and R.J. Hollingdale, Vintage Books, New York, 1968.

Notes

1 Letter to Ilse Blumenthal-Weiss, Chateau De Muzot Sur Sierre, 28 December 1921, in Rainer Maria Rilke, *Selected Letters 1902–1926*, translated by R.C.F. Hull, Quartet, 1987.
2 *QCT*, 112.
3 *UZS*, 91/10.
4 *Ibid.*
5 *PT*, 21. *An Introduction to Metaphysics*, translated by Ralph Mannheim, Yale University Press, New Haven, 1959.
6 *Ibid.*
7 *Pt*, 3.
8 *SZ*, 1.
9 Bryan Magee, *Men of Ideas*, Oxford University Press, Oxford, 1978.
10 *QCT*, 94.
11 *WP*, 2.
12 *TI*, 41.
13 WM, 109.
14 *ID*, 54.
15 *Ibid.*
16 *Ibid.*
17 *Ibid.*
18 *ID*, 59.
19 *GS*, 181.
20 *WP*, 23.
21 *QCT*, 82.
22 *GS*, 182.
23 *GS*, 58.
24 EP, 57.
25 *Ibid.*
26 *UZS*, 39.
27 *WHD*, 4.
28 The *Gestell* is the enframing of Being wherein Being is only viewed in a singular manner. It is Heidegger's claim that in our age Being is enframed in the mode of the technological. What this means is that nature comes to be viewed as a standing resource for the forces of technology; nature is literally set upon by these forces. See "The Age of the World Picture", in *QCT*.
29 *QCT*, 16.
30 *G*, 61.
31 *G*, 47.
32 *Die Gelassenheit zu den Dingen. Gelassenheit* is used in modern German to indicate "composure", "calmness". It does, however, have older meanings in relation to

the early German mystics such as Meister Eckhart. In this sense it means releasing the world and giving oneself up to God. Heidegger in using this word is suggesting that we might come into a different comportment with the world and our relationship with technology.

33 *AED*, 3.
34 *ID*, 72.
35 *Ibid.*
36 LH, 226.
37 *Ibid.*
38 LH, 230.
39 "Wendung" ("Turning-point"), in Maria Rainer Rilke, *Selected Poems*, translated by Stephen Mitchell, Picador, 1986.
40 *PT*, 15.
41 *QCT*, 112.
42 Richard Wolin (ed.) *The Heidegger Controversy: A Critical Reader*, MIT Press, Cambridge, MA, 1993, 43.
43 In Heidegger's work *Gelassenheit* he exhorts us to "Openess to the mystery" (*Offenheit für das Geheimnis*), *G*, 22.

7

EMMANUEL LEVINAS
God and phenomenology

Phillip Blond

It is not how things are in the world that is mystical but that it
exists.

(Ludwig Wittgenstein, Tractatus Logico-Philosophicus[1])

Part I Phenomenology and the denial of God to being

I must accomplish a *phenomenological reduction:*
I must exclude all that is transcendently posited.

(Edmund Husserl, The Idea of Phenomenology[2])

It was Husserl who, by wishing to locate the ground of Being wholly in beings,
forbade God to phenomenology, ending his Cartesian Meditations with
Augustine's Delphic motto, 'Do not wish to go out; go back into yourself.
Truth dwells in the inner man.'[3] The promise of phenomenology was for
Husserl a promise to save cognition from contradiction and scepticism. And
for Husserl cognition risked contradiction because knowledge divided itself
by attempting to reach beyond itself to something transcendent to it. Consequently Husserl sought to end the separation of transcendence from immanence by abolishing faith in any reality transcendent to human experience.
As a result, cognition was prevented from acknowledging anything external
to itself, and all that could not or would not present itself as evidence (*Evidenz*)
to immanent cognition was assumed not to be. In this respect phenomenology
remains a discipline founded on the prohibition of transcendence and theology, not least because God cannot show Himself to a human consciousness
that claims itself to be the sole determinate of all that it experiences. And this
erasure of God from phenomena takes place because for Husserl, and for the
new science of phenomenology, the world is now the creation of human
rather than divine intentionality.[4]

For Husserl had, in order to ascertain and reveal the human foundation
of phenomena by the Ego, bracketed out or placed under an *epoché* any
naive belief in an external world existing independently of the mind. Once
the mental – or rather intentional – constitution of phenomena had been

established, the world was returned to view with its cognitive foundation now secured.[5] This had the curious result that the restoration achieved after the phenomenological *epoché* was claimed to be a return to 'the things themselves' (*Sachen selbst*) in their true eidetic intentional form.[6] For though the phenomenological subject constitutes the world, the things therein are not simply the products of idealistic projection, since '[C]onsciousness is always consciousness of something', as Husserl puts it in his *Pariser Vortäge*.[7] Though the object of intentional consciousness does find its foundation not in itself but in transcendental subjectivity, since this subjectivity is intentional – in that it intends the objects whose essence it secures – the object and the subject are not for phenomenology thinkable apart from one another. This refusal to posit an ideality outside or beyond the relation of the mind to the world meant that the world was seen by Husserl as a fulfilment and completion of human intentionality, in which case Husserlian phenomenology, having abolished the idea of an external world (a world existing out there apart from me and my synthesis of it), reconstituted this world as existing only in and through the ideality of human consciousness and its *cogitationes*.

However, despite this act of worldly reconstitution Husserlian phenomenology soon found its transcendentalism questioned and indeed subsequently abolished. For Heidegger argued that the exhibition of the self-givenness (*Selbstgegebenheit*) of the phenomenon took place regardless of any transcendental constitution. Consequently the Husserlian return to the intentional foundation of the things themselves became instead a Heideggerian phenomenology of the things themselves (*zu den Sachen selbst*) – with the resulting injunction that whatever was seen was to be seen apart from, and in spite of, any attempt to transcendentally constitute it prior to the facticity of its own appearance.[8] However, with Heidegger the issue in manifestation is not so much that which is exhibited apart from us 'by itself and from itself', but rather that which 'lies hidden' in what is shown. Indeed, in spite of being concealed, this hiddenness belongs for Heidegger so essentially to the exhibited phenomenon 'as to constitute its meaning (*Sinn*) and its ground (*Grund*)'.[9] For Heidegger, of course, that which lies hidden in the phenomenon of beings is the Being (*Sein*) of beings (*Seiendes*).

From the point of view of theology and from the situation of these first few paragraphs, it seems as though theology should welcome the Heideggerian abolition of transcendentalism and the introduction of the language of concealment and the Being of beings. For it appears that Husserl's atheistic and transcendental assumptions about phenomena have been quickly rejected in favour of a greater faithfulness to the appearances themselves. Not least because to speak of the Being of beings seems to approach one of the first names of God; for Thomas Aquinas the questions of Being and God are inseparable since God 'is being itself', *Deus est Suum esse*, and moreover for Aquinas God is the highest being who encompasses all others as the '*summum ens*'.[10] In which case, after the abolition of Husserlian transcendentalism and

Heidegger's raising of the question of Being and his belief that Being shows itself in beings, one might think that phenomenology could not resist a corresponding consideration of God and a realisation of the possibility of His requisite presence and visibility in phenomena. Yet despite this shift of focus, no such opening of phenomenology to God occurred. Indeed, we are told by Heidegger in *Sein und Zeit* that 'the term "phenomenology" is quite different in its meaning from expressions such as "theology" and the like'.[11] And as I will go on to show, this separation of phenomenology from theology has only deepened and ossified over time, becoming in the end a division between God and Being that still remains to be adequately questioned. In respect of this issue, it is worth stating that for theology the inability of phenomenology to see God when the 'things themselves' are seen is at the very least questionable. Christianity has always maintained that God, 'however invisible', has 'been there for the mind to see in the things he has made' (Rom. 1:20); in which case theology should perhaps contest phenomenology in both its Husserlian and Heideggerian forms, as neither of these forms of phenomenology appear to hold that God in any way informs appearances or indeed has any relation with any essence that the things themselves choose to show.

But this sort of secular assumption about what phenomena are and what they can show is something that has been with phenomenology since the beginning. At its inception Husserlian phenomenology was determined not to separate ideality from reality precisely because if the ideal was allowed to transcend the real then knowledge of the real would not provide knowledge of the ideal. As a consequence Husserl formulated an a priori account of the 'essences' that were to be perceived, by construing any actuality as but one arbitrary fulfilment of a possibility that had already been ideally secured. What this meant was that any actuality, insofar as it was exhibiting eidetic (essential) characteristics, had been secured in advance by an investigation of its ideal possibility. In this way a phenomenological and transcendental account of possibility guaranteed and mapped the parameters of actuality before it ever became existent. Which means again that phenomenology, at least in its Husserlian beginning, was already a discourse of assumption about phenomena and lived actuality.

This transcendentalism, when coupled with a phenomenological claim that this a priori ideality actually showed itself in certain experiences, led furthermore to Husserl adopting a very critical view of the normal empirical sciences. For Husserl ordinary natural science took the primary actuality of an object as a sufficient proof of its indubitable and undoubtable nature, and since for this understanding the world is simply and unproblematically there, empirical science saw no need to secure the appearance of the object beyond the phenomenal reality it showed. Yet for Husserl necessary knowledge of the world is not possible or derivable from sensory experience, since there seems to be no necessary link between the objects themselves and their changing appearance; for Husserl therefore, empirical intuition simply reveals fact and not essence. As a result natural science risked becoming a merely descriptive chronicle of the arbitrary character of reality, with no account being given of why this actuality was existent in this form *x* rather than in another form *y*. And as empirical science was unable to secure the descriptions it gave of objects, in the sense that this science was unable to say whether what it described was necessarily true of the objects it studied, Husserl felt that the whole enterprise of knowledge was threatened by scepticism and contradiction. In response he positioned phenomenology as an ideal foundational science that would map out and secure the possibilities of all the other empirical sciences. And as the eidetic (a priori) sciences were claimed by Husserl to stand over and against the (a posteriori) natural sciences of fact as their foundation, then eidetic phenomenology, and only eidetic phenomenology, could determine what it was subsequently possible for the other empirical sciences to know and find. And in this respect theology did not differ from any other science, since along with the suspension of the natural world that accompanied the *epoché*, Husserl had also suspended the transcendence of God, and as neither God nor the natural world was found by consciousness when it achieved its eidetic state, then this eidetic state assumed its priority over both God and the world.[12]

Unfortunately, this a priori priority of phenomenology in respect of other disciplines and ontic sciences did not change with Heidegger. Instead, in *Sein und Zeit* this priority re-expressed itself in terms of Heidegger's inversion of Husserl and his redescription of phenomenology as the only discipline which allowed the primordial disclosure of the phenomenon to be seen on its own terms, apart from any prior transcendental constitution. And if for Heidegger it was only phenomenology that permitted this letting be seen (*Sehenlassen*) of that which shows 'itself from itself' (*von ihm selbst her*) then in a sense phenomenology in its Heideggerian form retains all of Husserl's assumption of privilege and position in respect of other inquiries.[13] For Heidegger still understood phenomenology as the primary mode for the investigation of the disclosure of phenomena, a path at one with Husserl's in the sense that it was equally at odds with the pretensions of any other 'method' to describe the world and its possibilities.

And it is not that one should reject this priority of phenomenology, it is rather that the initial, and I would say unfaithful, account of the possibility of phenomena that Husserl gave still dictates the character and shape of most of the subsequent accounts of phenomenality that we have been given. This is tantamount to saying that these subsequent writers, insofar as they thought for example that the possibilities of phenomena did not include any theological account of actuality, erroneously believed themselves to have been liberated from any and all transcendental assumptions. Unfortunately, and as a result, the phenomenological movement took itself to be embracing an authentic primordial experience, something uncorrupted and untouched by any transcendental scission of the world into the divided categories and intuitions of formal rationality. Which again is perhaps why for Merleau-Ponty, phenomenology was always 'from the start a disavowal of science'.[14]

If then for phenomenology a certain form of science, as it set empirical actuality over and against the priority of phenomenal possibility, was to be rejected and dismissed, then there was little doubt that theology was to be subjected to a similar *epoché*. This bizarre position was necessitated by the growing view that if the object of theology (God) was to be put in suspension by Husserl, along with the objects of the natural sciences, then for phenomenology perhaps theology was simply like every other form of empirical science. Indeed this was exactly the position that Heidegger adopted in 1927 when in his lecture 'Phänomenologie und Theologie' he claimed that theology was 'closer to chemistry and mathematics than philosophy' and as such had the status of a mere ontic science of being, as opposed to an ontological science such as philosophy which investigates Being as such.[15] If so, then for Heidegger theology as an ontic science is not able to investigate Being from the perspective of its region of being, and is not able to see or investigate the ontological possibilities shown by the phenomena themselves – this task apparently is reserved for phenomenology alone.

This was not, however, the end of the phenomenological relegation of theology; theology finally assumed the status of prime pejorative for 'phenomenology' (if one can still use this term in respect of the later Heidegger), when in 1957 Martin Heidegger advanced in a discussion of Hegel the thesis of an onto-theological constitution of metaphysics.[16] In this discussion theology is no longer seen as simply akin to the natural sciences; rather Heidegger admits of a new position and priority for theology in respect of ontology. Now he writes: '[W]estern metaphysics, however, since its beginning with the Greeks has eminently been both ontology and theology.'[17] Furthermore, in this 1957 lecture Heidegger points us towards his 1929 essay *Was ist Metaphysik?* in which he says he recognised the onto-theological character of metaphysics 'as the question about beings as such *and* as a whole'.[18] In his 1936 lectures on Schelling, Heidegger defines ontology as the study of 'beings as such' (*Seiendes als solches*), and theology as the study of 'beings as a whole' (*Seiendes im Ganzen*).[19] Metaphysics is then the unity of theology and ontology as onto-theology. Metaphysics is onto-theology because the ontological inquiry as the search for the most general 'ground-giving unity' of the Being of beings has become conjoined with the theological inquiry which is 'the unity of the all that accounts for the ground, that is the All-Highest'.[20] This means that the ontology which distributes ground generally to all beings is itself given a foundation by a theology which vouchsafes this distribution, since theology claims to account for all general distribution of being through providing an account of it as a whole on a higher level. However, because theology seeks to give an account of the ground of beings in *the whole*, as a *whole*, theology fulfils metaphysics for Heidegger when it departs from those beings in order to enclose them within its own account. Since this is assumed to be what theology does – lay claim to the whole whilst lying outside the whole – then the task of a non-metaphysical philosophy appears clear. It appears to be an elimination of a hitherto metaphysical theology, since the Heideggerian claim is that theology departs from what something is in order to give that thing a foundation and unity that we are told theology believes the thing does not show and would otherwise lack. Whereas for Heidegger in *Sein und Zeit*, since '"[B]ehind" the phenomena of phenomenology there is essentially nothing else'; there is nothing to depart from the phenomena for, consequently any liberation of ontology from metaphysics seems to require a similar liberation of ontology from theology.[21]

Phenomenology at both its most critical and its most unreflective obeys, almost by definition, this secular conflation of theology with metaphysics. Insofar as phenomenology seeks the unity of the whole of the whole, the Being of beings (*on he on*), then it must do so without theology. Theology, now perceived by phenomenology as this unwarranted structure of departure from phenomena, found itself no longer allowed even a regional account of being as it was finally excluded from any phenomenal description whatsoever. As such phenomenology had brought to logical fulfilment the method that it had inherited from Husserl, a method that inverted the traditional relation of immanence to transcendence, such that immanence became the ground or possibility for any transcendence. This immanence, figured first, and perhaps most strongly, in the open force of Husserlian intentionality, precluded even the transcendence of the in-itself from the for-itself. It followed that the being hidden from us was hidden from itself, and that the only being that could be said to be was that which presented itself to us through its appearance as such.

However, this exclusion of transcendence was also fatal to phenomenology itself and its attempt to give an unprejudiced account of phenomenal possibility. Husserl had levelled any account of possibility to an account of what it was possible for the ego to experience. As a result for phenomenology, that which would claim itself as the highest and the most general could only do so via a manifestation that would be on an equal par and terrain with every other manifestation. Such a situation precluded any theological actuality from being recognised by an account of possibility that believed itself to be able to secure all that could be known in a transcendental intuition in advance of specific givenness and manifestation. Husserl writes in *Ideas*, part 44: 'we can always see that transcendent Being in general whatever its genus may be, when understood as Being *for* an Ego, can become a datum only in a way analogous to that in which a thing is given, thus only through appearances.'[22] Having thus liberated ontological actuality from any theological possibility, Husserlian phenomenology believed itself to have secured all the possibilities of actuality in advance, preventing the arbitrary and insufficient character of actuality from threatening knowledge and immanentist coherence.

None the less even though phenomenology as first philosophy (*prôtê philosophia*), seeks unity and coherence in that which presents itself as primary, the encounter with the primary may not be an encounter with a coherent unity, since what is first may not present itself to us as a unified whole.[23] At many places in his work Husserl accepts that the encounter with pure phenomena is a confrontation with 'Heraclitean flux' – a situation which of course is what initiates Husserl's attempts to provide a transcendental unification of this dissonant experience of the visual.[24] Indeed, in this regard we are reminded of the Aristotelian insight that what is first in nature may not be what is first for us. And if it was the attempt to find unity within plurality that provoked Brentano (the man who turned Husserl's thinking towards intentionality), to inquire into any possible unity and ground that the first might have (his analysis of Aristotle's four categories of being), then by so doing Brentano's doctoral dissertation set phenomenology's horizon. Phenomenology became that which opens itself up upon the divergent manifold in order to locate the unity which inheres within the manifest possibilities of the sensible world.[25]

As Brentano noted, Aristotle wrote in the fourth book of the *Metaphysics*, that 'Being is said in many ways'; this saying in many ways produces in the seventh book of the *Metaphysics* the recognition that '[T]here are several senses in which a thing may be said to "be"',[26] a divergence at source that calls into question the project of origination itself and the quest for a non-metaphysical ground. Aristotle himself found this deeply problematic and though he sought unity in *ousia*, in a substance which underpinned the several senses with a common form (*eidos*), he always hesitated about its status. Unable to define it as either differentia or genus, Aristotle was forced to return to the 'original' manifestation of the fourfold, and invoke analogy for evidence of *ousia*'s primacy and presence.

It was precisely this problem, the problem of how to recover from ever-changing appearance the unity of essence, which provoked Husserl to give a transcendental account of how phenomena were able to hold a unified form, at the same time as he was accepting the absolute priority of the exhibition of this ideality in the phenomenon itself. Indeed, Husserl often found himself in the difficult situation of arguing for an intuited and phenomenological manifestation of essence whilst at the same time defending the thesis that the ground of this essence lay in the mind and not in the phenomenon itself. However, to investigate appropriately Husserl's complex understanding of essence, and also to suggest against the atheistic account of Husserl that I have so far presented that his work is defined less by an excess of immanentising intention and perhaps more by the presence of the transcendent inexhaustibility of the object, would lie outside the focus of this chapter. None the less, my focus might take greater shape via an elucidation of the following: this phenomenological opposition to theology, even before it was fully articulated or understood as such, was ensured by Husserl's transcendental erasure of transcendence from his account of phenomenal possibility, an erasure that was prompted, as I have said, by Husserl's desire to render immanent and internal all the elements necessary for full apodictic cognition. However, the phenomenological recovery of the question of what was first, even if it had eradicated the divergence of transcendence from immanence, had still to account for the seeming divergence and disjuncture of original primary experience. Moreover, if phenomenology had originally sought the unity of the ideal and the real in primary manifestation, and if this primary manifestation subsequently showed itself not to provide this assurance of unity, then one can perhaps ascertain at a deeper level the origin of Husserl's desire to secure phenomenality against this possibility by his account of transcendental subjectivity.

Yet leaving aside any understanding we might have of why Husserl believed that apodictic cognition had to eradicate transcendence from phenomena, we can in all honesty no longer accept the claims made for the potency of the (idealistically conceived) intentional act. If this is so, then it appears that phenomenology must forego a unified account of knowledge and descend into the realms of the many, becoming (eliding for now the exception of the Heideggerian deployment), a mere description and recognition of ever-changing appearance. Phenomenology so conceived would be unable to give an account of any deeper concordance between the mind and its object other than the mere description of the succession and juxtaposition of varied sense impressions on empirical intuition. Which would be to say that though phenomenology came to diagnose the ills of philosophy as arising from a theological relationship to phenomena – in the sense that theology as a false form of distanciation forbids, as Husserl might put it, 'cognition from touching its objects' – the exclusion of the transcendent in the name of the immanent requirements of secular cognition does not appear to have facilitated an eidetic relationship to essence. Indeed, the occlusion of the transcendent in the name of what it is possible for the transcendental ego to experience raises the question as to what it is possible for us to experience if the ego is also regarded as an unverifiable assumption that should be placed under an *epoché*.

All of which would be to say that the attempt to exclude theology from phenomenology appears to have reckoned without the irreducible persistence of transcendence. Apart from suggesting that theological accounts of transcendence and God are not reducible to the ready caricatures and assumptions of secular thinking, this thought raises the possibility that the theological presence in phenomena is either so positive that no *epoché* can remove it, or else so negative that it escapes any codification as a metaphysical positivism. In which case the theological dimension of phenomena would be there despite any acts of transcendental reduction, or in the case of Heidegger this dimension would be so original as to place at risk the priority and ascendancy of any fundamental ontology that sought to separate itself from theology. And to say this is to suggest that the atheistic attempt to find with Husserlian phenomenology a non-theological ground, unity or even meaning within divergent experience departs from the irreducibly theological nature of that experience in order to do so. Or conversely that when the foundational project of phenomenology was abandoned by Heidegger in favour of his account of ontological difference (the difference between Being and beings), this difference was apparently thought by him to be more than enough to separate both Being and beings from any relation to God. Indeed by separating Being from revelation Heidegger was able thereby to argue that Being was not an issue for faith as the sole subject for faith was revelation, as the analysis of the manifestation of Being in beings belongs apparently only to philosophy and not theology.[27] Yet this seems to be theologically problematic as it appears to leave the consummation and highest explication of a sphere of being to Being itself, a Being idolatrously assumed to be other than God. Whereas for theology it is God – and not this mystical pre-Christian account of Being – that lies at the origin of all being. And if the Heideggerian assumption that Being can manifest itself more essentially apart from God than it can with him appears dreadfully wrong, then we have perhaps already glimpsed that there must be – for theology – something more fundamental to Being and beings than any Godless account of ontology can capture. Not least because it is the recognition of God which makes ontology possible (in the sense that it is God who is Being, or rather God who includes Being within himself, and it is He who gives Being to beings), and not this atheistic and mystical account of ontology that gives God his possibility. Theology cannot accept that there is any aspect of the created world that is essentially more manifest apart from God than with Him, yet it is exactly this assumption that appears to have governed the accounts of the phenomenal world that both Heidegger and Husserl have given.[28]

This might be explained by the fact there seems to be in Husserl (most obviously) and Heidegger (less noticeably but perhaps no less decisively) a residual transcendentalism that prohibits the full theological self-disclosure of phenomena, since in respect of Heidegger, as Jean-Luc Marion has pointed out, in *Sein und Zeit* it is impossible to have a manifestation of Being apart from being.[29] And if the disclosure of Being relies to this extent on a being, then the account of the being for which Being is an issue (Dasein) seems perilously close to determining what is possible on the basis of Dasein's account of possibility. Now it seems that Heidegger believes that Dasein is not open to theological possibility, and for this reason one has great difficulty in seeing this atheistic construal of Dasein as anything but a residual transcendental assumption. For it is surely a transcendental assumption that Being can be precipitated off from God because it is an issue for beings, whereas God apparently is not an issue for beings and so not a possibility for Dasein.

Indeed, at the risk of making an assertion, it seems that these phenomenological projects cannot bring themselves to think the thought that their own constitutive assumptions, their own assumptions about possibility, their own assumptions about what it is possible for either the ego or Dasein to experience, betray a lack of faith in what appearances can bear and what phenomena can and do disclose. For if the search for origins, for the recovery of what was first, be it the drive for a primary foundational certitude, or be it the Heideggerian denial of any such commerce between phenomena and an *ens originarium*, dismissed theology as being of a piece with the metaphysical thinking that precluded any authentic discernment of origin, then the phenomenological refusal to take account of theology and its descriptions of the relationship that might pertain between created phenomena and their origin in the Creator seems to look ever more arbitrary and indeed ever more peculiar.

Part of the origin of this situation lies, in the fact that phenomenology has always viewed transcendence as a contradictory notion that disturbs the fundamentally immanentist nature of cognition. Perhaps this follows from phenomenology's insistence that consciousness is always *consciousness of* something and that an object is always an *object for* something. However, this *'consciousness of and this object for'*, whilst it includes every meaningful thing in its mutuality, fails to see an encounter which might also be present in such a reciprocality. This excluded term is as one might expect – transcendence. And it is questionable whether phenomenology, despite its many and manifold developments, ever escapes its fundamentally immanentist construal of the relation between the subject's intentionality and the giveness of its object.

However, it may be objected that neither Husserl nor Heidegger excluded transcendence from their accounts and from their phenomenology. There is no doubt that this is true; none the less the accounts of transcendence that one finds there are in the end accounts that are managed by a transcendentalism for which transcendence will always be a form of sublimity. For example, even though Husserl can be seen to readmit the possibility of transcendence (in the sense of the transcendence of the object over and above the immanence of the subject), through the very difference of the object from the subject, the transcendental subject still manages the transcendence of the object through the ego's own determinate intentionality, even though the phenomenological object is often thought by Husserl to be an almost sublime horizon of perceptual indeterminancy.[30] Similarly, even though Heidegger in *Sein und Zeit* did produce an account of transcendence, the relation between Being and Dasein is such that there can be no question of this transcendence eliding Heidegger's transcendental account of Dasein's possibility, nor his atheistic account of ontological difference, since transcendence is still understood as finite transcendence, that is, as the very finitude of the finite – being towards death (*Sein zum Tode*). And it is so interpreted precisely because, even for Heidegger, transcendence is still construed within the terms of this immanentist 'consciousness of and object for'. Transcendence is therefore defined via its manifestation *for us*, which is quite simply for any

finite subject that believes in nothing but its own account of possibility –
death. to say this is to contend that transcendental self-sufficiency still lies at
the heart of phenomenology, even after its Heideggerian revision and even
after a new non-original and indeterminate relationship is thought to pertain
between Being and beings, because it is now thought to be this peculiar relationship, rather than that of the Creator to his creatures, that is thought to
be the way to account for the ontological difference. All of which is to say
that theology, insofar as it refuses to be limited by any such ratio with finitude,
sees at the heart of phenomena an utter transcendence of self-sufficiency in
all its forms.

Despite such remarks, it is not a mistake to open the question of transcendence in the tradition of phenomenology, not least because theology should
agree with phenomenology that any account of possibility must indeed lie in
an adherence 'to the things themselves' (*zu den Sachen selbst*), and in a wish to
give a full account of what is truly given.[31] This is to say that if the most fundamental possibility of phenomenology does lie in its desire to give an account
of the real, in its wish to see everything that can be seen when the world is
allowed to show how things are, then this is a project that should be undertaken without prejudice or secular presupposition: not least because for theology there is a visible warrant to see the world and its possibilities quite
differently, even if this visibility has not yet been fully seen by the philosophy
that was founded on the possibilities of phenomena. And to open up phenomenology to theology suggests that such a project seeks to bring into conjuncture that which theology never divided – the principle of reality and the
principle of salvation. It suggests that this question, and more importantly
this search, would not necessarily terminate in an account of a phenomenal
world which is separable in principle or practice from transcendence and all
its possibilities. For a world which separates itself from transcendence and
from God finds that it can give no true explanation of itself or of its origin. As
a consequence, in any attempt to explain the world, immanentism finds itself
unable to produce its own closure (which it above all needs, to remain reflexively immanent) and transcendence always returns to fracture its phenomenal field. As a result immanentism culminates only in aporia and
ontological paradox. At worst, in the attempt to explain this incompleteness,
immanentist ontology turns itself into a warped and twisted form of theology
by hypostasising and worshipping this negation of completeness as a negativity that exists in-itself as the truth that lies behind all positive phenomena
as such.

Perhaps all this is because phenomenology had accepted too readily
Heidegger's claim that faith and phenomena are dimensions that manifest
themselves apart from each other. However, if one refuses to accept that revelation and phenomena are quite so separable, if one thinks that no phenomenon is self-sufficient and exists apart from its dependence upon God, and
if one thinks and sees that the phenomena themselves reveal their created

insufficiency and their dependency on the Creator, then one can have as it were a conjunction of faith and phenomena. Moreover, a phenomenology that has been brought to this accord with theology is one that would now seek to bring both God and phenomena together and so save each from metaphysics and onto-theology; a contention that would suggest that the phenomenological project still contains within itself possibilities – possibilities that have yet to be realised or fulfilled. The original phenomenological fear that transcendent possibility – the possibility of a non-immanent cognition – acts so as to negate actuality, is itself a misconstrual of the relation between actuality and transcendence.

For theology, actuality does not need to be secured by any transcendental account of its possibility; actuality is already secure in that its being is given and sustained by God. And as God is (in the Thomistic sense) the only fully actual being, then any actuality we or the world have is as a result of creatures already participating in and unconditionally receiving the being of the Creator. In this sense, for Christianity the ideal or the possible (what we might be) is given along with the actual. And as a result, when Christianity speaks of actuality and possibility, it is speaking of the situation that pertains to the created world, where any possibility that we might have is not prior to us but is rather the *very possibility of our actuality*, what we might become if we fulfil the form that we are given.

It is by contrast a nihilism, perhaps it is even the essence of nihilism, to posit possibility above actuality, as if in principle possibility is not the possibility of actuality. So when in *Sein und Zeit* Heidegger says '[H]igher than actuality stands possibility', there is another – as yet unexamined – sense in which his account does not itself escape either nihilism and metaphysics.[32] For if phenomenology cannot help separating possibility from actuality in order to break the hold of a naivety that sees actuality, or the natural world as described by science, as the only possibility, it fails to argue or see that this ontic account of actuality is not real enough. By failing to contest this ontic account of the real, phenomenology accepts that actuality is ontic and pursues the ideal (Husserl) or the ontological seen as identical with the *nihil* (Heidegger) apart from this actuality, and as such separates the actuality of the real from its own possibility. Consequently we should perhaps not be surprised that secular phenomenology cannot show why the possibilities that it has described and secured (be it Heideggerian Being or the Husserlian Ego) should have produced a world anything like ours at all.

For the real issue is why we allow these non-Christian accounts to insert themselves behind the actuality we are given, as if they are somehow more truthful and more disclosive than anything that we actually see. But theology is not in this position, since for theology, that which we are given bears a discernible relationship to, and participation in, that which gives, which means again that perhaps it is indeed only theology that can overcome nihilism and metaphysics. Even if Heideggerian phenomenology claims that Being is exhibited only in beings, this Being does not have any love of beings; it does not in principle care which being it is an issue for since such ontic concerns are not an issue for it. However, this is not true for Christianity; for Christianity *what is* matters. Since what God created is never negated or destroyed, created actuality has a genuine and non-arbitrary relationship with divine actuality, and as a result any possibility or potentiality that the actual has is committed to the created actuality that actually shows itself. Moreover, this potentiality (what this being can be) is itself shown there in the world as a phenomenon that is inseparable from its material accompaniment.

In this case theology would be more faithful to appearance than any version of phenomenology yet articulated, as it could in principle see that which is covered up and hidden from secular vision – that actuality itself stands in possibility. And the actuality seen by theology would be an actuality that was in visible analogy and proportionality with its supposedly unseen possibility, and here phenomenology would pass over to theology because the status of this invisible possibility would not be resolved on the side of visibility. This visibility would not be, for theology, a knowable realm over and against which an unknowable and unseen sublime would stand threatening the negation of the world that we know, and thereby as a result maintaining the finite and transcendental account of the visible world. No, our whole picture of what visibility and appearance might mean would be changed. We would suddenly realise what phenomenology has itself at times also grasped, that the visible world is not a phenomenon that is determinable by human beings and their account of what it is possible for them to experience. Visibility is rather a glorious participation in a plenitude of donation, a donation that is nothing but the attendance of possibility on actuality, and the becoming actual of the invisible, which means again that any 'essence' that the world shows and reveals will not reside in or derive from the world and its inhabitants, nor from some false nothingness behind what is given – but rather from what makes and gives the world to be. And there is no concealment here, for what is shown in the analogy that the visible has with the invisible is the revealed flow whereby God overwhelms the world and yet maintains it. Moreover, it is this structuration and harmony of the world that cannot be accounted for or described by a secular phenomenology. For the secular hands over the description of the world to a nihilistic and Manichaean variant of atheism which argues that God is not present in what He has created. And if phenomenology has, by and large, fallen into this account and failed thereby to keep pace with the world and what is shown there, this is because it has denied what theology has always seen – that the 'essence of the world' lies in the essence of God.

Part II Emmanuel Levinas

> We have already said that it is improper to affirm of God that he
> does anything, or that he cannot do it, of necessity. For all neces-
> sity and impossibility is under his control.
>
> (St Anselm, 'Cur Deus Homo'[33])

Otherness and theology

To doubt the soteriology involved for Heidegger in the question of Being, and
in the same gesture to raise the possibility of God (as that very salvation), is
not, however, an intimation that is wholly unknown in the phenomenological
tradition. Emmanuel Levinas, writing at the conclusion of his 'Note préliminaire' to the opening of *Autrement qu'être* states that

> to hear a God not contaminated by Being (*entendre un Dieu non con-
> taminé par l'être*) is a human possibility no less important and no less
> precarious than to bring Being out of the forgetfulness (*tirer l'être de
> l'oubli*) in which it is said to have fallen in metaphysics and in onto-
> theology.[34]

Though Levinas's later work may have culminated in an attempted reorien-
tation of the phenomenological horizon away from the recovery of Being, to
a God not contaminated by such a search, this refiguring presents us with a
major question. For initially, if not at first, Levinas's concern had been to
establish not the priority of God but rather that of ethics. Indeed the thesis of
ethics as first philosophy was amply demonstrated in 1961 with the publication of Levinas's enormously influential magnum opus *Totalité et infini*.[35] It is
only after the publication of *Totalité et infini* that God, although present in
Levinas's work beforehand, begins decisively to influence his phenomenological 'method'. This change is perhaps most marked by the publication in
1963 of Levinas's paper 'La Trace de l'autre', where God is brought into the
argument in order to provide a temporality transcendent to that of immanence in order to safeguard the phenomenon of the other human face. And
this alignment between the demands and obligations of God and the interests
of the Other in respect of the erasure and nihilation of difference and alterity
by, to use Levinas's language, 'the same' seems only, in the work published
after the development of the notion of the trace, to have strengthened. Since,
in his second major work, *Autrement qu'être*, published in 1974, and indeed in
the important essay 'Dieu et la philosophie' published soon after that in
1975, alterity and God are brought into a relationship of mutual concordance
and even identity.

Leaving aside for now questions as to whether Levinas's project succeeds in breaking with immanence through a phenomenological and ethical encounter by the ego with an Otherness grounded in the phenomenon of the human face and vouchsafed as such by God, I would like to focus on what for theology would be the decisive issue – the deemed congruence of interest between alterity and God. Perhaps theology should question whether God is subsumable under the thought of the Other (*Autrui*), for it is not immediately clear that phenomenology or theology should approach God through the face of the Other,[36] not least because the bringing together of 'otherness' and God suggests that God finds Himself more explicitly expressed in His absence from the world rather than through His revelation in it.

Levinas, of course, situates himself within the Judaic and not the Christian tradition, and he has published a large number of texts and Talmudic interpretations meditating on otherness as indicative of the Jewish relationship to God and ethics. However, these religious texts are not my concern; I will instead focus on his philosophical works. And this focus reflects not just a division in the texts that Levinas himself wished to make, but rather it takes seriously Levinas's claim that his philosophical work is primarily phenomenological and so gives a description of an event that is not defined by or limited to anything other than the 'experience' of the irruption of otherness in human life.[37] Moreover, it is not Levinas's Jewish writings that have captivated current thinking, but rather it is his phenomenological account of otherness that has impelled so much recent theological work to embrace this seeming conflation of alterity and God.

Despite having said all this, it is still surprising that there has been such a wide acceptance by Christian thinkers of Levinas's language and thought, since the Levinasian elision of any distinction between otherness and God lies at odds with much of Christian tradition.[38] For Christianity God is not, surely, utterly foreign and utterly other to us. As Paul said, 'in fact he [God] is not far from any of us since it is in him that we live and move and exist' (Acts 17:27–8). Indeed it is in the first book of the Hebrew Bible that we are reminded that we are not so utterly unlike God since we are made in his image and likeness (Gen. 1:26). However, this is not to say that Christianity is unable then to make any distinction between God and man, or rather God and creation, for though we are in God we are self-evidently not God, and though we are made in God's image we are not as a consequence indistinguishable from Him.

And since God is not so Other to creation that he does not allow creation to reveal and rejoice in Him, then Christian theology is, or should be, a language that refuses to see the existence of created natures as anything but good. Given that this is the case it will not surprise us that no less a figure than Augustine held in *De Natura Boni* that '[N]o nature is evil so far as it is naturally existent'.[39] For St Augustine the good is held by any created nature insofar as it has a nature at all, since all created nature comes from God and participates in the Creator. Or as St Thomas Aquinas was to put it some 850 years or so later, '[E]very being that is not God is God's creature. Now every creature of God is good (I.Tim.iv.4): and God is the greatest good. Therefore every being is good.'[40] To say this is to say then that the thought of God's otherness (his irreducibility to us) has already been accounted for by Christianity as the excess of His givenness to us, a profusion and immoderation of love and visible donation that we can never be equal to. It follows then that any privileging of the language of God's otherness and alterity at the expense of his 'oneness' with us and his love of us is theologically invidious. Because if alterity divides us and our world from God, then it risks dividing the Creator from his creatures and making incomprehensible the idea of God as a loving author of us and the world.

However, with Levinas the language of otherness is wholly appropriate to God because nothing is wholly appropriate to Him. For Levinas, God is absolutely Other. He writes in *Dieu et la philosophie* that God is not simply the 'first Other' (*premier autrui*), the 'Other par excellence' or the 'absolutely Other', but other than the Other (*autre qu'autrui*), other otherwise, other with an alterity prior to the alterity of the Other, prior to the ethical bond with another and different from every neighbour', indeed God is apparently so other that he is 'transcendent to the point of absence' (*jusqu' à l'absence*).[41] One reason perhaps why God is viewed as other to the world is that for Levinas the world is defined so pejoratively. Now by 'world' I am referring here both to what is worlded (beings) and what worlds (Being), and also to that which in the Levinasian vocabulary precedes the presence of Being in beings and constitutes as it were the facticity of Being without beings: the sheer brute category of existence itself – the *Il y a*.

This pejorative account of the world and our existence in it comes about through Levinas distancing himself from Heidegger's account of ontology and man's relation to Being. This inclination first found full expression in his 1947 publication *De l'existence à l'existant*, where in a famous remark about Heidegger's work Levinas writes of his 'profound need to leave the climate of that philosophy'.[42] In this text existence is considered by Levinas in terms of what he perceives as the absolute indifference of existence to whatever actually exists, so much so that existence itself is redescribed by Levinas as the simple brute positivity of the *there is* (*Il y a*) of Being. Indeed, Levinas claims the *Il y a* to be a more general and thus more basic account of what there is than Heidegger gave in *Sein und Zeit*, since he suggests that the bounds of the *Il y a* are marked not by any finitude of Dasein but rather by the overwhelming elemental positivity of undifferentiated existence that threatens to absorb anything that might exist back into itself; thus an 'inhuman neutrality', as Levinas calls it, haunts the beings that exist in Being.[43] Levinas goes on to suggest that as a consequence Being has 'some sort of underlying evil (*mal foncier*) in its very positivity'.[44]

It is against this undifferentiated horror that subjectivity, or what Levinas will later call ipseity, takes form. This subjectivity is formulated for Levinas through an upsurge from the nameless horror of undifferentiated Being, the *Il y a*. The *Il y a*, as the primordial facticity of an existence without existents, is interrupted by the forming of an existent. Against the primordial night and silence of the no-thingness of sheer presence, the ego (for that is what is being formed) must constitute itself by mastering and naming this 'being' as its own, or risk becoming again a neuter, dissolved in the indifference and disregard of Being in general. 'To be conscious', Levinas writes, 'is to be torn away (*être arraché*) from the there is'; it is to become 'a master of being' and thus a 'name in the anonymity of night'.[45] The existent then takes form in the instant of its self-affective constitution, opens up an interval or a private domain in amidst the horror of darkness, and in this realm separates itself from generalised Being by claiming some of this generalised Being for itself, and thus the ego makes out of Being in general a substantivity and universality for itself.

The *Il y a*, however, still circumscribes this self-formed creature, though the consciousness of the creature has of necessity no regard for what lies beyond itself. For the Levinas of *Totalité et infini*, the very elements liberated from undefined generality give themselves over to the enjoyment of the ego, and the ego 'in living from the world (*vivant du monde*) lives at home with itself'.[46] This creature feeds on the world so as to back up away from generalised Being and construct its own particular interiority and identity. After such an auto-constitution this ego opens out upon the world as a representational economy of labour which 'understands' the world as a series of manipulable objects to be possessed and consumed. This labour wrests matter from the elemental enjoyment that the ego first has with it, and makes matter into thing, such that labour prevents any absorption back into undifferentiation and thereby 'masters the future and stills the anonymous rustling (*bruissement*) of the *Il y a*'.[47] Having constituted itself the ego then moves through the world, stilling any threat to it from objective anonymity by making all Being or existence its own property and possession: '[I]n labouring possession reduces to the same what at first offers itself as other.'[48] The resulting economy is then entirely egoist, and yet for the Levinas of *Totalité et infini* this egoism is *what it is to be*; wresting itself out from anonymity the ego exists for itself alone. Indeed in the earlier *De l'existence à l'existant* Levinas writes that 'the verb to be is a reflexive verb: it is not just that one is, one is oneself' (*on s'est*).[49]

Otherness and the need for God

It is of course against this whole picture of selfhood that Levinas counterposes the idea of infinity or Otherness. And the absolute value accorded to this Otherness appears to stem directly from the depth and depravity of the immanentist situation that it is taken to redeem, which means again that for

Levinas his account of selfhood or immanence does not just have the value of being a local description pertaining to one aspect of human relationship, but has a universal scope and an apodictic value. Since all '[P]hilosophy is an egology', and all our thoughts and thinking are similarly constituted, there seems little possibility of immanentist subjectivity redeeming itself by its own powers; instead egology exhaustively captures for Levinas the overwhelming and unavoidable nature of immanence.[50] In a sense however, with his subsequent validation of 'otherness', Levinas sets the possibility of a 'realist' encounter over and against this immanentist and essentially idealist picture of consciousness. However, this 'realist' encounter with alterity does not function (as a realism normally does) so as to achieve a seamless correspondence and exactitude between the mind and its impression of external reality. On the contrary, it is for Levinas precisely the encounter with radical exteriority which fractures and shatters the structure of any such reflective narcissism.

In *Totalité et infini* (1961), Levinas located the site of this radical alterity in the 'phenomenal' capacity of the other human being to 'face' the representational ego and refuse its cognitive processes via the very modality of its appearance. However, in *Autrement qu'être* (1974), he appears to locate this transcendence closer to home, not outside in a phenomenon that refuses all the normal a priori forms of phenomenality, but in the heart of subjectivity itself. Rather than offering an account of an immanentist subjectivity broken down by a 'relation' with an absolute alterity external to it, he suggests that at the heart of this immanentist subjectivity there is already exteriority, an exteriority which lies closer to the subject than its own consciousness. This exteriority is now thought to supplant the primacy of enjoyment as the core of subjectivity. Recodified as the very sensibility of the subject, alterity is now found disturbing and reordering the most intimate level of the incarnated flesh and skin of human life. In this way interiorised life becomes for Levinas, by the time of *Autrement qu'être*, an ever more eviscerated existence, with an increasing sense that there is no subjectivity for oneself anymore. For Levinas oneself (*le soi-même*) is now another.[51]

Nevertheless, this alterity, despite its increasing encroachment, is still thought of as a good which provokes a transcendence out of 'the world of the same' towards a state of ethical responsibility – even though this state now constitutes our subjectivity as such and so problematically precedes any conscious 'taking responsibility' which ethics normally requires. Obviously then there has been, after the publication of *Totalité et infini* in 1961, a discernible alteration in Levinas's work. Otherness is still the issue, but the means of its transmission to the ego has been radically reconfigured. The radicalisation of the priority of the other and its encroachment on subjectivity goes hand in hand with a sudden intensification of the role of God. Indeed in the more recent work it appears as though God can now in some sense be 'given' to phenomenology. To put it as simply as possible, this further change consists, I believe, in a departure from the phenomenology of the face-to-face to a curiously tri-nodal structure whereby another term intervenes in the face-to-face relation in order to invest the Other with an alterity that Levinas now seems to think it would otherwise lack. This new 'phenomenon' is God, a God thought through a temporal disjuncture in appearance – an interruption called the trace.[52]

The rationale for this change is in some way obvious, since the new pivotal role accorded to God is due in no small part to the recognition by Levinas that he still spoke, prior to the radicalisation of the other via its congruence with the trace of God, the language of ontology instead of transcendence, the language, that is, of interiority as opposed to the sought-after language of exteriority.[53] By Levinas's own admission then, the project of *Totalité et infini* fails insofar as it is still too ontological, in that *Totalité et infini* did not allow for exteriority or infinity to be thought or experienced on its own terms, but only as the overcoming of interiority or totality. As a result of this, the other for the Levinas of *Totalité et infini* could never function as absolutely Other to the self, since both exterior Otherness and interior egoity seem to be thought only through their relation to each other, a relationality that would for Levinas undermine any hopes of according an absolute transcendent status to otherness. In this respect it seems understandable why Levinas – hoping to maintain the absolute quality of otherness – reconfigured his project and brought God into the self–other relation to radicalise and absolutise the previously human dimensions of the other.

It is important to recognise the nature and extent of the change that this embrace of God forced upon Levinas's work. For example and by way of contrast, in his 1946/7 lectures published under the title *Le Temps et l'autre*, Levinas writes of the nature of the relationship with the other, '[T]his is not a participation in a third term (*troisième terme*). . . . It is the face-to-face without intermediary.'[54] By 1963, however, in 'La Trace de l'autre', we find as I have suggested that the other has lost his specificity and uniqueness. Now, apparently, the other is not sufficient unto himself, and there appears to be a requirement on behalf of the other to move beyond himself, to go to that which gives to him and his face the qualities that make him what he is – the Other. In 'La Trace de l'autre' Levinas writes, '[T]he other proceeds from the absolutely Absent. His relationship with the absolutely absent from which he comes does not indicate, does not reveal this Absent; and yet the Absent has a meaning in a face.'[55] Whereas previously this 'absolutely Absent', whatever it may be, had no purchase outside of the face-to-face relation, now this Absent is distinguishable, if not discernible, apart from the structure of the face-to-face, such that the notion of a third term suddenly presses itself into the description. Levinas continues, '[T]he relationship which goes from a face to the absent is outside every revelation and dissimulation, *a third way* excluded by these contradictories' (my emphasis).[56] The third way reveals itself as a trace, and 'because a trace signifies beyond being', it brings to the structure of the self–other relation the notion of a

third who now inhabits this 'beyond being' and makes possible our orientation to it.[57] Almost immediately Levinas writes that

> *Beyond being is a third person* (*troisième personne*) which is not definable by
> the oneself by ipseity. It is the possibility of this third direction of
> radical *uprightness* (*irrectitude*) which escapes the bipolar play of
> immanence and transcendence proper to being, where immanence
> always wins against transcendence.[58]

If then it is only the status and situation of the third that enables the self–other
relation to escape the play of immanence, who or what is the third? For
Levinas, though, to ask 'who' or 'what' is to give the third what it does not
have – a name or a noun. Instead Levinas gives the third a pro-noun, putting
the third in the form of the masculine third person singular *Il* (in English
He), or in its equivalent neologism *Illeity*. None the less there seems little
doubt that the third person, the He (*Il*), is God. For example in *Dieu et la philosophie*, Levinas writes, '[W]e have designated this way for the infinite or for
God, to refer, from the heart of its very desirability, to the non-desirable
proximity of others, by the term illeity'.[59] Or again in *Autrement qu'être*, when
writing of *Illeity*, '[I]t makes the word God be pronounced without letting
(*sans laisser*) "divinity" be said'.[60]

Despite its reliance upon anything given by a third, the other is still, however, encountered as a face, as that which refuses through contestation any
codification into the presentation of the world to consciousness. None the
less, this facing is no longer interpreted by Levinas as a purely phenomenological refusal of the intentional act; rather the divinised face manifests itself
amidst phenomena via its interruption of phenomenology. The face now
loses the intensity and peculiar positivity previously accorded to it in the
pages of *Totalité et infini*, and as such the divinised face now risks its own phenomenal abstraction and erasure. The face no longer 'appears' by itself in an
unmediated fashion as an attendance of the speaker with the spoken, and as
such the face no longer accompanies its manifestation as it did in *Totalité et
infini*; instead the phenomenon of the face is now mediated by God, the face
having become a visage 'seen' via a God that it is not, and a phenomenon
made possible by a temporality that is not its own. The face then interrupts
visibility and yet is itself a form of visual refusal, and as a result of this curious
oscillation between, and indistinction of, God and the Other, alterity now
loses the integrity and phenomenality it was accorded in *Totalité et infini*; now
the face like the trace 'disturbs (*dérange*) immanence without settling into the
horizons of the world'.[61]

In *Totalité et infini* Levinas wrote that the nature of the Other *qua* Other 'precisely signifies the absence of a third party taking in me and the other'; at
this stage there was an 'impossibility of the exterior point of view', as alterity
was 'produced only in the speaker who, consequently himself *faces*'.[62] Now,

however, the face of the other appears as an abstraction because the face requires the attendance of something else, as the other in order to be the Other must stand in the trace of the third. The third or *Illeity* comes to the face-to-face relation, because without it the other could never escape the play of immanence, in which alterity always falls back into the same. Moreover, this is explicitly conceded by Levinas as early as 'La Trace de l'autre'. For here Levinas accepts that it is God who as the third provides the necessary and sufficient condition of irreversibility, the impossibility of recouping the relationship between self–other back into the play of the same and the world of the self-identical. Levinas writes, '[T]he *illeity* of the third person is the condition for the irreversibility'.[63] The conclusion appears clearly drawn: God alone is He who can prevent alterity falling back into the same. Indeed we are told that 'illeity is the origin (*l'origine*) of the alterity of being'.[64]

Levinas and the nihilation of the phenomenal world

The cardinal feature of gnostic thought is the radical dualism that governs the relation of God and world. . . . The deity is absolutely transmundane, its nature alien to that of the universe, which it neither created nor governs and to which it is the complete antithesis: to the divine realm of light, self-contained and remote, the cosmos is opposed as the realm of darkness. The world is the work of lowly powers which though they may mediately be descended from Him do not know the true God and obstruct the knowledge of Him in the cosmos over which they rule.

(Hans Jonas, *The Gnostic Religion*[65])

What though does all this mean? Have I not been arguing for the introduction of God to phenomenology, have I not been trying to suggest that phenomenology has no legitimate basis for excluding God from phenomena? Why then this implied critique of Levinas? Has he not more than anyone else brought God back into a relationship with a phenomenology, a discipline that had previously been unable to acknowledge, see or even experience Him? And moreover if God is God He cannot be anything like us or our world, so what other form than otherness can He possibly have? How can God be anything but other to us, unless, that is, what I am arguing for in respect of God is a form of pantheism or immanentism?

Yet for me it is still questionable whether Levinas has really broken with any of the traditional prejudices concerning God and phenomenology. For if the deepest of these atheistic and in the end essentially Manichaean prejudices is that God and phenomena, in order to preserve their true natures, must occur apart from and in contra-distinction to each other, then Levinas can only be seen as fulfilling to an extreme degree this deeply ingrained and deeply idolatrous opposition. However, what is remarkable and what is new in respect of this tradition is that Levinas has taken the side of God against phenomena rather than the side of phenomena against God, such that it is the phenomenal world that is erased in the name of God, instead of the more common erasure of God in the name of phenomena. This means that instead of opposing, as did earlier phenomenology, an ideal possibility over and against an arbitrary actuality Levinas opposes an idealised 'actuality' (albeit one 'beyond' the actual) actuality over and against any empirical possibility whatsoever, since for Levinas actuality has now passed from us to God and we now occupy with others the realm of the merely possible, a site that serves only to demonstrate the ascendency and absolute transcendence of this divine 'actuality' over any concern for us or our being. None the less, this Levinasian reversal still occurs within the same idolatrous opposition of God to His creatures, since it appears that for phenomenology creatures must either eradicate the Creator or the Creator must nihilate His creatures. And yet this antagonistic opposition is deeply idolatrous and flawed because it departs from the phenomenal relation that actually pertains between God and His creatures in order to reach this agon. Phenomenology refuses to understand or even see that St Thomas Aquinas was right, that God as pure act is pure actuality, and yet despite this God's actuality does not negate our possibility since our possibility is to be allowed to participate in His actuality and become more real as a result. And since God is a loving Creator, He is not indifferent to what He creates; He gives us the possibility of actuality. His actuality has a stake in ours; He wants us to fulfil our form and so understand that we are not the merely possible creations of an indifferent power but an actuality that reveals His glory. And of course if we step outside His love then we will indeed become nothing, since we would separate our actuality from Him and fail to see that what we are given is not indifferent to us and our highest possibilities. As such any attempt to separate what there is from what there might be is a nihilism that departs from actuality for nothing whatsoever. Hence to oppose God to phenomena is to complete nihilism by celebrating the triumph of nothing over something. Moreover, to oppose the Creator to His creation is to separate the God who saves (the God of redemption) from the God who makes the world (the God of creation); is to fulfil a Gnostic description of a world already so completely handed over to evil and darkness that its nihilation and absolute erasure appears absolutely justified.

This means again that when Levinas, after *Totalité et infini*, brought God into the phenomenology of the face-to-face, God is never accorded any positive relationship to, nor presence in, the phenomena that He transcends. Instead God becomes, in respect of the phenomenal, an absolute that has at the same time no visuality, an enigma to a phenomenal world that has for Levinas already been abandoned by any divinity. Indeed, in his 1965 essay 'Enigme et phénomène', Levinas argues once again that as '[T]he other can not appear (*apparaître*) without renouncing his radical alterity', then neither can the God that now sustains alterity, since He (God) is 'separate from the adventure of being which occurs in phenomena and in immanence'.[66] All of which is to say that Levinas accepts almost wholeheartedly Heidegger's idolatrous division of Being from God, except that now instead of Being separating itself from God, God separates Himself from Being, a point Levinas confirms when he asks '[I]s it not folly to ascribe plenitude of Being (*l'être*) to God who is always absent from perception'.[67] God conceived as this otherwise than Being assumes then the form of a chimerical universality whose ghostly presence disturbs the world of reality and appearance by the apocalyptic portent of the final dissolution and negation of all worldly essence.

However, just as it is less than obvious that a plenitude of Being is absent from perception, so it is less than evident that the essence of phenomena do not in some way lie in the essence of God. Perhaps Levinas's inability to perceive any other possibility lies not in the essence of appearance itself, but rather in his assumption that all phenomena are utterly pejorative. One reason for this may be that visibility is only understood by Levinas to be an intentional product of the ego. There appears to be for Levinas no dimension or domain essentially proper to what appears other than that of evil. Visibility and appearance are then by this account wholly immanentist, never able to produce, carry or convey transcendence. Perhaps again this is why we find in Levinas such extraordinary invectives against visual art and aesthetics. As early as 1948 we find in his work art being denigrated as a shadow of reality, for Levinas had argued in this regard that images disincarnate reality of its content by substituting for the real objects their visual images, images which are only shadows of the things which they depict.[68] Yet for a phenomenologist this is, in a sense, what reality is and can only be – imagistic appearance, which explains why, if for Levinas all phenomenality is irredeemably imagistic, all phenomenality is indeed irredeemable. But if all visual reality is an imagistic production of intentionality, that is, if all visual reality has fallen under the shadow of egoist projection or indeed the *Il y a*, then one can explain why Levinas departs from this visual reality in order to find the truly real beyond it, in which case we suddenly have a situation where that which is *not* visible has become the measure and site for the condemnation of visibility and all visibles. And even if this site is deemed to be that of the Other as God, then we suddenly have a position where a God annihilates the visible world, as it represents an idolatrous failure to adequately resemble or capture the reality of which He apparently is the only measure. Suddenly, however, this situation is starting to look perilously like what Levinas has described as 'the same'.

But in another sense this collapse back into 'the same' should not surprise us at all. It seems to be the natural result for an unresolved dualism. And Levinas's thought is deeply and utterly dualistic, a situation which has not changed for all this recent talk of the third. For it remains the case that the distinction between the 'otherness of the other', and the 'otherness of illeity' cannot be made – let alone maintained in any coherent fashion. They are both neither entirely absent nor visually present, and as such 'the other' and 'the third' are either both species of the same otherness or so other that they differ to such an extent that they cannot be thought to have anything to do with one another at all. This is to say that Levinas's dualistic and antagonistic account of the relation between self and other has not been changed markedly by the introduction of the third. The opposition of the face-to-face through the ceaseless demands of the always suffering and yet negatively transcendent Other remains the decisive fulcrum. However, the introduction of this third term, whilst not changing the essential structure of the self–other relation, has had the effect of intensifying the nihilation and negativity that the other always represented for the self. Indeed the introduction of God to Levinas's phenomenology has resulted not in the foundation or creation of anything at all, but rather in the almost complete eradication of any stable subjectivity whatsoever.

In the later work the very sensations that once gave themselves over to egoist selfhood and its joyful elemental immersion are experienced as the means whereby ethical accusation and alterity enters into our private life. The subject reconfigured as a 'pure passivity' whose essence lies in vulnerability, now exists without even the protection of labour and possession (which itself was another example of evil ontologised) from the ever-encroaching potency of the freshly divinised and increasingly horrific Other. Now subjectivity feels alterity as the pain of its own self-erasure, for the subject facing the other experiences a 'stripping beyond nudity', a 'being torn up from oneself', a 'being less than nothing'.[69] Subjectivity has become for Levinas by the time of *Autrement qu'être* the 'breaking point', where the self facing the 'impossibility of escaping (*se dérober*) responsibility' finally accepts the necessary surrender of his ego to the other and the interests of alterity.[70] Of course this 'break up of essence is ethics', since for Levinas the being that we have and are given is not a good, as 'goodness is *other* than being (*l'être*)'.[71] But in that case this goodness which comes to beings to nihilate them is obviously and necessarily violent, since if goodness is other than being then no being can by definition be good, and as a consequence there is for any being facing this goodness the necessity of its own 'sacrifice without reserve'. For the existent has now become the hostage of this goodness and 'the sacrifice of a designated hostage who has not chosen himself to be a hostage', but who has been 'elected by the Good' (*le Bien*), is apparently for Levinas the final triumph of goodness over the invidious nature and volition of the existent.[72]

If one thinks, however, that goodness should sustain and fulfil life rather than negate and sacrifice any existent creature, then, from Levinas's perspective, one will have misunderstood reality and existence. For Levinas ontologises evil and makes it the principle of all reality and Being. And if Being is wicked then so are the beings that participate and share in Being, hence the Manichaean and blasphemous need to negate and sacrifice the existence and existents of this world. The problem here is that having coded all reality and all phenomena as a negative – apart, that is, from the interruption of this reality by another negative phenomenon (and what is the Other now if not a negative phenomenon?) – it becomes increasingly clear that negativity or an absolute and total negation of all beings is the only result of Levinasian ethics. And let me be clear, to say this is to say that the Other and the *Il y a* have become *exactly the same phenomenon*. It follows then that Levinas's whole project of distancing himself from anonymity and an existence without existents has only succeeded in reiterating and reinstating in an ever more exact and explicit form the domination of the *Il y a*. Moreover, just as it is impossible in the realm of concepts to distinguish between the absolute anonymity of the *Il y a* and the absolute otherness of the Other, so it is also impossible to distinguish between their respective phenomenologies either. For if the *Il y a* is accompanied by the experience of the horror of anonymity, then so too is this divinised Other of *illeity*, since the Other, like the *Il y a*, is also in itself absolutely unknown and yet as it has a face without a face terribly present; as a consequence this Other also threatens to eviscerate us and reduce all our interiority and specificity to a horrific void where all living beings have vacated that which is essential to themselves. The project of transcendence centred around the Other has culminated then not in ethics but in the wholesale endorsement of an erasure of existents from existence. Moreover, Levinasian ethics never grew out of an affirmative model of human goodness and fulfilment, but only out of a reactive and secondary response to an ontology whose misery, violence and suffering are made inevitable and nihilistically necessary. For in reality Levinas has never really been interested in ethics itself, but only in ethics as a means to transcend and eradicate a world, a world that he has always idolatrously presumed to hand over to evil and wickedness. Indeed Levinas himself sometimes unthinkingly acknowledges this; he writes for instance in the fifteenth footnote to '*Dieu et la philosophie*' that it 'is the meaning of the beyond, of transcendence and not ethics' that his work 'is pursuing'.[73] But if transcendence finds its meaning in ethics and ethics finds its meaning in transcendence, and neither find their meaning in a world, then this is not only a circular means of validation but more terribly, only one side of a double nihilation. For if the world of beings is what is nihilated by Levinas, then it is a world that is nihilated on two sides, first by the beyond being of God, *illeity*, and second by the ever-present threat of negation back into Being in general, the *Il y a*, from which originally the world of existents arose.

This of course is to say that in reality the *Il y a* and *Illeity* are one and the same. For example, when one looks at *De l'existence à l'existant*, we find there (in this strangely prescient work from 1947) the following description:

Like the third person pronoun in the impersonal form of the verb. . . .
This impersonal, anonymous, yet inextinguishable 'consummation'

of being, which murmurs in the depths of nothingness itself we shall designate by the term *there is*. The *there is* inasmuch as it resists a personal form, is 'Being in general' (*être en général*).[74]

What then is the distinction from the *Il y a* of *Illeity*, this Levinasian God, this non-pejorative form of *il*, this good form of the third person? What then from the point of view of the creature is the difference between the threatening anonymity of the *Il y a* and the ethics of a God of absolute alterity who also threatens to eradicate the personal form of what is – presumably – his creation? What then does this say of a God for whom the world is so invidious that He must retreat into the absolute recesses of Otherness and alterity in order to annihilate what he has created? All of which suggests that, if *Illeity* is the good form of the third person, this is for Levinas because *Illeity* 'is somehow outside the distinction between Being (*être*) and beings (*étant*)'.[75] And goodness resides beyond this distinction precisely because beings no longer matter; all beings are pejorative, and Being itself inasmuch as it implies the very possibility of life (since as soon as you have Being you also have the possibility of beings), is also subjected to nihilation by the Other and the strange and perverse God that it has now become. For to be outside the distinction between Being and beings is to be nothing whatsoever, and the 'goodness' of this nothing must follow from the perception that the world and what exists in it are bad. And if that which we and others are is transcended and transcended without any account of us being also restored, redeemed and fulfilled, then this transcendence is only the completion of what Levinas had ostensibly opposed himself to all along, a total and complete absorption of beings by an empty and generalised universality.

And perhaps this was always obvious. Maybe Levinas represents the most extreme and yet the most logical culmination of the assumption that God does not give himself superabundantly to Being. And of course the resulting theological problems of accepting this idolatrous division of God from Being are many and perhaps even manifest. One can, if operating under this negative idolatry, give no account of why there is a world at all, nor any account of why there is for human beings the phenomenal presence and possibility of beauty, truth and goodness. For if one attempts to hold on to these qualities they must be given to the whole of creation and all of Being, since if one wishes to say that the world is wicked, whilst at the same time holding that one 'phenomenon' (Levinas's face for example) is good as it is Other to this world, that would mean that the rest of the world was utterly abandoned by God, and the resulting phenomenological chasm that this Otherness opens up between itself and every other nature would create an atheistic totality even as this Other claimed to transcend it, not least because the Other drains all the world of value in the name of value and denies God's phenomenal presence in order to testify to his absence. Hence the Other leaves the phenomenal world very much as both modernity and atheism have described it.

Yet from my perspective which reason must at least grant to be possible I would want to deny this whole story. I would want to say and see that all being insofar as it is created is good. I would want to accept the narrative of Genesis that after each and every act of creation God saw that which he had created and saw that it was good. For the image of God can never be destroyed; even if we do not yet fulfil it, we are in his image. To be, is to be in goodness, and to be in this sense is to be always in the image, an image or *imago* which as Irenaeus pointed out, represents our created form, which since it is God-given can never be negated or taken away. And if I have now shown the consequence of dividing Being from God, if I have correctly described the perverse and dreadful consequences of dividing God from Being as a divorcing of our possibility from any actuality that we might otherwise have, then a different imperative manifests itself out of the nihilation worked by the Levinasian Other. Phenomenology, it seems, must return to the visible world to show and discern how that which is given to us is not separated from that which we are given by Him. For phenomenology, that which is given to us is actuality as visibility, and since God is not reducible to the gifts given to us, He must in some sense be beyond visibility, that is, he must be in respect of the visible, *in*visible. However, if *in*visibility is not ultimately separable from visibility, and clearly if it is more than nothing it is not, then insofar as we are given actuality, God as the highest possibility of actuality must in some sense be visible to us. For if invisibility is not visibility's 'other', then that which is beyond visibility also gives itself to vision and appearance. Which means again that God as the invisible is not then separated from, nor indeed denied to, vision and manifestation. As such, this invisibility or possibility is that wherein visibility or actuality resides, for just as form is a gift made for content, so possibility is an actuality made for reality and invisibility is a donation that was made for vision. Which means again that God freely gives Himself to what is seen as a transcendent attendance of the highest possibility upon each and every actuality.

But here the human perspective inverts and reverses itself, because the possibility that God presents to us is suddenly revealed to be more real than any reality we might inhabit. Since God is the highest form of actuality – being in Himself the incomposite pure fullness of Being – He shows us that the actuality we have is nothing but the potential and possibility to become more real. And this donation and inundation of the highest reality shows itself as an attendance and superabundance of an ever more real invisibility on a participating visibility that strives to fulfil and complete the form that it has been given. As a consequence each visible uncovers its reality in the shape of an unfulfilled possibility and promise. Yet the unfulfilled possibility of this promise is not a negation or lack in each visible thing, nor does the reality and possibility of the invisible reside apart from visible actuality in a realm content with itself. On the contrary, the inability of each visible to be adequate to the plenitude which it is given shows the utter presence and attendance of the Father and His inexhaustable love for what He brought into being. As a consequence, just as a cause overwhelms and yet contains its effects, each visible fills up and spills over with transcendence, as God allows each and every existent being to reveal their participation in Him, His actuality and His glory.

Notes

1 Ludwig Wittgenstein, *Tractatus Logico-Philosophicus*, London: Routledge, 1974, 6.44, p. 73.
2 Edmund Husserl, *The Idea of Phenomenology*, tr. W.P. Alston and G. Nakhnikian, Dordrecht: Kluwer Academic, 1964, p. 4.
3 Husserl quotes from Augustine's *De Vera Religione*, 39, no. 72. See Edmund Husserl, *Cartesian Meditations*, tr. Dorion Cairns, The Hague: Martinus Nijhoff, 1969, p. 157. Hereafter abbreviated as *CM*. It is of course highly doubtful whether Augustine's Trinitarian model can be subsumed under the aegis of monological subjectivity. Though Husserl forbade God to direct experience in the sense of a noematic correlate to a noetic act, he still drew upon God as an *Idee* (Idea in the Kantian sense), a unifying and limiting horizon that whilst not an objective correlate of intentionality could provide the possibility of a 'final ground' for the synthesising acts of the transcendental ego, a site that was, 'in principle', accessible to subjectivity through its own activity.
   See section 58 of the first volume of *Ideen zu einer reinen Phänomenologie und phänomenologischen Philosophie*, Halle: Max Niemeyer, 1922. English edition *Ideas*, tr. W.R. Boyce Gibson, London: Collier Macmillan, 1962. Hereafter *Id I*. Here Husserl, through seeking the facticity of a pure constituting consciousness, had sought to exclude the transcendence of God from that facticity. See also the Dilthey-Husserl correspondence, published in translation in *Husserl: Shorter Works*, ed. P. McCormick and F. Elliston, Brighton: Harvester Press, 1981. Hereafter *HSW*. For a brief discussion of the development of phenomenology in the light of this relationship see Chapter 2 of Otto Poggeler's *Martin Heidegger's Path of Thinking*, Atlantic Highlands, NJ: Humanities Press, 1987; which outlines the relationship between the work of Husserl, Dilthey and Heidegger, concerning factical experience and Christian faith.
4 For Husserl, as for Kant, God cannot be an object of knowledge, a position which for both thinkers does not exclude 'metaphysics' (understood in the phenomenological sense as a source of being lying outside the consciousness of that being) as a subject of discussion and regulation, but refuses metaphysics as a ground for such an inquiry.
5 As Husserl writes: 'I must lose the world by epoché in order to regain it again by a universal self-examination' (*CM*: 157).
6 Edmund Husserl, *Logische Untersuchungen*, vol. 2, part I, 2nd edn, Halle: Max Niemeyer, 1913, p. 6. At the time of the *Logical Investigations*, 1900–1, Husserl conceived this sphere of indubitable self-givenness rather narrowly, that is, only within the domain of the intentional act itself. However, after about 1906 or so he began to consider the object of the act (its intentional correlate) as also revealing this self-givenness, since the object itself was never given in one sole and single act but rather in a 'constitutive' fulfilment of each act of intentional consciousness. Of course for Husserl the essence of this intentional object is not illusory, it is real; but the ground for its reality lies rooted not in the object itself but in consciousness. As a result, since it is only the *epoché* that can reveal the constituting power of

consciousness, entities can reveal themselves *as themselves* only as a result of the *epoché* and only in the light of this relation being exposed and revealed, a point Husserl made in his 'Inaugural lecture' at Freiburg in 1917: 'What remains to us [after the *epoché*] is the totality of the phenomena of the world, phenomena which are grasped by reflection as they are absolutely in themselves (*in ihrer absoluten Selbstheit*)' (*HSW*: 15). What is interesting is that for Heidegger, after the abolition of the transcendental *epoché*, the things themselves were given the capacity to reveal themselves.

7 Edmund Husserl, *The Paris Lectures*, tr. P. Koestenbaum, The Hague: Martinus Nijhoff, 1967, p. 13.

8 The Husserlian injunction 'To the things themselves' is explicitly accepted by Heidegger in 1927 in *Sein und Zeit* as a maxim of phenomenology. In this regard see Martin Heidegger, *Being and Time*, tr. J. Macquarrie and E. Robinson, Oxford: Basil Blackwell, 1962, p. 50. Hereafter *BT*. And also in German *Sein und Zeit*, Gesamtausgabe, vol. 2, Frankfurt: Vittorio Klostermann, 1977, p. 37. Hereafter *SZ*. In this respect see also *BT*: 58, *SZ*: 46.

9 *BT*: 59, *SZ*: 47.

10 *Summa Theologica* Q11 A4. I will not attempt to reinscribe the Heideggerian distinction of Being and being, back onto Aquinas.

11 *BT*: 58, *SZ*: 46.

12 Again this reference is to section 58 of Husserl's *Ideas*.

13 *BT*: 51, *SZ*: 38.

14 Maurice Merleau-Ponty, *Phénoménologie de la perception*, Paris: Gallimard, 1945: '*c'est d'abord le désaveu de la science.*' The quote is from the celebrated preface, p. ii.

15 See Heidegger's *Phänomenologie und Theologie*, Frankfurt: Klostermann, 1970, p. 15. This lecture, 'Phenomenology and Theology', was first given on 9 March 1927 in Tübingen. The English translation can be found in *The Piety of Thinking: Essays by Martin Heidegger*, tr. James G. Hart and John C. Maraldo, Bloomington: Indiana University Press, 1976, This reference p. 6.

16 See Heidegger's *Identität und Differenz*, Pfullingen: Verlag Günther Neske, 1957. English translation, *Identity and Difference* (English/German edn), tr. Joan Stambaugh, New York: Harper and Row, 1961. Hereafter *ID*. Even though the term 'onto-theology' receives perhaps it fullest explication and most influential focus in this 1957 lecture, the term did not originate there. Indeed, during the 1957 lecture Heidegger himself attempts to give us the origin of his use of this term. For example he refers us to the fifth edition of *Was ist Metaphysik?*, published in Germany in 1949, in which a new introduction explicitly refers to the onto-theological nature of metaphysics; however, he also indicates that it was with the publication of *Was ist Metaphysik?* in 1929 that we can detect the original (albeit unstated) use of the term (see *ID*: 54–5). This perhaps would make sense because it is with *Was ist Metaphysik?* that Heidegger first defines the metaphysical issue as that of 'the being of the whole'. It is later on in his 1936 lectures on Schelling that Heidegger identifies the question of beings as a whole as a theological one, as opposed to the question of being in general which he apportioned to ontology. It is here that Heidegger to my knowledge first makes and then brings these two distinctions together under the label of 'onto-theology'. For references to this see note 19 below. I remain grateful to my colleague Laurence Henning for our conversation in respect of this issue.

17 *ID*: 54.

18 *ID*: 54.

19 See Martin Heidegger, *Schelling's Treatise on the Essence of Human Freedom*, tr. Joan Stambaugh, Athens: Ohio University Press, 1985, p. 51; Martin Heidegger,

Schellings Abhandlung über das Wesen der menschlichen Freiheit (1809), Tübingen: Max Niemeyer, 1971, p. 62.

20 *ID*: 58.

21 *BT*: 60, *SZ*: 48. '"Hinter", *den Phänomen en der Phänomenologie steht wesenhaft nichts anderes*.'

22 *Id I*: 125.

23 It is interesting that Aristotle appears to view first philosophy, metaphysics and theology as virtually co-determinate terms. Especially since so much thinking which seeks to be first philosophy endeavours to exclude metaphysics and theology from its inquiries. What is also notable is that Aristotle appears to accept that the issue of theology is one of origin; he says of the first theologians that they made the Gods (Ocean and Tethys) the fathers of coming-to-be (see Ar. Met. 983b 29).

24 See for example Husserl's 1907 lectures in Göttingen, published as *The Idea of Phenomenology*, tr. W.P. Alston and G. Nakhnikian, Dordrecht: Kluwer Academic, lecture III, p. 37.

25 See Franz Brentano, *On the Several Senses of Being in Aristotle*, ed. and tr. Rolf George, Berkeley: University of California Press, 1975. It was Brentano's later work on psychologism that provoked Husserl, his pupil, to suggest that the ground and unity of the manifold lay in the intentional actions of human consciousness itself.

26 *Met*. IV.2.1003a33, *Met*. VIII.1.1028a10.

27 See for example Anstösse: *Berichte aus der Arbeit der Evangelischen Akademie Hofgeismar*, vol. 1, 1954, pp. 31–7. The actual conversation was recorded by Hermann Noack, reported to have taken place in December 1953, and was apparently approved as a record of the discussion by Heidegger before its German publication. See also the English translation 'Conversation with Martin Heidegger', tr. James G. Hart and John C. Maraldo, in the *Piety of Thinking*, Bloomington: Indiana University Press, 1976, pp. 59–71.

28 This is not to say that certain theologians have not accepted Heidegger's division of faith and Being. The best and finest example of this is Jean-Luc Marion's influential text *Dieu sans l'être: Hors texte*, Paris: Librairie Arthème Fayard, 1982. Now whilst Marion might take a distance from Being for reasons that it risks idolatry and that God is free in all matters, not least that of his own being, the question as to whether this move eclipses or allows for idolatry remains open, because it seems, to me at least, that Marion accepts too wide a scope for Heidegger's account of onto-theology and its metaphysical influence over Being. He thus fails to see that though the thesis of onto-theology and its thought of Being may well have a history that stretches back to the Greeks, this history is not necessarily the same history as that of theology and its account of being. For example, in the preface to the English edition of *Dieu sans l'être*, written in January 1991, the two domains of Being that Marion says he seeks to liberate God from are the '*ens commune*', of the objective concept of Being which gives the same Being to both God and His creatures, and the Being that Heidegger seeks to uncover. However, Marion does not take account of Aquinas' and perhaps theology's, most important point – that the being that God has is in an *analogical relation* with the being that we are given. Consequently for theology there has not been quite the danger of idolatry when thinking God and Being that both Heidegger's account of Being and the tradition of metaphysically interpreting the '*ens commune*' risks! For an analogical account of being there is no possibility of a direct and univocal proportion or relationship to obtain between (to use the Heideggerian type again) God's Being and the being we are given. This means quite simply that analogy is not subsumable under any thought of onto-theology. Consequently the undue separation of God from Being

or beings is an acceptance of, rather than a resistance to, a Heideggerian falsehood about how theology has thought the Being of God and the Being of beings. In respect of this see Jean-Luc Marion, *God Without Being*, tr. T.A. Carlson, Chicago: University of Chicago Press, 1991, p. xxiii.

29 This point is made by Jean-Luc Marion in *Réduction et donation*, Paris: PUF, 1989. See for example p. 249 – 'Le Rein et la revendication':

Si l'énigme de *Sein und Zeit* tient à la dissimulation en lui de la différence onto-logique par une 'différence ontologique' bornée à l'analytique du *Dasein*, son aporie revient toute entière à l'impossibilité d'accéder directement au 'phénomène d'être'.

30 Many commentators on Husserl and his concept of intentionality fail to recognise that much of Husserl's own work on the reciprocity of the intentional act and the intended object paradoxically risk displacing the primacy of the intending subject. Indeed, one may perhaps recognise that at the heart of Husserlian phenomenology, at the heart of absolute immanence, lies the recognition of the transcendence and essential indeterminability of the object.

In reference to this, see again section 44 of Husserl's *Ideas*, where he speaks of the essential indeterminancy of perception. He writes: 'A certain *inadequacy* belongs, further to the perception of things. . . . In principle a thing can be given only "in one of its aspects", and that means only incompletely' (*Id I*: 125).

31 *BT*: 50, *SZ*: 37.

32 *BT*: 63, *SZ*: 51–2. 'Höher als die Wirklichkeit steht die *Möglichkeit*.' Of course the actual is never just actual. I am not arguing here for a naive realism, but for a connection of the actual and possible that does not posit behind what is given some sort of negative and nihilistic account of its possibility, e.g., the actual is this but it could just as easily have been something else. So for me it is imperative not to accept that behind what there is, is some sort of causative a priori negativity that is not committed to what it produces as its effect.

33 St Anselm, 'Cur Deus Homo', *Basic Writings*, tr. S.N. Deane, 2nd edn, La Salle, IL.: Open Court Classics, 1962, p. 287.

34 From the 'Note préliminaire' prior to 'L'Argument', which is the opening exposition of Emmanuel Levinas, *Autrement qu'être ou au-delà de l'essence*, The Hague: Martinus Nijhoff, 1974, p. x. Hereafter *AE*. English translation: *Otherwise than Being or Beyond Essence*, tr. A. Lingis, The Hague: Martinus Nijhoff, 1979, p. XIii. Hereafter *OB*. English translation amended. It is perhaps worth noting that the phrases italicised here for being in another language were also italicised in the original French, an emphasis lost in the English translation.

35 It is probably a good idea to give an indication of the time-scale and relationship of some of the publications that I will go on to discuss.

Totalité et infini was first published in the Hague by Martinus Nijhoff in 1961.

Levinas's article 'La Trace de l'autre' first appeared in the *Tijdschrift voor Philosophie* in September 1963. It was the publication of this piece by Levinas that prompted many of Derrida's revisions for the 1967 version of his famous article on Levinas's 'violence and metaphysics'.

This article by Derrida, 'Violence et métaphysique' originally appeared in the *Revue de Métaphysique et Morale* in the form of a two-part essay in 1964; it was then subsequently reprinted (with several important revisions which predominantly took account of Levinas's notion of the Trace) in 1967 for Derrida's collection, *Ecriture et Différence*, Paris: Editions du Seuil.

Levinas's second major work, *Autrement qu'être ou au-delà de l'essence*, was published in 1974 (again by Nijhoff). Chapter IV of this work, 'La Substitution', is identified by Levinas in the preliminary note to the book as the centre-piece of the whole work. This chapter appeared as early as October 1968 when it was published under the same title in *La Revue philosophique de Louvain*. Indeed throughout 1970–2, other important parts of *Autrement qu'être* were published in various journals and collections.

Levinas's other major statement around this time on the relationship of his work to the question of God, '*Dieu et la philosophie*', was first presented by him in the form of a lecture given at the University of Lille on 13 March 1973. It was given a further five times, the last presentation before publication being on 4 March 1974 in Geneva. A revised text of these lectures was subsequently published in *Le Nouveau Commerce*, in 1975.

By virtue of the above we can see that 'God and Philosophy', though roughly contemporaneous in terms of publication with 'Otherwise than Being', was actually accomplished some considerable time after the main work for 'Otherwise than Being' had been completed.

36 Here I shall follow convention and translate Levinas's *autre/Autre* by 'other', and *autrui/Autrui* by 'Other'. I shall also follow established procedure by using the standard English translations of Levinas's work together with the French equivalents. However, where I do amend some of the English translations this is noted alongside the normal references.

37 Levinas makes this point very clear in an interview with Richard Kearney. He says, in answer to the question of how he might reconcile the phenomenological and religious dimensions of his thinking, the following: 'I always make a clear distinction, in what I write, between philosophical and confessional texts' (*Face to Face with Emmanuel Levinas*, ed. R. Cohen, New York: SUNY, 1986, p. 18).

38 I take it as given that the influence of this 'language of otherness' has passed wholesale into contemporary Christian thought and theology, so much so that I find it hard to think of any influential theological work of the last twenty years that has not in some way imported Levinas's concepts and language.

39 St Augustine, 'The Nature of the Good', *Earlier Writings*, ed. J.H.S. Burleigh, Philadelphia: Westminster Press, 1953, p. 331.

40 St Thomas Aquinas, *Summa Theologica*, Pt 1 Q.5 Art. 3.

41 Emmanuel Levinas, 'God and Philosophy', tr. R.A. Cohen and A. Lingis, *The Levinas Reader*, ed. Seán Hand, Oxford: Basil Blackwell, 1989, pp. 166–89. Hereafter *GP*. The French edition is found in Levinas's *De Dieu qui vient à l'idée*, Paris: Vrin, 1982, pp. 93–127. Hereafter *DVI*. The references for this quote are thus *GP*: 179, *DVI*: 115.

42 Emmanuel Levinas, *Existence and Existents*, tr. A. Lingis, The Hague: Martinus Nijhoff, 1988. Hereafter *EE*. *De l'existence à l'existant* (1st edn 1947), 2nd edn, Paris: Vrin, 1982. Hereafter *DEE*. This quote *EE*: 19, *DEE*: 19. We can also find similar remarks about the avoidance of the anonymity of Being in a 1935 publication by Levinas entitled *De l'évasion*, reprinted in Montpellier by Fata Morgana in 1982.

43 *DEE*: 12. Preface to the second edition, as yet untranslated into English.

44 *EE*: 20, *DEE*: 20.

45 *EE*: 60, *DEE*: 98.

46 Emmanuel Levinas, *Totalité et infini*, The Hague: Martinus Nijhoff, 1961. Hereafter *TeI*. *Totality and Infinity*, tr. A. Lingis, Pittsburgh: Duquesne University Press, 1969. Hereafter *TI*. *TI*: 147, *TeI*: 121.

47 *TI*: 160, *TeI*: 133. Prior to the commencement of labour there is for Levinas the enjoyment of the elemental, which itself requires mastering because it threatens a retreat back into rather than a separation from the *Il y a*.
48 *TI*: 175, *TeI*: 150.
49 *EE*: 28, *DEE*: 38.
50 *TI*: 44, *TeI*: 14.
51 *OB*: 8, *AE*: 9.
52 The trace of the other was – as I have said before – originally published in the *Tijdschrift voor Philosofie*, September 1963, pp. 605–23. The trace was however already prefigured in *Totality and Infinity* in the chapter concerned with the dwelling (*la demeure*), in a section devoted interestingly enough to the relationship between representation and the gift (*la donation*) *TI*: 168–74. It is even possible to follow the lineage of Levinas's formulation of the trace back to the 1946/7 lectures published as *Time and the Other* (see note 54 below).
53 A retrospective remark Levinas makes in 'Signature' concerning *Totality and Infinity*. See 'Signature', tr. A. Peperzak, *Research in Phenomenology*, 8 (1978: 189).
54 Emmanuel Levinas, *Le Temps et l'autre*, Paris: Quadrige PUF, 1983. Hereafter *TA*. *Time and the Other*, tr. R.A. Cohen, Pittsburgh: Duquesne University Press, 1987. Hereafter *TAO*. *TA*: 89, *TAO*: 94.
55 A copy of the paper can be found in Emmanuel Levinas, *En découvrant l'existence avec Husserl et Heidegger*, Paris: Vrin, 1997. Hereafter *EDE*. The English version is 'The Trace of the Other', tr. A. Lingis, in M. Taylor (ed.) *Deconstruction in Context*, Chicago: University of Chicago Press, 1986, pp. 345–59. Hereafter *TTO*. *TTO*: 355, *EDE*: 198.
56 *TTO*: 355, *EDE*: 198.
57 *TTO*: 356, *EDE*: 198.
58 *TTO*: 356, *EDE*: 199.
59 *GP*: 178, *DVI*: 113–14.
60 *OB*: 162, *AE*: 206.
61 *TTO*: 354, *EDE*: 197.
62 *TI*: 251, *TeI*: 229.
63 *TTO*: 356, *EDE*: 199.
64 *TTO*: 359, *EDE*: 202.
65 Hans Jonas, *The Gnostic Religion*, 2nd edn, Boston: Beacon Press, 1963, p. 42.
66 Emmanuel Levinas, 'Phenomenon and Enigma', tr. A. Lingis, *Collected Philosophical Papers*, The Hague: Martinus Nijhoff, 1987. Hereafter *PE*. Incidentally this collection mistakenly dates the French publication as 1957 in *Revue de Métaphysique et de Morale*, whereas 'Enigme et phénomène' actually first appeared in the June issue of *Esprit* in 1965. It was subsequently included in the 2nd edition of *En découvrant l'existence avec Husserl et Heidegger* (*EDE*) published in 1967, p. 203–16. *PE*: 64, *EDE*: 206; *PE*: 67, *EDE*: 209.
67 *PE*: 62, *EDE*: 204. English translation amended.
68 See Levinas's paper 'La Réalite et son ombre', *Les Temps Modernes* 38 (1948): 771–89.
69 *OB*: 15, *AE*: 18 and *OB*: 75, *AE*: 95.
70 *OB*: 12, *AE*: 15 and *OB*: 14, *AE*: 17.
71 *OB*: 14, *AE*: 17 and *OB*: 18, *AE*: 22.
72 *OB*: 15, *AE*: 19. English translation amended.
73 *GP*: 188, *DVI*: 114. '*C'est la signification de l'au-delà, de la transcendence et non pas l'éthique que notre étude recherche. Elle la trouve dans l'éthique.*'
74 *EE*: 57, *DEE*: 94.

75 *TTO*: 358, *EDE*: 201. English translation amended. Usually it is traditional to translate *étant* by 'existent' in order to avoid reproducing the Heideggerian distinction between *Sein* and *Seendes*, thereby preserving something of the insistence of Levinas's early work that sought to describe a subjectivity not overly determined by Being. However, in this case as I think Levinas has surrendered this distinction to Being; the translation of *étant* by being might be justified.

8

THE THEOLOGICAL PROJECT OF JEAN-LUC MARION

Graham Ward

Let me begin by outlining the postmodern horizons within which Marion's work is situated. The first horizon is the post-metaphysical; that is, philosophically Marion works within the critique of onto-theo-logic. In this, as Marion is aware, 'I remain close to Derrida' (*GWB* p. xxi). The second horizon is what I would identify as the theological horizon of much postmodernism – the concern with the other and the elsewhere, the concern with that which remains unresolved, remains in question, while the critique of onto-theo-logic is forever being accomplished: in fact, that which prevents there ever being a final accomplishment of the onto-theo-logical critique. For Marion, it is this transcendental trajectory which 'develops an ahistorical "deconstruction" of the history of metaphysics. At least it claims to outline this "deconstruction" within the framework of a phenomenology that is pushed to its utmost possibilities' (*GWB* p. xxii). It is this openness which forestalls the apocalyptic end of metaphysics, Derrida's 'promise' or 'yes, yes'. The first of these horizons is critical, and the second is ethical – the reinstallation of the question of the other. And we do not need to travel far into the work of Levinas, Kristeva, Irigaray or Derrida to discover the importance of this second horizon and its concomitant concern to establish a new ethics, an ethics of ethics, an analysis of love.

Marion, despite describing this second horizon in terms of 'deconstruction' believes that in tracing the phenomenological economy of *agape* his 'enterprise does not remain "postmodern" all the way' (*GWB* p. xxi). He believes that at a certain point he can move beyond postmodernity's concern with onto-logical difference. He runs his pen along postmodernism's post-secular horizon in order to indicate 'a point of reference all the more original and unconditional' (*RD* p. 303). But at this point a *volte-face* occurs and Marion proceeds to erase the horizon he has outlined and the postmodern project along with it. For in this *volte-face* Marion forecloses the postmodern questioning with an uncritical dogmatism. It is this dogmatism which marks Marion's theological, as distinct from his philosophical, project and it is this *volte-face*

229

which I am attempting to outline and understand in this chapter. The two horizons of the postmodern project, therefore, provide Marion with his Eucharistic site, but it is Marion-as-Conservative-Catholic who places upon that site the transubstantiated host elevated by an ecclesiastical authority. The postmodern site is used to draw attention to an *a priori* gift, *la donation*, but then Marion proceeds to a naming of the giver (as God) and the world as icon (the incarnated gift). In the work of Marion, therefore, the possibilities beyond postmodernity focus upon the question of legitimation. At a certain point in this work there is a turn, the explicit espousal of an authoritative given and an explicit commitment to what Bauman has termed an imaginary community.[1] As Bauman's thesis explains, this is a typical postmodern response.

If we wish to determine the scene of the *volte-face* more precisely, I would suggest that it lies in the centre of *God Without Being*. In French the title of this book is both equivocal and polemical. For the title is *Dieu sans l'être* – God without being and also, homophonically, God without the letter; which explains the second part of the title *Hors-texte*, beyond or outside the text. As Marion writes in his Introduction '*Hors-texte* indicates less an addition than a *deliverance*' (p. 3). What it is a deliverance from we shall have to examine later. For the moment it is sufficient to realise that, on the basis of Marion's argument for the God beyond logocentrism (an argument which is concluded in Chapter 5, 'Of the Eucharistic Site of Theology') it is necessary to move into the second part of the book, the *Hors-texte* which opens with 'The Present and the Gift'. The polemic lies in the way it turns Derrida's infamous dictum of *différance*, '*il n'y a pas de hors texte*', on its head. In the blank space between Part 1 and Part 2 of Marion's *God Without Being* we find a fulcrum point that has shifted the entire direction of his thinking.

Let me briefly rehearse the direction of that thinking. Marion's engagement with the question of Being issued in a *tour de force* published in 1977, when he was only 30, *L'Idol et la distance*. Here, Heidegger's ontological difference is challenged by Levinas's (and Maximus the Confessor's) concept of 'distance' and the Other than (*au-dela*) Being. Aided by Levinas's distance-in-relation, Marion proposes a space surpassing ontological difference in which the giving of the gift beyond Being, the gift also of Being, can be thought. Levinas's concepts, in their turn, are challenged by Derrida's *différance*, and Marion appropriates a space in which '*différance* seems to offer distance characteristics which distance required in order to think about itself' (*ID* p. 286). Derrida develops, and perfects, Levinas's thinking for Marion. This distance is now named '*distance du Père*' – the Father's distance and distance from the Father. Beyond ontology, maintaining ontology, is the rule of the Father who gives, who loves. The revelation of this loving is finally developed in terms of the economy of giving as it is sketched out in Heidegger's concept of *Ereignis*: 'creation corresponds to the gift (*Gabe, etant*) and the Father acts (as *Ereignis*) to give it' (*ID* p. 304).[2]

Postmodernism provides Marion then with the post-metaphysical structures whereby the distance of the Father and his gratuitous love can be thought beyond onto-theology. He pursues postmodern existential phenomenology, he employs postmodern hermeneutics (of *différence*, *différance* and *Ereignis*) and writes theology within the transcendental horizons they open up. Phenomenology folds in upon itself, opening a fourth dimension of love beyond knowledge and: 'The humble and unthinkable authority of the Father remains first and foremost that which puts at a distance Being as the icon of distance itself' (*ID* p. 315).

More recently, in 1991 Marion published *La Croisée du visible* in which he explores a phenomenology of perception. Again the idol, icon and the gift are foundational concepts for tracing the theology which constitutes 'an unimpeachable moment in all theories of pictures' (*CV* p. 8). The relation between the icon, the face of Christ and the sacrament is developed through analyses of visibility in terms of the image, the ectype and the prototype. He concludes that the icon

> breaks with the figured allocation of the visible in the perceptible face for the invisible in the intelligible, because it substitutes for imitation . . . a transition . . . this transition does not manage the visible and the invisible, but organises them with a view to revealing . . . charity . . . a movement from the Son to the Father prior to the passage from type to prototype, and visible to invisible . . . [C]harity reveals that the Father gives himself in and as the Son, that the prototype opens itself up in and as the visible. . . . The icon is completed in the paradox of an invisible sanctity, from which it is dispensed. Thus the icon even surmounts the metaphysical iconoclasm of our age.
>
> (*CV* p. 150)

Heavily reliant upon exegeses of the Early Church Fathers, Marion's thinking is moving along broadly Platonic lines. What is absent is any of the debates found earlier in his work for establishing the characteristics of the icon (and the idol) on the question of ontological difference and the possibility of thinking beyond the ontological question. Charity 'alone renders the icon possible' (*ibid.*). Marion is no longer attempting to examine an icon of distance as it is discovered in and as Being. The gift of Being does not become thinkable on the basis of an engagement in, with and through postmodern thinking. The project of Being has been replaced by the project of visibility,[3] ontology by aesthetics, and Marion appears to be moving towards a theology of the *sacramentum mundi*. It is a natural theology insofar as revelation occurs in all visibility. All visibility is founded upon that which is given by the invisible and bears the marks, the cross, the imprimator of the invisible. The cross is the icon for visibility itself. In a curious way, Marion has then embraced

231

the relation between seeing and knowing, the ocularcentrism so radically challenged by Foucault, Derrida and Irigaray.

A profound shift of thought between his early work and its later development is evident. There has been a shift in emphasis. In the early work the emphasis is upon the idol and its inextricable ties with ontology and the visible. Marion took seriously the dazzling attraction of the phenomenological. He recognised the difficulty of circumventing visibility or representation. Even in the early chapters of *God Without Being* Marion recognised the difficulties of withdrawing God from idolatry, from 'the will to power, hence metaphysics in its completion, hence finally. . . . Being itself envisaged as the Being of beings' (*GWB* p. 60). God had to be thought outside and was this possible? Was it possible to outwit Being? Marion engaged and struggled with the task these questions posed. But we move into much clearer water in his later work. Untroubled by the will-to-power and Being's all too visible idolatry, his French prose is washed in a more rarefied, mystical light. In the closing pages of *La Croisée du visible* the icon is defined in terms of the power it invokes to venerate the invisible and to pray. The result is a gnosticism. The dialectic of the idol and the icon has become the subsumption of the idol by the icon:

> the look . . . recognises in the visible paint the anterior and alternative reality (*reelle*) of an other (*autre*). . . . In effect, the icon only merits veneration to the extent that it shows an other than itself and thus becomes the pure type of prototype. . . . The image is snatched from idolatry by totally destroying the screen of its visibility in order to be poorer, like the pure sign of that which marks it.
>
> (*CV* p. 152)

Despite Marion's statements that 'the icon saves the image from auto-idolatry' (*ibid.*), the image (the visible, the phenomenological) is not 'saved' at all but effaced. Marion dissolves the postmodern crisis of representation in an apocalyptic light, '*un feu qui ne detruit plus*' (*CV* p. 154).

In Marion's later work, then, the icon and the invisible consume the problematic of Being and representation which he struggled with much earlier. No longer does 'Ontological difference . . . present itself thus as a *negative* propaedeuctic of the unthinkable thought of God' (*GWB* p. 45). The question of Being is not at all important. The question this chapter wishes to address is *why* it is no longer important. I think we can trace the answer by returning to *God Without Being* and those pivotal chapters, 5 and 6. For it is here that he first moves beyond the project of postmodernity. And his moves are both deft and illicit. Illicit insofar as much is left unsaid and unaccounted for in the moves he makes. Let me detail them briefly.

The dialectic of the *idol and the icon* in *God Without Being* develops in a way not evident earlier and not evident again later in Marion's work. It is developed here in terms of conceptualisation, whereas earlier and later the idol and the icon are understood in terms of two modes of visibility and reception. By this move, the idol and the icon are affirmed as modes of representation and Marion's project is related to the theological problem of divine predication and related also to the more general problematic of naming. What is absent is Marion's awareness that a certain metaphorical slippage takes place as we move from discussions of visibility – Athena on the Acropolis (*GWB* p. 10) – to discussions of the conceptual idol in which 'the measure of the concept comes not from God but from the aim of the gaze' (*GWB* p. 16). 'Gazing' here can only be metaphorical, likewise the use of 'idol'. We stumble across this rather typical move in Marion several times – the movement from the concrete, the *reelle*, into the metaphoric, where objects continually lose their specificity, their texture if you like.

This move occurs most profoundly in his account of transubstantiation in Chapter 6. Theology must be interpreted by or as the priest at the Eucharist, for in the Eucharist there is a recognition of 'the nontextual Word of the words' (*GWB* p. 150). The Eucharist in turn must be interpreted through the Scriptures (Luke's account of the Emmaus encounter)[4] and the theologian is exegete. In this circular hermeneutical practice, time and sign collapse into participation in a current liturgical event. But throughout that event there circulates an authority, a hegemony, which authorises going 'beyond the words as far as the Word' (*GWB* p. 153). The authority is both God's and the Church's, since 'All is given to the Church so the Church can return it . . . to the Word' (*GWB* p. 158). Theology as a textual practice, as writing, is subsumed beneath theology as liturgical praxis, as transubstantiation, as the 'place of the Word'. The theologian becomes priest and the priest is 'invested by the *persona Christi*' (*GWB* p. 153). Nothing and no one is what or who they are phenomenologically, objects become signs and signs take on 'spiritual meaning' (*GWB* p. 156). Marion informs us that the materiality of bread and wine becomes the body of Christ, 'a simple, perceptible medium' (*GWB* p. 167), and the sacramental body of Christ completes the oblation of the historically material body of Jesus. The material *body* of bread and wine becomes the sacramental *body*. This body issues from and completes the historical *body* which is then assimilated into the 'ecclesiastical *body*'. This ecclesiastical body is 'more real – than any physical *body*', for it constitutes the 'mystical *body*'. The italics throughout are mine, but in this economy what happens to the word 'body'? It dissolves, it becomes metaphorical, it becomes iconic.

There is a sliding scale of value implicit in Marion's presentation of the world – a hierarchy in which the physical is metaphorised, then iconised and finally vaporised. There is an implicit Platonism here more fundamental to Marion than any engagement with postmodernism.

If the idol becomes a metaphor, then the icon becomes a cypher (albeit from an alternative direction). For it is our intentionality which creates the idol, whereas with the icon 'the intention here issues from infinity' (*GWB*

233

p. 20). The affect is similar. The materiality of the icon – first in terms of its manufacture 'by the hands of men' and then in terms of the concept as 'intelligible medium' – is consumed by an insistence that 'the icon comes to us from elsewhere' (*GWB* p. 21), that it attains a certain transparency which 'summons to infinity' (*GWB* p. 24).

The analysis of the idol and the icon, then, is always slipping into metaphoricity and the metaphors are saturated with an eternal light to the point where they are purely translucent. The dialectical tension between them, instituted on the basis of human intentionality, its limitations and its narcissism, is continually being dissolved. One pole merges into the operation of the other. Both idol and icon are related by being respectively the low and high water marks of an all-encompassing divine.

The advent of this infinity has been, so far at least, the product of a phenomenological reduction similar to Levinas's. But Marion wishes to name the source of this infinite summons God the Father, to name this distance as Christ, and relate both to the project of Being through a love anterior to ontology. And such naming can only take place according to the logic of a discourse quite different from that of phenomenology; i.e. a theological discourse.[5] Since the advent is of nothing – that is, of distance issuing from a certain iconoclastic moment – a negative natural theology seems to emerge. It is a negative theology which Marion, following Balthasar, develops in *La Croisée du visible* in terms of the Cross as the watermark within reality. What is, is founded upon an absence, an excess, both a plenitude and a void. What is bears the mark of an irrecusable distance and distance is always '*la distance christique*' (*PC* p. 37). Hence the question of God's relation to Being. But since the advent is anterior to Being, an ontological investigation as such is not necessary, or can at least be bypassed. For in the advent of the infinite, 'the unthinkable taken as such is the concern of God Himself' (*GWB* p. 46). The advent then is not phenomenology's manifestation (*die Offenbarkeit*) but the 'irreducible heteronomy' of revelation (*die Offenbarung*). Marion can make all the moves to cross through Being therefore, but the passage itself is unnecessary, for as Heidegger wrote and Marion quotes: 'Faith does not need the thought of Being' (*GWB* p. 61). The *experience* of God no doubt flashes through Being, but Marion's concern lies with the God without Being, the God outside textuality. Revelation and faith are indifferent to Being and so gradually analyses of ontological difference give way to biblical exegesis. Marion's discourse moves from post-metaphysics to 'a difference more essential to being than ontological difference itself' (*GWB* p. 85), a difference testified to in 'biblical revelation'. We must understand what is at stake in this second move and what its consequences are.

I wish to emphasise two consequences of this move. The first is an evasion of the hermeneutical question. This is concomitant with an evasion of the economy of representation, an economy of exchange. Let me explain. Earlier in the book he had recognised that the difficulty with silence is understanding 'what silence says' (*GWB* p. 54). The far reaches of the ineffable therefore require interpreting. Similarly, for iconicity to emerge, there is a necessity for 'a hermeneutic that can read in the visible the intention of the invisible' (*GWB* p. 21). The advent of the unsayable requires interpretation; that is why there is a dialectic between the icon and the idol. But the biblical revelation is the hermeneutical key itself – here God is declared to be indifferent to ontological difference. The biblical revelation remains beyond interpretation; existing as a meta-critique of metaphysics. It lies outside critique as 'a discourse held about faith and on the basis of faith' (*GWB* p. 87). Its authority is self-affirming. Marion's *a priori* faith in the testimony of revelation itself confirms (proves?) a God beyond Being reinforces Marion's faith in his own interpretation of this testimony. Any boundary between, any attempt to distinguish, exegesis and eisegesis is obviated. There is no room for self-critique. In *Prolégomènes à la charité*, in a discussion on the reality of Satan, Marion emphasises that the free will is an axiom of personhood: 'the root of the person – that which unites a person with God in Christ, is the will' (*PC* p. 40). Faith is this assertion of the will which Satan wishes to tempt us to renounce. But Marion never relates the assertion or the nature of this will with that will-to-power which constitutes idolatry and the ontological difference. In order to read St Paul as a commentary on ontological difference or to state that 'the *ousia* of the prodigal son can resonate legitimately . . . with the echo of the *ousia* of the philosophers' (*GWB* p. 96), the very least which is required is a doctrine of scriptural inspiration which might legitimate such a reading. The move from phenemonology to dogmatism is evident in Marion's use here of the word 'legitimately'. For who is it who legitimates such a reading? Marion does not inform us.

The legitimation, the authority, issues from the gift, the purity of givenness without return. It is a givenness which is ineffable, which is God. The gift gives Being itself and is therefore prior to Being. But then the gift as pure gift can only be thought in terms of a divine hegemony read as the logic of love. It can only be conceived as an authority which cuts through Being, representation and the need for interpretation. Without entering Derrida's recent and dense analysis of giving,[6] does it make sense to speak of a gift outside of an economy of representation and human exchange? Surely a gift, surely giving itself, can only be understood within the economy of exchange, within the economy of Being, within the economy of representation. How else would we understand it *as* a gift? How else would we be able to receive it *as such*? Is the notion of a pure gift not only inexpressible and inconceivable, is it in fact possible? As Marion writes in his Preface, his dogmatism issues from the fact that '*agape* appears only as a pure given, with neither deduction or legitimation. But *in this way* the given appears all the more as given' (*GWB* p. xxiv). Later he admits that this gift 'does have to do with a violence' (*GWB* p. 105). The violence is perpetrated against hermeneutics and performs a tearing in his text. The book becomes dismembered so that Marion can begin again on the other side of Being and representation, on the other side of Chapter 5 – in the *Hors-texte*.

The move to the logic of another form of discourse – self-validating and self-legitimating exegesis – in order to think the unthinkably pure gift, leads directly to the vexed question of the bishop as theologian *par excellence*. Finally, Marion's appeal for the God beyond Being, the God beyond postmodernity, is an appeal to the circulation of a legitimation which is hierarchically ordained. There is God, God's Word in Christ and the Scriptures, the Eucharist, the bishop and finally the theologian. This appeal to authority invalidates, in fact cuts across, any ontological or phenomenological or hermeneutical investigation. So although he claims 'we can glimpse God only in the intermittent half-times of our idolatries' (*GWB* p. 108), his emphasis is increasingly upon dogmatically reinscribing the teachings of the Bible, the tradition and the Church. In theology there is no space for analysis, critique or interpretation. For theology is a sacrament. Theology directs an enquiry beyond the idolatries and beyond textuality to 'The spirit [which] undoes every reality in suspension . . . the more violently the spirit breathes, the more being becomes a shadow of itself' (*GWB* p. 125). And this is neither the subject nor the consequence of analysis, rather 'confirmation of this comes from the texts of the New Testament' (*GWB* p. 134). Biblical revelation provides proof-texts which argue against metaphysics.

These two illicit movements – the one from the empirical to the metaphorical and iconic, the other towards an evasion of the hermeneutical question – are both movements governed by a gnosticism, a movement towards the 'silent immediacy of abandoned flesh' (*GWB* p. 139). In Christ there is abolished the gap between the speaker and the sign and the sign and the referent. In Christ, the postmodern preoccupation with an ineradicable semiology is dissolved. Hence the way is open to a reinstatement of the doctrine of transubstantiation and theology as a Eucharistic site. 'The referent', we are told, 'transgresses the text to interpret it to us' (*GWB* p. 148). And the question of who interprets the referent is never raised, can never be raised, without stepping outside the structures of authority which determine the nature and the stature of that referent. Pierced by the light of such an authority the theologian's words become translucent: 'The theologian . . . lets the Word let him speak human language in a way that God speaks it in his Words' (*GWB* p. 144). Again a doctrine of divine inspiration lies waiting to be announced. But its announcement will never come – for such a doctrine would amount to an explanation of the mechanics, an interpretation of how the Word incarnates our words. With explanation and interpretation the gift could not appear as pure gift, as *agape* given 'without deduction or legitimation'. And so, in the analysis of charity and the gift, ineluctably we move towards the *Hors-texte*. The non-representation and hiatus of the pure gift occurs in the blank pages between Chapters 5 and 6. This is Marion's final and ultimate move, a leap in fact. The advent of God's pure giving occurs in the gap.

The moves, then, from the concrete to the metaphorical to the iconic (later from the image to the prototype), from phenomenological analysis to biblical dogmatics means that Marion has no further need to engage with the end of the metaphysics or ontological difference. And so his theological work in *Prolégomènes à la charité* and *La Croisée du visible* is separated from his philosophical work *Réduction et donation: Recherches sur Husserl, Heidegger et la phenomenologie.*[7] Marion does not push beyond the transcendental horizons of postmodernism. He works through and towards those transcendental horizons, but his God beyond Being is substantiated in the self-authenticating discourse of biblical revelation. Marion side-steps and dissolves postmodernity's problem of the body, the text. He turns the icon, the face, of Christ towards postmodernity, offering it a return to a pre- and post-secular cosmology: the world as a sacrament of love mediated by and on the authority of the community called the Church.

We return ironically to the typical postmodern response, the authority invested in communities by the 'overwhelming affective commitment of its self-appointed "members"'.[8] 'Postmodernity is weak on exclusion', Baumann rightly recognises, 'there is no court whose authority it recognises'.[9] But Marion's theology divorced from ontology, Marion's post-postmodernism, is a commitment to Catholic orthodoxy and firm authoritarian structures based upon reappropriation of the mystical fires of Maximus the Confessor.[10] Postmodernity can call this ideology, but it cannot pass any judgement upon such an ideology. It is one ideology among myriad. But concerning theology's engagement with postmodernity, Marion's work raises two important questions on the basis of a fundamental conclusion. His conclusion, which is implicit in the radical shift he has made, is that theology cannot embrace postmodernism unequivocally. The questions this raises are: first, whether his ideological commitment is any better or any worse than postmodernity's radical depoliticisation; and second, whether it is possible to write a theology which is able to operate dialectically with and upon the postmodern suspicions of authority and ideological commitment. Perhaps the term 'dialectically' here points a way forward.[11]

References

Translations for French texts except *GWB* are my own. Abbreviations for works by Marion are as follows:

CV	*La Croisée du visible* (Paris, La Difference, 1991).
ID	*L'Idol et la distance* (Paris, Grasset, 1977).
GWB	*God Without Being*, trans. Thomas A. Carlson (Chicago, University of Chicago Press, 1991).
PC	*Prolégomènes à la charité* (Paris, La Difference, 1986).
RD	*Réduction et donation* (Paris, PUF, 1989).

Notes

1 Cf. Z. Bauman's *Intimation of Postmodernity* (London, Routledge, 1992), p. xix. Bauman suggests that postmodernity is an 'age of the *imaginary community* . . . [C]ommunity is now expected to bring succour previously sought in the pronouncements of universal reason and their earthly translations: the legislative acts of the national state' (pp. xviii–xix). Rather than moving beyond postmodernism, Marion's response *is* postmodern.

2 It seems to me that Marion does not give an adequate account of the connection between *Ereignis* and ontological difference as Heidegger develops it, particularly in *On Time and Being*, trans. Joan Stambaugh (New York, Harper Torchbooks, 1972).

3 This emphasis upon the experience of the visibility of the phenomenal might be compared with and challenged by Derrida's remarks on Levinas's 'empiricism' in his essay 'Violence and Metaphysics', in *Writing and Difference* (Chicago, University of Chicago Press, 1978), pp. 139, 151–2.

4 This interpretation might profitably be compared to Nicholas Lash's reading of the story in *Theology on the Way to Emmaus* (London, SCM, 1986). Lash's emphasis in the story (see p. 201, although the theme is evident throughout the book) is upon the Church as always 'on the way' and Christ as the one who accompanies 'although they [the Church] cannot often understand their company'. His interpretation allows a doctrinal statement about the Church and its relation to Christ and the Eucharist to emerge, but clothed in shadow, metaphor and knowledge of what is unknown. His emphasis is not upon either certainties or identities. Although we do 'recognise him in the breaking of the bread', the 'him', like the one who accompanies, is curiously undefined and left to resonate where it will.

5 This is akin to the two 'logics' analysed by Balthasar. In *Mysterium Paschale* (Edinburgh, T. & T. Clark, 1990), human reasoning is viewed as other than Christ and 'a logic created by and identical with him' (p. 54). It is because of this logic that Balthasar claims only the 'believing theologian' (p. 79) can write theologically. There is an hiatus between human thinking and theological thinking which Marion endorses.

6 Jacques Derrida, *Given Time: I Counterfeit Money*, trans. Peggy Kamuf (Chicago, University of Chicago Press, 1992). Derrida's concern in this volume is to elucidate the double bind of the gift – to point out that the gift is both impossible and yet necessary.

7 In *Réduction et donation*, Marion is still concerned with Heidegger's ontological project as it develops Husserl's phenomenology. He is still concerned with the given (*la donation*). He attempts to argue in this book that 'the given is at the centre of reduction and therefore of phenomenology' (*RD* p. xxi). The given is *a priori*, but it is analysed philosophically rather than theologically. It is a given rather like Heidegger's *es gibt* but beyond Being. Marion unpacks a threefold reduction which takes place in a phenomenological analysis and in the third reduction we move towards 'a point of reference all the more original and unconditional' (p. 303). Speaking precisely, this point '*is* not, because what summons it and practises it most rigorously no longer issues from the horizon of Being (nor objectivity) but from the pure form of the summons itself' (p. 315). The summons 'gives the gift itself' (*ibid*). But that is where Marion concludes his study. The theology of this gift is for other books which have methodologically moved beyond philosophical analysis into the realm of revealed faith.

8 Bauman, *Intimation of Postmodernity*, p. xix.

9 Bauman, 'Postmodernity: Chance or Menace?', Centre for the Study of Cultural Values, Lancaster, 1992, p. 5.

10 One of Marion's first published works is an essay on Maximus the Confessor, in 1972. He builds upon von Balthasar's earlier work, *Kosmische Liturgie*, published in 1941. Maximus figures significantly in the margins of Marion's first book *L'Idol et la distance* and those who would understand Marion, I suggest, need to be more acquainted with *Ambigua* than Heidegger.

11 Cf. my essay 'Theology and the Crisis of Representation', in Gregory Salyer and Robert Detweiler (eds) *Literature and Theology at the Century's End* (Atlanta: Scholars Press, 1995), pp. 131–58.

9

METAPHYSICS AND MAGIC

Wittgenstein's kink

Fergus Kerr

Philosophy without theses

According to G.E.M. Anscombe (1954: 373), Wittgenstein once said of his later work: 'Its advantage is that if you believe, say, Spinoza or Kant, this interferes with what you believe in religion; but if you believe me, nothing of the sort.' Both theologians and philosophers, no doubt for a variety of reasons, would find this a strange remark. Many theologians would like to think that philosophy, properly introduced, strengthens and even provides intellectual foundations for their enterprise. Many philosophers, on the other hand, would think that philosophy's interference with religious belief is such that it undermines it completely. And it is easy to think of other ways in which philosophy might interact with religion. What is this turn in the history of philosophy, then, which apparently allows the philosopher to say something about religion without encroaching upon it in any way, either to improve or discredit it?

G.E. Moore (1959: 322), who took substantial notes at the time, was 'a good deal surprised' at claims Ludwig Wittenstein made about what he was doing in lectures in Cambridge during the academic years 1930–3. It was not just a stage in a continuous development, so Wittgenstein claimed, but a 'kink' in the history of philosophy comparable with what happened when Galileo and his contemporaries invented dynamics, or with the emergence of chemistry from alchemy: hyperbolic claims indeed, one might think, which the self-disparaging word 'kink' scarcely moderates. During the same years, moreover, in the chapter entitled 'Philosophy' in the so-called 'Big Typescript', written between 1930 and 1932, but only recently published, Wittgenstein made such perplexing remarks as the following (1991: 12): 'If one tried to advance *theses* in philosophy, it would never be possible to debate them, because everyone would agree to them' – a remark which survives in his *Philosophical Investigations* (1953: §128). Such a provocative statement would still perplex people interested in philosophy, if they paid it any attention. In practice, of course, now as then, a philosopher's work is commonly taken to be precisely nothing other than the advancing of some thesis in opposition to what someone has recently maintained, which someone else in the profession will in turn no doubt want to refute. The point of philosophical work, one might be inclined to say, is surely to discover profound truths which not everyone would agree to, at least initially, mainly because such truths naturally elude all but the deepest thinkers. How could Wittgenstein have seriously supposed that there would be no room for debate in his conception of philosophy because everyone would agree to whatever theses one advanced?

Far from unearthing hitherto unnoticed truths, whether by rigorous logical analysis or by imaginative metaphysical insight, philosophical work in Wittgenstein's wake becomes a largely non-deductive method of releasing people from alluring traps set by language. Thus, rather than a systematic exposition of metaphysical principles, work in philosophy becomes 'a battle', as Wittgenstein will say (1953: §109), 'against the bewitchment of our intelligence (*Verstand*) by the devices of our language (*durch die Mittel unserer Sprache*)'.

Radicalizing Kant

How Wittgenstein regarded the place of his remarks about religion within his philosophical work as a whole is hard to determine. On the face of it, the late work seems to be entirely concerned with the philosophy of language and the philosophy of psychology, with no detectable reference or relevance to ethics or religion. It is much disputed, on the other hand, whether the remarks in the *Tractatus* (1922) dealing with the inexpressible, which plainly have ethical and religious implications, are the climax of the book or simply an aberration. 'Whereof one cannot speak, thereof one must be silent', as C.K. Ogden rendered the concluding proposition, somewhat hermetically.

Writing in 1919, soon after his return to Vienna from a harsh year in a prisoner-of-war camp in Italy, Wittgenstein made this comment about the *Tractatus*:

> My work consists of two parts: the one presented here plus all that I have not written. And it is precisely this second part that is the important one. My book draws limits to the sphere of the ethical from the inside as it were.
>
> (Engelmann 1967: 143-4)

This is generally taken to mean that the distinction in the *Tractatus* between what can be said and what must be left in silence is intended to separate the realm of representable contingent facts from the realm of the meaning of life.

According to one of his favourite anecdotes (Monk 1990: 64), Bertrand Russell once asked Wittgenstein, who was in a state of high excitement, whether he was thinking about logic or about his sins – 'Both', the 23-year-old allegedly replied (this was in 1912). But the text of the *Tractatus* as we have it, effectively completed during a longish leave in the summer of 1918, is certainly the work of a very different man from the Cambridge student whose discussions with Russell of problems in formal logic gave rise to it. The famously obscure remarks towards the end are the precipitate of thoughts which were conceived during the terrible months in 1916 when the Austro-Hungarian army, in which Wittgenstein was serving (with some heroism), was driven back into the Carpathian mountains by a Russian offensive. He had given up the Catholic religion which he inherited from his mother but the nearness of death made him pray constantly. In the crisis of war, he clearly felt more challenged than at any other time in his life by traditional religious questions. In June 1916, as the surviving journal shows, the notes on logical matters suddenly gave way to reflections on God, the meaning of life, death and suchlike (1961: 72). His work broadened, as he noted himself on 2 August 1916, 'from the foundations of logic to the essence of the world' (1961: 79).

Logic, according to the *Tractatus* (6.13), is transcendental – that is to say: 'Logic is not a body of doctrine, but a mirror-image of the world (*keine Lehre, sondern ein Spiegelbild der Welt*).' From the beginning, Wittgenstein sought to break the grip of the venerable conception of logic as a deductive system in which theorems are inferred from self-evident principles. The only book review he ever published, in *The Cambridge Review* 34 (1912–13), was a caustic dismissal of *The Science of Logic* by P. Coffey, a typical example of the kind of neo-scholastic philosophy then current in Roman Catholic theological colleges (and still current fifty years later!). For Wittgenstein, in contrast, the purpose of a logical system, at this period in his career at least, was to exhibit the logic of ordinary language more perspicuously than it does itself. Language, logic and the world stand in line one behind the other, as it were, each equivalent to the other (cf. 1953: §96). Logic, the essence of thought, presents the a priori order of the world (1953: §97). It is not that the propositions of logic state what would traditionally be called transcendental truths. What Wittgenstein means is that they show something that pervades everything sayable – something itself unsayable. And it is not unsayable through any defect on our part – in our language, for example. 'The tacit conventions on which the understanding of everyday language depends are enormously complicated', as Wittgenstein noted (1922: 4.002). It is easy to see why: 'Everyday language', after all, 'is a part of the human organism and is no less complicated than it'. That is why, as he says in the same place, 'it is not humanly possible to gather immediately from [language] what the logic of language is'. But the logic *is* there – 'In fact, all the propositions of our everyday language, just as they stand, are in perfect logical order' (1922: 5.5563). And it is possible to give the essence of a proposition, which means in turn to give the essence of all description and so the essence of the world (1922: 5.4711). As Wittgenstein noted, human beings 'have always had a presentiment that there must be a realm in which the answers to questions are symmetrically combined – a priori – to form a self-contained system' (1922: 5.4541).

The Kantian reminiscence is unmistakable: 'Reason has a presentiment of objects which possess a great interest for it.' The question is how we are to account for 'our inextinguishable desire to find firm footing somewhere beyond the limits of experience' (Kant 1978: A 796, B 824). The *Tractatus* cannot be fully understood unless the reader feels the pull of this metaphysical demand for some perception of the a priori order which must be common to both world and thought (cf. 1953: §97). The later Wittgenstein (we may say) stood by his conception of everyday language – it is, on the other hand, this 'prejudice in favour of the crystalline purity of logic' that he sought to remove (cf. 1953: §§107–8).

Human reason, as Kant noted (1978: A vii), has this peculiar fate that it is burdened by questions which, as prescribed by the very nature of reason itself, it is not able to ignore, but which it is also not able to answer. Human beings, as Wittgenstein noted in the 'Big Typescript' (1991: 15), in a rather Kantian idiom, 'keep stumbling over the same puzzling difficulties and find themselves staring at something which no explanation seems capable of clearing up'.

These difficulties will arise, Wittgenstein says in the same passage (1991: 15), 'as long as there is a verb "to be" which seems to function like "to eat" and "to drink", as long as there are adjectives like "identical", "true", "false", "possible", as long as one talks about a flow of time and an expanse of space', and so on. And the sense of bafflement at these difficulties, he maintains, 'satisfies a longing for the supra-natural/transcendental/, for in believing that [we] see the "limits of human understanding" of course [we] believe that [we] can see beyond it'. His distinctly Kantian conception of philosophical work is plain: 'human reason . . . stands in need of a discipline to check its extravagances, and to guard it against the deceptions which arise therefrom' (Kant 1978: A 795, B 823). 'Our inextinguishable desire to find firm footing somewhere beyond the limits of experience', as Kant says, is accounted for by there being 'some source of positive modes of knowledge which belong to the domain of pure reason' which yet 'give occasion to error solely owing to misunderstanding' (1978: A 795, B 823). Wittgenstein, we may say, radicalizes Kant's conception of philosophy as a 'discipline for the limitation of pure reason' in the sense that he moves beyond seeing the positive modes of rational knowledge as occasionally giving rise to error to considering the positive resources of our language as readily giving rise to error – or rather, as he will say, to superstition (1953: §110).

Against *The Golden Bough*

Wittgenstein considered various ways of opening the book which engaged him from 1929 onwards, but which appeared posthumously as *Philosophical*

Investigations (1953). In 1930, for example, he noted his desire to start his book 'with books as it were' – the propositions written and spoken of all the philosophers whom he had read or heard (1980: 8). The following year, prompted apparently by Goethe's admonition that we learn more from getting out into the open air than from doing laboratory experiments, he was thinking of starting his book 'with a description of nature' (1980: 11). Thus he considered starting either from standard philosophical texts or from the natural world. In the end, of course, he chose the passage in the *Confessions* where Augustine described how he thought he learnt to speak (1953: §1). Instead of starting from philosophical literature or our physical environment, that is to say, he seized on the picture of language in the most celebrated autobiography in Christian tradition. But he had also considered beginning with remarks, stimulated by his reading of *The Golden Bough*, about 'metaphysics as a kind of magic', a proposal that deserves examination (1979: VI).

Frazer's work, first published in two volumes in 1890 but revised and expanded so much that the final version runs to twelve (1911–15), seemed as epoch-making at the time as Newton's papers or *The Origin of Species* in their day. For example, it revolutionized classical scholarship, particularly in Cambridge, and inspired writers as different from one another as T.S. Eliot and D.H. Lawrence. Although never taken quite seriously by professional anthropologists, *The Golden Bough*, with its evolutionary story of how magic gave way to religion and religion in turn to science, would still seem to most casual readers the right sort of thing to say about these matters, whether they were theistically minded or not.

In 1931 Wittgenstein began to read the first volume of *The Golden Bough* with a friend. They did not get very far. Wittgenstein's expostulations became his most substantial reflections on the nature of religion. But they evidently also played an important part in the revision of his philosophy. Even materially, a substantial section of what has been published as *Remarks on Frazer's Golden Bough* (1979) is identical with the recently published 'Philosophy' chapter in the 'Big Typescript' (1991). The criticisms of Frazer's rationalistic explanations of primitive religion, it is now possible to see, played an important part in generating Wittgenstein's later conception of philosophy – philosophy without substantive truths, as one might call it. Frazer's presuppositions about how human beings fit into the world seem to have been the catalyst in Wittgenstein's rejection of the traditional philosophical assumption that, as subjects of consciousness, we take our place among the items in the world primarily as the ones who have *ideas*. 'The characteristic feature of primitive man, I believe, is that he does not act from *opinions* (*Meinungen*) he holds about things (as Frazer thinks)' (1979: 12).

Magic and religious ritual, Frazer assumed, are practices founded on hypotheses about the world (which *we* know to be erroneous). But this is difficult to accept, Wittgenstein finds: 'It is very queer that all these practices are finally presented, so to speak, as stupid actions, *Dummheiten*' (1979: 1). There is something deeper than error here. Magic always rests, so Wittgenstein says, on a certain picture of signs (1979: 4). He was soon led to identify and examine the widespread and deeply entrenched natural assumption in our culture that our relationship to the world, and our relationship to other minds, is essentially a matter of *beliefs*. A religious symbol, Wittgenstein protested against Frazer, is not founded on any *Meinung* (1979: 3). But then neither are our reactions to one another: 'My attitude towards [a friend] is an attitude towards a soul (*Einstellung zur Seele*)', as Wittgenstein was later to write: 'I am not of the *opinion* (*Meinung*) that he has a soul' (1953: 178). In another version of the same thought Wittgenstein notes that instead of *Einstellung zur Seele* one might as well say *Einstellung zum Menschen*: 'attitude to the human being' rather than 'attitude to the soul [mind]' (1992: 38). And he goes on to ask what the difference is between an attitude and an opinion, *eine Einstellung* and *eine Meinung*, and suggests that 'the attitude comes *before* the opinion' (his emphasis). Prior to our beliefs about the world, or about this or that in the world, including other people, there are what he rather jejunely speaks of as *attitudes* – not, of course, attitudes one might existentialistically 'strike', dispositions one might adopt by voluntaristic decree, but just the opposite: natural reactions, antecedent to whatever views or theories there might arise – unhesitating acceptance of kinship, as one might say. Our presentness to one another, that is to say, is first of all a matter of perception (so to speak) rather than interpretation – of acknowledgement rather than knowledge, as Stanley Cavell (1969) would say. It is a symptom of the intellectualist assumptions about our way of being in the world that words like 'reaction' and 'attitude' seem barely adequate – we have a significantly meagre vocabulary for the ways in which we dwell in the world independently of, and antecedent to, theoretical cognition. (Is Heidegger's neologizing attempt, in *Sein und Zeit* (1927), to break the spell of the intellectualist myth, preferable?)

Critique of the idea that *Meinung* (opinion, view, belief, idea, meaning) lies at the bottom of all characteristically human activity might be said to be the most revolutionary move in Wittgenstein's later work. There is nothing more wrongheaded, as he said at the end of Part 1 of the *Investigations*, than calling meaning (*Meinen*) a mental activity (1953: §693). But it is very difficult to break free of the assumption that the meaning of what one says accompanies what one says, so he thinks (1967: §139). 'Ever and again comes the thought that what we see of a sign is only the outside of something within, in which the real operations of sense and meaning go on' (1967: §140). 'We are tempted to think that the action of language consists of two parts: an inorganic part, the handling of signs, and an organic part, which we may call understanding these signs, meaning them, interpreting them, thinking' (1958: 3). We have a strong inclination, in our culture, when we think about these matters, to picture language, and indeed all rational behaviour, as founded upon and issuing from radically hidden inward mental states or activities which are no doubt revealed in behaviour but certainly not constituted by it in any way. We are, after all, distinguished by being rational animals – which surely means (we should like to think) that our behaviour at its most distinctively human is the outcome of *thought* – and thought seems to be 'something immaterial, with properties different from all *mere signs*' (1958: 4, my emphasis). Oddly enough, as Wittgenstein says, one of the most philosophically dangerous ideas is the truism that we think in our heads – 'The idea of thinking as a process in the head, in this completely enclosed space, makes it something occult' (1967: §§605–6, retranslated). When we start philosophizing, that is to say, we immediately generate myths about our symbol systems or our mental processes (1967: §211). In effect, we deny the materiality of signs in the constitution of our minds.

One of Wittgenstein's main concerns was to bring us to see what is obvious – which is that it is our ways of acting, reacting and interacting, which give rise to our psychological states and attitudes. Or rather: our inner mental life is rooted in our interaction with the world as physical beings. 'The origin and the primitive form of the language game is a reaction; only from this can more complicated forms develop' (1980: 31). Again: 'I really want to say that discriminating reflection begins (has its roots) in instinct' (1967: §391). The language game we play does not originate in reflection – rather, reflecting is an element in the language game, which is of course why concepts have their home in the language game (1967: §391 retranslated). Language, as he would finally say (1969: §475), 'did not emerge from any kind of ratiocination'. Rather, by this stage (5 April 1951, three weeks before his death), noting that there was still a great gap in his thinking, Wittgenstein wanted to regard human beings as animals – 'as primitive beings to whom one of course (*zwar*: omitted in the English translation) grants instinct but not ratiocination' (1969: §475).

Wittgenstein's final conception of how human beings mesh with the world, as instinctively interacting agents rather than centres of rational consciousness, developed from his discontent with Frazer's conception of religious practices as based on beliefs. 'What makes the character of ritual action is not any view or opinion, either right or wrong, although an opinion – a belief – itself can be ritualistic, or belong to a rite' (1979: 7). His indefatigable endeavour to relocate our rationality in our animality, so to speak, evidently sprang from his dissatisfaction with Frazer's intellectualistic prejudices about religion. The superstition, Wittgenstein came to think, lay in Frazer's assumptions, rather than in the primitive rites – 'Frazer cannot imagine a priest who is not basically an English parson of our times with all his stupidity and feebleness' (1979: 5). His explanations of the primitive rites 'are much cruder than the meaning of the observances themselves' (1979: 8) – the meaning which will come out, so Wittgenstein seems to think, in a description of the rites: 'We can only *describe* and say: Human life is like that' (1979: 3). Alternatively: 'One would like to say: This is what took place here; laugh, if you can' (1979: 3).

In short, Wittgenstein's critique of the traditional philosophical emphasis on theoretical cognition as the primary mode of human relations with the world originated in his objections to Frazer's reductively rationalistic accounts of primitive religious practices. Historically, Wittgenstein's desire to liberate religion from subjection to Victorian-rationalist hermeneutics enabled him to break the spell of the received intellectualist picture of our way of being in the world.

Magical signs

To return to the question of how to start the work which eventually became his *Philosophical Investigations*, let us look at the conception of philosophical work inspired by *The Golden Bough* (1979: vi):

> I think now that the right thing would be to begin my book with remarks about metaphysics as a kind of magic.
>
> But in doing this I must neither speak in defence of magic nor ridicule it.
>
> What it is that is deep about magic would be kept. ——
>
> In this context, in fact, keeping magic out has itself the character of magic.
>
> For when I began in my earlier book to talk about the '*world*' (and not about this tree or that table), was I trying to do anything else but conjure up something of a higher order into my words?

Wittgenstein was dissatisfied with this passage (written in 1931). He later marked it 's' (for *schlecht*: bad), and did not have it typed. But it remains illuminating, even if undeniably obscure. He calls on a considerable range of metaphor in his later writings to locate what he wants to say about metaphysics. When we try to say something of philosophical importance about the nature of propositions, words and signs, for example, it proves difficult to keep our heads above water –

> to see that we must stick to things we think everyday, and not go down the wrong track where it appears as if we have to describe extreme subtleties, which we are however quite unable to describe with the means that we have.
>
> (1953: §§105–6)

But one of his preferred analogies for our plight when we engage in meta-physical reflection is the image of the mind's being bewitched by the devices of our language (1953: §109). Metaphysics is a kind of magic – and not easily or lightly dismissed.

In the *Tractatus*, he had come to think, he was still attempting to 'conjure into words something higher'. In saying, for example, that 'The world is all that is the case' (1922: 1), he was not, after all, saying anything very remark-able. Rather than the portentous metaphysical thesis it initially seems, it is just a grammatical remark – a thesis with which indeed nobody would disagree.

Consider, even more interestingly, the remark about the role of words like 'object' and 'complex' in the *Tractatus* at the end of the following paragraph (1979: 10):

> To cast out death or to slay death; but he is also represented as a skeleton, as in some sense dead himself. 'As dead as death.' 'Nothing is so dead as death; nothing is so beautiful as beauty itself.' Here the image (*Bild*) which we use in thinking of the reality is that beauty, death, etc. are the pure (concentrated) substances, and that they are found in the beautiful object as added ingredients of the mixture (*Beimischung*). – And do I now recognize here my own observations on 'object' and 'complex'?

The ordinary ways in which we speak about death and the like, in a religious context, contain a picture according to which dead or beautiful objects are granted a share of something which is in pure concentrated form on some other plane of reality. Our ways of talking, in effect, easily generate Platon-ism. Citing Plato's *Theaetetus* (201e–202b) on primary elements, Wittgenstein did indeed later suggest that the 'objects' in the *Tractatus* were at home only in a conception of the world in which forms are self-predicable, in the sense that only a form perfectly instantiates itself while any other object only par-ticipates in it (1953: §46). In retrospect, that is to say, he regarded his own early work as deeply metaphysical – in the sense that certain words are allowed to call things 'of a higher order' into existence, like an enchanter's spell. 'The idea', he says (1979: 4), is 'that one can beckon a lifeless object to come, just as one would beckon a person'. The principle at work, in meta-physics as in magic, is that of 'personification' (1979: 4) – animism, as we might say. We have a magical conception of our signs.

This may seem a wild claim, but consider some of Wittgenstein's examples. Among the devices of our language none is more mesmeric, he considered, than the demonstrative pronoun. Pointing to some object as we say the word 'This' easily tempts us into seeing naming as a charmed relationship with items in the world. Wittgenstein is reminded of Bertrand Russell's notion that the only thing necessary to understand the name for a particular is to be acquainted with that particular itself (1956: 202) – as if knowing were some kind of direct hook-up between thought and thing. No doubt he also remembered his own self-mocking feeling of awe – 'I can correlate all that I see, this landscape, the flight of seeds in the air, all this – with a *name*; indeed, what should we call a name if not this!' (1961: 53, 30 May 1915). Nothing seems more extraordinary than our power to give things names. One might even think naming to be some supernatural act – 'as it were baptizing an object' (1953: §38). It is as if language summoned the world into existence.

Wittgenstein recalled how G.E. Moore would stare at a house some twenty feet away and say, 'with a peculiar intonation': 'I *know* that there's a house!' (Malcolm 1984: 71). This was Moore's attempt to exhibit to himself what knowing something for certain feels like, or so Wittgenstein claimed. The more intensely one contemplates an object the more certain its existence becomes, or so it seems. It is at any rate not difficult to recall comparable experiences that philosophers have sought to describe – Roquentin's famous encounter with the roots of a chestnut tree in Sartre's novel *Nausea*, for example: supposedly a concept-free perception of sheer haecceity. The thought is, then, that one brings things into the realm of meaning by naming them, that one charms things as it were out of themselves by one's words. Or that our language casts a spell of meaning around what are otherwise simply brute data.

Propositions, to take another of Wittgenstein's examples, are of course important; but we are easily seduced into thinking that they must be achieving something extraordinary, something unique (1953: §93). 'Thought', we want to say, 'is something miraculous' – something as it were from beyond this world. To make such a fetish of thinking is not, Wittgenstein suggests, anything as simple as a mistake; rather, it is 'a superstition produced by grammatical illusions' (1953: §110). The devices of our language easily lure us into fantasies. Magic always rests on a certain idea of language – the idea that words have power to beckon things into existence or at least into our proximity. But it is precisely this magical conception of language that generates the illusions of metaphysics. That seems to be Wittgenstein's story. The difference between error and superstition in the case just quoted is presumably that the grammar of the concept of thinking, misunderstood in a certain way, engenders the feeling that thinking is a kind of magic.

Signs supposedly perform the astonishing feat of bridging the gap between our minds and world. But what if there is really no such gap? Do we have to picture knowing the world as a confrontation between the mind and some radically alien and essentially inaccessible reality? Why need we picture the knowing subject as so transcendent that it is out of the world? To make such a cult of propositions as the later Wittgenstein accused himself of having done in the *Tractatus* is already to etherialize representation altogether (1953: §94). Our forms of expression, perfectly all right if left to do their work, encourage us, in our philosophical moods, to pursue chimeras (1953: §94).

Weighing linguistic facts

What bearing does all this have on theology? Far from offering the meta-physical support which theologians from Origen to Thomas Aquinas may plausibly be thought to have expected of philosophy, but equally far from constituting the threat which theologians from Luther to Karl Barth have feared it to be, Wittgenstein's kink, in his work from 1930 onwards, profes-sedly leaves religious belief intact. 'Philosophy, as *we* use the word, is a fight against the fascination which forms of expression exert upon us', as he said, dictating in English in the session 1933–4 (1958: 27, my emphasis). The mis-takes Kant regarded as occasioned by reason, against which philosophical cri-tique is to guard, have become superstitions generated by misunderstanding of the standard devices of our language. Historically, it seems, Wittgenstein's dislike of Frazer's rationalistic explanations of religious practices in *The Golden Bough* led to his exposure of the intellectualist distortion of our way of being related to the world which philosophy has propagated – in terms, that is to say, of theoretical cognition. We are easily bewitched by the devices of our language: time and again, when we withdraw such linguistic resources as propositions, demonstrative pronouns and so on, from ordinary everyday conversation, we find them rapidly inflating into something chimerical. The philosopher's task, in Wittgenstein's view, is then to bring words back from their metaphysical to their everyday application (1953: §116). And this is no easy matter – we are as it were driven to misunderstand how our language works (1953: §109).

How 'driven' are we? 'A *picture* held us captive. And we could not get out-side it, for it lay in our language and language seemed to repeat it to us inexor-ably' (1953: §115). When philosophers of the pre-Wittgensteinian sort get to work on the concept of knowledge, for example, it soon appears as if knowl-edge – 'in the strict sense' – is humanly unachievable: it seems that we can never know anything beyond all possibility of doubt. We have an ideal – an idol – of knowledge, according to which all human knowing is defective. Again: the first-person pronoun 'I' easily generates the image of a mysterious immaterial entity, my 'real self', residing in but radically distinct from my body – from which putative situation a whole string of apparently exciting metaphysical implications follows. When philosophers use words like 'know-ing', 'being', 'object', 'I', 'proposition' and 'name', Wittgenstein says, and seek to get hold of the essence of the thing, they inevitably produce *Luftge-bäude*, structures of air (1953: §118). The Wittgensteinian response is to ask if the word in question is ever so used in the language in which it is at home (1953: §116).

One might claim – it has often indeed been claimed – that Wittgenstein's approach is consistent with what has often been standard philosophical prac-tice, if perhaps never quite so self-consciously. Claiming, for example, that Luther spoke of theology as the grammar of the word 'God' (Ambrose and

Macdonald 1979: 32), Wittgenstein took this to mean that, if people disputed how many arms God had and someone denied that one could speak of God's having arms, 'this would throw light on the use of the word'. In Moore's more detailed account (1959: 312), Wittgenstein apparently maintained that many controversies about God could be settled by saying that different religions 'treat things as making sense which others treat as nonsense, and don't merely deny some proposition which another religion affirms'. He illustrated this by saying that in certain religions it would make sense to say that the god had arms (like Shiva, perhaps, in Hinduism), while in others to say that 'God has so many arms' would be nonsense. 'Theology as grammar' (1953: §373) would thus mean drawing attention to such differences in the way that words fit into different contexts that contradiction is ruled out – but 'grammar tells us what kind of object something is'. Traditional theological reflection, it might be said, has indeed been concerned with deciding what may and may not be appropriately said about God – 'God is not a body', for example, as Aquinas argues (*after* his arguments for God's existence) – which may well tell us something about the kind of object God is. It might seem, then, that Wittgenstein was doing nothing all that new – at most he would have been reminding theologians that the only contribution philosophy could make to their discipline would be clarificatory – and not in any way substantive or foundational. What then becomes of Wittgenstein's description of his intervention in philosophy as a kink – some kind of breakthrough?

Another way of neutralizing his later work is to ridicule its lack of professional rigour. It operates at a level of such awful simplicities, one might say. Who is so bewitched by the first personal pronoun as to be committed to the notion of the soul as *ein gasförmiges Ding* (1967: §127)? Who is so bemused by similarities between the verb 'to eat' and the verb 'to think' as to have succumbed to the 'pneumatic' conception of thought (1953: §109)? Whose philosophical doctrines are linguistically generated illusions? How pervasive and inescapable is the mythology deposited in our language (1979: 10)? Why does Wittgenstein compare our condition when we philosophize to being bewitched? If metaphysics is a kind of magic how easy is it to break the spell?

Some of Wittgenstein's remarks about religion – at least about certain Christian doctrines – certainly look like attempts to bring words back to the context in which they are at home. The word 'proof', for example, in connection with proofs for the existence of God, if it were properly used, would mean something by means of which one could be convinced (1980: 85). Proof has to do with demonstration, certainty, knowledge and suchlike: that is where it fits, grammatically, as Wittgenstein would say. But, in this note made in 1950, he goes on to observe that when people who are already believers offer proofs of God's existence (and who else does so?) they are really just out to analyse and justify their faith by means of their reason (*Verstand*) – 'they themselves would never have come to believe as a result of such proofs'

(1980: 85). This observation leads Wittgenstein to suggest that, if you want to speak of 'convincing someone of God's existence', this would have to mean doing so 'by means of a certain upbringing, by shaping his life in such and such a way' (1980: 85). You might then say, he goes on in the next remark, that *life* can educate (*erziehen*) one to faith in God – 'life' as distinct from *Verstand*, presumably, and 'faith in God' rather than 'being convinced of his existence'. It would, then, be experiences which would teach one – not 'visions and other forms of sense experience' which show us the existence of this being, Wittgenstein at once adds, 'but e.g. sufferings of various sorts'. Such experiences would not enable us to perceive God in the way that we sense a physical object nor would they allow us to start hypothesizing. 'Experiences, thoughts – life can force this concept ["God"] on us', Wittgenstein concludes – finally remarking that it is thus perhaps similar to the concept of 'object' (1980: 86).

By that last remark he presumably means that, if certain similarities between items in the environment never struck people, the very idea of 'objects' would not arise – they would be content to speak of shoes, ships, sealing-wax, cabbages and kings, without having any need for the general term. Analogously, Wittgenstein is suggesting, the concept of God forces itself on people who have a certain upbringing or experience of life – but the suggestion is actually an invitation to look and see what is obviously the case.

Here Wittgenstein is doing his best simply to describe what it is to be convinced of God's existence – in the hope that the description releases us from the drive to misuse the word 'proof' in connection with God. At no point in his description does it appear what his personal beliefs might be – he is simply saying that, if you are going to talk about believing in God, then it is upbringing, experience of life, sufferings and so on, which are the relevant background, and (by implication) Christian apologetics of the rationalist kind is beside the point. Theoretical cognition of the divine as a metaphysical entity is thus sidelined.

It is not difficult to find other instances of how Wittgenstein, without ever revealing his own religious commitment, offers illuminating descriptions of how key words in theological discourse are actually used. He apparently brought up the word 'God' in connection with criticism of Frazer's assumptions in *The Golden Bough* and with criticism of Freud, all in the context of analogies between ethics and aesthetics (Moore 1959: 312). He invited us to regard 'the face as the soul of the body' (1980: 23). Christianity, he reminded us, is not 'a theory about what has happened and will happen to the human soul, but a description of something that actually takes place in human life' (1980: 28). He invited us to consider predestination as 'less a theory than a sigh, or a cry' (1980: 30). He drew attention, in a very remarkable passage composed in 1937, to the conceptual connections between belief in the resurrection of Christ and love (1980: 33), a passage headed by a pretty clear declaration of his personal lack of faith. Being religious has more to do with believing oneself wretched (*elend*) than merely inadequate (1980: 45). And so on. Time and again, often in a somewhat Kierkegaardian spirit – 'Kierkegaard was by far the most profound thinker of the last century' (Rhees 1984: 87), but also 'he is too long-winded, he keeps on saying the same thing over and over again' (Rhees 1984: 88) – Wittgenstein clears away persistent encrustations and allows us to see familiar things as if for the first time. It becomes possible to see how 'wild conjectures and explanations' might be replaced by 'quiet weighing of linguistic facts' (1967: §447).

But Wittgenstein's departure from traditional philosophical activity surely promises something a good deal more radical and iconoclastic than any of this. Sitting in a Cambridge garden watching G.E. Moore pointing to a tree and listening to him saying again and again 'I *know* that that's a tree' seems to have been a paradigmatic experience – 'Someone else arrives and hears this, and I tell him: "This fellow isn't insane. We are only doing philosophy"' (1969: §467). Wittgenstein often speaks of traditional philosophical activity as comical and even crazy. Sometimes it seems to be a neurosis – his own treatment of a philosophical question is like a therapist's treatment of an illness (1953: §255). The clarity for which he is striving means that the philosophical problems '*completely* disappear' (1953: §133), as obsessive illusions might with the help of a psychoanalyst. The drive we have to misunderstand the working of our language (1953: §109) is a *prejudice* – but 'not a *stupid* prejudice' (1953: §340). Like Frazer's savages whose religious practices should not be dismissed as *Dummheiten*, traditional metaphysical activity is not just a mistake. We are back with whatever Wittgenstein meant by describing metaphysics as a kind of magic.

When the standard devices of our language (demonstratives, pronouns and so on) bewitch the philosophically minded, Wittgenstein seems to think, weird and wonderful entities are conjured up which are actually only linguistic creations, although it goes against the grain to acknowledge this. We are not making a mistake which might be corrected; we are indulging in a superstition which has to be exorcized. The medium in which the traditional metaphysician works seems to be propositions about the world, theses about reality, the truth of which he seeks to establish by analysis or insight. But in fact, according to Wittgenstein, he manipulates language, or is manipulated by language, to generate myths which answer to deep and ancient needs, at least in our culture. It is appealing and compelling, for example, to regard our kind of knowing as radically defective. Moore's efforts to bridge the gap between his mind and the tree in his garden by an act of concentrated staring is a comical failure to see that there is no such gap in the first place. But there is something in us that wants there to be a gap between mind and world, thought and reality. Or again: it is a remarkable achievement when an infant learns to employ the personal pronouns correctly – an autistic child may never do so. Mastery of the use of the pronoun 'I' easily gives rise to privileged moments of putative self-experience and then to conceptions of the invisible soul which were better regarded as linguistic conceits. But then again, with something of the same desire, we feel drawn to the idea of the enclosed and isolated mind.

Consider this remark: 'Why are grammatical problems so tough and seemingly ineradicable? – Because they are connected with the oldest thought habits, i.e., with the oldest images that are engraved in our language itself' (1991: 14). The devices of our language, resolutely misconceived, conjure up the most ancient myths 'deposited in our language' (1979:10). When he spoke of the 'world' in the *Tractatus*, what else was Wittgenstein doing but summoning up some sublime reality by a sort of incantation, he asks himself (1979: vi). Metaphysics is a kind of magic in the sense that words, like talismans, have the power to recall and reveal the primitive images in language itself. 'Nothing shows our kinship to these savages better than the fact that Frazer has at hand a word as familiar to us as "ghost" or "shade" to describe the way these people look at things', Wittgenstein insists, with the rider that 'too little is made of the fact that we include the words "soul" and "spirit" in our own civilized vocabulary' (1979: 10). The entities conjured into existence by misinterpretation of our speech-forms at once seem to set us deep problems – problems which are deeply disquieting, we may say; but that is because they are rooted as deeply in us as the forms of our language are themselves (1953: §111).

Ceremonial, not theology

Wittgenstein clearly had a certain respect for the Christian religion and, as we have seen, sought, in a tentative but perhaps paradigmatic way, to elucidate some of the standard concepts. He did so by bringing words back to their ordinary use (as with the word 'proof') and by drawing attention to somewhat neglected but certainly not radically contestable links with other concepts (as with Christ's resurrection and love). He placed theology in proximity to ethics and aesthetics. Instructive as this all may be, it is hardly revolutionary. He was well aware that, in Christianity's own self-understanding, there is more to it than having sound doctrines – 'you have to change your *life*' (1980: 53). But, as we hear in conversations held in Vienna in 1930, he had no difficulty in imagining 'a religion in which there are no doctrinal propositions, in which there is thus no talking' (Waismann 1979: 117). 'When people talk [in a religion], then this itself is part of a religious act and not a theory', he goes on to say, which means that it 'does not matter at all if the words used are true or false or nonsense' (Waismann 1979: 117). The year before, talking to a friend in Cambridge, he made the following remark (Rhees 1984: 102): 'The symbolisms of Catholicism are wonderful beyond words. But any attempt to make it into a philosophical system is offensive.' Interestingly, when his friend mentioned von Hügel, Wittgenstein dismissed the modernist movement in Catholic theology – 'they misunderstand the nature of symbolism' (Rhees 1984: 107). Enigmatic and undeveloped as these remarks are, they help to show the sense that religion seems to have had for Wittgenstein.

He was capable of deep religious feeling. Passing a street evangelist in Cambridge he shook his head sadly: 'If he really meant what he was shouting, he wouldn't be speaking in that tone of voice' (Rhees 1984: 111). He went on: 'This is a kind of vulgarity in which at least you can be sure that the Roman Catholic Church will never indulge' – a judgment he immediately qualified when he remembered how the consecrated host was carried in Krupps-made bomb-proof containers by priests in the German lines during the First World War – 'This was disgusting. It should have had no protection from human hands at all.' 'Vulgarity', 'tone of voice' – his feelings here are close to something aesthetic. On another occasion, sitting in Westcott House chapel in Cambridge with a friend, he jumped up and left angrily when someone started to play a piano: 'Blasphemy! A piano and the cross. Only an organ should be allowed in a church' (Rhees 1984: 121). When the friend gave up his intention to become a priest (largely through Wittgenstein's influence, it seems) and ceased to attend the Holy Week and Easter ceremonies, Wittgenstein castigated him:

> When I wanted to dissuade you from becoming a parson I didn't mean that you should at the same time cease to attend your church services. That wasn't the idea at all. Though it may be that you have to learn that these ceremonies haven't the importance you once attached to them – but that doesn't mean that they have no importance.
>
> (Rhees 1984: 129)

There is much more evidence, anecdotal and in the *Nachlass*, to show that Wittgenstein detested *theology*, taking it to be inevitably a form of *theory* – principally because he regarded it as being destructive of religion. It is not just that he deplored philosophical attempts to provide rational foundations for religion – he clearly believed that *all* theorizing, and thus all theology and even doctrine, only undermined the religious feelings and practices for which he evidently had unbounded respect – '*All* religions are wonderful, even those of the most primitive tribes' (1980: 102, my emphasis). What appealed to him in the Christian religion was what it had in common with primitive religion – 'The religious actions of the priest-king [at Nemi, according to Frazer] are not different in kind from any genuinely religious action today, say a confession of sins' (1979: 4). What we have in the ancient rites is the institutionalized use of an extremely complex gesture-language (1979: 10). Time and again, in Wittgenstein's writings from about 1930 onwards, we are referred to the place of gestures – negation as a gesture of exclusion (1953: §550), the gesture that means 'and so on' (1953: §208), making a face with a gesture of resignation (1953: §330) and so on. Often he refers to the hand – 'the innumerable language-games involving one's hand' (1969: §374). He refers to the face, the eyes, looks and glances – 'One can terrify with one's eyes, not with one's ear or nose' (1967: §222). Philosophical states of mind can involve the face – 'My eyes were wide open, the brows not contracted. . . . My glance was vacant; or again *like* that of someone admiring the illumination of the sky and drinking in the light' (1953: §412).

In short, Wittgenstein's later work persistently returns us to 'our language-game':

> Being sure that someone is in pain, doubting whether he is, and so on, are so many natural, instinctive, kinds of relationship to other human beings, and our language is simply an auxiliary to, and further extension of, this way of behaving (*Verhalten*). Our language-game is an extension of primitive behaviour (*Benehmen*). (For our *language-game* is behaviour.) (Instinct.)
>
> (1967: §545)

Time and again, Wittgenstein reminds us that the rational animal's rationality is rooted in primitive and indeed animal and instinctive behaviour. This is, paradigmatically, how he deals with – dissolves – the traditional metaphysical problems about solipsism, knowing other minds, external-world scepticism and so on. It is how he dissolves problems in the philosophy of mathematics, in *Remarks on the Foundations of Mathematics*, a text he once hoped to integrate with his work on philosophical psychology. It is also how he brings in religion:

> When we watch the life and behaviour of human beings all over the earth we see that apart from what might be called animal activities, food gathering and so forth, they also perform actions which bear a character peculiar to themselves and these could be called ritualistic (*rituell*).
>
> (1979: 7)

He is even tempted to say that human beings are 'ceremonial animals'.

It comes back to our way of being in the world. Fire, like the sun, naturally makes a deep impression on human beings – which does not mean that there is something unique about them. On the contrary, 'no phenomenon is in itself particularly mysterious, but any of them can become so to us, and the characteristic feature of the awakening mind is precisely the fact that a phenomenon comes to have meaning for us' (1979: 7). Then we behave towards the world in certain ways –

That a man's shadow, which looks like a man, or that his mirror image, or that rain, thunderstorms, the phases of the moon, the change of seasons, the likenesses and differences of animals to one another and to human beings, the phenomena of death, of birth and of sexual life, in short everything a man perceives year in, year out around him, connected together in any variety of ways – that all this should play a part in his thinking (his philosophy) and his practices, is obvious.

(1979: 6)

What it is that is deep, about religious rituals as well as magic, is evidently that they bring us into significant relationship with these earthly mundane phenomena. That is what, in Wittgenstein's judgment, needs to be respected. But when the ancient rites become enveloped in doctrine and theory, so he seems to be suggesting, they lure us into the same kind of metaphysical illusions as the devices of our language when they are uprooted from their mundane context.

'If Christianity is the truth', Wittgenstein noted in 1949 (1980: 83), 'then all the philosophy that is written about it is false'. In effect, for Wittgenstein in his most radical mood, religion is natural and theology only gets in the way of seeing this.

Note

I am indebted to the students at The Colorado College with whom I read the Wittgenstein texts on religion in Block 7, 1992.

References

Ambrose, Alice and Macdonald, Margaret (1979): *Wittgenstein's Lectures: Cambridge 1932–35*, Blackwell, Oxford.

Anscombe, G.E.M. (1954): 'Misinformation: What Wittgenstein Really Said', *The Tablet*, 17 April, 373.

Cavell, Stanley (1969): *Must we Mean What we Say? A Book of Essays*, Charles Scribner's Sons, New York.

Engelmann, Paul (1967): *Letters from Ludwig Wittgenstein with a Memoir by Paul Engelmann*, edited by B.F. McGuinness, Blackwell, Oxford.

Kant, Immanuel (1978): *Critique of Pure Reason*, tr. Norman Kemp Smith, Macmillan, London.

Monk, Ray (1990): *Ludwig Wittgenstein: The Duty of Genius*, Jonathan Cape, London.

Moore, G.E. (1959): *Philosophical Papers*, George Allen & Unwin, London.

Malcolm, Norman (1984): *Ludwig Wittgenstein: A Memoir*, 2nd edn with Wittgenstein's letters to Malcolm, Oxford University Press, Oxford and New York.

Rhees, Rush (1984): *Recollections of Wittgenstein*, Oxford University Press, Oxford and New York.

Russell, Bertrand (1956): *Logic and Knowledge: Essays 1901–1950*, edited by R. Marsh, George Allen & Unwin, London.

Waismann, Friedrich (1979): *Wittgenstein and the Vienna Circle*, edited by Brian McGuinness, Blackwell, Oxford.

Wittgenstein, Ludwig (1922): *Tractatus Logico-Philosophicus*, Routledge & Kegan Paul, London.

—— (1953): *Philosophical Investigations*, Blackwell, Oxford.

—— (1958): *The Blue and Brown Books*, Blackwell, Oxford.

—— (1961): *Notebooks 1914–1916*, Blackwell, Oxford.

—— (1967): *Zettel*, Blackwell, Oxford.

—— (1969): *On Certainty*, Blackwell, Oxford.

—— (1979): *Remarks on Frazer's Golden Bough*, Brynmill, Retford.

—— (1980): *Culture and Value*, Blackwell, Oxford.

—— (1991): 'Philosophy': Sections 86–93 of the so-called Big Typescript (Catalogue number 213), edited by Heikki Nyman, translated by C.G. Luckhardt and M.A.E. Aue, *Synthese* 87, 3–22.

—— (1992): *Last Writings on the Philosophy of Psychology*, Vol. 2, Blackwell, Oxford.

10

JACQUES DERRIDA
The God effect

Kevin Hart

The question of context

'This is my starting-point', says Jacques Derrida, 'no meaning can be determined out of context, but no context permits saturation'.[1] What is at issue
here, he explains, is not the 'semantic fertility' of high canonical literature
such as the texts to which he has been referring, P.B. Shelley's *The Triumph of
Life* and Maurice Blanchot's *L'Arrêt de mort*, but rather 'the structure of the
remnant or of iteration', which applies to every text regardless of its aesthetic,
moral, political or religious values.[2] Doubtless Derrida could have added
more disjunctions – remnant *or* iteration *or* parergon *or* remark *or* supplement
or trace – for he has given this structure many nicknames over the years. One
could say without being at all grudging that he has done nothing else but
brood upon this structure as it variously conceals and reveals itself in writings
that answer the names of 'law', 'literature', 'philosophy', 'poetry', 'psychoanalysis' or 'theology'.

In 1977, for instance, we find Derrida *en courroux* chastising the speech act
theorist John Searle for missing the point about iteration:

> I repeat, therefore, since it can never be repeated too often: if one
> admits that writing (and the mark in general) *must be able* to function
> in the absence of the sender, the receiver, the context of production,
> etc., that implies that this power, this *being able*, this *possibility* is
> always inscribed, hence *necessarily* inscribed *as possibility* in the func-
> tioning or the functional structure of the mark.[3]

Any mark, and by extension any text, must be able to signify in the absence of
its original context and intended destination, though not, of course, in the
complete and total absence of any context whatsoever. It is always possible
for any text to arrive in an unforeseen place, to be read within a frame that
its author never felt appropriate or could never have imagined. What presents

itself as outside a text – a supplement, a parergon, or whatever – co-operates intimately with the inside; it reworks the writing from within, delicately adjusting each word, if only slightly, affecting what the text signifies and so disrupting any presumed self-identity of meaning. It is always possible. Not inevitable, to be sure, since the text may be so weak or kept so secret that it is never in fact repeated outside its original context. Or it may be read for a while and then fall into illegibility, its grammar having been lost or forgotten. No matter: this chance of radical repetition, and all that follows from it, is an enabling condition of a mark or a text in the first place.

It would be reassuring to call this state of affairs a background against which I can pose a problem, but the force of Derrida's contention is that a background can always flex itself and occupy the foreground as well. There is nothing that is not in principle exempt from being caught up in this play of text and context. With this endless performance in mind, I would like to relate and examine two instances of this intertwining of text and context: the circumstances that make 'Jacques Derrida' significant, and those that do the same for 'theology'. Or, more precisely, I would like to see how one of Derrida's words, 'deconstruction', has been charged with meaning by its first contexts, and how a fuzzy set of discourses that has long intrigued Derrida, 'negative theology', has been resolutely framed by another fuzzy set of discourses we can call 'philosophy' or 'the metaphysics of presence' or even, once we know what it means, 'onto-theology'. My broad concern can be outlined in three phases, two statements and a group of questions, and in making the statements I would like to take some time to thicken the descriptions on offer.

Deconstruction and atheism

From Derrida's first writings, deconstruction was received, especially in the English-speaking world, in contexts that were at the least secular and at the most determinedly atheistic. It could be shown from a study of early and influential expository works by Jonathan Culler, Gayatri Spivak and others that the invitation to grammatology came hand in glove with a reductive and even dismissive treatment of faith, mysticism and theology. The editorial to the Summer 1981 edition of *Diacritics* can stand as an emblem. Guest editors Timothy Bahti and Richard Klein devoted an issue of the journal to deconstructive readings of Kant and Hegel; they called it 'The Ghost of Theology' and their opening remarks cast theology in an invidious and in the end tedious role 'as a form, a content, and a performance'.[4] More generally, the first framings of deconstruction foreclosed on possible relations that Derrida's writings might have with religion or theology.[5] Derrida's religious views and intentions are plainly relevant here although they have only recently been indicated in print and, even so, are difficult to classify. In 'Circumfession' (1993) he evokes his:

religion about which nobody understands anything, any more than does my mother who asked other people a while ago, not daring to talk to me about it, if I still believed in God . . . but she must have known that the constancy of God in my life is called by other names, so that I quite rightly pass for an atheist, the omnipresence to me of what I call God in my absolved, absolutely private language being neither that of an eyewitness nor that of a voice doing anything than talking to me without saying anything.[6]

Scarcely a declaration of faith, this expression is also not a straightforward affirmation of atheism. It is one thing to be an atheist, quite another, perhaps, to 'rightly pass' (*passe à just titre*) for one while none the less admitting to a God effect in one's life. There are, as Derrida knows, mystics whose religious confession so 'resembles a profession of atheism as to be mistaken for it', even though he makes no claim to be one of these.[7] His confession is further compli- cated by the reference to an 'absolutely private language', since Derrida has keenly argued from his earliest writings against the hypothesis of a purely pri- vate language or an absolutely proper name while all the time desiring what remains very close to it – a unique idiom. And what, we might ask, is an absolved language? We know that absolution must come from an Other or the Other, and we know too that it erases a content, a list of omissions and/or commissions. A true absolution, however, also removes the obligation to make a return for what has been freely given: forgiveness, grace. Absolution requires us to think a gift outside or beyond the circuit of exchange, a scan- dalous thought because it is, at heart, a thought of faith, maybe *the* thought of faith, the thought that only faith can give. At any rate, an absolved lan- guage would be one that accepts what is offered to it and understands this strictly as a gift, with no return involved. Yet for this to happen the gift must somehow remove itself in advance from the circuit of exchange, for how could one who receives a gift absolve himself or herself from such a responsi- bility? To have a sense of an absolved language is to have a thought of God, even if 'God' here does not refer to a supreme being or to being itself. Even so, as I have suggested, what Derrida calls 'God' cannot be a wholly private affair, while at the same time there can be no guarantee that anyone else will fully grasp how 'God' functions for him in his idiom.

The subtleties of Derrida's religious commitment or lack of commitment can distract us from the purpose at hand when there is no need for that to happen. If he confessed himself to be an atheist in the clearest, directest and most forceful of terms, that would surely influence how his writings were received by believers and non-believers alike. It would not, however, rigor- ously determine the religious orientation of deconstruction. For by Derrida's own reasoning, there is always a chance that his writings might feature in alien situations. And in fact that chance was realised very early on. The styles of reading and writing we associate with him were primarily established in dialogues with Husserl and Heidegger; yet while the originary institutional context of deconstruction is more heavily marked by philosophy than by literature, its horizons of reception have so far been more 'literary' than 'philosophical'. Within the Anglophone academy, the word 'deconstruction' has been heard more often in Departments of English and Comparative Literature than in Departments of Philosophy, especially in those colleges and universities where analytic philosophy sets the pace and the tone.

In recent years the word 'deconstruction' has also been used in Departments of Religious Studies and in Faculties of Theology. Far from lamenting this as a card-carrying atheist might, Derrida has shown a sympathetic interest in the religious and theological opportunities of his work. When talking in 1985 about 'a deconstructive theology movement', he suggested that

> the point would seem to be to liberate theology from what has been grafted on to it, to free it from its metaphysico-philosophical super ego, so as to uncover an authenticity of the 'gospel', of the evangelical message. And thus from the perspective of faith, deconstruction can at least be a very useful technique when Aristotelianism or Thomism are to be criticized or, even from an institutional perspective, when what needs to be criticized is a whole theological institution which supposedly has covered over, dissimulated an authentic Christian message. And [the point would also seem to be] a real possibility for faith both at the margins and very close to Scripture, a faith lived in a venturous, dangerous, free way.[8]

The formula 'would seem to be', and the scare quotes around 'gospel', suggest that Derrida is entering into another's adventure or conviction. But it is a free entrance all the same and one he manages in this conversation with ease and generosity.

Negative theology and philosophy

From early days Derrida has intermittently expressed an interest in what theologians have long called 'negative theology', that is, attempts to conceive God outside or beyond being construed as presence. He has shown a vigilant awareness that his styles of writing are not the same as a negative theology's, or even a negative atheology's. In 1968 he took the opportunity in 'Différance' to stress that, occasional appearances to the contrary, *différance* has no theological dimension,

> not even in the order of the most negative of negative theologies, which are *always* [my emphasis] concerned with disengaging a super-essentiality beyond the finite categories of essence and existence, that is, of presence, and *always* [again my emphasis] hastening to

262

recall that God is refused the predicate of existence, only in order to acknowledge his superior, inconceivable, and ineffable mode of being. [9]

More recently, he has rightly observed that the expression 'negative theology' denotes a wide variety of discourses: a point which does not lessen his insistence that their negativity is invariably regulated by philosophy.

But what is philosophy? We will get nowhere unless we understand the particular inflection he gives to this word. 'Philosophy', for Derrida as for Heidegger, is best described as 'the metaphysics of presence'. Now presence can work in three registers: the ontic (a being's temporal status as present), the ontological (the determination of being as presence) and the epistemological (a subject's presence to itself or to another subject). The metaphysics of presence is therefore accorded a vast scope: it marks all philosophies as well as discourses that would hardly seem philosophical or indeed that set themselves against philosophy. At the same time, Derrida maintains that the metaphysics of presence does not and cannot form a unity. To the extent that any text affirms, bespeaks or assumes a notion of presence, it is in fee to metaphysics. And yet it will never be *simply* metaphysical. For Derrida also claims, and supports his contention with many close readings, that no text fully abides in the present. Any text refers to an immemorial past, and that reference is essential to its construction as text. Not only is a text *always* a fabric of traces of other texts, he argues, but at any time it is *already* such. The combination of these adverbs suggests the peculiarity of deconstruction: it is oriented by the *de facto* (and hence Derrida attends to the empirical details of a text) while it also answers to the *de jure* by dint of regarding textuality as a system of laws that precedes any personal encounter. A text may address you familiarly, in the second person singular, but this intimacy is conditioned by an impersonality to the extent that it addresses all readers in this way. [10]

This latter consideration will reappear more concretely towards the end of my discussion. The main point to stress now is that Derrida holds that negative theology is monitored by philosophy, understood in his special sense of the word. The God who is 'beyond being' turns out, he thinks, to enjoy a higher kind of being, a supreme mode of self-presence, a superessentiality. Now Derrida does not claim that this philosophy is the sole, inaugural context of these negative theologies, whether of the Pseudo-Dionysius, Meister Eckhart, Angeleus Silesius, Martin Heidegger or of the many others he does not list and examine. Nor does he hold that this broad framework exhausts their meaning and their importance. He acknowledges, rather, that there are 'original, heterogeneous elements of Judaism and Christianity' which 'were never completely eradicated by Western metaphysics. They perdure throughout the centuries, threatening and unsettling the assured "identities" of Western philosophy.' [11] And elsewhere he makes what seems to be a similar concession:

in effect I believe that what is called 'negative theology' (a rich and very diverse corpus) does not let itself be easily assembled under the general category of 'onto-theology-to-be-deconstructed'. Undoubtedly there are also the places of 'positive' theology, about which as much could be said.[12]

The expression 'Does not let itself be easily assembled' turns on 'easily' rather than on 'not'. He remains firm: no negative theology quite reaches a place that is not, in some way, overseen by philosophy.

Questions

Let us organise these remarks into two sets of questions, keeping in mind the position from which Derrida begins, that for meaning to occur a text needs at least one context but that no cluster of contexts exhausts the meaning of any text.

First set

Does deconstruction assume the necessity of at least one context – call it atheism, disbelief, scepticism or unbelief – in order to function? Is it committed in advance to a world-view in which there can be no God? Does it make God, insofar as it can acknowledge him, into an idol? Or can deconstruction work equally well in a theological framework? If deconstruction is not a negative theology, is there a deconstructive moment in negative theology?

Second set

Does Derrida convincingly show that theology is always and invariably answerable to philosophy, as he understands it? Must theology and negative theology appeal to philosophy overtly or covertly in order to be intelligible, let alone meaningful? Or does Derrida impose, or sketch in too heavily, a philosophical framework for negative theology in order to understand *it*? Could there be a theology that escapes or, deep down, does not need to answer to the contexts he would call 'philosophical'?

Theology and Theiology

Deconstruction has widely been understood in Nietzschean terms, as a celebration of God's death and an affirmation of atheism. First uttered with the urgency of prophecy, the expression 'God is dead' has become tired and doctrinaire. That it was spoken by a madman in search of God, is indebted to Hegel and others, and has competing reference points in epistemology, ethics, metaphysics and religion, has largely been forgotten. Rather than simply fold deconstruction into the three dark syllables 'God is dead', we need to ask how words such as 'atheism', 'divine', 'God', 'sacred' and 'theology' function in Derrida's writings. One cannot presume they follow the rhythms of *Thus Spake Zarathustra*, *Twilight of the Idols* or *The Anti-Christ*. Nor can one assume they always refer to the one religious constellation. Christianity, Judaism and paganism are all evoked in passing by Derrida. Or I should say Christianities, Judaisms and paganisms, since his interest has always been to uncover hidden or repressed possibilities in traditions.

Even though theology has not been one of Derrida's prime concerns, he has repeatedly touched on the question of God and its effects. It would be laborious to map all the nuances the word 'God', say, acquires in his discussions of Celan, Jabès and Levinas (all Jews but in quite different ways) or in his meditations on the Pseudo-Dionysius, Eckhart, Rousseau and Hegel (all Christians, though all singular in their Christianity). Nevertheless, it would not be hard to show that Derrida has a religious lexicon, perhaps a richer one than is usually thought, and that it is used to definite ends. Consider the word 'God'. For all its minute variations from text to text a broad pattern can be discerned if one moves back a step or two:

> God is the name and the element of that which makes possible an absolutely pure and absolutely self-present self-knowledge. From Descartes to Hegel and in spite of all the differences that separate the different places and moments in the structure of that epoch, God's infinite understanding is the other name for the logos as self-presence.[13]

Without making an issue of it, Derrida is pointing out that the word 'God' does more than signify a divinity men and women may worship. It also serves to ground a range of philosophical systems in a number of ways, and therefore marks the imagined end of any signifying chain. So when he observes in a vivid image that 'the intelligible face of the sign remains turned toward the word and the face of God', the point is that all sign systems have been underwritten, at some stage, by something outside or beyond these systems.[14]

Derrida's target is this absolute exteriority or interiority which has been repeatedly named and used to ground philosophical systems. One of the most important names it has been given is 'God'; but, as he shows, Nature and Self-consciousness have also been pressed into service from time to time. It is enough to make us look closely at his phrasing when writing about a religion or God. Here are two examples, both from *Of Grammatology*:

> The difference between signified and signifier belongs in a profound and implicit way to the totality of the great epoch covered by the history of metaphysics, and in a more explicit and more systematically

articulated way to the narrower epoch of Christian creationism and infinitism *when these appropriate the resources of Greek conceptuality.*

> Only infinite being can reduce the difference in presence. In that sense, the name of God, *at least as it is pronounced within classical rational-ism*, is the name of indifference itself. Only a positive infinity can lift the trace, 'sublimate' it.... We must not therefore speak of a 'theological prejudice', functioning sporadically when it is a question of the plenitude of the logos; the logos as the sublimation of the trace is *theological*.[15]

It is clear in the first passage that Derrida's critical object is metaphysics, not faith as such. Christianity is of interest because it offers a manageable example of a metaphysical state of affairs, but even so it is not a pure instance. Christian theologies become metaphysical 'when these appropriate the resources of Greek conceptuality', and while those borrowings may be steady and extensive they do not exhaust Christianity. The second passage confirms the first. Only when the concept of God is conflated with that of pure exteriority or interiority, as happens in 'classical rationalism', does it become metaphysical.

The import of this second passage is made more distinct in *Glas*, where Derrida momentarily overhears a dialogue between Mendelssohn and Hegel. 'Mendelssohn reckons it a high merit in his faith that it proffers no eternal truths', writes the young Hegel in 'The Spirit of Christianity and its Fate'.[16] And Derrida offers this gloss: 'Since God does not manifest himself, he is not truth for the Jews, total presence or parousia. He gives orders without appearing.'[17] Here the Jewish God as treated by Mendelssohn seems to slip outside the metaphysics of presence. Tempting as it might be, one cannot say, 'As in *Glas* for the Jews, so in *Of Grammatology* for the Christians', since Christianity is historically more complicit with Greek metaphysics than Judaism has ever been. 'Complicit with', though, does not have to imply 'dependent on'. And the point that 'God' and 'presence' are not necessarily coextensive remains: a crucial issue given that on Derrida's understanding all metaphysics revolves around presence. We can conclude that not only is Derrida's analysis not pivoted around 'God' but that it keeps open – for others, if not for himself – a possibility of thinking the divinity in a non-metaphysical manner. As he observes in a long meditation on Antonin Artaud, 'The death of God will ensure our salvation because the death of God alone can reawaken the Divine' and, with a similar paradoxical flair, 'The divine has been ruined by God'.[18]

All this goes a fair way toward explaining how the word 'theology' functions in the second passage and elsewhere. When Derrida alludes to 'the theological presence of a centre', this centre need not be named God but, like the philosopher's God, must be unique, beyond all displacement, exchange or substitution. And when he tells of the logos sublimating the trace and so being theological or of *différance* blocking 'every relationship to theology', the upshot is that there can be no undivided self-presence (whether natural or divine) in a world where every proposition is always open to be interpreted by another proposition.[19] Derrida's word 'theology' is plainly being used in a special sense. Given the Heideggerian cast of the passages I have been discussing, it should be no surprise that this sense originates with the German thinker. Toward the end of *Nietzsche*, Heidegger meditates on the fundamental question of metaphysics, 'Why are there beings at all, and why not rather nothing?' This, he tells us, 'is the question of the *theion*, a question that had already arisen at the beginning of metaphysics in Plato and Aristotle'.[20] I have already given one description of metaphysics according to Heidegger, and here is another that complements it. Metaphysics in Heidegger's view is the study of both beings in general, the *on hei on*, which is known as ontology, and the study of the ground of beings as a whole, and as the highest ground is called the *theion* it is known as theology. Thus when Heidegger and Derrida talk of metaphysics as theology, or about the onto-theological constitution of metaphysics, they are making claims about philosophy's internal logic and historical destiny, not about its relations – historical or conceptual, overt or covert – with religion.

Given all this, it would be helpful to distinguish between theiology, the study of highest grounds, and theology, the study of God. The one necessarily passes through a metaphysics of presence, while the other, at least in theory, is not obliged to do so. Whether it is constrained to do so in practice, as soon as one begins to speak of or to God, is another question. Certainly the distinction cannot be drawn smoothly and continuously, because even those theologies which assail a particular philosophy, or even philosophy in general, are not thereby automatically freed from metaphysical notions. An example: Tertullian tries to stretch the distance between Athens and Jerusalem as far as it will go, and yet he cannot stop himself from speaking Greek when specifying what he means by 'God'.[21]

One way in which theologians have sought to arrest the metaphysics in their theologies is by developing one or more negative theologies: stringent attempts to erase, limit or suspend the predicates one ascribes to the deity. As I have already mentioned, Derrida has often alluded to negative theology, and although it is only in a recent essay, 'How to Avoid Speaking', that he addresses the topic at length, he has always asterisked it as a problem or, better, as a cluster of problems. Thus in an early essay of Georges Bataille, he observes that

> Even in its discourse, which already must be distinguished from sovereign affirmation, this atheology does not, however, proceed along the lines of negative theology; lines that could not fail to fascinate Bataille, but which, *perhaps*, still reserved, beyond all the

rejected predicates, and even 'beyond being', a 'superessentiality'; beyond the categories of being, a supreme being and an indestructible meaning. *Perhaps*: for here we are touching upon the limits and the greatest audacities of discourse in Western thought.[22]

I emphasise Derrida's qualifications, those two uses of *perhaps* which are considerably more circumspect than the two *always*es I noted in his allusions to negative theology in 'Différance'. To weigh the relative importance of these words, let us recall the discussion following the presentation of his paper 'Différance' in 1968 to the French Society of Philosophy. Early in the piece Brice Parain suggested that *différance* 'is the God of negative theology' at which point Derrida interrupted, 'It is and it is not. . . . It is above all not.' A little later he replied more fully, saying, 'nothing in such a discourse strikes me as more alien to negative theology'. Immediately, though, there came a qualification: 'And yet, as often happens, this infinite distance is also an infinitesimal distance. That is why negative theology fascinates me . . . negative theology is also an *excessive* practice of language.'[23]

I will leave aside the question of whether Derrida and Parain are talking about negative theology or negative theiology, and what the distinction between these might be in this situation, and look instead at why Derrida is right to argue for the originality of *différance*. 'Originality', here, should not be taken at face value, for Derrida's word looks back and partly translates Heidegger's *Austrag* and Blanchot's *Neutre*, which themselves look back to pre-Socratic Greek.[24] That said, Derrida's concept is his own, as much as any idea this late in philosophical history can be one's own; and it is a long way from the God beyond being and even from the God effect that shimmers along the edges of his confession in 'Circumfession'. What Parain calls 'the God of negative theology' is the ground of being, which can be approached only by using a syntax of neither–nor. It is transcendent and transcendental, which means it forms the condition of possibility for the world and human beings to have meaning while also surmounting that world. *Différance*, by contrast, is a condition of possibility which, as 'meaningless play', is incapable of forming a solid ground; it is transcendental though not transcendent. Purely transcendent or purely transcendental: in terms of religious belief the difference is infinite; with regard to textual interpretation, infinitesimal. A Talmudic scholar or a Christian exegete might defend multiple or playful interpretations of scripture by pointing to the inexhaustible fullness of God's word. Yet Derrida can affirm the same styles of reading for sacred and secular texts alike by appealing to *différance*, which ceaselessly generates meaning while refusing to be reified into a being, let alone the highest being, the ground of being, or being itself.

In 'How to Avoid Speaking' Derrida distinguishes deconstruction from negative theology in similar terms. His project is both like and unlike those of the Pseudo-Dionysius and Meister Eckhart. What worries him about apophatic discourse is that, despite all its ruses and deferrals, it is committed in advance to a singular destination; it promises to lead one beyond being to the immediacy of a presence, God himself. No wonder then that Derrida takes the act of promising as his guiding thread through that labyrinth of problems we call 'negative theology'. He has often said he will explain himself more fully on the topic. 'I will speak of a promise, then', he says, 'but also within the promise'.[25] He has no choice but to speak 'within the promise', since by his own reasoning all texts are structured as promises. They make a promise to those who read them by their very structure; they may promise to convey emotion or knowledge, or just to speak in an idiom. They commit themselves to work in, around or against certain genres – the essay, the letter, the ode, the prayer, the treatise – to be 'philosophy', or 'theology', or 'literature' or whatever, and to be answerable to the laws of the Church or State. Moreover, they promise to be readable in the absence of author and intended audience.

We have encountered this last claim in *Limited Inc*, though it can be found much earlier, in *Speech and Phenomena*, where it is formulated in an arresting way: 'My death is structurally necessary to the pronouncing of the *I*.'[26] Now if a piece of writing functions by dint of its transcendental structure rather than by virtue of the presence of an author or an addressee, it cannot promise anything in the present. The promise it makes to be legible for others will have already been made in an immemorial past. One could say the same thing in another way: that texts promise to be unreadable, not to yield all their sense and significance in the present. It follows from either formulation that no text can be encoded with a singular destination. There must always be the possibility of a text being deflected from a simple or a single end, regardless of how forcefully that intention may be announced. It is as though each text has a tiny hammer hidden deep inside which can hit the author's intention, bend it a little, and send his or her text astray.

What promise does a text of negative theology make, *The Mystical Theology* of the Pseudo-Dionysius, for instance? We know that it is addressed to Timothy, a presbyter, who requires induction into the higher reaches of mystical experience. Yet the Pseudo-Dionysius does not begin with a greeting to Timothy but with a prayer; and, as Derrida observes, this is highly significant. Without this call to the Other there would be no guide to the apophatic way: the negations would be unmotivated, capable of heading in any direction. From the perspective of the mystic, the opening prayer is a way of smashing all idols in advance, of distinguishing the unknown and unknowable God of faith from the God of the philosophers and the gods of the pagans. Yet this does not provide us with an example of what Derrida regards as a pure prayer, an address to the Other as wholly other, for the prayer is supplemented at its origin by an encomium offered to the Trinity beyond being. The negativity risked by the Pseudo-Dionysius is released in the name of the Christian God and in the hope that he may 'direct us to the mystical summits'.[27] No Christian could do otherwise: the supplement is essential. And so *The Mystical Theology* promises, among other things, to be overseen by the Trinity.

Having established this, Derrida has no trouble in showing that the text in question cannot have a singular destination. It opens by addressing both the Other and the Christian God whose alterity is already compromised by doctrinal specifications. Moreover the Pseudo-Dionysius does not simply pray, he also quotes his prayer and does so while addressing Timothy. So, rather than beginning in the immediacy and simplicity of prayer, the work starts in the complexity of multiple addressees. And even if the prayer were uttered silently, in a hushed and intimate communion with God, the mystic would not be able to eliminate the possibility of inscription and all that follows from it. One cannot approach God by passing from language to silence; even a silent and unwritten prayer would be marked by *différance*. A moment ago I noted that for Derrida the possibility of the writer's and intended reader's deaths is written into a text. There is no doubt that *The Mystical Theology* announces the Areopagite's death. Can it also announce God's death?

In one situation the confession of God's death might be part of a Christian apologetics ('*God himself is dead*', wrote Hegel), while in another it might be a forthright atheism ('God is dead', say the Nietzscheans).[28] But how can the phenomenon of *writing* sway religious belief one way or the other? Derrida is not the only thinker to have made so sublime a claim. An author for whom he has the greatest respect, Maurice Blanchot, regards writing as

> an anonymous, distracted, deferred, and dispersed way of being in relation, by which everything is brought into question – and first of all the idea of God, of the Self, of the Subject, then of Truth and the One, then finally the idea of the Book and the Work.[29]

A bold claim, to say the least, and it is significant that God heads the list because it indicates how Blanchot conceives him: as everything that follows in his list gathered together and raised to a higher power. One finds this sense of God from time to time in Derrida's writings, especially in *Writing and Difference*, although he distances himself from talk of the death of God, knowing full well that a denial of God conceived as an elevated mode of presence is no less metaphysical than an affirmation of the same deity.[30]

To say that God dies means for Derrida no more than (and no less than) that he is unable to reveal himself in language. The point is made in the middle of a discussion of Husserl's account of meaning and representation:

> If the possibility of my disappearance in general must somehow be experienced in order for a relationship with presence in general to be instituted, we can no longer say that the experience of the possibility of my absolute disappearance (my death) affects me, occurs to

an *I am*, and modifies a subject. The *I am*, being experienced only as an *I am present*, itself presupposes the relationship with presence in general, with being as presence. The appearing of the *I* to itself in the *I am* is thus originally a relation with its own possible disappearance. Therefore, *I am* originally means *I am mortal*. *I am immortal* is an impossible proposition. We can even go further: as a linguistic statement 'I am he who am' is the admission of a mortal. The move which leads from the *I am* to the determination of my being as *res cogitans* (thus, as an immortality) is a move by which the origin of presence and ideality is concealed in the very presence and ideality it makes possible.[31]

It is breathtaking how quickly Yahweh, 'I am he who am', is transformed into the God of modern philosophers, a *res cogitans*; and we may well ask whether God is a subject in quite this way. I leave the question for the moment, and underline the general point that all inscription, even by God, must pass through the realm of *différance* or the *trace*.[32] As soon as the word 'God' enters a discourse it can never again be singular and unique; it begins to divide so that we can never be entirely sure whether a text refers to the deity or quotes his name without quotation marks. And if that is the case, no treatise of negative theology can confidently claim to be negating predicates in such a way that will lead one eventually to God.

This argument deserves serious examination. To highlight one of its facets, the status of *différance*, I will look briefly at Derrida's first study of Emmanuel Levinas, 'Violence and Metaphysics', where Levinas's notion of the trace is examined and adjusted. Inspired by Exodus 33 and by Franz Rosenzweig's critique of totality in *The Star of Redemption*, Levinas tries to rethink ethics by way of the trace of the Other in preference to intuition, utility, virtue or other touchstones of moral philosophy. His central claim concerns the relation between the other person and time: 'A face is in the trace of the utterly bygone, utterly passed absent, withdrawn into what Paul Valéry calls "the deep yore, never long ago enough", which cannot be discovered in the self by an introspection.'[33] One of the things at issue here is that I am always and already responsible for the other person. My obligation to him or her is not forged in the present moment, or even in a future present (the realisation of a better society, for example) but in an immemorial past. Levinas sometimes calls this 'deep yore' eternity, but it is not behind, beyond or above the phenomenal world; nor is it a knowledge revealed to me directly by God. Rather, I approach God only in recognising that the other person moves 'in the Trace of God'. In acknowledging that the other person is always in principle closer to God than I am, and in acting upon the precept that meeting his or her material needs will satisfy my spiritual hungers, I draw closer to the deity. In short, God appears within the horizon of ethics, not religion or metaphysics. And so eternity is glimpsed, as it withdraws, in the ethical imposition

271

of the 'always already'. I grasp that the other's past can never be made present to me, that any model of the other person I make on the basis of introspection will always be a reduction of his or her alterity, dignity and freedom.

This idea of an immemorial past is, as Derrida allows, a radical notion; it 'risks incompatibility with every allusion to the "very presence of God"'.[34] Levinas would not disagree with this, for he distinguishes phenomenological intelligibility (which answers to presence) from ethical responsibility (which does not), and insists that for him the latter transcends and interrupts the former, upsetting any totalising moves that might be astir. Levinas might disagree, though, when Derrida makes his next move and proposes that the thought of *Totality and Infinity* can be 'readily converted into atheism'. How could such a conversion take place? By reading Levinas against himself at the point where he determines the nature of the trace, that is, by recognising the trace as primary, as the transcendental condition for all polarities – presence and absence, God and man, subject and object – and by showing how Levinas arrests his insight into the trace and draws back from characterising it as the meaningless play of *différance*. Once this move is made Derrida can reasonably ask 'if God was an *effect of the trace*?'[35] Whether one answers yes or no to this question will depend on what one understands by the word 'God'. For Derrida, here, 'God' denotes a presence, a *res cogitans*. One cannot say the same for Levinas. It would be a difficult task to say exactly what 'God' means in his writings, and one I will not attempt here, but certainly the God of Levinas is to be thought otherwise than the Greek notion of being, which is always a mode of being present and which therefore effaces difference and separation in the names of simultaneity and unity. Against the Greeks, Levinas argues that God can be thought only in terms of ethical responsibility, in the recognition that the other person never coincides temporally with me point by point and that the relation between us is asymmetrical and always in the other's favour.

Derrida's response to this is well known. Levinas's apparent exit from ontology can be shown to depend at important points on what he claims to have abandoned. Levinas professes to have broken with the philosophy of Parmenides and with the very thought of *Dasein* cast in the neutre as elaborated by Heidegger. But for Derrida not even Plato could assassinate Parmenides, the sovereign thinker of being. And consequently Derrida asks, 'But will a non-Greek ever succeed in doing what a Greek in this case could not do, except by disguising himself as a Greek, by *speaking* Greek, by feigning to speak Greek in order to get near the king?'[36] The high stakes of this question become clear when we listen to Derrida pose the question that orients all his thinking and writing:

> If philosophy has always intended, from its point of view, to maintain
> its relation with the non-philosophical, that is the antiphilosophical,
> with the practices and knowledge, empirical or not, that constitute

its other, if it has constituted itself according to this purposive *entente* with its outside, if it has always intended to hear itself speak, in the same language, of itself and of something else, can one, strictly speaking, determine a nonphilosophical place, a place of exteriority or alterity from which one might still treat *of philosophy*?[37]

In the first question about how to get close to the king we can almost hear Derrida meditating how he would ease himself out of Levinas's predicament, while in the second question we hear him indicating a way. He knows that he must set metaphysics against itself, must play the game of philosophy with consummate skill but with an awareness that philosophy is itself caught up in a game it cannot fully control. Proceeding along these lines, he will uncover the strange realm from which philosophy can be questioned without thereby increasing its territory. The 'nonphilosophical place' is what Derrida calls *différance* in its transcendental register.

It may be that *différance* produces 'God' in the same way it originates 'identity', 'proper', 'speech' and 'truth', since *différance* generates all conceptual polarities, including those terms associated with presence. Here Derrida extends Nietzsche's quip, 'I fear we are not getting rid of God because we still believe in grammar'; it is the gnawing suspicion that linguistic structures encourage false dualistic thinking, that the very existence of the word 'man' opens the way for people to think of 'God', to misconstrue God as a reality.[38] The concept 'God' would therefore be an effect of the trace, and all theologies would be answerable to this 'God' effect. But not wholly answerable. When Blanchot suggests that writing brings everything into question, 'and first of all *the idea of* God [my emphasis]', his phrasing is careful and precise.[39] Like Blanchot, Derrida can strictly address only the word and the concept 'God' (which can never fail to divide and multiply once they enter discourse) and can make no rigorous judgement, positive or negative, about the divine reality professed by believers, whether that reality appears through ethics or religion. To be sure, deconstruction puts pressure on distinctions between word and reality and reorients our senses of both. Yet while Derrida shows the relations between 'reality', 'word' and 'presence' to be more complex and equivocal than we have thought and in ways that have not been thought, he does not deny material realities. He denies that their materiality is a mode of presence. Derrida writes far more often about materiality than spirituality, but so far as deconstruction goes the general point remains for both. He argues against God conceived, experienced or used as a mode of presence, though not against God as such. In Derrida's world there may be a God, and this God may be full self-presence, or may be otherwise than presence. These are open questions for him. But if there is a God and he presents himself immediately to consciousness the event cannot be discussed without the mystic's own words embarrassing the claim. 'We are dispossessed of the longed-for presence in the gesture of language by which we attempt to seize it', he says with respect to Rousseau, though the point has far wider import.[40]

Keeping all this in mind, let us assume for the sake of argument what, strictly speaking, cannot be risked outside the dimension of faith. Let us assume there is a God as evoked by the Pseudo-Dionysius. Now as Derrida cheerfully admits, everyday communication occurs between individuals even though no speech or writing can have a unique addressee. Conversations happen, meals are ordered, classes are taught, and so on, with structural undecidability impinging, to be sure, though without it being an insupportable burden that makes communication impossible. Deconstruction begins its labours when the possibility of deflection in any communication is suppressed or repressed. Or, equally, when it is noted that signification exceeds intended meaning. Communication is not abolished in Derrida's world but is reset in a new framework, one that does not appeal to a constitutive or regulatory presence. So God, if there is a God, can presumably hear and answer the Pseudo-Dionysius's prayer for guidance even though it necessarily contains the possibility of being deflected to other destinations, and even though it may signify more than he intends. It is worth noting that, in the terms of this argument, we are not obliged to regard God as a mode of presence, let alone pure self-presence, a *res cogitans*. Communication occurs between people who, on Derrida's understanding, are not and cannot be self-present. Insofar as communication is the question, then, one need not go so far as to claim that God be self-present in order to hear and answer prayer.

To the divine idiom

The Mystical Theology promises, Derrida thinks, to lead us to a place above or beyond being. Can it keep this promise? He thinks not. 'It is doubtless the vision of a dark light, no doubt an intuition of "more than luminous [*hyperphoton*] darkness", but still it is the immediacy of a presence'.[41] When the Pseudo-Dionysius claims that the divinity is beyond [*hyper*] being, his statement 'has the double and ambiguous meaning of what is above in a hierarchy, thus both beyond and more', and so his apophatic theology never quite escapes the metaphysics it calls into question.[42]

The Pseudo-Dionysius is not the only writer who promises to lead us beyond being. When discussing negative theology Derrida reminds us of Plato (who evoked the *Chora*, the placeless place where the Demiurge inscribes the Forms) and Heidegger (who tried to grasp *Ereignis*, that which grants being by way of time and time by way of being). Now Derrida concedes that these quests are by no means simply metaphysical; they contain motifs which unsettle the will to ground. The *Chora* thwarts logics of exclusion ('neither–nor') and inclusion ('both–and'); it belongs to a 'third genus' which frustrates the usual movements of Platonism. Similarly, *Ereignis* slips between being and beings because it is the event which grants being to thought and so gives rise to metaphysics and the overcoming of metaphysics. Why do Plato and Heidegger differ from the Pseudo-Dionysius? Because the author of *The Mystical Theology* remains committed to a superessentiality above being while Plato and Heidegger try to think places that are neither interior nor exterior. In doing so they glimpse, in different ways, *différance*, the quasi-concept which bespeaks a promise made in an immemorial past.

I would like to make two responses to this. In the first place, while Derrida acknowledges that the Greek prefix *hyper* can mean both 'above' and 'beyond' he dwells on the first of these when contemplating being, namely 'that which is more' rather than 'that which is beyond'. There is no doubt that the Pseudo-Dionysius provides an ambiguous text about God, that it makes both metaphysical and non-metaphysical gestures at the same time. His account of God may therefore be trammelled in metaphysics at any given moment, but it need not be wholly and simply metaphysical, and not just because of the *différance* at work within his writing: the thought that God is beyond being cannot be reduced without remainder. It may not be possible to say anything, at least in propositional terms, about this God, but that is another matter.

In the second place, it would be quite possible to grant that *différance* provides the condition of possibility for all discourse, and still to believe in a God who abides above or beyond being. To ask God to guarantee determinate meaning and to maintain metaphysical hierarchies would be to mistake the relationship that humans can have with the divinity. Imagine someone praying for God to change the laws of inscription! Indeed, a theology would be the dream of God doing just that, and far from questioning metaphysics a negative theology would be at one with it, a privileged way of isolating the *theion*, as Derrida correctly realised in 'Différance'. By contrast, theology would be the working out of God's calls and gifts to men and women in a life of faith. It would never be a simple matter, for theology can never reflect on faith without involving religion. And as Paul Ricoeur argues, 'metaphysics makes God into a supreme being; and religion treats the sacred as a new sphere of objects, institutions, and powers within the world of immanence'. The life of faith inexorably tends to turn *signs* of the sacred into sacred *objects* and, as Ricoeur suggests, 'This diabolic transformation makes religion the reification and alienation of faith'.[43] In one of its gestures, negative theology would be what returns to theology in order to identify and, so far as possible, arrest this dark transformation. One of its tasks would be to remind theology of the promise in which it abides: to speak of the eternal God and not of idols.[44]

Consequent as it is in many respects, *The Mystical Theology* is not all of a piece. It braids together a metaphysical and a non-metaphysical theology, the one being required to make 'God' intelligible and the other necessary if we are to pass from a propositional knowledge of God to God himself. A full analysis of this text would do one thing that Derrida does not do in 'How to Avoid Speaking', namely read the Pseudo-Dionysius along this very ridge.

There is no reason to expect him to have done this. When he reads Bataille or Levinas against themselves it is to clarify the status, scope and strength of *différance*; and when, in *Of Spirit*, he follows the same strategy with Heidegger it is to show how only a thoroughgoing deconstruction of *Geist*, a movement from *geistig* to *geistlich*, could have saved him from his catastrophic political error in the 1930s.[45] In reading the Pseudo-Dionysius or Meister Eckhart, one of Derrida's interests is in identifying differences between deconstruction and negative theology. Principally, his concern is to show that the *texts* of negative theology always presuppose a presence, that at one level or another they invariably use a philosophical vocabulary, regardless of what the mystics actually experienced, regardless of whether God (or experience of him) is or is not a mode of presence beyond beings or being.

Not having heard or responded to the call of faith – 'I quite rightly pass for an atheist', he says, despite the subtleties of his *credo* – Derrida would have no motivation to follow the darkened, criss-crossing paths from the God of metaphysics to the unsayable God of Love along which a deconstruction tries to run in *The Mystical Theology*. Yet he understands the logic which operates once the call of faith has been received. When asked in a discussion of Walter Benjamin's theory of translation whether sacred texts are necessary, he answered:

> a sacred text, if there is such a thing, is a text that does not await the question of whether or not it is necessary that there be such a thing: if there is a sacred text, then there is a sacred text. You are wondering whether or not the sacred text is necessary: this is a question which that text couldn't care less about. The sacred text happens, it is an event.[46]

Which calls for two points. The first is merely a comment on the context of this response: an oral improvisation to a question. Had there been more time in this symposium, many qualifications could have been made. The valencies of 'sacred' in different faiths, and in any particular faith, would have to be accounted for to give substance and pertinence to 'sacred'. And the second point is a comment on 'If there is such a thing'. The conditional allows room for the sacred to be conceived by way of sacralisation. One sees that the text resists translation at certain moments, that its uniqueness is supremely valuable and its idiom can never be reconstituted in another code, and at that point the text becomes sacred. (One might say of some texts that they become literary, not sacred; but let us pass the question of the relations between sacred and secular writing without disturbing it.[47]) For the faithful, though, there can be no 'if' about sacred texts, the Gospels for example: they commemorate and explore a foundational event, they are *sui generis*, and even though they remain susceptible to sacralisation, and are partly sacralised themselves, they cannot in principle be naturalised.

A sacred text elaborates itself at an extreme limit; its idiom resists reduction at every point. Idiom? The word has come up before, and Derrida charges it with high value. I will limit myself to one quotation, from his analysis of Nicholas Abraham and Maria Torok's *Cryptonomie*. Having just found difficulties with a view of 'conscious representations of "words" and "things" for a self speaking within the "internal" system of language', Derrida explores another way of conceiving writing:

> But the situation would be quite different if we focused on what is produced in speech or in writing by a *desire for idiom* or an *idiom of desire*. There, a system is wrenched open within the system, general (national) codes are diverted and exploited, at the cost of certain transactions, in a type of economy which thenceforth is neither purely idiomatic (the absolutely undecipherable) nor simply commonplace (conventional and transparent).[48]

Taking this as our cue, a sacred idiom would be neither natural nor supernatural, neither literal nor metaphoric. If we say it comes from the divine, it is surely mediated by an individual, a community or a tradition: so it is neither exterior nor interior, and for the same reasons, neither fact nor fiction. That eerie quality of originality, of authority, one finds in sacred writings can never be accommodated in conceptual oppositions, the very mechanisms that Nietzsche thought had produced metaphysics. Rather, this quality lingers between, around, beside and against those oppositions.[49] The importance of a sacred text's message requires that it be translated, while its singularity testifies to the impossibility of adequate translation. A Christian will regard the Gospels as containing, in a more or less encrypted form, the divine idiom; and will see himself or herself as addressed there, by something in the words and yet withdrawing behind them. One might say that a Christian is someone who chooses to regard himself or herself as uniquely addressed by the Gospels, in the full knowledge that the proclamation is not reserved for any one individual. The Christian chooses God, then becomes aware of having been chosen. However one figures the logic of responding to God's call, to believe that scripture or tradition speaks here and there – fleetingly, perhaps, and certainly in spite of contamination – in a divine idiom is to live and move within the God effect.

In the same way, one could think of *The Mystical Theology*, or any thoroughgoing negative theology, as a quest for the divine idiom. By definition, this idiom would be undecipherable and unspeakable, both in fact and by right. In revelation, however, the divine idiom is given to language, to a peculiar semantics and syntax, and so must engage with all kinds of codes: generic, legal, linguistic, national, ritual and so forth. What the Pseudo-Dionysius calls the 'divine names' – Good, Light, Beauty, Love – function in an economy which circulates between the cryptic and the communicable. Within theology these names are empowered to appropriate themselves even as they move among us, that is, to declare themselves proper. Hence negative theology: the doubled process of exposing that reappropriation while gradually contracting the scope of the economy so that we can move from the sayable in the direction of the unsayable. It is a dark passage from religious codes to the divine idiom, from 'God' to God, and one that is never able to be fully traversed.

Negative theology cannot lead us silently into the immediate presence of a deity regarded as *res cogitans*. Its function is otherwise: to remind us that God escapes all programmes, even the many subtle ones developed by philosophers and theologians. God is possible, says the positive theologian, meaning that the divine is revealed if only we would see (and the terms of seeing are then spelt out). God is impossible, says the negative theologian, meaning that God always exceeds the concept of God. Each theology claims priority: without negative theology God talk would decay into idolatry, yet without positive theology there would be no God talk in the first place. It is a permanent task of religious thought to keep the negative and the positive in play, to demonstrate that the impossible is not in contradiction with the possible. What Derrida helps bring into focus is that the possible and the impossible are not to be resolved dialectically or logically: they arrange and rearrange themselves in the negative form of an aporia. Religious experience pulls a person in different directions at the same time, demanding we attend both to the possible and the impossible; and in negotiating this aporia one's conscience is never satisfied. This experience of desire, dissatisfaction, insufficiency and uncertainty is a part of the God effect.

Notes

I wish to thank Phillip Blond, Mark C. Taylor and Brayton Polka for criticisms of an earlier version of this paper.

1 Jacques Derrida, 'Living On', *Deconstruction and Criticism*, ed. Geoffrey H. Hartman (London: Routledge and Kegan Paul, 1979), 81.
2 Derrida, 'Living On', 81. Derrida remarks in 'Afterward: Toward an Ethic of Discussion' that the much quoted expression 'there is nothing outside the text' means 'there is nothing outside context', *Limited Inc* (Evanston: Northwestern University Press, 1988), 136.
3 Derrida, *Limited Inc*, 48. The essay 'Limited Inc' was first published in *Glyph* in 1977.
4 Editorial, *Diacritics*, 11:2 (1981), 1.
5 See my *The Trespass of the Sign: Deconstruction, Theology and Philosophy* (Cambridge: Cambridge University Press, 1989), 43f.
6 Derrida, 'Circumfession', *Jacques Derrida*, by Geoffrey Bennington and Jacques Derrida (Chicago: University of Chicago Press, 1993), 154–5. It is also worth quoting in this context an extract from a letter by Derrida:

Modestly and in my own way, I try to translate (or to let myself be involved, carried along, perhaps elsewhere, by and perhaps without) a thought of Heidegger that says: 'If I were still writing a theology – I am sometimes tempted to do that – the expression "Being" should not figure in it.... There is nothing to be done here with Being. I believe Being can never be thought as the essence and the bottoming of god.

Letter to John P. Leavey', *Semeia*, 23 (1982), 61

7 Derrida, 'Post-Scriptum: Aporias, Ways and Voices', *Derrida and Negative Theology*, ed. Harold Coward and Toby Foshay (Albany: SUNY, 1992), 283.
8 James Creech *et al.*, 'Deconstruction in America: An Interview with Jacques Derrida', *Critical Exchange*, 17 (1985), 12.
9 Derrida, *Margins of Philosophy*, trans. Alan Bass (Chicago: University of Chicago Press, 1982), 6.
10 The familiar form of address is '*tu*'; however, in French the law uses that form in an impersonal sense.
11 Richard Kearney, 'Deconstruction and the Other', in his *Dialogues with Contemporary Continental Thinkers: The Phenomenological Heritage* (Manchester: Manchester University Press, 1984), 117.
12 Derrida, 'Letter to John P. Leavey', 61.
13 Derrida, *Of Grammatology*, trans. and intro. Gayatri Spivak (Baltimore: Johns Hopkins University Press, 1976), 98.
14 Derrida, *Of Grammatology*, 13.
15 Derrida, *Of Grammatology*, 13, 71. My emphasis in both quotations except for the final word in the second passage.
16 G.W.F. Hegel, *Early Theological Writings*, trans. T.M. Knox, intro. Richard Kroner (Philadelphia: University of Pennsylvania Press, 1971), 195–6.
17 Jacques Derrida, *Glas*, trans. John P. Leavey, Jr. and Richard Rand (Lincoln: University of Nebraska Press, 1986), 51a.
18 Jacques Derrida, *Writing and Difference*, trans. Alan Bass (London: Routledge and Kegan Paul, 1978), 184, 243.
19 Jacques Derrida, *Positions*, trans. Alan Bass (Chicago: University of Chicago Press, 1981), 14, 40.
20 Heidegger, *Nietzsche IV: Nihilism*, trans. Frank A. Capuzzi, ed. David Farrell Krell (San Francisco: Harper and Row, 1982), 209.
21 See Hart, *The Trespass of the Sign*, 98f.
22 Derrida, *Writing and Difference*, 271. My emphases.
23 Jacques Derrida, 'The Original Discussion of "Différance" (1968)', *Derrida and Différance*, ed. David Wood and Robert Bernasconi (Warwick: Parousia Press, 1985), 130, 132.
24 See Heidegger's discussion of 'Moira' in *Early Greek Thinking*, trans. David Farrell Krell and Frank A. Capuzzi (San Francisco: Harper and Row, 1975) and Maurice Blanchot, *The Infinite Conversation*, trans. Susan Hanson (Minneapolis: University of Minnesota Press, 1993), 47.
25 Derrida, 'How to Avoid Speaking', *Languages of the Unsayable: The Play of Negativity in Literature and Literary theory*, ed. Sanford Budick and Wolfgang Iser (New York: Columbia University Press, 1989), 14. Also see Derrida's remarks on Michel de Certeau's *La Fable mystique* in 'A Number of Yes', *Qui Parle*, 2: 2 (1988), 120–33.
26 Jacques Derrida, *Speech and Phenomena: And Other Essays on Husserl's Theory of Signs*, trans. and intro. David B. Allison, pref. Newton Garver (Evanston: Northwestern University Press, 1973), 96.

27 Pseudo-Dionysius Areopagite, *The Divine Names and Mystical Theology*, trans. John D. Jones (Milwaukee: Marquette University Press, 1980), 211.

28 Hegel's remark comes by way of arguing against Gnosticism. See his *Lectures on the Philosophy of Religion*, ed. Peter C. Hodgson, trans. R. F. Brown *et al.* (Berkeley: University of California Press, 1985), vol. III, 219. Nietzsche's similar statement occurs in his story of the madman in *The Gay Science*, trans. Walter Kaufmann (New York: Vintage Books, 1974), §125.

29 Blanchot, *The Infinite Conversation*, xii.

30 See Derrida, *Of Grammatology*, 68.

31 Derrida, *Speech and Phenomena*, 54.

32 Derrida suggest that '*The (pure) trace is différance*', *Of Grammatology*, 62.

33 Levinas, 'The Trace of the Other', *Deconstruction in Context: Literature and Philosophy*, ed. Mark C. Taylor (Chicago: University of Chicago Press, 1986), 355.

34 Derrida, *Writing and Difference*, 108.

35 Derrida, *Writing and Difference*, 108.

36 Derrida, *Writing and Difference*, 89.

37 Derrida, *Margins of Philosophy*, xii.

38 Nietzsche, *Twilight of the Idols and The Anti-Christ*, trans. R.J. Hollingdale (Harmondsworth: Penguin, 1968), 38.

39 Blanchot, *The Infinite Conversation*, xii.

40 Derrida, *Of Grammatology*, 141.

41 Derrida, 'How to Avoid Speaking', 9.

42 Derrida, 'How to Avoid Speaking', 20.

43 Paul Ricoeur, *Freud and Philosophy: An Essay on Interpretation*, trans. Paul Savage (New Haven: Yale University Press, 1970), 530.

44 See Hart, *The Trespass of the Sign*, Ch. 6.

45 Jacques Derrida, *Of Spirit: Heidegger and the Question*, trans. Geoffrey Bennington and Rachel Bowlby (Chicago: University of Chicago Press, 1989).

46 Jacques Derrida, *The Ear of the Other: Otobiography, Transference, Translation*, ed. Christie V. McDonald and trans. Avital Ronell and Peggy Kamuf (New York: Schocken Books, 1985), 147.

47 The distinction receives more attention in my essay 'Poetics of the Negative', Chapter 6 of *Reading the Text: Biblical Interpretation and Literary Theory*, ed. Stephen Prickett (Oxford: Basil Blackwell, 1991).

48 Derrida, 'Fors: The Anglish Words of Nicolas Abraham and Maria Torok', trans. Barbara Johnson, intro. to *The Wolf Man's Magic Word: A Crytonomy*, Theory and History of Literature series, 37 (Minneapolis: University of Minnesota Press, 1986), xlvi–xlvii.

49 Stephen Prickett provides an exemplary account of how biblical language evades these polarities in his reading of I Kings 19: 8–12 and its translation history, *Words and 'The Word': Language, Poetics and Biblical Interpretation* (Cambridge: Cambridge University Press, 1986), Ch. 1.

11

FREUD'S GOD

Regina M. Schwartz

> The distortion of a text is not unlike a murder. The difficulty lies not in the execution of the deed but in doing away with the traces.
>
> (Freud, *Moses and Monotheism*)

Modernism was born as the institution of the Secular, with the great critics of religion – Nietzsche, Marx, and Freud – laying the cornerstones of its philosophy. "Why atheism nowadays?" Nietzsche would have asked, "'The father' in God is thoroughly refuted; equally so 'the judge,' 'the rewarder.'" "Criticism of religion is the premise of all criticism," according to Marx, "the abolition of religion as the illusory happiness of the people is required for their real happiness."[1] Freud warned us that "civilization runs a greater risk if we maintain our present attitude to religion than if we give it up."[2] The modernist Freud was above all a scientist, investing all authority (all faith) in science: "Scientific work is the only road which can lead us to a knowledge of reality outside ourselves"[3] – and within ourselves, adds psychoanalysis. Because of his faith in the explanatory power of science, this secular Freud is paradoxically compatible with the onto-theological tradition, with its search for origins, for meaning for purpose, for truth.

> Confronting religion, psychoanalysis shows itself for what it is: the last great formulation of nineteenth-century secularism, complete with substitute doctrine and cult – capacious, all-embracing, similar in range to the social calculus of the utilitarians, the universal sociolatry of Comte, the dialectical historicism of Marx, the indefinitely expandable agnosticism of Spencer. What first impresses the student of Freud's psychology of religion is its polemical edge. Here, and here alone, the grand Freudian animus, otherwise concealed behind the immediacies of case histories and the emergencies of practical therapeutics, breaks out."[4]

And when it broke out, the founder of psychoanalysis not only told us that religion is nonsense, but that it is a mass neurosis. Inversely, the secular

Freud was the modernist Freud, characterizing a world of alienation and fear and maintaining that the way to gain mastery over this anxiety (and the drive toward mastery is no small part of his modernism) is through reason. Reason insists that God is only a projection of infantile wishes for a protective father. Reason suggests that religion is contemptible for trying to mask the terror of the human condition before the hostile forces of nature.

But if, from his pulpit of secularism, the high priest of reason inveighs against religious myths as so many projections of infantile fears and wishes, there is another Freud: not the secular scientist, but the genuinely religious thinker. Here I will argue that *Totem and Taboo* and *Moses and Monotheism* are essentially myths in which Freud writes psychoanalysis in a new key – not as the child of science after all, but of religion. While Freud's first hostile forays into religion sprang from his modernist pose – his effort to understand the subject without recourse to the transcendent, a self-sufficient godless subject who has science at his command – at the end of his career, Freud no longer speaks as a secular atheist. He writes of monotheism as the institution of ethics. He writes of the subject as the trace of something that recedes infinitely, and he writes a collective rather than a case history whose origins elude him. He also rewrites the oedipus complex as, not a private history of the self, but an ancient religious myth of the communal slaying of Moses, an explicitly rewritten Bible that confers monotheism (and patriarchy) upon us as surely as its biblical prototype.[5] There is irony here. At the very moment when biblical authority had eclipsed, when higher criticism had definitively replaced divine with human authorship, Freud reinvented the biblical myth for our time. It is called psychoanalysis, and initially he thought it was everything religion was not: rational not superstitious, courageous not fearful, empirical not delusional. But the scope of *Moses and Monotheism* was so sweeping – an account of the origin of culture, of morality, of law, and of our drives – that it gathered up his past psychoanalytic work into it, recontextualizing psychoanalysis within the purview of this vast ancient myth. Freud concluded his life's work by rewriting psychoanalysis as religious myth. And *Moses and Monotheism* was the final instalment in Freud's Bible.

In my reading, this religious Freud is closer to a postmodernist Freud: a proposition considerably less apparent than the cliché of the secular modernist. But instead of a vast gulf separating these understandings of Freud, the difference is subtle, even one of style. The unfillable gaps of history that are a source of frustration to the modernist Freud free the postmodern thinker in him for deflections, displacements, and finally, for a new genre: an "historical novel." And where the modernist Freud may accept ambivalence with resignation, the postmodernist celebrates it for stirring the creation of our cultural and ethical codes. If the modernist Freud laments the loss of a coherent history, a coherent self, the postmodernist Freud affirms the randomness, the fragments, the incoherence. He exhibits the "suspensive" irony that, according to Alan Wilde, characterizes postmodernism: "an indecision about the meanings of relations of things is matched by a willingness to live with uncertainty, to tolerate, and in some cases, to welcome a world seen as random and multiple, even, at times, absurd."[6] Still, we should stop short of celebrating a Freud who celebrates uncertainty for there is something he is certain about: authority. Despite his embrace of ambivalence, Freud unambivalently invests authority in Moses – and because Moses is the authority whose monotheism institutes ethics, it is the love and hatred of him that becomes the key to culture. And yet even with Moses, Freud does not simply cling to authority conservatively; he plays with the identity of his authoritative figure. Who is Moses? He is not the Same, but the Other, not the Other, but Another. Such play radically subverts authority at its core – by subverting identity. And so *Moses and Monotheism*, wherein origins recede infinitely and indefinitely, is postmodern in its embrace of uncertainty and it is post-secular in that it seeks the explanations for our desire and torment in a religious myth rather than in a scientific truth, in explanations that dissolve into a deep and thoroughgoing ambivalence beyond resolution.[7]

The modernist Freud

In *The Future of an Illusion*, Freud writes a story of heroic confrontation with the tragedy of loss suffered by the modern subject. He depicts a world in which man is alienated from himself and from nature, set adrift and undefended amidst its raging violence. In this world, Freud sees man clinging to religion for safety:

> Man's self-regard, seriously menaced, calls for consolation; life and the universe must be robbed of their terrors. . . . Impersonal forces and destinies cannot be approached; they remain eternally remote. But if the elements have passions that rage as they do in our own souls, if death itself is not something spontaneous but the violent act of an evil Will, if everywhere in nature there are Beings around us of a kind that we know in our own society, then we can breathe freely, can feel at home in the uncanny and can deal by psychical means with senseless anxiety. We are still defenceless, perhaps, but we are no longer helplessly paralyzed.[8]

Religion is the palliative for a dreadful human condition. The gods

> must exorcise the terrors of nature, they must reconcile men to the cruelty of Fate, particularly as it is shown in death, and they must compensate them for the sufferings and privations which a civilized life in common has imposed on them.[9]

Ill-prepared and ill-protected, we long for that divine paternal protection from the terrors of such a world: "The defense against childish helplessness is what lends its characteristic to the adult's reaction which *he* has to acknowledge – a reaction which is precisely the formation of religion."[10] The scientist, however, resolutely refuses such solutions. He drags belief through an inquisition in the court of empiricism, exposing its failure before all-judging proof:

> We ought to believe because our forefathers believed. But these ancestors of ours were far more ignorant than we are. . . . The proofs they have left us are set down in writings which themselves bear every mark of untrustworthiness. They are full of contradictions, revisions and falsifications, and where they speak of factual confirmations they are themselves unconfirmed.[11]

Our knowledge of the secrets of the universe may be scanty, but "There is no appeal to a court above that of reason,"[12] asserts Freud, who goes on to wonder what the psychological (i.e., reasonable) explanation is for the powerful hold unreasonable religion has on us. His answer, that religious convictions are "illusions, fulfillments of the oldest, strongest and most urgent wishes of mankind"[13] is written in the voice of a man staunchly facing rather than shirking the difficult truth: "we shall tell ourselves that it would be very nice if there were a God who created the world and was a benevolent Providence, and if there were a moral order in the universe and an after-life; but it is a very striking fact that all this is exactly as we are bound to wish it to be." This modernist manifesto concludes with a classic paean to secularity and science:

> Our god Logos is perhaps not a very almighty one, and he may only be able to fulfill a small part of what his predecessors have promised. If we have to acknowledge this we shall accept it with resignation. We shall not on that account lose our interest in the world and in life, for we have one sure support which you lack. We believe that it is possible for scientific work to gain some knowledge about the reality of the world, by means of which we can increase our power and in accordance with which we can arrange our life. . . . No, our science is no illusion. But an illusion it would be to suppose that what science cannot give us we can get elsewhere.[14]

And yet, what science could not give him, Freud sought elsewhere – as *Moses and Monotheism* so urgently attests.

Freud and history

Why does Freud, in the last years of his life, embark on the bizarre, decidedly unscientific project we know as *Moses and Monotheism*? Why does a thinker who was an avowed atheist and who called himself a godless Jew care at all about monotheism? And why does he, at the risk of sounding logically absurd, historically tenuous (at best), and in contradiction to key tenets of his own psychoanalytic theory, insist that "the man Moses, the liberator and lawgiver of the Jewish people, was not a Jew, but an Egyptian"?[15] What madness makes him, at a time when he must flee Nazi Germany for his life, want to assert anything that could remotely be interpreted anti-semitically? Freud marshals any proof he can borrow or invent to make this assertion despite a storm of protest: he calls upon etymology (Moses is an Egyptian name), biblical authorities (however specious their evidence), and a theory of myth (leaning on Otto Rank's work on the birth of the hero), to try to demonstrate what he confesses must seem monstrous even to imagine – that Moses was not a Hebrew. Friends begged him not to publish it and even he acknowledged that the risk was too great to see the project to completion in Vienna, only to take it up again in England, writing and publishing the final section there in the final year of his life, knowing full well that it would evince a storm of hostile criticism. He was not disappointed in this. Among the chilly reactions, Martin Buber dismissively confined his remarks on Freud's book to a footnote, calling it a "regrettable performance, based on groundless hypotheses." Father Vincent McNabb was less circumspect, writing in the *Catholic Herald* of London that "Professor Freud is naturally grateful to 'free, generous England' for the welcome it has given him, but if his frank championship of atheism and incest is widely recognized we wonder how long the welcome will remain in an England that still calls itself Christian."[16] From America, threatening language was hurled less delicately:

> I read in the local press your statement that Moses was not a Jew. It is to be regretted that you could not go to your grave without disgracing yourself, you old nitwit. We have renegades like you by the thousands, we are glad to be rid of them and we hope soon to be rid of you.[17]

While Freud's relation to Judaism, the effect of the Holocaust on his life and thought, the character of nineteenth-century Viennese Jewry, and his relation to his own father all impinge on our understanding of his *Moses* and on why he wrote it,[18] I want to turn to another curious aspect of the work: Freud's insistence that in *Moses and Monotheism* he is writing history, embracing historical veracity and not the productions of the psyche. Throughout *Moses and Monotheism* he speaks obsessively of truth and facts: an event *actually* happened in the past and it determined all subsequent history. The event in question is the murder of Moses. "Let us adopt . . . the surmise that the Egyptian Moses was killed by the Jews, and the religion he instituted abandoned. It allows us to spin our thread further without contradicting the trustworthy results of historical research."[19]

> At this point I expect to hear the reproach . . . that I have built up this edifice of conjectures with too great a certainty, for which no adequate grounds are to be found in the material itself. I think this reproach would be unjustified.[20]

This emphasis on history is not some aberrant lapse on Freud's part. His entire career is marked by oscillation between levels of explanation, between on the one hand, the individual psyche with its fantasies of the family drama, and on the other, events that occurred in the life of the mass community, in either prehistoric or historic time. We know, for instance, that he shifted modes of explanation in the seduction theory, moving in 1897 from his conviction that his clients were really seduced by their fathers or brothers to his belief that such seductions occurred only in the realm of fantasy.[21] Hysteria was simply too widespread to be accounted for by the historical level of explanation; Freud wrote uncomfortably that "in all cases, the father had to be accused of being perverse, my own not excluded."[22] And this shift of his conviction that the historical fact was instead psychic truth became the essential factor for his development of psychoanalytic theory with its descriptions of our inner lives. But it was no conclusive flight to the inner sanctum of the mind. In *Totem and Taboo*, published in 1912, he returned to constructing prehistory, a mythic drama of universal significance. He asserts that the primal hoard rose up to destroy their oppressive father, murdered and devoured him, and subsequently worshipped a substitutive totemic animal and instigated the incest taboo in guilty atonement. This response to the father is marked by its ambivalence. The sons hated and feared their father but they also loved and worshipped him; hence they murdered and subsequently deified him, literally devouring the father to identify with him. While this account was prehistoric, even mythic, none the less, it was important to Freud that it occurred – and not just in the mind. But it was not until *Moses and Monotheism*, after Freud has fully elaborated his version of the psychic apparatus, the oedipus complex, the drive theory, and painstakingly offered case histories to explore the role of analysis, that this urge to locate the explanation for our culture in the historical rather than the psychic was fully fleshed in – with abandon, with self-indulgence, and with wildly imagined "historical" detail. As ontogeny recapitulates phylogeny (and Freud's Darwinian cultural inheritance has been noted[23]), so the individual's family dramas repeat the ancient dramas of mankind. When the repressed returns, it is from a collective mythic past. The murder of Moses is the key to our inner life, explaining our guilt for parricidal urges. And a collective historical event – the sacrifice of Jesus – is culture's guilty response to that event.

None the less, this history eludes him. Freud tells us that "deeper knowledge of the historical and psychological conditions of the origin [of monotheism] would be of inestimable value," but he despairs that he cannot reach that origin because it is lost, forgotten.

[N]othing available concerning Moses can be called trustworthy. It is a tradition coming from one source, not confirmed by any other, fixed in writing only in a later period, in itself contradictory, certainly revised several times and distorted under the influence of new tendencies, while closely interwoven with the religious and national myths of a people. Thus one undertakes to treat each possibility in the text as a clue and to fill the gap between one fragment and another according to the law, so to speak, of least resistance, that is – to give preference to the assumption that can claim the greatest probability.[24]

Even when he rallies to assert confidence in the certainty of his history, he ends up dissolving into tentativeness:

The objection is likely to be that the circumstances of the origin and transformation of legends are too obscure to allow of such a conclusion as the preceding one, and that all efforts to extract the kernel of historical truth must be doomed to failure in face of the incoherence and contradictions clustering around the heroic person of Moses and the unmistakable signs of tendentious distortion and stratification accumulated through many centuries. I myself do not share this negative attitude, but I am not in a position to confute it.[25]

This collapse of Freud's faith in the capacity of history to recover the past with certitude gives way to a new, more speculative history: fiction. The original subtitle of *Der Mann Moses und die monotheistische Religion* called attention to precisely that fictional quality: *Ein Historischer Roman*, an historical novel. Furthermore, the original manuscript opens with an introduction – never published – in which he sets out to explain the subtitle:

As the sexual union of horse and donkey produces two different hybrids, the mule and the hinny, so the mixture of historical writing and free invention give rise to different products which, under the common designation of historical novel sometimes want to be appreciated as history, sometimes as novel.[26]

A contemporary historian (John Vernon) recently wrote,

Those with a passionate interest in the past always feel sooner or later that history's ultimate unknowability mocks them. This could be just paranoia, but it is more: it is the powerful feeling that history is simultaneously there and not there, real and illusory – a ghost forever tailing behind, which vanishes when we turn around . . . history is full of missing pieces and indecipherable shards that are the material counterparts of human forgetting.

And then Vernon offers the payoff: "To be sure, such a view of history enables novelists like myself shamelessly to mix history and fiction."[27]

Freud moves history from the realm of a verifiable, scientific truth into the realm of fiction, more specifically aetiological myth. In this latter, myths of explanation are the domain of religion. Indeed, apart from delineating identity boundaries through ritual and offering credos of faith, religions are characterized by myths of revelation and transmission of revelation – how Moses received the word and disseminated it, how Christ revealed the word and his apostles bore witness, how Mohammed received the word and promulgated it. These are religions' ancestral myths, aetiologies of human life. These narrative myths (or ancient fictions) are the pillars upon which rest ritual and faith, explaining what the ceremonies mean and what the faithful believe. Neither a mass nor a credo are constitutive of Christianity alone: the New Testament offers multiple *narratives* of the incarnation, passion, and resurrection.

In *Moses and Monotheism*, Freud is offering just such a religious myth. For him, "the oedipus complex of the individual is too brief and too indistinct to engender the gods; without an ancestral crime as part of our phylogenetic past, the longing for the father is unintelligible; *the* father is not *my* father."[28] His is an account of the first slaying of Moses which he believed gave rise to religion (as surely as Christ's passion gave rise to Christianity). And for him, the slaying of Jesus is only the return of the repressed earlier event. "There is some historical truth in the rebirth of Christ, for he was the resurrected Moses and the returned primeval father of the primitive horde as well – only transfigured, and as a Son in the place of his Father."[29] In Freud's aetiological narrative, our lives are shaped by the repressed memory of that murder and its inevitable return. This is the stuff of religion. And while he claims that this past truth is "historical," for Freud, something is believed because it has a core of some forgotten truth, and he embarks on these reconstructive imaginings of the past precisely because for him, at the core of faith is some "piece of forgotten truth."[30] "Such a kernel of truth – which we might call historical truth – must also be conceded to the doctrines of the various religions."[31]

> Every memory returning from the forgotten past does so with great force, produces an incomparably strong influence on the mass of mankind, and puts forward an irresistible claim to be believed, against which all logical objections remain powerless – very much like the *credo quia absurdum*.[32]

Because it is forgotten, it cannot ever be recovered, hence, these imaginative narratives about the past, these "historical fictions" as he called his *Moses and Monotheism*, are approximations, and hence, his historical fiction is littered with apologies for the inexact nature of his admittedly speculative version of the past.

Paul Ricoeur, who has written so powerfully about time and narrative,[33] is ultimately attentive to the fiction in Freud's historical fiction. But when Ricoeur insists that Freud held fast to historical veracity, his Freud remains a modernist:

> An essential element of the Freudian interpretation is that this murder actually occurred in the past either once or several times, and that there exists an actual memory of it inscribed in the hereditary patrimony of mankind. . . . Through the course of the years, Freud kept reinforcing the notion that the memory of the primal killing is a memory of a real event.[34]

He claims that Freud "deliberately turns his back" on the tradition from Schelling to Bultmann that deprived myths of any aetiological function "in order to restore to them their mytho-poetic function capable of leading to a reflection or speculation."[35] But I would argue that for Freud, and this is crucial, the aetiological and the mytho-poetic function are one and the same; that is why the aetiological myth of *Moses and Monotheism* can ground an entire religion – all religion, for that matter. Ricoeur goes on to distinguish between the "truth" of memory and the "distortions" of imagination, which have a status like dreams, rationalizations, and superstitions. But memory cannot be so rigidly separated from imaginative productions, for the distinction between the former as "accurate" and the latter as "distortions" will not hold. Freud distinguishes between the work of hypnosis which claims to recover the past "accurately" and the work of analysis or interpretation, repetitions of past events with that important difference of the analytic context. Only a simplistic version of psychoanalysis understands the future as dependent upon our recovery of a repressed past, a version that characterized the early days of analysis when the "old technique" of hypnosis prevailed.

> In these hypnotic treatments the process of remembering took a very simple form. The patient put himself back into an earlier situation which he seemed never to confuse with the present one, and gave an account of the mental processes belonging to it.[36]

But Freud was eager to replace this reversion to the past with transference, in which the past can never be retrieved identically, in which the process of interpreting the past is carried on in the conscious present. "We cannot speak of an 'accurate' memory, as though memory could recover the contents of the past. All we have, all we can have are reconstructions, re-, and we must include that hyphen, memberings."[37] But Ricoeur falls prey to the modernist logic in his discussion of Freudian repetition. In Ricoeur's account of the role of repetition, Freud is misguided, that is, guided away from a religious sensibility to a rationalistic one: "for Freud, religion is the monotonous repetition of its own origins. It is a sempiternal treading on the grounds of its own archaism." Hence, he says "Freud's exclusive attention to repetition becomes a refusal to consider a possible epigenesis of religious feeling, that is to say, a transformation or conversion of desire and fear."[38] But although he later revised this claim,[39] Ricoeur oversimplifies here. Freud does not posit identical repetitions: the first Moses is Egyptian, the second, Hebraic. The first monotheistic deity is Aton, the next, Jahve. And Jesus' slaying is not the same as any of the Moseses; in fact, Freud claims that his death was believed to allay the guilt of the earlier slayings. Fear is not just revisited. It is transformed. Desire is not just reawakened. It assumes new shapes. Consequently, faith, and with it the "piece of forgotten truth" at its core, the "kernel of truth" that "must be conceded to the doctrines of the various religions" cannot be merely reduced to a single historical event. The forgotten truth is that sum of returns, and the urgency to return with inevitable difference to that mysterious, forever lost, past.

In *Prophets of Extremity*, Allan Megill contrasts the crisis of history with the crisis of faith.

> In the "theological" view, the dominant metaphor for crisis is the abyss: the metaphor of humanity stranded in a world without God or other absolutes on which we can depend. In my "historical" reading of crisis, the dominant metaphor is that of the break. This presupposes something to be broken, namely history; and in order to conceive of the possibility of history's breaking, one needs to think of it as a line or movement. In the theological reading of crisis, historicism is the product of crisis. . . . In my reading, historicism is the precondition of crisis, for only when one conceives of history as linear is it possible to think in terms of its being broken. . . . Firstly and most importantly, modernism and postmodernism emerge out of the collapse of historicism; only very indirectly do they come out of an earlier "loss of transcendence."[40]

The breaking of the historical thread characterizes not only the genre but the substance of the Freudian historical model. But it is the theological crisis, the loss of the abyss, of God, that propels Freud, again and again, out of history, into myth, and away from cogent explanations into intractable mysteries. It is that yawning theological abyss, fear of being stranded in a world without God, that characterizes both the genre and the substance of the Freudian religious model.

From one perspective, in *Moses and Monotheism* (and earlier in *Totem and Taboo*), Freud only historicizes the oedipal drive. Aggression against the father is *enacted*, not just wished, and culture develops – including religion and morality – from the guilty response. This is both disappointing and fascinating from my point of view. Disappointing, because he only reinscribes the myth of monotheism: instead of the father killing the son – Yahweh kills Moses in the Bible; having handed him the potent rod of leadership, he takes it away – in Freud's version, the sons kill the father. Freud would triumph over the biblical myth of paternal domination, but only to identify with a Moses who is defeated by his sons. Fascinating, as a striking demonstration of the way religious discourse is transformed into secular culture: the biblical myth of monotheism – wherein collective identity is forged in violence, against the other, against the past and against the future – is recapitulated in the story of psychoanalysis. Under its regime, instead of imagining the Egyptians versus the Israelites, we are asked to imagine killing the father or being killed, killing the son or being killed. As the myth of monotheism has been secularized externally into nationalism, so psychoanalysis is the shape it has assumed to describe our inner life. In both, we are condemned to desire an object that we must compete for, one that is figured as scarce: land, resources, the object of libidinal desire. Throughout his work, Freud only imagines one breast. The competition is fierce, the stakes are potency or castration, life or death. Murder and deification of the omnipotent father become the only way for the son to seize potency. Even when Freud, chafing under the biblical myth of paternal victory, inserts a circumscribed triumph of the son, he still depicts desire as a *contest*, with fundamental losers and winners. And the spiral of ambivalence that emerges from such a contest, the aggression joined to guilt, become for Freud the foundation of law and culture.[41]

But if the competition of the oedipus complex offered a satisfactory explanation for our cultural formations, why was Freud driven to "historicize" it with the slaying of Moses? And what is the effect of such historicizing, not only for psychoanalysis but also for religion? Before I can pursue these questions, I want to question the presupposition that gives rise to them. The formulation I have just offered – "in *Moses and Monotheism* Freud historicizes the oedipal drive" – is made, of course, from Freud's point of view, rather, from one of his points of view, the one that prevails when he writes that "at bottom, God is nothing other than an exalted father," a projected father.[42] It is the point of view that informs the *Future of an Illusion* where religion has its infantile prototype in the feeling of helplessness one has as a small child in relation to one's parents: "One had reason to fear them, and especially one's father; and yet one was sure of his protection against the dangers one knew."[43] His cynical summary of a religious sensibility barely disguises his contempt. "Here is the gist of the matter" he wrote jeeringly:

Life in this world serves a higher purpose; no doubt it is not easy to guess what that purpose is. . . . Everything that happens in this world is an expression of the intentions of an intelligence superior to us, which in the end, though its ways and byways are difficult to follow, orders everything for the best. . . . Over each of us there watches a benevolent providence which is only seemingly stern and which will not suffer us to become a plaything of the overmighty and pitiless forces of nature. Death is not extinction, is not a return to inorganic lifelessness, but the beginning of a new kind of existence which lies on the path of development to something higher . . . the same moral laws which our civilizations have set up govern the whole universe as well, except that they are maintained by a supreme court of justice with incomparably more power . . . in the end, all good is rewarded and all evil punished, if not actually in this form of life than in the later existences that begin after death. In this way, all the terrors, the sufferings, the hardships of life are to be obliterated. The superior wisdom that directs such things comes to be concentrated in monotheism, in the divine which laid open to view the father who had all along been hidden behind every divine figure as its nucleus.[44]

If we were to take this reductive understanding of religion to heart, then, Freud would fall victim to his own unmasking, and *Moses and Monotheism*'s elaborate account of the origins of monotheism would simply lay bare the wish to murder the father which had all along been its nucleus: "Now that God was a single person, man's relations to him could recover the intimacy and intensity of the child's relation to his father."[45] The intensity of the oedipal struggle would issue in the projection of parricide, into the primitive remote past and eventually on to the not-so-remote heaven.

Freud and scripture

I am going to launch a critique of this reductive Freudian reading of Freud and I will use a more subtle Freud to do it. We only read *Moses and Monotheism* as a lapse from his scientific rationalism into a dark realm of superstitious religious myth if we privilege one text over the other, *The Future of an Illusion* (1927) over *Moses and Monotheism* (1939) – as I believe Ricoeur was tempted to do in his reading of Freud – if, that is, we privilege the psychological over the religious level of explanation; but it is precisely that which Freud cannot and will not do. In fact, his own disavowal of *The Future of an Illusion* was swift and explicit; he called it "childish," "feeble analytically, inadequate as self-confession" and in October of 1927, promising a friend a copy as soon as the proofs came back from the printer, he noted that "the analytic content of the work is very thin and in other ways too it is not worth very much."[46] In contrast, his investment in *Moses and Monotheism* was deep and lasting, lasting enough to resume work on it again after the crisis of fleeing the Nazis in Vienna, and deep enough to withstand the assaults against it without recanting. And his method is radically different in the later work. In *Moses and Monotheism* he does not put religion on the couch, he does not set out to explain a defensive mass neurosis by means of infantile feelings; he subjects our drives to an aetiological explanation in what is virtually a religious myth about the origins of monotheism. Simply put, in *Moses and Monotheism*, Freud does not psychoanalyze the Bible, he rewrites it – complete with myths of genesis, collective history, and prescriptions of ritual. He may call these ambivalence, latency, and identification but that does not make this last complete work of Freud's any less scriptural. In his first paper on religion, "Obsessive Actions and Religious Practices," Freud made connections between the rituals of obsessive neurotics and the rituals of religion, concluding that both work as defensive measures, that "in view of these correspondences and analogies one might venture to regard obsessional neurosis as a pathological counterpart of religious formation, neurosis as an individual religion, religion as a universal obsessional neurosis."[47] But if in Freud's first incursions into religion he defines religion as neurosis, in his last, he comes to see our psychic life as having its very source in religion.

The Darwinian logic that ontogeny recapitulates phylogeny also structures religious thought: an "original sin" lay behind each individual's sinful nature and Christ's atonement for that sin must be repeated, in the sacrifice of the Mass, in confession and contrition, by each individual. This explains Freud's odd fascination with spinning out the peregrinations of monotheism from an Egyptian to a Midianite Moses and thence to the Jews, to the murder of Moses repressed by the Jews and admitted by Christians who expiate their guilt by sacrificing the son. His version may or may not be more wildly speculative than the ancient versions of Western religious myth we have inherited – versions that tell of Eve eating an apple offered by a serpent, that tell of Moses saved from the Egyptians in a basket to be raised by an Egyptian princess, that tell of the immaculate conception of the Son of God – but in his story, Freud has recourse to the same manner of narrative explanation. In Freud's account, religion is born in an original crime instead of in an original sin – but that difference may not be so very great. With its repeated retreats from psychoanalytic explanations, which he gives only the status of an analogy to his sweeping historical drama, *Moses and Monotheism* emerges either as a challenge to his entire analytic apparatus or as a wholesale reconceptualization of it.[48] I believe it is the latter.

We can see the psychological level of explanation collapsing under the weight of prehistory in just one sentence, a remarkable sentence to be sure, one that elides any distinction between the individual and the collective, between the psychological and the historical levels of explanation:

> From then on [since the writing of *Totem and Taboo*, 1912], I have never doubted that religious phenomena are to be understood only on the model of the neurotic symptoms of the *individual*, which are so familiar to us, as a return of long-forgotten important happenings in the *primeval history of the human family*, that they owe their obsessive

character to that very origin and therefore derive their effect on mankind from the historical truth they contain.[49]

The neurotic symptoms of the individual give way to the historical truth of the human family's primeval history. But perhaps, and more productively, *Moses and Monotheism* is Freud's testimony to the subtle, dynamic, and inextricable relation between these two categories of thinking, the personal and the historical, and to the power they have to structure religions.

Here, then, is Freud's Bible, an account of religion that is less glib if more fantastic than his secular account in *The Future of an Illusion*. Monotheism had its origins in Egyptian imperialistic ambitions when a specific sect led by Amenhotep in 1385 BC declared that there were no other gods but Aton, banished all magic and sorcery along with polytheism, established high spiritual and ethical standards, and forced this new religion upon a disgruntled people. When Amenhotep, who had renamed himself Iknaton, died, the religion fell into disfavor and all but traces of it were obliterated. Nonetheless, one of its high priests (who happened to be named Moses) kept it alive by adopting a band of Semites and converting them to it. They murdered Moses and joined another band of Semites who worshipped another deity, Jahve. In contrast to the spiritual conception of God that originated in Egypt – "a single God who embraces the whole world, one as all-loving as he is all-powerful, who averse to all ceremonial and magic, set for humanity as its highest aim a life of truth and justice"[50] – the deity Jahve was a "rude, narrow-minded local god, violent and bloodthirsty."[51] He was a Midianite deity, extolled by a Midianite priest who, as it so happened, was also named Moses. In time, the memory of the values associated with Egyptian monotheism returned and transformed the religion of Yahweh; the Egyptian Moses who led the people out of Egypt was conflated with the Midianite priest; and the guilt for the murder of Moses was acknowledged and atoned for in Christianity by the sacrifice of the son, exacted for having murdered the father.

I want to pause in this narrative to point out that for an ontogenetic explanation, the beginnings of monotheism and the murder of Moses are awfully slippery, marked by the kinds of deflections and displacements we might expect of the psyche rather than of history. No sooner does Freud speak of the radical origin of Egyptian monotheism during the reign of Amenhotep III than he seeks it further afield among the priests of the sun cult of On, only to slip in that monotheism may have come from Syria. The first Moses was murdered, the religion of Aton forgotten, another Moses appears, this time a Midianite rather than an Egyptian priest, another god appears, Jahve, and we sense there will be more Moseses and more gods. Furthermore, he has split rather than resolved the ambivalent responses to the father into two deities, one, the despicable bloodthirsty Jahve, is loathed and feared; the other, the spiritual Aton, is all-loving and loved. Freud wrote about the

origins of monotheism with his remarkable collection of "idols" from anti-
quity lined up before him on his desk; it is little wonder that his treatise on
monotheism is so strikingly polytheistic.

When Freud tries to reconstruct the historical fragments for his story of
the forgetting and remembering of Egyptian monotheism, he does rely on
the psychic apparatus – for analogy. Like the individual's emotional life, his
myth is characterized by ambivalence – splitting the responses to the father
into the loved and hated deities – by latency – here the long delay is hundreds
of years in which the memory of the traumatic murder was repressed only to
resurface in the distorted fashion of guilt formation – and by identification –
Freud must correct the genealogy of Moses because he feels it pressing to identify with him.[52] In identification, the religious impulse surfaces once again,
distinguishing religious narratives from secular narratives of origin and collective history. The believer finds *his* story, not someone else's, in a religious
narrative. Identification also purports to bridge the gulf between the self and
the Other – whether the primal Father, the historical Moses, or the human/
divine Christ. The believer is both like Jesus – allegorically living the life of
Jesus – and the historical descendant of Jesus, tracing his genealogy back to
Jesus' story of origin. The same holds for Moses: Freud is both like Moses,
slain by his sons who forget and deny him and his descendant.[53] Furthermore,
his story is our story. Freud insists that, like so many religious narratives,
psychoanalysis condenses allegory and genealogical history. That is why
Freud felt compelled to change the genealogy of Moses. if Moses is not his
ancestor, Freud need not live his life and his death. This leader of a movement
may not have to be slain by his followers and have his memory forgotten.
When Freud labors to prove that Moses was an Egyptian and not a Jew,
when he invests so much in that genealogy, it is to attenuate his overwhelming
allegorical identification. But Moses is part of the Freudian genealogy and
the genealogy of Judaism, after all. For while Freud has moved Moses from
ancient Israel to Egypt, it is only to bring him back to adopt the Israelites,
thereby replacing a relation by blood with one by adoption. And so Moses'
story is Freud's story after all, but at one remove – presumably, at a safer
distance.

This distancing procedure marks Freud's sacred history elsewhere. Freud's
Bible takes the distinguishing features of ancient Israelite religion, the very
ones that, according to him, fundamentally separate Israel's religion from
Egypt's, and he attributes them all to a sect in Egypt – Israel's Other and old
enemy: the Hebraic prohibition against graven images, against magic, lack
of interest in the afterlife, embrace of monotheism and divine universalism.
Having asserted that Israelite religion is so different from Egyptian religion
that it must have developed in contrast to Egyptian polytheism, he then
moves the source of Israelite monotheism to Egypt where he discovers, in a
particular Egyptian sect, the very characteristics he had defined as uniquely
Israelite. Why? It is tempting to see him as deconstructing the opposition

between Egypt and Israel, but instead, Freud only reinscribes the opposition *within* Egypt.[54] It turns out that it was this Egyptian sect of radical mono-theism, and not ancient Judaism, that developed in contrast to the dominant Egyptian polytheism with its emphasis on magic and the afterlife.[55] Nonethe-less, instead of maintaining this internal division within Egypt in order to claim that Egypt, Israel's Other, is the source of monotheism and leaving it at that, Freud's next move is to show that this Egyptian monotheism gave rise to monotheism in Israel when Moses the Egyptian adopted the Israelites as his people. This leads him to the remarkable conclusion that Egypt led Israel out of Egypt: "the exodus passed off peacefully and without pursuit" for it had an Egyptian at its head.[56]

If Israel ends up monotheistic anyway, why this massive displacement onto Egypt and then back? Why rewrite the genealogy of ancient Israel to put a foreigner, rather, The Foreigner, at its head? One thing Freud achieves with this roundabout logic is the assertion that ancient Israel does not flee Egypt, it is adopted by Egypt (by Moses), and subsequently adopts Egypt (mono-theism). Israel thereby becomes part-Egyptian; what had been antagonism between Israel and Egypt turns into a peaceful inheritance as Israel's enemies become – almost – its forebears.

This is also the contorted logic – far but not too far, near but not too near – by which he tries to disentangle religious identity, and with it, the tragedy of anti-semitism, from religious faith. If the first Moses was an Egyptian, rather than a Hebrew, then the founder of monotheism is no longer one of the "chosen," but the progenitor of a universal religion whose founder neither Judaism nor Christianity can claim. Projecting an Egyptian Moses before a Hebrew one takes not only the triumph but also the sting out of the following assertion:

> I venture to say this: it was one man, the man Moses, who created the Jews. To him this people owes its tenacity in supporting life; to him, however, also much of the hostility which it has met with and is meet-ing still.[57]

Similarly, the Egyptian god, the first monotheistic deity, was not a god of one people, but a universal god – "a single God who embraces the whole world, one as all-loving as he is all-powerful, who averse to all ceremonial and magic, set for humanity as its highest aim a life of truth and justice."[58] This is the God that Freud the persecuted Jew longed for, wishing that this deity of justice would be everyone's ancestor so justice could reign.

This convoluted myth not only expresses a wish for Israel and its others to live together in more harmony; it also dramatizes the unrelenting ambiva-lence of the oedipal conflict. Displacing the father of monotheism onto Egypt means that Freud can both slay the father – it is not his father, after all – and express filial piety toward him – he did not slay his father. In all this genealogical and allegorical identification, the status of the Other is incredibly destabilized: now it is the Same and now it is the Other, and now it is the Other giving birth to the Same which thereby becomes the Other – or does it?

Similarly, the Egyptian Moses becomes a radically ambiguous figure, victimized by his people – but they are not *his* people – who slay their father – but they do not slay *their* father, they slay the Other. It gets more involuted still: Freud will not rest with an Egyptian monotheistic deity, Aton, and his priest, Moses, adopting the Hebrews and being slain by them. He institutes more displacements: another deity of the Midianites, Jahve, and another priest named Moses, and the Hebrew people soon adopt this fierce volcanic deity, Jahve. By proliferating multiple Moseses, Freud is able to move the father he has distanced closer to home – but over time – to move him in stages from Egyptian to Midianite to Hebrew ancestry until eventually they become one Moses, and Freud can in turn become one with them. We can hear the initial binarism of his thinking:

> I think we are justified in separating the two persons from each other and in assuming that the Egyptian Moses never was in Qadesh and had never heard the name of Jahve, whereas the Midianite Moses never set foot in Egypt and knew nothing of Aton. In order to make the two people into one, tradition or legend [rather, Freud] had to bring the Egyptian Moses to Midian.[59]

Freud has repeated the same gesture with the Egyptian and the Midianite Moseses that he had with Egypt and Israel. They were radically different, radically separate, radically Other, but they become One. We can also hear his assertion that this project of conflating Moseses, like that of conflating Egypt and Israel, entails fitting his sacred history into the biblical one, however jarring the fit:

> I may now express my conclusion in the shortest formula. To the well-known DUALITY of that history [biblical history] – TWO peoples who fuse together to form one nation, TWO kingdoms into which this nation divides, TWO names for the Deity in the source of the Bible – we add two new ones: the founding of two new religions, the first one ousted by the second and yet reappearing victorious, two founders of religion, who are both called by the same name, Moses, and whose personalities we have to separate from each other.[60]

Separate only in order to recombine, "my sole purpose having been to fit the figure of an Egyptian Moses into the framework of Jewish history."

Freud has come such a long way in his argument that we must remind ourselves that Moses, a Hebraic Moses, was already fitted firmly into the framework of Jewish history until Freud took him out – only to make it his sole purpose to put him back in. Freud makes the business of religion to make the two Moseses, foreign and native, ONE, just as the effect of his entire displacement of monotheism onto Egypt is to make the two nations, Egypt and Israel, radically separate, ONE: "For some 800 years," writes Freud,

> from the exodus to the fixing of the biblical text by Ezra and Nehemiah, the religion of Jahve had undergone a retrograde development that had culminated in a fusion (perhaps to the point of actual identity) with the original religion of Moses.[61]

And this is Judaism, he tells us, born in the labored process of latency, the return of the repressed and, in the end, identification. Needless to say, the displacement and identification that once characterized psychic processes now describe religious myth. Freud has left the sphere of projection, wherein infantile fantasies of protection are cast onto omnipotence, to enter a far more complex and rich arena of religious sensibility, in which myths of the past – not projections onto the heavens – recede into a horizon of infinite origins. Both long ago and far away, this is his distance, this, his version of transcendence. The forever receding murder of a spiritual guide who is both the same and the other, an identity whose birth is both away from home, Egypt (the biblical house of slavery), and at home, Israel (the biblical promised land): these infinite manifestations constitute both Freud's subject and his god.

Freud treated theology with contemptuous neglect, bothering only to accuse the philosophers of religion of dissembling, disguising the emotional basis of their abstractions. "The conceptual God was simply a pale abstraction of the living God."[62] He turned instead to primeval deities, savage rituals, obscure myths, and primitive religion for in these could be discerned the true nature of the religious impulse: "White peacock and bull father, totems marched out before tribal brothers, sovereign kings of families covenanted together, communion rites and fertility images – these are religion."[63] Here could be discovered the explanation for the religious impulse, the murder of the primal father, the repression of the hideous deed with the institution of morality, and the subsequent atonement and identification with him.

> Totemic religion arose from the filial sense of guilt, in an attempt to allay that feeling and to appease the father by deferred obedience to him. All religions are attempts at solving the same problem, only varying according to the stage of civilization in which they arise.[64]

Far from claiming that the myth of slaying the totemic father was a projection – of infantile oedipal impulses, of course – Freud deliberately put it the other way around: the child carries the racial memory of that murder, a murder that condemns him to parricidal urges as surely as Adam's sin condemns the Christian.

Murder's traces

While *Moses and Monotheism* is ostensibly concerned with the murder of Moses and, as Freud says repeatedly, the return of that repressed murder shapes religion, it barely conceals another murder, the murder of a text. Amid Freud's speculations about the biblical evidence for his theory, he digresses into a discussion of the biblical text. As he imagines it, the text, like the father, has been treated with ambivalence, with both aggressive hostility and piety; it has been both rudely distorted, "maimed" and lovingly preserved.

> How far the [biblical] accounts of former times are based on earlier sources or on oral tradition, and what interval elapsed between an event and its fixation by writing, we are naturally unable to know. The text, however, as we find it today tells us enough about its own history. Two distinct forces, diametrically opposed to each other, have left their traces on it. On the one hand, certain transformations got to work on it, falsifying the text in accord with secret tendencies, maiming and extending it until it was turned into its opposite. On the other hand, an indulgent piety reigned over it, anxious to keep everything as it stood, indifferent to whether the details fitted together or nullified one another. Thus almost everywhere there can be found striking omissions, disturbing repetitions, palpable contradictions, signs of things the communication of which was never intended. *The distortion of a text is not unlike a murder. The difficulty lies not in the execution of the deed but in doing away with the traces.*[65]

In a work about the murder of Moses, Freud depicts himself as committing the murder of Moses' text. Tying religion to the compulsive murder of the paternal figure issues in an amazing feat: Freud murders the Bible. And like all murders of the father, he thereby pays the greatest homage to it, keeping its legacy alive forever, with all the potency of repression and guilt. Freud's comments about his own text so closely echo his remarks about the Bible that he must have seen his own project as a reincarnation of it; both are marked by "gaps," "repetitions," and efforts to preserve earlier versions, even at the risk of extremely awkward prose. In a work where Freud repeatedly argues that the "heroic victim's demise generates the survival of the victim's legacy,"[66] Freud murders the Bible only to rewrite the Bible. *Moses and Monotheism* may be "maimed" and "distorted," but it has traces of its parent and of the murderous deed.

> One could wish to give the word "distortion" the double meaning to which it has a right. . . . It should mean not only "to change the appearance of," but also "to wrench apart," "to put in another place." That is why in so many textual distortions we may count on finding the suppressed and abnegated material hidden away somewhere, though in an altered shape and torn out of its original connection. Only it is not always easy to recognize it.[67]

It is not always easy to recognize the Bible in *Moses and Monotheism*. Where the Bible depicted filial piety instead of aggression, with God the father successfully prohibiting his son's entry to the promised land, with Moses unable even to speak unless it is at the behest of his heavenly father, Freud now wrote of a people slaying the father. Until *Moses and Monotheism*, Freud had to turn to Greek mythology for a masterplot of the murder of the father. The Hebrew Bible would not yield it. For there, God the omnipotent father destroys the aspirations of Babel, dispersing mankind; Ham curses his son's impiety, setting the brothers against one another; Abraham wields a knife against his son; the sons of Abraham, Isaac, and Jacob are all set against one another – even the first sons, Cain and Abel, betray a murderous rivalry – and the sons of Israel are all marked by circumcision in a symbolic castration. The Bible's sons do not rise up collectively against their father; they are set against each other by him in a dominant motif of sibling rivalry.[68] But when, in his last years, Freud finally murdered the text, he rewrote it, maimed, distorted, and torn away from its original context, to describe Moses slain, not by his father, but by his sons. And this slaying enabled the triumph of his religion, psychoanalysis, over the old one, for the guilty sons would cherish Freud's/Moses' memory in everlasting piety – until, that is, the return of the repressed murder would urge on the murder of Freud's Bible as it had urged Freud to murder Moses' Bible.

Moses and Monotheism was the preoccupation of the last five years of Freud's life, but it was not his sole preoccupation.

> Preoccupied with his own mortality, preoccupied with the survival of the Jewish people and with the survival of psychoanalysis, preoccupied with *Moses and Monotheism*: perhaps this was in fact a single preoccupation, and the feverish but fitful work on the book became a way of coping with the anguish over whether and how his movement would survive his death. . . . In the very essay which vigorously psychologized and otherwise relativized some of the most treasured verities of Judaic and Christian traditions, Freud may also have

been participating in his own way, in one of the most traditional of religious activities, the quest for an afterlife.[69]

And so *Moses and Monotheism* offers the traces of the murder that all along was the enabling condition of the religion of psychoanalysis.

Is the religious Freud guilty of precisely the sins he has accused the philosophers of religion of, substituting a pale psychoanalytic myth to rewrite the living God? Has he only erected a counter-myth, after all, to the inherited religious ones he scorned – replacing worship of the father with slaying of the father, replacing piety toward tradition with debunking tradition? Is he only another philosopher *qua* psychologist of religion, or is there something more lofty here, something that transcends either of the religious myths, biblical or Freudian-biblical? Freud confessed that there is another feature of totemism, other than filial guilt, that is preserved unaltered in religion: emotional ambivalence, and it may offer the key.

> The tension of ambivalence was evidently too great for any contrivance to be able to counteract it; or is it possible that psychological conditions in general are unfavorable to getting rid of these antithetical emotions? However that may be, we find that the ambivalence implicit in the father-complex persists in totemism and in religions generally. Totemic religion not only comprised expressions of remorse and attempts at atonement, it also served as a remembrance of triumph over the father.[70]

As even Ricoeur astutely discerned in the end, "one does psychoanalysis a service, not by defending its scientific myth as a science, but by interpreting it as myth." And his description sounds remarkably like a Western religion:

> The ethical history of mankind is not the rationalization of utility, but the rationalization of an ambivalent crime, of a liberating crime, which at the same time remains the original wound; this is the meaning of the totem meal, the ambiguous celebration of mourning and festival.[71]

It says in Deuteronomy that no one knows where the bones of Moses lie and I would argue that Freud has resurrected him in a post-secular key where he forever performs a disappearing act – now an Egyptian, now a Midianite, now a leader of the Hebrews, now you see him and now you don't, returning in distorted guises, murdered by a rationality that reappropriates the murdered, maiming its victim beyond recognition even as he is so piously preserved. Freud's Moses expresses an unyielding ambivalence between, not just aggression and love, but also the near and the far, the immanent and the transcendent, the historical and the universal, and it is his resolute refusal to take final refuge in one model that enables the distinctly subtle Freudian explanation of our condition, a condition that hovers, ambivalently, and I might add heroically, between theory and belief. And it may well be that heroic ambivalence, rather than some clearer faith (illusion) or easier atheism (disillusion), that distinguishes a post-secular philosophy.

Notes

1 Karl Marx and Frederick Engels, *On Religion* (New York: Shocken Books, 1964) pp. 41–42.
2 Sigmund Freud, *The Future of an Illusion*, ed. James Strachey (New York: W.W. Norton, 1961) p. 35.
3 Freud, *The Future of an Illusion*, p. 31. Philip Rieff writes, "Regardless of how far he ranged outside the recognized boundaries of experimental science Freud was anxious to preserve the image of himself as a solid scientist rather than a free-lance explorer poking around savage hinterlands of the civilized mind" (*Freud: The Mind of the Moralist* (Chicago: University of Chicago Press, 1959) p. 23).
4 Rieff, *Freud: The Mind of the Moralist*, p. 257.
5 On biblical monotheism, see Regina Schwartz, *The Curse of Cain: The Violent Legacy of Monotheism* (Chicago: University of Chicago Press, 1997). For a discussion of the Bible in relation to Freud, see especially Chapter 3, "Kinship," pp. 102–120.
6 Allan Megill, *Prophets of Extremity* (Berkeley: University of California Press, 1985) p. 322.
7 To argue for a "religious" Freud is not to argue for a Freud who claims a religious identity – a Jewish identity – nor is it to claim that Freud subscribed to any single doctrine. Not arguing for a religious, or post-secular Freud, but imagining a post-modern one, Allan Megill writes

> The postmodernist Freud propounds no doctrine, conveys no message. He is not a moralist in any sense but is rather (like Nietzsche) an antimoralist. He teaches us not how to live but how to read. In short, the postmodern Freud is Freud the interpreter – not the interpreter of dreams, or of the psyche, or of culture, but the interpreter tout court.
> (Megill, *Prophets of Extremity*, p. 325)

8 Freud, *The Future of an Illusion*, pp. 16–17.
9 *Ibid.*, p. 18.
10 *Ibid.*, p. 24.
11 *Ibid.*, pp. 26–27.
12 *Ibid.*, p. 28.
13 *Ibid.*, p. 30.
14 *Ibid.*, pp. 54–56.
15 Freud, *Moses and Monotheism* (New York: Alfred Knopf, 1939) p. 16.
16 Quoted in Peter Gay, *Freud: A Life for our Time* (New York: Doubleday, 1989) pp. 646–647.
17 *Ibid.*
18 Marthe Robert, *From Oedipus to Moses: Freud's Jewish Identity*, trans. Ralph Manheim (Garden City, NY: Anchor Books, 1976); Marianne Krull, *Freud and his Father* (Munich: C.H. Beck, 1979); Dennis B. Klein, *Jewish Origins of the Psychoanalytic Movement* (Chicago: University of Chicago Press, 1981); Yosef Hayim Yerushalmi, *Freud's Moses: Judaism Terminable and Interminable* (New Haven: Yale

University Press, 1991); Emmanuel Rice, *Freud and Moses: The Long Journey Home* (Albany: State University of New York Press, 1990).

19 Freud, *Moses and Monotheism*, p. 43.
20 *Ibid.*, p. 35.
21 Jeffrey Masson, in *The Assault on Truth: Freud's Suppression of the Seduction Theory* (New York: Farrar, Straus, and Giroux, Inc., 1984), argues that Freud deliberately suppressed his early hypothesis that hysteria was caused by sexual abuse in infancy.
22 Letter to Fleiss, 21 September 1897, *The Complete Letters of Sigmund Freud to Wilhelm Fleiss 1887–1904*, ed. and trans by J. Masson (Cambridge, MA: Belknapp Press, 1985) p. 264.
23 Arthur L. Caplan and Bruce Jennings (eds), *Darwin, Marx, and Freud: Their Influence on Moral Theory* (New York: Plenum Press, 1984).
24 Yosef Hayim Yerushalmi, "Freud on the 'Historical Novel,'" *International Journal of Psychoanalysis*, 70(3), pp. 375–395, p. 379.
25 Freud, *Moses and Monotheism*, p. 14.
26 Transcribed and translated by Yerushalmi, "Freud on the 'Historical Novel,'" p. 379.
27 John Vernon, "Exhuming a Dirty Joke," *New York Times Book Review*, July 12, 1992, p. 35.
28 Paul Ricoeur, *Freud and Philosophy* (New Haven: Yale University Press, 1970) p. 537.
29 Freud, *Moses and Monotheism*, p. 114.
30 *Ibid.*, p. 107.
31 *Ibid.*, p. 108.
32 *Ibid.*
33 Paul Ricoeur, *Time and Narrative*, trans. Kathleen McLaughlin and David Pellauer (Chicago: University of Chicago Press, 1984–1988) 3 vols.
34 Ricoeur, *Freud and Philosophy*, p. 537.
35 *Ibid.*
36 Sigmund Freud, *The Standard Edition of the Complete Psychological Works of Sigmund Freud*, trans. James Strachey (New York: W.W. Norton, 1961) vol. 12, p. 148.
37 Schwartz, *The Curse of Cain*, p. 163.
38 Ricoeur, *Freud and Philosophy*, p. 534.
39 *Ibid.*, pp. 536–551.
40 Megill, *Prophets of Extremity*, p. xiii.
41 Schwartz, *The Curse of Cain*, pp. 106–119.
42 Freud, *The Future of an Illusion*, p. 22.
43 *Ibid.*, pp. 18–19.
44 *Ibid.*, p. 19.
45 *Ibid.*
46 Gay, *Freud: A Life for our Time*, p. 524.
47 Freud, *The Standard Edition of the Complete Psychological Works of Sigmund Freud*, vol. 9, pp. 126–127.
48 Many have remarked on the troubling relation between the individual history and the collective one in Freud, the relation of the psyche to the social. Positions range from Voloshinov's Freudianism (V.N. Voloshinov, *Freudianism: A Critical Sketch*, trans. I.R. Titunik and ed. with Neal H. Brass (Bloomington: Indiana University Press, 1987) which takes it to task as being socially unresponsive to Barbara Johnson who reiterates the sense that many share that he only speaks of the social in a forced analogy to the individual (Barbara Johnson, "Moses and Intertextuality," in *Poetics of the Americas: Race, Founding, and Textuality*, ed. Bainard Cowan and

Jefferson Humphries (Baton Rouge: Louisiana State University Press, forth-coming). I do not see this analogy as forced, but as springing from a common source, one that operates at both the social and individual levels.

49 Freud, *Moses and Monotheism*, p. 71, my italics.

50 *Ibid.*, p. 61.

51 *Ibid.*

52 Freud's identification with Moses has been long noted. He made it explicit, among other places, in a letter to Jung dated January 17, 1909: "We are certainly getting ahead; if I am Moses, then you are Joshua and will take possession of the promised land of psychiatry, which I shall only be able to glimpse from afar" (W. McGuire (ed.), *The Freud/Jung Letters: The Correspondence Between Sigmund Freud and C.G. Jung*, The Bollingen Series 94 (Princeton, NJ: Princeton University Press, 1974), pp. 196–197).

53 "They were, to Freud, not father and son . . . but fellow fathers, hence, fellow victims" (James E. Dittes, "Biographical/Theological Exegesis of Psychological Texts: The Case of Freud's Search for 'After-Life,'" *Religion and Social Order*, 1, 1991, pp. 37–51, p. 37).

54 Freud, *Moses and Monotheism*, p. 64.

55 Barbara Johnson speaks of this internal division in Egypt as "self-difference," noting that "by introducing a difference between Moses and the people he liber-ates, [Freud] places difference at the root of the foundational story" (*Moses and Intertextuality*, p. 19 in manuscript).

56 Freud, *Moses and Monotheism*, p. 32.

57 *Ibid.*, p. 136.

58 *Ibid.*, p. 61.

59 *Ibid.*, p. 49.

60 *Ibid.*, p. 64.

61 *Ibid.*, p. 57.

62 Rieff, *Freud: The Mind of the Moralist*, p. 264.

63 *Ibid.*

64 Sigmund Freud, *Totem and Taboo* (New York, W.W. Norton, 1950) p. 145.

65 Freud, *Moses and Monotheism*, p. 52, my italics.

66 Dittes, "Biographical/Theological Exegesis of Psychological Texts," p. 48.

67 Freud, *Moses and Monotheism*, p. 52.

68 Schwartz, *The Curse of Cain*, pp. 113–119; Yael Feldman, "'And Rebecca Loved Jacob,' But Freud Did Not," in *Freud and Forbidden Knowledge*, ed. Peter Rudnytsky and Ellen Handler Spitz (New York: New York University Press, 1994) pp. 7–25.

69 Dittes, "Biographical/Theological Exegesis of Psychological Texts," p. 41.

70 Freud, *Totem and Taboo*, p. 180

71 Ricoeur, *Freud and Philosophy*, pp. 208–210.

12

LACAN AND THEOLOGY

Charles E. Winquist

Theological discourse

Thinking theologically is a complication in the study of religion that needs to be examined in both the analysis of religion and in the assessment of the possibilities for the study of religion. On a very basic level theological thinking is a practice akin to ritual practices, the veneration of saints, or the recitation of sacred texts. Like many other practices, it is a modality of religious experience that, without giving it special privilege, falls within the range of any phenomenologically based study of religion. However, it is unlike other modalities of religious experience in that at least some of the conditions of its possibility are epistemically isomorphic with the conditions that make the study of religion possible. It is possible that the deracination of theology in a postmodern sensibility may have implications for the study of religion that are more far-reaching than attention to theology alone would indicate.

A veil of suspicion has obscured the meaning of theological discourse in the twentieth century and that veil itself must be analyzed as part of an assessment of the possibilities for theological thinking. Certainly theology has long not been able to assume a realist epistemological base for its development, but in American culture it was the radical theologies of the 1960s that first made it clear that theological judgments were suspect as adjudications of reality, that theological judgments lacked a clear domain of reference, and that theological interrogations have turned from traditional doctrinal questions to the question of theology's own possibility as a meaningful discursive practice. There is a notable discrepancy between the descriptive and ostensive uses of language in most ordinary discourse and the extreme formulations of theological discourse. That than which nothing greater can be conceived, God as wholly other, Allah as Lord of the worlds, or Lao Tzu's mother's impregnation by a shooting star are not subject to the dominant empirical canons of verification or justification that have characterized the Enlightenment project of modernity. Theology since the Enlightenment can appear from a secular perspective as a vast quilt of *reductio ad absurdum* arguments convoluting in their own extreme formulations.

This statement might appear to suggest that theology is an anachronism and that its time as a meaningful discursive practice is over. However, surprisingly, in a remarkable quotation from one of the appendices of Gilles Deleuze's *The Logic of Sense*, he says:

> it is our epoch which has discovered theology. One no longer needs to believe in God. We seek rather the "structure," that is, the form which may be filled with beliefs, but the structure has no need to be filled in order to be called "theological." Theology is now the science of nonexisting entities, the manner in which these entities – divine or anti-divine, Christ or Antichrist – animate language and make for it this glorious body which is divided into disjunctions. Nietzsche's prediction about the link between God and grammar has been realized.[1]

Is there any way to make sense out of this audacious claim by Deleuze?

First, it appears that Deleuze has made a transcendental turn in the interrogation of theological discourse. Instead of asking "What does theology think?" priority is given to asking "What are the formal conditions that make theological thinking possible?" Second, Deleuze's transcendental turn is not simply a Kantian interrogation of the conditions of objective knowledge grounded in a Cartesian understanding of the self as subjectivity. The force of his inquiry is not marked by apodictic certainty. The formal conditions have genealogies and describe a more general heterological infrastructure for subjectivities profoundly influenced by the nineteenth-century hermeneutics of suspicion. The door to transcendental inquiry was both further opened and confused by the interrogations of Nietzsche, Marx, and Freud. The multiple expressions of the unthought in Nietzsche, Marx, and Freud moved transcendental inquiry beyond the bounds of the onto-theological tradition that identified reality with objective presence to consciousness.

The hermeneutics of suspicion brought closure to the book of the onto-theological tradition and with its closure proclamations of the death of God, the end of history as a meaningful explanatory paradigm, and the displacement or loss of the self.[2] It is the displacement or loss of the self that is of most interest to me in this chapter because it is that loss that has the most immediate ramifications within a Cartesian ordering of things where the self defined as subjectivity is the arbiter of meaning. And it is only in the disruption and defamiliarization with the common order of things that we can grasp why Deleuze can refer to our epoch as an epoch that has discovered theology. The displacement or loss of the self is most commonly associated in the twentieth century with the name Freud.

Of course the name Freud is a metaphorical condensation of many Freuds. The Freud that I want to turn to in the analysis of the displacement of the self as subject is the often unthought Freud of the unthought. This is a Freud that is increasingly thought of as a French Freud in contrast to the Anglo-

American Freud of ego psychologies. This is a Freud that has been particularly but not exclusively discovered in the work of Jacques Lacan.

Reading Lacan

A turn to Jacques Lacan is a return to Freud and most importantly a return to what is unassimilable in Freud. Lacan's reading of Freud has a debt to surrealism.[3] This reading might even be characterized as a "strong misreading" and this is its profundity. Elizabeth Grosz says that:

> Lacan's work is far from a dutiful commentary or secondary text *on* Freud's primary texts. Lacan's work is not parasitic on Freud's, for it produces a certain Freud, a Freud perhaps more bold and threatening than the cautious Viennese analyst.[4]

It is Lacan's reading and understanding of the subversion of the subject in Freud that has severe implications for theories of psychological and theological discourse. It is a move behind the adaptive strategies of Americanized ego psychologies to originary wounds where the "it" of the unconscious is marked.

What we first notice when we turn to Lacan and the secondary literature about the work and life of Lacan is that everyone has trouble reading Lacan. Muller and Richardson "call Lacan's writings a rebus. . . . Lacan not only explicates the unconscious but strives to imitate it."[5] "Lacan cultivates a deliberate obscurity. . . . Lacan works largely by indirection, circularity, ellipsis, humour, ridicule, and word-play."[6] We have no simple understanding of "Who is speaking?" when we read Lacan. We do not simply interrogate the text but we are interrogated by the text. This belongs to style. Lacan is teaching style. "Lacan's style is deliberately provocative, stretching terms to the limits of coherence, creating a text that is difficult to enter and ultimately impossible to master."[7] Jane Gallop suggests that Lacan's *Ecrits* are writerly texts "written not to be read."[8] The reader is implicated in a perpetual struggle of production. It is not a benign *agon*. The rebus is not a parlor game puzzle that is to be undone or put together. In reading Lacan we assume our inevitable castration in language.[9] Lacan's style is "the man to whom one addresses oneself" and as Gallop suggests

> The violence of Lacan's style is its capacity to make the reader feel nonidentical with herself as a reader . . . to make the reader feel inadequate to her role as "the man to whom Lacan addresses himself," that is, inadequate to Lacan's style.[10]

Lacan develops a style of analytical discourse that fixates a concept of the subversion of the subject which is at the same time an oxymoronic requirement

307

for slippage in speech and writing leaving cuts, gaps, and spaces on the record-ing surface of experience. Reading Lacan is a lesson in Lacanian reading. A Lacanian reading is not a search for hidden significations but is an insistence on the letter of the text in the specific dialectic of text production. It would be a shallow misreading of Lacan to begin to search for hidden symbolic meanings in a literary text or for specific Lacanian concepts in a theological text. The real loss in a theological assimilation of Lacanian concepts would be the loss of the loss we experience in Lacanian discourse. When theological concepts are used to mirror rather than interrogate reality, the unrestricted scope of these concepts can transumptively relocate figurations of lack on a surface that seems to fill in the lack. For example, Lacan's formula for athe-ism, "God is unconscious," can be psychologically tamed and epistemo-logically neutered if it is relocated from the Freudian unassimilable "it" into a discourse assimilating it into the more familiar theological formulation of God as wholly other. Here, there could be a falling back on a *specular* figure of otherness and wholeness so that when the "it" of the unconscious God is remarked in symbolic discourse, it has been transposed into a different discur-sive situation that is not Lacanian. The formulation can lose its transgressive force within the discourse. Assimilation is the problem. Reading Lacan is reading what is unassimilable in reading Freud.

Reading Freud

In *Ecrits*, Lacan writes that "Freud's discovery puts truth in question, and there is no one who is not personally concerned by the truth."[11] Putting "truth into question" is a theme in Lacan's reading of Freud that is of particu-lar importance for assessing the importance of Lacan and Freud in under-standing the possibilities for theological discourse. Freud's discovery of the unconscious unveils that there is a "secret" in our epistemic processes. It is not, however, a secret content or a secret knowledge that is to be deciphered by a proper hermeneutic. In commenting on a fundamental homology of interpretive procedure in Marx and Freud, Slavoj Žižek writes: "the 'secret' to be unveiled through analysis is not the content hidden by the form [the form of commodities, the form of dreams] but, on the contrary, the 'secret' of this form itself."[12] The secret of the form is an epistemological wound and it is because of the infliction of this wound that Marx and Freud join Nietzsche in the circle of the hermeneutics of suspicion.

Analyses of religion and theology from a Freudian or Lacanian perspective must begin with their detailing of the epistemological problem of the secret of the form and not with their more explicit analyses of religion and culture if we want to understand the radicality of the latter analyses. It is the epi-stemological problem that prevents easy assimilation into alternative frames of theological thinking.

Paul Ricoeur points out in his study of Freud:

> the exegesis of culture is simply an application of psychoanalysis
> by way of analogy with the interpretation of dreams and the neur-
> oses. . . . Everything psychoanalysis says about art, morality, and
> religion is determined in two ways: first by the topographic-economic
> model which constitutes the Freudian "metapsychology," and
> second by the example of dreams, which furnish the first term of
> a series of analogues that can be drawn out indefinitely, from the
> oneiric to the sublime.[13]

The topographic-economic model and the dream-work in Freud's *Interpretation of Dreams* both present an epistemological aporia that is prior to and
important for Freud's interpretations of religion and culture. Freud never
passes through this aporia (impassable passage) and in a very important way
this aporia remains embedded in his thought all the way to *Civilization and its
Discontents*.

Ricoeur refers to Freud's metapsychology as an adventure of reflection that
leads to a wounded Cogito – "a Cogito that posits itself but does not possess
itself: a Cogito that sees its original truth only in and through the avowal of
the inadequacy, illusion, and lying of actual consciousness."[14] This wounded
Cogito is implicit in Freud's understanding of the dream-work and exfoliated
as an epistemological problem in the metapsychological studies.

The delineation of the dream-work is Freud's first full articulation of the
problem of psychic representation as a disjunctive mixing of force and meaning. The rebus of the dream cannot be untangled by correlating latent
dream thoughts with a manifest dream content. A work has occurred that
has formally intertwined the dark forces of desire with the light of consciousness. The representation of the dream cannot be reduced to either its manifest
content or deciphered latent dream thoughts. There are mechanisms of a
primary process in which

> desire attaches itself to the dream, it intercalates itself in the inter-
> space between the latent thought and the manifest text . . . its only
> place is in the *form* of the "dream": the real subject matter of the
> dream [the unconscious desire] articulates itself in the dream-work.[15]

The mechanisms of the dream-work (condensation, displacement, and representation) are forced substitutions that mark the making of a dream and are
remarked in its secondary revision or conscious reflection.

The epistemological aporia in Freud's thought is the constant combinant
disjunction of force and meaning in conscious representation. At the core of
this problem is the primacy of the theory of drives or instincts. Freud himself
has written that "[t]he theory of instincts is so to say our mythology."[16] The

theory of the instincts is integral and not alongside of a theory of consciousness. Ricoeur says that

> [a]t a certain point the question of force and the question of meaning coincide; that point is where the instincts are indicated, are made manifest, are given in a psychical representative, that is, in something psychical that "stands for" them; all the derivatives in consciousness are merely transformations of this psychical representative, of this primal "standing for."[17]

Freud calls this point *Reprasentanz* in contrast to *Vorstellung*. It is a process that involves the forces of primal repression and as Ricoeur suggests, this means that consciousness is always "in the mediate, in the already expressed, the already said."[18] The semantics of meaning is always implicated in the economics of force without ever being able to overcome force as a constituent element of the mediate domain of expression. The remainder of ideas is the realm of affect. "[A]ffects 'represent' instincts and instincts 'represent' the body 'to the mind.'"[19] The theory of *affects* marks the extreme point of distension between a semantics of meaning and an economics of force.[20] In Lacan's theoretical formulations this point of distension marks the surplus in the gap between the real and its symbolization.

The imaginary, the symbolic, and the real

In the development of Freud's thought we see the emergence of two topographies that function heuristically to articulate and differentiate the relationship between basic drives and psychic representation. The first topography is the distinction between the systems unconscious and preconscious/conscious. The second topography is a further development differentiating the id, the ego, and the superego. It is in the interstices of these topographical differentiations where the work of psychic differentiation occurs – the making of dreams, the making of consciousness in its ordinary and pathological manifestations. The interstices are processional gaps where force is intercalated with meaning in constituting imaginary or symbolic representational economies.

To accommodate insights from Saussurian linguistics, structuralism, and Freud's two topographies, Lacan has developed a third topography differentiating domains of the imaginary, the symbolic, and the real. This third topography functions heuristically to emphasize the aporetic relationship between the systems unconscious and preconscious/conscious, and understand ego and superego formations in relationship to the id.

In Lacan's early work the domain of the imaginary is understood in relationship to what he calls the mirror stage. Some time in that interval of infancy between 6 and 18 months, the child is able to recognize its own image in a mirror. The mirror stage is an identification and marks a transformation of the subject when the subject assumes an image. As Lacan says, "the *I* is precipitated in a primordial form."[21] A substitution occurs. The love of the image of the whole body is substituted for the autoerotic relationship to the partial objects of the fragmented body. The subject is separated from the primacy of perception of the fragmented body in the reflection of the primordial image of the whole body. The mirror image can be thought of as a referential fantasy, figural *gestalt*, or imago for a transcendental unity of apperception that is outside of the empirical subject. This unification and totalization of this idealized form of the "I" is virtual and alienated. The mirror image cannot be touched. Only the mirror can be touched. The image can be indexed only on an imaginary register. The mirror image is the reflection of a projection and as such is the privileged experience of structuring projections. The subject transcends and loses the molecular multiplicity of the subject. There is an imaginary mastery in the naming and idealistic unification of the image. The mirror is a surface and the image can be unified and total and have no depth. The surface of the mirror is a recording surface that lacks depth, lacks organs, lacks being.

It is in the mirror stage that the subject is reified as an image outside of intersubjective structures that are themselves a play of differences. Lacan's order of the imaginary becomes a realm where the play of differences (e.g. the interrelationship of the fragmented body with the (m)other) is covered over by mirroring.[22] This appears to be a heuristic qualification to help explain how a tendency toward idealization can have empirical credibility. Empirical credibility is important because the mirror image substitutes for a lack in the relationship with the sometimes absent mother. The mirror image allows the child to be differentiated from the (m)other in this imaginary realm.

The mirror image is a first stage of substitute differentiation. Julia Kristeva places primal repression in a pre-mirror stage and understands it as a condition for imaginary or figural representation.[23] There is a loss and a lack in the mirror image. If Kristeva is correct we can better understand Gallop when she says, "Lacan's writings contain an implicit ethical imperative to break the mirror, an imperative to disrupt the imaginary in order to reach the symbolic."[24] There will in Lacan's later work be an imperative to disrupt the symbolic to keep open the gap between the real and its symbolization;[25] but at this time the move is toward the symbolic as a concatenation of the real to compensate for the lack in the imaginary. Gallop goes on to suggest that the symbolic can only be reached as a tear in the fabric of the imaginary.[26] The move to the symbolic register is through the imaginary. When the imaginary is understood to be imaginary and no longer an empirical refuge, it is then located in a discursive situation that is symbolically intersubjective and differential. The imaginary experience is linked to the symbolic order as soon as it is given over to discourse. What is imaginary must have voice in the symbolic order if it is to be anything other than a mute repetition of its scene of origination.

The identification of the imaginary order with the mirror stage and the accession to the symbolic can be understood as a strategy for differentiating language and symbolic discourse from a mimetic function. The goal of thinking is not an adaptation to the order of the real because the domain of the real is outside of the representation of the subject, be it through the imaginary ego or through the representational play of the symbolic. The truth of the subject is found in the locus of the Other.

This claim only makes sense if we see how Lacan understands differential play in the symbolic order. It is here that we also see the originality of Lacan's use of linguistics to articulate his return to what is unassimilable in Freud. Lacan accepts the Saussurian distinction between the signifier and the signified. Meaning is made determinate in the interrelationship and play of differences between signifiers. The signified is itself in a web of signification which is always a play of signifiers. Unlike Saussure, Lacan emphasizes the bar separating the signifiers from the signified in the Saussurian algorithm. The circle or ellipse that embraces and unifies the Saussurian algorithmic expression of the barred relationship between signifier and signified is erased. The signified is absent in the present play of signifiers. There is no mimetic reference to the real. The bar is an aporia. Symbolic identity is in difference. The symbolic order is the possibility for deferral and difference. This is what it means to represent an identity.

This means that the Lacanian algorithm is a formula of separateness that does not admit of a reciprocity between the signifiers and the signified. This has a remarkable implication for the representation of the Freudian unconscious. "The unconscious is structured like a language."[27] We are never conscious of the unconscious as unconscious. It can only be known in an overdeterminate structure of language manifested symptomatically. The unconscious must be structured like a language, a play of signifiers, to have the referential motility that characterizes its formations. This is in Freud's language a consideration of representability. Lacan says that the linguistic structure "assures us that there is, beneath the term unconscious, something definable, accessible and objectifiable."[28] This is not the Freudian unconscious but it does designate that it is in the symbolic order that we will encounter the unconscious. It will be in the symbolic order that the written or spoken sentence will stumble. There will be gaps and as Lacan understands Freud, "the discovery" is in these gaps.[29] The imaginary and the symbolic speak their own lack.

What is discovered is not what is present. What is discovered is an absence. Quoting from Lacan, "the reality of the unconscious . . . is not an ambiguity of acts, future knowledge that is already known not to be known, but lacuna, cut, rupture inscribed in a certain lack."[30] The unconscious is what is unthought in thinking. It is where the fabric of the text gapes. It is in the sensuality of the trace – in what appears through what disappears. We might say that Lacan's return to Freud is a return of the repressed. We are back to the "it" of the unconscious and "it" is anti-conceptual and thus unassimil-able. It resides in a domain that is always other. Repression delineates a domain of otherness.

There is a possible trap in this language that could lead to a theological mis-reading of Lacan. When Lacan talks about a grand Other, there is a tempta-tion to objectify the other and name it God. It is then too easy to fill in the gap that is the importance of otherness. Lacan is concerned about the subject. The Other is an object of the interrogation of the subject – "Who is speak-ing?" Lacan refuses to comment explicitly on what he means by the grand Other.[31] But, I think Žižek is correct when he identifies the grand Other with the symbolic order itself.[32] In this sense the grand Other is somebody who is already presumed to know; but, the problem is that the interrogation of the Other reveals a lack. The Other is barred as the subject is barred. There is an otherness that represents what the grand Other lacks. In the phe-nomenality of the representation of desire the lack is the petite other of partial objects – an anus, a nipple, faeces, the gaze, the phoneme, the nothing.[33] These petite objects do not represent a whole; they are what escapes the sub-ject. They are the lack in the grand Other. They are the lack in the Other that constitutes the subject as subject. The limit of the unconscious is the con-cept of lack.[34] The lack, the gap, the fissure paradoxically marks a surplus. Symbolization fissures because it cannot contain the real.

Theology and symbolic transgression

Žižek, in a discussion of the death instinct (drive) and the symbolic order notes that there are three periods in Lacan's thinking about the function and importance of the symbolic order.[35] In the first period the word is a death when reality is symbolized (imagined). Analysis responds by seeking nar-rative integration of the word into the full speech of the symbolic. In the second period the symbolic realm itself wounds the subject, imposes a lack that must be accepted. In the third period the symbolic order is understood to have at its center an unassimilable reality. There is in this third period a shift in emphasis from the symbolic to the *real*. The strategic task is to keep open the gap between the *real* and its symbolization.[36] The strategic task is continually to transgress the symbolic.

Surprisingly, Lacan may in this third period have defined a task that is more readily aligned with the arts and even with theology than with psychotherapy as a professional practice. It is the gap the harbors the "secret" of the real and its quasi-transcendental relationship with psychic or conscious represen-tations. It is in the gap that desire is intercalated with meaning. It is the gap that gives access to desire and thereby witnesses to the chora of the real.

In this chapter I am particularly interested in what these claims about representational economies mean for theology and the study of religion. It should now be clear that a theology in the wake of Lacan will be a theology

313

of desire. That is, what we encounter in Lacan that is immediately relevant for a theory of theological discourse is that its speech will always speak a lack and that the domain of its discourse is barred so that the otherness of reality does not belong to description but to desire. Theology must develop strategies of desire in language if it is meaningfully to speak of otherness.

What we need is an articulation of textual strategies that accept responsibility in their own reflexivity for the representational repression of otherness that is at the same time, ironically, constituted in the otherness of reality. These are textual strategies that do not compensate for loss by a fascination with exotica but work through themselves toward the significance of otherness. Desire references what discursive representations are not – the extra-textual reference – but at the same time desire is itself only known discursively. The problematic of desire in language is to acknowledge extra-textual reference and yet stay within an internal play of linguistic signification.

It is here that we can discern a new warrant for theological thinking and place its importance within the study of religion. Theological thinking is relevant because it is other than ordinary discourse and is itself a discourse that can display the otherness of its semantic achievement. This is already part of the achievement of the theological tradition. Historically, the fundament in theology has been unrestricted – God, ultimate reality, Brahman and other metonymic intrusions of unconditional formulations – and even though an objective and descriptive literalism is no longer credible, the definition of theology as a discursive discipline includes responsibility for unrestricted inquiry. As we have already noted, notions of "that than which nothing greater can be conceived" violate intelligible closure to achievements of understanding within the symbolic order. We could characterize theology as a deconstructive agent and theological thinking as a deconstructive act within the symbolic order. Questions about what we take seriously without any reservation may not have answers but they transgress the boundaries of semiotic captivity.

A post-Lacanian theology would not be defined by the object of its inquiry. It is the form of inquiry, the form of interrogation, that instantiates a loss, constitutes knowledge of a lack, and fissures the completeness of symbolic expression. Theology harbors no secret knowledge and has no access to a hidden order of things. It does not provide knowledge in the symbolic order that other disciplines lack.

This means that theology is textual production in which the author is written into the work as a theologian by implicating the text in the exigencies of the unrestricted scope of theological inquiry by juxtaposing within the text unconditional formulations or interrogations that cannot be contained within the scope of the symbolic order. They challenge the completeness of the symbolic order. We will still be reading a text but the text will be marked and sometimes remarked by fissures wrought by limiting questions, poetic

314

indirections, and figures of brokenness. Theological inverbalization and inscription will be a dangerous supplement to ordinary thinking. We might even think of theology as a supplementary valuation of the otherness that is present only by its absence in the textual articulation of experience within the symbolic order. It is in its postmodern articulation a strategy of hesitation on the surface, the fold, the skin, and the appearance of reality, so that there can be an acute recognition of the complexity of process in the emergence of our symbolically constructed worlds. There is in this recognition a consent to alterity – a primal sense of reality or *numinosum* – that is always in danger of being repressed and exploited by systems of thinking.

Theological text production can be a negative dialectic within language that prevents the symbolic order from closing in on itself or tightening the weave of its differential play into a seamless fabric. This is important because language can cover up its forgetfulness unless there is a commitment to subvert the closure of language from within language. The trajectory of the theological use of language is to produce an extreme distension within the symbolic domain.

The lesson of Lacan for the theologian is that systematic theology can never come to completion in the symbolic order and that foundational theology is not a meta-analysis. Theology cannot stand outside of itself to envision its radical possibilities. It is reflexively immanent. Its radical possibilities for discursive extremities are an achievement of its internal subversion. It cannot become a system because it works against the completeness of a system if it sustains its radical interrogative structure.

Theological thinking is an ongoing experiment and a permanent critique. It may be an experiment with the truth but it is more importantly an experiment of desire. Theology with its radical conceptuality implicates desire in the full range of textual achievements. It would appear that theology can have a place even within postmodern discourse without being an a/theology. Theology continues to have a special role in its capacity to transgress any closure of the symbolic order. Theological interrogations are transgressions of the symbolic order that continually reference the depth of experience as the unthought darkness of desire.

This reference to the unthought darkness of desire is how Lacanian thought "puts truth into question"; and theology complements the Lacanian project by marking the domain of the symbolic with ineradicable gaps. Theology's unrestricted interrogations show a dimension of the otherness of reality that does not belong to description but to desire.

There are many implications of the Lacanian interrogation of "truth" for both theology and the study of religion that are more radical and more important than his explicit statements about religion. For example, the complexity of theological discourse as an act implicates the study of religion in this same complexity if its analyses are to be interpretively adequate to the object of its study. To exclude theology from the study of religion is to falsify the range of interrogations in the study of religion and deliberately skew the practices of some religious communities. To include theology is to include the problematic of the wounded Cogito in the study of religion's own reflexivity. That is, there is no longer a credible second naivety on which to build the study of religion as a purely descriptive science when theology is included as an object of study. The study of religion can no more think itself out of the aporia of representational consciousness than can theology. It cannot escape the unthought darkness of desire. That is, the study of religion is always already implicated in the problematic and in the exigencies of theological thinking.

Lacan is asking "Who is speaking?" This is a question that must be asked by theologians and students of religion as well as by psychoanalysts and philosophers. It is the question that displaces simplistic notions of the subject and simplistic notions of thinking. After Lacan, we cannot avoid accounting for an epistemic wound in the dispersal and complexification of the subject.

Notes

1 Gilles Deleuze, *The Logic of Sense*, trans. Mark Lester (New York: Columbia University Press, 1990), p. 281.
2 Cf. Mark C. Taylor, *Erring: A Postmodern A/theology* (Chicago: University of Chicago Press, 1984), Part I.
3 Elizabeth Roudinesco, *Jacques Lacan and Co.: A History of Psychoanalysis in France, 1925–1985*, trans. Jeffrey Mehlman (Chicago: University of Chicago Press, 1990), p. 26.
4 Elizabeth Grosz, *Jacques Lacan: A Feminist Introduction* (London and New York: Routledge, 1990), p. 9.
5 John P. Muller and William J. Richardson, *Lacan and Language: A Reader's Guide to Ecrits* (New York: International Universities Press, 1982), p. 3.
6 Grosz, *Lacan*, pp. 13–14.
7 Grosz, *Lacan*, p. 17.
8 Jane Gallop, *Reading Lacan* (Ithaca: Cornell University Press, 1985), p. 46.
9 Gallop, *Reading Lacan*, p. 20.
10 Gallop, *Reading Lacan*, p. 117.
11 Jacques Lacan, *Ecrits: A Selection*, trans. Alan Sheridan (New York: Norton, 1977), p. 118.
12 Slavoj Žižek, *The Sublime Object of Ideology* (London and New York: Verso, 1989), p. 11.
13 Paul Ricoeur, *Freud and Philosophy: An Essay in Interpretation*, trans. Denis Savage (New Haven and London: Yale University Press, 1970), pp. 153–4.
14 Ricoeur, *Freud and Philosophy*, p. 439.
15 Žižek, *Sublime Object of Ideology*, p. 13.
16 Sigmund Freud, *The Standard Edition of the Collected Works of Sigmund Freud*, 24 vols, trans. James Strachey (London: Hogarth Press, from 1953), vol. 22, p. 95.
17 Ricoeur, *Freud and Philosophy*, p. 135.
18 Ricoeur, *Freud and Philosophy*, pp. 140–1.
19 Ricoeur, *Freud and Philosophy*, pp. 150.
20 Cf. Ricoeur, *Freud and Philosophy*, p. 151.
21 Lacan, *Ecrits*, p. 2.
22 Gallop, *Reading Lacan*, p. 59.

23 Grosz, *Lacan*, p. 158.
24 Gallop, *Reading Lacan*, p. 59.
25 Žižek, *Sublime Object of Ideology*, pp. 230–1.
26 Gallop, *Reading Lacan*, p. 60.
27 Jacques Lacan, *The Four Fundamental Concepts of Psycho-Analysis*, trans. Alan Sheridan (New York: Norton, 1978), p. 20.
28 Lacan, *Four Fundamental Concepts*, p. 21.
29 Lacan, *Four Fundamental Concepts*, p. 25.
30 Lacan, *Four Fundamental Concepts*, p. 153.
31 See his translator's note in Lacan, *Four Fundamental Concepts*, p. 282.
32 Žižek, *Sublime Object of Ideology*, p. 133.
33 Lacan, *Four Fundamental Concepts*, p. 315.
34 Lacan, *Four Fundamental Concepts*, p. 26.
35 Žižek, *Sublime Object of Ideology*, pp. 131–3.
36 Žižek, *Sublime Object of Ideology*, pp. 230–1.

KRISTEVA'S FEMINIST
REFIGURING OF THE GIFT

Philippa Berry

In the continuing task of that deconstructing or 'overcoming' of Western metaphysics which contemporary thought has inherited from Heidegger, as well as Nietzsche, it is becoming apparent that the redefinition of Western models of 'thinking' is inseparable from the articulation of a new position and 'subject' of knowledge.[1] While in the first instance this implies that the current discourse in relation to or around philosophy cannot avoid a simultaneous engagement with some version of psychoanalytic discourse (specifically, with the legacy of Lacanian psychoanalysis, which began so influentially to extend the phenomenological critique of Western metaphysics to the unified subject of metaphysical speculation, the 'subject who is supposed to know'), several of the most recent contributions to this interrogation of subjectivity point beyond the established boundaries of psychoanalysis, as well as of philosophy, in the direction of states and experiences which both these discourses have typically treated with mistrust. Thus the intersection of psychoanalysis with philosophy, although it was first explicitly negotiated by Lacan, has borne some of its most challenging fruit in the works of Julia Kristeva and Luce Irigaray, who have both, to different degrees, gone beyond the Lacanian limit, in exceeding the master's conception of his project. Although these thinkers have often been contrasted in recent years, it is my view that the intersection between key aspects of their work is far more extensive than their commentators have suggested.

Both Kristeva and Irigaray have founded a critique of the rationalism of Western society since the Renaissance upon the psychoanalytic space of the pre-oedipal; although each accords a different priority in her writing to philosophy and psychoanalysis respectively. And as I have suggested elsewhere, Kristeva and Irigaray have each made vital contributions to a feminist restructuring of that pre-oedipal space by deploying notions of 'opening' and 'spacing' which are derived from phenomenology and deconstruction respectively in order to point towards the possibility of another psychic structure.[2] Such a structure, their work suggests, would differ from that mapped by

Freud and Lacan, above all in its different figurations of law and paternity, but also in the different valency which it would accord to a triadic psychic organisation, as a system that could promote psychic growth and mobility along with a capacity for love, rather than stasis, restraint and despair. It is Kristeva's version of this intervention, as articulated in her discussion of the *père imaginaire* – the Imaginary Father of 'la pré-histoire individuelle' – in *Histoires d'amour*, with which I will be concerned in this essay. But the importance accorded by her to this figure has, I believe, a striking affinity to the role accorded by Irigaray to the angel in 'La Croyance même' and *Ethique de la Différence Sexuelle*, as a bearer and facilitator of love who occupies the place *between*.[3] Certainly, Irigaray's recent emphasis upon questions of love has been of equal importance to the work of Kristeva in redirecting intellectual interest to the complex relationship of love with the category of woman.

Through her work on the attributes of this space of the pre-oedipal, which (significantly) she renamed as the semiotic *chora*, Julia Kristeva has for more than twenty years been engaged in elaborating – and simultaneously critiquing – key aspects of the Lacanian project: most importantly, against Lacan's account of the unconscious as 'structured like a language', Kristeva has often stressed the non-verbal affinities of *chora*. In the process, she has made a subtle yet extremely important contribution to the expansion of contemporary conceptions of 'thinking'. In the text which was first published in French in 1983 as *Histoires d'amour*, and translated in 1987 as *Tales of Love*, she points to the need to found a new subjectivity upon a discourse around identity which privileges affect and the giving of love, instead of an endless quest for the absolutes of objective knowledge. Such a discourse, Kristeva suggests, is urgently needed, in order to 'take the place of this religious discourse that's cracking now'.[4] Moreover, in *Tales of Love* she implies that the new discourses and structures of subjectivity can only be elaborated via a reassessment of the now discarded religious paradigms which pre-dated the emergence of modernity.

As a number of thinkers have recently begun to demonstrate, continental thought since Nietzsche combines with its apparent nihilism a striking concern to reassess and redefine the relevance to its thinking, not only of a previously degraded sphere of feeling, but also of themes of the sacred, numinous or uncanny.[5] *Tales of Love* is an important example of this trend, and offers insights into its complexity as well as its importance for the contemporary rethinking of subjectivity. For one of Kristeva's central concerns in this book (as also in *In the Beginning was Love*) is to elaborate a new analytic stance which she specifically identifies as an antidote to nihilism. She contends that: 'What today's analyst must do . . . is restore to illusion its full therapeutic and epistemological value'.[6] My concern in this chapter is with the implications of these quasi-religious themes in Kristeva's attempt to define a new philosophy – and experience – of love, a love which exceeds or differs from Freud's influential model of desire in important respects. Such a knowledge or state, she suggests, can help to cure the crises of the modern era, through the construction of a new psychic structure and a new capacity for idealisation.

In drawing upon the psychoanalysis of Freud and Lacan in order to pass beyond it, Kristeva is by implication influenced by the Nietzschean conception of going beyond (*übergehen*), as well as by French reformulations of the concept, above all in the writings of Blanchot and Derrida, as *le pas au delà*; at the very beginning of *Tales of Love*, she refers to 'an exaltation beyond (*au-delà de*) eroticism'. But at the same time, in a manner which both resembles and yet is different to the Nietzschean meditation upon time which complements this going beyond, Kristeva also associates her exploration of love with a return to the questions of temporality which she had addressed in 'Women's Time',[7] referring to 'the non-time of love', and asserting that 'love and the loved one erase the reckoning of time' (TL, 5). Blanchot wrote of the curious relationship between time and 'the step beyond' that: '*le pas au-delà*, which is not accomplished in time, would lead outside of time, without this outside being timeless.'[8] Thus if, as the French title of Kristeva's book suggests, love or '*amour*' is embedded in and inseparable from history, insofar as the '*histoires*' or tales of the title are 'of' love, they also depend upon and are subordinate to it; love, like the 'father of pre-history' who is here delineated as its source, is consequently implied to come, if not first, at least before historical time (as indeed love once did, when it was held to have emerged from chaos in the ancient Greek cosmogony of the Orphics). Moreover, Kristeva's *Tales of Love* fissures the singularity of a linear model of history. It does this not only by converting history into a series of tales, but also by its claim for the relevance of past epochs of Western cultural history to our possible future(s), by turning back to the pre-modern in order to think the postmodern. In this respect Kristeva is echoing the preoccupation of Heidegger in *On Time and Being* with 'the time space of true time', which 'consists in the mutual reaching out and opening up of future, past and present'.[9] Indeed, like much contemporary continental thought, whose paradoxical historicity is only now beginning to be recognised, *Tales of Love* is deeply embedded in Western intellectual history, looking back by implication to the nineteenth-century intellectual agendas of Saint-Simon and Comte (both of whom sought to reconnect intellect with feeling), as well as of Feuerbach (who repositioned love as a mediating but material and human concept in his anti-Hegelian discourse in a way which anticipates the thought of Heidegger, Irigaray and Kristeva), to Platonism and Neoplatonism, and also to the theology of the Middle Ages. It is the Middle Ages, however, which enjoy a privileged position in Kristeva's eclectic and sketchy cultural history of love (this is even implied, incidentally, in her selection of a medieval depiction of love for the cover of her book). In this respect, her rethinking of key Freudian concepts deviates quite markedly from the cultural preferences of Freud himself; as Carl E. Schorske has shown, Freud had nothing but horror when he encountered the remnants of medieval Catholicism in Rome: 'I found almost intolerable the lie of salvation which rears its head so proudly to heaven.'[10]

Yet it is figuratively consistent with Kristeva's interest in the 'between', or middle, that crucial aspects of her argument about love as a third term derive from her readings of texts of the *medium aevum* or Middle Ages of Western culture. The idea of the turn or return which haunts so much contemporary writing is indelibly marked by association with the return of Nietzsche's Zarathustra, with its perplexing connotations of a non-teleological – but enclosed and circular – model of temporality. Yet in more recent texts this Nietzschean 'turn' is often refigured as a turn to the between or middle. Versions of this demi- or half-turn (which is more of a turn aside or *écart* than a return) appear in the writings of Heidegger, Derrida, Irigaray and others, and even seem to have been anticipated in the works of those early nineteenth-century philosophers whose influence, acknowledged or not, also seems to overshadow current thought: Comte, Saint-Simon, Hegel.[11]

In *Tales of Love*, Kristeva points out that the vital psychic space which modernity has destroyed was constituted at the beginning of the Christian era, and notes that the death of the Christian God (as articulated by Nietzsche) was in a sense synonymous with the death of love, since it removed a ternary psychic structure (of father, mother and child) from the realm of what Lacan has called the imaginary, leaving only an uneasy binary relationship between mother and child to dominate the pre-oedipal psyche (TL, 61). It is for this reason that, in the *middle* of the book, she returns to medieval Christian mysticism to explore what she believes is now an anachronistic, triadic model of love, which she characterises as 'a *disinterested gift*' (*don gratuit*). Earlier, she has asked: 'Are not two loves essentially individual, hence incommensurable, and thus don't they condemn the partners to meet at a point infinitely remote? Unless they commune through a third party: ideal, God, hallowed group' (TL, 3). And now she claims that the rejection, during the Renaissance, of a definition of identity in terms of love had disastrous consequences for Western subjectivity. She suggests that when the *Ego affectus est* of a medieval thinker such as St Bernard of Clairvaux was replaced by the Cartesian *Ego* (as) *cogito*, the resultant definition of identity, which was of course in terms of rational thought, produced a profound narcissistic crisis – a crisis whose consequences we have only really seen in the twentieth century. As a result, she argues, modern Western culture cannot elaborate the complex triadic structure of primary narcissism. And in particular, it cannot ground narcissism in a productive encounter with otherness.

There is a difficulty here in Kristeva's argument, which is fundamental to any use of the pre-oedipal phase to explore psychic space: the analysand, poet or writer can never wholly recover '*le temps perdu*' of childhood, but can only half-remember and reconstruct it, as '*histoire*', as they too turn backwards in order to move forwards. In *Tales of Love*, as in all her other work, she is therefore much concerned with the reconstruction of this state or space through aesthetic representations – representations which not only facilitate access to long-forgotten, infantile psychic states, but which also apparently have the capacity to refigure these states to good or bad effect. Hence there is often an indecision apparent in much of her work as to what has priority: the infantile experience, or its cultural refigurations in religion, art, philosophy – and in the psychoanalytic encounter. In any case, it is to cultural, and specifically religious, representations that Kristeva turns in order to theorise a forgotten or buried psychic potential for love. Freud too had figured this capacity in terms of religion, and in Kristeva's account of the 'primary identification' which engenders this experience, faith is seen as a characteristic, if unsatisfactory metaphor. But her preferred metaphor in her rethinking of the religious refiguring of this concept is that of the gift, and in the use of this figure for primary identification, I see *Tales of Love* as articulating an unacknowledged, yet extremely important dialogue with key aspects of the thought of Nietzsche and Heidegger, as well as with Derrida.

This love which can facilitate the first encounter of a subject-to-be with alterity is significantly differentiated by Kristeva from desire. She notes the typical feeling, 'during love, of having had to expend *if not give up* desires and aspirations' (TL, 1, my emphasis). Thus she writes of love or 'affect' in St Bernard of Clairvaux:

> As bond between man and externality, God, and things, the affect is a notion closely related to *desire*. The difference between the two may reside in the following: *desire*, as we shall see, emphasizes the *lack*, whereas *affect*, while acknowledging the latter, gives greater importance to the movement toward the other and to mutual *attraction*.
>
> (TL, 155)

While desire or *eros* is active, Kristeva stresses that the human experience of love (as *affect* or the Christian *agape*) is initially passive. Here love as an outside force acts upon the psyche, and thereby produces movement; this movement is a response to rather than a search for love: 'An outside agent is needed for the soul, thus set in motion, to show an affect in response' (TL, 156). In the opening pages of *Tales of Love*, Kristeva figures this agency in the impersonal and abstract guise of 'a call', thereby hinting from the beginning at the intersection of her amatory discourse with Heidegger's thinking of *Dasein*, which he described as responding to a 'call' to authenticity (TL, 5). Later, however, she will link this agency with the anthropomorphic god of Christianity. This God was idealised, according to Kristeva, precisely *because* he was seen as loving. And he was consequently identified with. She explains this process with reference to Freud's notion of the *Einfühlung* or primary identification with the father of individual pre-history. But she sees the opportunity for idealisation and identification as typically unavailable to the modern psyche, with most damaging consequences: 'a psychic structure that lacks an identifying metaphor or idealization tends to realize it in that embodied object called somatic symptom' (TL, 37–8). In Christian theology, notes Kristeva, *agape* descends in the form of a sacrificial (and an ultimately *edible*, assimilable) gift, which is the incarnation of Christ. Nietzsche's Zarathustra, on his descent from the mountain at the beginning of *Thus Spake Zarathustra*, had stressed the difference of the 'gift' (*Geschenk*) which he brought to man from the love offered by the god of Christianity: 'What did I say of love? I am bringing mankind a gift.'[12] In re-emphasising – and reinterpreting – the association of love with giving, Kristeva rejects this Nietzschean formulation; at the same time, she implicitly alludes to the enigmatic association between giving and Being in the later work of Heidegger, as well as to more recent meditations on that move. Heidegger's aphoristic remark that 'It gives Being' (*Es gibt Sein*) has exercised a number of French thinkers in recent years, most notably Maurice Blanchot, Jacques Derrida and the Heideggerian theologian Jean-Luc Marion. In one of Derrida's earliest references to the Heideggerian gift, in *Glas* (1974), he suggests that this gift or present cannot escape that logic of presence which he sees as permeating even the later works of Heidegger; he alludes there to the gift which 'upsurges "before" philosophy', asserting that this gift 'has for its destination or determination, for its *Bestimmung*, a return to self in philosophy'.[13] Yet Gerard L. Bruns has suggested in *Heidegger's Estrangements* that the step back (or turn aside) in the direction of an earlier thought, *pace* Heidegger, is valuable precisely because it facilitates a letting go (*Gelassenheit*), and a receptive listening to difference.[14] And in Heidegger's return to his key concepts of Being and time in his late work, *On Time and Being*, with a discussion of the *Es gibt Sein* and the *Es gibt Zeit* (It gives Being/There is Being, etc.), it is precisely this act of giving which is held to elude those metaphysical and onto-theological speculations that he admits have continued to overdetermine his thinking of Being and time:

> To think Being explicitly requires us to relinquish Being (*Sein*) as the ground of beings (*des Seinden*) in favour of the giving which prevails concealed in unconcealment, that is, in favour of the It gives (*Es gibt*). As the gift of this It gives, Being belongs to giving. As a gift, being is not expelled from giving. Being, presencing is transmuted. As allowing-to-presence, it belongs to unconcealing; as the gift of unconcealing it is retained in the giving. Being *is* not.[15]

It is therefore Heidegger's incorporation of giving into his thinking of Being which enables him to say 'Being *is* not'. His account of the gift is expressly intended to circumvent the teleology and regulation later attributed to it by Derrida in *Glas*.[16]

In according a new psychic specificity to *Es gibt*, through its affiliation with a hitherto unexplored aspect of her semiotic *chora*, Kristeva also gives a new significance to its uncanny capacity to elude or reconfigure those concepts of regulation and definition which Derrida implies must always confine the 'free' gift, in relation to a restricted economy; much later, in *Given Time I*, Derrida will associate these forces with 'the time of the king': in other words, with the father's law.[17] In *Tales of Love*, the difference putatively opened up by this trace of the Heideggerian gift is very much oriented to an unspecified, 'open' future which is multiple rather than singular. In *Powers of Horror*, Kristeva indirectly alludes to the project of the late Heidegger in relation to the gift when she comments that the only place proper to the analyst is *'the void*, that is, the unthinkable of metaphysics'.[18] And in *Tales of Love*, she defines this place as that of the Imaginary Father. She further suggests that if 'the old psychic space, the machinery of projections and identifications that relied more or less on neurosis for reinforcement, no longer hold[s] together . . . it may be because another mode of being, of unbeing, is attempting to take its place'. But, she contends, 'We should not attempt to give it the outlines of the "own proper self"' (TL, 379–80). Instead, she suggests we should see this crisis as 'a work in progress' whose outcome may not as yet be defined. Yet in looking forwards, *à l'avenir*, Kristeva accords to psychoanalysis the task of enabling the psyche to experience a state comparable to, yet not identical with, Christian *agape* or love in a secular era.

Lacan's account of the formation of the ego at the mirror stage, which has been enormously influential, stresses the specular character of that beginning. But the self-love with which Kristeva is concerned in her rethinking of love, the self-love which she believes can restore a lost psychic space to the melancholy narcissists of contemporary culture, crucially precedes specularisation as well as access to language. Just as the child of the Lacanian mirror stage accords an imaginary and illusory wholeness to its image as first perceived in the mirror, so Narcissus misrecognises himself in the watery mirror in which he eventually drowns: in the Ovidian version of his story, from the *Metamorphoses*, this end has been pre-determined by Nemesis (or Fate) as a punishment for his self-love. In theorising an earlier moment of self-love (primary narcissism), Kristeva is attempting to excavate and reclaim a different, and less destructive model of (self-)recognition through the other, one which is not tragic in its implications, since seemingly it has the capacity to transform the relationship of the emergent individual to abjection and hence to the death drive – a force which Freud as well as Kristeva sometimes figures as Fate or Necessity.[19] (Necessity is a term which Freud borrowed from the Greeks, and perhaps specifically from the tragic dramatists, who wrote of the tragic hero as being under 'necessity's yoke'. The feminine gender of the several Greek concepts associated with fate or necessity – *ananke*, *moira*, *parca* – has been picked up by Sarah Kofman in her critique of Freud's half-repressed association of the mother with the death drive.[20]).

Kristeva therefore goes back to Freud – to *Totem and Taboo* as well as to *The Ego and the Id* – in order to find a place for what she terms paternal love in the pre-oedipal psyche. From Freud, she recovers what he called the archaic father of pre-history. Yet this disinterment is not so much the rediscovery of a person as of a *place* or state – an *opening* in the pre-linguistic space of *chora* which creates a space *between* the symbiotic dyad of mother and child. In an ecstatic experience of sensuous immediacy, the child's attention is diverted and turned away from the mother through the creation or intervention of this third position, whose interpellation clearly anticipates the severe father who intervenes at oedipalisation, but with an important difference. The Imaginary Father is identified as the source of a mysterious and unsolicited profusion of love that leads to what Freud calls primary identification (*Einfühlung*). In this transferential process, the emergent subject merges with or empathetically assimilates the Imaginary Father, whose capacity to own yet simultaneously transmute the death drive through this sacrificial process is aptly figured in Kristeva's stress on his *ghostly* or non-existent character, as a signifier or metaphor who (like the gift of Heidegger's Being) is not. Here the chasm which opens up at the beginning of differentiation from the mother is transferred to the place of the Imaginary Father, who thereby anticipates, Kristeva contends, the metaphoric character of all signification.

Since this moment of self-discovery and self-love in relation to alterity precedes the mirror stage, it is described by Kristeva as impossible to apprehend in terms of a centred or focused vision; she reminds us of Freud's comment in *Totem and Taboo* about 'the sun-drenched face of the young Persian god', Mithras, which 'has remained incomprehensible to us'. Freud compared this god, as well as Christ, to the subject of *Einfühlung*, since each had, in a different way, replaced the father without generating an Oedipal feeling of guilt in the collective because of this act. Kristeva interprets the 'luminous *jouissance*' associated by Freud with the face of Mithras as a central metaphor of primary identification, reminding us that '*Einfühlung* with the Phallus which is desired by the mother 'amounts neither to being the mother's Phallus nor [to] entering the Oedipal drama'. And in elaborating Freud's fleeting comments about the 'halo of light surrounding' the young Persian god, she re-emphasises the spiritual or numinous qualities attributed to this position.[21] For apparently this present of love confers, through the immediacy of identification, what Kristeva, in a Hegelian formulation, calls *parousia*, or 'the presence of the Absolute in knowing' (TL, 39). This 'presencing of the present' (as *eonta* or what is present, as well as *das Geschenk*, the gift) was associated by Heidegger with the activity of fate or Moira.[22] And as he noted, the process simultaneously involves a movement of withdrawal or concealment – a theme to which Kristeva appears to allude in her emphasis upon the metaphoric character of this place or state.

In *Glas*, Derrida has played on the punning – but at first sight most unlikely – relationship between the *Sa* of Hegel's Absolute knowledge (*Savoir Absolu*) and the *ça* or id of the Freudian unconscious, which dominates the process before ego formation. A similar metamorphosis (albeit without the puns) is implicit in Kristeva's account of the *parousia* associated with the Imaginary Father. For while at oedipalisation *Sa* implicitly manifests itself in *Sa*turnian and devouring form, as the harsh father who embodies judgment, here it shows a different, benign face, as an 'It' (*ça, Es*) which creates Saturnalia as it paradoxically anticipates the law of the oedipal father through its inversion. It (*ça*) is multiple and heterogeneous, rather than singular in effect, effacing and mysteriously negating itself in an unmerited gift requiring no exchange (Heidegger's *Es gibt*). From a religious perspective, this gift amounts to grace, forgiveness, blessing, in a suspension (which is none the less both literally and metaphorically *avant la lettre*) of the judgmental father or *père sevère*.[23] Thereby, It (*ça*) constitutes 'the basis of imagination itself', enabling a new, metaphoric and playful relationship to that unrepresentable, uncanny nothing or void which subtends and makes possible representation – as well, Kristeva asserts, as the structure of primary narcissism (TL, 45). The mysterious affinity noted by Freud between the id (German: *Es*) and the superego associated with the oedipus complex is thereby hinted at.[24] Yet the subject which emerges from this process of identification is importantly different from conventional (post-Lacanian) notions of the subject, in that in figurative terms it has accepted death, through an immediate and ecstatic identification with the self-sacrificing giver of love.

But to what extent does the Imaginary Father represent a love which is significantly different from the maternal *jouissance* which brings it into being? As Gayatri Spivak has pointed out in an essay on *Glas, Sa/ça* also evokes *sa* as 'a pronoun possessing an undefined feminine object'.[25] And Derrida has recently noted that *Es gibt* in French is *ça donne*: a version of the verb 'to give' which re-emphasises woman as donor.[26] This suggests an affinity, hinted at by Kristeva, between the lady of the troubadours (often addressed in verse as 'midons' or my lord) and the Imaginary Father; she cites a poem by Arnaut Daniel, where the poet declares that:

> A thousand masses I hear and proffer [or: I utter]
> And I burn a light of wax and oil
> So that God may give me a good outcome
> From her, against whom fencing is no protection.

(TL, 285)

How, then, are we to interpret this installation of the Imaginary Father within the space of the semiotic *chora*, whose determining (if ultimately self-effacing) influence Kristeva has elsewhere shown to be the figure of the mother? I observed earlier that this third term corresponds more to a place than to a person, as well as to the differential activity of the sign. While the Imaginary Father is closely linked with the 'oral stage' in which the child is still at least partially dependent upon the mother's body (an association which is consistent with the child's figurative *consumption* of this 'father' in assuming his place), this opening in the *chora* is clearly *elsewhere* in relation to the mother's body. But while the Imaginary Father has many of the attributes of Derridean *différance* (including its deconstructive relationship to the between or *entre*) it rises up or intervenes both before the accession to language and *before* the imposition of sexual difference as such (with oedipalisation). Freud saw 'him' as equivalent to both parents, and Kristeva defines the 'archaic unity' of the Imaginary Father as 'a coagulation of the mother and her desire' (TL, 41). Moreover, in writing of *agape*, the feminine gender of the noun leads her to refer to this gift of God as '*elle*'. Nonetheless, Kristeva's elaboration of Freud's hints about *Einfühlung* (with the help of Klein) points, as Freud does not, to the priority of (an idea of) the mother in enabling this event. And it is, of course, the Virgin Mary whom she persistently cites as an image of motherhood which, for all its deficiencies, facilitated or figured something akin to this process in medieval Christendom. At the same time, she argues that a recovery of the position of the Imaginary Father has important implications for the status of the mother's image in the emerging psyche. In particular, she suggests that it can protect the future subject from that abjection of the mother as the corporeal representative of death or necessity which, as she herself has shown elsewhere, plays such a vital part in the hatred of women. This gift of love therefore sublimates narcissism and protects it from illness or abjection by giving it a (pre-)'object' of identification which is its 'salvation', assisting the emergence of a more or less healthy subjectivity.

For just as abjection occurs before the establishment of any clear distinction between subject and object, so too does the possibility of identification with the Imaginary Father. In *Polylogue* it is already clear that it is only the Phallic Mother – the fantasy of the mother as substantial and all-powerful – which Kristeva believes it necessary to abject. And *Powers of Horror* suggests that there is an escape from the tragic dichotomy of maternal *jouissance* and its abjection. Here Kristeva notes that there is another version of the confrontation with the feminine: one which accepts its emptiness, and is even willing briefly to occupy its empty place. It only appears, however, 'in a few rare flashes of writing', for by implication, this encounter is more bodily than textual. It requires an attitude 'that, going beyond abjection, is enunciated as ecstatic'. The individual who seeks it must: 'Know the mother, first take her place, thoroughly investigate her jouissance and, without releasing her, go beyond her.'[27] In 'Stabat Mater', an essay written in 1977, but reproduced in *Tales of Love*, Kristeva notes that the great Christian mystics occupied this negative and liminal place of the mother, using it to replace concrete icons of faith with a much less easily definable object of adoration: 'Freedom with respect to the maternal territory then becomes the pedestal (*socle*) upon which love of God is erected.'[28] What is implied by this is an idea of the maternal place as stepping stone towards or pedestal of an even more abstract ideal. The Virgin mother is here seen as the vital facilitator of access to that beyond or *au-delà* which is the gift of love. This ideal is none the less implied to have a phallic character, in the fleeting (and unexpectedly oriental) evocation of love as obelisk or column which repeats a central motif of *Glas*. But its evocation also points to the indeterminate character of the experience of alterity to which it alludes. For the column is merely a marker, a sign of meeting, like the pillar erected by Jacob at the place where he dreamed of the angelic ladder: 'And Jacob rose up early in the morning, and took the stone that he had put for his pillows, and set it up for an altar, and poured oil upon the top of it.'[29] Subsequently, Derrida has suggested that a postmodernism which ended modernism's plan of domination 'could develop a new relationship with the divine that would no longer be manifest in the traditional shapes of the Greek, Christian, or other deities, but would still set the conditions for architectural thinking'.[30] His preference (in a text such as *The Truth in Painting*) is implicitly for Judaic (non-)figures; but the monument or marker which I would wish most closely to associate with the Imaginary Father, as a *père imaginaire* of *pré-histoire individuelle* (and hence a Papa whose initials spell *pi*), is not the Egyptian obelisk, Roman column or Jewish pillar, for these offer nothing in the way of an opening, and so remain mere phallic markers. Rather it is the pre-historic gate of horn or stone dolmen, as Π, whose architecture gives shape to the balance between bounded and open space that this recovery of a triadic version of love facilitates, yet which simultaneously marks an opening, a limen or boundary between different states. And indeed, in her repetition – with a difference – of the two columns of *Glas* which Kristeva performs in 'Stabat Mater', where her text divides between personal experience and a critical, quasi-theological commentary on motherhood, the text begins with this structure, as its opening paragraph, which stresses the need for a new conception of motherhood, overarches and links the practice and theory columns beneath it. As G. Rachel Levy demonstrated some years ago, such gateways were associated with goddesses of birth and death in many pre-historic societies.[31] This imaginary construct in the pre-oedipal consequently escapes from the restricted circular logic of the gift figured as a turning around a phallic column or pillar, to which Derrida alludes in *Glas*, testifying to the possibility of a new and less restrictive relationship between our re-imagined pasts and our possible futures.

In *Tales of Love*, Kristeva claims that 'without the maternal diversion towards a third party, the bodily exchange is abjection or devouring' (TL, 34), and she further suggests that it is the child's identification with the Imaginary Father which in a sense endows the mother with existence. Yet mysteriously, it is only the mother who is able to bring the Imaginary Father into the child's field of awareness. Commenting in *Spurs* on Nietzsche's aphorism in *The Gay Science*, 'Women and their Action at a Distance', Derrida writes: 'there is no essence of woman, because she diverts and is diverted from herself': this distancing of woman is linked, again via Nietzsche, to woman as an enigmatic '*coup de don*'.[32] For Kristeva, it is similarly a diversion or turning away of the mother from her maternal place which paradoxically makes possible that gift of love which endows her with existence. Some years before she wrote *Tales of Love*, Kristeva had noted with fascination the peculiar gazes of Bellini's Madonnas, several of whom contemplate, not their child, but some undefined object outside of the pictorial frame: 'The faces of his Madonnas are turned away (*détournées*), intent on something else that draws their gaze to the side, up above, or nowhere in particular, but never centres it in the baby.'[33] The prominence in recent French thought of the concept of the *écart*, the turn or deviation which is also a gap or opening, clearly owes much to the later work of Merleau-Ponty; as I have argued elsewhere, it seems to me to draw as well on Heidegger's conception of the *Kehre* or turning. Irigaray and Derrida both use *écart* in relation to woman; but only fleetingly, in 'Motherhood According to Bellini', does Kristeva speak of the Virgin represented by Bellini as *écartelait* by her exile in a numinous 'elsewhere'. Nonetheless, her sidelong glance certainly allies Bellini's Mary with Kristeva's later evocation of the mother who 'can indicate to her child that her desire is not limited to her offspring's request' (TL, 40). And although Kristeva here uses the word 'desire', we might rather contend, within the terms of Kristeva's argument in *Tales of Love*, that the angled gaze of Mary is itself a response to a gift of love, as is the luminosity which the painters attributed to her. In 'Giotto's Joy', Kristeva had hinted at the connection of this radiance with primary identification, by suggesting that the colourism associated with Renaissance paintings of the Virgin actually lessened the child's dependence on the mother:

> all colors, but blue in particular . . . have a noncentered or decentering effect, lessening both object identification and phenomenal fixation. They thereby return the subject to the archaic moment of its dialectic, that is, before the fixed, specular 'I,' but while in the process of becoming this 'I' by breaking away from instinctual, biological (and also maternal) dependence.[34]

If Mary's function here is therefore implied to be as a bodily mirror of the radiance of alterity, then it is comparable to that diversion or *écartement* of the mother's role as mirror which Luce Irigaray effects in *Speculum*, where she angles or turns that mirror aside, in order to free woman from a patriarchal logic of similitude and resemblance. For as is shown in the central chapter of *Speculum*, '*La Mystérique*', the turn or tilt of Irigaray's maternal mirror or speculum opens up a space 'beyond' the mother which is a space of mystical self-love also, although here what is discovered is the self-love of a daughter freed from the burden of the maternal role.[35] In this respect, reading Kristeva alongside Irigaray hints at the feminine character of her own 'sublation' of narcissism through love (TL, 32). And as Kristeva suggests in 'Stabat Mater', in the doctrine of Mary's bodily assumption into heaven this liberation of the mother from a solely maternal role points to a potential transformation of our relationship to the death drive, delineating the possibility of a *herethics* which owns yet transforms death (*mort*) through its assimilation into love (*amour*) as *a-mort* or undeath. Mary's defiance of death and assumption to the place of God, as daughter and bride, is indeed the theme of the 'Stabat Mater', whose music, Kristeva contends, 'swallows up the goddesses and removes their necessity' (TL, 263). While this move repeats the connection between the goddesses of love and death made in Freud's 'Three Caskets' essay, through the play on *amour* it gives priority to love rather than to death.[36]

Thus while Kristeva declares at one point in *Tales of Love* that she considers it a 'necessity' to maintain the authority of a severe father in the modern world, elsewhere in that work she suggests that the unsettling (*ébranlement*) of this severity, far from leaving us orphans, or inexorably psychotic, can reveal 'multiple and varied destinies' for the archaic and metaphorical paternity which she describes. Such destinies or directions, she contends, could be manifested by the clan as a whole, as well as by the priest or therapist (TL, 46). While she stresses here that the object of *Einfühlung* or identification is always metaphoric, Kristeva urges the analyst to accept this place of non-being, of the Imaginary Father, in the course of the therapeutic transference, and so act as a figure who can introduce difference rather than resemblance into the psyches of the doomed narcissi of the modern world. (In order to do this, however, she implies, as early as *Powers of Horror*, that s/he must play the part of the mystic. Indeed, given her remarks in 'Stabat Mater' and elsewhere, it seems that the analyst could only assume the position of an Imaginary Father if s/he had a relation to a certain maternal *jouissance*.) In this respect, Kristeva's gift of love escapes from the determinations of time as perpetual present (always the same) which were criticised by Heidegger in *Time and Being*. For in its evocation of an *avant* which is imagined and not originary, it simultaneously opens up what is yet to come, as an *à-venir* which escapes from the closed circle of gift as obligation or contractual exchange.

In her return to Freud's *Einfühlung*, therefore, I see Kristeva as tracing a philosophical as well as an analytical move. In the many echoes of Heidegger's project of thinking which are apparent in *Tales of Love*, Kristeva is according a new psychic specificity to that rethinking of giving which recent French thought has inherited (however ambivalently) from his works, as well as from Nietzsche. In the process, she seems to be pointing towards a necessary redefinition of philosophy as well as of psychoanalysis, in which thinking might recover its relationship to feeling; Emmanuel Levinas has similarly suggested that philosophy should be 'the wisdom of love at the service of love'.[37] But Kristeva is also, less directly, reopening those questions of time and law which, as Derrida has reminded us, are allied to the rule of the severe father as Saturn or Chronos. For her account of the gift locates it outside this sphere, in another space-time whose character is never clearly specified. As she begins *Tales of Love* by declaring: 'L'amour est le temps et l'espace où "je" se donne le droit d'être extraordinaire' (Love is the time and space where 'I' give myself the right to be extraordinary) (TL, 12).

Notes

I would like to thank John Peacocke and Monique Rhodes Monoc for the stimulus provided by several conversations on questions related to this essay. All quotations from *Tales of Love* (TL) are from the translation of Leon S. Roudiez (New York: Columbia University Press, 1987).

1 See for example, *Who Comes After the Subject?* (eds) Eduardo Cadava, Peter Connor and Jean-Luc Nancy (London: Routledge, 1991).
2 See Philippa Berry, 'Woman and Space according to Kristeva and Irigaray', in *Shadow of Spirit: Postmodernism and Religion* (eds) Philippa Berry and Andrew Wernick (London: Routledge, 1993), and 'The Burning Glass: Paradoxes of Feminist Revelation in Irigaray's *Speculum*', in *Engaging with Irigaray* (eds) Margaret Whitford, Naomi Schor and Carolyn Burke (London: Routledge, 1994).
3 Luce Irigaray, 'Belief Itself' ('La Croyance même'), in *Sexes and Genealogies*, trans. Gillian C. Gill (New York: Columbia University Press, 1993), pp. 23–53; and 'La Différence sexuelle', in *Ethique de la différence sexuelle* (Paris: Editions de Minuit, 1984), pp. 13–25. The first oral presentation of these essays is dated by Irigaray as 1980 and 1982 respectively; thus the elaboration of these ideas by Irigaray co-incided strikingly with Kristeva's work on *Histoires d'amour* (Paris: Denoel, 1983).
4 Julia Kristeva in conversation with Rosalind Coward, in *Desire*, ICA Documents (ed.) Lisa Appignanesi (London: ICA, 1984), p. 25.
5 See for example Edith Wyschogrod, *Saints and Postmodernism* (Chicago: University of Chicago Press, 1990); Berry and Wernick, *Shadow of Spirit*; *Derrida and Negative Theology* (eds) Harold Coward and Toby Foshay (New York: SUNY Press, 1992).
6 Julia Kristeva, *In The Beginning was Love*, trans. Arthur Goldhammer (New York: Columbia University Press, 1982), p. 21.
7 'Women's Time', in *The Kristeva Reader* (ed.) Toril Moi (Oxford: Basil Blackwell, 1986).
8 Maurice Blanchot, *Le Pas au-delà* (Paris: Gallimard, 1973), p. 8.
9 Martin Heidegger, *On Time and Being*, trans. Joan Stambaugh (New York: Harper and Row, 1972), p. 14.
10 Carl E. Schorske, 'Freud's Egyptian Dig', in *The New York Review of Books*, 27 May 1993, pp. 35–40. See also Schorske, *Fin-de-Siècle Vienna* (New York: Knopf, 1980), Chapter 4.
11 See for example Berry, 'The Burning Glass'; Lawrence Dickey, *Hegel, Religion, Economics and the Politics of Spirit* (Cambridge: Cambridge University Press, 1987); Ernest Benz, *Les Sources mystiques de la philosophie romantique allemande* (Paris: Vrin, 1968).
12 Friedrich Nietzsche, *Thus Spake Zarathustra*, trans. R.J. Hollingdale (Harmondsworth: Penguin Books, 1969), p. 40.
13 Jacques Derrida, *Glas*, trans. John P. Leavey, Jr and Richard Rand (Lincoln: University of Nebraska Press, 1986), p. 243.
14 Gerard L. Bruns, *Heidegger's Estrangements* (New Haven: Yale University Press, 1981), Chapter 2.

15 Heidegger, *On Time and Being*, p. 6.
16 Significantly, Derrida articulated this critique with reference to the early Heideggerian term of *Bestimmung*, whose unstable function in *Being and Time* is apparent in Heidegger's later use of *Stimmung* or moodedness. Rodolphe Gasché, in 'Floundering in Determination', in *Commemorations: Reading Heidegger* (ed.) John Sallis (Bloomington: Indiana University Press, 1993), stresses the 'floundering' or 'incoherence' of *Stimmung* (and hence of *Bestimmung*) in Heidegger's thought:

> If thought flounders when we try to come to grips with determination, it is because the very necessity of formulating an originary synthesis such as *Stimmung*, for instance, cannot avoid producing a proliferation of precisely what has to be derived – a plurality of not only improper but also sharply different notions of determination . . . different because of tone, style, tense, and, in particular, levels of argumentation.
>
> (p. 17)

17 Jacques Derrida, *Given Time I*, trans. Peggy Kamuf (Chicago: University of Chicago Press, 1992).
18 Julia Kristeva, *Powers of Horror*, trans. Leon S. Roudiez (New York: Columbia University Press, 1982), p. 209.
19 In *Totem and Taboo*, trans. James Strachey (London: Routledge and Kegan Paul, 1950), Freud describes the emergence of primitive religious belief as a submission to the death drive (or Necessity) which simultaneously denies it, and thereby changes its meaning (p. 93).
20 In 'The Theme of the Three Caskets' (1913), Freud associated the mother with the first of the three Fates (or Moirae), Clotho, and distinguished her from Atropos, the death goddess who cuts the thread of life, whom he rather associated with Mother Earth. But in her discussion of Freud's own fantasies and dreams, Sarah Kofman has shown how his mother was fused with ideas of fate and necessity:

> far from being a representation of untrammeled spontaneity, she stands for law and necessity: of time, Death, *difference*. A figure of necessity, Parca, Moira, or Ananke, she is the one who silently teaches her child to resign himself to the inevitable, unacceptable, and stupefying necessity of Death.
> (*The Enigma of Woman: Women in Freud's Writings*, trans. Catherine Porter Ithaca: Cornell University Press, 1980, p. 74

The mother as Moira, Kofman contends, teaches that 'every gift, every share of life, has to be paid back, that the gift of life is always simultaneously a gift of death' (p. 75).
21 Freud, *Totem and Taboo* p. 153.
22 Martin Heidegger, 'Moira', in *Early Greek Thinking*, trans. David Farrell Krell and Frank A. Capuzzi (New York: Harper and Row, 1975), pp. 79–101. The implications of this essay are very interestingly drawn out by Gillian Rose in *Dialectic of Nihilism* (Oxford: Blackwell, 1984), p. 75.
23 See Derrida, *Glas*.
24 Sigmund Freud, *The Ego and the Id*, trans. Joan Riviere (London: Hogarth Press, 1961), pp. 34–6.
25 Gayatri Spivak, 'Glas-Piece: A Compte Rendu', in *Diacritics* 7(3) (September 1977), pp. 22–43.
26 Derrida, *Given Time I*, pp. 22–3.
27 Kristeva, *Powers of Horror*, p. 59.

28 Julia Kristeva, 'Stabat Mater', in *The Kristeva Reader* (ed.) Toril Moi (Oxford: Blackwell, 1986), p. 162.
29 Genesis 28: 18.
30 Jacques Derrida, 'Architetture ove il desiderio può abotare', *Domus* 20 (1986); this quotation is translated in Mark Taylor, *Disfiguring* (Chicago: University of Chicago Press, 1992), p. 266.
31 G. Rachel Levy, *The Gate of Horn* (London: Faber and Faber, 1948).
32 Jacques Derrida, *Spurs: Nietzsche's Styles* (Chicago: University of Chicago Press, 1978).
33 Julia Kristeva, 'Motherhood According to Bellini', in *Desire in Language*, trans. Leon S. Roudiez *et al.* (Oxford: Blackwell, 1980), p. 247.
34 Julia Kristeva, 'Giotto's Joy', in *Desire in Language*, p. 225.
35 See Berry, 'The Burning Glass'.
36 Freud, 'The Theme of the Three Caskets', in *The Standard Edition of the Complete Psychological Works*, trans. James Strachey, XII (1911–13) (London: Hogarth Press, 1958), pp. 289–302.
37 Emmanuel Levinas, *Otherwise than Being or Beyond Essence*, trans. Alphonso Lingis (Dordrecht: Kluwer, 1991), p. 162.

14

LUCE IRIGARAY

Divine spirit and feminine space

Alison Ainley

A burning glass is the soul (*l'ame*) who in her cave joins with the
source of light to set everything ablaze that approaches her
hearth . . .

(Irigaray[1])

To think about otherness, or relations with the other, at the interface between
theology, philosophy and feminist theory may have the incendiary effect
Luce Irigaray suggests in the above quote. By the illumination of such a
blaze it might be possible to look at the issues in a different light, particularly
when questions about sexual difference intersect with questions concerning
divine alterity.

There is no doubt about the centrality of feminist thinking to Irigaray's
work. At the beginning of her 1984 book *The Ethics of Sexual Difference*,[2] she
states her belief that sexual difference is

> one of the major philosophical issues, if not the issue, of our age.
> According to Heidegger, each age has one issue to think through . . .
> sexual difference is probably the issue in our time which could be
> our 'salvation', if we thought it through.

Attending to this issue could herald 'the production of a new age of thought,
art, poetry and language: the creation of a new *poetics*'.[3] But, she suggests,
woman has occupied, literally and symbolically, the role of mirror for the
masculine subject, and has become reflexively 'the other'. Being trapped in
the role of reflecting 'the same' of the Western intellectual tradition – in a flat-
tened and constricting fashion – results in the impoverishment of contemporary forms of living, for both sexes. The otherness with which woman
is associated is either as a secondary complement, the ostensibly equal but
devalued half which makes up an illusory whole; or as negative, absent black

hole, Freud's mysterious dark continent or unknowable an-Arche. Woman as Other is not only, as Simone de Beauvoir suggested in *The Second Sex*,[4] a subjectivity denied its autonomy and freedom, but also through a symbolic alignment with negativity, chaos and abyssal darkness, an ex-centric excess 'other' even to otherness. Irigaray begins to think through the site of subjectivity opened by such ambivalence, suggesting a feminine philosophy of the subject functioning as 'other' to the onto-theological tradition which has resulted in repressive and inappropriate formations of subjectivity and restrictive modes of thought. To open up such otherness might allow for more fertile ethical and cultural fulfilment. Irigaray's characterisation of fulfilment or flourishing (*s'epanouir*) 'corresponds to the three translations for the etymology of the verb "to be" that Heidegger gives: "to live, to emerge, to linger or endure." It means to accomplish one's form.'[5]

Many feminist writers of recent years have dissected the remains of patriarchal culture, picking amongst the ruins for evidence of the obscure – or not so obscure – mechanisms of its economies. To aid this effort it has been necessary to borrow or steal the tools most appropriate for critical exploration. Irigaray's image of the *speculum* is most apposite in this respect, bringing together speculative philosophical investigation with meticulous explorations of the materiality of the body and its 'hidden' resources, and casting this double reflection back with the dark illumination of her feminist perspective. The imagery of the interior of the cave (Plato's originary philosophical space), the recesses of the body and the feminine gender of the soul (*l'ame*) provide her with poetic metaphors which allow her to rethink the oppositional split between, for example, carnal body and sacred spirit (and particularly when woman is equated with the body and man with spirit). Irigaray's project extends ambitiously over the Western intellectual tradition, from the pre-Socratic thinkers onwards through the diverse and complex strands of its historical legacy, and demands nothing less than 'a revolution in thought and ethics' for its fulfilment.

> In order to make it possible to think through, and live, this difference, we must re-consider the whole problematic of space and time.
>
> In the beginning there was space and the creation of space, as is said in all theogonies. The gods, God, create space. And time is there, more or less in the service of space. Philosophy then confirms the task of the gods or God. Time becomes the *interiority* of the subject and space its *exteriority* (as developed by Kant in the *Critique of Pure Reason*). The subject, the master of time, becomes the axis of the world's ordering, with its something beyond the moment and eternity: God.[6]

Here she suggests a different approach to the phenomenological structures which open the world and provide its grounding. In keeping with any attempt to explore the possibilities and consequences of anti-foundational thinking, the theological issues which press at the philosophical interface with epistemology, ontology and metaphysics must also come under consideration. It is not surprising that many feminists have tended to emphasise the continuity between metaphysical foundationalism and the tradition of a (male) monotheistic God who represents the supreme principle – Truth, Light, Good. The continuity established – by who knows what historical accident or biological chance – between singularity and masculinity is often described as 'phallo-logo-centrism' or 'the metaphysics of presence'.[7] The particular structuring of thought created and perpetuated by eliding these concepts together in order to provide an apparently seamless and coherent narrative is characterised by Irigaray as 'isomorphism' – the shape of thought and the shape of perceived body identity (morphology) are somehow made acceptably congruent. To suggest such an economy is historically contingent or has only local application is part of the questioning of meta-narratives to which feminist theory brings its own perspective. In this way, Irigaray suggests that identity has been constructed as masculine, using the horizon of the divine or infinite in the service of making a genre for men.

> Man has been the subject of discourse, whether in theory, morality or politics. And the gender of God, the guardian of every subject and every discourse, is always masculine and paternal, in the West.[8]

> Man is able to exist because God helps him to define his gender (genre), helps him orient his finiteness by reference to infinity. . . . In order to become, it is necessary to have a gender or an essence (consequently a sexuate essence) as horizon. Otherwise, becoming remains partial and subject to the subject.[9]

An awareness of the nature of the horizons or limits against which self-definition takes place is necessary so that women can begin to compensate for the lack of a subjectivity of their own. But another means of approaching otherness needs to be sought. To negotiate the symbolisation of the feminine or the figure of the mother as threatening destruction, the woman who 'threatens by what she lacks', 'a relation with the divine, death, the social and cosmic order'[10] needs to be effected for and by women. The means by which identity has been previously achieved has been at the expense of the construction of woman as negative, silent, without a place. The established relations between individuals, or between an individual and his God; the 'sense of belonging' which is the articulation of kinship or genre as ostensibly neutral, has been articulated, Irigaray suggests, according to a masculine logic. 'What poses problems in reality turns out to be justified by a logic that has already ordered reality as such. Nothing escapes the circularity of this law'.[11] Such an organisation guarantees its continuity by exclusion or suppression of that which

Irigaray identifies symbolically as 'the feminine'. In her essay 'Women, the Sacred and Money',[12] she draws upon the work of René Girard to show the sacrificial nature of many religious practices, the violence at the heart of the sacred which demands a cathartic immolation, consuming or cleansing to perpetuate a dominant order. Whether this is rite and ritual pertaining to social order, or the process of tension, discharge and return to homeostasis within the organism as described by Freud, the economy of sacrifice demands the symbolic consumption or degradation of nature or the materiality of the body. The consequences of figuring the symbolic economy in this way may leave women as victims or as paralysed and excluded from participation and ceremony.[13]

The methodological approach which permits this analysis is part of an historical account of religion which shows how it is implicated in social power relations. The critical resources of anthropology, sociology and history engage sceptically with religion as a material phenomenon to bring it under the epistemological microscope of reason. Religion is then seen simply (and somewhat reductively) as 'man-made'. Such analysis does, however, provide the means to question the alignment between masculinity and the transcendent. How did this alignment come to dominate ways of thinking so comprehensively in the West? If God is the concept which precedes all conceptualisation, why is the imagery of Fatherhood conflated with the singular, unique status of the infinite, the genre and horizon of human life as such?

The initial promise of humanism to question, if not unravel, such patterns of thought is not fully kept if the framework of 'masculine logic' remains untouched. From a feminist perspective, it might be as well to match scepticism about the original meta-narrative with scepticism about what replaces it. The thinking of the transcendent as material immanence can be seen, *pace* Nietzsche, as an attempt to find a solution to the 'failure' of divine otherness to remain absolutely other. The transvaluation of ethics presents an explanation of religion as a human phenomenon while substituting the self in the place of the divine. But the Promethean self is still masculine, the ostensibly 'human' neutralising the extent to which it is still complicit with the old order it came to replace. The collapse of the infinite into the finite by reason's critique could be seen as an act of appropriation to yet another manifestation of the machinery of a certain (masculine) epistemological logic.

The account which Feuerbach[14] gives of God as the projection of perfection, an abstraction into a place where aspirations are accomplished, illustrates the humanistic explanation of religious discourse in terms of the fulfilment of human need. The expansion of the will to eternal dimensions can then act as a narcissistic mirror for the (masculine) subject. Feuerbach is unusual in exploring the consequences of this process for sexuality and relations between the sexes. His account of the relations between humans, God, Son and Holy Spirit explicitly suggests a set of mediations between man and divine at the expense of any specific place for the feminine, which is 'veiled out'.[15] The only role for the feminine is that of a maternal function which is severely limited, constrained and given merely a supporting role. If religion is 'a relation based on the affections, which until now has sought its truth in a fantastic reflection of reality', a proper place for the feminine must be created. For Feuerbach, 'sex love assumes the material realisation of this relation',[16] and it is through the full recognition of this dual (sexual) relation that religion can come to its highest realisation, in keeping with the etymology of the word *religare* (Lat.); a bond.

As Marx pointed out, however, Feuerbach produces an essentialised, ahistorical notion of what it is to be human.[17] Feuerbach wants the sensuous (and sexed) human form, but abstracts an idealised content to produce a human essence. Although Irigaray might sympathise with Feuerbach's critique, she seeks a theoretical account of the self which can allow for historical and unconscious determinations. Psychoanalysis casts doubt on human reason or even the social/historical structures of power as foundational substitutes, suggesting that 'the rational and the real' may be constructions of the individual or social imaginary, and just as prey to delusions and paranoia. The illumination of Enlightenment rationality is darkened once again by the shadows of the unconscious.

The 'dark' side of Freud which Lacan seizes upon in his 'rereading' of Freudian texts[18] allows him to rewrite the scientific aspects of the rational will and biological drives into an 'other' dimension, a mysterious heteronomy which is already fractured by (linguistic) excess. The irreducibility of such otherness generates desire and difference, but remains ineradicably *in absentia*. Lacan playfully compares his Other with God, but resists identifying it with 'the good old God of all times': he refuses to accept wholly 'the myth of the death of God', but does not intend to return to the theologically orthodox either. God as complete absence would be, for him, a repetition or mirror image of God as full presence. Rather, for Lacan, 'God is not dead but unconscious'.[19] This formulation might sound like an attempt to embody the divine in the physical being of the subject, except the divine cannot be simply reducible to the materiality of the body. As Lacan puts it, memorably:

> What was tried at the end of the last century, at the time of Freud, by
> all kinds of worthy people in the circle of Charcot and the rest, was
> an attempt to reduce the mystical to questions of fucking. If you
> look carefully, that is not what it's all about.[20]

The endless displacements of the unconscious, neither wholly biological nor wholly linguistic; a site of slippage of meanings which remains material and yet unrepresentable; replaces or displaces both the all-knowing omnipotent God and the reflexive self-conscious, self-present subject. The absent Other is always something more, not all or not at all, the 'third party'[21] which undoes dualisms, the difference of difference. And Lacan goes further, and plays upon the symbolic equation between the Other and the Woman as ideal construct or as fluid plurality – both forming a projection for the masculine self. 'And why not interpret one face of the Other, the God face, as supported by feminine jouissance?'[22]

Irigaray might share some sympathy with this thinking of the divine as secular transcendence, but as a dissenting daughter from the Lacanian orthodoxy, she also articulates her feminist questions about this schema. For example, what suggests this dark otherness is symbolically parallel with the feminine? Is such a parallel useful or dangerous for women? If the political agenda of these questions is a well-charted territory by now, it still does not lessen their importance. It is true that Irigaray remains within this particular economy of thought and as such is not absolved from a certain philosophical thinking of 'the same'. From a theological perspective which seeks to establish utter, unthinkable alterity as an excess even to the circuits of immanent-transcendent otherness, she is caught back in an almost exact repetition of the modernist narrative of subjectivist politics – the search for emancipation. But her feminist perspective demands that the otherness she has gestured towards has to be interrogated in terms of questions of sex and gender. To suggest a version of Lacan's plural and heteronomous immanent-transcendent otherness should really leave its possibilities necessarily indeterminate. To presume to speak or represent 'on behalf of' is already to assume a questionable authority. What legitimates this voice after all? Perhaps Irigaray goes too far in sketching in her feminist version of its instantiation. At times she seems to want to stress that it is not simply the substitution of a male God by a female Goddess that she is seeking: 'I am far from suggesting that today we must once again deify ourselves as did our ancestors with their animal totems, that we have to regress to siren goddesses, who fight against men Gods.'[23] In other places, however, it seems that she is urging the deification of a feminine future when she writes, for example: 'A *female* god is still to come.'[24]

However, the event of this otherness may still open the thresholds of the body, the ethically unexpected, new transitions into different ways of life. Perhaps parallels could be drawn with Heidegger's revealing-concealing light of Being at this point, to indicate the ways in which recent anti-humanist thinking rejoins or deepens the historically earlier theological forays into thinking God or the divine in this fashion. Irigaray's often revelatory poetic language, which conveys a sense of sacred song or dancing syntax, evokes Heidegger's later writing. Her imagery of angels and birds suggests how they can act as mediating forces through the element of air and the space of breath, voice and song, finding new configurations of space.

> As if the angel were a representation of sexuality that has never been incarnated. A light, divine gesture (or tale) of flesh that has not acted or flourished. . . . These swift angelic messengers, who

transgress all enclosures in their speed, tell of the passage between the
envelope of God and that of the world as micro- or macrocosm . . .
they represent and tell of another incarnation, another parousia of
the body.[25]

For Irigaray, religious discourse also presents a unique opportunity to examine the price paid in submitting to the symbolic order, the cost of forging an
identity. As part of the networks of social practice, religious discourse characterises the point of submission as belonging to the celebration of orthodoxy
and constraint. But in terms of ecstatic experience, the point at which order
and hierarchy are challenged by love, abandonment, testimony and revelation, a force also seems to threaten such order and constraint. Julia Kristeva
describes this moment in the following way.

> The sacrifice of one's identity in the delight of being swept away by
> passion and so not to exist . . . to be for the other, to be lost, to be
> transformed. A risk of death which is also a chance of life.[26]

Descriptions of the experiences of mystic saints might correspond to this characterisation of the loss of identity as transformative. Such experiences seem
to be reconscripted and recoded to ensure they are kept under control, safely
occupying a position preordained by existing cultural symbolism. 'The love
of God has often been a haven for women. They are the guardians of the religious tradition. Certain women mystics have been among those rare women
to achieve social influence, notably in politics.'[27] It is 'uniquely . . . a place in
the history of the West in which woman speaks and acts so publicly . . .
where the poorest in science and the most ignorant were the most eloquent,
the richest in revelations'.[28]

 The experiences of revelation lie at the limit edge of meaning or at the point
where meaning is all but broken or split apart; where liminal equivocation
creates a potential residue or excess. Such excess, persistently escaping codification, might create potential transformations of existing practices. In other
words, by attending to 'deviant' or 'ex-centric' practices or experiences, the
orthodoxy of normal practice is opened for scrutiny, as is the *process* by which
dominant practices come to occupy apparently self-evident status. From a
feminist perspective, to address this territory is to look aslant at the constitution of canons and ways of knowing which comprise, for example, philosophy
and theology. In Irigaray's multifaceted exploration of 'La Mysterique' (the
central chapter in *Speculum of the Other Woman*) she not only foregrounds the
feminine elements of mysticism, hysteria and mystery in one semantically
condensed term, but also suggests a dark, obscure tradition of an alternative
story about knowledge which might present spaces for women to create
their own voice(s): speaking (as) woman (*parler femme*). In this sense
her work is not only an interrogation of the exclusive constrictions of onto-

theology but an attempt to develop a notion of what a feminine genre or gender might mean – the creation of a still as yet hypothetical space for women to become.

> We women, sexed according to our gender, lack a God to share, a word to share and to become. Defined as the often dark, even occult mother-substance of the word of men, we are in need of our *subject*, our *substantive*, our *word*, our *predicates*; our elementary sentence, our basic rhythm, our morphological identity, our generic incarnation. To be the term of the other is nothing enviable. It paralyses us in our becoming. As divinity of and for man, we are deprived of our own ends and means. It is essential that we become gods *for ourselves* so that we can be divine for the other, not idols, fetishes, symbols that have already been outlined or determined.[29]

One way in which Irigaray begins to suggest the articulation of the excluded otherness is to focus on a 'heretical' notion within Lacanian orthodoxy; that of a specific form to feminine pleasure, a *jouissance* uniquely feminine. According to Lacan's economy of desire, pleasure can only be thought or conceptualised within the (masculine) terms of the Symbolic. The precondition for the appearance of identity structured in social and cultural terms is the overcoming of diffuse, heterogeneous pleasure, an indeterminate fluidity which is symbolically feminine. This experiential pleasure is 'elsewhere' to the linguistic structures which shape meaning as communicative sense. Lacan denies that it can be represented at all, since this would suggest an alternative symbolic order, almost a parallel universe. If feminine pleasure is allowed to exist at all, it is, as Lacan implies in 'God and the Jouissance of (the) Woman', only as silent, excessive bliss, a transport of joy glimpsed on the transfixed face of Bernini's statue of St Theresa in Rome. This pleasure is for Lacan 'beyond the phallus',[30] beyond communication. But, as Irigaray suggests, this definition of pleasure is also a way of silencing the woman and retaining mastery. 'Pleasure without pleasure; the shock of a remainder of silent body matter that shakes her in the interstices, but of which she remains ignorant. 'Saying' nothing of this pleasure, after all, thus not enjoying it.'[31]

Irigaray's female mystics experience irradiation by the flames of the divine, the madness which 'slips away unseen from the light of reason' into the soul's night to be illuminated by a different blaze of light. The mystic is, in St Theresa's words, a 'burning glass' which refracts the loss of subjectivity in a luminous fluidity.

> Fires flare up in the inexhaustible abundance of her underground source and is matched with opposing but congruent flood which sweeps over the 'I' in an excess of excess. Yet, burning, flowing along in a wild spate of waters, yearning for even greater abandon,

the 'I' is empty still, ever more empty, opening wide in a rapture of soul.[32]

The hysterical mimicry of subjectivity – 'subjectivity undone by being over-done'[33] as Toril Moi puts it, might act as a displacement and subversion at the very heart of the onto-theological tradition, and provide a provisional articulation of a language for the feminine. The experience of fluidity, the poetic/prophetic revelatory form is described by Irigaray as 'the double syntax', overplaying 'the masquerade of femininity' to allow women to 'appear' or to speak.

> [W]hat a feminine syntax might be is not simple or easy to state, because in that 'syntax' there would no longer be either subject or object, 'oneness' would no longer be privileged, there would no longer be proper meanings, proper names, 'proper' attributes. . . . Instead, that syntax would involve nearness, proximity, but such an extreme form that it would preclude any distinction of identities, any establishment of ownership, thus any form of appropriation.[34]

It might be objected that Irigaray trusts too much to the established circuits of linguistic meaning, and that it is not clear that it is wholly by conventional systems of representation that such changes could be achieved. It often appears that it is simply by another aspect of representation, 'another writing',[35] that Irigaray thinks the feminine genre could be created. How-ever, the body cannot simply be 'written into being' if writing is a neutral or even polysexual medium, since Irigaray's project requires the acknowledge-ment of the specificity of women. In this respect, her deployment of the meta-phoric fluidity and indeterminate plurality of the feminine sex does provide a poetic rendering or symbolic articulation in her work, through which to sug-gest changes to the existing order.[36] Conversely, Irigaray is not suggesting that the fluid syntax of mystical experience is an essentialist language of the female body. The creation of a feminine gender/genre is not the uncovering of a hidden 'essence' of Woman but an active construction or creation, with the emphasis on becoming rather than Being.

So far it is clear that Irigaray's analysis of onto-theology takes place from a materialist perspective. Her references to Feuerbach and Heidegger suggest the revising of religion from within, to reconstruct a 'sensible trans-cendental'[37] – so that the horizon of self-perfecting can be opened up for women. 'Without the possibility that God might be made flesh as a woman, through the mother and the daughter, and in their relationships . . . there can be no possibility of changing.'[38] To allow speaking (as) woman to be incarnated requires a version of the incarnation in the feminine. As Irigaray says: 'Our theological tradition presents some difficulty as far as God in the feminine gender is concerned. There is no woman god, no female trinity:

mother, daughter, spirit.'[39] Does this approach restrict the area of enquiry to a politics of the subject? As we have seen, if God is defined as the perfecting horizon or limit of human self-transcendence, then it seems God is no more than a projection of humanity and therefore defined within the terms of what it is possible to think. Nevertheless, without some form of cultural and historical resources (a *genealogy*) it is difficult to envisage a genre for feminine subjectivity being able to come into existence. The requirements of such a genre must include the images which allow self-representation, separation and articulation for the subjects who presently lack such resources. If such a proposal simply suggests a repetition of the existing circuits of meaning, drawing its apparent innovations from the cultural residues which have been devalued or overlooked in the past, it may seem to be restricted within the onto-theological constrictions it was seeking to circumvent.

Equally, to suggest the origin or condition of subjectivity and sexuality must be by definition wholly outside or beyond the circuits of conceptualisation is once again to raise questions about the nature and approachability of such otherness. It may be conceded that only an absolutely transcendent God could be other enough to provide the unconditional by which phenomenology and other forms of philosophical-foundational thinking can function. The revelatory status of a divine origin circumvents the epistemological problems of self-reflexive consciousness (which must know itself before it knows otherness or else rely on otherness to found it). But the relational networks by which a divine origin is with or within the world still need to be thought. The encounter with otherness still throws up disconcerting questions. How is it actualised? By whom? These questions do not fade away simply by nominating a priori unconditionals which are ethical in and of themselves. The conditions under which values are instantiated have perhaps not yet been made explicit enough to trust an unknown absolute to be ethical for us. That the absolute condition for all subjective politics is alterity, absolutely other, may be granted, but does not preclude the work of practical change, which strives to recast the relations to and about otherness into more ethical terms.

In an echo of Heidegger, Irigaray's acknowledgement that 'God alone can save us, make us safe . . . inspire our projects'[40] may be her awareness of a divine alterity. But in order to bring about a space for women to become, to relate to themselves, to others and even to God it is necessary to imagine, provocatively, what God 'in the feminine gender' might be.

> God in the feminine gender . . . an other we still have to make actual, as a region of life, strength, imagination, creation, which exists both within and beyond, as our possibility of a present and future.
>
> Is not God the name and the place that holds the promise of a new chapter in history and also denies that this could happen? Still invisible? To be incarnated? Archi-ancient and forever future.[41]

Notes

1 Luce Irigaray, *Speculum of the Other Woman*, Ithaca, Cornell University Press, 1985, tr. G. Gill (*Speculum de l'autre femme*, Paris, Minuit, 1974), p. 197.

2 Luce Irigaray, *The Ethics of Sexual Difference*, London, Athlone Press, 1993, tr. C. Burke and G. Gill (*Ethique de la différence sexuelle*, Paris, Minuit, 1984).

3 Irigaray, *Ethics*, p. 5.

4 Simone de Beauvoir, *The Second Sex*, Harmondsworth, Penguin, 1984, tr. H.M. Parshley (*Le Deuxième Sexe*, Paris, Minuit, 1949).

5 Martin Heidegger, *An Introduction to Metaphysics*, New Haven and London, Yale University Press, 1959, tr. R. Mannheim, p. 72. Cited in Luce Irigaray, *Sexes and Genealogies*, New York, Columbia University Press, 1993, tr. G. Gill (*Sexes et parentes*, Paris, Minuit, 1987), fn. 4, p. 66.

6 Irigaray, *Ethics*, p. 7.

7 Jacques Derrida's name is perhaps most familiarly associated with these terms. See for example Jacques Derrida, *Eperons/Spurs, the Styles of Nietzsche*, Chicago, University of Chicago Press, 1978, tr. B. Harlow (bilingual text).

8 Irigaray, *Ethics*, p. 6.

9 Irigaray, *Sexes*, p. 61.

10 Irigaray, *Ethics*, p. 9.

11 Luce Irigaray, *This Sex Which is Not One*, New York, Cornell University Press, 1985, tr. C. Porter and C. Burke (*Ce sexe qui n'est pas un*, Paris, Minuit, 1974), p. 88.

12 Luce Irigaray, 'Women, the Sacred and Money' in *Sexes*, pp. 73–88.

13 But, Irigaray suggests, this destructive circuit is only sustained if it is *sacrifice* rather than *sharing* which is given priority. The future of a 'fertile and amorous exchange' for the sexes may be articulated if the debt owed to otherness can be acknowledged.

14 Ludwig Feuerbach, *The Essence of Christianity*, New York, Harper Torch Books, 1957, tr. George Elliot, first published 1841. Irigaray refers the reader to Feuerbach for an exact understanding of her essay 'Divine Women' in *Sexes*, fn. 3, p. 61.

15 Ibid., p. 73.

16 Ibid., p. 92.

17 Karl Marx, *Theses on Feuerbach*, in David McLellan (ed.), *Karl Marx: Selections*, Oxford, Oxford University Press, 1988.

18 See Jacques Lacan, *Ecrits: A Selection*, London, Tavistock, 1977, tr. A. Sheridan, and *The Seminar of Jacques Lacan Book II: The Ego in Freud's Theory and in the Technique of Psychoanalysis 1954–55*, ed. Jacques-Alain Miller, Cambridge, Cambridge University Press, 1988, tr. S. Tomaselli.

19 Jacques Lacan, *Four Fundamental Concepts of Psychoanalysis*, Harmondsworth, Penguin, 1979, tr. A. Sheridan, p. 59.

20 Jacques Lacan, 'God and the Jouissance of (The) Woman', in Juliet Mitchell and Jacqueline Rose (eds), *Feminine Sexuality, Jacques Lacan and the Ecole freudienne*, London, Macmillan, 1982, p. 147.

21 Ibid., p. 139. For further discussion of these issues see Edith Wyschogrod *et al.* (eds), *Lacan and Theological Discourse*, New York, SUNY Press, 1989.

22 Ibid., p. 147.

23 Irigaray, *Sexes*, p. 60.

24 Ibid., p. 67.

25 Irigaray, *Ethics*, p. 16.

26 Julia Kristeva, *Tales of Love*, New York, Columbia University Press, 1987, tr. L. Roudiez (*Histoires de l'amour*, Paris, Editions Denoel, 1983), p. 6.

27 Irigaray, *Sexes*, p. 93.

28 Irigaray, *Speculum*, p. 192.

29 Irigaray, *Sexes*, p. 71.
30 Lacan, 'God and the Jouissance', p. 145. Lacan uses the example of St Theresa for his account of feminine *jouissance*, but as Irigaray ironically comments: 'In Rome? So far away? To look? At a statue? Of a saint? Sculpted by a man? What pleasure are we talking about? Whose pleasure?' *This Sex*, p. 91.
31 Irigaray, *This Sex*, p. 96.
32 Irigaray, *Speculum*, p. 195.
33 Toril Moi, *Sexual/Textual Politics*, London, Methuen, 1985, p. 137.
34 Irigaray, *This Sex*, p. 134.
35 Ibid.
36 See for example Irigaray's references to the two lips or *le mucu* (mucous), *passim*, metaphoric renderings of feminine thresholds of the body which, as 'neither one thing or another' capture the linguistic indeterminancy of a possible feminine syntax.
37 See Margaret Whitford, *Luce Irigaray: Philosophy in the Feminine*, London, Routledge, 1991, p. 154.
38 Irigaray, *Sexes*, p. 71.
39 Ibid., p. 62. See also Leonardo Boff, *The Maternal Face of God: The Feminine and its Religious Expressions*, London, Collins/Flame, 1989, and Janet Martin Soskice, 'Trinity and the Feminine Other', *Catholic Theological Association of Great Britain*, 1–4 September 1993.
40 Irigaray, *Sexes*, p. 67.
41 Ibid., p. 72.

15

JEAN BAUDRILLARD

Seducing God

Andrew Wernick

It was the year when they finally immanentised the Eschaton.
(Robert Shea and Robert Anton Wilson, *Illuminatus!* Trilogy
(1975: 7))

Like every generation that preceded us, we have been endowed
with a *weak* Messianic power.
(Walter Benjamin. 'Theses on the Philosophy of History'
(1969: 254))

In the opening pages of *Fatal Strategies* (1990a: 14–16) Baudrillard cites with
approval the following passage from Canetti:

> A painful thought: past a certain point, history has not been real.
> Without realising it, the whole human race seems to have suddenly
> left reality behind. Everything that is supposed to have happened
> since then would no longer be true, but we wouldn't be able to realise
> it. Our task and our duty would now be to uncover this point, and
> until we did we would have to persist in our present destruction.

Baudrillard evidently endorses this scenario. He too posits the present as an
epoch in which the real, as the referent of any representation, has disappeared. But, he remarks, 'Canetti's wish is a pious one, even if his hypothesis
is radical. The point he refers to is by definition impossible to find, for if we
could grasp it, time would be given back to us.'

The void into which we have fallen is epistemological as well as political.
The classical categories of understanding founder in a world in which effects
precede causes and the territory comes after the map. Perhaps, indeed, the
confounding is originary, and all that has happened in the fateful but unloca-
table rupture to which Canetti refers is the final dissipation of the Enlightenment illusions (about subject/object, cause/effect, rational praxis, etc.) that
were holding the void at bay. Nor can we hope to redeem things through

some future radical intervention, that is, by effecting 'a deceleration which would allow us to come back into history, the real, the social'. For 'beyond this point there are only inconsequential events (and inconsequential theories), precisely because they absorb their sense into themselves. They reflect nothing, presage nothing' (Baudrillard 1990a: 16–17). From a redemptive standpoint the diagnosis is even bleaker than in the earlier laments of the Frankfurt School, whose depoliticised echo Baudrillard is sometimes taken to be.[1] The founding project of social emancipation has not merely been deferred, but rendered unthinkable. Thus for Baudrillard there is no *aufhebung* along the way of contemporary critique, only deepening nihilism; no great refusal, no successor to the proletariat, no aesthetic dimension, indeed no transcendentalist element or force surviving in the culture, and only the simulation of a political sphere within which corrective strategies – even if conceivable – could (not) be deployed. Wisdom, today, begins with recognising that the stasis of an ever-developing capitalism is forever where we are.

And yet a kind of light flickers behind the darkness of this closed horizon. For in that very same text, somewhat like the ecstatically melancholic Pascal wagering on God, Baudrillard invokes the possibility that 'fatal strategies' – and chief among them, his own brand of mimetically excessive 'ironic theory' – might yet provide a salvific opening. Elsewhere (1990b: 91) he speaks of such theory as offering 'a challenge to the powers of the world, including the gods', to appear once more. Of course, this reappearance is not to be taken literally, and the parallel with Pascal cannot be pressed too far. The intent of Baudrillard's 'theory', insofar as it can be plausibly deciphered, is not to evoke the divine in the form of a real presence, as incarnation, miracle or the personal answer to a prayer, but to conjure up a metaphorical power. Nor, at the same time, is the otherness Baudrillard would provoke into being pitched in an unreachable beyond. For – at least on his sociological side (the side that has assimilated Bataille's notions of symbolic exchange, ritual violence and the sacred) – this power, or powers, which theory would seduce, would challenge into existence, derives from alterities which, however secretive and however invisible through a traditional 'materialist' grid, are ontologically in and of the world. There is a crucial difference, finally, between the bad infinities which provoke Pascal and Baudrillard to throw their respective dice. The ground of Baudrillard's metaphysical anguish is not the desert of infinite space, and the designification of the individual subject it seems to presage. It is the desert of the social, that black hole of the life-world, into which the post-God Western transcendentals of society, history and above all, the Revolution, have, in the obscene, obese, ecstatic and falser than false culture of late capitalism, irretrievably vanished.

Baudrillard situates himself, in fact, rather like Nietzsche's madman in the marketplace. He perversely seeks – or seeks to seduce – that which he names as 'God' but knows, and declares, to be dead. But Baudrillard's reprise of the

Nietzschean problematic is not a simple repetition. In contemporary ideological conditions the lost object of a defunct rhetoric (and thwarted desire)
is not the traditional deity, but that deity's equally metaphysical and equally
ressentiment-charged successor. Baudrillard's (updated) preoccupation, in
short, is with a second death of God, or rather – it amounts to the same thing
– with the death of a second deity: 'God' secularised and decoded, projected
into the idealised space of the human subject (individual and collective), and
apprehended as a kind of Good Absolute, immanent in the species. After
Hegel, classical social and political theory conceived this figure in a diversity
of related forms – from Comte's Humanity, Feuerbach's Man, Marx's 'social
humanity, or human society', to Durkheim's Society. Today, though cultu-
rally and conceptually undermined, it lingers on: both as a casual hypostasis
of the social (or national), and – more radically – in the often confounded
registers of populism, socialism, existentialism and New Ageism wherein is
expressed that recurrent craving for *communitas* which has hovered close to
the sometimes millenarian surface of every outbreak of 'movement' consciousness in the advanced industrial world.

For those to whom Nietzsche's parable of the ultimate man still speaks, and
who have been touched, in the second half of the twentieth century, by both
the eruption and the eclipse of a Promethean will to world-redemption (the
pseudo-apocalypse of 'the Sixties'), Baudrillard's demolition of these secular-
humanist idols has a special significance. It engages the 'weak messianic
power' (Benjamin) of the generation to which Baudrillard speaks and (at
least by adoption) belongs.[2] As such, its interest lies not only in its trajectory,
its ideological and theoretical line of flight: *away* from Marx, Freud, French
Structuralism and a sympathy for revolutionary politics. It also lies in the
positions through which that trajectory takes him, positions which in the
very extremity of what they propose stake out an entire field within the
barely explored *topos* of irreligious religiosity that marks the post-secular as
precisely that.

The absconding of the humanist deity

From *Système des objets* to *La Seduction* and beyond, Baudrillard's thinking
unfolds what he ironically describes as a 'dialectic of subject-object' (1990c:
18). Ironically, because both within the movement of his thought and within
the 'real' historical movement it determines, these terms finally change
places. Thus, simulating the (seemingly) actual splintering and depletion of
subjectivity as a force in the world, Baudrillard is increasingly impelled to
stake his bets not on any recuperation (as active, autonomous, redeeming,
self-infinitising, etc.) of the individual or collective human agent, but on the
fatal 'passion' and 'strategy' of the Object itself.

This startling exchange of places, however, did not involve a clean
break. Even after Baudrillard's initial move of substituting a transgressive

counter-logic of 'symbolic exchange' for the dialectical one of expropriating the expropriators, his early work, culminating in the critique of 'the political economy of the sign', was, he confesses (1990c: 18), shadowed by a neo-Marxist preoccupation with the constitution and overcoming of alienation. Moreover, while Baudrillard's critique of Marx's concepts of needs, use-value and commodity fetishism[3] aimed to make this shadow definitively disappear, the conceptual excision of the (dis)alienated Subject left a missing centre, a nagging absence, that was subsequently symptomatised by the surfacing of a kind of God-talk, elsewhere, in the margins of his discourse. To grasp the significance of the latter, then, we must begin by looking at the (ambiguously) abandoned problematic itself. And here, what matters is less the category of alienation as such than the place of this notion in the Situationist analysis of the spectacle through which, most proximately, Baudrillard received – and displaced – it.

The clearest presentation of that analysis is in Debord's *Society of the Spectacle*, a text which is prefaced by a quote from Feuerbach[4] and whose critique of consumer capitalism is cast in explicitly Feuerbachian terms. Capitalism has turned the world of human objectifications into a publicity show which, conversely, represents the highest form of the commodity. In being dazzled by the show, *le spectacle*, we worship human creation and human powers in alienated form.

> The spectacle is the material reconstruction of the religious illusion. Spectacular technology has not dispelled the religious clouds where men had placed their own powers detached from themselves; it has only tied them to an earthly base. The most earthly life becomes opaque and unbreathable. It no longer projects into the sky but shelters within itself its absolute denial, its fallacious paradise. The spectacle is the technical realisation of the exile of human powers into a beyond; it is separation perfected within the interior of man.
>
> (Debord 1977: thesis 20)

For Debord, the reversal of this state of affairs, the dissipation of the media illusion, the negation of the condition in which '[E]verything that was directly lived has passed away into a representation' (1977: thesis 1), would coincide with the inauguration of a truly human society and history.

To be sure, this is not Feuerbach pure and simple. It is Feuerbach's parable of exile and homecoming, of Man assuming the mantle of the idolised Power upon which he had projected his nature-transcending qualities and capacities, as reconfigured by (young) Marx. If the world, as a matter of ideological fact, is separated into a real and fantasmatic realm, this can only be explained as the effect of an earthly split. That is: of a social division between rulers and ruled, exploiters and exploited, in which objectified human power is appropriated by the dominant and converted into power over its original producers. Salvation, correspondingly, is not just a matter of illumination and changed consciousness. The social relations of domination must themselves be overcome for the subjective side of alienation, the hell of human self-separation, to be redeemed.

We are, moreover, a century and a quarter further on. With capitalist development, the site of the 'religious illusion' has shifted. For Debord, in effect, the duplication of alienated life into an earthly and heavenly realm has been resurrected, outside the fading and hysterical remnants of traditional religion, by the rise to ideological power of the culture industry. Resurrected, indeed, with a vengeance. For the commodification of culture, combined with the rise of mass reproductive technologies, has led to an even more intractably alienated state of affairs than the dominance of the God-out-there illusion contested by Feuerbach. Echoing the reduplicative realism of the (media) image, the scene of life has itself become a copy of this copy. The real has become spectacular and the spectacle has become real. A similar bad unity associated with the rise of capitalism was depicted by Marx in his notion of commodity fetishism. But for Debord – wherein he follows Adorno and Marcuse[5] – the tendency for the commodity-system to erect a false mirror has been taken to the limit in the transformed conditions of advanced capitalism; conditions in which the organisation of consumption and the fusion of commodities with the publicity process wherein they are circulated has become a dominant and strategic feature of socio-economic life.

Baudrillard's entire work can be read as an elaboration of these theses, but with a crucial difference. While key aspects of Debord's culturo-economic analysis are retained (the merger of signs and commodities, the eclipse of social reality by simulation and the hyper-real), the transformist hope for dis-alienation that drives the analysis along is placed in abeyance by conceptually deprivileging (as itself a simulacrum internal to the ideological reproduction of early capitalism) the man/god figure at its fideistic centre. Feuerbach/ Marx – together with their foundational post-God 'God' – is made to disappear from the Situationist brew. That this disappearance nevertheless left a trace in Baudrillard's thought is to be accounted for in terms of the complex, and essentially substitutive, manoeuvre that brought it about. In effect, Baudrillard makes two moves.

First: while Baudrillard retains from Debord and the whole modern revolutionary tradition a profound sense that contemporary social reality, however monolithic it may seem, is riven by contradictions, the locus of that contradictoriness is repositioned. Debord's society of the spectacle was confronted by (and depicted from the point of view of) an active subject which, even in its mesmerised passivity, carried the potential for a world-redeeming self-transformation. The counter-logic that Baudrillard seizes on, as he works his way out of the Marxist paradigm, is the non-teleological principle of symbolic exchange. This principle, which metamorphosises into what Baudrillard later calls seduction and challenge, derives from French sociology via

Durkheim, Mauss and Bataille.[6] Through this substitution, there is not only a change in register – from the historical to the sociological, the diachronic to the synchronic; the replacement problematic is also appropriated from an appropriation (Bataille's cultural anthropology), which itself has torn free from a substantialist (and implicitly transcendentalist) social ontology.[7] The principle that sacrifice makes sacred, and that the Gods must continually have sacrifices to stay alive, rests on an impersonal and functional group dynamic and presupposes no God-identified collective mind. There is no place on this map for the big-s Subject, whether in the form of Feuerbach and ('young') Marx's Man or in that of Durkheim's Society. Nor indeed is it possible on this basis to sustain any grand narrative of History as Self-realisation, and the latter as theodicy.

At the same time, the religious interest which had been tangled up with the revolutionary-dialectical position which Baudrillard's atheism-of-the-left deconstructs, continues on in another form. In place of a Messianic eschatology in which Man becomes God in historical time, a truly free community is established, and the riddle of history is solved, the radical hope and dissatisfaction which this expresses transmutes into the terms of a primal and, it would seem, cyclical anthropology. The gift and counter-gift of symbolic exchange constitutes a mechanism and dynamic that exceeds the dominant (semiotic and exchangist) logics of late capitalism. Society, History and the Revolution may be dead, but the operations of symbolic exchange – with their irrational symbols, rituals and ecstasies – cannot fail continually to resurrect buried experiences of alterity. 'Even signs can burn' (Baudrillard 1981: 163).

On the one hand, then, the God term projected onto the human subject, whether as Man, the revolutionary proletariat, or Society, disappears along with its simulacrum. But on the other hand, the gestural place for a pointing towards 'that' beyond 'this' is preserved. It lives on in the irrepressibility of the counter-gift, of the sacrifice, of the violence that makes sacred, which even the most thorough disenchanting of the world cannot suppress. Indeed, the very movement of disenchantment, associated as it is with commodification and the generalisation of the sign-form, puts life itself in debt to death and provokes a reciprocal symbolic violence (in urban terrorism and inner-city riots, or, less dramatically, in bloody-minded electoral apathy) in the same process wherein material conflicts, and the social/political projects to which they give rise, are emptied of any but a simulated significance.[8]

Thus the crypto-religious question of the traditional political left – how can we, in becoming 'we', actualise the ideal qualities and aspirations projected into the heavens? – is less obliterated than transformed. In Baudrillard's mutant matrix it is, more precisely, posed in reverse. The question becomes: how can the autonomised movement of the human object-world – an Object that now includes the non-agentic humans themselves caught in its coils – elicit (collective and individual) manifestations of otherness, despite the

351

dead subject, through the unconscious reciprocities of symbolic exchange? How, through 'fatal strategies' which identify with the destining of late capitalism's world-made-object, can the gods be made to 'reappear'?[9]

The iconoclastic controversy revisited

It is in just this context that Baudrillard (in a formulation he repeats in several writings and interviews from the mid-1970s on[10]) rethinks his way into the current cultural situation by means of a striking parallel from religious history, one drawn in fact from the time of Pascal himself.

For Baudrillard, the debate about mass media in the late twentieth century replays, in certain essentials, the iconoclastic controversy of the seventeenth. Contemporary rage against the image, as a duplicitous distortion of and deflection from the real, recalls Protestant rage against the idolatrous iconography and ceremonial of the Roman Church. Moreover, just as puritan attacks on religious theatre combined with attacks on secular theatre, as if theatre itself were the devil's work, moralistic critiques of tabloid TV, of porno, of bad representations, flow over into attitudes of hostility towards 'the media' as such. A promotionalised politics evinces a demand for 'issues not images'. A sickness with the illusory promises of commodity imaging sustains a yearning for the natural and the original which was evident in back-to-the-land counter-culture and has come to mark the consumer style of the metropolitan middle class. For Baudrillard himself, in his *gauchiste* phase, the media were not to be reformed but smashed. The practical point of Situationism had been to stop the show in order to create a (revolutionary) situation.

As against all this, the later Baudrillard, in a curious way like McLuhan (a Catholic convert, after all), reverses loyalties. Quoting Rivarol's dictum that 'the people [in 1789] didn't want a Revolution, only the spectacle of it' (1990a: 75), he rejects the current equivalent of Protestantism in favour of the Counter-Reformation, the Jesuits and the Baroque. That is, he moves from a posture of implacable opposition to the glittering superficiality of mass culture to one of ironic embrace.

The iconoclasts, 'whose millennial quarrel is with us still' (Baudrillard 1987: 8), believed that the experience of God, and more generally of the sacred, was cheapened through iconic representation. For them, Christian belief could only be preserved as a living idea if the old Jewish prohibition against mimesis was maintained. Their deepest fear was that God might disappear in the multiplication of his simulacra. This was not groundless. Indeed, compared with 'the iconolaters who saw in them only reflections and were content to venerate God at one remove' (1987: 9), the iconoclasts manifested a strikingly modern appreciation for the (liquidating) power of the image. Yet they were naive. For if God seemed, to European intellectuals of the seventeenth and eighteenth century, to have gone into hiding, this was for good historical reason. The surge of other-worldliness that accompanied the cataclysmic disintegration of the feudal order had waned. Those who sought to retrieve the hidden deity from idolatrous falsification by returning to a pure and unembellished faith were engaged, then, in a futile mission.

The Jesuit iconolaters, who wanted still more embellishment, more icons, more theatre, knew better. A magic show, which semiotically staged the death and resurrection of the deity not just in the Mass, but in the whole panoply of ritual practice, was essential if popular religion was to be saved. And not just as a pedagogical concession to those (the masses) who could only live 'the idea of an altered truth'.[11] For they knew – or at least their leading minds knew – that the religious image concealed not the infinite otherness of an unrepresentable deity, but the fact that (as many had begun to suspect) no such ultimate reality existed, that precisely nothing 'out there' corresponded to the (triune) image of God.

Today, similarly, the prevalence, in the double mirror of life and its mediatised representation, of a false representation of Love, Desire, the human community, etc., conceals that these versions of 'the real' do not exist either; that in third-order simulation, the simulation of ideals, indeed of any referent, is the only existence they are granted. The hollowness through which we sense this renders pointless any moralistic critique of capitalist culture's 'altered reality'. Wisdom lies in following the iconolaters; that is, in going over to the side of the Object, which now (as sign-commodity) radiates with all the obscene hyperreality of the spectacle. 'We are no longer in the drama of alienation, we are in the ecstasy of communication' (1990a: 67).

Yet there are difficulties with the analogy. These begin when we try to pin down the precise aspect of the Jesuit position with which Baudrillard identifies in the transposed context of contemporary capitalism. His identification is evidently not with the noble lie that ensures species survival. Still less is it with the ignoble lie which masks and perpetuates the rotting carcass of a still-oppressive *ancien régime*. Nor, in fact, is the relative validity of iconolatry a matter of ideology, of truth and falsehood, or, more generally, of representation at all.

> All of Western faith and good faith was engaged in this wager on representation: that a sign could refer to the depth of meaning, that a sign could *exchange* for meaning and that something could guarantee this exchange – God of course. But what if God himself can be simulated, that is to say reduced to signs which attest his existence? then the whole system becomes weightless.
>
> (1983a: 10)

The question strikes at the root of Catholic realism no less than of Protestant nominalism. Yet, for Baudrillard, it is precisely the placing of this interrogatory mark that gives the Jesuit moment its importance. 'The transition from

353

signs which dissimulate something to signs which dissimulate that there is nothing marks the decisive turning point' (1983a: 12). By no means, of course, was this dissolvent truth of the image official Church doctrine. It was merely secreted (for those with eyes to see[12]) in the instinctive rationality of those who championed a liturgical strategy.[13] Thus to the Jesuits' 'visible theology' – in which signs of the sacred participate in the grace which they mediate – Baudrillard counterposes 'the divine irreference of images', the esoteric principle according to which God, the Real, Revolution, etc., have never been more – nor less – than mirages precipitated, seductively, on the 'sacred horizon of appearances' (1990b: 53). What connects the one position with the other is that the former is treated as an alibi for the latter, with just the dialectical difference that the causal order of the symbol and the Real is turned on its head.

In sum, what draws Baudrillard towards the Jesuit embrace of theatre – especially religious, but also secular – is what he takes to be its implicit affirmation of the simulative spectacle's performative power, Iconolatry, in its intelligent form, discloses a kind of Machiavellian magic. If God really is only an effect of the gestures and signs which simulate 'Him', then these same simulations can create what, ostensibly, they only denote. As Pascal put it: 'Move your lips in prayer and you will believe' (cited in Althusser 1971: 158). But Pascal was a Jansenist, and even this formulation risks a misrecognition, as though what Baudrillard calls the 'Jesuit' strategy is to be conceived – banally – as merely an instrumentalism, a calculated means to an end. For Baudrillard, rather, the religious *trompe d'oeil* of the Counter-Reformation was seductive.[14] It was, that is, a move within a kind of game: a game of appearances (as between potential lovers) in which each player seeks to lure the other into the mirror of their own desire, and, in so doing, challenges the other to defer that expression through a counter-challenge of their own. The practice of seduction, so conceived, is neither unilateral nor, despite its libidinous alibi, motivated by desire at all. It is not even, in religious context, motivated by such a desire as underlies Pascal's existentially driven *foi*.[15] To seduce is already to have entered into a regime of absolutely fixed rules. And, of course, precisely because it is a game there is more than one player. Even solitaire pits the self against Lord Chance.

But this is not all. The cycle of seduction begins with a provocation, just as its every move, designed to test the resistant will of the other, also has a provocative character. Seduction itself, then, is an instance of an even more general ludic form: that of the challenge, a dynamic exemplified by duels and wagering, in which one disequilibrium (of risked face and honour) engenders another, and the loser (whatever the material outcome) is the one who quits, or finally reveals their hand. To pray, in short, is not just to produce the signifier in order to construct a signified by which one can wilfully fall prey to the illusion that the ritual act corresponds to the reality it pretends to address. As fantastic as it might seem – and precisely so, since we are in the field of the imaginary – the ceremonial which simulates the referentiality of the Ideal is a challenge to God really to appear.

Here, though, we come to further difficulties. For, as Baudrillard tells the tale, the Jesuits sponsored theatrical illusion and its seductions both as a matter of deliberate policy, and in the distinct form of a cultural institution whose revival (for a while) they spearheaded. In contrast, the contemporary spectacle arises blindly, as a determined consequence of the fusion of signs and commodities in an economy of general exchange. It is orchestrated by no one. Moreover, whereas the Jesuits championed the visible Church as an antidote to secular disenchantment, for Baudrillard it is the fallen world which has itself become the equivalent of the ecclesiastical apparatus, and it is upon this, not on a counter-institution like the Party or the Movement, that he stakes his bets. It is as if, for him, in the ultra-commodified epoch of the spectacle, the secular order itself challenges the (transcendentally) real, whose absence it conceals, to come into existence. For that reason, too, doxa and militancy have no place. The movement towards this epiphanic destiny is indirect. It operates through a spiral of response and counter-response, through 'fatal strategies' (of the Object as well as of the Subject) which mimic the mime in the mirror and force its illusory illusoriness to unveil itself through the reverse movement of the subject's own seductive sacrifice.

But what kind of seduction is this? The Jesuit strategy, as Baudrillard reads it, was to conjure God into being through a theatre which evoked the living eminence and virtue of the divine. In which terms his own strategy of seduction is perverse. It embodies not the church, as the mystical body of Christ, but a 'society of the spectacle' that repels transcendence and does not even have the appearance of the Good. It is a morbid seduction, in which an abjection calls forth an abjection, and which elicits, at the limit, an absolute abjection as a death that would reverse death. In this parodic inversion of 'I am the Life and the Way', any progressive political engagement has been left behind. As with the disruptive overconformism of the silent masses, Baudrillard's 'fatal' theory is not a call to arms, but an invitation to ecstatic surrender. Which leads us to wonder, finally, not only about the dark character of the power by which Baudrillard's God is to be seduced, but also about that God itself. In the epoch of the sign-commodity, simulation and general exchange, the grand seduction in play is not simply of the human subject by its objectifications, and vice versa, but of a third term by both. So what live power is it that Baudrillard imagines that the dead power of the contemporary image can conjure up? Who, or what, is Baudrillard's 'God'?

The evil powers of the world

I said, however, that Baudrillard's reconfiguration of Situationist motifs involved two moves, and if we are to follow the ambiguous path down which these final questions lead, we must turn to the second.

Baudrillard's second move was, in effect, to identify the collapse of the real into its image in the society of the spectacle with a diabolical version of Nietzsche's 'greatest noontide'.[16] For Nietzsche, noontide was the dance of the free spirits, the final emancipation from Platonism and Christianity, the moment in which the apparent world, recognised as the only one in existence, was valorised as the valorisation of life itself. Even more than that, it initiated a movement in which the whole dichotomy fell to the ground. 'We have abolished the real world: what world is left? the apparent world perhaps? . . . But no! *with the real world we also have also abolished the apparent world!*' (Nietzsche 1990: 51, emphasis in the original). For Baudrillard, the fusion of signs and commodities, the absorption of the habitus into its image, the impenetrable mutual mirroring of TV and life, have similarly collapsed the distinction between the real and the apparent. Echo and Narcissus have become their own insubstantial doubles. Henceforth, there are only simulations, copies without an original. By the same token, though, the Nietzchean figure is made to stand on its head. The merger of the real (i.e., the ideal) with the apparent in the 'postmodern scene'[17] has taken place not simply on the ground of the apparent – as the rise of science and the restored value of the senses – but on the ground of the copy. The triumph of the apparent has been the triumph not of Life, but of its reduction to digitality and the code.

At first sight, this is still Debord. That is: an elaboration (in dystopian terms) of the Marxist theme of ideology, particularly as linked (via Chapter 1 of *Capital*) to a theory of (capitalist) mystification. It is in that vein, we may add, that Baudrillard invokes the memory of Bacon's idols and of Descartes's great deceiver (the 'evil genie of images'[18]), both – in a bad end to the dialectic of consciousness that never was – victorious at last. But we must be careful. For Baudrillard, precisely because he has inscribed himself within a Nietzschean definition of the situation, the capturing of culture by reproducibility and abstract exchange is not to be grasped as simply the accumulation of (ever more profoundly) mystifying effects.

If all that remains of the modern's 'big reals' (the social, desire, will-to-freedom, etc.) is their simulation in a discourse and symbology which the dispersed circuitry of power no longer needs, then these metaphysical shibboleths, too, are on their way to dissolution. For those who would philosophise with a hammer, this is progress. Contra the piety of the religiously correct, there is something emancipatory about the fading and discrediting of even the most progressive humanist attachments. But by this very movement, the transcendentals appealed to in any legitimation of the revolutionary project (Marx's *or* Nietzsche's) are themselves undermined – and with them the grounding for any such demystifying interest. 'True consciousness', 'true needs' and the paradise of natural transparency in which they are imagined to come into their own, unveil themselves as no more than determined sociocultural effects. With that knowledge, their motive power dissolves.

It is, indeed, this very demystification of demystifaction, at the hands of an objective nihilism wholly other to the acting/knowing subject, which gives a diabolical character to what is, for Baudrillard, the actually existing dawn of Nietzsche's longest day. In what was projected to be the crowning, and reversing, moment in the process of detranscendentalisation, the nihilism Nietzsche had identified with Plato and Christianity is not brought to an end (Derrida's 'cloture de la metaphysique'[19]) but deepened. Just at the point when other-worldliness is dissolving through the movement of its own will-to-nothingness, and the way is prepared for an affirmative transvaluation, another 'uncanny guest' enters the scene. It is indeed even uncannier than the first. For the fatality of which this (postmodern) nihilism is the cause, harbinger and symbol is not spiritual – the self-extinction of *ressentiment* – but socio-economic: generalised exchange, pan-simulation, and the collapse of modernity's referential imaginary.

Accordingly, Baudrillard's reworking of the Nietzschean problematic involves not only the thinking of a new moment, but a new thinking; a thinking which, in its a/sociologism, registers (in the mode of mimesis) a 'real' shift in the character of modern capitalism. For Nietzsche, the drama of (Western) culture was internal to the human subject: sickness unto death, and convalescence in the depths of the abyss. For Baudrillard, that game (if it ever meant anything) is over. It is so, moreover, through the operation of culturo-economic forces whose existence Nietzsche did not even suspect. The self that would overcome itself (to become a 'self-propelling wheel') has been definitively eclipsed by the rise of the object (as spectacle, sign-commodity), and by the related dissolution of the life-world into a heteronomous imitation of itself. The 'death of Man' that coincides with the catastrophe point of this development is thus more abyssal than the divine death whose mere after-shock it might seem to be. On the one hand, any place for the subject, and hence for will-formation, has been evacuated. On the other, an irreversible kind of negativity has come to rule, the 'objectal' effect of a spreading ultra-capitalism that Sartrians would recognise as a special form of the practico-inert, and that Baudrillard himself comes to describe – with explicitly Manichaean overtones[20] – as a principle of evil.

In the Manichaean imaginary, the sensory world was ruled by an evil deity, identified with the biblical God of Creation, with which a higher Power was locked in combat. It was only through the divine light of this latter – a god of pure spirit – that release was possible from ignorance and suffering. In one variant, though, this did not rule out the paradox that the path to the empyrean might first lead downwards, through sinful matter and commerce with the Evil One himself.[21] To be sure, Baudrillard no more 'believes' in the one deity than the other. His flirtation with Manichaean symbology is (to use a term he borrows from Jarry) 'pataphysical': a hypothesis of an evil demiurge running the world which is faithful to a certain (darkly ironic) experience of it, and which is essayed to see what features of our current condition this might illuminate. Yet it is a flirtation that is seriously intended, and

Baudrillard does not mask the perversity of the strategy which it emboldens him to espouse.

Citing Mandeville's slogan of 'Private vices, public virtues',[22] and basing himself on the martial arts approach of strategic indirection, he insists on the wisdom of a cynicism that would resist resistance to the endlessly fascinating blandishments of a culture that has totally put an end to integrity and depth. It is as if effective resistance to the triumphant Object can only come through identification with it. Indeed through an excessive identification, one that affirms precisely what a left-humanist sensibility would take to be its evil implication.

> We need to reawaken the principle of Evil active in Manicheism and all the great mythologies in order to affirm, against the principle of Good, not exactly the supremacy of Evil, but the fundamental duplicity that demands that any order exists only to be disobeyed, attacked, exceeded, and dismantled.
>
> (1990a: 77)

Baudrillard's recourse to the Manichaean picture is selective and fragmentary. If he insists on the illuminating virtues of its model of absolute cosmic duality, he tends to highlight only one of its dualistic terms. The ethereal realm imagined beyond the evil powers of the world stays in the shadows, together with any redemptive hope to which it might beckon. Yet, even here, the dialectical (despite itself) cast of Baudrillard's speculations directs them away from a merely monochromatic indifference or despair. In line with Nietzsche's revaluation of what the Judaeo-Christian world calls sin (pride, egotism, lust, aggressiveness) Baudrillard offers his own revaluation of various manifestations of the 'evil' that contemporary moralists take the spirit of TV-age capital to have installed as a dominant principle of life. He writes 'in praise of the Sexual Object' (1990a: 119–27), and of the postauratic superficiality brought to an art-form in drag-ball fashion and Warholian pop iconography. In these falser than false representations he sees a 'feminine' principle, seduction incarnate, which – much more than the contemporary feminism he detests – stands over and against a destructively phallocratic Reason.

In any case, as Heidegger's commentary on Nietzsche suggests, if nihilism means, precisely, 'the weakening of the highest values hitherto',[23] and if those values are themselves reactive, then – as an actual historical process – the degenerative movement of this weakening cannot itself be all bad. Embracing the rise of what a timid, mediocre and moralistic consensus considers evil is a step towards completed nihilism, i.e., towards a beyond of moral value that transcends not only the old antinomies, but the subjectivistic and positivist-tinged self-inflation of 'value-positing' as such. The very excessiveness of the hyperproductive sign/commodity economy is its potential undoing. Too many signs chase too little meaning. The stockpiled tokens of exchangeable value undermine the currency that gives them value, and ultimately the very meaningfulness of the meaning they purport to represent. The more real than real, the more scenic than scenic, etc., draws us out of a dead-brain sobriety into the ek-stasis of a game that is much older than the market, a game that is always already liable to transgress its homogenising commutability, and restore the play and counter-play of the symbolic to its full, fatal and non-identitarian power.

From God to gods

So the God that Baudrillardian theory aims to seduce is neither the resurrected spirit of a dead transcendental humanism nor the spirit of its murderer, the 'principle of Evil', whose reawakening is none the less indispensable to the cycle of challenge and counter-challenge through which the divine figure(s) to which Baudrillard makes rhetorical appeal might be induced to appear. Nor again, since Baudrillard de-existentialises Nietzsche and eschews his self-affirmative vitalism, is this divinity to be thought of as the spirit of vertiginous ecstasy from which a pop-cultural epicurean might derive pleasure in the 'achieved utopia'[24] of a postmodern capitalism in which the ideational has disappeared into the actuality of an hallucinatory, simulative, reality. Baudrillard's God, then, is neither the Crucified, nor Satan, nor Dionysus.

Perhaps the undecidability of Baudrillard's meaning, and his refusal to disambiguate it, is to be accounted for simply in terms of the cognitive interest that, even in its rhapsodic tendencies, lends consistency to a project that began, after all, with an examination of commodity logic in the contemporary world. For all its 'metaphysical' preoccupations, that is, Baudrillard remains a sociologist, resolutely seeking the truth of a social reality within which, as the effect of a real social development, neither the social nor the real retain a semblance of more than metaphysical meaning. Nevertheless, as hints towards the delineation of an a-religious religiosity adequate to the current epoch, there are two other possibilities worth drawing out.

The first is (as it were) Buddhist. Baudrillard's God – the Other of the Evil Genie of Objects – is no-God, an imaginary goose in an imaginary bottle which can be released, along with all the spiritual energy it locks up, by releasing ourselves (in line with the disenchantment wrought by the ascendancy of 'third-order simulation') from the tyranny of all such metaphors. To read Baudrillard in this way, though, is to ignore what he has learned from Bataille: the power of the metaphor itself, and the irrepressible energy of the sacred, at once destructive and constructive, to which that metaphor refers. It also eliminates the essential ambiguity of Baudrillard's practical stance. His is a mysticism of the disillusioned revolutionary; a mysticism which, moreover, in its very flight from practice, refuses to let go entirely of the transformist impulse that animated the initial challenge his early work trenchantly offered to 'la société de consommation' and its diabolical 'système des objets'.

A second possibility recalls Nietzsche's scornful comment in *The Antichrist*. 'Almost two millennia, and not a single new God!' (Nietzsche 1990: 141). Which is to speak not of *one* God, who lives and dies, but of a whole succession of them. And if a succession, why not a plurality? For if we are, in such discourse – indeed in all discourse – walled up in a world of metaphor, the issue is not which God is the true one, but whether singularity itself is an adequate meta-metaphor in which to express the manifold richness of a sacred realm whose only limits are those imposed by the social imaginary we happen to have inherited. A nodal point in Rushdie's *Satanic Verses* is the episode in which, over his mischievous protests, Haroun's inner Allah insists on suppressing all deities but one. Similarly, we might say, Baudrillard's nihilist dismantling of the substantialist pretensions of post-God foundational categories like Man, Society, Desire, the Real, etc., is aimed especially at their unicity. In which respect, moreover, this dismantling is of a piece with his magical attempt to reawaken the principle of Evil, and so 'challenge the real' to reappear (1987: 124–5). Again, the target is a Good construed as that which would reconcile all in the one. Against general exchange, universal semiosis and the hyperreal collapse of idealities and realities into one another, what Baudrillard proposes is a seduction of the sacred as such, which can only be properly conceived as a seduction of a multiplicity, an archaic sorcery, an activist polytheism whose theism, of course, just as much as that of the mono-worshippers it seeks to exceed, is under erasure.

From this angle, we might add, though Baudrillard is not remotely drawn down such a path, there is no reason why past gods too might not be welcomed at the table, including the dead Christian one the earlier Jesuits had sought to resurrect. If all deities are symbols of the symbolic, then they all have their necessity, as well as their limitations. Baudrillard's disregard for the God (or gods) of the Christians, and Jews, which surfaces in a visceral hostility towards all manifestations of what the media and the right call 'political correctness', symptomises a fundamental lack of compassion. Besides, the absolute Other of the established order projected within his Manichaean pataphysics would not be absolutely Other if it were only a different version of the same cruel principle (as 'chance', 'fate', 'destiny', etc.). Why, then, should we retain the starkness of a choice, which Baudrillard, seemingly still ranting in Nietzschean fashion against the anti-life God of the West, saw no way to soften? Why not invoke both Dionysus and the crucified? Past the 'dead point', with all the representational realism sucked from our codes, has not the very necessity of such a choice, like the defunct monotheism which insists on it, revealed itself to be banal?

This is not necessarily to argue for a lazy relativism in which the paradox of incommensurability is valued as such and allowed to relax into indifference. If we are to keep faith with the anguished disillusionment which Baudrillard's writings exemplify, the tension between warring gods must be preserved – not only as a guide, but as a puzzle. The transcendence of modern nihilism would transcend the opposition between Christianity and paganism which a whole lineage of Western thought, from Kierkegaard and Nietzsche to Bataille and Daniel Bell, have presented as an irreconcilable choice. In the last analysis, then, the religio-moral significance of Baudrillard's work, indeed of the whole post-1960s Nietzschean turn in radical French thought, may lie precisely here: in the reconciliation it points towards, but fails to achieve, in that space wherein overlaps, impossibly, a social Messianism, a groundless mysticism and a Bacchanalian dance with the spirits of death and rebirth.

Notes

1 This view of Baudrillard has been developed by Doug Kellner (1989).
2 Baudrillard's formation (he was born in 1929) was in the 1950s. A lecturer at Nanterre from 1966 to 1987 he was influential less on the 68ers than on the disillusioned generation that followed. While Mark Taylor, in *Disfiguring* (Chicago and London: University of Chicago Press, 1992) and other works, has described him as the intellectual counterpart of pop art, it might be more accurate to see him as parallel to the decadent/nihilist pop-cultural current which runs from the Velvet Underground to punk. In *Homo Academicus*, Pierre Bourdieu classifies him among the 'minor heresiarchs' in the French post-1960s university scene (1988: xxvi and n. 15).
3 The principal texts in which Baudrillard conducts his critique of Marxism (especially of its 'productivist' philosophical anthropology) are *For a Critique of the Political Economy of the Sign* (1981) and *Mirror of Production* (1975).
4

> But certainly for the present age, which prefers the sign to the thing signified, the copy to the original, fancy to reality, the appearance to the essence . . . *illusion only is sacred, truth profane*. Nay sacredness is held to be enhanced in proportion as truth decreases, so that the highest degree of illusion comes to be the highest degree of sacredness.

Debord's citation is taken from the Preface to the Second Edition of Feuerbach's *Essence of Christianity* (1956: xxxix).
5 In Horkheimer and Adorno's *Dialectic of Enlightenment*, the accent is on the triumph of total administration and instrumental reason; for Marcuse, in *One Dimensional Man*, it is on that of the immanent actuality of the established order. The allegedly totalitarian character of advanced capitalism was a common coin of 1950s social critique, and mirrored by the rise of functionalism, convergence theory and 'end of ideology' ideology in mainstream social science.
6 Moments in the development of the idea of symbolic exchange would include: the theory of ritual and social reproduction in Durkheim's *Elementary Forms of the Religious Life*; Mauss's theory of the gift in the classic of that name (Mauss 1967); Lévi-Strauss's exchangist conception of kinship systems and structures; and Bataille's account of violence, the sacred and the 'accursed share' (Bataille 1988–91).
7 Within the modern French tradition of *sciences humaines*, the break with the notion of a Society-subject, inherited from Comte and De Bonald, has three identifiable

moments: (1) the detachment of the concept of social structure (synchronics) from that of social development (diachronics); (2) the consignment of the latter, as history, to the realm of contingency (see Lévi-Strauss's introductory essay to Mauss's *The Gift*, reprinted as Chapter 1 of Lévi-Strauss, *Structural Anthropology*, New York: Basic Books, 1967); (3) the emergence, in structural anthropology, of the notion of a 'structure without a subject', whose vertiginous implications (held in abeyance by Lévi-Strauss's ambiguous Kantianism) have been drawn out, philosophically, by Derrida.

8 It is this theme which relates Baudrillard's identification of capital's gift and counter-gift with *thanatos* in *Symbolic Exchange and Death* to the political thesis (the radicality of apathy) advanced in *In the Shadow of the Silent Majority* (1983b). See, too, the comments on hostages in *Fatal Strategies* (1990a: 34–50).

9 For characteristically elusive comments on the theme of appearance and disappearance see the interviews with Lotringer (1987: 123–50) and Guy Bellavance (1990c: 21–4). See also 'The Secret and the Challenge' in 1990b: 79–84.

10 Baudrillard's most extended comment on the Jesuits and the iconoclastic controversy is in *Simulations* (1983a: 8–14). See also 1990b: 91–4 and 1987: 118–19.

11 For Baudrillard, 'altered truth' is all anyone can live. 'It is the only way to live in conformity with the truth. Otherwise life becomes unbearable (precisely) because the truth does not exist' (1990b: 59).

12 For Baudrillard's discussion of *trompe d'oeil* see 1990b: 60–7.

13 'Thus faith in the religious sphere is like seduction in the game of love' (1990b: 142).

14 These eyes evidently did not include Hegel, at least not in the terms in which he championed the Reformation and the *innerlichkeit* it brought to the fore:

> The corruption of the Church was a native growth; the principle of that corruption is to be looked for in the fact that the specific and definite embodiment of the Deity which it recognises, is sensuous – that the external in a coarse form, is enshrined in its inmost being . . . henceforth it [the merely Spiritual] occupies a position of inferiority to the World-Spirit; the latter has already transcended it, for it has become capable of recognizing the Sensuous as sensuous, the merely outward as merely outward.
>
> (G.W.F. Hegel, *Philosophy of History*, New York: Dover, 1956)

15 The slippage occurred on the site of what Baudrillard takes to be the dichotomous dualism of the Jesuit conception of faith and reason:

> For the Jesuits – and this is their basic proposition – it is impossible to establish a proof of God's existence. So all right, God exists, grace exists, but it has nothing to do with us because what we're dealing with is a strategic worldliness.
>
> (1987: 119)

16 Nietzsche's formulation of this issue in *Twilight of the Idols* ('How the "Real World" at last Became a Myth – History of an Error'), and its influence on Heidegger and the various currents of 'poststructuralism' deserves much greater attention from commentators than it has so far been given.

17 A phrase coined by Arthur Kroker. See Kroker and Cook (1986).

18 Baudrillard's most extended discussion of the 'evil genie' is in *Fatal Strategies* (1990a: 91–112).

19 See the discussion of the closure of metaphysics in *Of Grammatology* (Derrida 1976). Note that for Derrida, as for Baudrillard, the moment of historical rupture (with logocentrism and the representational value/concept of language) is prolonged and suspensive. 'The sign and divinity have essentially the same place and time of birth. The age of the sign is essentially theological. Perhaps it will never end. Its historical closure is, however, defined' (1976: 14).

20 The following, from *Fatal Strategies* (1990a: 72), make the heretical implications of the Manichaean allusion particularly clear:

> Would God have fallen into this strategy, unworthy of him, of reconciling man with his own image, at the end of a Last Judgment that would bring him indefinitely closer to his ideal goal? Fortunately not: God's strategy is such that he maintains man in suspense, hostile to his image, elevating Evil to the power of a principle and marvellously sensitive to any seduction that turns him away from his goal. . . . Beyond the ecstasy of the social, sex, of the body, information, the Evil Principle keeps watch, evil genie of the social, the object, irony of passion.

21 As the strange religious career of Sabbatai Z'vi in the late seventeenth century exemplifies, the antinomian notion that the path to salvation (for the World, as well as of the soul) lies through moral transgression, even to the point of blasphemy, sacrilege also became an important ingredient of Messianic Kabbalism. See Gershom Scholem, *Major Trends in Jewish Mysticism* (New York: Schocken Books, 1961).

22 'Neither the morality nor the positive value system of a society makes for progress, but rather its immorality and vice' (1990a: 72). No more exact precis of Mandeville's *Fable of the Bees* (Harmondsworth: Penguin, 1970) can be imagined.

23 See especially 'On the Word of Nietzsche: "God is Dead"' in Heidegger 1977.

24 Baudrillard's America, as seen through the eyes of a European: 'The US is utopia achieved. . . . Ours is a crisis of historical ideals facing up to the impossibility of their realisation. Theirs is the crisis of an achieved utopia, confronted with the problem of its duration and permanence' (1988b: 77).

References

Althusser, Louis (1971), *Lenin and Philosophy and other Essays*, London: New Left Books.

Bataille, Georges (1988–91), *The Accursed Share: an Essay on General Economy*, New York: Zone Books.

Baudrillard, Jean (1968), *Le Système des objets*, Paris: Gallimard.

Baudrillard, Jean (1975), *The Mirror of Production*, St Louis: Telos Press.

Baudrillard, Jean (1981), *For a Critique of the Political Economy of the Sign*, St Louis: Telos Press.

Baudrillard, Jean (1983a), *Simulations*, New York: Semiotext(e).

Baudrillard, Jean (1983b), *In the Shadow of the Silent Majority*, New York: Semiotext(e).

Baudrillard, Jean (1987), *Forget Foucault and Forget Baudrillard* (interview with Sylvère Lotringer), New York: Semiotext(e).

Baudrillard, Jean (1988a), *The Ecstasy of Communication*, New York: Semiotext(e).

Baudrillard, Jean (1988b), *America*, London: Verso.

Baudrillard, Jean (1990a), *Fatal Strategies*, New York and London: Semiotext(e) and Pluto Press.

Baudrillard, Jean (1990b), *Seduction*, London: Macmillan and New World Perspectives.

Baudrillard, Jean (1990c), *Revenge of the Crystal: Selected Writings on the Modern Object and its Destiny, 1968–83*, ed. and tr. Paul Foss and Julian Pefanis, London and Concord: Pluto Press.

Baudrillard, Jean (1993a), *The Transparency of Evil*, London: Verso.

Baudrillard, Jean (1993b), *Symbolic Exchange and Death*, London: Sage.

Benjamin, Walter (1969), *Illuminations*, New York: Schocken Books.

Bourdieu, Pierre (1988), *Homo Academicus*, Stanford: Stanford University Press.

Debord, Guy (1977), *Society of the Spectacle*, Detroit: Black and Red.

Derrida, Jacques (1976), *Of Grammatology*, tr. Gayatri Spivak, Baltimore and London: Johns Hopkins University Press.

Durkheim, Emile (1995), *The Elementary Forms of Religious Life*, New York: Free Press.

Heidegger, Martin (1977), *The Question Concerning Technology and Other Essays*, New York: Harper and Row.

Kellner, Douglas (1989), *Jean Baudrillard: From Marx to Postmodernism and Beyond*, Cambridge: Polity Press.

Kroker, Arthur, and Cook, David (1986), *The Postmodern Scene: Excremental Culture and Hyperaesthetics*, Montreal and New York: St Martins Press.

Lévi-Strauss, Claude (1969), *The Elementary Structures of Kinship*, Boston: Beacon Press.

Marcuse, Herbert (1996), *One Dimensional Man: Studies in the Ideology of Advanced Industrial Society*, Boston: Beacon Press.

Mauss, Marcel (1967), *The Gift: Forms and Functions of Exchange in Archaic Societies*, New York: Norton.

Nietzsche, Friedrich (1990), *Twilight of the Idols/The Anti-Christ*, Harmondsworth: Penguin.

Wilson, Robert Anton and Shea, William (1975), *The Illuminatus! Trilogy*, New York: Dell.

INDEX

365